CHAPMAN
GREAT
SAILING SHIPS
OF THE WORLD

CHAPMAN
GREAT SAILING SHIPS
OF THE WORLD

OTMAR SCHÄUFFELEN

Hearst Books
A Division of Sterling Publishing Co., Inc.
New York

Translated from the German by Casey Servais

Library of Congress Cataloging-in-Publication Data Available

10 9 8 7 6 5 4 3 2 1

Published by Hearst Books
A division of Sterling Publishing Co., Inc.
387 Park Avenue South, New York, NY 10016
Published in 2002 by Delius Klasing Verlag
Siekerwall 21, D-33602 Bielefeld
Under the title DIE LETZTEN GROSSEN SEGELSCHIFFE,
(10th edition) Copyright © by Delius, Klasing & Co. KG, Bielefeld
English translation copyright © 2005 by Sterling Publishing Co., Inc.

CHAPMAN and CHAPMAN PILOTING and Hearst Books are
trademarks owned by Hearst Communications, Inc.

Distributed in Canada by Sterling Publishing
c/o Canadian Manda Group, 165 Dufferin Street
Toronto, Ontario, Canada M6K 3H6

Distributed in Great Britain by Chrysalis Books Group PLC
The Chrysalis Building, Bramley Road, London W10 6SP, England

Distributed in Australia by Capricorn Link (Australia) Pty. Ltd.
P.O. Box 704, Windsor, NSW 2756, Australia

Printed in China
All rights reserved

Sterling ISBN: 1-58816-384-9

Contents

Foreword ix

How This Book Came
About xi

The Great Sailing Ships . . xiii

The Tonnage and Dimensions
of Ships xix

Types of Sailing Ships . . . xxi

The Rig xxiii

Argentina **1**
Libertad 1
Presidente Sarmiento 2
Uruguay 3

Australia **4**
Alma Doepel 4
Amity 5
Bounty III 6
Challenge of
Outward Bound 7
Duyfken 7
Endeavour 8
Enterprize 9
Falie 10
Golden Plover 11
James Craig 11
Lady Nelson 12
Leeuwin II 13
One and All 14
Our Svanen 14
Polly Woodside 15
Solway Lass 16
South Passage 17
Sovereign of the Seas . . . 18
Spirit of the Pacific 19
Windeward Bound 19
Young Endeavour 20

Bahamas **21**
Concordia 21
Wind Star/Wind Song/
Wind Spirit 22
Wind Surf 22

Belgium **23**
Mercator 23
Ragnborg 24

Bermuda **25**
Creole 25
Shenandoah 26

Brazil **27**
Cisne Branco 27

Bulgaria **28**
Kaliakra 28
Patriot 28
Veslets 28

Canada **29**
Black Jack 29
Bluenose II 30
Fair Jeanne 31
Hector 31
Nonsuch 32
Pacific Swift 33
Pathfinder 34
Robertson II 34
Spirit of
Chemainus 35
St. Lawrence II 36
St. Roch 37

Cayman Islands **38**
Phocea 38

Chile **39**
Esmeralda 39
Huascar 40
La Sirena 40

Columbia **41**
Gloria 41

Cook Islands **42**
Picton Castle 42

Denmark **43**
Aaron 43
Bonavista 44
Brita Leth 45
Carene Star 46
Danmark 46
Den Store Bjørn 48
Elinor 48
Freia 49
Fulton 50
Fylla 51
Georg Stage 52
Halmø 53
Havet 54
Isefjord 54
Jens Krogh 55
Jylland 56
Lilla Dan 57
Madonna 58
Marilyn Anne 59
Midsummer 59
Nordboen 60

Ecuador **126**
Guayas 126

Equatorial Guinea **62**
Flying Cloud 62
Legacy 63
Mandalay 64
Polynesia II 65
Yankee Clipper 66

Finland **67**
Albanus 67
Helena 67
Jacobstads Wappen 68

Linden 69
Pommern 70
Sigyn 71
Suomen Joutsen 72

France **73**
Bel Espoir II 73
Belem 74
Club Med II 75
Duchesse Anne 76
Frya 77
La Belle Poule and
L'Etoile 78
La Cancalaise 79
La Recouvrance 80
Le Renard 81
Rara Avis 81

Germany **82**
Albatros 83
Albin Köbis 83
Alexander von
Humboldt 84
Amphitrite 85
Aquarius 86
Arny Maud 86
Aschanti IV
of Vegesack 87
Astarte 88
Atalanta 88
Atlantic Tramp 89
Bartele Rensink 90
Birgitte 90
Blue Sirius 91
Bremer Hanseatic Cog . . 91
Carmelan 92
Carola 92
Dagmar Aaen 93
Dora av Raa 94
Elbe 3 94
Elbe 3 (FS Weser) 94
Falado 95
Freedom 95

Fridtjof Nansen 96
Friederike 97
Fulvia af Anholt 97
Gesine von Papenburg . . 98
Gorch Fock II 98
Greif 100
Grethe Witting 101
Grönland. 102
Grossherzogin
Elisabeth. 103
Hanseatic Cog–Kiel . . . 104
Hordatral 105
Jachara 105
Johann Smidt 106
Lili Marleen 107
Lilleholm 108
Mary-Anne. 108
Nobile. 109
Norden 110
Passat 111
Pippilotta 113
Rakel 113
Rickmer Rickmers 114
Roald Amundsen 115
Ryvar 116
Sælør 117
Schulschiff
Deutschland 118
Seute Deern 120
Seute Deern II 121
Solvang. 122
Thor Heyerdahl 122
Ubena von Bremen. . . . 123
Undine 124
Valdivia 125
Vegesack BV2 126
Vidar. 127
White Dune 127
White Shark 128
Wyvern von
Bremen. 129
Zuversicht. 130

Great Britain **131**
Activ. 132
Adix 132
Baboon 133
Carrick 134
Carrie 135
Cutty Sark 136
De Wadden 137
Discovery 138
Earl of Pembroke 139
Eye of the Wind 140
HMS Gannet 141
Glenlee 141
Golden Hinde 142
Grand Turk 143

Great Britain. 144
Helga 145
Irene 146
Jean de la Lune. 146
Ji Fung 147
Julia 147
Kaskelot 148
Kathleen & May. 148
Lord Nelson 149
Matthew 150
Phoenix. 151
Queen Galadriel 152
Raphaelo. 152
Result 153
Return of Marco Polo. . 154
Ring-Andersen 155
Royalist 155
Saint Kilda 156
Søren Larsen 157
Spirit of Winestead. . . . 158
St. Barbara Ann 158
Stavros S. Niarchos/
Prince William 159
Tenacious 160
HMS Trincomalee 161
HMS Unicorn. 162
Unicorn. 163
HMS Victory 163
HMS Warrior 165
Yankee Trader 166
Zamoura of Zermatt . . . 166
Zebu 167

Greece **168**
Eugenios Eugenides . . . 168

India **170**
Tarangini 170
Varuna 171
Indonesia. **172**
KRI Arung Samudera. . 172
KRI Dewarutji 173
Ireland, Republic of . **174**
Asgard II 174
Dunbrody 175
Jeanie Johnston 176

Israel **177**
L'Amie 177

Italy **178**
Amerigo Vespucci 178
Croce del Sud 180
Palinuro 180
Puritan 181

Japan. **182**
Akogare 182

Belle Blonde. 183
De Liefde 183
Kaisei 184
Kaiwo Maru II 185
Kanko Maru 186
Kanrin Maru. 186
Meiji Maru 187
Nippon Maru I and
Kaiwo Maru I 188
Nippon Maru II 189
Prins Willem 190
San Juan Bautista 191
Unyo Maru 192

Luxemburg **193**
Royal Clipper 193
Star Clipper/
Star Flyer 194

Madeira **195**
Anny von Hamburg . . . 195

Malaysia **196**
Tunas Samudera 196

Malta. **197**
Black Pearl. 197
Charlotte Louise 197
Sea Cloud 198
Sea Cloud II 200

Mexico **201**
Cuauhtémoc 201

Monaco **202**
Xarifa 202

The Netherlands **203**
Abel Tasman. 204
Abel Tasman. 205
Albert Johannes 206
Amazone 206
Amsterdam. 207
Antigua. 208
Aphrodite 208
Artemis. 209
Astrid 210
Atlantis 210
Atlantis 211
Batavia 212
Bisshop van Arkel 213
Bonaire 214
Brabander 214
Brandaris 215
Catherina 215
De Liefde 216
Eendracht II 217
Elegant 218

Elisabeth Smit 218
Elizabeth. 219
Europa 220
Fleurtje 220
Frisius van Adel 221
Grootvorst 221
Hendrika Bartelds 222
Hoop doet Leven 223
Horizon. 224
Ide Min. 224
Jacob Meindert. 225
Jantje 225
J. R. R. Tolkien. 226
Koh-I-Nor. 227
Linde 227
Loth Loriën 228
Luciana. 229
Maartinus 229
Mare Frisium 230
Minerva 231
Mon Desir 231
Mondrian 232
Morgana 233
Nil Desperandum 233
Noorderlicht. 234
Oosterschelde. 235
Oostvogel 236
Pacific Swift. 237
Pedro Doncker 237
Pollux 238
Radboud 239
Rainbow Warrior 239
Regina Maris 240
Rembrandt van Rijn . . . 241
Sir Robert
Baden-Powell. 241
Sodade 242
Stad Amsterdam 243
Stedemaeght 244
Store Baelt 245
Swaensborgh 245
Swan fan Makkum 246
Tecla 247
Thalassa 247
Tsjerk Hiddes 248
Urania. 248
Vliegende Hollander . . 249
Vrouwe Geertruida
Magdalena 249
Willem Barentsz. 250
Wytske Eelkje/
Willem 250
Zeelandia 251
Zuiderzee 252

New Zealand **253**
Breeze. 253
Edwin Fox 254

R. Tucker Thompson . . 255
Spirit of
New Zealand 256
Tui 257

Norway **258**
Anna Kristina 258
Christian Radich 259
Christiania 260
Fram 261
Johanna 262
Sørlandet 263
Statsraad Lehmkuhl . . . 264
Svanen 266

Oman **267**
Shabab Oman 267

Polen **268**
Dar Mlodziezy 268
Dar Pomorza 269
Fryderyk Chopin 270
General Zaruski 271
Iskra II 271
Kapitan Glowacki 272
Oceania 273
Pogoria 273
Zawisza Czarny II 274

Portugal **275**
Boa Esperança 275
Condor de Vilamoura . . 276
Creoula 277
D. Fernando II
e Gloria 278
Leão Holandês 279
Sagres II 280
Santa Maria Manuela . . 281

Romania **282**
Mircea 282

Russia **283**
Alevtina and Tuy 283
Alpha 284
Courier 284
Elena Maria Barbara . . 285
Horisont 286
Kronwerk 287
Kruzenshtern 288
Meridian/Sekstant/
Tropik 289
Mir 290
Nadeshda 291
Pallada 292
Sedov 293
Shtandart 294

Sviatitel Nikolai 295
Triumph 296
Yunyi Baltiets 297
Zarja 298

The Seychelles **299**
Sea Pearl 299
Sea Shell 300

Spain **301**
America II 301
Carmen Flores 302
Don Juan de Austria . . . 302
Gefion 303
Juan Sebastian
de Elcano 304
Niña 306
Pinta 306
Santa Maria 307

St. Vincent/
Grenadines **309**
Peace 309

Sweden **310**
Af Chapman 310
Älva 311
Amorina 312
Baltic Beauty 312
Blå Marité af Pripps . . . 313
Blue Clipper 314
Falken and Gladan 315
Götheborg III 316
Gratia of Gothenburg . . 316
Gratitude of
Gothenburg 317
Gretel 317
Gunilla 318
Hamlet 318
Hawila 319
Jarramas 319
Lady Ellen 320
Lady Ellen IV 321
Najaden 321
Najaden 322
Shalom 323
Vida 324
Viking 324
Wasa 326

Ukraine **328**
Druzhba 328
Khersones 329
Towarischtsch 329

Uruguay **331**
Capitan Miranda 331

USA **332**
Adventure 333
Alabama 334
Alvei 335
America III 336
American Pride 337
American Rover 337
Amistad 338
Ariel 339
Balclutha 339
Barba Negra 340
Beaver II 341
Bill of Rights 342
Black Pearl 342
Bounty II 343
Bowdoin 344
C. A. Thayer 345
Californian 346
Caribee 346
Carthaginian II 347
Charles W. Morgan . . . 348
Clipper City 349
Constellation 350
Constitution 351
Coronet 353
Corwith Cramer 354
Denis Sullivan 354
Eagle 355
Elissa 356
Falls of Clyde 357
Friendship 358
Gazela of
Philadelphia 358
Half Moon 359
Harvey Gamage 360
Hawaiian Chieftain . . . 360
Jamestown Ships
(replicas) 361
Joseph Conrad 362
Kalmar Nyckel 363
L. A. Dunton 364
Lady Maryland 365
Lady Washington 366
Le Pelican 367
Lettie G. Howard 367
Liberty 368
Liberty Clipper 369
Lisa 369
Margaret Todd 370
Mary Day 370
Maryland Dove 371
Mayflower II 372
Moshulu 373
Mystic Whaler 374
Nathaniel Bowditch . . . 375
New Way 375
Niagara 376

Niña 377
Ocean Star 378
Peking 378
Perseus 380
Pilgrim 380
Pioneer 381
Polynesia 382
Pride of Baltimore II . . 383
Providence 384
Regina Maris 385
Rose 386
Sea Lion 387
Shenandoah 387
Soundwaters 388
Spirit of
Massachusetts 388
Star of India 389
Stephen Taber 390
Swift of Ipswich 391
Tabor Boy 392
Te Vega 393
Timberwind 393
Tole Mour 394
Unicorn 395
Victory Chimes 396
Wavertree 396
Wawona 397
Westward 398
Windy 399
Young America 399

Venezuela **400**
Simon Bolivar 400

Yugoslavia **401**
Jadran 401

Appendices
Glossary 403
The Museum Harbor of
Oevelgönne 406
The Sail Training
Association (STA) 407
Pamir and Passat 408
Acknowledgments 409
The Photographs 413
Register of Ships 416

Foreword

This book cannot—and does not wish to—claim to be completely up-to-date in all of its parts. Things change too rapidly for that to be the case. Because of communication difficulties that cannot necessarily be attributed to the author, it was also not possible to get all of the data for some of the ships. The author asks the reader's forebearance with respect to the lower limit placed on the size of the ships included in the book. Some types of ships receive only token representation; otherwise the scope of the book would have become completely unmanageable.

A new feature is the inclusion of ships that illustrate the development of the rig in exemplary fashion, such as the reproductions of the cogs. Computer technology has opened a new chapter in the history of sailing-ship construction. As a result of such technology, traditional principles of sailing-ship design have been completely abandoned, especially with respect to the rig. Examples are the *Club Med I* and the *Wind Song*. Automated systems operate the sails. A computer determines the position of the sails and the sail area. On these ships the communal work, be it on deck or in the rigging, that once made the operation of a large sailing ship so attractive, no longer exists. Thirty years ago, when the idea of assembling this book first came to me, it was impossible to foresee the renaissance that large sailing-ship travel would experience in the years that have since passed. At that time the profitability of sailing freighters had become irrelevant, because motorized ships had long dominated the freight trade.

The sailing school-ships of the navies were in part old, long-serving ships. New constructions in this area were an exception. These circumstances led the author and the publishing company to give the book its somewhat melancholy title. Since then, the world's fleet of large sailing ships has grown significantly. The intention of bringing all these ships together for a rendezvous, at least literarily, has remained the same in the new edition of the book of this title.

Only some of the new and reconstructed ships of recent years have been pure school-ships. The uses of the ships that don't fall into this category are extremely diverse. We find adventure school-ships, cruise ships, large private sailing ships, research ships, and sailing ships that are used for social work. The political changes of recent years have made it possible for sailing ships of every flag to visit every port in the world as a matter of course. Who would have ever believed that it would one day be possible to embark as a paying guest on a Russian sailing school-ship?

The descriptions in this book are authentic. This means that information had to be requested from all parts of the world. The level of cooperation was for the most part unprecedented, and I would like to take this opportunity to express my heartfelt thanks to Erik Christian Abranson of the Mariners International Club, London, and to Hans-Joachim Gersdorf and Reinhard Nerlich, both of Hamburg. They contributed much to the book, often in a completely spontaneous manner.

Dr. Otmar Schäuffelen
(1932–2001)

How This Book Came About

"The two four-masted barks *Pamir* and *Passat* have departed on their first postwar journey to South America." That small notice appeared in a daily newspaper in 1952. It provoked my interest. Short reports about the progress of the sailing ships continued to appear occasionally, and I collected them. The tragic loss of the *Pamir* on September 21, 1957, resulted in a plethora of illustrated reports in all newspapers and magazines. The texts often demonstrated a shocking lack of knowledge of the relevant issues. Without providing exact information, they often simply pointed with great pathos to the danger and uselessness of sailing-ship travel.

What had really happened? What were and are the preconditions for up-to-date training aboard a sailing school-ship? How many large sailing ships still exist, and to whom do they belong? Research into these topics ultimately transformed someone who at first had been merely curious into a true "ship lover," as the English so accurately express it.

First there arose a short list of a handful of sailing school-ships, but hardly containing more than the usual information.

A number of specialized books were at my disposal, but the larger the number of books, the larger the number of inconsistencies and contradictions I encountered. This was especially the case with respect to the dimensions and the question of whether a particular ship was still in existence and to whom it belonged. Only the ship's current owner could really help with these questions. The first letter with a premade questionnaire was sent to the famous frigate *Constitution* in Boston. Barely ten days had gone by when the reply came. It contained more photographic material and information than I had requested. Similar responses occurred almost regularly. This encouraged me, especially since as time passed direct contacts arose all over the world. Often all I knew by way of an address was the name of the ship and its home port. Through contacts I acquired details about other ships of which previously only the names had been known. One day a response came from South America that asked when and where the finished "book" would available.

This new idea (no one had thought about a book up to this point) got the ball rolling. The material at hand was appropriate for this purpose. In the case of a few ships, small additions were necessary, but they were not difficult to acquire at this point. As the work continued, countries that had never before provided technical information in such detail for a purpose of this kind offered their assistance. Thus there came about in the course of a few years a descriptive compendium of the last great sailing ships, which at first was arranged only for private use, and indeed in such as manner that the ships could easily be compared with one another. The publishing company adopted this same basic concept, for which I am grateful, and used it to create a book that will certainly answer many open questions.

More than fifty new ships have been included in the expanded and updated tenth edition—ships that have recently been completed as new constructions or whose restorations are finished. A number of large sailing ships have been renamed and now sail under a different flag, such as, for example, the *Regina Katharina* from the Netherlands. She now sails under the name *Sea Pearl* in the waters off the Seychelles.

Other ships were eliminated because they had sunk or been scrapped. A number of ships were sold (for example, the *Winston Churchill* from Great Britain), and it wasn't possible to acquire new data because the owner and home port are unknown. In a case like this, the ship was not included, and we hope that for the eleventh edition of the book we will have more exact information and will once again be able to show the ship.

In the age of the computer, in which information quickly becomes obsolete, the Internet offers the opportunity to provide current information. Descriptions of (large) sailing ships and links to individual home pages can be found, for example, at www.tallship-fan.de, www.ista.co.uk, and www.sta-g.de.

A visit to one of these sites reveals that many ships now have their own home pages. In addition to photos and more exact descriptions of the sailing ships current, route plans are often provided—with the possibility of booking a passage. At some sites there are even job announcements. Large sailing ships can also be located by way of the Internet sites of chartering and shipping companies.

It continues to be the case that technical details about traditional sailing vessels from different sources diverge. The reason for this may lie in the modifications to which older sailing ships are continually subjected, but may also simply lie in calculation errors made in converting from English to metric units.

The Great Sailing Ships

Nowadays, a visit by a great sailing vessel to a port in any country of the world is an event of the first order. Both the print media and television report extensively on it, and even newspapers print stories about the ship and its crew on their back pages. The level of general interest is so high that daily papers report about a sailing ship even when it belongs to a foreign country and even when the visit takes place on another continent. Many of the large school-ships are well known, and their voyages through the world's oceans are followed attentively.

When a large sailing ship makes a stay in a foreign port, the public usually has an opportunity to visit it. An example will demonstrate how enthusiastically people respond to this friendly gesture. When, in the summer of 1963, the newly built Argentinean sailing school-ship *Libertad* visited Europe, 30,000 visitors boarded the ship in the course of her 15-day stay in Hamburg.

Many specialized works about these sailing ships have been published, especially in English. These consist primarily of technical works about the history of the ships, their design, the types of rigging they employ, and the different sails they use, along with analyses of their often very lengthy voyages. Books that

The 4-masted bark Magdalene Vinnen *(launched 1921 at the Krupp-Germania shipyard).*

narrate stories about the glorious epoch of the square-rigged sailing vessels are less common.

What is the source of the strong interest in these ships, which one finds even among people who have seldom or never been able to see a large sailing vessel with their own eyes, much less to see one "in action," that is to say, under sail?

The sail is one of the oldest tools of the human race. In its more than 6000-year history, the sailing ship has evolved in a constant and logical manner to which scarcely any other technical achievement of the human race can compare. Many vehicles have a long his-

tory, for example, the wagon. Yet in the case of the wagon, the propulsive force that was used to keep the vehicle in motion changed constantly. This necessarily led to an erratic development of the technology.

In the case of the sailing ship, the propulsive force, the wind, has remained the same. It is true that shipbuilders and shipyards utilize technological innovations and improved materials, but only with the aim of using the same combination of natural forces to power ever-better, ever-faster ships. In this context the word "fast" is synonymous with the word "elegant," and hence also with the word "beautiful," a fact that is demonstrated by the ships

themselves. There are few other cases in which a tool of such vast dimensions constructed by human beings for motives that are clearly economic has achieved so much beauty and aesthetic charm. This may be one of the main reasons why the fascination of these ships is irresistible and why they are as much in the public eye today as they were in the past.

The great sailing ships had their golden age in the last two decades of the nineteenth century. By that time the epoch of their most beautiful representatives, the clippers, had already passed. The rapid development of the steam engine and the motor soon brought an end to the square-riggers as well. While the power of the machines driving the steam ships was impressive, these newer vessels lacked the visual appeal that had characterized their elegant predecessors. The improvement of the self-propulsion systems was initially thought to be more important than the form of the hull and its superstructure, which were neglected at first. Only more recently has it become clear that the hull of a motor-powered ship can also be beautiful. The performance of these powerful ships depends on the influence of the wind and water, just as is the case with sailing vessels. When these factors are taken into consideration in the design process, aesthetic forms are the necessary result.

Only seven decades ago, there were so many sailing ships in the world's harbors that people spoke of a "forest of masts." These were exclusively cargo and passenger vessels. Combined school-ships and freighters appeared slightly later, but pure school-ships of the kind we have today were virtually unknown. With respect to maritime trade and the functioning of commercial harbors, very little of importance has changed between then and now. Freighters come and go in ever-greater haste, because time is money. But the commodities they carry are for the most part the same as before. Efficient modern facilities stand ready to load and unload ships, reducing to a minimum the length of a freighter's stay in the port.

Naturally, the people who work on the ships have not changed fundamentally. The decisive transformation has not been in the sailor but rather in his equipment, the ship.

Even if there is still an impressive number of square-rigged sailing vessels in the world for us to wonder at, there is really no longer a great wind-powered freighter of the kind that used to rigorously train and shape its crew. The disappearance of the great sailing ships and of the type of men who used to earn their living aboard them has led to the formation of a completely new professional group, at least in the case of the merchant marine. The working conditions that exist for sailors now are in many ways similar to those on land. There is much emphasis on health and other types of benefits the sailors legitimately demand and that make

The full-rigged ship Grossherzogin Elisabeth, the first ship built by the German School-Ship Association (launched 1901 at Tecklenborg/Geestemünde).

life on board reasonably attractive to the seaman.

That is not to say, however, that the old sailing ships in all cases endangered the lives of their crews. On the contrary! Many types of colds and infectious diseases were completely unknown aboard sailing vessels on the high seas. Admittedly, food preservation was a problem in the days before refrigeration.

At the same time as the steam engine and the internal combustion engine developed, private life also started to become increasingly easy and pleasant as a result of improved technology. The mere fact that the development of reliable and punctual means of transportation allowed schedules to be established and maintained brought with it decisive changes in the life of the individual. The modern communications system allows us today to establish connections quickly and easily anywhere in

the world. It is understandable that sea travel in particular made immediate use of the available technological innovations. As a result, the level of risk faced by the seaman in the exercise of his profession has decreased quite significantly. He is now acquainted with the ship's schedule and knows when he will return home. He has a right to vacation time, and it is worth his while to establish a life on land as well as on the ship. His workplace is like a floating engine room with a corresponding workshop. The damp quarters of the old sailing ships, with all their discomforts, have disappeared.

Comfortable, well-lit cabins and berths have taken their place. Modern navigational instruments guarantee a relatively predictable course to the journey. Without these facilities and many other similar amenities, no sailor today would agree to serve aboard a

ship. For this reason, however, the profile of the seaman has changed dramatically. His bond with the vessel is minimal, because the vital, reciprocal relationship between man and ship as we know it from the time of the great sailing ships has almost completely disappeared. Today, machines and reliable automatic systems assist the human beings aboard the ship.

When a seaman enlisted aboard a large sailing freighter, he knew very well that he had to submit to an order not found in any profession on land—even the military, at least in peacetime. The period of service was over when the ship reached its destination, and that could often be more than half a year. Even the strictest regulations and the hardest training served, in the final analysis, to secure the safety of the ship and its crew. Order as an end in itself was a foreign concept aboard these

The 4-masted bark Parma: *The watch laying out on a yard.*

ships. Only when everyone knew his place, when everything was properly prepared, could a sailing maneuver be completed quickly and reliably in all situations, but especially at night.

In spite of the burdens and hardships in comparison to life on land, good ships were always able to find a crew. Especially the fast, ambitious sailing ships had no difficulties in this regard. Aboard one of the large old sailing vessels, all work was done by hand. When it came to handling the sails, this meant that human beings had to have the strength to move gigantic sail areas and yards weighing tons. It is true that these tasks were sometimes made easier with tackles and sometimes with steam winches, but even then a single man could not complete them by himself. Only a community in which everyone knew that success ultimately depended

on him, in which every person could count on every other, was in a position to bring such a ship to life.

In their own way, large sailing ships are living beings. Nothing on them is static; everything demonstrates dynamism. The entire ship functions like a body that can be anatomically dissected. What makes this fascinating is that nothing remains hidden. All of the organs are recognizable. In the centre stands the skeleton of the masts, topmasts, and yards. The extremely diverse system of innumerable ropes and lines, which on the one hand have support functions but primarily serve to transfer the forces on deck to the yards and sails, look like linear filigree. The corporality of a large sailing ship becomes particularly striking when the powerful sailing towers are fully rigged.

Such a complex organism can move forward in a mean-

ingful way only if it is centrally steered. The leadership is supported by the crew, which must dutifully follow and execute all requests and commands. If this is not the case, then the ship and its entire crew will find themselves in grave danger. Through the interaction of man and ship and through the mutual dependence of the crew members, a type of community arose on ships that is unknown elsewhere. The ship served the humans, the humans the ship, and they loved it. They were proud of "their" sailing ship when it rested at the pier following a fast journey and the newspapers reported about the good voyage. Every one of them had played a role in the success.

Most sailing ships were not only identified by their names but also bore lovingly carved figureheads that stood in some relation to those names. These figures gave each ship a face of its own. The seamen were well aware of the uniqueness of their ships. It is remarkable that a tool received this kind of recognition and respect even while it was in use. Usually this occurs from a different perspective than that of the workmen, and only after the object in question has taken on historical significance. The many pictures and models that

captains and sailors painted and crafted likewise demonstrate how closely connected these men were to their ships.

Even with the last two German commercial school-ships, the *Pamir* and the *Passat,* it was still the case that during boat drills the young men were not just supposed to familiarize themselves with the rescue procedures. The captains considered it valuable for the future officers to have the opportunity to see the ship in its full splendor on the open sea. For most of them this was no doubt an unforgettable experience. It was meant to instill a sense of belonging and no doubt had this effect on many of the young men.

Today all of the great windpowered freighters have vanished from the world's oceans. Steamers and motorized ships have eliminated them in the course of a tough competitive struggle. In terms of modern standards for the profitability of seafaring ships, the size of the crew in the classical type of sailing ship was too large relative to the carrying capacity. It was not the sail area that was decisive in determining the size of the crew, however, but rather the number of masts. In many maneuvers, the sails have to be moved as simultaneously as possible so that the ship does not lose too much

The everyday life of a seaman: caulking . . .

maritime space or come into danger. This means, however, that a specific number of seamen are needed for every mast. The largest square-riggers had five masts, but all of them were under 6000 tons gross, which is not a very large carrying capacity in comparison to a motorized freighter. Yet for a 4-masted sailing ship, a crew of 48 men was necessary. If one had wanted to increase the carrying capacity of the ships, the number of masts would have had to have been increased to six or seven. It is true that such ships existed, but for technical and economic reasons they were no longer practical.

Today, motorized ships travel according to schedules that for the most part they are able to keep. Economic competition dictates that commodities must arrive as quickly and punctually as possible. It is true that wind-powered freighters traveled on many routes with astounding regularity. For individual voyages, however, this regularity could not be guaranteed in advance. Lulls and storms had too great an influence on the sailing ship.

Under certain conditions, large sailing ships could operate at a profit even today. Yet the long-term risk is too great. The traditional materials used

to make sails and ropes retain their firmness and elasticity only as long as they are in constant use. If a set of sails is then lost in a storm, the cost of the damage would significantly exceed fifty thousand euros in the case of a large ship. In contrast to a motorized ship, a sailing vessel constantly exposes its most sensitive parts to the destructive influences of wind and weather. Very few shipowners could afford to equip their ships with Perlon rigging and sails made of synthetic fibers.

Of the great sailing ships, today only school-ships and luxury ships still travel the oceans of the world. Some of the last freighters lie in various harbors as museum ships firmly at anchor. It is desirable that at least these ships be saved for the future. Obviously, they must serve some purpose in order to survive. The large spaces under the deck offer sufficient space for the most diverse activities.

The last freight-carrying school-ships of all were the two German four-masted barks the *Pamir* and the *Passat.* In their case an attempt was made to compensate for the substantial maintenance costs through profits made from hauling freight. In the end, the ships could be kept in service only because 40 German shipown-

Keckling the cables on the Passat.

ers created the *Pamir* and *Passat* Foundation and assumed responsibility for the entire enterprise. The tragic loss of the *Pamir* in 1957 then brought the active life of the *Passat* to an end as well.

Pure school-ships have existed within the merchant marine only since the beginning of the twentieth century. The German School-Ship Association was a leader in the training of future generations of officers for the merchant marine. Its first ship, the full-rigged ship *Grossherzogin Elisabeth,* was launched in 1901. She had been built to serve purely as a school-ship. The subsequent sailing ships of the society likewise carried no cargo.

The sailing school-ships found—and find—themselves in a situation completely different from that of the freighters. It makes no difference whether we're talking

about a school-ship of the merchant marine or of the navy. These ships are economically independent. They have a yearly budget at their disposal that is sufficient to cover their regular expenses and that above all makes it possible to keep the ships in an optimal state of operational safety. How often, by contrast, did one of the old freighters come into danger because costs had been cut in the wrong places?

This is the case particularly when it comes to stability. The new ships are able to right themselves from angles of heel of different degrees. This problem is much more difficult to deal with in the case of sailing ships with their tall riggings than in the case of motorized ships. The long lever arms of the masts work much more powerfully against the stabilizing forces in the hull than do the shorter superstructures of a motorized ship. It

. . . and replacing the planks.

The Schulschiff Deutschland *was launched in 1927 as a full-rigged ship.*

used to be that stability was guaranteed by the weight of the load or, in the case of an empty ship, by ballast that could be removed again before the ship was loaded. The modern sailing school-ships are always stable. The necessary ballast consists primarily of reinforced concrete and is firmly embedded in the body of the ship. Thus there is room in the hold itself for training and living rooms.

With this financial backing, it is possible for modern school-ships to replace individual parts much earlier than is necessary. The health of the crew members is the highest priority. This is also the expla-

nation for the extreme rarity of accidents on large sailing ships. Along with this material security, the large number of crewmembers also allows them to keep the ship in the best of shape. Not everyone agrees unconditionally with the need to provide future ship's officers with training on sailing ships. There are always voices that speak against this type of training. Admittedly, the supposed "danger" of this type of training is so minimal that it is hardly mentioned. Instead, the main argument of its opponents is that in the age of modern motorized ships the time aboard a sailing school-ship is obsolete and superflu-

ous. The example that is often used is that in the age of automobiles one does not, after all, use a horse-drawn carriage to practice driving. Derogatory words like "romantic" and "lust for adventure" are often used to drive home the uselessness of this training.

Yet service aboard a large sailing ship is anything but romantic. Precisely when the young men are fulfilling their duties with great enthusiasm they demonstrate that they approach their profession soberly, honestly, and without false pathos. The training to become a seaman does not tolerate stragglers or dreamers. For the well-being of the ship and of his comrades, everyone must engage himself fully with his task from the very beginning. We should note with joy that in our technical and sober world there is still a place for sailing vessels, which in their construction are not only highly practical but also beautiful.

All the arguments against the use of sailing school-ships serve to demonstrate that their opponents have absolutely no idea what is at stake in this type of training. The goal is not for the young men to learn how to operate or pilot a sailing ship. Although most of them are future officers, the point of their being aboard the ship in not even for them to learn how to lead men. The fundamental goal is, first of all, to accustom the young people to integrating themselves into a large community that is living together in a very

small space. In this living and work situation consideration, camaraderie, and helpfulness are so urgently necessary that in a very short time they become second nature to everyone.

That the work high above in the masts and on the yards requires courage, decisiveness, and circumspection is obvious. The communal life on the ship and the daily handling of the sails generate possibilities for building character that are available only on a large sailing ship.

Along with the work in the rigging, most of the other tasks aboard a sailing school-ship also take place on deck. In the process it is possible to gain a much more intimate relationship to weather and sea than would be the case on a motorized ship. An exact knowledge of the elements of nature is still necessary today for the steady handling of a ship, regardless of its size. In recent years serious ship catastrophes have occurred—not in spite of the fact that the ships had the most modern navigational aids at their disposal, but because people chose to rely on these.

In addition to their educational purpose, the large sailing school-ships have an additional use. Almost all of these ships represent their nations during visits to other countries. They do this in a remarkable and enduring manner, and certainly it is better to use a much-admired sailing ship for this purpose than a heavily armed warship.

The Tonnage and Dimensions of Ships

As long as it was necessary for each human being to make his tools himself (and as long as he was in a position to do so), he remained independent of designers, workshops, sale prices, and other economic issues. This was naturally also the case with boats and ships, especially for small hunting vessels. It was not necessary to calculate the size of these ships in any way, not even when they were trading vessels that were built through communal work. The ships met one's own needs.

The intended use, the skill of the builder, and the available material determined the size of the vessel. Even today among some peoples, individual users build their own ships and boats. It wasn't until the emergence of shipyards at which ships were commissioned to be built for pay that a more exact system of measuring size became necessary in order to determine the sale price. If the ship was intended to earn money as a trading vessel it was necessary to determine its cargo-carrying capacity.

Measurements of size became an urgent necessity for modern shipping. The size of a ship determines insurance premiums, canal and port fees, and so on. In busy harbors no berth can be provided if length, width, and draft are not known precisely.

In the course of time different methods of measuring arose, a fact that still causes inaccuracies to occur today. Thus it is often not indicated whether a measurement corresponds to the decimal system or to English units. Measurements of length can also differ because different points of reference are assumed. Hence, for example, the measurement "length over all" of a ship, especially a sailing ship, can have different values in the literature depending on what is meant by this term. And this is the case with a measurement whose very name seems to determine its meaning quite unambiguously.

A very old measurement for the cargo-carrying capacity and thus also, approximately, for the size of the ship was the "tun." This measurement was often used in the Middle Ages. The "ton" (= casket) was at that time purely a measurement of volume. Only later did it evolve into a measure of weight, unfortunately. In the metric system 1000 kilograms make a metric ton (t). The English ton (t, ts; here: "long ton") corresponds to 2240 pounds (lbs) (one pound being equivalent to 453.6 g) = 1016 kilograms. The "ton register" then became an international unit of measure for the volume of ships. It consisted of 100 English cubic feet, which corresponds to 2832 cubic meters.

The possibilities for measuring the size and capacity of a ship are described in detail here.

Ton register: Obsolete unit for the tonnage of a ship: 1 TR = 100 English cubic feet = 2832 cubic meters (Oslo tonnage). Tons register, a measurement of volume, has been replaced by the dimensionless gross register tonnage (GRT).

Tons gross: This value is determined through a measurement of all the spaces below the main deck, plus the superstructures that reach from side to side. This value is then indicated as "tons gross."

Net register tonnage: Formerly, this was the total volume of a ship in tons gross, minus the engine, living, and mechanical rooms. Today the method of measuring is different, and tons gross is an obsolete measurement. The net register tonnage is also measured differently.

Gross register tonnage: With the implementation of the 1969 *International Convention on Tonnage Measurement of Ships* in the year 1982, and following a transition period from 1982 to 1994, gross register tonnage and/or net register tonnage have definitively replaced tons gross as a measurement of tonnage. Gross register tonnage, unlike register tonnage or cubic meters, is a dimensionless number and not a measurement of volume. Nonetheless, it is based on the volume of the ship as measured in cubic meters.

The new value is given by the formula $GT = k \times V$. V is the total volume in cubic meters, k a variable dependent on the size of the ship but lying between 0.22 and 0.32.

The net register tonnage is no longer given by a process of subtracting from the gross register tonnage but rather by a complicated formula in which the holds, the number of passengers, and other factors appear as variables.

Burden: The weight of the cargo that a ship can carry without exceeding its maximum permitted draft.

Load: The volume of the cargo that a ship can carry without exceeding its maximum permitted draft.

Deadweight (tons dead weight, tdw or ts dw): The carrying capacity of a ship including bunkers and supplies. This measurement can be expressed in 1000 kg metric tons (t) or in 1016 kg long tons (ts).

Displacement: The quantity of water displaced by the underwater portion of the ship. In the metric system the displacement is measured in cubic meters, the weight of the displaced water in 1000 kg metric tons (t) or, more often, in 1016 kg long tons (ts).

Ship's weight: The underwater portion of the ship measured in cubic meters (quantity of water displaced), multiplied by the specific weight of the water displaced.

Thames measurement: Formula used primarily for sporting vessels, similar to a formula used by the British admiralty as early as the fourteenth century:

$$\text{Tons TM} = \frac{[(L - W) \times W \times \frac{1}{2} W]}{94}$$

The original formula was:

$$\frac{[\text{Length} \times \text{Width} \times \text{Depth to deck}]}{100}$$

Today, instead of the depth to deck, the half width is used and the product divided by 94.

Warships are almost always measured only in terms of their displacement in long tons. Two values are given, separated by a fraction stroke. The number above the line expresses the displacement of the fully armed ship without fuel, while the number beneath the line expresses the increase in the displacement caused by the bunkered fuel. For warships the displacement is also often indicated in terms of "standard displacement" (ts stdd) as measured in long tons.

Well into the seventeenth century, shipbuilding was a craft that depended solely on the experience and skill of a particular master. Plans were used neither in the design nor in the construction process. Occasionally a model could give the person commissioning the construction of the ship a general idea of its external appearance, but even this was not binding. The final dimensions of a ship could be determined only once it had been built. Gradually, people learned to sketch designs prior to construction. The demands placed on the different types of ships were becoming greater. Eventually, seagoing ships were designed in advance and drawings were made for the shipyard. Shipbuilding had thus become a technical process of the first order. The main point in making designs of the hull was to project the three principal planes:

1. Profile view

2. Half-breadth plan or waterline plan

3. Body plan

Every point and every line of the hull can be determined in this three-dimensional system of coordinates. A milestone in the use of preparatory drawing and designing was the work *Architectura Navalis Mercatoria* by the Swedish shipbuilder Frederik Henrik af Chapman, which appeared in 1768 in Stockholm.

For the design itself as well as for calculating the size of the ship, a number of measurements are extremely important. Additionally, these measurements make it possible to get an idea of the size and approximate shape of a ship. The reference points for these measurements are tied to the lines of the hull and its boundaries. In the case of sailing ships, there is an additional factor, which is that, even disregarding masts and yards, the hull alone does not determine the total size of the ship. The bowsprit and the mizzen boom must also be taken into consideration.

The waterline plan of a ship is developed from the baseline, the bottom of the ship. The waterlines (WL) lay vertically, one above the other. One of these waterlines is the loaded waterline (LWL) or designed waterline (DWL). It is the line or plane at which the ship is designed to float when loaded (or, in the case of a warship, armed). Admittedly, one must take into account that in the case of freight ships the floating waterline does not need to be identical to the DWL. The specific weight of the water varies depending on the salt content and the temperature, and the ship's draft and its floating waterline vary with it.

Vertical lines drawn perpendicular to the baseline produce the body plan. In the case of a large sailing ship with a vertical sternpost, the aft edge of the sternpost lies on the first cross section; in the case of ships with engines the forward edge of the sternpost is used. The foremost and hence last of these numerous cross sections cuts across the stem at the DWL. Thus two vertical lines are established on the baseline, known as the perpendiculars—more precisely, the fore and aft perpendiculars. The distance between these two lines is the "distance between perpendiculars," one of the main values used in determining the dimensions of a ship.

In the case of smaller ships on which the sternpost does not stand straight perpendicular to the baseline, the aft perpendicular cuts across the sternpost at the DWL. The shape and length of the rudder blade is not considered when measuring the length between perpendiculars. If the measurement "length of the waterline" is given, then in many cases this means that the rudder blade has been included in the measurement.

The measurement "length hull" gives the length of the hull as measured from the bow ornamentation and/or figurehead to the stern railing. This is often referred to as the "length overall." In the case of sailing ships, however, this value must not be confused with the total length of the ship, from the end of the jibboom and/or bowsprit to the end of the mizzen boom or, if it does not rise above the body of the ship, the stern railing.

The "greatest width" indicates the total width of the hull. It is measured by way of the planks. On old sailing warships the greatest width usually lay at half the depth to deck, because the body of the ship was sharply tapered upwards toward the bulwark. This made it possible to defend against boarding and to keep the guns in action in battles when one found oneself side by side with an enemy ship.

"Depth to deck" is measured at the ship's midpoint. It measures the distance from the lower edge of the hull (in the case of steel ships) or from the outer edge of the keel rabbet (in the case of wooden ships) to the upper edge of the deck beams of the uppermost continuous deck. The "depth in hold" indicates the height of the ship's usable interior spaces. It is measured from the upper edge of the floor plate to the upper edge of the uppermost deck beams midships. In the case of old warships with multiple decks, the "depth in hold" indicates only the height of the lowermost open interior space, the height between the floor plate and the upper edge of the deck beams of the lowermost deck.

The "draft" of a ship is the distance of the floating waterline from the lower edge of the keel. On larger ships there are draft marks on the sternpost and stem. Roman numerals are used to indicate the value in decimeters or English feet.

Types of Sailing Ships

In this short description of the individual types of sailing ships, only those basic types were taken into consideration that can still be found today and that are represented in this book.

Square-rigged ships are distinguished by the number of masts and by the way in which the yards are distributed. The 3-masted full-rigged ship or full-rigged ship became the classic form. On this type of ship all three masts are "fully" rigged; every mast carries a full set of square sails. This type of ship became so synonymous with large sailing ships that in the English language the word "ship" is simply used for it. Larger types were the 4-masted full-rigged ship, and the largest full-rigger ever built was the 5-masted *Preussen* at 5081 tons gross.

Because the size of the crew for a full-rigger always had to be very large in relation to the profitability of the ship, shipping companies preferred the bark for commercial trade. On a bark, the last mast, the mizzenmast, set exclusively fore and aft sails, usually gaff-sails that can be operated by a small number of men while the ship is maneuvering. In addition, another advantage of the bark is that a bark, because of the sails on the mizzenmast, is easier to steer. During steering and steadying, they play a role similar to that of the side rudder on an aircraft.

The navy did not need to settle for limitations in terms of the number of sails. The crews were always large enough to operate full-rigged ships (*Constitution; Victory*).

In addition to the 3-masted barks for which the name "bark" is used, it was primarily the 4-masted barks that at the end of the nineteenth century promoted world trade and forged close connections among the continents. The "Flying P-Liners" of the Hamburg shipping company Ferdinand Laeisz played a large role in this process. The last representative of this type of ship in German possession is the 4-masted bark *Passat,* which today lies moored at Travemünde.

The largest sailing ship ever built was the 5-masted bark *France II,* which measured 5633 tons gross, belonging to the shipping company of Antonin Dominique Bordes in Bordeaux.

If a sailing ship has a full-rigged foremast and at least 2 additional masts with fore-and-aft sails, it is described as a barkentine or a schooner bark.

Four-masted barkentines were rare, but nonetheless there were even 6-masted barkentines, such as the *E.R. Sterling* (1883). This unwieldy rig deprived the ships of elegance, however. The 2-masted brig was one of the smaller square-rigged sailing ships on which the 2 masts were fully rigged. If only the foremast is fully rigged, one speaks of a brigantine or a schooner brig. Unfortunately, the elegant brigs have largely vanished from the world's oceans.

In addition to the square-rigged sailing ships, the schooners were the second largest group of large sailing vessels. A common feature of all schooners is the presence of fore-and-aft sails on every mast. These can be gaff-sails, staysails, or Bermuda sails. The most basic type of schooner is a 2-masted vessel on which the larger mast stands aft and sets the mainsail.

In order to make better use of following winds, some schooners set square sails rather than fore-and-aft topsails on the foremast, although these square sails are also called topsails in this case. These ships are then called square-rigged schooners or topsail schooners. The main difference between a square-rigged schooner and a barkentine or schooner bark is the fact that the barkentine has no fore-and-aft sails on its foremast. This sail, when on the foremast of a schooner, is called a schooner sail.

The corresponding sails on the other masts are named after the name of the mast, thus, for example, mainsails and mizzen sails. The largest fore-and-aft schooner ever built was the 7-masted *Thomas W. Lawson* at 5218 tons gross, which was operated by 16 men. It is an important advantage of schooners that even when there is a large sail area, only a small crew is needed to operate the sails, because almost everything can be accessed from on deck. This fact was of great importance for the profitability of trading vessels. Modern sailing school-ships are almost all square-rigged, however, because the size of the crew plays no role and because for training and educational purposes as many work places as possible should be available. A square foresail is often used as an additional square sail on the various schooners. It is then usually deeper cut than a normal foresail.

Staysail schooners have staysails only on the lower stays, and usually with a boom. In the triangular space between the lower stay and the mast in front of it trysails are set. A notable rigging peculiarity can be observed in the case of the Polish 3-masted staysail schooner *Zawisza Czarny.* Each of the trysails stands between two bent gaffs. Thus these sails get an optimal curvature. This type of rig is referred to as a "wishbone rig" because it was probably used by the former Brazilian navy school-ship *Albatross* (formerly the *Wishbone*). The idea originated in the United States.

On a ketch, the smaller mast, the mizzenmast, stands aft. In order to supplement the descriptions of the individual types of ships, a specific ship shown in the book is indicated below, the picture of which shows the main characteristics of the type of ship in question particularly clearly.

Full-rigged ship: *Georg Stage*
Four-masted bark: *Kruzenshtern*
Bark: *Gorch Fock*
4-masted barkentine: *Esmeralda*
3-masted barkentine: *Palinuro*
Brig: *Royalist*
Brigantine: *Greif*
4-masted topsail schooner: *Juan Sebastian de Elcano*
3-masted topsail schooner: *Eugene Eugenides*
Topsail schooner: *La Belle Poule*
3-masted Bermuda schooner: *Álva*
3-masted fore-and-aft schooner: *Belle Espoir*
Fore-and-aft schooner: *Falken*
3-masted staysail schooner: *Zawisza Czarny*
Ketsch: *Seute Deern II*
Lateen sail: *Mayflower II*

The Rig

The oldest known representation of a sailing vessel comes from the fourth century B.C.; it is located on an Egyptian clay urn. One may safely assume, however, that human beings had already succeeded much earlier in harnessing the wind to power their boats or rafts. Observations of floating objects being pushed along by the wind probably led to the construction of wind-catching devices based on this principle. They were most certainly not sails in our sense. But branches with many leaves, large leaves, skins, or mats were probably adequate for the initial requirements. These simple vessels sailed in front of the wind, that is to say, with the wind at their backs. In the course of time it then became possible, by changing the position of the sail, to make use of wind from the sides.

The prototype of the sail is the square sail that is attached to a spar that is hung horizontally, perpendicular to the long axis of the ship. In this basic position it offers a large area of resistance to the wind, such that the ship is easily driven forward when the wind blows aft.

By modifying the position of the sails, it is also possible to sail when the wind is blowing from the side in back or from the side in front. Until approximately the middle of the fifth century A.D. all ships sailed with square sails. This type of sail was found on ships from northern lands as well as on the ships of the Egyptian queen Hatshepsut, the dromons of the Phoenicians, the Greek triremes, and the Roman war and trading ships. Warships to a large extent did without sails during battles, because the ships were much faster and more maneuverable when driven with oars.

While the further development of shipbuilding techniques in the northern lands is for the most part well known, almost nothing is known about shipbuilding techniques in the Mediterranean from the fifth to the ninth centuries A.D. Hence it is all the more astounding that from this period on representations appear in this region in which a completely new type of sail can be seen—the lateen sail. This type of sail undoubtedly originated in the Mediterranean region, but it is not known who invented it. In contrast to the square sail, the lateen sail has a triangular shape. It is attached to a sloping spar that runs parallel to the length axis of the ship. The lateen sail was the first fore-and-aft sail, and from it evolved all sails that are set parallel to the length axis of the sip. Classic examples of lateen rigging are the galleys and the galleasses of the fifteenth and sixteenth centuries, Columbus's caravels as well as

Lateen Sail

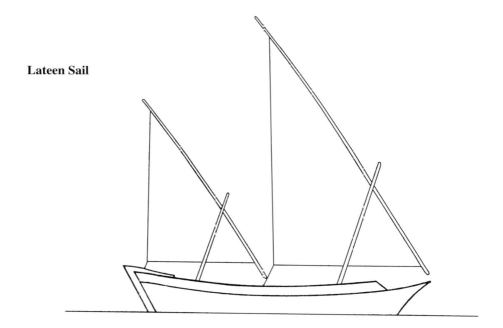

the large Arab dhows that still exist today.

From the fourteenth century on, the square sail reasserts itself in the Mediterranean as well. At the end of this century both types of sails were combined in the north as in the south, and indeed always in such a manner that the forward masts carried square sails and the rear masts lateen sails. At the beginning of the fifteenth century this rigging was standard everywhere.

The Netherlands developed into the most important seafaring nation in the sixteenth century. Here the most renowned shipbuilders of the period ushered in an extraordinary high point in the history of ship construction. One of the most important innovations in the rigging of ships was the invention of the staysail, which was originally set only as a forestaysail on the forestay, but gradually started to appear on the stays and the topmast stays of the other masts as well. The jib likewise belongs to this group. Starting in approximately 1660, all large sailing ships had staysails.

Gaff-sails have been in use since the middle of the seventeenth century. Here the sail is attached to a spar, the foot of which touches the mast. In order to secure the position of the spar, its end is forked, which caused the spar to be called a "gaff." Already in the seventeenth century, gaff-sails had become the primary sails of fast ships, especially yachts. Sailing ships rigged in this way could be brought close to the wind, and hence they became largely independent of the direction of the wind.

Along with the numerous fore-and-aft schooners with multiple masts engaged in trade during the nineteenth and into the twentieth century, almost all sporting vessels at the beginning of the twentieth century made use of gaff-sails. Since then, however, the gaff-less jib-headed or Bermuda sail has achieved almost exclusive dominance among sporting vessels. Nonetheless ships can still be found on all the world's oceans that still make use of every type of rig ever developed.

Because the size of the ships grew constantly as time went on, the sail area also had to become larger. Even on ships with multiple masts, the square sails became so large that when the weather was bad they could only be operated with great difficulty. Many opportunities for reefing and also the strips of sail that could be attached to the feet of the square sails (laced studding sails) no longer sufficed to deal with these difficulties. Additional square sails had to be introduced. Columbus's *Santa Maria* is one of the first ships of which we know for certain that it had a topsail above the mainsail.

The tower of sails continued to grow. The topsail was followed by the topgallant, and in the second half of the eighteenth century the first royals appeared. Finally, the introduction of the skysail came in the nineteenth century and, in isolated cases, moon-sails, although these hardly served a practical purpose any longer. In the 1860s the topsail was divided into a lower and an upper topsail, and shortly after, the topgallants were similarly divided. A full-rigged mast could hence have, in the most extreme case: a foresail, lower and upper topsails, lower and upper topgallants, a royal, a skysail, and a moon-sail. Certainly, studding sails have also been in use just as long as staysails. These are square sails on spars that can be moved to either side of the respective yard. They were used especially in areas where there was little wind. Warships, which during an attack or while fleeing had to make use of every little breeze, almost always used studding sails.

Ketch

1. Jib
2. Forestaysail
3. Mainsail
4. Main gaff-topsail
5. Mizzen sail
6. Mizzen gaff-topsail

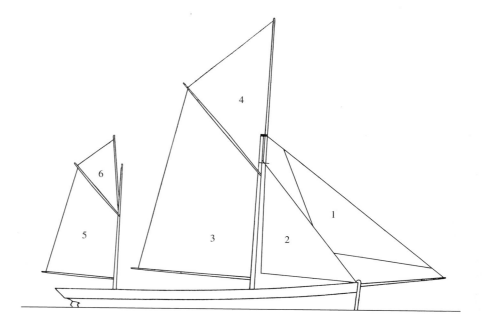

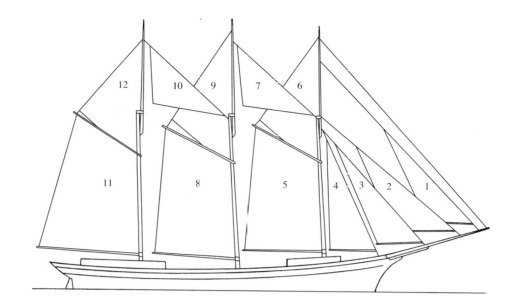

3-Masted Schooner

1 Middle staysail (flying jib)
2 Outer jib
3 Inner jib
4 Forestaysail
5 Foresail
6 Fore gaff-topsail
7 Main-topmast staysail
8 Mainsail
9 Main gaff-topsail
10 Mizzen-topmast staysail
11 Mizzen sail
12 Mizzen gaff-topsail

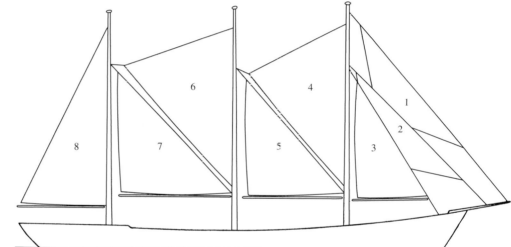

3-Masted Staysail Schooner

1 Jib topsail
2 Jib sail
3 Forestaysail
4 Foretrysail
5 Main staysail
6 Main trysail
7 Mizzen staysail
8 Mizzen sail

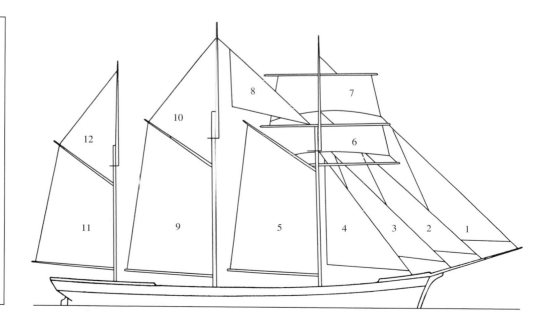

3-Masted Topsail Schooner

1 Middle staysail (flying jib)
2 Outer jib
3 Inner jib
4 Forestaysail
5 Fore lower topsail
6 Fore upper topsail
7 Fore upper topsail
8 Main-topmast staysail
9 Mainsail
10 Main gaff-topsail
11 Mizzen sail
12 Mizzen gaff-topsail

Brigantine

1 Middle staysail (flying jib)
2 Outer jib
3 Inner jib
4 Fore-topmast staysail
5 Forestaysail
6 Foresail
7 Fore lower topsail
8 Fore upper topsail
9 Fore topgallant
10 Fore-royal
11 Main staysail
12 Lower main-topmast staysail
13 Upper main-topmast sail
14 Main-topgallant staysail
15 Mainsail
16 Main gaff-topsail

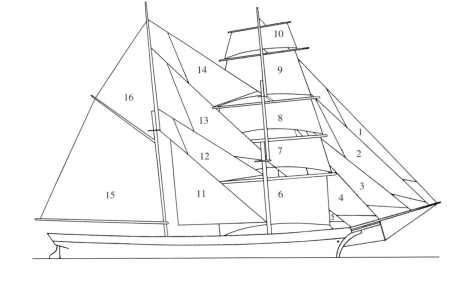

Brig

1 Middle staysail (flying jib)
2 Outer jib
3 Inner jib
4 Fore-topmast staysail
5 Foresail
6 Fore lower topsail
7 Fore upper topsail
8 Fore topgallant
9 Fore-royal
10 Main-topmast staysail
11 Main-topgallant staysail
12 Main-royal staysail
13 Mainsail
14 Main lower topsail
15 Main upper topsail
16 Main topgallant
17 Main royal
18 Trysail

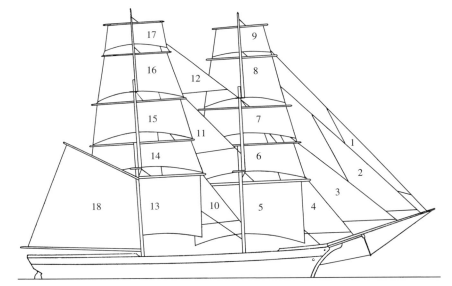

Barkentine

1 Middle staysail (flying jib)
2 Outer jib
3 Inner jib
4 Fore-topmast staysail
5 Foresail
6 Fore lower topsail
7 Fore upper topsail
8 Fore lower topgallant
9 Fore upper topgallant
10 Main staysail
11 Main-topmast staysail
12 Main-topgallant staysail
13 Mainsail
14 Main gaff-topsail
15 Mizzen-topmast staysail
16 Mizzen staysail
17 Mizzen gaff-topsail
18 Topmast staysail
19 Mizzen sail
20 Gaff-topsail

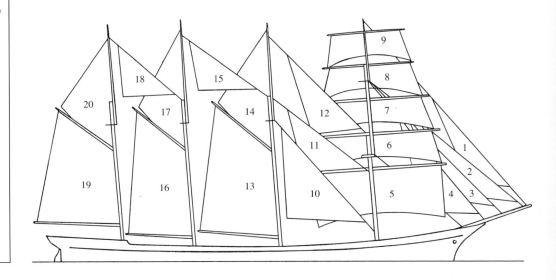

Bark

1 Middle staysail (flying jib)
2 Outer jib
3 Inner jib
4 Fore-topmast staysail
5 Foresail
6 Fore lower topsail
7 Fore upper topsail
8 Fore-topgallant
9 Fore-royal
10 Main-topmast staysail
11 Main-topgallant staysail
12 Main-royal staysail
13 Mainsail
14 Main lower topsail
15 Main upper topsail
16 Main topgallant
17 Main royal
18 Mizzen staysail
19 Mizzen-topmast staysail
20 Mizzen-topgallant staysail
21 Lower mizzen sail
22 Upper mizzen sail
23 Gaff-topsail

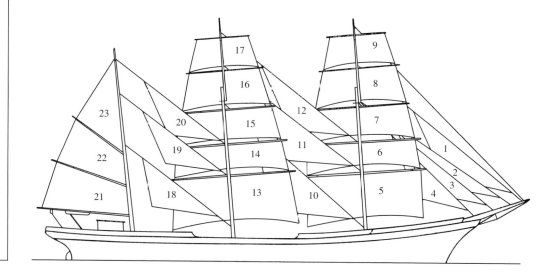

Full-Rigged Ship (ideal rigging)

1 Middle staysail (flying jib)
2 Outer jib
3 Inner jib
4 Fore-topmast staysail
5 Forestaysail
6 Foresail
7 Fore lower topsail
8 Fore upper topsail
9 Fore-topgallant
10 Fore-royal
11 Main staysail
12 Main-topmast staysail
13 Main-topgallant staysail
14 Main-royal staysail
15 Mainsail
16 Main lower topsail
17 Main upper topsail
18 Main topgallant
19 Main royal
20 Main skysail
21 Main spencer
22 Lower mizzen-topmast staysail
23 Upper mizzen-topmast staysail
24 Mizzen-topgallant staysail
25 Mizzen-royal staysail
26 Crossjack
27 Mizzen lower topsail
28 Mizzen upper topsail
29 Mizzen topgallant
30 Mizzen royal
31 Mizzen sail

Full-Rigged Ship (*Christian Radich*)

1 Middle staysail (flying jib)
2 Outer jib
3 Inner jib
4 Fore-topmast staysail
5 Foresail
6 Fore lower topsail
7 Fore upper topsail
8 Fore-topgallant
9 Fore-royal

10 Main-topmast staysail
11 Main-topgallant staysail
12 Main-royal staysail
13 Mainsail
14 Main lower topsail
15 Main upper topsail
16 Main topgallant

17 Main royal
18 Mizzen-topmast staysail
19 Mizzen-topgallant staysail
20 Mizzen-royal staysail
21 Mizzen lower topsail
22 Mizzen upper topsail
23 Mizzen topgallant
24 Mizzen royal
25 Mizzen sail

a Bowsprit
b Figurehead
c Bow
d Rudder
e Stern
f Taffrail

g Backstays
h Shrouds
i Stay
k Foremast
l Mainmast
m Mizzenmast

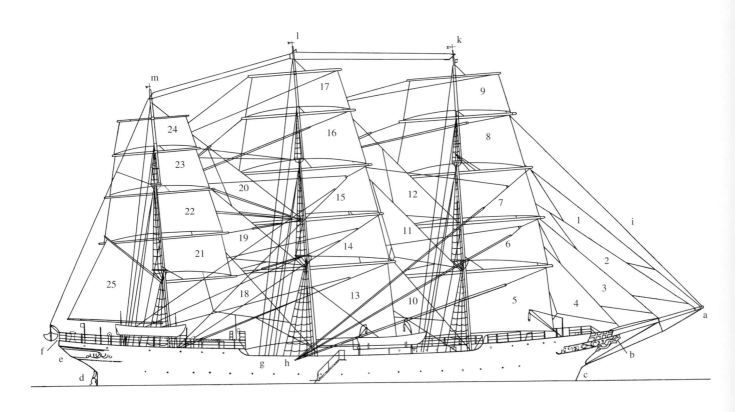

Argentina

Libertad   Presidente   Uruguay
                  Sarmiento

Libertad

Type: full-rigged ship, steel

Nation: Argentina

Owner: battle fleet, Argentinean navy

Home port: Buenos Aires

Years of construction: 1953–56; keel laid December 11, 1953; launched May 30, 1956.

Commissioned: May 28, 1960

Shipyard: A.F.N.E Astilleros Navales (Argentinean state shipyard), Rio Santiago

Tonnage: $\frac{3765}{2740}$ ts displacement

Dimensions:
Length overall: 103.00 m
Length of hull: 91.75 m
Length between perpendiculars: 80.00 m
Width: 13.80 m
Draft: 6.65 m

Sail area: 2643 square meters

Rigging: 27 sails; 5 foresails; double topsail, single topgallant, royals

Masts: all masts with one topmast; height of foremast: 48.66 meters; mainmast: 49.80 meters; jigger mast: 43.17 meters

Auxiliary engine: two Sulzer diesel motors, 1200 horsepower each;

both engines drive a single shaft by way of a Vulcan hydraulic coupling; speed with engine, 13.5 knots

Crew: 351 people in total; 24 officers, 49 cadets, 39 "aspirants" from the maritime mechanical engineering school, 239 petty officers and regular crew members

Use: school-ship under sail

The full name of this remarkable, newly constructed school-ship is *Frigata A.R.A.* (Armada Republica Argentina) *Libertad*. In the summer of 1963 the ship departed from Buenos Aires on her six-month maiden voyage. The major stops on this voyage were San Juan, Bermuda, Lisbon, Le Havre, Hamburg, London, Cadiz, and Dakar. During the ship's 15-day stop in Hamburg, approximately 30,000 visitors came aboard.

The *Libertad* was adapted to the modern requirements of training aboard a school-ship. She has a flush deck and, between the foremast and the mainmast, a bridge with wings similar to that of a motorized ship. The smokestack stands between the mainmast and the mizzenmast. In addition to her main engines, the ship has two 500-kilowatt, 380-volt generators, and one 85-kilowatt, 300-volt auxiliary gen-erator.

The following boats are found on board: two wooden jollyboats with one metal double cabin (equipped with a 4-cylinder, 400-horsepower Thornycroft engine; each boat can carry 15 men); a wooden loading jollyboat with a 4-cylinder, 400-horsepower Thornycroft engine (which can carry 30 men); a boat with sails and oars; and a boat with sails only. Naturally, the ship also carries automatic life rafts.

Because the sails are not very deep cut, they do not billow very much in the wind; for this reason, and because the 3 masts on the long hull stand far apart, baggywrinkle on the stays is not necessary to pre-vent chafing. Originally, the coat of arms of the Argentinean navy was the ship's only ornamentation. Later a figurehead depicting a female figure was added.

The *Libertad* has continuously proven herself to be a fast sailing vessel. On a voyage in 1966, a top speed of 18.5 knots was logged. In 1976, during the opening regatta of the U.S. Bicentennial Tall Ships Race to New York, she had a spectacular collision with the Spanish ship *Sebastian de Elcano*.

Presidente Sarmiento

State-owned school-ships not only train future naval officers but are also responsible to an especially high degree for representing their states abroad. This task of "showing the flag" makes such ships into ambassadors for their nations. Very few school-ships of this type have done this as intensively and as long as the Argentinean *Presidente Sarmiento* during her 63 years of active service. When she arrived in a foreign port, emperors, kings, and presidents were guests on board. She was present at the coronations of Edward VII,

George V of England, and Alfons XIII of Spain, as well as at the inaugurations of Presidents Taft of the United States, Alessandri of Chile, and Alvaro de Obregon of Mexico.

In the year 1894 the Argentinean naval captain D. Martin Rivadavia proposed to the government and the president that Argentina have a modern sailing school-ship built for its naval officer candidates. A sailing ship had already been used for this purpose from 1884 to 1891, namely the corvette *La Argentina,* which had been built in Trieste. Ad-

Type: full-rigged ship (frigate), steel	Width: 13.32 m Depth to deck: 7.32 m
Nation: Argentina	Sail area: 3358 square meters (with studding sails)
Owner: battle fleet, naval museum ship (Buque-Museo Fragata A.R.A. Presidente Sarmiento)	Rigging: 23 sails, plus 12 studding sails; 4 foresails; typical naval rig; single topsails (set very deep); single topgallants; royals on the fore- and mainmasts; instead of topmast staysails gaff-sails (spencers) without a boom
Home port: Buenos Aires	
Year of construction: 1897; launched August 31, 1897; commissioned July 20, 1898	
Shipyard: Camell Laird, Birkenhead (near Liverpool, England)	Masts and spars: height of mainmast over the deck: 49.80 meters; bowsprit with jibboom and outer jibboom
Tonnage: 2750 ts displacement	Auxiliary engine: steam engine, 4 boilers, 2800 horsepower; speed with engine, 15 knots
Dimensions: Length overall: 85.05 m Length of hull: 76.50 m Length between perpendiculars: 72.60 m	Crew: up to 400 people when under sail Use: museum ship

mittedly, this ship had made only 5 voyages during that period. In keeping with a decision by the president, Luis Sáenz Peña, a commission of naval officers was formed in 1895 to organize the construction of a new sailing school-

ship. An English shipyard was commissioned to carry out the construction work. The ship received the name of President D. Domingo Faustino Sarmiento (February 13, 1811, to September 12, 1888, president from 1868 to 1874). This president had been a particularly strong advocate for the officer candidates and was also the founder of the naval academy. After his death, the largest ship in the fleet, the cruiser *Los Andes,* was supposed to receive his name. Instead, it was given to the new school-ship. The *Presidente Sarmiento* is a large steam corvette like those of the nineteenth century. The stern gallery, which can be accessed only by way of the officers' living quarters, is particularly typical of this kind of ship. Also characteristic are the baroque bow and stern ornaments. In order to house the large crew, the poop was ex-

tended all the way to the ship's middle. The forecastle was also lengthened and reaches past the foremast. The hull is made of steel but is covered with a layer of teakwood, which on the underwater portion is in turn covered with a layer of copper to protect against teredo. One of the torpedo tubes opens in the stem, just above the waterline. On July 20, 1898, the Argentinean flag was raised for the first time on board. Lieutenant D. Enrique Thorne had the command during the voyage to Argentina. On September 10, 1898, the *Presidente Sarmiento* arrived in Buenos Aires.

The first long voyage lasted

from January 12, 1899, to September 30, 1900. It followed a route of 49,500 nautical miles around the world. The frigate captain D. Onofre Betbeder had the command at that time. As of December 1938, the ship had made 37 long voyages with a total length of 576,770 nautical miles. During this period more than 1500 officer cadets were trained on board. Each year the cadets in their last year at the naval academy came aboard the sailing ship. In 1938 the *Presidente Sarmiento*'s first period of service as a school-ship came to an end. From that time on, with the exception of two long voyages, only shorter

training cruises were undertaken. In addition to the officer cadets, regular sailors were also trained on board. On January 26, 1961, the ship was retired from active training service. She had logged a total of 1.1 million nautical miles. Her successors today are the full-rigged ship *A.R.A. Libertad* and the cruiser *La Argentina.* Today the *Presidente Sarmiento,* a national and cultural memorial, lies in the harbor of Buenos Aires. Not without reason, she is considered a *reliquia histórica* of the Argentinean people.

Uruguay

Type: corvette (rigged as a bark)	Dimensions: Length overall: 46.36 m Width: 7.63 m Depth to deck: 5.40 m Draft: 3.50 m
Nation: Argentina	
Owner: battle fleet, maritime museum ship	Auxiliary engine: steam engine (2 boilers), 475 horsepower
Home port: Buenos Aires, Puerto Madero	Armaments: four 7-inch guns on iron mounts
Year of construction: 1873	
Shipyard: Laird, Birkenhead, England	Crew: 14 officers, 100 petty officers and regular crew members
Tonnage: 550 ts displacement	Use: museum ship

The *Uruguay* became famous because of the rescues of the Swedish Nordenskjöld expedition (Otto Nordenskjöld) in the year 1903. This expedition had departed in 1901 aboard the converted whaling ship *Antarctic* (formerly the *Cap Nor*) with the goal of investigating the geology of the

southwestern region of the South Shetland Islands. The *Antarctic* was lost in the ice on February 12, 1902. The *Uruguay,* which had rushed to help, brought all of the members of the expedition back to the Falkland Islands after they had, spectacularly, passed the winter in separate camps. The

Uruguay served as a survey ship until 1930. After her retirement, the Argentinean navy used her as a depot ship. Since about 1982 the bark has been moored without an engine in Buenos Aires as a museum ship. She is cared for by the Argentinean navy. A special exhibit in the ship commemo-

rates the rescue in the icy southern sea. A unique feature of the ship is the iron hull planked with teakwood, in addition to which the underwater portion is covered with zinc plates.

Alma Doepel
Amity
Bounty III
Challenge of
    Outward Bound
Duyfken
Endeavour
Enterprize

Falie
Golden Plover
James Craig
Lady Nelson
Leeuwin
One and All
Our Svanen
Polly Woodside

Solway Lass
South Passage
Sovereign
    of the Seas
Spirit of the Pacific
Windeward Bound
Young Endeavour

Alma Doepel

Type: 3-masted topsail
schooner, wood

Nation: Australia

Owner: Sail & Adventure, Ltd.,
Victoria

Home port: Hobart

Year of construction: 1903;
launched October 10, 1903

Shipyard: Bellingen N.S.W.

Tonnage: 150.69 tons gross

Dimensions:
Length overall: 45.20 m
Length of hull: 35.90 m
Length between
perpendiculars: 31.60 m
Width: 8.00 m
Depth in hold: 2.30 m
Depth to deck: 2.50 m
Draft: 2.20 m

Sail area: 557 square meters

Rigging: 10 sails; no square
foresail

Masts: height of mainmast
over the deck: 31 meters

Auxiliary engine: LC3 Gardner
diesel, 247 horsepower

Crew: 11 persons, 40 cadets

Use: sailing school-ship

The *Alma Doepel,* which was named after the daughter of its builder, Frederick Doepel, was Australia's last cargo-carrying square-rigger. By means of a centerboard attached fore and aft, the relatively shallow-going ship could also cruise through the shoals of coastal waters. As a freighter she received a great deal of attention for her record-breaking voyages.

In 1917 the schooner was sold to the Henry Jones, Ltd., marmalade factory. As a member of the "mosquito fleet," she continued to make fast voyages between Hobart, Tasmania, and the Australian continent. In 1937 the ship was unrigged, and after 1947 she was put into service by the American army as an AK 82 for the Australian army in New Guinea.

After the war the ship was rerigged as a pole-masted schooner. The *Alma Doepel* once again sailed the route between Tasmania and Melbourne as a freighter. In the 1960s she transported limestone between Southport and Electrona, Tasmania. In 1976 she was lying there unused when Sail & Adventure, Ltd., purchased her in order to restore her and employ her for its purposes. The conversion work was all-encompassing; even a new keel was installed.

Today the ship is available as a training ship to the youth of Australia (boys and girls), providing all the benefits that a sailing ship can without emphasizing the training of professional seamen.

Amity

Type: brig, reproduction, wood

Nation: Australia

Owner: city of Albany, Western Australia

Home port: Albany

Year of construction: 1976

Shipyard: built on her dry berth

Tonnage: 100 ts displacement; 142 tons gross

Dimensions:
Length overall: 35.30 m
Length of hull: 24.30 m
Length between perpendiculars: 22.90 m
Width: 6.50 m
Depth in hold: 3.50 m
Depth to deck: 3.90 m
Draft: 3.30 m

Sail area: 545 square meters

Rigging: 15 sails

Masts: height of mainmast over the deck: 22.80 meters

Crew: originally 8 persons in the active crew

The brig is an authentic reconstruction of a trading vessel of the same name that brought the first British settlers to Western Australia on December 25, 1826. This ship was also used as a research vessel, animal transporter, and whaling vessel. She was lost in a storm north of Tasmania in 1845. The current reconstruction has become a national monument in the region. She was built on a massive stone foundation.

Because the brig is not in the water, special structural factors had to be taken into consideration in the construction of the hull.

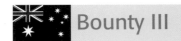

Type: full-rigged ship, wood (steel), reproduction of an eighteenth-century trading vessel

Nation: Australia

Owner: Bruce Reid, Bounty Cruises, Sydney

Home port: Sydney

Years of construction: 1978–79

Shipyard: in Whangarei, New Zealand

Tonnage: 387 ts displacement; 247 tons gross; 168 tons net

Dimensions:
Length overall: 42.00 m
Length of hull: 28.00 m
Length between perpendiculars: 26.00 m
Width: 8.00 m
Depth in hold: 4.60 m
Draft: 3.90 m

Sail area: 743 square meters

Rigging: 18 sails

Auxiliary engine: two Kelvin diesel (8-cylinder turbo), 415 horsepower each

Crew: 14-person active crew

Use: day cruises in the harbor area of Sydney

For the history of the *Bounty*, see also *Bounty II* (USA).

The original *Bounty* was built as a coal transporter with the name *Bethia* on the Humber in northeast England in 1783. The British navy acquired the ship four years later in order to equip her as an expedition ship. The figurehead remained on the ship. It depicted the wife of the first owner, Lady Bethia.

The admiralty feared for the morality of its sailors and sea soldiers, because it was well known that the inhabitants of the South Sea Islands wore little clothing. In order to show the natives how one behaved in "civilized" England, the figurehead was made to wear a chaste riding habit.

The hull of this reconstruction is made of steel but covered with wood above the waterline. The necessary equipment was added for the ship to be used in films. The ship became a floating film studio with all of the relevant technology. With the help of side balance tanks, for example, the ship was able to achieve a stronger angle of heel. In 1986 the *Bounty* was sold to Bounty Voyages, Ltd., Sydney, and registered in England. She was subsequently used in additional films. The ship returned to Tahiti for a se-

ries of documentaries about the voyages of Captain Cook. After taking part in the festivities for Australia's bicentennial, the *Bounty* sailed in Polynesian waters. Captain Bligh-Ware had the command. Exactly 200 years after the infamous mutiny he symbolically handed the ship over to his helmsman, Gerry Christian, a descendant of Fletcher Christian. The current owner acquired the ship in 1991.

Challenge of Outward Bound

Previous name: *Sha Numa*	Dimensions: Length overall: 30.70 m Length of hull: 23.70 m
Type: 3-masted fore-and-aft schooner, wood	Width: 5.30 m Depth to deck: 2.30 m Draft: 2.00 m
Nation: Australia	
Owner: Australian Outward Bound Foundation	Rigging: 5 sails
Home port: Sydney	Masts: height of mainmast over the deck: 16.40 meters
Year of construction: ca. 1974	Auxiliary engine: Detroit diesel, 175 horsepower
Shipyard: in Thailand	
Tonnage: 85 tons gross	Crew: 4-person active crew, 20 trainees
	Use: sailing school-ship

The schooner, with her typical Asiatic hull shape, was built as a fishing vessel. She arrived in Darwin in the early 1980s with one hundred refugees on board.

There she was rigged as a schooner. Since 1993 she has belonged to the Australian Outward Bound Foundation.

Kurt Hahn held the first Outward Bound course in 1941 in Scotland. In addition to training aboard the ship, which serves as a floating classroom, mountain tours with climbing courses are also offered. The courses are divided by age group. Adults are also allowed to participate.

Duyfken

The *Duyfken,* which sails for the Vereinigde Oost-Indische Compagnie (VOC), can claim to be the first European ship to have discovered the Australian coast, in 1606. While searching for a legendary land of gold, Captain Willem Janszoon rounded New Guinea and eventually found the Cape York Peninsula. He drew the first maps of the Australian coastline.

The construction of the *Duyfken* included Latvian oak, which had been brought to Fremantle specifically for this purpose. In keeping with an old Dutch construction method, the planks, which had been bent over steam, were assembled, and only after that were the ribs added. An expert described the construction as a whole as "an exquisite piece of furniture." A red lion decorates the long "beak," and the coat of arms of the city of Fremantle adorns the square stern. The *Duyfken* has proved to be extremely seaworthy.

Type: Dutch yacht (ca. 1600), wood, reproduction

Nation: Australia

Owner: Duyfken 1606 Replica Foundation

Home port: Fremantle, Western Australia

Years of construction: 1997–99; keel laid January 11, 1997; launched January 24, 1999

Shipyard: Western Australian Maritime Museum, Fremantle

Tonnage: 100 ts displacement

Dimensions:
Length overall: 30.60 m
Length of hull (including the "beak"): 25.30 m
Length between perpendiculars: 20.00 m
Width: 2.40 m
Depth in hold: 2.40 m
Depth to deck: 3.20 m
Draft: 2.40 m

Sail area: 290 square meters

Rigging: 6 sails (including sprit sail)

Masts: height of mainmast over the deck: 19.50 meters

Auxiliary engine: two diesel motors, 80 horsepower each

Crew: 20-person active crew, 12 guests

Use: museum ship, chartered ship

Endeavour

Type: full-rigged ship, wood, reproduction of the *Endeavour*, eighteenth century

Nation: Australia

Owner: HM Bark Endeavour Foundation Pty., Ltd.

Home port: Sydney, Australia

Year of construction: keel laid October 1988; launched December 9, 1993; commissioned April 16, 1994

Shipyard: Mews Road, Fremantle

Dimensions:
Length overall: 43.70 m
Length of hull: 30.92 m
Length between perpendiculars: 33.53 m

Width: 9.25 m
Depth in hold: 33.50 m
Depth to deck: 6.39 m
Draft: 3.40 m

Sail area: 1461 square meters, of which the studding sails account for 531 square meters

Rigging: 25 sails, bowsprit with 2 sprit sails

Masts: height of mainmast over the deck: 28 meters

Auxiliary engine: Caterpillar (two of the 3406 B model), 404 horsepower

Crew: 14-person active crew, 32 trainees, 10 guests

Use: sailing museum ship

The ship is a reconstruction of the bark HM *Bark Endeavour*, aboard which James Cook (1728–1779) undertook his famous exploratory voyages between 1758 and 1779. The designation "bark" was the official designation at that time. The ship has the rig of a full-rigged ship.

The original was built in 1764 as a coal ship with the name *Earl of Pembroke* in Whitby, Yorkshire. In 1768 she was purchased by the British admiralty and received the name HM *Bark Endeavour*. In addition to other voyages, Captain James Cook commanded the ship during his voyage around the world from 1768 to

1770. Cook lost his life in Hawaii during an altercation with the natives. His ship ended up as a whaling vessel in Newport, Rhode Island. The reconstruction is charming because of her solid construction and splendid outfitting. As one of the best navigators of his time, Cook would certainly have been enthusiastic about

the navigational aids of our time that are at the disposal of the officers. Following a voyage around Australia with stops in many ports, the *Endeavour* sailed from Fremantle to London in 1996. A voyage around the world was also undertaken at that time.

Today she is a sailing museum ship.

Type: 2-masted topsail schooner, wood

Nation: Australia

Owner: Enterprize Ship Trust, Williamston

Home port: Melbourne

Years of construction: 1991–97; keel laid August 8, 1991; launched August 30, 1997 (completely finished)

Shipyard: Melbourne Maritime Museum (previously Duke & Orrs)

Tonnage: 68 ts displacement

Dimensions:
Length overall: 26.96 m
Length of hull: 16.04 m
Length between perpendiculars: 14.26 m
Width: 6.09 m
Depth in hold: 2.58 m
Depth to deck: 4.36 m
Draft: 2.94 m

Sail area: 185 square meters

Rigging: 10 sails

Masts: height of mainmast over the deck: 15.50 meters

Auxiliary engine: Cummins-diesel, 180 horsepower

Crew: 6-person active crew, 10 trainees

Use: chartered ship

The original *Enterprize* was built in 1829 in the Tasmanian port of Hobart. She belonged to the fleet of coastal sailing ships that transported trading goods along the southern shore of Australia because the system of roads was not very well developed at that time. Once she had 300 sheep on board. In August 1835, she sailed with settlers to the Port Phillip District in order to look for a suitable settlement area there. She discovered the Yarra River and founded a settlement on its banks, out of which the modern city of Melbourne developed. Continuing in the trading business, the ship was wrecked and lost in 1845.

The current *Enterprize* was built in memory of this episode in early Australian history. Exclusively wood taken from demolished wooden structures was used in the construction of the hull. Hence, the jarrah wood, for example, came from a wool warehouse in Fremantle. The ship is unusual in that she was already fully rigged when she was launched. Her main sailing areas are the Port Phillips Bay and the southeastern coast of Australia.

Previous name: *Hollands Frouw*

Type: gaff-ketch, steel

Nation: Australia

Owner: FALIE Project, Ltd.

Home port: Port Adelaide

Year of construction: 1919

Shipyard: Richter uit den bog Aarot, Maassluis, the Netherlands

Tonnage: 244 ts displacement; 227 tons gross; 115 tons net

Dimensions:
Length overall: 45.70 m
Length of hull: 36.50 m
Width: 6.70 m
Draft: 3.10 m

Sail area: 595 square meters

Rigging: 7 sails

Masts: height of mainmast over the deck: 30.10 meters

Auxiliary engine: National 5-cylinder turbo diesel, 250 horsepower

Crew: 9-person active crew, 20 guests

Use: chartered ship

Until 1923, the former freighter sailed European waters. Her new home then became Australia, with her home port at Port Adelaide. Grain, wood, and artificial fertilizer were the main cargoes that the ship transported along the coasts of Australia for 59 years. During World War II the Royal Australian Navy claimed the ship. The *Falie* lay as a guard ship at the entrance to the harbor at Sydney. For a time she served as a supply ship in the waters of New Guinea.

After the war, the ship delivered explosives to all the states on the continent. She was not retired from service as a cargo ship until 1982. The government subsequently purchased the veteran ship. The restoration took two years and was generously supported by private donations.

In 1986 the *Falie* was a flagship at the festivities in honor of South Australia's sesquicentennial. In addition to her use as a cruise ship, the sailing ship is also displayed to the public during visits to many ports.

Golden Plover

In 1910, what is now a brigantine was first built as steam-powered tug that could also carry cargo. For several years she lay sunk in the Maribyrong River in Melbourne. After she was raised, a German family set to work modifying and rerigging her. The *Golden Plover*, as she was called from then on, made a voyage to Europe and after that entered service in England. In 1982 she was put up for sale.

James Craig

Previous name: *Clan Macleod*	Tonnage: 646 register tons
Type: bark, iron	Dimensions: Length: 54.70 m
Nation: Australia	Width: 9.70 m Draft: 5.30 m
Owner: Sydney Maritime Museum	Depth to deck: 5.30 m
Home port: Sydney	Use: museum ship after rerigging
Year of construction: 1874	
Shipyard: Bertram, Haswell & Company, Sunderland, England	

As a wind-powered freighter, this bark was the first of the famous "Clan" sailing ships that Thomas Dunlop had built for himself. For many years she sailed on the world trade routes and had many successful voyages. In 1887, she was acquired by Fa. Russel & Co. in Glasgow. Later the bark found her way to New Zealand, where her new owner rechristened it *James Craig*. In 1912 she became a hulk; due to a shortage in shipping capacity, however, she was once again rigged. In the 1920s it was idle once more. As a coal hulk, she made her way to Hobart, Tasmania, where she eventually ran aground. The ship lay there for more than 30 years, after which she was raised and badly repaired. In 1981, the *James Craig* was towed to Sydney. Now the ship lies in a floating dock in Sydney's Darling Harbor. She is being thoroughly overhauled, restored, and rerigged.

The ship has now been restored to the point that she can sail again.

Lady Nelson

Type: brig, wood

Nation: Tasmania (Australia)

Owner: Tasmanian Sail
Training Association

Home port: Hobart

Years of construction:
1985–87

Shipyard: Ray Kemp,
Woodbridge, Tasmania

Tonnage: 60 ts displacement

Dimensions:
Length overall: 25.76 m
Length of hull: 16.00 m
Width: 5.34 m
Draft: 2.74 m

Rigging: 9 sails

Masts: height of mainmast
over the waterline: 17.45
meters

Auxiliary engine: diesel
engine

Crew: 3-person active crew,
overnight accommodations
for 12–14 trainees, 25–30
trainees on day tours

Use: sailing school-ship
(adventure school-ship)

The modern-day *Lady Nelson* is an exact reproduction of a ship of the same name built in 1798 in Deptford, England. Her small proportions soon earned the brig the nickname "tinderbox." Her small draft, for which a centerboard could compensate, allowed for use in shallow coastal waters and rivers. The admiralty bought the ship in 1799. She made history during the early European exploration and settlement of Australia, Tasmania, and New Zealand. The brig be- came the most important ship in the early history of Australia. Between 1800 and 1825 she took part in numerous enterprises. She was not involved in just exploration, however; she also had settlers and goods on board. She has a unique place in the history of Tasmania. In 1803 and 1804 she sailed from Australia to the large island, in the process entering and exploring rivers.

At that time, the first European settlements, Hobart and Port Dalrymple, were estab- lished on Tasmania. The ship met her end in 1825 off the island of Baba near New Caledonia. The crew was murdered by the natives because of its aggressive behavior. The ship was stranded and burned.

The modern-day *Lady Nelson* is supposed to keep the memory of this history alive while at the same time offering the youth of Tasmania the opportunity to experience the world of sailing.

Leeuwin II

Type: barkentine, steel

Nation: Australia

Owner: Leeuwin Sail Training Foundation, Ltd., Fremantle

Home port: Fremantle

Year of construction: 1986; launched August 2, 1986

Shipyard: Australian Shipbuilding Industries Pty., Ltd., South Coogee, W.A.

Tonnage: 236 tons gross

Dimensions:
Length overall: 55.00 m
Length of hull: 41.50 m

Length between perpendiculars: 33.40 m
Width: 9.00 m
Draft: 3.40 m

Sail area: 810 square meters

Rigging: 14 sails

Masts: height of mainmast: 33 meters

Auxiliary engine: two Detroit NA6, 671, 6-cylinder diesel engines

Crew: 5-person active crew, 8 volunteers, 40 trainees

Use: sailing school-ship

The *Leeuwin* sails for the Sail Training Association of Western Australia. The ship was built upside down, with the keel up. The hull was rotated during the launch. The *Leeuwin* is available to be used by all residents of Western Australia. The only requirements are good health and a minimum age of 16.

The ship got her name from the famous Dutch galleon *Leeuwin* ("Lion"). In 1622 this ship rounded Australia's southwestern cape, which was later named Cape Leeuwin. The "II" in the current name does not refer to this galleon, but rather to a yacht that was already entered under this name in Australia's ships' register. The crew of the Japanese school-ship *Kaisei* was trained aboard this barkentine.

One and All

Primarily schools charter this ship as an educational and training aid. The *One and All* was completed just in time for the 150th anniversary of the first European settlement of Southern Australia. A distinguishing feature of this sailing ship is her almost 13-meter-long bowsprit.

Type: brigantine, wood

Nation: Australia

Owner: Sailing Ship Trust of South Australia

Home port: Port Adelaide

Year of construction: launched December 1, 1985; commissioned April 5, 1987

Shipyard: W. G. Porter & Son, Port Adelaide

Tonnage: 206 tons gross; 36 tons net

Dimensions:
Length overall: 42.60 m
Length of hull: 29.80 m
Length at the waterline: 26.50 m

Width: 8.20 m
Draft, centerboard up: 2.60 m; centerboard down: 3.90 m

Sail area: 451 square meters

Rigging: 12 sails

Masts: height of mainmast over the deck: 27 meters

Auxiliary engine:
Volvo 6-cylinder diesel, 400 horsepower

Crew: 10-person active crew, 29 trainees

Use: sailing school-ship

Our Svanen

Previous names: *Svanen, H. C. Andersen, Pacific, Mathilde*

Type: barkentine, wood

Nation: Australia

Owner: Laurie Kalnin, Sydney

Home port: Sydney

Year of construction: 1922

Shipyard: K. Andersen, Frederikssund, Denmark

Tonnage: 100 tons gross; 250 tdw

Dimensions:
Length overall: 39.60 m
Length of hull: 27.40 m
Width: 7.20 m
Draft: 3.00 m

Sail area: 550 square meters

Auxiliary engine:
250-horsepower Caterpillar diesel engine

Use: passenger cruises

The ship was launched under the name *Mathilde* as a 3-masted fore-and-aft schooner for use in the Baltic trade. Frequent changes of name and ownership followed. The ship received her first engine in 1938. For several years she was employed by the Tuborg Brewery in Copenhagen to transport malt.

The purchase by the Havers, a Canadian married couple, in the early 1970s put an end to her time as a freighter. *Our Svanen,* as the ship was now called, was converted into a barkentine in Denmark and in 1977 registered in Stornoway in the Hebrides. Until 1985 the ship was a privately sponsored school-ship for cadets of both sexes from the Royal Canadian Sea Cadets. After that she was sold to Sail Pacific Charters, Ltd., of Vancouver. The ship took part in the bicentennial Australian First Fleet Re-enactment along with other ships from England and Australia. Following the end of the festivities she was acquired by the Sail Training Association of South Wales as a replacement for its barkentine *New Endeavour,* which had been scrapped in 1987.

For financial reasons Laurie Kalnin, a businessman from Sydney, purchased *Our Svanen* in May 1990 in order to use her for cruises around the harbor in Sydney and to observe whales.

Polly Woodside

Previous names: *Rona, Polly Woodside*

Type: bark, iron

Nation: Australia

Owner: Melbourne Maritime Museum

Location: Graving Dock, Yarra River, Melbourne

Year of construction: 1885

Shipyard: Workman, Clark & Company, Ltd., Belfast

Tonnage: 694 tons gross; 610 tons net

Dimensions:
Length overall: 70.00 m
Length of hull: 61.10 m
Length between perpendiculars: 58.40 m
Width: 9.10 m
Depth to deck: 5.20 m
Depth in hold: 4.90 m

Rigging: 20 sails; probably double topsail, single topgallant, royals

Masts: height of mainmast over the deck: 33.50 meters

Auxiliary engine: none

Crew: 11 to 15 persons (with deck boys)

Use: museum ship

Many large sailing ships could have been preserved to serve as museum pieces without much expense. Nonetheless, economic considerations brought about the demise of almost all wind-powered freighters. At the last minute, ship enthusiasts are now attempting to rescue the few remaining ships—even when all that is left is a mastless hulk, as is the case with the *Polly Woodside.*

Australia, which played such a large role in the heyday of sailing-ship travel, possesses only this *Polly Woodside* as its last large sailing ship. Thus it was not surprising that the plan to restore the ship met with great interest in diverse circles.

The bark was built for the ship owner W. J. Woodside (Bark Polly Woodside Company) in Glasgow. It was said of her that she was the most beautiful vessel ever launched in Belfast. For many years she sailed for her owner as part of the general freight trade. After running aground off New Zealand in the year 1903, she was purchased by the firm A. H. Turnball & Company of New Zealand and rechristened *Rona.* (She got her new name from Miss Rona Munro, whose father was the naval su-

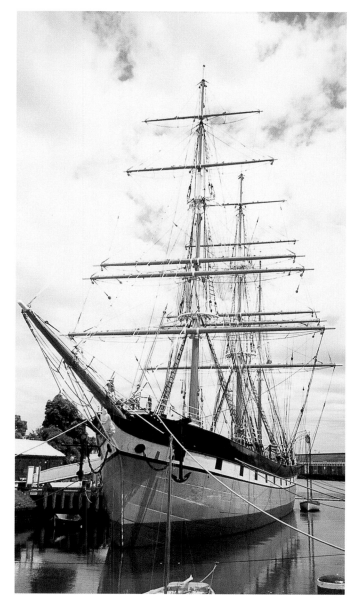

perintendent of the Canterbury Steamship Company, New Zealand). During this period she sailed as a freighter between New Zealand, the Pacific Islands, and Australia. She lost her figurehead and bowsprit in a collision in San Francisco harbor on a voyage to the United States during World War I.

After the war, the shipping firm G. H. Scales of Wellington acquired the bark. In 1921 she was stranded on Barratt's Reef at the entrance to Wellington harbor. Since this accident, the ship has not had any masts.

The Adelaide Steamship Company acquired the ship and used her as a coal-lighter. Her last owners, who likewise used her as a coal ship, were Messrs. Howard Smith, Melbourne. In December 1967, the heads of the firm donated the ship to the National Trust of Australia (Victoria). In the meantime a committee had formed which through its many subcommittees prepared for the ship's restoration. The restoration finally began in 1974, when the *Polly Woodside* entered the dry dock and the first new planks were laid in her deck. Today the rigging procedures have also made great progress. Since Easter 1977 the ship has been open to visitors. The bark cannot leave her current berth because a bridge has been built downstream in the Yarra River.

Solway Lass

A ship that is over 95 years old can look back on a long history. The *Stina,* which was built as a pure sailing ship at German expense and rigged as a ketch, supplied foodstuffs to the island of Helgoland from 1902 to 1905. She undertook trading cruises in the North and Baltic seas until 1913 under the name *Adolf.* At the beginning of World War I the owner lost his ship to the English. Taken as a prize, she was converted into an auxiliary cruiser and deployed to observe submarines.

Between 1919 and 1937 she was once again deployed as a trading ship under the British flag. In 1924 the ship's home was at Solway Firth and the ship was given the name *Solway Lass.* In the meantime a diesel engine had been installed. In 1938 the ship started to sail under the Danish flag.

During World War II the sailing ship was deployed as an icebreaker under German command. An impact with a mine caused her to run aground in shallow water. After the war the ship was once again engaged in commercial trade. Hence she received the names *Bent* and *Sundeved* while under the Danish flag. In 1972 the *Sundeved* was sold to Suva (Fiji Islands). Under the British flag she passed through the Panama Canal and began service as a copra carrier in the South Sea. There she received the new name *Tui-Na-Savu Savu* ("Lord of Savu Savu"). In the meantime she had been rigged as a topsail schooner. In 1983 the current owner acquired the ship. In three years of work she was modified in Sydney for its new use. On November 17, 1985, she was made available for passenger cruises. Today the ship is a gem.

Previous names: *Tui-Na Savu Savu, Lawedua, Sundeved, Bent, Solway Lass, Adolf, Stina*

Type: 2-masted topsail schooner, steel

Nation: Australia

Owner: Tim & Jillian Lloyd, Sydney (Matilda Cruises)

Home port: Sydney

Year of construction: 1902

Shipyard: Bodewes Shipyard, Martenshoek, the Netherlands

Tonnage: 115 ts displacement; 104 tons gross

Dimensions:
Length overall: 38.00 m

Length of hull: 31.90 m
Width: 5.92 m
Draft: 2.50 m

Sail area: 510 square meters

Rigging: 10 sails; foremast with topsail and topgallant

Masts: height of mainmast over the deck: 27 meters

Auxiliary engine: Caterpillar 3306, 6-cylinder diesel, 189 horsepower

Crew: 5-person active crew, up to 60 guests

Use: chartered ship for fine dining in the harbor area of Sydney

South Passage

Type: 2-masted fore-and-aft schooner, aluminum

Nation: Australia

Owner: Queensland Sail Training Association, Inc.

Home port: Brisbane, Queensland

Year of construction: 1993; launched September 23, 1993

Shipyard: John Gilbert

Tonnage: 64 ts displacement; 52 ts gross; 16 tons net

Dimensions:
Length overall: 30.50 m
Length of hull: 25.00 m
Length between perpendiculars: 20.00 m
Width: 5.78 m
Depth in hold: 2.30 m
Depth to deck: 3.57 m
Draft: 2.30 m

Sail area: 270 square meters

Rigging: 4 sails

Masts: height of mainmast over the deck: 23.50 meters

Auxiliary engine: AIFO-Fiat-diesel, 93 kilowatts

Crew: 6-person active crew, 24 trainees

Use: sailing school-ship

The preferred sailing areas of the privately owned schooner are the Moreton Bay and the coastal waters of Queensland. Handicapped young people are able to take part in the training cruises. A mermaid (full figure) adorns the hull, which is made of welded aluminum.

Type: barkentine, wood

Nation: Australia

Owner: Ashronia Christian Cadet & Mission Ship Association, Fremantle

Home port: Fremantle

Years of construction: 1999–2000

Shipyard: in Transfield near Fremantle

Tonnage: 400 tons gross

Dimensions:
Length overall: 61.00 m
Length of hull: 56.00 m

Width: 11.50 m
Draft: 4.30 m

Sail area: 830 square meters

Rigging: 23 sails, of which 6 are studding sails

Masts: height of mainmast over the deck: 33.50 meters

Auxiliary engine: Yanmar T220 (2 propellers)

Crew: 13-person active crew, 13 trainees

Use: sailing school-ship, transport of humanitarian aid, providing for the needy

The model for this ship was the Norwegian bark *Barden*, which was built in 1892 and used primarily to transport wood. The heavy wood jarrah, a type of eucalyptus, was used in the construction of the current barkentine.

As a school-ship she is also available for the use of physically handicapped young people. One of her major tasks is to provide useful goods of all kinds to needy people in the most disparate ports. For this reason there is also a 10-bed hospital on board. This use of a sailing ship as a mission ship is unique.

Spirit of the Pacific

Previous name: *Spirit of Adventure*

Type: 2-masted topsail schooner, steel

Nation: Australia

Owner: Captain Cook Cruise Line

Home port: Sydney

Year of construction: 1973

Shipyard: Vos and Brijs, Auckland

Tonnage: 120 ts displacement; 99.6 tons gross; 84.6 tons net

Dimensions:
Length overall: 32.00 m
Width: 6.50 m
Draft: 3.30 m

Sail area: 531 square meters

Rigging: 12 sails

Masts: height of mainmast over the deck: 27 meters

Auxiliary engine: Cummins NT355 6-cylinder turboloaded diesel, 350 horsepower

Crew: 10-person active crew, 26 trainees

Use: sailing school-ship

The ship is primarily for the use of female and male students from New Zealand, who are able to stay on board for 10 days. Adults can also sail along on specific weekends. The support of numerous organizations and firms in New Zealand made the construction of the ship possible.

Windeward Bound

Type: brigantine, wood

Nation: Australia

Owner: Windeward Bound Trust, Hobart, Tasmania

Home port: Hobart

Year of construction: launched March 1996

Shipyard: large warehouse at Pavillion Point in Hobart

Tonnage: 100 ts displacement

Dimensions:
Length overall: 33.00 m
Width: 6.00 m
Draft: 3.20 m

Masts: height of mainmast over deck: 24.50 meters

Crew: 12-person active crew, 10 trainees

Use: sailing school-ship

The construction of this ship was the result of a private initiative. No public funds were used. Private citizens, firms, and the Rotary and Lions clubs provided sustained financial support. Many disadvantaged young people were able to assist in the construction and hence receive training in the relevant trades. Aside from the hull, which is made of new wood, much wood from demolished buildings and old ships was used. The masts come from the schooner *New Endeavour*, which was scrapped in 1987.

Type: brigantine, steel

Nation: Australia

Owner: Royal Australian Navy

Home port: Sydney

Year of construction: 1987; launched June 2, 1987

Shipyard: Brooke Yachts International, Lowestoft, England

Tonnage: 239 ts displacement; 175 tons gross; 51 tons net

Dimensions:
Length overall: 44.00 m
Length of hull: 35.00 m
Length at the waterline: 28.30 m
Width: 7.80 m
Depth to deck: 5.60 m
Draft: 4.00 m

Sail area: 511 square meters

Rigging: 10 sails

Masts: height of mainmast over the deck: 32 meters

Auxiliary engine: two Perkins diesel V8 M200 TI engines, 165 horsepower each

Crew: 10-person active crew, 30 trainees

Use: sailing school-ship

The ship was a gift from England to Australia in celebration of the 200-year anniversary of the first British settlement of the country. Her voyage to Australia in the summer of 1987 passed through Rio de Janeiro, Tristan da Cunha, and Antarctica.

The *Young Endeavour* is a sister ship of the Malaysian *Tunas Samudera*, which was built by the same designer at the same shipyard.

Twenty 10-day cruises along the Australian coast are usually undertaken each year, including a number of trips for handicapped young people.

Bahamas

| Concordia | Wind Star/ Wind Song/ Wind Spirit | Wind Surf |

Concordia

Type: barkentine, steel

Nation: Bahamas

Owner: West Island College International, Inc., Montreal, Calgary

Home port: Nassau

Year of construction: 1992; launched April 26, 1992

Shipyard: Colod, Ltd., Scenic (Stettin), Poland

Tonnage: 495 ts displacement; 413 tons gross

Dimensions:
Length overall: 57.50 m
Width: 9.00 m
Draft: 4.20 m

Sail area: 900 square meters

Rigging: 15 sails

Masts: height of mainmast over the waterline: 35 meters

Auxiliary engine: MAN diesel, 600 horsepower

Crew: 16-person active crew, 48 trainees

Use: sailing school-ship

The private educational institution West Island College was founded in 1974 by Terry Davies. Both campuses, in Montreal and in Calgary, have a total of 600 students. A trip around the world is undertaken yearly with the *Concordia*, which belongs to the school. The students are able to register for this voyage.

Primarily political science, natural sciences, and anthropology are taught aboard the ship. Not least important, the 16- to 19-year-olds become familiar with the problems of the countries they visit.

Wind Star/Wind Song/Wind Spirit

Because the communal work of handling the sails is almost completely absent, these powerful ships have almost nothing in common with the classic sailing vessels of the past. An extremely effective computer has completely replaced human judgments about wind and weather conditions. All sails can be furled or unfurled in a minute's time. The pulsing life of a square-rigger has given way to the restful and quiet atmosphere of a floating grand hotel.

Type: 4-masted staysail schooner, steel

Nation: Bahamas

Owner: Windstar Cruises, Seattle, Washington

Home port: Nassau

Years of construction: 1986–88

Shipyard: Ateliers et Chantiers du Havre, France

Dimensions:
Length overall: 134.00 m
Width: 15.80 m
Draft: 4.10 m

Sail area: 2000 square meters

Rigging: 6 sails

Masts: height of masts over the waterline: 62 meters

Auxiliary engine: diesel-electric

Crew: 10 officers, 12 sailors, 160 passengers

Use: cruise ship

Wind Surf

The ship has abandoned the classic design of a great sailing vessel. Seamanship is no longer in demand, but rather a pleasant cruise on a floating luxury hotel offering a wide variety of leisure activities. *Wind Surf* has a computer-controlled rolling device for the sails. With this a sail can be furled or unfurled on a minute-by-minute basis. While the ship is cruising, sails and motors can be used simultaneously. The ship is divided into eight decks and contains two swimming pools and two tenders, which are similar to landing boats. The ship's equipment includes bow and stern rudders, a pitch-control mechanism, and fin stabilizers. All 196 external cabins and 5 suites feature satellite telephone jacks.

Previous name: *Club Med I*

Type: 5-masted staysail schooner, steel

Nation: Bahamas

Owner: Windstar Cruises, Seattle, Washington

Home port: Nassau

Year of construction: 1989

Shipyard: Ateliers et Chantiers du Havre, France

Tonnage: gross register tonnage 14,754

Dimensions:
Length overall: 187.00 m
Width: 20.00 m
Draft: 5.00 m

Sail area: 2500 square meters

Rigging: 7 sails

Masts: height of masts over the deck: 50 meters

Auxiliary engine: four 3000-horsepower Wärtsilä diesel; two 280-kilowatt alternating-current generators (diesel-electric power)

Crew: 163-person standing crew, 308 passengers

Use: cruise ship

Mercator   Ragnborg

Mercator

Type: barkentine, steel

Nation: Belgium

Owner: trading fleet of the Association Maritime Belge

Home port: Ostend—Mercator Dock

Year of construction: 1932; handed over on April 7, 1932

Shipyard: Ramage & Ferguson, Ltd., Leith

Tonnage: 770 tons gross; 159 tons net

Dimensions:
Length overall: 78.50 m
Length of hull: 68.00 m
Length between perpendiculars: 57.90 m
Width: 10.60 m
Draft: 5.10 m

Sail area: 1260 square meters

Rigging: 15 sails; 4 foresails; foremast: double topsail, single topgallant; large and mizzenmasts: gaff-sail, gaff-topsail

Masts: height of mainmast over the keel: 39 meters; foremast: top- and topgallant masts; mizzenmast: topmast

Auxiliary engine: diesel engine, 500 horsepower

Crew: formerly, when the ship was in service, about 100 people, including around 45 boys

Use: museum ship

Before the *Mercator* was built, the private, but state-subsidized Association Maritime Belge, S.A., owned a different school-ship, the four-masted bark *L'Avenir*, and also the stationary school-ship *Comte de Smet Naeyer*, formerly the *Linlithgowshire*. Nonetheless, the Belgian government ordered the construction of the state-owned *Mercator*. In the process, the association lost its subsidies, and hence to a large extent its economic base. Both of its ships had to be sold. *L'Avenir* ended up in Gustaf Erickson's fleet in Mariehamn.

The *Mercator* was originally rigged as a topsail schooner: foremast with one topmast, foresail, boom fore-sail, a single topsail, and a single topgallant. The passage to Ostend following the completion of the ship's construction did not go well. The ship ran aground, which caused damage to her rigging and a leak in the bow. The ship was refitted as a barkentine at a shipyard in Normandy.

For seven years prior to World War II, the *Mercator* made extended voyages to all corners of the globe. During a long voyage that lasted from 1934 to 1935, she brought many of the famous monolith sculptures from Easter Island back to Belgian and French museums. In 1936 the barkentine sailed up the Amazon as far as Manáos—a distance of more than 1200 kilometers from the mouth of the river.

Beginning in February 1940, the ship found herself on a voyage to the West Indies and South America. On her passage home, she was detained off the West African coast because of the war. The crewmen journeyed home on other vessels. The barkentine was used for a while on hydrographic expeditions. In Boma, in the former Belgian Congo, she was handed over to the British navy on January 11, 1943. She sailed as a British ship to Freetown (Sierre Leone), where she was deployed as a submarine depot ship. She was returned to Belgium in 1948.

On January 20, 1951, following an extensive refitting and modernization, the *Mercator* set sail on her first postwar voyage. In recognition of the ship's service during the war, the British navy covered some of the cost of the reconstruction work. The Association Maritime Belge once again undertook the care and supervision of the ship.

Since 1961, the *Mercator* has been laid up. Following overhaul work in Antwerp she arrived in Ostend as a museum ship. In 1967 she visited Rotterdam for three months.

On July 28, 1967, she returned to Ostend. The old Second Trading Dock in Ostend was renamed the Mercator Dock in her honor. In 1993 she once again undertook a short voyage from Ostend to Antwerp. Since October 1996, the *Mercator* has been a Belgian national monument.

Ragnborg

Type: 5-masted fore-and-aft schooner, wood

Nation: Belgium

Owner: A. S. B. L. Vent Debout, Lüttich

Home port: Lüttich

Year of construction: 1948

Shipyard: in Sibbo, Finland

Tonnage: 160 ts displacement; 300 tons gross; 140 tons net

Dimensions:
Length overall: 42.40 m
Length of hull: 33.00 m
Length between perpendiculars: 30.00 m
Width: 8.05 m
Draft: front 1.45 m
Draft: 2.80 m

Sail area: 516 square meters

Rigging: 12 sails

Masts: height of mainmast over the deck: 27 meters

Auxiliary engine: General Motors diesel engine, 250 horsepower

Crew: 20-person active crew, 12 trainees

Use: sailing school-ship

Until 1970 the ship was a lumber transporter. After that, she passed into private hands as a yacht with a significantly reduced rig. In 1987 the Vent Debout organization purchased the ship. The time-consuming conversion work had not yet been completed as of 1996. She might be rigged as a topsail schooner. The sailing ship will primarily serve the needs of girls and boys with social problems.

Bermuda

Creole   Shenandoah

Creole

Type: 3-masted staysail schooner, composite construction

Nation: Bermuda

Owner: Gucci family, Italy

Home port: Hamilton, Bermuda

Year of construction: 1927; launched October 1927

Shipyard: Camper & Nicholsons, Ltd., Gosport

Tonnage: 697 ts displacement; 433.91 tons gross; 272.06 tons net

Dimensions:
Length overall: 65.30 m
Length of hull: 57.80 m
Length between perpendiculars: 50.80 m
Width: 9.40 m
Depth in hold: 5.00 m
Draft: 5.60 m

Sail area: 2040 square meters (total)

Rigging: 10 sails (total); 3 foresails (plus spinnaker); foremast: trysail; mainmast: staysail, trysail; mizzenmast: spanker (jib-headed sail)

Masts: height of mainmast over the deck: 39.50 meters; all masts are one piece

Auxiliary engine: two diesel motors with a total of 3000 horsepower

Crew: 25 people; accommodations for 10 additional people as a private yacht

Use: private yacht

The *Creole* is one of the largest and most beautiful high-sea yachts ever built. The shipyard built her for Alex Smith Cochrane. After her completion, however, she belonged to Major Maurice Pope and Sir Connop Guthrie.

During World War II the schooner was requisitioned by the British Admiralty and cruised the Scottish waters as an auxiliary ship. After the war the *Creole* was retired from service and returned to her shipyard. She remained there until 1951, when the Greek shipowner Stavros Niarchos purchased her.

For the great sailing-ship regatta of 1956, from the Torbay to Lisbon, Niarchos lent his ship to a British team. The *Creole* also raced under the British flag.

The hull of the schooner consists of steel frames and 10-centimeter strong teak planks. Beneath the waterline the ship's body is covered with a layer of copper.

In 1980 the ship was sold to the merchant marine school in Nyborg, Denmark. From there she undertook training cruises.

In 1983 the Italian fashion designer Maurizio Gucci purchased the schooner. The ship's thorough refitting and conversion into a luxury yacht cost 2 million pounds.

The *Creole* is currently moored in Mallorca, where she is undergoing a thorough overhaul that is expected to last 2 years and will cost 2 million pounds.

Previous names: *Atlantide, Shenandoah, Lasca II, Shenandoah*

Type: 3-masted fore-and-aft schooner, iron

Nation: Bermuda

Year of construction: 1902

Shipyard: Townsend & Downey, Shooters Island, New York

Tonnage: 280 tons gross; 225 tons net

Dimensions:
Length overall: 44.20 m
Length at the waterline: 30.48 m
Width: 8.17 m
Draft: 4.11 m

Sail area: 613 square meters

Auxiliary engine: two 6-cylinder Volvo Penta TAMD 120 B diesel engines, 750 horsepower each

Crew: 10 people

Use: private yacht

The schooner bears a close resemblance to the yacht *Meteor III*, which was built at the same shipyard for Kaiser Wilhelm II. Her first owner was the American financier Gibson Fahnestock.

In 1912 District President Walther von Brüning acquired the ship. She received the new name *Lasca II*, and Kiel became her homeport. At the outbreak of World War I the ship happened to be anchored in Cowes. The English immediately confiscated her.

Following several changes of ownership, Prince Spado Veralli, who was governor of Rome at that time, acquired the ship in the late 1920s. The ship received the new name *Atlantide*. Additional changes of ownership followed.

In 1972 the French ballpoint-pen manufacturer Bich purchased the ship and gave her back her original name. A thorough overhaul took place in 1974. In the process the ship acquired the most modern navigational equipment and every conceivable comfort. In 1986 the Swiss businessman Phillipe Bommer became the owner of the *Shenandoah*. Finally, in 1990, the ship passed into Japanese hands. She has changed owners at least ten times in her long life, and after 1990 she also had a German owner.

The complete restoration of the *Shenandoah* was one of the largest projects of recent years at the McMullen & Wing shipyard in Auckland, New Zealand. The wooden masts and the rig used in this process were delivered from England.

In 1998 the ship took part in the Nioulargue in Saint Tropez. In 2000 she sailed off Auckland, New Zealand, during the America's Cup.

Brazil

Cisne Branco

Cisne Branco

Type: full-rigged ship, steel

Nation: Brazil

Owner: Brazilian navy

Home Port: Rio de Janeiro

Year of construction: 1999; launched August 4, 1999; commissioned December 1999

Shipyard: Damen Shipyard, Gorinchen, the Netherlands

Tonnage: 1038 ts displacement; 698 tons gross

Dimensions:
Length overall: 76.00 m
Length of hull: 60.50 m
Length at the waterline: 55.60 m
Width: 10.50 m
Depth to deck: 6.45 m
Draft: 4.80 m

Sail area: 2195 square meters (with studding sails); 1899 square meters (without studding sails)

Rigging: 29 sails; foremast: double topsail, single topgallant, royal-sail; mainmast: double topsail, single topgallant, royal-sail, skysail; mizzenmast: single topsail, double topgallant, studding sails on foremasts and mainmasts

Masts: height of mainmast over the deck: 46.40 meters

Auxiliary engine: Caterpillar, 746 kw

Crew: 22-person active crew (7 officers), 58 trainees

Use: sailing school-ship

The first sailing school-ship of the Brazilian navy was the *Guanabara,* formerly the *Albert Leo Schlageter.* This ship, a completely identical sister ship to the *Horst Wessel,* which today sails under the name *Eagle* for the U.S. Coast Guard, was launched on October 30, 1937, at the Blohm & Voss shipyard in Hamburg. After being used as a stationary training ship she was put into service for the first time in 1944. In the same year she ran into a mine in the Baltic, resulting in fifteen deaths. Her sister ship, the *Horst Wessel,* towed her to Swinemünde. At the end of the war she was taken as a prize by the victorious powers. She was transferred to the United States.

Because of overcapacity, the United States gave the ship to Brazil. She received the new name *Guanabara.* In 1961 Portugal acquired the sailing ship, which from then on was called the *Sagres* and since then has been a permanent part of the Portuguese navy.

With the construction of the *Cisne Branco* ("White Swan"), Brazil once again has a sailing school-ship for its navy. She is a clipper in the style of the nineteenth century and can be considered a sister ship of the Dutch *Stad Amsterdam.* As a result, all South American navies now have sailing school-ships.

The goal was to complete the sailing ship in time for the 500th anniversary of the discovery of Brazil by Cabral. Pedro Alvares Cabral, a Portuguese seafarer (ca. 1468–1526) reached the east coast of Brazil on April 22, 1500, and claimed it for Portugal. In the further course of his voyage he reached Southeast Asia by way of the Cape of Good Hope.

Bulgaria

Kaliakra   Patriot   Veslets

Kaliakra

Type: barkentine, steel

Nation: Bulgaria

Owner: Navigation Maritime Bulgare

Home port: Varna

Year of construction: 1984; launched February 28, 1984

Shipyard: Stocznia Gdanska (Danzing shipyard), Gdansk

Tonnage: 386 ts displacement; 299 tons gross

Dimensions:
Length overall: 48.50 m
Length of hull: 43.20 m
Width: 8.20 m
Draft: 3.30 m

Sail area: 1000 square meters

Crew: 45 people

Use: sailing school-ship

The model for and sister ship of the *Kaliakra* is the Polish *Pogoria*. Characteristic of these newly constructed sailing ships is the flat stern.

The figurehead is a woman's figure. She represents the Bulgarian national heroine Kaliakra, who jumped to her death in the fourteenth century in order not to fall into Turkish hands.

In spite of the long distance that must be covered in order to leave the Black Sea, the ship is a frequent guest at rendezvous of large sailing vessels. For economic reasons, the *Kaliakra* was laid up in 1990 and 1991. She was once again present at the Columbus Regatta in 1992. Subsequently the ship once again lay anchored, but was once again able to take part in a regatta in 1998.

Patriot

Previous names: *N. I. Vaptsarov, Gorianin*

Since the founding of the Bulgarian navy in the year 1879 following the War of Independence against the Turks, five sailing school-ships have been in service: the iron brigantine *Assen* (1891–1904), the wooden *Yawl Strela* (1906–41), the steel fore-and-aft schooner *Assen II* (1927–56), the wooden schooner *Veslets* (1949–72), and the wooden 3-masted fore-and-aft schooner *N. I. Vaptsarov*

(1951–59). The last two still exist today and are scheduled to go back into service.

The 3-masted schooner was built in 1943 in Tsarevo (now Michurin) and sailed originally as a trading ship. In 1951 she was modified to serve as a school-ship. In 1959 the ship was rerigged and continued to serve as a school-ship. In 1981 the *Patriot*, as the ship was henceforth known, was turned over to the Bulgarian youth organization. Following her rerigging she is to sail as a school-ship once more.

Veslets

Previous names: *Vola, Milka*

The schooner was built in 1942 in the Greek city of Kavalla for the Bulgarian shipowner Todo Szeliabov as a trading ship. In 1949 the Bulgarian navy purchased her and converted her into a sailing school-ship for the naval school in Varna. In 1959 the *Veslets* became a civilian school-ship, until she was laid up in 1979 for financial reasons. Since 1977 she has been a stationary club ship. Her restoration is under way.

Canada

Black Jack	Nonsuch	Spirit of Chemainus
Bluenose II	Pacific Swift	St. Lawrence II
Fair Jeanne	Pathfinder	St. Roch
Hector	Robertson II	

Black Jack

The *G. B. Pattie* was in use for almost 50 years as a tree-trunk hauler for the Upper Ottawa Improvement Company. Captain Thomas G. Fuller of Ottawa acquired her in 1952 and converted her into a brigantine for his private use.

Since 1984 the ship has sailed under the flag of Bytown Brigantine Inc., a company started by Captain Fuller to which the brigantine *Fair Jeanne* also belongs (Ottawa was founded in 1827 as Bytown). The *Black Jack* sails primarily on the rambling Ottawa River. She has become an icon of Canada's capital city. School and university students are trained on board.

Previous name: *G. B. Pattie*

Type: brigantine, steel

Nation: Canada

Owner: Jeanne Fuller

Home port: Ottawa, Canada

Year of construction: 1904

Shipyard: in Scotland

Tonnage: 40.50 ts displacement

Dimensions:
Length overall: 26.50 m
Length of hull: 20.70 m
Length at the waterline: 17.30 m
Width: 4.60 m
Draft: 1.80 m

Sail area: 278 square meters

Rigging: 10 sails, foremast: foresail, topsail, and topgallant

Masts: height of mainmast over the deck: 24.40 meters

Auxiliary engine: Detroit diesel, 235 horsepower

Crew: 6-person active crew, 20 trainees

Use: sailing school-ship

In 1921 the schooner *Bluenose* was built. She is a well-known type of the famous fishery schooner of Nova Scotia, which sails to the Great Banks to fish for cod. But even at that time it was no longer just a matter of achieving high market prices for the catch by sailing home quickly. The ship was primarily used for competitive schooner races between Canada and the United States (International Fishermen's Race). The *Bluenose* succeeded in winning the cup for Canada several times. In the process she became a Canadian symbol like the maple leaf, appearing on stamps and coins. Later the ship had to be sold.

As a freighter between the islands of the West Indies she ran aground on a coral reef in 1946 and was completely lost. To preserve her memory the *Bluenose II* was built in 1963 at the same shipyard and according to the original plans. The only difference is in the interior furnishings. Instead of storage holds there are now comfortable cabins for guests and crew. The most modern navigational instruments are available on board. During the winter months the schooner sails as a chartered ship for vacationers in the Caribbean. In the summer she cruises in Canadian waters. The name *Bluenose* is a nickname for the fishermen of Nova Scotia used especially by the fishermen of Gloucester (Massachussetts) to designate their rivals. The hardest racing also took place between these two groups of fishermen.

Whenever the schooner is in Halifax, she undertakes three 2-hour cruises a day with up to 80 passengers aboard.

Type: 2-masted fore-and-aft schooner, wood

Nation: Canada

Owner: Oland & Son Ltd., Halifax, Canada

Home port: Lunenburg (Nova Scotia)

Year of construction: 1963; keel laid February 27, 1963; launched July 24, 1963

Shipyard: Smith & Rhuland Ltd., Lunenburg, Nova Scotia; designer: William Roue

Tonnage: 286 ts displacement; 191 tons gross; 96 tons net

Dimensions:
Length overall: approx. 54.00 m
Length of hull: 43.50 m
Length at the waterline: 34.00 m
Width: 5.10 m
Depth to deck: 5.10 m
Draft: 4.80 m

Sail area: 1012 square meters

Rigging: 8 sails; 3 foresails; foremast: foresail, fore gaff-topsail; mainmast: mainsail, main gaff-topsail, fisherman's staysail

Masts: height of mainmast over the deck: 38.30 meters

Auxiliary engine: two diesel motors, 250 horsepower each; speed with engine, 10 knots

Crew: 12-person active crew, accommodations for 12 guests in cabins

Use: private ship for passenger cruises

Type: brigantine, composite construction

Nation: Canada

Owner: Jeanne F. Fuller

Home port: Kingston, Ontario

Year of construction: 1982

Shipyard: designed by Captain Thomas G. Fuller

Tonnage: 125.24 ts displacement

Dimensions:
Length overall: 33.50 m
Length of hull: 25.00 m
Length at the waterline: 18.90 m
Width: 7.40 m

Draft:
Centerboard up: 1.80 m
Centerboard down: 3.60 m

Sail area: 418 square meters

Rigging: 10 sails; foremast: foresail, topsail, and topgallants

Masts: height of mainmast over the deck: 24.40 meters

Auxiliary engine: Detroit diesel, 235 horsepower

Crew: 10-person active crew, 22 trainees

Use: sailing school-ship

Captain Thomas G. Fuller built the brigantine as a private yacht; steel was used for the ribs and fiberglass for the planks. She sailed on the oceans worldwide. After the owner's death the ship came under the flag of Bytown Brigantine Inc., an enterprise founded by Captain Fuller that sails the Great Lakes and the Saint Lawrence River with the brigantine *Black Jack*. During the winter months the ship visits the Caribbean.

The young men and women ages 13 to 24 who come on board do not only receive training in seamanship; general school subjects are also taught. A figurehead, the bust of a blond woman, points the ship's way.

The original was built as a wind-powered freighter in Holland. Equipped modestly as an emigration vessel, she carried Scottish emigrants to the new world even before her historic voyage. Most of the emigrants disembarked in Boston. At that time the *Hector* belonged to the businessman Mr. Pagan of Greenock, Scotland. Under the command of Captain John Spiers she left Scotland from Greenock and Loch Broom on July 1, 1773. More than 170 people from the Scottish highlands, including many children, were on board. Poverty and hunger had forced them to emigrate. They had been promised free passage, provisions for a year, and a farm. The voyage was ill-fated. A storm off Newfoundland 36 pushed the ship far off course to the east. It took 14 days to return to the point it had reached before the storm. Eighteen children died of dysentery. The *Hector* dropped anchor in Pictou (Newfoundland) in September of 1773 after an 11-week voyage. Its passengers were suffering great privations by the end of the journey. Their disappointment was great, because the cultivated land they had been promised was not available.

The modern reproduction of the ship is a memorial to the difficult period of the country's settlement. The reconstruction, which was followed with great interest, took place outdoors. Under the eyes of an exceptionally large public, the ship was lowered into the water, sliding down sideways, on September 17, 2000.

Type: Dutch flute, wood, reproduction

Nation: Canada

Owner: city of Pictou, Nova Scotia

Home port: Pictou

Year of construction: keel laid 1990; launched September 17, 2000

Shipyard: Hector Heritage Quay

Tonnage: 100 tons carrying capacity

Dimensions:
Length overall: 37.50 m
Length of hull: 25.90 m
Width: 6.70 m
Depth in hold: 3.60 m
Draft: 2.40 m

Sail area: 562 square meters

Masts: height of mainmast over the deck: 29.50 meters

Auxiliary engine: twin diesel engines, 165 horsepower

Crew: unknown, 50 day guests

Use: museum ship, chartered ship

Nonsuch

Type: square-rigged ketch, wood (oak)

Nation: Canada

Owner: Manitoba Museum of Man and Nature, Winnipeg—Manitoba

Home port: Winnipeg

Year of construction: 1968; launched August 1968

Shipyard: J. Hinks & Son, Appledore, Devon, England

Tonnage: 65 ts displacement

Dimensions:
Length overall: 22.80 m
Length of hull: 16.30 m
Length between perpendiculars: 15.30 m
Width: 2.10 m
Depth to deck: 2.10 m
Depth in hold: 2.10 m
Draft: 2.10 m

Sail area: 176 square meters

Rigging: 6 sails; 2 foresails; mainmast: mainsail, topsail; mizzenmast: square topsail, lateen sail

Masts: height of mainmast over the deck: 22.50 meters

Auxiliary engine: Perkins diesel, 95 horsepower

Crew: approx. 12 people

Use: museum ship

In the year 1668 the first ship of the Hudson Bay Company, the *Nonsuch*, sailed to North America with trading goods on board for the Indians. The ship made it as far as the James Bay. There the ship spent the winter in a house built on land. In the following year the *Nonsuch* returned to England with a full load of beaver pelts. The *Nonsuch* was built in 1650 at the shipyard of Mr. Page in Wivenhoe (Essex). After her return King Charles II officially sanctioned trade with the Hudson Bay Company on May 2, 1670.

For the celebration of the 300th anniversary of the Hudson Bay Company, an exact reproduction of the *Nonsuch* was commissioned at J. Hinks & Son in Appledore (Devon).

This shipyard was chosen because the dexel, a type of ax, is used in the shipbuilding process there. The plans were carefully prepared with the help of the National Maritime Museum in Greenwich. The shipyard crafted the ship in the classical manner. Only large wooden nails were used. The result is striking. It is not just that a ship of that time with her fine lines and ornamentation has come into being, but we have a fitting monument to the pioneering acts of the trading company before us. Naturally, there were much larger trading ships at that time. But the *Nonsuch* was the freighter in whose wake the Hudson Bay Company was able to expand its area of influence to the point that it encompassed the entire western hinterland of Canada by the time Canada purchased the sovereignty rights in 1869.

The well-known figurehead sculptor Jack Whitehead from Wotton (I.O.W) completed the ornamentation, of which the poop ornamentation and the mermaids in particular should be mentioned. The mermaids support the prow on either side of the bow.

Following an extended visit to the United States in the years 1969 and 1970 the ship was donated to the Manitoba Museum in Winnipeg. By modern standards, the *Nonsuch* would actually have to be classified as a brig. Her classification as a ketch is based on seventeenth-century terminology. The cost of the reconstruction came to 70,000 English pounds.

Pacific Swift

This schooner was built before the eyes of the public during Expo '86. Thirty thousand spectators witnessed her launch. The model for this ship was the brig *Swift* from the year 1778. She was a predecessor of the famous Baltimore clippers. The sharp lines of the *Pacific Swift* reveal her to be a fast sailing ship. A praying woman adorns the bow as a figurehead.

Type: 2-masted topsail schooner, wood

Nation: Canada

Owner: Sail and Life Training Society, Victoria, B.C.

Home port: Victoria, B.C.

Year of construction: launched October 11, 1986; commissioned May 1988

Shipyard: Vancouver, B.C.

Tonnage: 98 ts displacement

Dimensions:
Length overall: 33.70 m
Length of hull: 24.30 m
Width: 6.20 m
Draft: 3.20 m

Sail area: 278 square meters

Rigging: 9 sails

Masts: height of mainmast over the deck: 25.80 meters

Auxiliary engine: Isuzu diesel, 160 horsepower

Crew: 5-person active crew, 30 trainees

Use: sailing school-ship

Pathfinder

This brigantine is the exact sister ship of the *St. Lawrence II* from Kingston and of the *Playfair*. Only the arrangement of the interior rooms is somewhat different, because the *Pathfinder* has to accommodate more youngsters. Toronto Brigantine Incorporated is a completely civilian enterprise to which citizens of Toronto belong. All boys and girls between the ages of 14 and 18 are eligible for the courses. These usually last for 1 week in the summer, while only day cruises are undertaken in the autumn. In the winter the ship is usually laid up in Toronto. All of the voyages take place on the Great Lakes and visit their port cities.

Type: brigantine, steel

Nation: Canada

Owner: Toronto Brigantine Incorporated

Home port: Toronto

Year of construction: 1963; launched May 6, 1963

Shipyard: Kingston Shipyards, Ltd.; design: F. A. MacLachlan, Naval Architect

Tonnage: 50 ts displacement; 36 tons gross; 32 tons net

Dimensions:
Length overall: 21.70 m
Length of hull: 18.10 m
Length between perpendiculars: 14.60 m

Width: 6.60 m
Depth in hold: 2.60 m
Depth to deck: 3.30 m
Draft: 2.50 m

Sail area: 250 square meters

Rigging: 8 sails; 2 (3) foresails; foremast: foresail, single topsail; mainmast: mainsail, gaff-topsail, main staysail, main-topmast staysail

Masts: height of mainmast over the waterline: 16.50 meters

Auxiliary engine: Volvo diesel, 150 horsepower

Crew: 10-person active crew, 18 trainees

Use: sailing school-ship

Robertson II

Type: 2-masted fore-and-aft schooner, wood

Nation: Canada

Owner: Sail and Life Training Society, B.C.

Home port: Victoria, B.C.

Year of construction: 1940

Shipyard: in Shelburne, Nova Scotia; design: McKay

Tonnage: 180 ts displacement; 99 tons gross

Dimensions:
Length overall: 39.50 m
Length of hull: 31.90 m
Length at the waterline: 26.40 m

Width: 6.70 m
Draft: 3.50 m

Sail area: 510 square meters

Rigging: 7 sails

Masts: height of mainmast over the deck: 30.40 meters

Auxiliary engine: General Motors diesel, 200 horsepower

Crew: 5-person active crew, 30 trainees (as a fishing vessel 20 people, 8 dories)

Use: sailing school-ship

The *Robertson II* is one of the last fishing vessels to have been built in Canada. The ship fished with eight dories in the Grand Banks off Newfoundland into the 1970s. In 1974 the Quest Star Society purchased the schooner and moved her to Victoria in British Columbia. There she was converted into a 3-masted staysail schooner and equipped for the training courses of the Sail and Life Training Society.

In 1980 a thorough overhaul took place, and since 1982 the *Robertson II* has once again become an elegant 2-masted fore-and-aft schooner with her original rig.

Spirit of Chemainus

Type: brigantine, wood

Nation: Canada

Owner: Sail and Life Training Society, Victoria, B.C.

Year of construction: launched September 14, 1985; commissioned May 1986

Shipyard: in Chemainus, Vancouver Island

Displacement: 45 ts displacement; 35 tons gross

Dimensions:
Length overall: 28.00 m
Length of hull: 20.60 m
Width: 5.40 m
Draft: 2.90 m

Sail area: 232 square meters

Rigging: 13 sails

Masts: height of mainmast over the deck: 19.70 meters

Auxiliary engine: Perkins diesel, 120 horsepower

Crew: 5-person active crew, 18 trainees

Use: sailing school-ship

The Royal Canadian Sea Cadets Corps St. Lawrence has existed since 1942. It is overseen by civilians and by the navy. Nonetheless, the main goal of the corps' ship is not to train future officers for the navy. She is supposed primarily to give 14- to 18-year-old boys the opportunity to learn how to live in a mutually dependent community in a small space. As of the year 1964, more than 1000 Canadian boys had already attended the courses and had thus become "sea cadets." In 1952 the corps decided to have a ship of its own built. The new ship received her name from the 112-canon 3-deck HMS *St. Lawrence*, which was built in 1814 by the Point Frederick naval shipyard in Kingston.

The "active crew" and the "petty officers" are chosen from among the senior cadets. They must commit to stay aboard the ship for an entire sailing season. The boys leave the 140-day courses with different ranks depending on ability and inclination. Multiple courses are necessary in order to achieve leadership positions on board. The brigantine sails exclusively on Lake Ontario. Three 3.5-meter dories can be found on board, which provide the boat service. A white streak adorns the sides. During the winter months the ship is laid up in Kingston.

In July of 1964 the ship took part in "Operation Sail" in New York. Unrigged, she sailed under her own power down the Oswego Canal and the Hudson to the parade of tall sailing ships in New York.

The Sea Cadet Corps uses the ketches *Minstrel, Rosborough*, and *Privateer* in conjunction with the *St. Lawrence II.*

Type: brigantine, steel	Shipyard: Kingston Shipyards, Ltd.; design: F. A. MacLachlan, naval architect	Depth to deck: 3.30 m Draft: 2.30 m	Auxiliary engine: diesel engine, 72 horsepower
Nation: Canada		Sail area: 231 square meters	Crew: 22 officers and cadets
Owner: Brigantine Incorporated, Kingston, Royal Canadian Sea Cadets Corps St. Lawrence	Tonnage: 39–42 ts displacement; 34.30 tons gross; 30.87 tons net	Rigging: 8 sails; 2 foresails: foresail, single topsail; mainmast: mainsail, gaff-topsail, main staysail, main-topmast staysail	Use: sailing school-ship
Home port: Kingston, Ontario	Dimensions: Length overall: 21.70 m Length of hull: 18.10 m		
Year of construction: 1953; launched December 5, 1953; officially commissioned July 1957	Length between perpendiculars: 14.60 m Width: 6–60 m Depth in hold: 2.60 m	Masts: height of mainmast over the waterline: 16.10 meters	

♦ St. Roch

Type: 2-masted fore-and-aft schooner, wood

Nation: Canada

Owner: Maritime Museum, Vancouver, B.C.

Home port: Vancouver, B.C.

Year of construction: 1928; launched April 1928

Shipyard: Burrard Drydock Company, Ltd., North Vancouver, B.C.

Tonnage: 323 ts displacement; 193.43 tons gross; 80.60 tons net

Dimensions:
Length between perpendiculars: 31.70 m
Width: 7.50 m
Depth to deck: 3.90 m
Depth in hold: 3.30 m
Draft (fully equipped): 3.90 m

Sail area: 226 square meters

Rigging: 3 sails; 1 foresail, 1 gaff-sail each

Masts: height of mainmast over the deck: 18.90 meters

Auxiliary engine: Union diesel engine; 1928, 150 horsepower; since 1944, 300 horsepower

Crew: 9 people

Use: museum ship

As soon as one hears the name Royal Canadian Mounted Police (RCMP), one thinks automatically of the red-uniformed horsemen with wide-brimmed hats who are world-famous for their riding and shooting abilities. It is a little-known fact, however, that this police force also maintains its own maritime division. Until a few years ago the *St. Roch* was still known for her daring arctic voyages.

The schooner, built specially for arctic conditions, is the second ship to have sailed through the Northwest Passage from west to east (only the third voyage through the passage as of that time); she is the first ship to have sailed through the Northwest Passage in both directions and, finally, the first ship to have sailed all the way around the continent of North America, using the Panama Canal. The first of these great voyages began on June 23, 1940, in Vancouver and ended twenty-eight months later, on October 11, 1942, in Dartmouth, Nova Scotia. In 1944 the *St. Roch*, equipped with a more powerful engine, sailed back to Vancouver from east to west. Staff-Sergeant Henry A. Larsen, RCMP, had the command during these arctic voyages. St. Roch is a community in the voting district Quebec East.

In 1954 the *St. Roch* returned definitively to Vancouver. The government donated the ship to the city of Vancouver for its maritime museum. In the meantime the museum has built a tent-shaped shelter that is 36 meters long, 15 meters wide, and 18 meters high for the remarkable schooner. The masts and the rigging, which were shortened and changed in the course of the ship's years of service, have been returned to their original conditions.

Cayman Islands

Phocea

Previous name: *Club Méditerranée*

Type: 4-masted schooner, steel

Nation: Cayman Islands

Home port: Georgetown

Year of construction: 1976

Shipyard: DCAN, Toulouse

Dimensions:
Length overall: 74.20 m
Width: 9.60

Sail area: 1648 square meters

Rigging: Bermuda rigging with staysails, 8 sails

Auxiliary engine: Pielstick diesel engine, 600 kw

Use: cruise yacht

Alain Colas had the ship built in 1976 in Toulon under the name *Club Méditerranée.* He wanted to use her to win the transatlantic race OSTAR, in which each entrant sails his ship single-handedly. Michel Biogin designed this 72-meter racing yacht on the basis of the principle that "length is speed." A couple of years later the ship was used for day tours for tourists in French Polynesia.

In 1982 the businessman Bernard Tapie purchased the ship. He had a designer rebuild

her and lengthen her to 74.20 meters. The luxurious cruise ship then decayed at the quay of the International Yacht Club of Antibes.

The current owner, Mouna al-Ayoub, a Lebanese woman, acquired the ship in 1997 and had her completely overhauled at the Lürssen shipyard in Bremen-Vegesack in 1998–99. There were problems, however, finding a crew that would sail the ship to Bremen. Her condition is said to have been catastrophic: on board there were winches that were rusted

stiff and water tanks that stank like cesspools.

Butch Dalrympe-Smith was responsible for the architecture, including the rig. The grate booms were replaced with conventional booms, which work not with bulkheads but rather with a hydraulic system that lies between the mast and the boom. The *Phocea* now has a dark blue hull. Jörg Beiderbeck designed the interior.

The 4-masted schooner can sail at up to 30 knots. It took her 8 days, 3 hours, and 29 minutes to cross the Atlantic

(North America to England). The ship probably still holds the speed record for a one-hulled yacht.

The *Phocea* is one of the largest private sailing yachts. She is used for luxury cruises. The *Phocea* can also be chartered for about 200,000 dollars per week.

38

Esmeralda

In the 1879 War of the Pacific against Bolivia and Peru the Chilean warship *Esmeralda* fought successful engagements with the opposing fleet. The current Chilean sailing school-ship got her name from this historic ship. The barkentine was built in 1946 as the *Juan d'Austria* for the Spanish navy. During the construction process fire destroyed a large part of the ship. For this reason she couldn't be launched until 1952. The Chilean navy acquired the ship under the name *Esmeralda* in 1954 for the purpose of training its future officers. Like her almost identical sister, *Juan Sebastian de Elcano*, the barkentine uses the old, original schooner rig, which means that all gaffs are hoisted and lowered. The sails are bent to the mast with cringles. There are fundamental differences from the sister ship when it comes to the rigging of the foremast and the hull construction.

The *Esmeralda* doesn't use a schooner sail and hence must be categorized as a barkentine. The square sails are peaked up to the yardarms and not to the middle of the yard as is the case on her sister ship. The poop reaches to the mizzenmast, and the very long forecastle almost to the mainmast. The deckhouse, located near the middle of the ship, has a small navigation bridge on its roof. The *Esmeralda* has the most modern navigational instruments at her disposal. In addition to the boats in davits and chocks there are eight fully equipped rubber boats, which are lashed to the lower shrouds above the bulwark and above the rail. A powerful,

Previous name: *Juan d'Austria*

Type: 4-masted barkentine, steel

Nation: Chile

Owner: Armada de Chile, Buque Escuela "Esmeralda"

Home port: Valparaiso

Year of construction: keel laid 1946; launched 1952; commissioned 1954

Shipyard: Messrs. Echevarrietta y Larrinaga, Cadiz

Tonnage: 3500 ts displacement (armed)

Dimensions:
Length overall: 113.00 m
Length of hull: 94.00 m
Length between perpendiculars: 79.00 m
Width: 13.00 m
Depth in hold: 8.70 m
Draft: 6.00 m

Sail area: 2852 square meters

Rigging: 21 sails; 6 foresails; foremast: fore and double-topsail, single topgallant, no schooner sail; mainmast: gaff-sail, gaff-topsail, staysail, topmast staysail, topgallant staysail; mizzenmast: gaff-sail, gaff-topsail, topgallant staysail

Masts: the mizzen lower mast serves to divert exhaust gases; height of mainmast over the waterline: 48.50 meters

Auxiliary engine: 6-cylinder Fiat diesel engine, 1500 horsepower; speed with engine, 12 knots

Armaments: four 5.7-cm rapid-fire cannons

Crew: 332 officers, petty officers, midshipmen, cadets, and regular crew members

Use: sailing school-ship

beautifully painted condor, the Chilean coat of arms in its talons, adorns the bow.

The *Esmeralda* is one of the sailing ships that logs the largest average number of miles traveled each year.

Huascar

Type: steamship rigged as a brig

Nation: Chile

Owner: Chilean maritime museum

Home port: Talcahuano

Year of construction: 1865

Shipyard: Baunmer 321 Laird Brothers, Birkenhead, Great Britain (hull)

Tonnage: 1130 ts displacement

Masts: 2

Use: floating museum ship, memorial for naval seamen

This steamship rigged as a brig, built in 1865, was built as a warship and became famous in 1877 when, under the flag of the Peruvian rebels, she defeated the Chilean *Esmeralda*. It was from the latter ship that the current Chilean school-ship *Esmeralda* got its name. In the ensuing battles the *Huascar* was captured by Chilean units. Today she belongs to the Chilean maritime museum in Talcahuano.

La Sirena

In Puerto Montt lies the largely unrigged full-rigged ship *La Sirena*, formerly the *Allerton*. The 2088 tons gross ship was built in 1884 by the shipyard Oswald, Morduant, and Co. in Southampton for the shipping firm R. W. Leyland & Co. She was one of the largest freighters of her time.

Dimensions:
Length of hull: 83.10 m
Width: 12.30 m

Colombia

Gloria

Gloria

Type: bark, steel

Nation: Colombia

Owner: Armada de Colombia

Home port: Cartagena

Years of construction:
1967–68; launched
December 2, 1967; delivered
by shipyard September 7,
1968

Shipyard: Astilleros y Talleres
Celaya, S. A., Bilbao, Spain

Tonnage: 1330 ts
displacement

Dimensions:
Length overall: 76.00 m
Length of hull: 64.60 m
Length between
perpendiculars: 56.10 m
Width: 10.60 m
Depth to deck: 6.60 m
Depth in hold: 4.20 m
Draft: 4.50 m

Sail area: 1250 square meters

Rigging: 23 sails; 5 foresails;
double topsail, single
topgallant, royals;
mizzenmast: mizzen sail,
mizzen topsail

Masts: height of mainmast
over the deck: 36 meters

Auxiliary engine: Naval Stork
RHO 216, 530 horsepower;
speed with engine, 10 knots

Crew: 9 officers, 5 officer
trainers, 30 petty officers, 80
cadets, 12 regular crew
members, 9-person auxiliary
crew

Use: sailing school-ship

The construction of the *Gloria* proves that nations continue to recognize and take advantage of the great practical value of training aboard sailing schoolships, even in cases in which the country in question does not have a great seafaring tradition, or perhaps especially when this is the case.

In her basic features, the bark was built according to the plans for the *Gorch Foch I*. Admittedly, the shape of the hull deviates significantly from this basic type. It is also impossible to miss the compact construction of the bridge, which meets modern demands and which could already be found on the Argentinean *Libertad*. The design of the ship was tested in the wind tunnel of the National Institute of Technical Aeronautics in Madrid.

The *Gloria* is able to stay at sea for 60 days at a time and is not dependent on external supplies during this period. She is able to take 53 tons of fresh water on board and store 23,330 gallons of fuel, which also keeps the 180-kilowatt onboard power station in operation.

The figurehead received particular attention. It personifies Gloria, a winged female figure who in one hand carries a laurel bow and in the other the table of immortality.

The bark's first long voyage began on January 3, 1970, in Cartagena. It took her around the world; Sydney was a main destination. Numerous large sailing ships met there to take part in the celebrations surrounding the 200th anniversary of the discovery of the east coast of Australia by Captain Cook. Since entering service, the *Gloria* has also repeatedly visited European ports. The *Gloria* is the first of a series of four barks built in Bilbao for Latin American navies. She was followed by the *Guayas* for Ecuador in 1976, the *Simon Bolivar* for Venezuela in 1979, and the *Cuauhtemoc* for Mexico in 1982.

Cook Islands

Picton Castle

Picton Castle

Previous names: *Dolmar, Picton Castle*

Type: bark, steel

Nation: Cook Islands

Owner: Windward Isles Sailing Ship Company

Home port: Avatin, Rarotonga, Cook Islands

Year of construction: 1928

Shipyard: Cochran's Shipyard, Selby, Yorkshire, England

Tonnage: 565 ts displacement; 284 tons gross; 85 tons net

Dimensions:
Length overall: 54.40 m
Length of hull: 45.00 m
Length at the waterline: 39.50 m
Width: 7.30 m
Draft: 4.30 m

Sail area: 1156 square meters

Rigging: 19 sails, double topsail, single topgallant, royals

Masts: height of mainmast over the deck: 30.40 meters

Auxiliary engine: Burmeister & Wain alpha diesel, 690 horsepower

Crew: 14-person active crew, 34 trainees (paying guests)

Use: sailing school-ship, ship for guests

The current bark was built as a British steam trawler. During World War II she served as a minesweeper for the Royal Navy. After 1945 she was once again active as a fishing vessel. In 1955 the ship was sold to Norway. She sailed in the coastal trade under the new name *Dolmar* until 1991. A two-year period of inactivity followed. The ship has be-longed to the current owners since 1993. Her conversion into a bark took place in Lunen-burg, Nova Scotia. The *Picton Castle* became well known as the result of a voyage around the world for paying guests, which took 18 months to circle the globe. Trading goods were also carried on this voyage. The costs per person came to 32,500 dollars.

Denmark

Aaron
Bonavista
Brita Leth
Carene Star
Danmark
Den Store Bjørn
Elinor
Freia

Fulton
Fylla
Georg Stage
Halmø
Havet
Isefjord
Jens Krogh
Jylland

Lilla Dan
Madonna
Marilyn Anne
Midsummer
Nordboen

Aaron

Type: 2-masted fore-and-aft schooner, wood

Nation: Denmark

Owner: Kristian Lund, Svendborg

Home port: Svendborg

Year of construction: 1906

Shipyard: L. J. Bager jun., Marstal

Tonnage: 100 ts displacement; 61.25 tons gross; 39 tons net

Dimensions:
Length overall: 32.50 m
Length of hull: 21.22 m
Length between perpendiculars: 5.65 m
Width: 2.10 m
Draft: 2.65 m

Sail area: 320 meters

Rigging: 12 sails (square foresail)

Masts: height of mainmast over the deck: 22 meters

Auxiliary engine: Gardner diesel, 110 horsepower

Crew: 2-person active crew, 12 guests

Use: chartered ship

The *Aaron* is one of the famous "Marstal schooners," which proved themselves to be extraordinarily effective as wind-powered trading vessels in the service of Denmark.

She was first removed from service as a trading ves-sel in 1968 and converted into a chartered ship by her current owner. In 1976 Kris-tian Lund received the award for the best preserved and restored ship of the year from the Danish veterans' ship club.

Bonavista

The ship name *Bonavista* comes from a small port on the west coast of Newfoundland from which a great deal of stockfish was shipped to Europe. The Newfoundland trade—stockfish to Portugal, salt from Portugal to Newfoundland—was a domain of the Danish freighters. The schooner *Bonavista* was built very strong for the Newfoundland trade. The outbreak of World War I put an end to this trade.

The ships were then employed as tramping vessels in the North and Baltic seas until they reached an age at which they could be used only for the shorter coastal trade. The ship received her first engine in 1926. In 1972 the ship's cargo-carrying days were over.

She was preserved out of an interest in cultural history. An extensive modification followed during which the ship was equipped for its current use.

Brita Leth

Previous names: *Hilfred, M. A. Flyvbjerg, Brita*

Type: 2-masted fore-and-aft schooner, wood

Nation: Denmark

Owner: Otto Bjørn Leth, Århus

Home Port: Århus

Years of construction: 1910–11

Shipyard: J. Ring-Andersen, Svendborg

Tonnage: 87 tons gross; 44 tons net

Dimensions:
Length overall: 33.00 m
Length of hull: 22.00 m
Width: 6.50 m
Draft: 2.60 m

Sail area: 420 square meters

Rigging: 13 sails (square foresail)

Masts: height of mainmast over the deck: 23 meters

Auxiliary engine: Scania-Vabis diesel, 230 horsepower

Crew: 2–4-person active crew, 12 trainees, 30 guests on day cruises

Use: chartered ship, sailing school-ship, film ship

Like most Danish sailing ships still in use today, this schooner was built as a freighter. Extensive modifications were necessary before she could be used for her present purpose.

An extremely dramatic accident took place in the year 1941. A hurricane ripped the rig off and the hull sprang leaks in numerous places. The crew tried to land the ship on the sand near Samsø, and an ordinary seaman from the three-man crew lost his life in the process. The ship ran aground in water 22 meters deep. She was raised and put back in working order. With a large engine and the new name *M. A. Flybjerg*, she worked again as a freighter. In 1972 the Leth family acquired the ship.

The training program for the boys and girls consists not only of activities related to the handling of the ship but also and especially of instruction in various academic subjects. Great emphasis is placed on achievement in various athletic activities, including mountain climbing.

Previous names: *Lars, Mona, Hanne Hansen, Karna, Argus, Carene, Mistralen*

Type: 3-masted topsail schooner

Nation: Denmark

Owner: Amba Thomas Brocklebank

Home port: Rømø

Year of construction: 1945

Shipyard: J. Ring-Andersen, Svendborg

Tonnage: 119 tons gross; 36 tons net

Dimensions:
Length overall: 40.84 m
Length of hull: 30.18 m
Length between perpendiculars: 26.70 m
Width: 7.04 m
Draft: 3.00 m

Sail area: 540 square meters

Rigging: 13 sails; foremast (square foresail), single topsail, single topgallant

Masts: height of mainmast over the deck: 24 meters

Auxiliary engine: Scania-Vabis diesel, 230 horsepower

Crew: 5-person active crew, 10 trainees, 3 guests

Use: sailing school-ship for young people with social problems

After the sale of the *Viking* and after the tragic loss of the *København* in December 1928, the Danish government had the state-owned full-rigged ship *Danmark* built. She became a school-ship for future officers of the merchant marine. Initially it was possible to take 120 young men on board. After her modernization in 1959 this number was reduced to 80. Some of the boys, who came aboard at the age of 15 to 18, came from the full-rigged ship *Georg Stage.*

The *Danmark* displays the lines of a classic commercial sailing ship. Tall superstructures are absent, and the two deckhouses are barely visible. The ship has stock anchors on both sides. Six lifeboats hang in davits; two of them have motors. In addition there are automatic rubber boats and liferafts. The active crew sleeps in berths; the young boys sleep in hammocks. Modern navigational equipment is available for training purposes. The *Danmark* is steered from the poop, in front of the charthouse, with a double wheel. Behind the charthouse stands the emergency steering system.

Until World War II, training voyages were undertaken regularly. In 1939 the *Danmark* sailed to the world's exhibition in New York, where the war overtook her. The ship's commanders received instructions not to return to Europe because of the risk. The ship was moored for a while in Jacksonville, Florida, until she was placed at the disposal of the U.S. government upon America's entry into the war. The *Danmark* served as a U.S. Coast Guard school-ship in New London (Connecticut)

until the end of the war. A total of 5000 cadets were trained during this time. The use of the *Danmark* as a school-ship provoked the U.S. Coast Guard to commission the *Eagle*, formerly the *Horst Wessel*, after the war. Today a plaque aboard the *Danmark* expressing the gratitude of the Coast Guard serves as a reminder of this time.

On November 13, 1945, the Danish sailing ship returned home. Danish trainees were back on board already the following year. Since that time the ship has been regularly under sail.

In 1990 a third of the ship was thoroughly overhauled. The training program has

Type: full-rigged ship, steel

Nation: Denmark

Owner: merchant marine (state-owned); Ministry for Trade, Shipping, and Industry, Copenhagen

Home Port: Copenhagen

Year of construction: launched November 19, 1932; commissioned June 1933

Shipyard: Nakskov Skibs, Nakskov (Lolland); design: Aage Larsen

Tonnage: 790 tons gross; 216 tons net; 150 tdw

Dimensions:
Length overall: 77.00 m
Length of hull: 64.00 m
Length between perpendiculars: 54.50 m
Width: 10.00 m
Draft: 4.20 m

Sail area: 1636 square meters

Rigging: 26 sails; 4 foresails, double topsails, single topgallants, royals

Masts and spars: All masts have topmasts and topgallant masts; bowsprit with jibboom; height of mainmast over the waterline: 39.60 meters; length of the main yard: 20.10 meters

Auxiliary engine: diesel engine, 486 horsepower; speed with engine, 9.5 knots

Crew: in addition to the active crew and instructors, 80 boys and girls

Use: sailing school-ship

been reduced in the meantime. Because the contract with the shipping company A. P. Møller, which has stopped training its future officers aboard sailing ships, was not renewed, only 1 training voyage a year is undertaken now. This means that only the permanent active crew now sails aboard the *Danmark*.

Den Store Bjørn

Previous name: *Feuerschiff Nr. 18*

Type: 3-masted fore-and-aft schooner, wood

Nation: Denmark

Owner: the Small School, the Sailors (Småskolen Fremtidens, Denmark/Søfolkene)

Home port: Nyborg

Year of construction: 1902

Shipyard: F. N. Hansen, Odense

Tonnage: 420 ts displacement; 169 tons gross; 53 tons net

Dimensions:
Length overall: 47.00 m
Width: 6.50 m
Draft: 3.60 m

Sail area: 525 meters

Rigging: 10 sails

Masts: height of mainmast over the deck: 31.50 meters

Auxiliary engine: Alpha-diesel, 210 horsepower

Crew: 8-person active crew (including 3 teachers), 12 trainees

Use: sailing school-ship

As a lightship, the *Den Store Bjørn* ("The Great Bear") received a strong hull. She was one of the largest ships to be used for this purpose in Danish waters. After her retirement, the ship was rigged as a schooner in Hobro. The most advanced students of the Small School now use it as a training vessel to supplement the curriculum. The young people study at this school for three years.

Elinor

Previous names: *Alta, Sörkyst, Fuur, Agnete, Elinor*

Type: 3-masted fore-and-aft schooner

Nation: Denmark

Owner: Sejlskibskommanditselskabet ALTA, Gentofte, Denmark

Home port: Copenhagen

Year of construction: 1906

Shipyard: Otto Hansen, Stubbekøbing

Tonnage: approx. 120 ts displacement; 71.48 tons gross; 38.37 tons net

Dimensions:
Length overall: 36.00 m
Length of hull: 25.00 m
Length between perpendiculars: 23.00 m
Width: 6.00 m
Depth in hold: 2.20 m
Depth to deck: 2.50 m
Draft: 2.10 m

Sail area: 450 square meters

Rigging: 15 sails

Masts: height of mainmast over the deck: 22.40 meters

Auxiliary engine: 8-cylinder Deutz diesel engine, 155 horsepower

Crew: 4–6-person active crew, 12 guests

Use: chartered ship

As a trading ship, the young *Elinor* earned her money in the Newfoundland trade. For most of her career, however, she sailed in the Scandinavian coastal trade. In the process she was transformed evermore into a motorized ship. The current owners purchased her in 1967 and returned her to her original condition, including her original rig. The *Elinor* is available for chartered cruises, sailing to the Caribbean in addition to other destinations. Young people with learning disabilities also sail on board.

Type: 2-masted fore-and-aft schooner

Nation: Denmark

Owner: David and Kirsten Thomas, Svendborg, Denmark

Home port: Svendborg

Year of construction: 1897

Shipyard: Bornholms Maskinfabrik, Rønne

Tonnage: 72 tons gross; 48 tons net; 110 tdw

Dimensions:
Length overall: 32.30 m
Length of hull: 23.80 m
Length at the waterline: 21.00 m
Width: 5.90 m

Depth in hold: 2.20 m
Draft: 2.10 m

Sail area: 310 square meters

Rigging: 8 sails; 4 foresails; schooner mast: schooner sail, schooner topsail; mainmast: mainsail, main topsail

Masts: height of mainmast over the waterline: 25.80 meters; both masts have topmasts

Auxiliary engine: Hundested 2-cylinder Hot Head diesel engine, 90 horsepower

Crew: captain, boatswain (cook), 10 guests

Use: chartered ship

The *Freia* is a typical Baltic trading vessel. As a fast sailing ship with a clipper bow (the famous *Cutty Sark* was the model for the construction of the hull), she spent most of her life carrying freight in the Baltic and North seas. The owner changed repeatedly. The name remained the same, and Rønne was always the home port. In 1921 the schooner received its first engine. In 1935 the rig was reduced to that of a galleass. Since 1978 the *Freia* has carried guests.

In 1987 her current owners acquired her. During the subsequent two years she underwent a general overhaul and was equipped with radar and perfect safety equipment at the J. Ring-Andersen Shipyard in Svendborg in keeping with the strict requirements of the Danish seamen's professional association. All cruises leave from and return to Kiel-Holtenau.

Type: 3-masted fore-and-aft schooner, wood

Nation: Denmark

Owner: National Museet, Skibshistorisk Laboratorium, Roskilde

Home port: Marstal

Year of construction: 1915; launched March 26, 1915

Shipyard: C. L. Johansen, Marstal

Tonnage: 98 tons gross; 35 tons net

Dimensions:
Length overall: 34.70 m
Length of hull: 26.44 m
Length between perpendiculars: 25.10 m
Width: 6.90 m
Depth in hold: 2.50 m
Draft: 2.50 m

Sail area: 483 square meters

Rigging: 13 sails

Masts: height of mainmast over the deck: 23.20 meters

Auxiliary engine: Scania Vabis diesel, 6 cylinders, 200 horsepower

Crew: 11-person active crew, 30 boys and girls

Use: sailing school-ship used for social work

As a freight schooner, the ship carried cement and grain to Newfoundland. Later the *Fulton* also found use in the Swedish coastal trade, in which the sails were scarcely used. Since May 1970 she has belonged to the Danish National Museum. Primarily young pupils are gathered on the ship in the context of a social reintegration, boys and girls being equally represented.

Previous names: *Polar Freeze, Arctic Freezer, Fylla, Fyn*

Type: 3-masted fore-and-aft schooner, wood

Nation: Denmark

Owner: Fyns Amtskommune, Svendborg

Home port: Odense

Years of construction: 1922–23

Shipyard: Drejer, Nyborg

Tonnage: 122 tons gross; 88 tons net

Dimensions:
Length overall: 42.00 m
Length of hull: 28.30 m
Length between perpendiculars: 24.00 m
Width: 7.50 m
Depth to deck: 2.90 m
Draft: 2.50 m

Sail area: 480 square meters

Rigging: 11 sails

Masts: height of mainmast over the deck: 26 meters

Auxiliary engine: Scania-Diesel, 234 horsepower

Crew: 3-person active crew, 33 guests and/or students

Use: chartered ship, school field trips

The *Fylla* was built as the freighter *Fyn* and was registered in Marstal. In 1932 Captain H. P. Rasmussen of Svendborg purchased her. A year later the firm Den Kongelige Grønlandske Handel purchased her.

With the new name *Polar Freeze*, the ship transported sheep, fish, and reindeer in the waters off Greenland. In 1979 the municipality of Fyns purchased the ship and had her modified for her current use. Primarily school classes come on board the schooner. She sails among the Danish islands.

Georg Stage

In the year 1882, the Danish shipowner Carl Frederik Stage started the Georg Stage's Minde Foundation and do-

nated to it the full-rigged ship *Georg Stage*. Both foundation and ship received their names from the shipowner's deceased

only son. In 1935 the ship was replaced by the somewhat larger *Georg Stage II*. (The original *Georg Stage* still ex-

ists today under the name *Joseph Conrad*.)

Unique features of the current *Georg Stage* include 2 through decks, 5 bulkheads, a double bottom, 145 tons of fixed ballast (iron and stones), room for 23 tons of water ballast, 4 lifeboats stowed outboard in davits, 1 motorboat, and 1 dinghy. She has a stock anchor on the starboard side and a stockless anchor on the port side, an anchor capstan on the forecastle deck, lighting by oil lamps, heating by ovens, and a bust of Georg Stage as a figurehead.

The fore- and mainsail as well as the spanker can be reefed. The young men sleep

---

Type: full-rigged ship, steel

Nation: Denmark

Owner: merchant marine, Georg-Stage-Stiftung, Copenhagen ("Georg Stage's Minde")

Home port: Copenhagen

Years of construction: 1934–35

Shipyard: Frederikshavn's Vaerft & Flydedok A/S, Frederikshavn

Tonnage: 298 tons gross; 185 tons net

Dimensions:
Length of hull: 41.00 m
Length between perpendiculars: 37.60 m
Width: 8.40 m
Draft: 3.80 m

Sail area: 860 square meters

Rigging: 20 sails; 3 foresails, double topsail, single topgallant sail, royals

Masts and spars: All masts have top- and topgallant masts; lower masts, lower yards, and top yards: steel; all yards and

spars: wood; height of mainmast over the waterline: 30 meters

Auxiliary engine: diesel engine, 122 horsepower; speed with engine, approx. 5 knots

Crew: captain, first, second, and third mates, purser, machinist, radio operator, steward, doctor (only for Atlantic voyages), 4 petty officers, 80 boys

Use: sailing school-ship

in hammocks, which during the day are rolled up and stowed in bulwark nets. In February of each year the young men for the coming training period are recruited by the directorship. The majority of them pay approximately 100 euros for the season. (The yearly budget of the entire ship comes to about 80,000 euros). Some of the young men receive financial aid. Their ages range between 15 and 18. In order to achieve a certain equality in their treatment, the young men on board are referred to by number. The training begins each year in April. Initially the ship drops anchor every night. The voyages then become increasingly longer. In keeping with tradition, the *Georg Stage* visits ports in Sweden, Norway, and Scotland during the summer. Normally she returns to Copenhagen by the beginning of September. There the young men unrig her themselves as a part of their training. During the winter the ship remains laid up in the Royal Danish Naval Shipyard in Copenhagen. Here she is rerigged in the spring. The young men switch to motorized ships in the autumn. Approximately 30 of them are transferred to the state-owned school-ship *Danmark* each year.

The full-rigged ship takes part in the windjammer regattas only when the training program allows for it. Her first voyage across the Atlantic, in 1989, took her to the Caribbean and from there to the East Coast of the United States as far north as Mystic Seaport, where the original *Georg Stage*, today the *Joseph Conrad*, is moored. In 1992 she sailed in the Columbus regatta.

Previous names: *Marie af Sæby, Halmø*

Type: 2-masted fore-and-aft schooner, wood

Nation: Denmark

Owner: Freddy and Bent Jörgensen

Home port: Copenhagen

Year of construction: 1900

Shipyard: Rasmus Møller, Fåborg, Denmark

Tonnage: 120 ts displacment; 58 tons gross; 16 tons net

Dimensions:
Length overall: 32.00 m
Length of hull: 21.00 m
Width: 6.00 m

Sail area: 258/353 square meters

Rigging: 7 to 11 sails

Masts: height of mainmast over the waterline: 22 meters

Auxiliary engine: Alpha diesel 343 90/110 horsepower

Crew: 3-person active crew, 12 berths, 28 deck guests

Use: chartered ship

The *Halmø* got her name from a small island in the vicinity of Marstal. Until 1930 she sailed as a freighter in the Baltic. In 1927 she received her first engine and was rigged as a galleass. From 1930 until 1970 the ship sailed under the name *Marie* as a coasting vessel, serving as a ship of the line between Sæby and Copenhagen.

In 1974, her current owner purchased her. After a process of rebuilding and reconstruction lasting 11 years, the schooner was turned over in 1986 to her current function.

The *Halmø* has once again taken on the typical appearance of a Marstal schooner.

Havet

Previous name: *Edvord Hansen*	Year of construction: 1953	Sail area: 480 square meters	
Type: galleass, wood	Shipyard: Holbæk Skibs- & Bådebyggeri, Holbæk	Auxiliary engine: 142 horsepower	
Nation: Denmark	Tonnage: more than 100 tons gross	Rigging: 5 sails, and in addition 2 topsails	
Owner: Svend + Gitte Hansen, Helsingør	Dimensions: Length overall: 37.50 m	Use: chartered ship	
Home port: Helsingør	Width: 7.10 m Draft: 2.60 m		
Location: Marstal			

The *Havet* ("the Sea") was designed for the Greenland trade. Under her first name the galleass carried freight goods, primarily grain and livestock feed, on the route Copenhagen to Bornholm.

The city of Copenhagen acquired the sailing ship in 1972 and employed the *Havet* in the passenger trade. In 1991 the ship was thoroughly overhauled in Marstal and rigged in the original manner.

Isefjord

Previous names: *Minna, Skagen*	Shipyard: H. V. Buhl's Skibsvaerft, Frederikshavn	Rigging: 9 sails
Type: 2-masted fore-and-aft schooner, wood	Tonnage: gross register tonnage 30; 16 tons net	Masts: height of mainmast over the deck: 17.50 meters
Nation: Denmark	Dimensions:	Auxiliary engine: Bukh diesel, 65 horsepower
Owner: Baron Erik Gyldenkrone-Rysensteen	Length overall: 25.00 m Length of hull: 17.50 m	Crew: 2-person active crew, 24 guests
Home port: Copenhagen	Width: 4.30 m Draft: 1.90 m	Use: chartered ship
Year of construction: 1874	Sail area: 300 square meters	

Twice a day in Copenhagen the *Isefjord* invites guests to a cruise in Danish waters lasting several hours. The wooden 2-masted fore-and-aft schooner was built in 1874 as the *Skagen* in Frederikshaven. As a freighter the ship brought fish from northern Jutland to Copenhagen and transported bulk goods back to Jutland. In summer the sailing voyages also went to Norway, Sweden, and Iceland. In 1937 the *Minna*, as the ship had been called since 1920, ran aground on a sandbank and sank. The diver Valdemar Jensen from Lynæs raised the schooner and gave her the name *Isefjord*. During World War II, the *Isefjord* helped the resistance movement and transported munitions from Sweden to Denmark. Many Jews were able to escape across the Øresund to safety in Sweden.

Since 1971 the ship has belonged to Erik Gyldenkrone-Rysensteen of Copenhagen. At great expense he had the ship rebuilt and equipped for her current purpose. Her guests are allowed to help with navigation, steering, and setting the sails.

Jens Krogh

Previous names: *Ulla Vita, Ida, Jens Krogh*

Type: ketch, wood

Nation: Denmark

Owner: FDF Ålborg Søkreds (Ålborg Seepfadfinder)

Home port: Ålborg

Year of construction: 1899; launched June 22, 1899

Shipyard: H. V. Buhl's Shipyard (now Danyard), Frederikshavn

Tonnage: 59 ts displacement; 34.40 tons gross

Dimensions:
Length overall: 24.20 m
Length of hull: 18.60 m
Length between perpendiculars: 16.40 m
Width: 5.00 m
Draft: 2.20 m

Sail area: 215 square meters

Rigging: 7 sails

Masts: height of mainmast over the deck: 21 meters

Auxiliary engine: Gardner Marine Diesel 6LX, 170 horsepower

Crew: 3-person active crew, 16 trainees

Use: sailing school-ship (also for children)

Built for two traders and a captain, the *Jens Krogh* was registered in Frederikshavn in 1907.

The ketch fished for many years in the North Sea and in the Kattegat, mostly under wind power. From 1912 to 1957 she was registered in Esbjerg. Later Grenå and Sæby were her home ports. In 1973 a youth organization purchased the sailing ship and converted her into a school-ship in three years' work. From April to October the ship is under sail, primarily making visits to foreign countries.

Type: steam frigate (full-rigged ship), wood

Nation: Denmark

Owner: City of Ebeltoft, Frigate Jylland Foundation

Home Port: Ebeltoft (Jutland)

Year of construction: 1857; keel laid June 11, 1857; launched November 20, 1860

Shipyard: Orlogsværft Nyholm, Copenhagen

Tonnage: 2450 ts displacement

Dimensions:
Length overall: approx. 95.00 m
Length between perpendiculars: 64.10 m
Width: 13.20 m
Draft: 6.00 m

Sail area: 1881 square meters

Rigging: originally 18 sails (not counting studding sails); 4 foresails, single topsails, double topgallants (royals), gaff-sails on all masts, studding sails on fore-, topgallant, and lower topgallant yards; later the topgallants and studding sails are absent

Masts and spars: height of mainmast over the waterline measured from the masthead truck: 54 meters; main yard with studding sail spars: approx. 42.50 meters; main yard approx. 28 meters; main topsail yard approx. 24 meters; main topgallant yard: approx. 14 meters

Auxiliary engine: 2-cylinder steam engine (horizontal) from Baumgartner & Burmeister, 400 horsepower (nominal); 1300 horsepower (rated); speed with engine, approx. 12 knots

Crew: 437 men

Armaments: forty-four guns (smooth bored); battery deck thirty 30-pound guns, upper deck fourteen 30-pound guns; caliber 16.2 cm. After conversion in 1863–64 on the upper deck eight 18-pound and four 12-pound (rifled bores); later also a number of rifled breechloaders.

Use: museum ship

Three battleships of the Danish fleet bore the same name before the frigate *Jylland* (1704, 1739, 1760). The frigate was built at the famous navy shipyard on the island Nyholm in Copenhagen. Approximately 1600 120- to 200-year-old oak trees had to be felled for the construction. For the first time in the history of Danish shipbuilding, wire was used for the standing rigging. The beautiful figurehead with a shepherd's staff, a net, ears of grain, and mussels symbolizes the fertility of Jutland and its coast. The rich ornamentation on the stern also reflects this theme.

The ship was first commissioned on May 15, 1862. At first the frigate was a pure cadet ship. Before the outbreak of the war with Prussia and Austria the ship was armed in anticipation of the possibility of war in the winter of 1863–64.

The declaration of war took place on February 1, 1864. On May 9, 1864, off Helgoland the *Jylland,* along with the rest of the Danish squadron under the command of Admiral Suenson, fought a successful engagement against the Prussian and Austrian squadron, which included the steam frigate *Fürst Felix Schwarzenberg* under the

command of Tegetthoff. After the war the ship made numerous voyages in European waters. In 1874 King Christian IX sailed with the frigate to Iceland, and in 1876 to Saint Petersburg. The last great voyage was to the West Indies in 1886–87. At that time Prince Charles, the later King Haakon VII of Norway, was on board as a volunteer cadet.

In the year 1892 the *Jylland* became an exercise and cadet ship. On May 14, 1908, she was retired. The towboat of a German salvage company had already arrived in Copenhagen when the decision was made to keep the frigate after all. Unfor-

tunately, at this point all of the masts and yards had already disappeared. From that point on use was made of the somewhat too weak corvette rig of the retired *Dagmar.* In the following years the *Jylland* was used as an exhibition ship with different exhibits aboard and in this capacity traveled from port city to port city. In August 1912 the estate owner E. Schou purchased the ship and brought her to Juelsminde. There the 50th anniversary of the battle of Helgoland was celebrated on May 9, 1914.

During World War I, the frigate was briefly put into use again as a barracks ship. Until

Schou's death she remained in Juelsminde. Afterward, in 1925, she was towed to Holmen. In 1926 the founding of the "Komitéen til Fregatten Jylland's Bewarelse" came about. As a result, restoration work began, only to be interrupted by the war. In 1935 the ship was brought to Copenhagen. From 1944 to 1945 German refugees lived aboard, and after that English military personnel as well. The ship ran aground in December 1947 as the result of a leak. After the war the restoration work was resumed. Since 1957 the National Museum has also contributed to it.

Several different cities in Jutland sought to acquire the *Jylland*. The city of Ebeltoft ultimately had its offer accepted. The frigate was towed there without masts on September 20, 1960.

The restoration work began in 1984. On August 11, 1984, the ship sailed on her own keel into a specially built dock, which was subsequently pumped empty. On March 24, 1994, the restoration was completed and the newly rigged frigate was presented to the public.

On board the *Lilla Dan* the students of the Kogtved merchant marine school learn practical seamanship. Originally the ship was built for the shipping firm of J. Lauritzen in Copenhagen as a training ship for its own future officers. In 1967 the Kogtved merchant marine school took over the ship. The training cruises lead primarily to the waters around Fünen. The living and sleeping quarters of the young men are located in the ship's hold. Eight berths are located on each side. The salon and the captain's living quarters are located in the stern.

Behind the mainmast stands a deckhouse in which the chart and navigation room is located. The raised quarterdeck is adjacent to this. The hull,

equipped with a rounded bow and a transom stern, was built of Danish oak. Two lifeboats hang in davits on the quarter deck, and a dinghy hangs athwartship over the stern. The gaff-sails are bent to the mast with cringles, and the gaffs are lowered. Ten tons of lead and two tons of stone give the ship the necessary stability. The young men are trained on board in the use of all modern navigational instruments.

At first the initials of the shipping company, Lauritzen, were included on each bow as a coat of arms. These coats of arms were removed following the acquisition by the sailing school and are now located in the impressive collection of figureheads and name plates of the shipyard J. Ring-Andersen in Svendborg. Only on the lower topsail of the *Lilla Dan* is the Lauritzen coat of arms still painted today.

Since 1996 the ship has been used increasingly as a chartered ship as well as for day cruises. The Kogtved merchant marine school has largely given up on instruction aboard sailing ships.

Type: 2-masted topsail schooner, wood	Tonnage: 95 tons gross; 12 tons net; 140 tdw	sails, gaff-topsails, topmast staysail
Nation: Denmark	Dimensions: Length overall: 32.50 m	Masts: height of mainmast over the waterline: 23 meters; both masts with topmast
Owner: merchant marine, "Kogtved Søfartsskole," Kogtved near Svendborg (Fünen)	Length of hull: 25.80 m Length at the waterline: 23.90 m Width: 6.30 m	Auxiliary engine: Alpha 2-cylinder diesel engine, 90/100 horsepower; speed
Home port: Kogtved	Depth to deck: 3.10 m Depth in hold: 2.40 m Draft: approx. 2.50 m	with engine, 7.5 knots
Year of construction: 1950; keel laid May 1950; launched October 28, 1950	Sail area: 280 square meters	Crew: captain, helmsman, 6 boys
Shipyard: J. Ring-Andersen, Svendborg	Rigging: 10 sails; 4 foresails; foremast: double topmasts, schooner sails; mainmast: gaff-	Use: sailing school-ship, chartered ship

Madonna

The former cargo-carrying three-masted schooner received the name *Talata* and was sold to the shipowner Per Henriksen in 1974. He had the ship rigged as a topsail schooner. In 1977 the ship was rechristened the *Mercantic II.* For tax-related reasons, the sailing ship was sold to a buyer in San Francisco in 1985 and received the name *Jacqueline.*

In 1991 the ship was once again up for sail. Per Hendriksen exercised his option on the ship and brought her back to Denmark. Following a general overhaul at the Ring-Andersen shipyard the ship was put back into service in 1992 under the name *Else Dorthea Bager,* named after the shipowner's mother. In 1996 the Tuborg Brewery purchased the ship and since then has used her for advertising purposes. Because in Denmark a bottle opener is often referred to as a "Madonna," the schooner received this name.

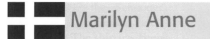

Marilyn Anne

Previous names: *Vest, Vestvåg, Frem*

Type: 3-masted fore-and-aft schooner, wood

Nation: Denmark

Owner: Herning-Holstebro Kommuner & Ringkjøbing Amtskommune

Home port: Struer

Year of construction: 1919; launched June 7, 1919

Shipyard: E. Eriksen, Marstal, Denmark

Tonnage: 280 ts displacement; 136 tons gross; 40 tons net

Dimensions:
Length overall: 38.16 m
Length of hull: 29.16 m
Length between perpendiculars: 26.30 m
Width: 7.60 m
Depth to deck: 3.31 m
Draft: 2.70 m

Sail area: 480 square meters

Rigging: 11 sails

Masts: height of mainmast over the deck: 25.80 meters

Auxiliary engine: Scania diesel, 256 horsepower

Crew: 4-person active crew, 16 trainees, 20 guests (without trainees, 36)

Use: sailing school-ship

This Marstal schooner was built for fishing off Newfoundland. In 1939 the ship was sold to a buyer in Sweden and received the new name *Vestvåg*. As a coastal trader the schooner now transported cement, coal, and wood. In 1958 she returned to Denmark with the name *Vest*, only to be sold to a buyer in Los Angeles in 1968 under the name *Marilyn Anne*. In 1978 the city of Struer acquired the ship. The name was not changed again. The work of converting her into a school-ship was finally completed in 1985. The sailing ship is used primarily to teach schoolchildren about life at sea.

Midsummer

Previous names: *Helge, Johanna Jacoba*

Type: 2-masted fore-and-aft schooner, steel

Nation: Denmark

Owner: Michael Kiersgaard

Home port: Troesne

Year of construction: 1910

Shipyard: Gebr. van der Windt, Vlaardingen, Holland

Tonnage: 94 tons gross

Dimensions:
Length overall: 35.50 m
Length of hull: 27.00 m
Width: 6.10 m
Draft: 3.00 m

Sail area: 550 square meters

Rigging: 7 sails

Auxiliary engine: diesel, 150 horsepower

Crew: 3-person active crew

Use: chartered ship

The herring lugger *Johanna Jacoba* fished with 15 men on board, primarily off the east coast of Scotland. By the 1930s this type of fishing was no longer profitable, and the ship, like many others, was sold to a foreign buyer. This lugger ultimately arrived in Denmark with the name *Helge*.

Unrigged and completely run down, the ship was finally moored in Odense. From 1979 to 1981 the sharply formed sailing hull was converted into a schooner yacht by the current owner in Troense. She sails mostly in the Danish islands.

Nordboen

Type: 2-masted fore-and-aft schooner, wood

Nation: Denmark

Owner: Lilli and Captain Ivan Olsen

Home port: Skagen

Year of construction: 1933

Shipyard: J. Ring-Andersen, Svendborg

Tonnage: 38.61 tons gross

Dimensions:
Length overall: 28.30 m
Length of hull: 21.00 m
Width: 5.30 m
Draft: 3.10 m

Sail area: 405 square meters

Rigging: 7 sails

Auxiliary engine: diesel

Crew: 2-person active crew, 5 berths

Use: chartered ship

The *Nordboen* ("North Land Inhabitant") was used as a fast fish transporter to the Lofoten. Her current owner purchased her in 1970 and equipped her for charter cruises.

A specialty of J. Ring-Andersen was the construction of "Kvasen." These are wooden fishing vessels whose cargo holds are filled with seawater so that the fish can be brought to port alive.

Ecuador

Guayas

Guayas

Type: bark, steel

Nation: Ecuador

Owner: Armada del Ecuador

Home port: Guayaquil

Year of construction: launched October 22, 1976; commissioned July 23, 1977

Shipyard: Astilleros y Talleres Celaya "Astace," Bilbao, Spain

Tonnage: 1300 ts displacement

Dimensions:
Length overall: 78.40 m
Length of hull: 62.40 m
Length between perpendiculars: 56.10 m
Width: 10.16 m
Depth to deck: 6.60 m
Depth in hold: 4.40 m
Draft: 4.40 m

Sail area: 1410 square meters

Rigging: 23 sails; double topsails, single topgallant; royals

Masts: height of mainmast over the deck: 38 meters

Auxiliary engine: General Motors diesel, 700 horsepower

Crew: 60-person active crew, 84 cadets

Use: sailing school-ship

This ship, belonging to the Ecuadorian navy and bearing a condor as a figurehead, received the name *Guayas* for three reasons:

1. Guayas was the name of a chief. He belonged to the Huancavilca tribe that lived in the vicinity of the port city of Guayaquil.

2. Guayas is the largest river in Ecuador.

3. Guayas was the first steamship to be built at the Guayaquil shipyard in the nineteenth century.

The *Guayas* and the Colombian *Gloria* are sister ships. The *Guayas* can be distinguished from the *Gloria* on the basis of her open flying bridge, whereas the *Gloria* has a closed wheelhouse.

Equatorial Guinea

Flying Cloud	Legacy	Polynesia II
	Mandalay	Yankee Clipper

Flying Cloud

Previous names: *Tuxtla, Oiseau des Isles*

Type: barkentine, steel

Nation: Equatorial Guinea

Owner: Didicated Holdings, Ltd.

Home port: Malabo

Shipyard: Chantiers Dubigeon, Nantes

Tonnage: 637 ts displacement; 452 tons gross; 370 tons net

Dimensions:
Length overall: 63.40 meters
Length of hull: 56.00 meters
Length between perpendiculars: 49.80 meters
Width: 9.70 meters
Draft: 4.80 meters

Sail area: 1090 square meters

Rigging: 11 sails

Auxiliary engine: 420 horsepower

Crew: 25-person crew, accommodations for 78 guests

Use: chartered ship for cruises (Windjammer Barefoot Cruises, Miami Beach)

Not much is known about the history of this ship. The *Oiseau des Isles* was a French school-ship. In 1955 she was sold to a buyer in Mexico and sailed there for ten years as a freighter with the name *Tuxtla*.

Today this large ship with the sharp clipper bow sails from Tortola as a cruise ship through the Virgin Islands.

Previous name: *France II*

Type: 4-masted trysail schooner, steel

Nation: Equatorial Guinea

Owner: Windjammer Barefoot Cruises, Ltd., Miami Beach

Home port: San Juan, Puerto Rico

Year of construction: 1959

Shipyard: Forges et Chantiers de la Méditerrannée, Le Havre

Tonnage: 1740 ts displacement

Dimensions:
Length overall: 89.40 m
Length of hull: 79.50 m
Length between perpendiculars: 68.50 m
Width: 12.30 m
Draft: 6.90 m

Sail area: 1848 square meters

Rigging: 11 sails, trysail

Masts: height of mainmast over the waterline: 51.80 meters

Auxiliary engine: three 8-cylinder Paxman Diesel/Electrics, 865 horsepower each

Crew: 43-person active crew, 122 guests

Use: cruise ship

For many years the *France II* served the French government as a meteorological research vessel. In 1989 she was acquired by the fleet of the Windjammer Cruises. In 1997 the schooner received her current name. The name is a tribute to the founder of the organization, Captain Michael Burke, whose likeness decorates the bow as a figurehead. With his Hawaiian shirt and a bottle of rum, his features are unmistakable. The powerful schooner meets all standards for luxury. The *Polynesia II*, the *Mandalay*, the *Flying Cloud*, and the *Yankee Clipper* also belong to the fleet.

Mandalay

Previous names: *Vema, Hussar*

Type: barkentine, steel

Nation: Equatorial Guinea

Owner: Hoveton, Ltd.

Home port: Malbo

Year of construction: 1923

Shipyard: Burmeister & Wain, Copenhagen

Tonnage: 743 ts displacement; 533 tons gross; 234 tons net

Dimensions:
Length overall: 71.70 m
Length of hull: 61.40 m
Length between perpendiculars: 56.20 m
Width: 10.00 m
Draft: 4.50 m

Sail area: 1190 square meters

Rigging: 11 sails

Masts: one-piece, steel; height of mainmast over the deck: 42.50 meters

Crew: 28-person active crew, accommodations for 60 guests

Use: chartered ship for cruises (Windjammer Barefoot Cruises, Miami Beach)

The *Vema* was built as the private yacht *Hussar* for Edward F. Hutton. Later Unger Vetlesen purchased the ship and renamed it the *Vema*. As a yacht she often distinguished herself through her speed. In 1941 she was taken over by the U.S. Maritime Commission. The schooner was converted into a school-ship.

At the end of the war the U.S. government sold the ship to Captain Louis Kennedy from New Scotland, who used her as a chartered ship for cruises. In 1953 Columbia University in New York purchased the ship. From then on she served the Lamont Geological Observatory and its students as a research ship for oceanography. The ship no longer sailed under wind power at that time. Only the lower masts and the streamlined hull were still reminiscent of the fast sailing ship she had been.

Today the ship belongs to the fleet of the Windjammer Barefoot Cruises company. The deck superstructures from her period as a research vessel were removed, and the entire interior was luxuriously furnished.

Polynesia II

Previous name: *Argus*

Type: 4-masted staysail schooner, steel

Nation: Equatorial Guinea

Owner: Bimba, Ltd.

Home port: Malabo

Year of construction: 1938

Shipyard: De Haan & Oerlmans

Tonnage: 820 ts displacement; 696 tons gross; 413 tons net

Dimensions:
Length overall: 75.40 m
Length of hull: 61.70 m
Length between perpendiculars: 51.60 m
Width: 10.90 m
Draft: 5.40 m

Sail area: 1323 square meters

Rigging: 13 sails

Masts: height of mizzenmast over the waterline: 55 meters

Auxiliary engine: Sulzer Diesel, 475 horsepower

Crew: 45-person active crew, accommodations for 126 guests

Use: chartered ship for cruises (Windjammer Barefoot Cruises, Miami Beach)

The *Argus* became famous as a Portuguese bank schooner.

At that time 72 fishermen with 53 dories sailed aboard her. Alan Villiers dedicated the biography *Quest of the Schooner Argus* to her, in which he also described the life of the entire bank schooner fleet. Since 1975 the ship has belonged to the Windjammer fleet in Florida. Extensive work was necessary in order to make the former fishing vessel into a cruise ship able to meet the highest standards. The cabins for the passengers are now located on two new decks. In addition to the new rig, the former 4-masted fore-and-aft schooner also received a complete teak upper deck.

The *Mandalay,* the *Flying Cloud,* and the *Yankee Clipper,* among other ships, also belong to the Windjammer Barefoot Cruises fleet.

Yankee Clipper

Previous name: *Cressida*

Type: 3-masted staysail schooner, steel

Nation: Equatorial Guinea

Owner: Magnolia Investments

Home port: Malabo

Year of construction: 1927

Shipyard: Fr. Krupp Germania Shipyard, Kiel

Tonnage: 600 ts displacement; 350 tons gross; 180 tons net

Dimensions:
Length overall: 59.50 m
Length of hull: 52.20 m
Length between perpendiculars: 9.10 m
Width: 3.30 m
Draft: 5.10 m

Sail area: 950 square meters

Rigging: 7 sails; 3 (4) foresails; foremast: fore trysail; mainmast: main staysail; mainsail (Bermuda rigging)

Masts: height of mainmast over the deck: 33.50 meters

Auxiliary engine: two General Motors diesel engines, 280 horsepower each

Crew: 23-person active crew, accommodations for 70 guests

Use: chartered ship for cruises (Windjammer Barefoot Cruises, Miami Beach)

The great yacht *Yankee Clipper* was built as the *Cressida* for the Vanderbilt family. She served primarily as a luxury yacht for long voyages and especially for exploratory expeditions. The idea for the Windjammer Cruises originated with Captain Mike Burke of Miami Beach (Florida). After World War II he purchased three exceptionally large yachts, the *Cressida*, the *Elk*, and the *Caribee*. (The *Elk* sails today under the name *Polynesia II*.) They were converted to be able to accommodate a large number of passengers and now undertake vacation cruises year-round for paying guests to the islands of the West Indies and to the Bahamas. The *Yankee Clipper* sails twice a month in the waters of the West Indies (Leeward Islands and Windward Islands).

During her stays in port the ship serves as a hotel. The guests have the opportunity to take part in the sailing maneuvers with their own hands.

Finland

Albanus
Helena

Jacobstads Wapen
Linden
Pommern

Sigyn
Suomen Joutsen

Albanus

Type: galleass (one-and-a-half-master), wood

Nation: Finland

Owner: the Albanus Association

Home port: Mariehamn

Year of construction: 1987; launched July 24, 1988

Shipyard: Albanus shipyard, Mariehamn

Tonnage: 80 ts displacement

Dimensions:
Length overall: 30.00 m
Length of hull: 21.70 m
Width: 6.20 m
Draft: 1.90 m

Sail area: 303 square meters

Rigging: 8 sails

Masts: height of mainmast over the deck: 25 meters

Auxiliary engine: Volvo Penta TAMD 71, 230 horsepower

Crew: 2- to 4-person active crew, 20 trainees

Use: sailing school-ship

The model for this reconstruction was a freighter of the same name that was built in 1904. The current *Albanus* is used primarily to instruct school-children and youth groups in traditional sailing techniques with all of the associated educational benefits.

Helena

In the summer the *Helena* sails primarily in the Baltic Sea. In the winter she visits the Caribbean.

Type: 2-masted staysail
schooner, steel

Nation: Finland

Owner: Sail Training Association
Finland

Home port: Uusikaupunki

Year of construction: 1992;
launched July 7, 1992

Shipyard: Uusikaupunki
Shipyard

Tonnage: 110 ts displacement;
79 tons gross; 49 tons net

Dimensions:
Length overall: 38.70 m
Length of hull: 31.00 m
Length between
perpendiculars: 23.30 m
Width: 6.50 m

Depth to deck: 2.60 m
Draft: 3.10 m

Sail area: 1120 square meters

Rigging: 10 sails (when fully
rigged)

Masts: height of mainmast over
the deck: 29.50 meters

Auxiliary engine: SACM UD-19,
6-cylinder diesel, 320
horsepower

Crew: 4-person active crew, 24
trainees

Use: sailing school-ship

 # Jacobstads Wapen

Type: galleass, wood,
reproduction

Nation: Finland

Owner: Jakobstads Gamla
Hamn AB

Home port: Jakobstad

Years of construction:
1988–1994; launched July
1994

Shipyard: Jakobstads Gamla
Hamn

Tonnage: 176 ts displacement;
128 tons gross; 40 tons net

Dimensions:
Length overall: 40.00 m
Length of hull: 23.90 m
Length between
perpendiculars: 6.80 m

Width: 6.80 m
Depth in hold: 2.20 m
Depth to deck: 3.90 m
Draft: 2.40 m

Sail area: 480 square meters

Rigging: 8 sails: 3 foresails;
mainmast: gaff-sail, single
topsail, single topgallant;
mizzenmast: gaff-sail, single
topsail

Masts: height of mainmast over
the deck: 29 meters

Auxiliary engine: two Volvo
Pentan engines, 350
horsepower each

Crew: 5- to 10-person active
crew, 50 guests

Use: public tours, public
charter

In the second half of the eighteenth century two ships were built in Jakobstad (Pietarsaari) in the Gulf of Bothnia that both bore the name *Jakobstads Wapen*. One of them was a galleass built in 1767. The plans for her, which still exist, came from the famous Swedish ship designer Fredrik Henrik Chapman (later af Chapman). This galleass was a trading vessel that transported primarily tar and wood. Jakobstad was an important trade center at that time.

The reconstruction was a national event, because the trading voyages of the Finnish ships, and the *Jacobstads Wapen* in particular, were able to significantly alleviate the restrictions to which Finland was subject after World War II. The galleass was one of the first Finnish ships to sail through the Øresund and was sold in a North Sea port after delivering her cargo.

Linden

Type: 3-masted fore-and-aft schooner, wood

Nation: Finland (Åland Islands)

Owner: Rederi AB LINDEN

Home port: Mariehamn

Year of construction: 1992; launched August 1992

Shipyard: LINDEN Varvet, Mariehamn

Tonnage: 353 ts displacement; 277 tons gross; 111 tons net

Dimensions:
Length overall: 49.00 m
Length of hull: 36.00 m
Length between perpendiculars: 32.30 m
Width: 8.70 m
Depth to deck: 4.30 m
Draft: 3.00 m

Sail area: 630 square meters

Rigging: 11 sails

Masts: height of mainmast over the deck: 31.50 meters

Auxiliary engine: Volvo TAMD 161, 550 horsepower

Crew: 9-person active crew, overnight accommodations for 30 guests, 75 guests on day cruises

Use: chartered ship

The *Linden* is one of the most beautiful newly built wooden sailing ships of recent years as a result of the exceptionally fine sheer line of her deck and the aesthetics of her coloration. The shrouds are made fast outboard with chain plates in the traditional manner. The model for the reconstruction was a similar schooner that was launched in 1920 in Mariehamn.

Previous name: *Mneme*

Type: 4-masted bark, steel

Nation: Finland

Owner: city of Mariehamn, Åland Sjöfartsmuseum

Home port: Mariehamn

Year of construction: 1903

Shipyard: J. Reid & Company, Ltd., Glasgow, Whiteinch

Tonnage: 2413 tons gross; 2266 tons net

Dimensions:
Length overall: 106.50 m
Length of hull: 96.00 m
Length between perpendiculars: 87.50 m
Width: 13.20 m
Depth in hold: 7.50 m
Draft: approx. 6.50 m

Rigging: 27 sails; 4 foresails, double topsail, double topgallant, no royals

("baldheader"); mizzenmast: mizzen sail, mizzen topsail

Masts and spars: all square-rigged masts are the same height; height of mainmast over the deck: 46.30 meters; length of the main yard: 27.70 meters; length of the main upper topgallant yard: 17.70 meters

Auxiliary engine: none

Use: museum ship

The 4-masted bark was built in 1903 in Glasgow as the *Mneme* (Greek: "memory") for the shipping firm of B. Wencke and Sons in Hamburg. To save money, she was built as a "baldheader" without royals; also, the yards were interchangeable. The ship did not have a main deck, and hence a very wide deck area typical of nineteenth-century trading vessels emerged between the poop and the forecastle. The large deckhouse stands between the fore- and mainmasts. In addition to the crew's living quarters, it contains the kitchen and the boiler. A smaller deckhouse stands between the mizzenmast and the poop. A short gangway connects it to the poop deck. The sailing ship was steered from the poop in the classic manner, so that the helmsman was not sheltered by a wheelhouse. A full-sized figurehead adorns the bow. It personifies the Greek muse.

In 1906 the "Rhederei Actiengesellschaft von 1896" purchased the ship. In the year 1907 the F. Laeisz shipping company of Hamburg acquired her. As a "P-Liner" the ship got the new name *Pommern*. Until World War I the *Pommern* sailed to South America in the saltpeter trade. She was in Valparaiso at the outbreak of the war. Not until 1921 did she return to Europe along with other sailing ships and was unloaded in Delfzijl. She had to be delivered to Greece as a reparations payment, although the Greeks had no use for the ship.

In 1923 the shipowner Gustaf Erikson of Mariehamn in the Åland Islands purchased the *Pommern*. From then until World War II she sailed mostly in the grain trade to Australia. During the war she was initially laid up in Mariehamn. Later she served as a granary in Stockholm. After the end of the war she returned to Mariehamn but was not put back into service.

In 1952 the Gustaf Erikson shipping company donated the ship to the city of Mariehamn. Since then the *Pommern* has belonged to the Ålands Sjöfartsmuseum. She is moored immediately adjacent to the museum in the harbor at Mariehamn.

Sigyn

Type: bark, wood	Sail area: as a bark originally approx. 800 square meters
Nation: Finland	
Owner: Sjöhistoriska Museet vid Åbo Akademi	Rigging: as a bark 20 sails; as a barkentine 16 sails; 3 foresails, double topsails, single topgallants, royals, gaff-sail, gaff-topsail
Home Port: Åbo, Aura quay	
Year of construction: 1887	
Shipyard: Gamla Varvet, Göteborg	Masts, topmasts, and spars: pitch pine; foremast: top- and topgallant masts; main- and mizzenmasts with one topmast each; height of mainmast over the deck: 30 meters (as a bark 32 meters); bowsprit with a jibboom
Tonnage: 550 ts displacement; 359 tons gross; 301 tons net	
Dimensions: Length overall: 55.00 m (as a bark originally): 59.00 m Length of hull: 47.50 m Length between perpendiculars: 42.50 m Width: 9.30 m Depth in hold: 3.80 m Draft (fully loaded): approx. 4.00 m	Auxiliary engine: none
	Crew: as a bark 11-person active crew; as a barkentine 8 to 9 people; in addition 2 to 4 boys
	Use: museum ship

Few ships have changed owners as many times in the course of their lives as the *Sigyn*. She was built in 1887 as a wooden bark for A. Landgrens Enka of Göteberg. In 1905 Anders Svensson of Halmstad (Sweden) bought her; he sold her in turn to the firm C. T. Jonasson & Salsakers Angsags AB in Råå (Sweden). After 1921 Salsakers Ansags AB was the sole proprietor. In the year 1925 Sigfried Ziegler of Råå bought the ship, only to sell her to Arthur Lundqvist of Wardö, Åland, in 1927. In 1935 the *Sigyn* became the property of Fredrik Eriksson of Wardö. Since 1939 she has belonged to the Sea-Historical Museum of the Åbo-Academy (Sjöhistoriska Museet vid Åbo Akademi).

The ship made her first voyage to China; she then sailed for years as a freighter in all the oceans of the world. In 1913 during a storm the *Sigyn* was torn loose of her anchor chain off the Norwegian coast near Kristiansand and was stranded and seriously damaged. She was able to be repaired but was rerigged as a barkentine.

In World War I she made numerous voyages across the Atlantic. The last one took her to Pensacola (Florida) in 1916. Until 1937 she sailed mostly in the Baltic Sea. In the autumn of 1937 she sailed for the last time as a freighter from Frederiksund (Denmark) to Wardö (Åland). Afterward she was retired.

The Åbo-Academy purchased the barkentine in the spring of 1939 in order to preserve her as a museum ship. The *Sigyn* sailed one more time, however, from August until September 1954, when she was used in the making of a film. Since then she has been moored as a museum ship at the Aura quay in Åbo.

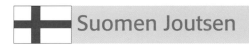

Suomen Joutsen

Previous names: *Oldenburg, Laennec*

Type: full-rigged ship, steel

Nation: Finland

Owner: merchant marine, maritime school Turku

Home port: Turku, Aura quay

Year of construction: 1902; launched October 16, 1902

Shipyard: Chantiers et Ateliers de Saint Nazaire

Tonnage: 2900 ts displacement; 2260 tons gross

Dimensions:
Length overall: 96.00 m
Length of hull: 88.70 m
Length between perpendiculars: 80.00 m
Width: 12.29 m
Draft: 5.15 m

Sail area: 2250 square meters

Rigging: 27 sails; 4 foresails; foremast, mainmast: double topsails, double topgallants, royals; mizzenmast: double topsails, single topgallant, royal

Masts, spars: all masts with top- and topgallant masts; height of mainmast over the waterline: 52 meters; on the mizzenmast no gaffs, but instead small flag gaff on the crosstrees

Auxiliary engine: two Scandia diesel engines, 200 horsepower each; speed with engine, approx. 6 km

Crew: today, as a stationary school-ship, 150 people (including boys)

Use: stationary school-ship

The full-rigged ship was built as the *Laennec* for the Societé Anonyme des Armateurs Nantais. At that time the ship carried saltpeter in addition to other cargo. Under her first owner the *Laennac* was involved in many, in part very serious, accidents. This pattern repeated itself throughout her entire career. Because no profitable cargoes could any longer be found, the society had to lay the ship up in 1921 in La Martinière near Nantes. In 1923 the shipping company of Hans Hinrich Schmidt in Hamburg purchased the ship, named her *Oldenburg,* and converted her into a freight-carrying school-ship. At that time the *Oldenburg* was involved primarily in the saltpeter trade.

In 1928 the Bremen school-ship company Sea Travel purchased the ship. Without a change of name the ship continued to sail as a freight-carrying school-ship. In 1931 the *Oldenburg* was sold to the Finnish government. She received the new name *Suomen Joutsen* ("Swan of Finland") and was converted into a school-ship for the Finnish navy. Living quarters for 80 to 90 cadets emerged on the between deck. Portholes were cut in the sides. The ship received a significantly higher freeboard in the reconstruction. The most important change was the introduction of two auxiliary engines, however. Until World War II the ship made regular training

cruises. During the war the sailing ship served, unrigged, as a barracks ship. After the war there were a few more voyages. Today the *Suomen Joutsen* serves the Finnish merchant marine as a stationary school-ship.

Since the time of the ship's construction, a peculiarity of the way the deck is laid out has been the fact that it connects the long forecastle with the forward deckhouse. The poop was connected to the forward deckhouse, the forecastle, and the deckhouse aft of the great mast by means of a gangway. The crew at that time lived in the forward deckhouse. In addition to a galley and donkey boiler, there was even a cafeteria for the crew inside, which was highly unusual for the time.

France

Bel Espoir II
Belem
Club Med II

Duchesse Anne
Frya
La Belle Poule
  and L'Etoile

La Cancalaise
La Recouvrance
Le Renard
Rara Avis

Bel Espoir II

Previous names: *Prince Louis II, Peder Most, Anette S., Nette S.*

Type: 3-masted topsail schooner, wood

Nation: France

Owner: Les Amis de Jeudi-Dimanche, Paris

Home port: Brest

Year of construction: 1944

Shipyard: J. Ring-Andersen, Svendborg, Denmark

Tonnage: 189 tons gross; 79.75 tons net

Dimensions:
Length overall: 35.50 m
Length of hull: 27.40 m
Width: 7.00 m
Depth in hold: 2.10 m
Draft: 2.60 m

Sail area: 465 square meters (without square foresail)

Rigging: 9 sails; 3 foresails; foremast: boom foresail, gaff-topsail (square foresail); mainmast: gaff-sail, gaff-topsail; mizzenmast: gaff-sail

Masts: all masts have one topmast; height of mainmast over the deck: 24.50 m

Auxiliary engine: diesel engine, 170 horsepower

Crew: captain, teacher, boatswain, machinist, cook, 24 trainees

Use: sailing school-ship

In 1944 the Danish shipping company A. C. Sørensen commissioned the *Nette S.*, later the *Peder Most*. The ship was supposed to be used for the transportation of cattle and was equipped accordingly. On her voyages between Copenhagen and Hamburg she carried up to 200 head at a time.

The schooner has the typical Scandinavian round bow. The sails are bent with cringles to the mast.

All gaffs are lowered. The dinghy, which in ships of this kind usually hangs over the stern, in this case is located in chocks athwartship on the quarterdeck behind the wheelhouse.

In 1955 the Outward Bound Trust of London purchased the ship as a substitute for the retired *Prince Louis I*. The Outward Bound Trust owns a number of schools in England. The students are not supposed to be explicitly trained as future seamen. Each school-ship be-

longing to this organization is in the first instance a means to encourage camaraderie, adaptability, courage, and similar qualities.

In addition to the interior reconstruction, the ship at that time received a new deck, because the large dormer windows had to be closed. On June 30, 1955, in Glasgow the flag and the name were ceremoniously changed in the presence of His Royal Highness Prince Philip.

The *Prince Louis II* belonged for many years to the Outward Bound Moray Sea School in Burghead, Elgin (Scotland). In 1967 she was transferred to Dartmouth (Devon). The ship had become too small for the school's re-

quirements. For that reason she was sold on May 9, 1968, to the French society Les Amis de Jeudi-Dimanche. The schooner afterward took on the name *Bel Espoir II*.

This French youth organization encourages recreational activities for schoolchildren. The name arose from the fact that French children have half of Thursday and, naturally, also Sunday off from school. The *Bel Espoir II* is supposed to offer children from families of modest circumstances the opportunity to become acquainted with the open sea and with foreign countries as part of a community.

An extensive overhaul took place in 1993–94 in Camaret. The ship was replanked and got new masts and a new set of sails.

The ship was built as the bark *Belem* ("Bethlehem") for the shipping company Denis Crovan & Company. The main cargo at that time consisted of cocoa beans, which the ship transported from Para (Belem, Brazil) to Nantes for a Parisian chocolate factory. Later the *Belem* sailed under the flag of H. Fleuriot & Company (Société des Armateurs Coloniaux). In 1913 the ship was sold to the duke of Westminster. He had the bark converted into a seagoing yacht but left the name unchanged. Significant changes included auxiliary en-

gines, electric light, and an enlargement of the deckhouse. The iron poop railing was replaced by a somewhat ponderous teak balustrade. The white streak was retained but was painted below the deck line in the English manner. For new decks and deck structures teak wood was used exclusively.

In 1921 the *Belem* was sold to Sir A. E. Guinness. Under the new name *Fantome II* she sailed once again as a yacht. After the death of her owner in 1950 she was put up for sale. In 1951 she was acquired by the Italian foundation Giorgio Cini in

Venice, whose name she also received. Her rerigging as a barkentine followed, although the square sails were not set. Modern navigational instruments were available for training purposes. The ship has an anchor winch on the forecastle, boats in davits, and a stockless anchor. A centrally located deckhouse carries the smaller charthouse on top. The roof of the deckhouse was extended to the bulwark. Hence a sort of main deck was created from which the ship was steered at that time. On the poop stands the emergency wheel.

The foundation primarily looked after orphans of sailors and fishermen. It was left up to the young men whether they wanted to remain in the maritime trades. The students wore uniforms similar to those of the Italian navy. During this period the ship had her dock immediately in front of the school buildings on the island of San Giorgio in Venice. On January 20, 1979, the French organization Association pour la Sauvegarde et la Conservation des Anciens Navires Francais acquired the barkentine and once again gave her the

Previous names: *Giorgio Cini, Fantome II, Belem*

Type: bark, steel

Nation: France

Owner: Fondation BELEM, Paris

Home port: Nantes (Cherbourg)

Year of construction: 1896

Shipyard: A. Dubigeon, Nantes

Tonnage: 611 ts displacement; 562 tons gross

Dimensions:
Length overall: 58.00 m
Length of hull: 51.00 m
Length at the waterline: 48.00 m
Width: 8.80 m
Depth in hold: 4.60 m
Draft: 3.50 m

Rigging; as a bark 21 sails; as a barkentine 13 sails; 2 foresails, foremast: foresail, double topsails, single topgallants, royals; mainmast: mainsail, main topsail, main staysail, main topmast staysail, main topgallant; mizzenmast: spanker (no mizzen topsail—exhaust pipe)

Masts, spars: lower masts, mizzen topmast, booms: steel; yards, fore-, main topmasts and all other spars: wood; lower mizzenmast expels exhaust gases; mainmast is lowered

Auxiliary engine: two Fiat diesel engines, 300 horsepower each

Use: sailing school-ship

old name *Belem*. After being towed for 34 days she arrived on September 17, 1979, in Brest. She was once more rigged as a bark.

For the journey to Paris the ship had to be fully unrigged once again. This relocation did not go smoothly, because various ports in Brittany objected to the ship's removal to Paris.

The *Belem* is the last authentic large French sailing ship.

In 1985 the *Belem* left Paris. In Le Havre and Caen the ship was equipped to sail once again. Her first trial runs occurred in the same year. Today the ship regularly makes voyages under wind power. She had her hundredth birthday in 1996.

Club Med II

These ships have abandoned the classic design of a great sailing vessel. Seamanship is no longer in demand, but rather a pleasant cruise on a floating luxury hotel offering a wide variety of leisure activities. *Wind Surf* has a computer-controlled rolling device for the sails. With this a sail can be furled or unfurled on a minute-by-minute basis. While cruising, sails and engines can be used simultaneously. The ship is divided into eight decks and contains two swimming pools and two tenders, which are similar to landing boats. The ship's equipment includes bow and stern rudders, a pitch-control mechanism, and fin stabilizers. All 196 external cabins and five suites feature satellite telephone jacks. The *Club Med I* has sailed for Windstar Cruises, Ltd., Seattle, since the beginning of 1998 under the new name *Wind Surf.*

Type: 5-masted staysail schooner, steel (combined sail and motor ships)

Nation: France

Owner: Club Mediterranée et Societé Havraise Services et Transports

Home port: Nassau

Year of construction: 1989 and/or 1992

Shipyard: Ateliers et Chantiers du Havre

Tonnage: gross register tonnage 14,754

Dimensions:
Length overall: 187.00 m
Width: 20.00 m
Draft: 5.00 m

Sail area: 2500 square meters

Rigging: 7 sails

Masts: height of mainmast over the deck: 50 meters

Auxiliary engine: four 3000-horsepower Wärtsilä diesel engines; two 280-kilowatt alternating-current generators (diesel electric power)

Crew: 222-person active crew, 410 passengers

Use: cruise ship

Duchesse Anne

Previous name: *Grand Duchess Elisabeth*

Type: full-rigged ship, steel

Nation: France

Owner: city of Dunkirk

Home port: Dunkirk

Year of construction: 1901; launched March 1901

Shipyard: J. C. Tecklenborg, Geestemünde (Bremerhaven)

Tonnage: 1260 tons gross; 721 tons net

Dimensions:
Length overall: approx. 92.00 m
Length of hull: approx. 80.00 m
Length between perpendiculars: 69.00 m
Width: 11.90 m
Depth in hold: 6.30 m

Rigging: 24 sails; 3 foresails, double topsail, single topgallant, royals

Masts, spars: height of mainmast over the deck: 40 meters; length of the main yard: 22 meters; length of main-royal yard: 11.50 meters; bowsprit with jibboom

Auxiliary engine: none

Crew: under sail a total of 180 to 200 persons

Use: museum ship

The German School-Ship Association, founded in 1900, owned three sailing school-ships until the beginning of World War I, the construction of which had been commissioned by the association. The ships were pure school-ships and accordingly didn't carry any freight. They received their names from members of the House of Oldenburg, whose grand duke had generously contributed to the training of future seamen aboard sailing school-ships. The first of these ships was the *Grand Duchess Elisabeth* (today the *Duchesse Anne*), which was launched in 1901. She was followed in 1909 by the *Princess Eitel Friedrich* (today the *Dar Pomorza*) and in 1914 by the *Grand Duke Friedrich August* (today the *Statsraad Lehmkuhl*).

The *Grand Duchess Elisabeth* was one of the first sailing school-ships that did not carry freight. These ships were consciously equipped for a large number of young men in order to habituate them, in addition to other exigencies, to communal life in a very confined space. The German sailing school-ships were all painted according to a shared color scheme. The white hull was bordered on top by a light ochre-colored poop and forecastle. For this reason the hull appeared exceptionally elegant, because the even, sheer line appeared to be uninterrupted. This coloration was retained in the modern *Gorch Fock*.

The *Grand Duchess Elisabeth* served as a school-ship for a total of 44 years. Her shorter cruises in the summer generally led to the North Sea or the Baltic, while the destinations in the winter were generally South Africa, South America, and above all the West Indian waters. The ship was seriously damaged in 1928 by a fire that broke out in the sail locker. A further incident occurred in 1931, when the ship collided with the Latvian sailing ship *Evermore*. Both ships suffered damage above the waterline.

Shortly before World War II the *Grand Duchess Elisabeth* was transferred to the German Seaman School in Hamburg without a change of name. In 1945 she had to be turned over to France as a reparations payment. At first it appeared that she would remain in training service under the new name *Duchesse Anne*. Later plans were announced to use her as a stationary school-ship in Lorient (Brittany). But this plan also fell through.

In 1946 the ship was unrigged to the lower masts and remained unused until 1951. At the end of 1951 the *Duchesse Anne* was towed to Brest. There she remained for many years as a barracks ship of the French navy. After her retirement she was towed to the Atlantic port of Lorient, where, in disrepair, she confronted an uncertain future. The city of Dunkirk intervened to preserve her. There she is being restored and rerigged in order to become a tourist attraction in the harbor.

Frya

Previous names: *Freia, Petsmo, Marij, Olaf Petersen*

Type: 3-masted topsail schooner, steel

Nation: France

Owner: Jacques Buret, Dunkirk

Home port: Dunkirk

Year of construction: 1906

Shipyard: Bondegard & Jespersen, Marstal, Denmark

Tonnage: 84.49 tons gross; 52.25 tons net; 125 ts TM

Dimensions:
Length overall: 27.50 m
Length of hull: 24.40 m
Length between perpendiculars: 22.80 m
Width: 5.60 m
Depth in hold: 2.60 m
Draft: 2.50 m

Sail area: 242 square meters

Rigging: 9 sails (Dacron); 3 foresails, all masts; gaff-sails, gaff-topsails

Masts: height of mizzenmast over the deck: 20 meters; bowsprit and masts: steel; topmasts: wood

Auxiliary engine: Modag-Krupp, 2-stroke diesel engine, 100 horsepower

Crew: 3-person active crew, 12 guests, students

Use: private ship for passenger cruises and sailing school-ship

As the first steel ship to leave the shipyard in Marstal, the former *Olaf Petersen* sailed primarily in northern waters. The shipping company belonged to H. M. Petersen and J. C. Albertsen. The ship also provided the postal service between Iceland and Spain for a time. In 1910 Oerum Wulff of Copenhagen purchased her. Under the name *Marij* the ship carried grain between Scandinavia and Russia. A small auxiliary engine of only 18 horsepower assisted it.

After 1929 the schooner sailed under the German flag with the names *Petsmo* and *Freia*. In the 1950s all of her masts were removed. The *Freia* had become a freight-carrying motorized ship. Her last German owners were Richard Hübner and, until 1961, Nikolaus Köln from Burgstaaken auf Fehmarn.

Her former Dutch owner discovered her in Burgstaaken. Through many years of work a new *Frya* took shape, one that met all the requirements of a modern cruise ship. This is the case both for the living accommodations and for the navigational equipment. The *Frya* sails not only for paying guests but is also available to serve as a sailing school-ship.

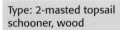
Type: 2-masted topsail schooner, wood

Nation: France

Owner: Marine Nationale Ecole Navale, Lanvéoc-Poulmic/Brest

Home port: Brest

Year of construction: 1932; launched January 1932

Shipyard: Chantiers Naval de Normandie, Fécamp

Tonnage: 227–275 ts displacement

Dimensions:
Length overall: 37.50 m
Length between perpendiculars: 25.30 m
Width: 7.20 m
Draft: 3.60 m

Sail area: 424 square meters

Rigging: 9 sails; 3 foresails (plus outer jibboom); foremast: boom foresail, single topsail; mainmast: gaff-sail, topsail, topmast staysail

Masts: height of mainmast over the waterline: 32.50 meters; both masts with topmast

Auxiliary engine: Sulzer diesel, 300 horsepower

Crew: 3 officers, 5 petty officers, 12 regular crew members, 30 cadets

La Belle Poule is the fourth ship of the French navy to bear this name. Her predecessors were frigates of the eighteenth and nineteenth centuries. Napoleon's exhumed corpse was brought to France aboard the frigate *La Belle Poule* in 1840, 20 years after the emperor's death. A famous privateer who served the navy in Bordeaux was the origin of the name.

Like her sister ship *L'Etoile*, the schooner was specially built for the merchant marine school. The schooners of Paimpol, which fished near the islands, served as a model.

The deep topsail is furled with the help of a roller reefing system. The gaffs are lowered. By this means, all of the sails can be handled from the deck. Both gaff-sails as well as the topsail are bent with cringles to the mast. One deckhouse stands aft of the foremast, a second aft of the mainmast. The band on the caps of the students bears the inscription "Ecole des Mousses." *L'Etoile* is the fifteenth ship in the French fleet since 1622 to bear this name.

The two ships undertook various voyages in English waters in the period from 1940 to 1944. The *La Belle Poule* was involved in military engagements during which casualties were sustained on board. Today the regular training cruises take place mostly in European waters.

La Cancalaise

A typical characteristic of the unconventional construction and rigging design of the bisques, in addition to the lug rigging, was the completely vertical stem and the wide, jutting stern. Between the turn of the century and the 1920s as many as 300 bisques (French for "crab soup") frequented the bays of Saint Michel and Saint Malo as fishing vessels. Because of their exceptional sailing qualities, regattas were sailed with them until the outbreak of World War II. After that most bisques were laid up or scrapped. After plans for the *Perle* were found, citizens of the city of Cancale founded the Association Bisquine Cancalaise in 1984. This laid the foundations for the reconstruction of one of these fascinating fishing vessels.

Type: bisque (lug rigging), wood, reproduction

Nation: France

Owner: Association Bisquine Cancalaise, Cancale

Home port: Cancale

Year of construction: 1987; launched April 18, 1987

Shipyard: Labbé-Leclerc et Fresneau, Cancale

Tonnage: 45 ts displacement

Dimensions:
Length overall: 30.00 m
Length of hull: 18.10 m
Width: 4.80 m
Depth to deck: 4.20 m

Depth in hold: 1.95 m
Draft: 2.50 m

Sail area: 350 square meters

Rigging: 10 sails; all 3 masts with lug sails

Masts: height of mainmast over the deck: 23 meters

Auxiliary engine: General Motors diesel, 180 horsepower

Crew: 2-person active crew, 14 trainees (25 guests on day cruises)

Use: cruise ship, day cruises

Type: 2-masted topsail schooner (Aviso-Goélette), wood

Nation: France

Owner: Association Goélette La Recouvrance

Home port: Brest

Year of construction: 1992; launched July 14, 1992

Shipyard: Chantier du Guip, l'Ile-aux-Moines, Brest

Tonnage: 130 ts displacement

Dimensions:
Length overall: 41.60 m
Length of hull: 24.90 m
Width: 6.40 m
Depth in hold: 3.22 m
Draft: 3.60 m

Sail area: 430 square meters

Rigging: 9 sails; foremast (square foresail): topsail and topgallant

Masts: height of mainmast over the deck: 28 meters

Auxiliary engine: diesel, 320 horsepower

Crew: 5-person active crew plus 5–6 helpers, 20 trainees during longer cruises, 30 trainees on short cruises

Use: chartered ship, reception ship

The French naval engineer Jean-Baptiste Hubert (1781–1845) drew the plans for a heavily armed topsail schooner in 1817. The first ship to be built according to these plans was the *Iris*. As armaments she carried six 24-pound carronades. This type of ship proved to be so effective that within 30 years six more schooners of this type had been launched. As a result of their exceptionally sharp lines and the size of their sail area, these ships were very fast and

maneuverable. For this reason they were used primarily to combat the slave trade in the Gulf of Guinea and to protect French trade routes from Africa to the West Indies. Up to 70 sailors and soldiers served aboard one of these ships at any given time.

This modern reconstruction of one of these schooners is one of the most striking ships built in recent years. The ship has often demonstrated the anticipated speed and seaworthiness.

Recouvrance means "happy

return." Significantly, a district in Brest also bears this name. Many seamen lived and live in this part of the city.

Naturally, the weaponry was not included in the reconstruction. Only the painted gun ports are reminiscent of the martial prowess of the ship's predecessor. The rake of the masts is a typical characteristic of a fast ship. A woman's bust with flowing hair adorns the flat bow as a figurehead.

Le Renard

The original cutter *Le Renard*, which was heavily armed for its size, was the last privateer to be equipped in what at that time was the infamous pirate city of Saint Malo. The ship was commissioned by the famous pirate Robert Surcouf, whose exploits at the beginning of the nineteenth century, which took him as far as the waters off India, made him one of the wealthiest shipowners in France. As late as 1813 the fast cutter sank the schooner *Alphea* of the Royal Navy. The deck plan and the ten cannons of the reconstruction are in keeping with the design principles of the early nineteenth century.

Type: topsail cutter, wood, reproduction

Nation: France

Owner: Association du Cotre Corsaire, Saint Malo

Home port: Saint Malo

Year of construction: 1991; launched May 18, 1991

Shipyard: Quai Vauban, Saint Malo

Tonnage: 70 ts displacement

Dimensions:
Length overall: 30.00 m
Length of hull: 19.00 m
Width: 6.00 m
Depth to deck: 2.80 m
Draft: 2.80 m

Sail area: 464 square meters

Rigging: 8 sails

Masts: height of mainmast over the deck: 26 meters

Auxiliary engine: Perkins, 230 horsepower

Crew: 3-person active crew, overnight accommodations for 12 people; 27 guests on day cruises

Armaments: original: ten 8-pound carronades

Use: chartered cruises, cruises in the waters around Saint Malo

Rara Avis

Type: 3-masted Bermuda schooner, steel

Nation: France

Owner: Les Amis de Jeudi-Dimanche, Paris

Home port: Toulon

Year of construction: 1957

Shipyard: in Terneuzen, Holland, completed at Groves & Guttridge, Cowes, England

Tonnage: 147 ts displacement; 198 tons gross

Dimensions:
Length overall: 30.00 m
Length of hull: 26.00 m
Width: 7.00 m
Draft: 1.50–4.00 m (centerboard)

Sail area: 500 square meters

Crew: 8-person active crew, 30 trainees or guests

Use: sailing school-ship, social therapeutic sailing, chartered ship

A notable feature of the *Rara Avis*'s hull is its variable draft. The ship was constructed as a private yacht for use in shallow waters. Three axially arranged center boards prevent drifting during cruises in deeper waters. In 1972 the ship passed into the hands of the present owner. Until then she had belonged to the department-store owner Hamon. During the summer the *Rara Avis* sails the coastal waters off southern France and in winter the Caribbean.

Germany

Albatros
Albin Köbis
Alexander von
    Humboldt
Amphitrite
Aquarius
Arny Maud
Aschanti IV of
    Vegesack
Astarte
Atalanta
Atlantic Tramp
Bartele Rensink
Birgitte
Blue Sirius
Bremer Hanseatic Cog
Carmelan
Carola
Dagmar Aaen
Dora av Raa
Elbe 3
Elbe 3 (FS Weser)

Falado
Freedom
Fridtjof Nansen
Friederike
Fulvia af Anholt
Gesine von
    Papenburg
Gorch Fock II
Greif
Grethe Witting
Grönland
Grossherzogin
    Elisabeth
Hanseatic Cog–Kiel
Hordatral
Jachara
Johann Smidt
Lili Marleen
Lilleholm
Mary-Anne
Nobile
Norden

Passat
Pippilotta
Rakel
Rickmer Rickmers
Roald Amundsen
Ryvar
Sælør
Schulshiff
    Deutschland
Seute Deern
Seute Deern II
Solvang
Thor Heyerdahl
Ubena von Bremen
Undine
Valdivia
Vegesack BV2
Vidar
White Dune
White Shark
Wyvern von Bremen
Zuversicht

Albatros

Previous names: *Esther Lohse, Iris Thy, Dagmar Larssen*

Type: 3-masted topsail schooner, wood

Nation: Germany

Owner: CLIPPER—German Youth Work at Sea

Home port: Bremerhaven

Year of construction: 1942

Shipyard: K. A. Tommerup, Hobro, Denmark

Tonnage: 109 tons gross; 58 tons net

Dimensions:
Length overall: 35.70 m
Length between perpendiculars: 24.90 m
Width: 6.90 m
Draft: 3.40 m

Sail area: 292 square meters

Rigging: 7 sails; foremast: no square foresail, topgallant

Masts: height of mainmast over the deck: 24.50 meters

Auxiliary engine: Alpha diesel, 120 horsepower

Crew: 5 people, plus room for 22 guests

Use: club ship

Before the German Youth Work at Sea assumed ownership of the *Esther Lohse*—a name she had received in honor of the wife of her owner at that time—she carried freight to Iceland from the early 1950s until 1973. This was followed by a modification for charter and film purposes. In addition to other films, the streamlined schooner could be seen in *The Onedin Line*.

An excerpt from the CLIPPER bylaws explains the mission of the ship's current owners: "The goal of the association is to give all young people interested in sailing the opportunity to learn the traditional skills of seamanship under expert pedagogical guidance and aboard appropriate ships."

Albin Köbis

This fore-and-aft ketch came into being from 1985 to 1990 from the conversion of a fishing cutter that had been designed in 1936. Originally planned as a dragnet fishing vessel with an auxiliary rig and a small auxiliary engine, the oak hull is characterized by sharp lines.

From 1947 to 1952, 360 ships designated as fishing cutters of Type D are supposed to have been built at 17 shipyards in Mecklenburg-Vorpommern and 1 shipyard in Berlin, over 230 of which were then given to the USSR as reparations payments.

The hull of the *Albin Köbis* is clearly the only cutter of this type that continues to sail under wind power. All of the round timbers are made of larch wood; the topmast on the mainmast and the jibboom can be removed.

Type: gaff-ketch, wood

Nation: Germany

Owner: Gaff-Ketch Albin Köbis Association, Kiel

Home port: Kiel

Year of construction: 1948

Shipyard: Shipyard Sanitz, Barth, Vorpommern

Tonnage: 38 tons gross

Dimensions:
Length overall: 24.00 m
Length of hull: 18.00 m
Length between perpendiculars: 15.00 m
Width: 5.00 m
Draft: 2.20 m

Sail area: 240 square meters

Rigging: 7 sails; 3 foresails; mainmast: mainsail, topsail; mizzenmast: mizzen sail, mizzen staysail.

Masts: height of mainmast over the waterline: 22 meters

Auxiliary engine: 6-cylinder Cummins diesel, 140 horsepower

Crew: 2-person active crew, 10–12 guests

Use: club chip, chartered cruises in the Baltic Sea

Alexander von Humboldt

Previous names:
Confidentia, FS Kiel, FS Reserve Holtenau, FS Reserve Sonderburg

Type: bark, steel

Nation: Germany

Owner: German Foundation Sail Training, Bremerhaven

Home port: Bremerhaven

Year of construction: launched September 10, 1906

Shipyard: Shipyard AG "Weser," Bremen, serial number 155

Tonnage: 829 ts displacement; gross register tonnage 396

Dimensions:
Length overall: 62.50 m
Length of hull: 54.00 m
Length between perpendiculars: 46.60 m
Width: 8.00 m
Depth to maneuver deck: 7.70 m
Draft, with cargo: 4.80 m

Sail area: 1035 square meters

Rigging: 25 sails; 5 foresails; mainmast: mainsails, double topsails, single topgallants, royal sails, sky sails; mizzenmast: lower mizzen sails, upper mizzen sails, mizzen topsails

Masts: height of mainmast over the waterline: 32 meters

Auxiliary engine: 8-cylinder 4-stroke MAN diesel, 375 kw

Crew: 20-person active crew, 35 trainees

Use: sailing school-ship, "Windjammer for Youth"

Stationary lightships must be able to stand up to the sea even better than their traveling sisters. That means that the form of their hulls must stand in the time-tested tradition of the great sailing ships. Their sharp underwater forms and their elegant, seemingly cutting clipper stems make this apparent.

This distinctive hull form was decisive in the conversion of the former lightship *Kiel* into a square-rigger following her retirement from service in 1986. The lightship had functioned as a "reserve ship" at many positions in the North Sea and the Baltic. Her last position, which she held until May 21, 1982, was at the German Bay Station. On September 30, 1986, the Sail Training Association Germany was able to acquire the ship. During her short voyage from Wilhemshaven to her new home port of Bremerhaven it bore the name *Confidentia*.

The ship's conversion into a bark according to the plans of the famous Polish sailing ship designer Zygmunt Choren commenced in the Motorenwerk in Bremerhaven. An intervening maneuver deck was inserted between the poop and the midship superstructure.

In addition to the modification of the interior to accommodate a large crew, the ship received a modern set of steering, radio, and navigational equipment.

Especially noteworthy is the wastewater purification unit. One hundred tons of cemented iron ballast provide the ship with the necessary stability. The exhaust pipes of the diesel motors pass through mizzenmast. A bow thruster supports the work of the rudder blade.

The green of the hull and of the synthetic fiber sails are reminiscent of the traditional color of the Richmers shipping company in Bremerhaven. In October 1998 the *Alexander von Humboldt* set off on a voyage to South and Central America in memory of her namesake's voyage of discovery 200 years before. The 7-month voyage was divided into 15 stages of 2 to 3 weeks each. Approximately 800 young people joined the active crew on board. In 2000 the ship took part in the Sail Bremerhaven event.

Amphitrite

Previous names: *Hinemoa, Joy Farer, Dolores, Amphitrite*

Type: 3-masted fore-and-aft schooner, wood

Nation: Germany

Owner: CLIPPER—German Youth Work at Sea

Home port: Bremen; summer: Travemünde

Year of construction: 1887

Shipyard: Camper & Nicholsons, Gosport, England

Tonnage: 110.84 tons gross; 61.60 tons net

Dimensions:
Length overall: 44.33 m
Length at the waterline: 29.00 m
Width: 5.70 m
Draft: 3.70 m

Sail area: 534 square meters

Rigging: 10 sails; 4 foresails, 2 gaff-sails, 1 square foresail, mizzen gaff-sail, 2 topsails

Masts: height of mainmast over the deck: 28 meters; all masts with a topmast

Auxiliary engine: 2 Mercedes diesel motors, 180 horsepower each, 2 propellers

Crew: 29 berths

Use: youth voyages in the Baltic Sea

The schooner was named after Amphitrite, the wife of Poseidon. Because the ship has almost always been in private hands and the logs no longer exist, very little is known about her history. *Amphitrite* belonged successively to the British Colonel Mac Greggor, the duke of Harwood, the duke of Arran, and the Swede Hans Ostermann. In 1969 she became the possession of the Frenchman François Spoerry (and of his sailing school), and in 1970 of the Horst Film Company in Berlin. After 1971 she belonged to the Amphitrite Sailing Company, and after 1974 to the CLIPPER German Youth Work at Sea.

The ship underwent a thorough overhaul at the French navy shipyards in Toulon and Travemünde in 1971–72. The interior accommodations testify to the refined taste of hers previous owners. The guest is greeted by a mahogany atmosphere that is astonishing in its juxtaposition with the technical equipment of our age. The ship possesses radar, echo sounding, radio system, hydraulic steering, telephone, radio direction-finding, and a weather map device. In addition, there are air-conditioning units, fully tiled shower facilities, electric powered toilet facilities, showers on deck, and a fully automatic kitchen. The sea emergency equipment includes more elements than would strictly speaking be necessary. The most modern safety devices are on board. The ship became famous by way of the TV series *Graf Luckner* and *The Secret of Mary Celeste*. CLIPPER offers young men and women the opportunity to experience all the nuances of communal life at sea aboard its sailing ships. An additional, equally central goal is the promotion of international understanding.

Aquarius

Previous names: *Te Quest, Black Douglas*

Type: 3-masted staysail schooner, steel

Nation: Germany

Owner: unknown (does not want to be identified)

Year of construction: 1930

Shipyard: Bath Iron Works, Bath, Maine

Tonnage: 500 ts displacement; 371 tons gross; 232 tons net

Dimensions:
Length overall: 62.50 m
Length of hull: 48.00 m
Length between

perpendiculars: 39.50 m
Width: 9.70 m
Draft: 3.60 m

Sail area: 1059 square meters

Rigging: 8 sails; 3 foresails; foremast: trysail; mainmast: trysail, staysail; mizzenmast: staysail, jib-headed sail

Masts: height of mainmast over the deck: 39.20 meters; all masts one piece

Auxiliary engine: two Volvo Penta TAMD 120B, 360 horsepower each

Crew: 22 girls, 33 boys (as the *Te Quest*)

Use: private yacht

Te Quest was built as a private yacht for Robert Roebling. He even sailed with her around Cape Horn. The first word, *Te*, connotes an especially elevated form of praise. Later, the ship became property of the state. She served in the Department of Fisheries and during the war in the navy. The portholes were closed and the entire rig was removed. Large guns stood on deck. The yacht had become a warship.

From 1972 to 1982, the ship belonged to the Flint School in Sarasota, Florida. Teaching and training for the charges of the school were conducted on board. In 1982, the yacht passed into German hands. She was converted into a luxury yacht at the shipyard of Abeking & Rasmussen.

Arny Maud

Previous names: *Finkampen, Laksen, Arny Maud*

Type: 2-masted staysail schooner, wood

Nation: Germany

Owner: Laurenz A. Shettler

Home port: Georgetown, Cayman Islands

Year of construction: 1904

Shipyard: in Dajord near Bergen, Norway

Dimensions:
Length overall: 28.35 m
Length of hull: 18.26 m
Width: 5.85 m
Draft: 3.00 m

Sail area: 210 square meters

Rigging: 6 sails

Auxiliary engine: Normo semi-diesel, 140 horsepower/103 kilowatts

Use: private ship, tours with school classes and groups of at-risk youth

The ship, which was built of Norwegian pine on an oak frame, sailed as a freighter in the Norwegian coastal waters. As a sealing vessel she also reached the coasts of Greenland and Spitzbergen. In 1924 the schooner got her first engine, which is still in use today. Anders Kolbenshavn, the first owner, sold his ship to Stainar Berge, who gave her the name *Laksen,* in 1953. The ship's use as a freighter remained the same. An additional change of ownership took place in 1974. The ship received the name *Finkampen* from the new owner. A 9-person consortium of owners purchased the sailing ship in 1979. In the meantime she had ended up in a lamentable condition. In 1980 she was acquired by the current owner, who has personally performed years of work in order to return the vessel to a seaworthy condition.

Aschanti IV of Vegesack

Previous names: *Achanti of Saba, Marie Pierre, Afaneti, Aschanti IV*

Type: 2-masted staysail schooner, steel

Nation: Germany

Home Port: Vegesack

Year of construction: 1954

Shipyard: Ernst Burmester, Bremen-Burg; design: Henry Gruber

Tonnage: 135 ts displacment; 177.79 tons gross; 140.94 tons net

Dimensions:
Length overall: 31.40 m
Length of hull: 31.40 m
Length at the waterline: 22.00 m
Width: 6.38 m
Draft: 4.20 m

Sail area: 550 square meters

Rigging: 8 sails; mainsail, 194 square meters

Masts: height of mainmast over the waterline: 34.60 meters

Auxiliary engine: MTU diesel, 504 horsepower

Crew: 7-person active crew, 8 guests

Use: chartered ship (worldwide)

The *Aschanti of Vegesack,* with her elegant lines, was built by Ernst Burmester as a regatta schooner and took part in international regattas for 10 years with great success. From 1954 until 1967 she functioned as a presidential yacht during Kiel Week. After Burmester's death she ended up in French hands twice, and in the process the interior was fundamentally changed. Since 1984 the ship has belonged to the current English owner. Before her deployment as a chartered ship a second interior remodeling took place, which gave the schooner the character of a luxury ship. Every year the ship takes part in sailing events in North America such as the Greater Schooner Race in Maine and in Gloucester, as well as the Classic Regattas in Newport and Antigua. The schooner got her name from a Sudanese tribe in central South Ghana famous for its valuable gold work.

A construction contractor from Bremen purchased the schooner and had her completely overhauled at the Lürssen shipyard in Bremen-Vegesack in 1994. In the process the yacht was newly outfitted with modern materials, but in the traditional style.

Astarte

Type: fore-and-aft cutter, wood

Nation: Germany

Owner: Schiffergilde Bremerhaven

Home port: Bremerhaven (old harbor)

Year of construction: 1903

Shipyard: August Albers, Finkenwerder

Tonnage: 36.84 tons gross; 11.52 tons net

Dimensions:
Length overall: 36.84 m

Length of hull: 28.80 m
Length between perpendiculars: 17.51 m
Width: 6.05 m
Draft: 2.08 m

Sail area: 234 square meters

Rigging: 7 sails

Masts: height of mainmast over the deck: 19.50 meters

Auxiliary engine: DAF diesel, 150 horsepower

Crew: 4-person active crew, 20 guests on day cruises, 12 on longer cruises

Although the *Astarte* cannot be counted among the truly large sailing ships, she deserves to be presented here as an unusually rigged high-seas cutter. These vessels fished in large numbers in the North Sea at the beginning of the twentieth century. Their seaworthiness and the hardiness of their crew members was legendary. In 1912, the *Astarte* (the name comes from the Phoenician goddess of the moon) received a 12-horsepower auxiliary engine. Her owner at that time, a man named Külper, continued to fish in the North Sea until 1952. The cutter was then sold to the Senkenberg Institute in Wilhelmshaven. She continued to do service as a fishery research vessel.

In 1978 the Mariners' Guild of Bremerhaven purchased the ship as the last of her kind. In the following years she was converted back to her original condition. The technical equipment of the *Astarte* meets current standards. She has modern safety equipment at her disposal.

The ship now usually carries young people in the German Bay, on the Weser, and on the Elbe. She is especially closely tied to the Sail Training Association, which has become an important vehicle for international understanding. The city of Bremerhaven, with its traditional ships belonging to the Mariners' Guild, has been a major German supporter of the association's work.

Atalanta

At the turn of the twentieth century, the Hamburg Senate owned six piloted schooners of the type passed down to us in the *Atalanta*. Future Elbe pilots had to serve as pilot's assistants aboard these ships and under the most adverse of conditions transport the real pilots with rowboats to the entering and departing freighters and passenger shippers.

After 28 years of service as a pilot schooner, the *Cuxhaven*, as she was known at the time, was sold to a Berlin industrialist. In 1929 at the Schlichting shipyard in Travesmüde she was converted into a high-seas yacht. Since that time she has borne the name *Atalanta*. After the bankruptcy of her owner in Berlin the ship became the possession of the House of Rosenthal. In the mid-1930s she was sold to the High Seas Sports Association of Glücksberg. Since 1950 she has been in the possession of the Alferra, whose mother company is the baking house of M. M. Warburg-Brinckmann, Wirtz & Company in Hamburg.

Since 1993 the Schooner Atalanta Association has cared for the ship. The ship has been thoroughly overhauled in the course of several ABM projects. The work was completed in 2001. The *Atalanta* makes educational voyages for young people and is also chartered to companies and others.

Previous name: *Cuxhaven* (Pilot Schooner Nr. 1)

Type: 2-masted fore-and-aft schooner, wood

Nation: Germany

Owner: Förderverein Schoner ATALANTA, Wismar

Home port: Wismar, old harbor

Year of construction: 1901

Shipyard: Junge, Wewelsfleth

Tonnage: 86.11 tons gross; 49.93 tons net

Dimensions:
Length overall: 36.10 m
Length of hull: 24.63 m
Width: 6.18 m
Depth in hold: 3.16 m
Draft: 2.80 m

Sail area: in the wind 333 square meters

Rigging: 7 sails; 3 foresails, gaff-sails, gaff-topsails

Masts: height of mainmast over the deck: 26 meters

Auxiliary engine: Deutz diesel BF/6/10/15, 200 horsepower

Crew: under sail 3-person active crew, 15 guests

Use: tradition and youth ship

Atlantic Tramp

Type: gaff-ketch, steel

Nation: Germany

Owner: Harald Hans

Home port: Bremen-Vegesack

Year of construction: 1871

Shipyard: North German Shipbuilding Company, Kiel-Gaarden

Dimensions:
Length overall: 29.00 m
Width: 5.10 m
Draft: 3.20 m

Sail area: 245 square meters

Rigging: 7 sails

Auxiliary engine: Deutz diesel, 118 kilowatts

Crew: 2-person active crew, 10-person accompaniment

Use: private ship

The ketch was built as a freighter for transports in the Baltic Sea. In 1952 it was converted into a seawater tanker. Her current owner acquired her in 1982 and converted her for her present use.

Bartele Rensink

Built as a fish lugger, the *Luchtstraal* entered service in 1910. The lugger was then registered as the freighter *Greta* in Hamburg in 1927.

In 1938 Captain Heinrich Behrens of Moorrege purchased the motorized sailing ship and continued to sail her under the name *Heinz Helmut*. In 1952 the ship was length-ened by 8 meters and modernized. Two additional changes of owner and name followed, although Stade remained the home port.

After the *Ursel Beate*, as the ship was now called, was removed from the register in 1971, the Dutch couple Frank and Wieke Vlaun of Amsterdam acquired her in 1978. Her conversion into the 3-masted schooner *Bartele Rensink*, which was used for charter purposes, followed. Two large deckhouses serve as messes and recreation areas. The cabins are located in the former cargo holds.

Since 1996 the ship has belonged to its current owner, Oliver Wipperfürth. She has been refitted as a 3-masted topsail schooner with a completely new rig.

The interior accommodations and the technical equipment were adapted to modern standards and requirements. The ship's area of operations, with Rostock as her point of departure, is primarily the Baltic Sea. Since 1997 the schooner has sailed under the German flag.

Previous names: *Ursel Beate, Lotte Nagel, Heinz Helmut, Greta, Luchtstraal*

Type: 3-masted topsail schooner, steel

Nation: Germany

Owner: Oliver Wipperfürth, Kiel

Home port: Rostock

Year of construction: 1910

Shipyard: Scheepswerf "Industrie," Alphen a/d Rijn

Tonnage: 225 ts displacement; 168 tons gross; 149 tons net

Dimensions:
Length overall: 46.00 m
Length of hull: 35.20 m
Width: 6.60 m

Depth in hold: 2.60 m
Depth to deck: 3.10 m
Draft: 2.50 m

Sail area: 700 square meters

Rigging: 12 sails, 4 foresails, fore-, top, and topgallant

Masts: height of mainmast over the deck: 25.40 meters

Auxiliary engine: DAF 1160, 240 horsepower

Crew: 5-person active crew, 26 guests, 60 guests on day cruises

Use: chartered ship

Birgitte

Type: galleass, wood

Nation: Germany

Owner: Berns, Stein, and Warkocz

Home port: Hamburg

Year of construction: 1957

Shipyard: Andersen Shipyard, Vildsund, Denmark

Tonnage: 40-ton cutter

Dimensions:
Length overall: 22.65 m
Width: 5.36 m
Draft: 2.50 m

Sail area: 200 square meters

Rigging: 7 sails

Auxiliary engine: Perkins, 6-cylinder, 110 kw

Crew: 4-person active crew, 6-person accompaniment

The ship was built as a fishing vessel for use in the North Sea. Her main fishing areas were on the Dogger Bank and in the waters off Greenland. The current group of owners acquired her in 1981. Subsequently they used their own labor to convert the ship at the H. Behrens shipyard in Hamburg-Finkenwerder and H. Hatecke in Freiburg for her present use.

Since 1984 the *Birgitte* has belonged to the S.T.A.G. (Sail Training Association Germany). The association seeks to give young people, including young handicapped people, the opportunity to sail.

Blue Sirius

Type: 2-masted fore-and-aft schooner, wood	Dimensions: Length overall: 29.00 m Width: 5.00 m
Nation: Germany	Draft: 2.90 m
Owner: M. Beil	Sail area: 260 square meters
Home port: Lübeck	Rigging: 4 sails
Year of construction: 1907	Masts: Height of mainmast over the deck: 21 meters
Shipyard: Björn Alvdal, Brekke, Norway	Use: private ship

The ship was built as a freighter and among other things carried salt between England and Norway. Later she was used for fishing. In the early 1970s the hull was acquired by a German businessman from Bergen and expanded into a chartered ship.

After changing owners two times and undergoing numerous modifications, the schooner is now in private use.

Bremer Hanseatic Cog (original from 1380)

Type: cog, wood	Dimensions: Length with castle deck: 23.27 m Length over the stem: 22.65 m Length keel/lower edge: 15.60 m
Nation: Germany	
Owner: German Maritime Museum Bremerhaven	Fore overhang: 4.81 m Aft overhang: 2.36 m Greatest width: 7.62 m
Home port: German Maritime Museum Bremerhaven, dry	Depth to deck from the lower edge of the keel, including washboard: 4.26 m Draft without cargo: approx. 1.25 m
Year of construction: 1380	Draft with cargo: approx. 2.25 m
Tonnage: approx. 60 tons	
Size of cargo hold: approx. 143–160 cubic meters	Sail area: approx. 200 square meters
Mass of cargo: approx. 76–84 tons	Masts: one mast, approx. 21 meters
	Use: museum ship

When, on October 8, 1962, a shipwreck was discovered during dredging operations in the Weser and identified as a Hanseatic cog, this was a golden moment in the history of maritime archeology.

The cog was the ship with which the Hanseatic League achieved greatness. The history of this ship is much older than the Hanseatic League itself, however. The Frisians developed the cog as a wool transporter for the coastal trade.

The individual pieces were laboriously raised with the help of divers and cranes. Time played an important role. The water-saturated wooden pieces were placed in tanks filled with a liquid preservative consisting of polyethylenglycol. If the wood had been allowed to dry without this preservative, it would have disintegrated immediately.

Originally, the conservation process was projected to take thirty years. With the help of a new method this time was reduced to six or seven years. Today the cog stands in a specially designed hall in the museum in Bremerhaven.

Seaworthy reproductions are the *Ubena von Bremen* and the *Hanseatic Cog–Kiel*.

Carmelan

Previous names: *Ene, Kristian*

Type: fore-and-aft ketch (Skagen galleass), wood

Nation: Germany

Owner: Hagen and Ute Weihe, Alt-Duvenstedt

Home port: Flensburg (in the winter Rendsburg)

Year of construction: 1927

Shipyard: Hjørne & Jacobsen, Frederikshavn

Tonnage: 34 tons gross

Dimensions:
Length overall: 25.50 m
Length of hull: 18.80 m

Length at the waterline: 16.80 m
Width: 4.80 m
Depth in hold: 1.90 m
Draft: 2.30 m

Sail area: 254 square meters

Rigging: 8 sails

Masts: height of mainmast over the deck: approx. 24 meters

Auxiliary engine: 6-cylinder Scania diesel, 180 horsepower/132.48 kilowatts

Crew: 2-person active crew, 10–12 youth

Use: social therapeutic sailing

The former Danish fishing cutter was modified, rerigged, and reconstructed for her current use in 1979. In addition to private use, the ship is employed in the owner's social pedagogy efforts. Her area of activity was formerly Norwegian, Swedish, and Danish waters.

Carola

Previous names: *Fortuna, Rauna, Annemarie Grenius*

Type: galleass—fore-and-aft ketch, wood

Nation: Germany

Owner: Youth Sailing Association, Plön (North Elbe Youth Work)

Home port: Kiel

Year of construction: 1900

Shipyard: Randers, Nyköbing

Tonnage: approx. 120 ts displacement; 53 tons gross

Dimensions:
Length overall: 25.00 m
Length between perpendiculars: 18.20 m
Width: 5.00 m
Depth in hold: 1.80 m
Draft: 2.40 m

Sail area: 290 square meters (including stay- and square foresail)

Auxiliary engine: Volvo Penta, 150 horsepower

Crew: 12 people

Use: ship for international youth encounters; project ship for youth work

The *Carola* was built as a freighter. She is one of the Marstal schooners, whose name comes from the famous shipyards in Marstal on Ærø. These especially seaworthy ships were employed in the cargo and fishing trades in North European waters well into the twentieth century.

In 1975 Hans Edwin Reith, the owner of the Orion Shipping Company, purchased the ship and had her converted into a training vessel. Shr got a powerful engine, and her cargo weight was replaced by a nine-ton ballast keel. A further fundamental overhaul took place in 1986. In the summer of 1996 the *Carola* entered the first Baltic Sea Encounter Tour for her present owner.

Dagmar Aaen

Type: shark cutter, wood	Shipyard: N. P. Jensen, Esbjerg, Denmark	Sail area: 220 square meters	Crew: variable depending on the expedition (12 persons)
Nation: Germany		Rigging: 8 sails (including trysail and storm foresail)	
Owner: Arved Fuchs	Dimensions: Length of hull: 18.00 m		Use: expedition ship
Home port: Wewelsfleth, berth in Flensburg	Width: 4.80 m Draft: 2.60 m	Auxiliary engine: 3-cylinder Callesen diesel 425 CO, 180 horsepower	
Year of construction: 1931			

The Danish shipowner Mouritz Aaen had the ship built for his freight company. He named her after his wife. Her conversion into an expedition ship by Arved Fuchs took place at the Danish shipyard of Skibs & Bådbyggerie in Gråsten. The equipment for the expeditions included a long list of instruments, radio, safety, and diving equipment as well as, obviously, rescue devices. Even a flying boat, as well as a hot-air balloon, has been on board.

Following a failed attempt to sail through the Northeast Passage, Arved Fuchs's expeditions led the shark cutter, after 1991–92, through the Northwest Passage (1993) and around the American continent (1995–96).

After that she went to Greenland for two arctic summers. Finally, the *Dagmar Aaen* was used as an escort vessel during the Shackleton 2000 tour in the Antarctic.

Altogether the ship has survived being frozen in the ice repeatedly, endured several Arctic winters, twice rounded the feared Cape Horn, and logged more than 150,000 sea miles.

In 2001 the rig was converted for new expeditions; the square foresail was removed, while middle staysails and topsails were added.

Dora av Raa

Type: fore-and-aft cutter, wood

Nation: Germany

Owner: Heinrich Kramer

Home port: Flensburg

Year of construction: 1887

Shipyard: in Raa, Sweden

Dimensions:
Length overall: 21.00 m
Width: 6.00 m
Draft: 2.46 m

Sail area: 230 square meters

Rigging: 6 sails, lower square sails and topsails in addition to gaff and gaff-topsails

Auxiliary engine: Ford diesel, 58 kilowatts

Crew: 2-person active crew, 8-person accompaniment

Use: private ship, sailing school-ship

The former customs cutter collected tolls for the Swedish treasury for many years in the Øresund. In the 1970s she was converted for her present use in Bremen. The unmistakable ship demonstrated its remarkable speed at many regattas.

Elbe 3

The ship was built for royal water inspection service in Tönning. At that time she was moored as a station ship in the mouth of the Elbe. The oldest lightship of this station had been a wooden, round-bellied galiot. Her successors were called "Eider galiots" after her. This name is obviously not appropriate for a ship of the *Elbe 3*'s type. She is a true sailing ship with clipper bow and a rounded stern. In contrast to later ships, the *Elbe 3* never possessed an auxiliary engine. In the event of a broken chain she was able to bring herself to safety with the help of the sails, which in the first instance were storm sails. During World War II she served as a positioning vessel in the Baltic Sea. From 1944 to 1966 she was anchored as a lightship at Position Elbe 3 in the mouth of the Elbe. Since 1967 she has lain as a museum ship in Bremerhaven.

Previous name:
Bürgermeister Abendroth

Type: lightship, Eider pilot galiot, steel

Nation: Germany

Owner: German Maritime Museum, Bremerhaven

Home port: Bremerhaven (old harbor)

Year of construction: 1909

Shipyard: Eiderwerft AG, Tönning

Tonnage: 450 tons gross

Dimensions:
Length overall: 44.00 m
Width: 7.00 m
Draft: 2.70 m

Crew: 16 people

Elbe 3 (FS Weser)

Previous name: *FS Weser*

Type: lightship, steel

Nation: Germany

Owner: Museum Harbor Oevelgönne

Home port: Hamburg/Oevelgönne

Year of construction: 1880

Shipyard: Johann Lange, Vegesack

Tonnage: 612 ts displacement

Dimensions:
Length overall: 45.10 m
Length of hull: 7.20 m
Width: 7.20 m
Draft: 3.95 m

Auxiliary engine: MWM 6-cylinder, 300 horsepower

Use: museum ship

The ship entered service under this name as a 3-masted schooner for the Weser station. In 1900 a "1" was added to her name. In 1925 the first modernization took place. The ship was electrified and received a radio beacon in addition to other equipment. A further fundamental regeneration took place in 1936–37 at the Seebeck Shipyard in Bremerhaven-Geestemünde. During World War II the ship lay at the Bremen station. In 1943 she was brought in to port because of the danger of air attack and replaced by a light buoy. After 1966 she once again fulfilled her duty as the *Elbe 3* at her position. In 1977 the ship was retired. A large automatic buoy had taken her place.

A group of members of the museum harbor Oevelgönne is to thank for the fact that the *Elbe 3* has been preserved as a maritime memorial to this day. It should especially be noted that the engagement of Jugend in Arbeit (Youth at Work) contributed significantly to making possible the ship's restoration at the Jöhnk-Werft Shipyard.

Falado

The *Falado* was built as a cutter and rerigged as a brigantine in 1969. From the very beginning the goal was to sail the ship for the benefit of young people. The owner, Dr. Herbert Hörhager, brought together youth groups in the Federal Republic, and after his death in 1972 these groups took over ownership of the ship and financed her by means of the Brigantine *Falado von Rhodos* Association. In September 1977 the *Falado* collided with a Danish coasting vessel in the Øresund. She was badly damaged in the process and ran aground. A costly repair followed. In June 1988 the brigantine's first circumnavigation of the globe began and lasted three years. A dolphin, according to legend, an enchanted sea robber, decorates the elegant bow.

Type: brigantine, wood

Nation: Germany

Owner: Brigantine Falado von Rhodos Association, Paderborn, Schloss Neuhaus

Home port: Schleswig

Berth: Kiel (KYC)

Year of construction: 1968; launched November 1968

Shipyard: Mastro Petros Xalkidos, Rhodos, Greece

Tonnage: 25.4 tons gross; 21.1 tons net

Dimensions:
Length overall: 22.00 m
Length of hull: 16.00 m
Width: 4.90 m
Draft: 2.60 m

Sail area: 210 square meters

Rigging: 12 sails

Masts: height of mainmast over the deck: 23 meters

Auxiliary engine: 6-cylinder MTU diesel, 99 kilowatts

Crew: 12 people total

Use: young people's sailing ship

Freedom

Previous name: *Gdynia 16*

Type: 2-masted topsail schooner, steel (fore-and-aft schooner)

Nation: Germany

Home port: Rostock

Year of construction: 1959 (as a herring lugger)

Shipyard: Gdansk, modified 1985 in Kolobrzeg (Kolberg)

Tonnage: 210 tons gross

Dimensions:
Length overall: 35.60 m
Length at the waterline: 24.00 m
Width: 6.80 m
Draft: 3.80 m

Sail area: 560 square meters

Rigging: 8 sails

Masts: height of mainmast over the waterline: 26 meters

Auxiliary engine: 6-cylinder Leyland diesel, 160 horsepower

Crew: 6-person active crew, 10 passengers—trainees

Use: chartered cruises worldwide, youth and group cruises, training cruises for the cadets at the maritime school in Szczecin (Stettin)

Fridtjof Nansen

Previous names: *Edith, Frederik Fischer, Gertrud II, Fridtjof Nansen*

Type: 3-masted topsail schooner, steel (jackass-bark, polka-bark)

Nation: Germany

Owner: Haus Temme, Hamburg (Traditional Sailing Ship Fridtjof Nansen, Association)

Home port: Wolgast

Year of construction: 1919

Shipyard: Kalundborg Skibsvaerft, Denmark

Tonnage: approx. 360 ts displacement; 247 tons gross; 74 tons net

Dimensions:
Length overall: 51.00 m
Length of hull: 43.33 m
Length between perpendiculars: 37.52 m
Width: 3.00 m
Draft: 2.80 m

Sail area: 850 square meters

Rigging: 15 sails; foremast (square foresail) and mainmast with topsails and topgallants

Masts: height of mainmast over the deck: 32 meters; steel lower masts; wood topmasts and spars

Auxiliary engine: Callesen diesel, 240 horsepower

Crew: 8-person active crew, 36 trainees

Use: sailing school-ship (youth cruises)

The current schooner was built as a motorized cargo-carrying sailing ship. In 1991 she was towed in a desolate condition to Wolgast.

The restoration of the ship and her conversion into a special type of topsail schooner began at the Peene shipyard in the context of the ABM project *Fridtjof Nansen*. The launch took place on March 25, 1992.

The ship was intentionally kept simple in her construction, but also equipped with all the most modern safety devices and means of communication. Electricity and heat are generated on the basis of the combined heat and power principle by a 44-kilowatt auxiliary unit.

The body of the ship consists of riveted steel and has 80 tons of permanent external ballast in a very deep keel. A hospital is available to deal with illnesses.

The ship is primarily used to benefit the environment and canvasses in the polar regions that her namesake explored. Since 1996 an Eskimo throwing a spear, created in Birgit and Klaus Hartmann's famous maritime sculpture studio on the island of Harriersand in the Weser, has adorned the elegant bow as a figurehead. In the winter the schooner sails the waters of the Canary Islands.

Friederike

Type: brig, wood

Nation: Germany

Owner: City of Papenburg (Homeland Association Papenburg)

Home port: Papenburg

Year of construction: 1986

Shipyard: Meyer Shipyard, Papenburg

Tonnage: 75 Commerzlasten = 225 TR

Dimensions:
Length overall: 38.28 m
Length of hull: 29.74 m
Length at waterline: 25.68 m
Width to chain plates: 6.74
Depth in hold: 2.72 m
Draft: 2.23 m

Masts: height of mainmast over the deck: 23.78 meters

Use: museum ship, conference ship

In 1865 the brig *Berge* was built at the H. W. Meyer shipyard in Papenburg. In 1871 she disappeared with a load of wood during a voyage from Quebec to Falmouth. The *Friederike* was built on a smaller scale according to the still extant plans. The ship is supposed to commemorate the seafaring tradition of the city of Papenburg.

Fulvia af Anholt

Previous names: *Allan Juel, Gudrun, Anna Elisabeth*

Type: galleass, wood

Nation: Germany

Owner: Jörn Eckermann

Home port: Hamburg

Year of construction: 1898

Shipyard: J. Koefoed, Fakse Ladeplads, Denmark

Tonnage: 31.87 tons gross; 22.16 tons net

Dimensions:
Length overall: 22.10 m
Length of hull: 17.10 m
Width: 5.30 m
Draft: 2.00 m

Sail area: 280 square meters

Rigging: 10 sails (square foresail)

Auxiliary engine: 6-cylinder Ford marine diesel, 110 horsepower, 80.96 kilowatts

Crew: 2-person active crew, 8-person accompaniment

Use: private ship

For many years this galleass earned her living as a mail and passenger ship traveling between Grenå and the island of Anholt. She also transported wood. A loading hatch in the bow is still reminiscent of this use. She received her first engine in 1919. In the 1940s she worked as a "stone fisher," usually with no rig. In 1975 the ship was completely restored at the Ring-Andersen shipyard in Svendborg. In the process she once again received her original rigging. In 1982 the current owner acquired the galleass. She received the new name *Fulvia*. She has proven her exceptional sailing capacities in regattas numerous times.

Gesine von Papenburg

Type: Frisian schmack, steel

Nation: Germany

Owner: Homeland Association Papenburg

Home port: Papenburg

Year of construction: 1985

Shipyard: Meyer Shipyard, Papenburg

Dimensions:
Length overall: 18.50 m
Width: 5.10 m
Draft: 1.55 m

Sail area: 242 square meters

Rigging: mainmast with square foresail and topsail

Auxiliary engine: MAN 6-cylinder, 146 kilowatts

Crew: 2-person active crew, 10-person accompaniment

Use: tradition ship

Schmacks, with flat bottoms and leeboards, were once commonly used cargo vessels in Wadden Sea. Their shallow drafts allowed them to enter tide harbors. Local wood always served as the building material.

The *Gesine* was reconstructed according to models as a project for apprentices. Twenty-five tons of ballast provide stability. The remarkable ship with her two square sails represents a piece of East-Frisian maritime history in a striking way.

Gorch Fock II

The insights and experiences won during the construction and operation of the sailing school-ships of the former navy, the *Gorch Fock, Horst Wessel,* and *Albert Leo Schlageter,* were taken into account in the construction of the new *Gorch Fock.* All of the ships were built according to the same basic design. They differed somewhat only in their dimensions. The greatest possible safety was the foremost consideration in the design process. By appropriately stowing permanent ballast, a remarkable level of stability was achieved. Counting the *Mircea,* which was built for

Romania at the same time, all four ships of the same type are still in use today, plus the fifth sailing ship, the *Gorch Fock II.*

The ship got its name from the writer Johann Kinau, who wrote sea stories under the name Gorch Fock. He fell in the battle in the Battle of Jutland (Skagerrak) in 1916. The deckhouse of the *Gorch Fock* is connected with the forecastle. The weighing of the anchor can take place either with machine power or by hand. To allow the trainees to get as much practice steering as possible, the main helm consists of three large steering wheels.

It is located on the poop in front of the charthouse.

The bark carries four boats—two in davits on the poop, two lashed to the deckhouse—of which one is a motor launch. In addition there are several automatic inflatable lifeboats. Three training missions take place yearly. The shorter ones lead mostly to ports on the North Sea coast, the larger ones on the Atlantic (the Canaries, the Antilles, New York, and so on). During the winter months the ship is moored in Kiel.

The *Gorch Fock* has been brought to the shipyard several times to be thoroughly modernized. In 1985, for example,

a water purification unit and a more powerful desalination device, among other things, were installed. In 1991 she received a 1660-horsepower engine as well as an air conditioner, in addition to other improvements. In December 2000 a 9-month regeneration began at the cost of 11 million euros: More powerful generators were installed, the living quarters were re-designed, and the formerly riveted steel plates were welded, and rivet heads were added to preserve the previous appearance.

In September 2001 the first 19 female officer candidates came on board. Previously, since 1989, women had been trained only for medical service aboard the *Gorch Fock*.

Since 1960 the *Gorch Fock* has participated very successfully in international large sailing-ship rendezvous and regattas and has encouraged intercultural contacts in the process.

Type: bark, steel

Nation: Germany

Owner: German navy

Home port: Kiel

Year of construction: 1958; launched August 23, 1958; commissioned December 17, 1958

Shipyard: Blohm & Voss, Hamburg

Tonnage: 1760 ts displacement

Dimensions:
Length overall: 89.32 m
Length of hull: 81.26 m
Length between perpendiculars: 70.20 m
Width: 12.00 m
Depth to deck: 7.30 m
Draft: 5.25 m

Sail area: 2037 square meters

Rigging: 23 sails; 4 foresails, double topsails, single topgallants, royals; mizzenmast: lower spanker, upper spanker, mizzen topsail

Masts: height of fore- and mainmast over KWL, 45.30 meters; height of mizzenmast over KWL, 40 meters

Auxiliary engine: Deutz MMM diesel BV6M628, 1660 horsepower

Crew: 269 persons; commandant, 9 officers, doctor, meteorologist, 36 petty officers, 21 regular crewmembers, 200 officer and junior officer candidates

Use: sailing school-ship

Greif

Previous name: *Wilhelm Pieck*

Type: brigantine, steel

Nation: Germany

Owner: Hansestadt Greifswald, nonprofit association

Home port: Greifswald

Year of construction: keel laid February 27, 1951; launched May 26, 1951; commissioned August 2, 1951

Shipyard: Warnow Shipyard, Warnemünde

Tonnage: 290 ts displacement

Dimensions:
Length overall: 41.00 m
Length of hull: 35.00 m
Length between perpendiculars: 32.00 m
Width: 7.40 m
Draft: 3.60 m

Sail area: 570 square meters

Rigging: 13 sails; 4 foresails; foremast: single topsail, single topgallant, royal, skysail; mainmast: gaff-sail, gaff-topsail, staysail, topmast staysail, topgallant staysail

Masts: both masts with topmasts; height of mainmast over the waterline: 32 meters

Auxiliary engine: MTU marine diesel, 171 kilowatts

Crew: 8-person active crew, up to 35 passengers

Use: sea cruises with young people, chartered cruises

The ship is the last of the true brigantines to be built and one of the few that still sails today. The fast and hard-sailing type of ship was very popular in the nineteenth century for coastal smuggling. Obviously, it was simultaneously the most important tool for protecting the coasts. The number of crew members necessary to handle the sails was small, and for that reason there were enough hands left over to man the guns.

The ship was originally named after the first president of the German Democratic Republic. The deckhouse on the main deck contains, in the first instance, the galley; secondarily also smaller storage rooms. In front of the charthouse on the raised quarterdeck stands the main wheel with the compass. The stockless anchors are raised to the stern with only the windlass. In addition to automatic life rafts the ship carries two service boats in davits. The mainsail is set on a boom. On her training expeditions the brigantine sails primarily in the Baltic Sea.

The former school-ship of the Society for Sport and Technology (German Democratic Republic) was turned over to the city of Greifswald on January 31, 1991, by the government trust responsible for disposing of East German state property. On February 25, 1991, the city founded the association Museum Harbor Greifswald e. V.

Grethe Witting

Previous names: *LT 685, Norford Suffling, YH 45, Ifka of Odense*

Type: Lowestoft lugger, ketch rig, wood

Nation: Germany

Owner: Wim Ruiter

Home port: Rostock

Year of construction: 1914

Shipyard: Cosberg Brothers, England

Tonnage: 170 ts displacement; 70 tons gross; 40 tons net

Dimensions:
Length overall: 37.15 m
Length of hull: 29.95 m
Width: 5.80 m
Depth in hold: 3.05 m
Depth to deck: 1.30 m
Draft: 3.20 m

Sail area: 437 square meters

Rigging: 8 sails

Masts: height of mainmast over the waterline: 26.15 meters

Auxiliary engine: Scania, 175 horsepower

Crew: 2–3-person active crew, 16 guests in berths, 140 on day cruises

Use: historical sailing ship, cruises for guests

Between the years 1874 and 1920 approximately 1000 highly seaworthy wooden ships were built in Lowestoft, England, to be used as fishing vessels. Three of these robust vessels, which wrote an important chapter in maritime history, are still preserved today. One of them is the *Grethe Witting.* Under different names and with various owners, the ketch spent most of her life fishing on the open sea. In 2001, another change of flags took place, the Dutch flag being replaced by the German. The ship offers comfort and safety to all of her passengers.

Grönland

Type: Nordic yacht, wood

Nation: Germany

Owner: German Maritime Museum Foundation—Bremerhaven

Home port: Bremerhaven

Years of construction: 1867–68

Shipyard: Tolleff Tolleffsen and Helge Johannsen in Skonevig, Norway

Tonnage: 85 ts displacement; 48.05 tons gross; 29.53 tons net

Dimensions:
Length overall: 29.30 m
Length of hull: 19.70 m
Length between perpendiculars: 18.10 m
Width: 6.06 m
Depth in hold: 2.30 m
Draft: 2.20 m

Sail area: 283 square meters

Rigging: 7 sails (2 square sails)

Masts: height of mainmast over the deck: 19.84 meters

Auxiliary engine: Deutz diesel, 6-cylinder, 120 horsepower

Crew: 12 people

Use: sailing museum ship

Although the *Grönland* does not count as one of the "great" sailing ships, she deserves to be mentioned, because she made history. In 1868 she was the ship of the first German North Pole expedition of the geographer Dr. Petermann from Gotha and his expedition leader Captain K. Koldewey.

Grossherzogin Elisabeth

Previous names: *Ariadne, San Antonio, Buddi, Santoni, San Antonio*

Type: 3-masted top-gaff schooner, steel

Nation: Germany

Owner: School-Ship Association Grossherzogin Elisabeth

Home port: Elsfleth

Year of construction: 1909

Shipyard: Jan Smit, Ablasserdam, the Netherlands

Tonnage: 463 tons gross; 267 tons net

Dimensions:
Length overall: 66.00 m
Length between perpendiculars: 46.00 m
Width: 8.30 m
Depth to deck: 4.00 m
Depth in hold: 2.80 m
Draft: 3.00 m

Sail area: 1000 square meters

Rigging: 12 sails; 4 foresails, all masts, gaff-sails, and gaff-topsails

Masts: height of mainmast over the deck: 30.50 meters with a topmast

Auxiliary engine: Caterpillar diesel

Crew: 62 people

Use: sailing school-ship

The *Grossherzogin Elisabeth* was built as a 3-masted schooner at Dutch expense. She received her current name in 1982 in honor of the full-rigged ship *Grossherzogin Elisabeth*, built in 1901 for the former German School-Ship Association. She was the first sailing ship to receive a diesel engine rather than a steam engine. As a freighter the schooner sailed for 30 years between North and West Africa. In the 1940s the ship was unrigged and sailed under the Swedish flag with the name *Buddi* in the coastal trade.

In 1973, Captain H. Paschburg found the ship laid up in a small Swedish harbor. With the support of Hamburg shipowners and businesspeople, the *Ariadne*, as she was henceforth called, was rebuilt according to the original plans, and her exterior was once again made to resemble that of her time as a sailing vessel. She received a completely new rig. Her name recalls the daughter of the king of Crete who helped Theseus out of the labyrinth. The ship's interior was remodeled so that she could serve as a private ship for passenger cruises. At this time the ship flew the flag of Panama.

During this period the sailing excursions led to the islands of the Baltic (including the Turku archipelago), to the Mediterranean, and to the Caribbean. In 1977 the ship served as the headquarters of the German Admiral's Cup team during the regattas off Cowes.

Since 1982 the schooner, with a new name, has served the merchant marine school in Elsfleth as a dormitory during the winter semester.

Today a figurehead of the ship's namesake adorns the bow. The old figurehead is located in the Skillinge Museum in Sweden.

Type: cog, reproduction of ship from 1380, wood

Nation: Germany

Owner: Youth in Labor Association, Kiel

Home port: Kiel

Years of construction: 1987–89; launched October 30, 1989

Shipyard: Bootswerft Rathje, Kiel

Tonnage: weight of ship 60 t; ballast 26 t; 86 ts displacement

Dimensions:
Length overall: 23.27 m
Keel length: 15.60 m
Width: 7.62 m
Depth to deck: 3.14 m
Draft: 2.25 m

Sail area: 200 square meters

Rigging: 1 sail (3 studding sails)

Masts: 1 mast; height over the deck: 25 meters

Auxiliary engine: two Volvo Penta diesel TAMD 41 HD engines, 145 horsepower, which power two Schottel pump jets, type SPJ 22

Crew: 10-person active crew, up to 35 guests on day cruises

Use: cruises on the routes of the old Hanseatic League in the Baltic region, primarily with young people with the purpose of promoting intercultural understanding; also excursions with school classes

The cog was the main ship of the Hanseatic League. These fat-bellied trading vessels with a square sail and stern rudder were in use beginning in the thirteenth century. The representations of them on the city seals of Elbing (1242) and Kiel (1365) give a good impression of the appearance of these ships. After the Viking ships, this was the first appearance of the square sail in Northern Europe. At that time the sail area could be enlarged or reduced by attaching or removing strips of cloth (studding sails). This was the beginning of the development of the square sail. The enlargement of the sail area made a subdivision necessary, so that ultimately the fast sailing ships of the nineteenth and twentieth centuries had up to seven sails (skysails) one above the other.

In October 1962 during dredging work in the former bed of the Weser ship, planks were found that, as it turned out, belonged to a cog. On the starboard side she was almost completely preserved from the keel to the handrail of the aftercastle.

This reconstruction embodies the classic image of the cog. It is not a hypothetical reconstruction—it is completely authentic in form and construction method. Typical features of the hull are a straight, flat keel plank and straight fore- and aftstems. The keel plank and the stems are attached to one another by means of sternfeet. The external surface of the hull is carvel built at the bottom and clinker built on the sides. The side planks are attached to one another with flat, square nails.

The seams between the planks were caulked primarily with tow, which was pressed into the joints with a last. The planks were then held together with clamps.

The reconstruction was carried out in the context of a work-creation program in cooperation with the German Maritime Museum in Bremerhaven, such that in the process the young workers were trained to be skilled craftsmen.

Hordatral

Previous names: *Gardar, Sweetheart*

Type: barkentine, Thomas iron

Nation: Germany

Owner: Matthias Zeug, Trasbol

Home port: Wilster, Schleswig Holstein

Year of construction: 1885

Shipyard: Hewett & Company, London

Tonnage: 150 ts displacement; 97 tons gross; 29 tons net

Dimensions:
Length overall: 39.70 m
Length of hull: 30.50 m
Length between perpendiculars: 27.20 m
Width: 6.10 m
Depth in hold: 2.40 m

Depth to deck: 3.40 m
Draft: 3.20 m

Sail area: 620 square meters

Rigging: 17 sails; foremast: foresail, double topsails, single topgallant

Masts: height of mainmast over the deck: 24 meters

Auxiliary engine: Deutz diesel, 630 horsepower

Crew: 5-person active crew, during maneuvers the 21 guests are integrated with the crew

Use: passenger ship

The name of this ship, which was converted into a barkentine by its current owner starting in 1985, is a combination of the name of the district Hordaland in southwestern Norway and traler ("trawler"), the term used to designate a fishing vessel that uses a dragnet. The *Hordatral* was built in 1885 as a sailing herring lugger for use in the rough seas around Iceland. At this time the ship had only sails, no engine.

After 2 years of service under the English flag with the name *Sweetheart*, the lugger was sold to the Norwegian shipowner Halsteinsen. It sailed in the herring trade for this firm for 90 years under the new name *Gardar*. During this period 10.6 million hectoliters of herring were brought to port. A small shipping company that acquired the *Gardar* during the 1970s and renamed her the *Hordatral* sold its operation after being in business for only 3 years.

In 1980 a Norwegian shipyard acquired the ship in order to cannibalize and scrap her. In 1945 the hull had been lengthened by 10 meters and the ship had received a powerful engine as well as the superstructures of a modern trawler.

The ship's acquisition by her current owner prevented her destruction. During her conversion into a barkentine all nonoriginal features were eliminated, and the lengthening of the hull was also undone.

Jachara

Previous name: *Skarvholmen*

Type: 2-masted fore-and-aft schooner, wood

Nation: Germany

Owner: North Elbe Society for Diakonie

Home port: Eckernförde

Year of construction: 1951

Shipyard: Bardset, Nordmøre, Norway

Tonnage: gross register tonnage 49.93

Dimensions:
Length overall: 28.20 m
Length of hull: 22.20 m
Width: 5.79 m
Draft: 2.52 m

Sail area: 230 square meters

Rigging: 5 sails

Auxiliary engine: GM Detroit, 230 horsepower

Crew: 3-person active crew, 10 young people

Use: pedagogical school-ship

Even though she is only a small sailing ship, the *Jachara* should be mentioned because she serves as a pedagogical learning aid in the education of physically and mentally handicapped young people. The Deacon's Work Schleswig-Holstein uses her for the benefit of young people from its own facilities. The name *Jachara* means "much luck."

Johann Smidt

Previous name: *Eendracht*

Type: 2-masted fore-and-aft schooner, steel

Nation: Germany

Owner: CLIPPER—German Youth Work at Sea

Home Port: Bremen

Year of construction: 1974; launched June 1, 1974

Shipyard: Cammenga, Amsterdam

Tonnage: 174.84 tons gross; 101 tons net

Dimensions:
Length overall: 35.94 m
Length of hull: 32.39 m
Length between perpendiculars: 27.24 m
Width: 8.03 m
Depth to deck: 4.94 m
Draft: 3.64 m

Sail area: 548 square meters

Rigging: 8 sails (with square foresail)

Masts: height of mainmast over the deck: 34 meters

Auxiliary engine: G. M. Detroit diesel, 400 horsepower

Crew: 6 persons, 31 students

Use: sailing school-ship

The schooner belonged to the Dutch association Stichting Het Zeilende Zeeschip until October 1989. The *Eendracht*'s primary purpose was to offer young citizens of the Netherlands the opportunity to experience sailing. The ship demonstrated her excellent sailing capacities in many S. T. A. regattas. During SAIL '80 in Amsterdam she was the flagship in the parade. In 1989 she was acquired by her current owner. The *Eendracht* has been replaced in Holland by the 3-masted fore-and-aft schooner *Eendracht II*. The ship was named after the Bremen mayor Johann Smidt.

Lili Marleen

Previous name: *Jules Verne*

Type: barkentine, steel

Nation: Germany

Owner: SSD Sailing Ship Society Deilmann & Company

Home port: Neustadt in Holstein

Year of construction: 1994; launched May 28, 1994

Shipyard: Elsflether Shipyard

Tonnage: gross register tonnage 704; net register tonnage 243

Dimensions:
Length overall: 73.98 m
Length of hull: 65.00 m
Length between perpendiculars: 56.46 m
Width: 9.50 m
Depth to deck: 4.35 m
Draft: 3.90 m

Sail area: 1200 square meters

Rigging: 15 sails; foremast; foresail; double topsails; single topgallant; royals

Masts: height of mainmast over the deck: 35 meters

Auxiliary engine: MAN D 2842 LYE, 660 kilowatts

Crew: 25-person active crew, 50 guests (25 passenger cabins)

Use: cruise ship

Usable parts from the hull of the French three-master *Jules Verne,* built in 1987, served as the foundation for the *Lili Marleen.* In 1993 the schooner, having left from Sete, arrived at the shipyards in Elsfleth.

The name of the sailing cruise ship comes from the poem of the same name by Hans Leip, which was set to music by Norbert Schulze, and which for shipowner Peter Deilmann is synonymous with "the whole world's longing for peace." The American winner of the Nobel Prize for Literature, John Steinbeck, confessed that for him "Lili Marleen" was the most beautiful love poem of all time.

The designers of the ship thus had to compete with the beauty of the poem. The barkentine has become a yacht of the sonderclass. All the amenities of a modern cruise ship can be found on board. Obviously, the safety features also meet the highest standards. The guests are allowed to take part in the operation of the ship if they desire and ultimately are able to participate in sailing maneuvers.

Lilleholm

Previous names: *Martana, Martin, Fremad, Dorothea*

Type: 2-masted staysail schooner, wood

Nation: Germany

Owner: group of owners in Lilleholm

Home port: Lübeck

Year of construction: 1893

Shipyard: Hansen, Marstal, Ærø, Denmark

Dimensions:
Length overall: 21.00 m
Width: 5.00 m
Draft: 2.40 m

Rigging: 5 sails

Auxiliary engine: 6-cylinder Ford diesel, 150 horsepower, 100.40 kilowatts

Use: private ship

The Marstal schooner with the characteristic transom stern was built at German expense. Under the German flag and, after numerous changes of ownership, also under the Danish flag, the ship sailed primarily in the Baltic as a freighter carrying the most diverse cargoes. In the 1960s the sails scarcely played a role any longer, because an auxiliary engine had been installed. The ship passed back into German hands in 1965 under the name *Lilleholm*. Its conversion into a first-class passenger ship took place in Frankfurt am Main but landed the new owner in financial difficulties. The ship had to be sold. Since she was taking on a lot of water, the current owners had to thoroughly overhaul her at great expense and with much of their own labor. The hull received a second layer of reinforced concrete. In 1993 the *Lilleholm* received a new keel.

Mary-Anne

Built on the model of the fast clippers of the turn of the century, which distinguished themselves with their particularly good sailing qualities, the barkentine, with her sleek lines and luxurious furnishings, offers an exceptional setting for every type of event. If they desire, guests are able to take part in handling the sails, navigating, and manning the helm. Trailboards on the bow bearing the ship's monogram add a personal touch.

Type: barkentine, steel

Nation: Germany

Owner: Segeltouristik Meyer zur Heyde, Ltd., & Company KG, Laboe

Home port: Kiel

Years of construction: 1995–96; launched 1995

Shipyard: Radunia, Danzig and the Brothers Friedrich, Kiel; designer: Herward W. A. Oehlmann, Travemünde

Tonnage: 480 ts displacement; gross register tonnage 404; 150 tons net

Dimensions:
Length overall: 65.85 m
Length of hull: 53.60 m
Length between perpendiculars: 43.20 m
Width: 7.95 m

Depth to deck: 5.50 m
Draft: 4.40 m

Sail area: 960 square meters

Rigging: 16 sails; foremast: foresails, double topsails, single topgallants, royal sails

Masts: height of mainmast over the deck: 34 meters

Auxiliary engine: Klöckner Humboldt Deutz diesel, Bf 8M 816, 660 horsepower

Crew: 12-person active crew, 50 guests when all berths are occupied, 120 guests on day cruises

Use: club sailing ship of the Sailing Ship Mary-Anne Association, passenger cruises

Nobile

Previous names: *Jødnafjell, Kathleen*

Type: fore-and-aft cutter, steel

Nation: Germany

Owner: city of Wolgast

Home port: Wolgast/Kröslin

Year of construction: 1919 (modified 1994)

Shipyard: Oulton Broad, Lowestoft, England

Tonnage: 80.14 tons gross; 40.34 tons net

Dimensions:
Length overall: 38.50 m
Length of hull: 26.00 m
Length between perpendiculars: 24.30 m
Width: 5.60 m
Draft: 2.90 to 6.10 m (leeboard)

Sail area: 500 square meters, 950 in the wind (spinnaker)

Rigging: 5 sails plus spinnaker

Masts: height of mainmast over the keel: 36 meters

Auxiliary engine: Caterpillar Turbo diesel, 300 horsepower

Crew: 6-person active crew, 14 trainees, 25 guests on day cruises

Use: youth sailing ship (Baltic Sea/North Sea) (Learn to Live on Sailing Ships Association, "Umberto Nobile" project)

It may seem strange to count a 1-masted vessel as a "great sailing ship," but with a sail area of 950 square meters the *Nobile* qualifies.

She was built as a 2-master with the name *Kathleen*. In 1947 she was sold to a buyer in Norway. Haugessund became its home port. After her transfer to Kristiansund, the *Jødnafjell*, as she was known in Norwegian, was employed in fishing, albeit now without masts.

In 1985 Trondheim became her new home port. The ship was employed as a dynamite transporter from this point on. Starting in July 1993 she was converted into a racing cutter on the model of the America's Cup ships as part of a work-creation program in association with the organization Learn to Live on Sailing Ships in Wolgast. Since January 1995 the city of Wolgast has owned the ship.

The ship got her name from the Italian polar explorer and aeronautic engineer Umberto Nobile (1885–1978). In 1926 Nobile flew over the North Pole in the airship *Norge* along with Roald Amundsen and Lincoln Ellsworth.

The sleek underwater lines and the very large sail area give the *Nobile* astounding speed. At wind velocities of barely Beaufort 4, the ship logged 8.5 knots. Stability is provided by an eight-ton rotating drop-keel that can be moved with the help of the hand-powered centerboard winch in the centerboard case located midships. Everyone is welcome to sail aboard the ship.

Norden

Type: Nordic yacht

Nation: Germany

Owner: Peter Fleck

Home port: Lübeck

Year of construction: 1870

Shipyard: in Skonevig, Norway

Tonnage: approx. 30 ts displacement

Dimensions:
Length overall: 28.50 m
Length of hull: 5.95 m
Draft: 2.40 m

Sail area: 259 square meters

Rigging: 5 sails

Auxiliary engine: Deutz diesel, 150 horsepower

Crew: 6-person active crew, up to 16 passengers

Use: private ship, chartered ship

The *Norden,* a robust smaller sister of the *Grönland,* primarily transported wood and salted cod during her time as a freighter. At times she also made runs between Bergen and the Lofotes. At the end of her time as a freighter she sailed with a motor only, the rig having been removed. In 1978 the ship was converted back into a sailing ship in Bremerhaven, receiving a 28.5-meter mast in the process.

In 1988 the current owner purchased the yacht. His motto, which he uses to woo his guests, is "Sailing today like it was yesterday."

The *Passat* was built at Blohm & Voss as serial number 206 for the shipowner F. Laeisz in Hamburg (together with her sister ship the *Peking,* serial number 205). Her price was 680,000 marks. In the year 1912 the *Passat* departed on her first voyage to Chile. Until World War I she made an additional 5 voyages as a saltpeter trader. At the beginning of the war she was moored with other sailing ships in Iquique. It wasn't possible to undertake the voyage to Marseille with 4700 tons of saltpeter until May 27, 1921. After arriving in Marseille, the ship had to be turned over to France.

The French had no use for the large 4-masted bark at that time, however. For that reason, Laeisz was able to buy his ship back for 13,000 pounds in 1921. The German crew went on board on January 3, 1922. After being put back into working order in Hamburg, the *Passat* was once again used in the saltpeter trade. In 1927 she was equipped as a freight-carrying school-ship.

After the *Passat*'s collision with the French steamer *Daphne* in August 1928 in the English Channel, the steamer sank after a few minutes. A further collision in the channel with the British steamer *British Governor* in June 1929 caused significant damage to the *Passat.*

After both collisions she had to sail to Rotterdam for repairs. In 1932 she was sold to the Finnish shipowner Gustaf Erickson of Mariehamn for 6500 pounds. The ship sailed under the Finnish flag in the Australia trade until World War II.

During the war she was initially laid up in Mariehamn. On July 6, 1944, the *Passat* was

Type: 4-masted bark, steel

Nation: Germany

Owner: Sports Bureau Lübeck (city of Lübeck, Save the Passat Association)

Home port: Travemünde, on the Priwall

Year of construction: 1911; keel laid March 2, 1911; launched September 20, 1911; ready for sea November 25, 1911

Shipyard: Blohm & Voss, Hamburg (Slipway I of the old shipyard on the North Elbe)

Tonnage: 3180.61 tons gross; as a sailing ship without an engine 2870 tons net, 4750 t carrying capacity; as a school-ship with a motor 2593 tons net, 4223 t carrying capacity

Dimensions:
Length overall: 115.00 m
Length of hull: 106.40 m
Length between perpendiculars: 96.01 m
Width: 14.40 m
Depth in hold: 8.08 m
Draft (with a load of saltpeter): 6.70 m

Sail area: 4100 square meters

Rigging: 34 sails; 4 (5) foresails, double topsails, double topgallants, royals; mizzenmast: lower mizzen sail, upper mizzen sail, mizzen topsail

Masts: height of mainmast over the deck: 52 meters; fore-, main-, mizzenmasts each have one topmast: mizzenmast is one piece

Auxiliary engine: 6-cylinder Krupp diesel engine, 900 horsepower (since the modification in 1951); speed with engine 6.5 knots; 16.4 knots was logged as the maximum speed under wind power

Crew: after the modification in 1951 a total of 80 to 90 people, including approximately 50 to 55 young men and deck boys

Use: events with the possibility of staying overnight; exhibit about the golden age of the square-rigged sailing ships

towed to Stockholm and there used as a grain storage unit until 1946. The first voyage after the war had South Africa and Australia as its destinations. The cargo on the voyage home consisted of 56,000 sacks of wheat, which were intended for England. The *Passat* and the *Pamir* then lay idle for a period of time in Penarth near Cardiff. In January 1951 it became known that both ships had been sold to a Belgian salvage company.

Captain Helmut Grubbe joined with the shipowner Heinz Schliewen to buy back both sailing ships. This occurred just in time. Schliewen was the new owner, and the new home port was Lübeck.

On June 20, 1951, the *Passat* arrived at Travemünde. A thorough overhaul and modernization followed at the Howaldt Works in Kiel. The costs for this came to 2.7 million marks (auxiliary engine, watertight bulkheads, two deckhouses, gangways, brace and halyard winches on the deck, etc.). Her classification by the German Lloyd was + 100 A 4, the best score. On February 12, 1952, the *Passat* sailed with cement to Brazil

and Argentina. At the end of June it returned home with a load of grain. The second voyage began in July 1952. It likewise had South America as its destination. From February 1953 to June 1955 the ship was laid up in Travemünde. Schliewen had had to stop making payments. The state bank of Schleswig-Holstein appointed Captain Grubbe as the trustee for the *Pamir* and the *Passat*.

In the second half of the year 1954, approximately 40 German shipowners formed the "Pamir and Passat Foundation." Both ships now flew the flag of shipowner Consul Thomas Entz's firm Zerssen & Company, which was located in Rendsburg. By 1957 the *Passat* had made 5 additional voyages to South America under Captain Grubbe's command. On the final voyage her cargo of grain (barley) shifted. A dangerous angle of heel resulted. The ballast tanks, which were filled with wheat, had to be flooded. In Lisbon the ship was emptied in order to allow these tanks to be cleared out. On December 8, 1957, the sailing ship returned to Hamburg with a full cargo.

The final long voyage lasted from July 18, 1957, to December 8, 1957. After the ship's 2-year stay in Hamburg, the foundation sold the *Passat* to the city of Lübeck. On January 5, 1960, she was towed to Travemünde through the canal from the North to the Baltic sea. At the Priwall she served the State Training Center for Future Seamen as a living and training ship. In 1965 the *Passat* was docked at the Flender Works in Lübeck. In the same year the school gave the ship back to the city of Lübeck. The *Passat* is now used for various sailing and sport courses.

The main lower topsail, which was made in 1936 for the *Kommodore Johnsen*, is on display in the exhibit area. It is a gift from the *Sedov*. In 1997–98 expensive refitting work took place at the Flender Works in Lübeck.

Passat-Sailing, a group of enthusiasts in Lübeck–Travemünde, set itself the goal of putting the *Passat* back into service. This proposal was rejected by a decision of the citizens of Lübeck in the spring of 2001 following a long debate. Passat-Sailing is now planning the construction of a 3-masted

bark fully in the P-liner tradition of the Laeisz shipping company, which was formerly the largest windjammer company. The bark, which is already on the drawing board and has already undergone computer simulations, is supposed to have a classic rig and classic lines. At the time of publication of this book, the project was still the object of negotiations with sponsors. The new bark will probably be moored in Rostock and have the following dimensions: length overall 62.80 m, length of hull 54.70 m, width 9.40 meters, draft 4.00 meters, height of the masts 36 meters, sail area approx. 1260 square meters. The ship would be sailed by an active crew of 22 and would be able to take 44 trainees along on board (plus 14 trainees who would be able to sleep in hanging hammocks as they did earlier). The estimated cost for the project is approximately 6 million euros.

Pippilotta

The *Pippilotta* began her sailing career as a 2-masted herring lugger with the name *Erika*. Her area of activity was the North Sea. At that time 12 to 15 of these modern luggers were built at different shipyards in the North Sea. The schooner is the only one of its kind that has been preserved. In 1955 it was sold to a buyer in Norway, where its home port was Haugesund. Its conversion into a freighter followed, including the installation of a new engine (Wichmann, 240 horsepower). For a time the vessel was also a supply ship for the oil platforms of the Norwegian coast.

The *Erika* remained in service as a coastal freighter until 1988; then she was laid up in the little port of Stord and decayed. In 1990 the current owner acquired the ship. After an extensive renovation she was rigged as a 3-masted fore-and-aft schooner. Astrid Lindgren's "Pippy Longstocking," with her many, in some cases scurrilous names, served as godmother at the christening. The voyages, which leave from Kappeln, not only go to the North and Baltic seas, but have also reached the Pacific and the South Sea. School classes are frequent guests aboard the ship.

Previous name: *Erika*

Type: 3-masted fore-and-aft schooner, steel

Nation: Germany

Owner: Hartwig Schröder, Ekenis

Home port: Hamburg (Kappeln)

Year of construction: 1933

Shipyard: Elsflether Shipyard

Tonnage: 260 ts displacement; 156 tons gross; 46 tons net

Dimensions:
Length overall: 44.00 m
Length of hull: 33.00 m

Length between perpendiculars: 30.00 m
Width: 7.20 m
Depth in hold: 3.50 m
Draft: 3.10 m

Sail area: 586 square meters

Rigging: 13 sails

Masts: height of mainmast over the deck: 25.50 meters

Auxiliary engine: Caterpillar diesel, 390 horsepower

Crew: 3–7-person active crew, 28 guests (also trainees)

Use: chartered ship

Rakel

Type: fore-and-aft ketch, wood

Nation: Germany

Owner: Falk Pfau

Home port: Bremerhaven

Year of construction: 1896

Shipyard: Colin Archer, Larvik, Norway

Dimensions:
Length overall: 27.00 m
Width: 5.30 m
Draft: 2.60 m

Sail area: 211 square meters

Rigging: 7 sails

Auxiliary engine: 6-cylinder MWM diesel, 112 kilowatts

Crew: 2-person active crew, 10 passengers

Use: private ship, chartered ship

The famous Norwegian ship-builder Colin Archer built the *Rakel* for Laurits S. Larsen of Alesund. The ship, with her typical stern that runs together to a point, proved herself to be exceptionally seaworthy under the most adverse conditions. She was even used as an ice-breaker in later years. The *Rakel* served as a fishing vessel in Norwegian waters for decades. Engines increasingly replaced wind power. In 1977 Petter Kjølleberg of Borhaug purchased the ship and used her to fish for cod, which he then sold to Nigeria as stock-fish. In 1980 the current owner acquired the *Rakel*. The ship was restored and rerigged according to plans preserved in the maritime museum in Oslo. The work lasted four years. Today the ship sails mostly in the North and the Baltic seas, but longer voyages can also be undertaken.

Rickmer Rickmers

The shipyard Rickmers had the *Rickmer Rickmers* built as a full-rigged ship in 1896. She was employed primarily as a trading vessel in the East Asia trade. On the voyage out the ship mostly loaded coal, on the voyage home rice and the much-sought-after commodity bamboo. Eventually she also sailed in the saltpeter trade. After serious damage was done to the rig during a storm in 1905, the ship had to be rigged as a bark for financial reasons. A notable feature of the hull is that the upper edge of the very high bulwark reaches almost the same height as the forecastle and poop deck. This gives the ship a supple sheer and a very elegant appearance.

In 1912 Rickmers sold the bark with the new name *Max* to the C. Krabbenhöft & Bock in Hamburg. From then on she sailed exclusively in the saltpeter trade. When Portugal entered the war against Germany in 1916, the ship was docked in the Portuguese port of Horta in the Azores on her way home with a load of saltpeter. The *Max* was commandeered by the Portuguese. Under the name *Flores* the ship transported war materials across the Atlantic until the end of the war. In 1924 she was converted into the school-ship *Sagres* of the Portuguese navy. The figurehead, which represented Rickmers, was replaced

by a depiction of Prince Henry the Navigator. All of the square sails as well as the mizzen sail bore a red cross on a white field.

The large size of the active crew is explained by the fact that instruction in all nautical and military disciplines was given aboard the ship. The orders were given in part over loudspeakers. All modern navigational instruments were available for instructional purposes. In 1931 two auxiliary diesel engines were installed. The ship took part in S. T. A. regattas in 1956 and 1958. In 1962 the *Sagres I* was replaced by the *Sagres II* (formerly the *Guanabara* and the *Albert Leo Schlageter*).

The *Rickmer Rickmers* was moored for many years as a supply and depot ship in the harbor of Alfeite (Portugal). Through the mediation of the German embassy's naval attaché, the association Windjammers for Hamburg succeeded in acquiring the partially unrigged bark in 1983 in exchange for a smaller sailing vessel. The former *Rickmer Rickmers* arrived in tow in Hamburg just in time for the 794th birthday of the harbor. Following a very careful restoration lasting several years, the ship is now moored as a landmark in the Hamburg harbor. The *Rickmer Rickmers* has become a museum and restaurant ship.

Previous Names: *Santo André, Sagres I, Flores, Max, Rickmer Rickmers*

Type: bark, steel

Nation: Germany

Owner: Windjammers for Hamburg Association

Home port: Hamburg

Year of construction: 1896

Shipyard: R. C. Rickmers, Geestemünde (Bremerhaven)

Tonnage: 3067 ts displacement; 1980 tons gross

Dimensions:
Length overall: 97.00 m
Length of hull: 86.00 m
Length between perpendiculars: 79.00 m
Width: 12.20 m
Depth in hold: 7.70 m
Draft: 6.00 m

Sail area: 3500 square meters

Rigging: 24 sails; 4 foresails, double topsails, double topgallants, royals; mizzenmast: mizzen sail, mizzen topsail

Masts: Fore- and mainmast with topmast and topgallant mast; mizzenmast with 1 topmast

Auxiliary engine: 2 Krupp diesel motors, 350 horsepower each; speed with engine, approx. 10 knotts

Crew: As a school-ship 12 officers, 22 petty officers, 140 regular crew members, up to 200 cadets

Use: museum ship

Roald Amundsen

This ship was commissioned on the Elbe to serve as a fishing lugger. While she was still under construction the People's Army of the former German Democratic Republic decided to convert her into a tank lugger, a ship equipped with large tank capacities. As Project 235, she received the name *Vilm*. The vessel then served for many years as a tank and supply vessel and supplied navy units with fuel, water, and equipment. Her base was always Peenemünde.

In the 1970s the ship was converted into a bilge water transporter. At regular intervals she visited the bases of the People's Navy in order to pump bilge water out of the ships at each base and bring it to a central collection point for treatment. This service came to an end at the turn of the year 1989.

Previous name: *Vilm*

Type: brig, steel

Nation: Germany

Owner: city of Wolgast; operator: Learn to Live on a Sailing Ship Association, Hamburg

Home port: Wolgast

Year of construction: 1952

Shipyard: Elbe Shipyard, Rosslau

Tonnage: gross register tonnage 252

Dimensions:
Length overall: 50.20 m
Length of hull: 41.00 m
Length between perpendiculars: 37.60 m

Width: 7.20 m
Depth to deck: 4.40 m
Draft: 4.20 m

Sail area: 850 square meters

Rigging: 18 sails; 4 foresails, 3 staysails between the masts, mizzen sails; masts: lower sails, double topsails, single topgallant, royal sails

Masts: height of mainmast over the keel: 34 meters

Auxiliary engine: Buckau Wolff diesel, 300 horsepower

Crew: 14-person active crew, 32 trainees, 50 guests on day cruises

Use: youth sailing ship, sailing school-ship

After being laid up for a year, the ship was towed to Neustadt in Holstein and served the naval base at Neustadt as a barracks ship for the guard detail. At the auction disposing of former GDR property in Frankfurt am Main, the master shipbuilder Detlev Löll and Captain Hanns Temme won the bidding for the ship. Her conversion into a brig in Wolgast in the context of a work-creation program followed, a project that provided work for 208 people. The ship entered service in July 1995.

The organization Learn to Live on a Sailing Ship was founded in Hamburg in 1989 with the goal of providing young people with educational experiences aboard traditional sailing ships (see also *Fridtjof Nansen*). Luxury was intentionally avoided. The safety equipment is state of the art, however.

Ryvar

Previous names: *Svegrunn, Meta Buck, Helga, Flevo I, Mervede, De Maas RO 16*

Type: herring lugger (rigged as a ketch), steel (riveted)

Nation: Germany

Owner: Joachim Kowalski

Home port: Museum Harbor Flensburg

Year of construction: 1916

Shipyard: D. & Joh. Boot, Alphen, the Netherlands

Dimensions:
Length overall: 38.30 m
Length of hull: 28.60 m
Length between

perpendiculars: 24.90 m
Width: 6.64 m
Draft: 2.90 m

Sail area: 360 square meters

Rigging: 7 sails

Masts: height of mainmast over the deck: 28.60 meters

Auxiliary engine: Caterpillar diesel, 365 horsepower

Crew: 2-person active crew, 28 trainees, 28 guests

Use: historic sailing ship, passenger cruises

The *Ryvar* was built in 1916 as a sailing lugger for the fisheries in the Netherlands. In her 85-year life she has largely remained faithful to this profession. She has often changed names and owners in the process.

A life-threatening accident took place in 1931 when the ship ran aground on Lillegrund in the Øresund. In 1932 it was possible to raise the ship, and she was towed to Copenhagen for repairs. After additional changes of ownership the ship was ultimately sold to Germany. The current owner had her converted and expanded into a comfortable traditional sailing vessel in 1995. Youth groups, associations, and families, as well as educational groups and seminars, are the primary target groups for the *Ryvar*.

Sælør

Previous names: *Bygda, Sælør*

Type: galleass, wood

Nation: Germany

Owner: Uwe Landschoof

Home port: Heikendorf-Möltenort

Year of construction: 1917

Shipyard: in Kragerö, southern Norway

Dimensions:
Length overall: 25.00 m
Width: 6.60 m
Draft: 2.60 m

Sail area: 260 square meters

Auxiliary engine: Volvo ship's diesel engine, 206 horsepower

Use: chartered cruises

The *Sælør* was built as a freighter. She got her name, which means "Seal Island," from the group of islands that lies south of Farsund. She primarily transported building materials in the southern Norwegian waters and fjords. In the 1930s she sailed as a coasting vessel with the name *Bygda*. In 1946 a thorough overhaul took place. Until the end of the 1960s the ship continued to be employed in the freight trade. Since 1980 she has once again born its original name.

The ship was completely overhauled in the years 1981 to 1983, and she received a new keel as well as a new keelson made of oak. She also received copper plating on her whole underwater surface. She was once again rigged as a galleass according to plans from the maritime museum in Oslo. Since then the *Sælør* has sailed as a charter ship in the waters of the North and Baltic seas.

After World War I the German School-Ship Association, founded in 1900, had to give up its sailing school-ship, the *Princess Eitel Friedrich,* to France. The substitute for this ship was the newly constructed *Schulschiff Deutschland,* completed in 1927. For reasons of tradition, all school-ships belonging to the society were registered in Oldenburg. The former grand duke of Oldenburg had taken a particular interest in the association and was one of its greatest promoters and benefactors. The S. S. *Deutschland* was designed to be a pure school-ship without cargo. Indicative of the large crew and the corresponding number of instructors is the long poop. The forecastle is connected to the deckhouse. Originally the hull was painted white. The ship has two through decks and six waterproof bulkheads. She carries 560 tons of permanent ballast.

The first long voyage lasted from September 1927 until February 1928 and had South America as its destination. Until 1939 the ship regularly made summer voyages to the Baltic and winter voyages to North, Central, and South America, as well as to South Africa. The ship returned to Germany shortly before the outbreak of World War II. In the winter of 1939–40 she was moored in Elsfleth. Training continued in spite of the war. In April 1940, the sailing ship was removed to the Baltic and spent the following winter

moored in Stettin. In 1941 there were once again training courses on board during short voyages in the Baltic. During the winter of 1941–42 the ship was moored in Lübeck. In Kiel in 1942 she was equipped

with magnetic self-protection against mines. Another winter in Lübeck followed. In 1943 the S. S. *Deutschland* sailed in the Baltic once again. Her final summer voyage took her to the area around Bornholm. During

the winter of 1944–45 she was once again in Lübeck. Before the war had ended she became a medical ship. For this reason, the ship was spared during the occupation. The wounded left the ship in June 1945. From

that point on it lay idle in Lübeck.

Eventually the S. S. *Deutschland* was towed to Cuxhaven. Until January 1, 1948, she provided living quarters to members of the German Mine Search Association. After that she was returned to the German School-Ship Association In the summer of 1948 it came to Bremen and from March 1949 on served as a youth hostel there in the Europa Harbor. On April 1, 1952, she became a school- and stationary training ship for the association. Since 1956 she has belonged to the maritime school in Bremen (a professional school). There is room for 114 trainees on board. The training is provided by three officers (Master's Certificate A 6), two boatswain instructors, and a captain as the head of the school. The active crews of the *Gorch Foch II* and of the Indonesian barkentine *Dewarutji* were trained aboard the ship.

Following a complete renovation at the Bremen Vulkan shipyard, the ship, her hull once again painted white, was towed to her current berth in a procession on July 14, 1996.

The S. S. *Deutschland* is the only still-existing maritime school in Germany, and thus a special piece of the maritime history of the free Hanseatic city of Bremen.

Type: full-rigged ship, steel

Nation: Germany

Owner: merchant marine, German School-Ship Association, Seaman's School Bremen

Home port: Bremen-Vegesack, mouth of the Lesum

Year of construction: 1927; launched June 14, 1927

Shipyard: J. C. Tecklenborg, Geestemünde (Bremerhaven)

Tonnage: 1257 tons gross; 770 tons net

Dimensions:
Length overall: 88.20 m
Length of hull: 73.50 m
Length between perpendiculars: 65.20 m
Width: 11.96 m
Depth in hold: 6.30 m
Draft: 5.00 m

Sail area: 1900 square meters

Rigging: 25 sails; 3 foresails, double topsails, double topgallants, royals

Masts: only a topgallant mast; height of foremast: 50 meters; height of mainmast: 52 meters; height of mizzenmast: 48 meters

Auxiliary engine: none

Crew: as a school-ship under sail 6 officers, 1 doctor, 1 purser, 12 petty officers, approx. 120 boys

Use: stationary school-ship, site for holding events

Seute Deern

Previous names: *Pieter Albrecht Koerts, Seute Deern, Bandi* (4-masted schooner), *Elisabeth Bandi*

Type: bark, wood

Nation: Germany

Owner: German Maritime Museum Bremen

Home port: Bremerhaven, Old Harbor

Year of construction: 1919

Shipyard: Gulfport Shipbuilding Company, Gulfport (Mississippi)

Tonnage: schooner: 767 tons gross; 658 tons net

Dimensions:
Length between perpendiculars: 54.40 m
Width: 11.03 m
Depth in hold: 4.57 m

Sail area: as a bark 1486 square meters

Rigging: 23 sails; 4 foresails, double topsails, single topgallant, royals; mizzenmast: lower mizzen, upper mizzen, mizzen topsail

Masts and spars: wood bowsprit, jibboom, and mizzenboom, all others made of steel; foremast and mainmast with topgallant masts

Auxiliary engine: none

Crew: as a school-ship approx. 30 people

Use: museum ship, restaurant ship

The ship was built in 1919 for the Marine Coal Company of New Orleans as the 4-masted schooner *Elisabeth Bandi* and was used primarily in the lumber trade. Already on her first voyage the schooner suffered a serious leak due to teredos. The ship didn't have an outer layer of copper plates to protect it from damage of this kind. There was an additional problem on this first voyage. The captain vanished without a trace while the ship was at sea, and the crew deserted.

After returning home, the ship entered a dock in Philadelphia for repairs. Nonetheless there continued to be leaks on future voyages. By 1925 the costs for repairs had become too high. The ship was sold to the firm of Walter E. Reid in Bath (Maine). In 1931 the Finnish shipowner W. Uskanen of Sotkoma purchased the schooner, changed her name to *Bandi* and em-ployed her almost exclusively in the lumber trade from Finland to England. The cold water of the Baltic quickly eliminated the teredos. In 1935–36 the *Bandi* was sold to the Finnish shipping company Yrjänen & Kumpp in Rauma. She remained in the lumber trade.

In November 1938 the Hamburg shipowner John T. Essberger purchased the ship. At Blohm & Voss in Hamburg she was converted into a bark. On May 15, 1939, the work was completed. Under her new name *Seute Deern,* she became a freight-carrying school-ship for Essberger's shipping company. The conversion involved major modifications: new additions included a white streak, a figurehead in the shape of a girl, and 70 tons of fixed ballast; lower rigging and backstays were added to the bulwark and attached to the chain plates outboard. The forecastle and the deckhouse were connected to each other. The ship received stockless anchors in hawses. The hull below the waterline was covered with plates. Shortly after the conversion the sail area was increased by widening all four topsails as well as the topgallants.

Following a brief stay in the Baltic, the *Seute Deern* carried her first cargo under the German flag to Finland. The war broke out while she was returning home with a load of wood. The bark entered a Danish port and remained there until the end of the war with Poland. During the first war years, shorter trade voyages (salt, wood) were undertaken in the Baltic Sea. In the winter the ship was laid up in Lübeck or Stolpmünde.

During the voyages, the shipowner Essberger trained future crews for his own fleet.

Each crew consisted of 10 to 12 regular sailors and 10 to 12 boys. At the end of September 1944, the *Seute Deern* was transferred to Lübeck. This is where she was located at the end of the war. The topmasts and yards had been removed at that point. Following the Allied occupation she temporarily served as an English guardhouse. In 1946 she was towed to Travemünde, where she was newly rigged at the Schlichting shipyard. From 1947 to 1954 she was then moored to Ferry VII in Hamburg as a hotel and restaurant ship. At the beginning of 1954 the ship was sold to the American A. J. Koerts, who was of Dutch descent. He in turn donated the *Seute Deern,* now under the new name *Pieter Albrecht Koerts,* to his native city of Delfzijl to serve as a youth hostel. On April 19, 1954, she was towed out of Hamburg.

In December 1964 the gastronome E. Hardisty of Emden purchased the bark in order to once again convert her into a restaurant ship. On December 3 the ship was towed from Delfzijl to Emden. The plans fell through, however. In the meantime the hotel owner H. Richartz of Helgoland had purchased the ship, in order to put her to the same use, but in Bremerhaven. At the Schröder shipyard in Emden, the sailing ship was thoroughly refitted and prepared for her new use. From 1966 on the bark was moored as a restaurant ship in Bremerhaven under her old name *Seute Deern.* Since 1972 she has belonged to the German maritime museum.

Previous names: *Noona Dan, Havet*

Type: fore-and-aft ketch, wood

Nation: Germany

Owner: German School-Ship Association (charter)

Home port: Travemünde

Year of construction: 1939

Shipyard: J. Ring-Andersen, Svendborg

Tonnage: 425 ts displacement; 105.36 tons gross; 25.72 tons net

Dimensions:
Length overall: 36.20 m
Length of hull: 29.90 m
Length between perpendiculars: 26.25
Width: 2.90 m
Depth to deck: 2.90 m
Depth in hold: 2.20 m
Draft: 3.05 m

Sail area: 332 square meters

Rigging: 7 sails; 4 foresails; main-, mizzenmast: gaff-sails, gaff-topsails

Masts: both masts with topmast; height of mainmast over the waterline: 26.25 meters

Auxiliary engine: Alpha-diesel, 165 horsepower

Crew: 6-person active crew, 24 students

Use: sailing school-ship

A Danish shipyard built the modern-day *Seute Deern* as the galleass *Havet.* Following World War II she was purchased by the Lauritzen shipyard in Copenhagen. In the process she received the name *Noona Dan.* In 1961 the ship brought a Danish expedition to the Salomon Islands and to the Australian coast. Shortly after her return the German School-Ship Association, along with the Foundation for Training Ships, purchased her. Extensive conversion work followed in order to allow the ship to be used for training purposes. In honor of the John T. Essberger shipyard's former school-ship *Seute Deern,* the ketch received the same name.

The official commissioning took place on July 22, 1964. At that time the ship undertook weekly voyages in the western Baltic during the warm months of the year. On these voyages the students of the maritime schools of Bremen, Bremerhaven, Elsfleth, Hamburg, Leer, and Lübeck were given the opportunity to perfect their theoretical knowledge by gaining experience in practical seamanship. The students of the S.S. *Deutschland* also took part in the voyages.

Since 1973 the *Seute Deern* has belonged to CLIPPER— German Youth Work at Sea. Even today the voyages with young people have the Baltic Sea as their destination; visits to foreign countries are part of the program.

Solvang

In Old Norwegian, *solvang* means "place in the sun." The ship was built as a freighter. During World War II she was requisitioned by the British navy and served as a command ship in the Shetland Islands. From 1945 to 1979 the *Solvang* sailed as a coasting vessel on the Haugesund–Lofotes route. The ship has been thoroughly restored since then and today uses the original rigging.

Type: galleass, wood

Nation: Germany

Owner: Werner Muffler, Wigand Freiherr von Salmuth

Home port: Lübeck

Year of construction: 1939

Shipyard: Aasheim, Sagvaag, Norway

Dimensions:
Length overall: 35.50 m
Length of hull: 24.41 m
Width: 5.86 m
Draft: 3.92 m

Sail area: 316 square meters

Rigging: 8 sails

Auxiliary engine: DAF diesel, 300 horsepower

Crew: 4-person active crew, 9 students, 30 day guests

Use: chartered ship, sailing school-ship

Thor Heyerdahl

Built in 1930 in Holland as a motorized ship, the *Tinka,* as she was known at that time, had her home port in Hamburg; later she was called the *Marga Henning* and the *Silke.* In 1951 the hull was lengthened by several meters midships, which increased her carrying capacity to 300 tons. At the end of the 1970s she was retired from service as a freighter. Two German shipowners converted the rundown coasting vessel into a 3-masted topsail schooner; in 1982 her restoration was completed and she was given a new name. On May 7, 1983, the ship undertook a trial voyage with her namesake.

(The ship was named after the Norwegian explorer Thor Heyerdahl, who received worldwide attention primarily for his voyage from South America to Polynesia with the raft *Kon-Tiki*). Since then the ship has made long voyages reaching as far as the Caribbean. The voyages for young people are designed to provide learning experiences. Since 1993 school classes have been taught for seven months at sea (Project High Seas High School).

Previous names: *Minnow, Silke, Marga Henning, Tinka*

Type: 3-masted topsail schooner, riveted iron

Nation: Germany

Owner: Thor Heyerdahl Association, Kiel

Home port: Kiel

Year of construction: 1930

Shipyard: Smidt & Son, Westerbroek, the Netherlands

Tonnage: 211.21 tons gross

Dimensions:
Length overall: 49.83 m
Width: 6.52 m
Draft: 2.25 m

Sail area: approx. 730 square meters

Rigging: 12 sails; middle staysail, outer jib, inner jib, forestaysail, 3 gaff-sails, 2 gaff-topsails, main topmast staysails, topsails, and topgallants

Masts: wood; height of mainmast over the deck: 26.50 meters

Auxiliary engine: 6-cylinder Deutz diesel, 215 horsepower, built in 1951; in addition, three auxiliary diesel engines to power devices on board

Crew: 8 people, room for 36 passengers

Use: chartered ship

Ubena von Bremen

Type: cog, reproduction of a ship from 1380, wood

Nation: Germany

Owner: Hanseatic Cog Shipyard Association, Bremerhaven

Home port: Bremerhaven

Years of construction: 1989–90

Shipyard: Hanseatic Cog Shipyard, Bremerhaven

Tonnage: 120 ts displacement

Dimensions:
Length overall: 23.23 m
Length of keel: 15.60 m
Width: 7.62 m
Depth to deck: 3.14 m
Draft: 2.25 m

Sail area: 150–200 square meters

Rigging: 1 sail (2 studding sails)

Masts: 1 mast; height of mainmast over the deck: 22.90 meters

Auxiliary engine: MWM-Deutz-V8 diesel, 204 kilowatts (reduced)

Crew: 10-person active crew, up to 35 guests on day cruises

Use: cruises on the routes of the old Hanseatic League; mutual understanding between peoples on a maritime basis

In the summer of 1991 the cog left her home port for the first time for a voyage on the traditional route of the old Hanseatic ships. Her name was chosen because the spice company Ubena supported the project with a substantial sum of money.

The name *Ubena* is directly related to the spice trade and designates an East African tribe that lives in modern Tanzania. The German East Africa Line named all of its ships after East African tribes.

The first *Ubena*, built during the 1920s, entered the history books early in 1945 as one of the ships that carried a total of 2 million refugees from what was at that time East Prussia from Danzig Bay to western ports. On 7 voyages, a total of 27,000 people were rescued by the *Ubena* alone. All of the children that were born aboard the ship during these voyages received Ubena as a middle name.

Undine

Previous names: *Nordstrand I, Gerd-Ute, Annelies, Palmyra, Franziska*

Type: 2-masted fore-and-aft schooner, steel

Nation: Germany

Owner: Gangway e.V., Hamburg

Home port: Hamburg, old customs pontoon, Reiherstieg (November 1 to April 30)

Year of construction: 1931

Shipyard: Gebr. Niestern, Delfzijl, the Netherlands

Tonnage: 130 ts displacement (empty); gross register tonnage 99; net register tonnage 38

Dimensions:
Length overall: 37.70 m
Length of hull: 28.80 m
Length between perpendiculars: 25.00 m
Width: 5.80 m
Depth in hold: 2.40 m
Draft (empty, middle): 2.10 m

Sail area: 420 square meters

Rigging: 9 sails

Masts: height of mainmast over the deck: 27.70 meters

Auxiliary engine: German Works Type 4 M 36, year of construction 1937, 120 horsepower

Crew: 4-person active crew (including 2 teachers), 8 young people

Use: cargo-carrying sailing school-ship; social group work

The *Undine* served as a freighter until 1980, originally as a $1^1/_2$-master, and after having her bow lengthened in 1940 as a motorized ship. From 1940 to 1945 the navy required the *Franziska,* as the ship was known at that time, to perform supply runs between Kiel and Norway. In the spring of 1945 Captain Werner Mehl brought her to Königsberg, which was occupied by Russian troops at that time. On the voyage home he took 100 refugees on board and brought them safely to Kiel. The large number of previous names demonstrates how often the ship has changed owners. After 1980 the current owner carried out the ship's restoration and conversion into a schooner in Glückstadt.

Since 1984 the sailing ship has been used as a freight-carrying school-ship for at-risk young people. The ship is an official freighter and is subject to the requirements of the maritime professional association and of the German Lloyd. In addition to other goods, sea salt from France and Portugal is transported for the food industry.

The youths remain on board for half a year in order to prepare themselves for a regular professional education, often in a maritime field.

Since 1999 the ship has been the property of the Gangway Association in Hamburg. She is still being used as a freight-carrying school-ship. The association works with the Youth Office in Hamburg.

Valdivia

Previous name: *Vanadis*

Type: 2-masted fore-and-aft schooner, wood

Nation: Germany

Owner: Uwe Kutzner

Home port: Hamburg

Year of construction: 1868

Shipyard: Södra Varvet, Stockholm

Tonnage: 50 ts displacement; 27.21 tons gross

Dimensions:
Length overall: 29.00 m
Length of hull: 20.00 m
Width: 5.10 m
Draft: 2.80 m

Sail area: 283 square meters

Rigging: 7 sails

Masts: height of mainmast over the waterline: 21 meters

Auxiliary engine: Daimler Benz diesel, type OM 352

Crew: 8 individual cabins, 1 double cabin

Use: chartered ship

Schooners with a streamlined form like the *Valdivia*'s were used primarily for fishing in the waters off Newfoundland. They became known as New-foundland schooners. Thus it is unusual that this particular ship, at that time called the *Vanadis,* was commissioned as a private yacht for a Swedish manufacturer. The owner later donated his ship to the Swedish navy. An expedition was under-taken and led all the way around the world in 1898–99. After that the *Vanadis* sailed as a courier, a pilot schooner, and a smuggling patrol ship.

Around 1914 she became a yacht belong to the Swedish navy. After being converted, the ship then belonged to the Royal Swedish Yacht Club after 1925.

In the winter of 1939–40 the schooner once again passed into private hands and earned her money as a chartered ship.

After the war the ship was sold to a buyer in the Federal Republic of Germany and reg-istered in Hamburg. She re-ceived the new name *Valdivia.* She has belonged to the cur-rent owner since 1975. Fol-lowing thorough repair work, rebuilding, and modernization, the *Valdivia* has been available for chartered cruises since 1982. The voyages take place primarily in the waters of the Baltic Sea.

Vegesack BV2

Previous names: *Nostra, Monika Harssen, Lilli, Lili, BV2 Vegesack*

Type: fore-and-aft ketch, iron

Nation: Germany

Owner: Maritime Tradition Vegesack Nautilus Association, Bremen

Home port: Bremen-Vegesack

Year of construction: 1895

Shipyard: Bremer Vulkan

Tonnage: gross register tonnage 75

Dimensions:
Length overall: 35.40 m
Length of hull: 5.40 m
Draft: 2.50 m

Sail area: 430 square meters

Rigging: 6 sails

Auxiliary engine: Volvo Penta diesel, 108 horsepower

Crew: 3-person active crew, 25 day guests

Use: chartered ship

The *Vegesack* (BV stands for Bremen-Vegesack) was the first ship built at the Bremen Vulkan shipyard. Her christening took place on April 29, 1895. Until World War I the ship fished for herring with gill nets in the North Sea. She spent the war in Vegesack. In 1921 an engine was installed. Prior to her sale to a buyer in Sweden in the year 1939 the ship earned her money in the coastal trade.

With the new name *Nostra* she continued to take part in the freight trade. Beginning in 1966 the sailing ship belonged to a merchant marine school in Härnösand for a number of years. In 1979 the *Nostra* was sold to a group of owners in Hamburg.

The ship was employed in youth work after an additional change of ownership. Since 1989 the ketch has belonged to the Maritime Tradition Vegesack Nautilus organization in Bremen.

Vidar

Type: 3-masted fore-and-aft schooner, wood

Nation: Germany

Owner: Wilhelm Ehlers, Büsum

Home port: Büsum

Year of construction: 1877

Shipyard: Johann Selsvik, Hardangerfjord, Norway

Dimensions:
Length overall: 40.00 m
Width: 7.00 m
Draft: 3.00 m

Sail area: 560 square meters

Rigging: 13 sails

Masts: height of masts: 27.50 m (all masts are the same height)

Auxiliary engine: MB 846 Mercedes diesel, 320 horsepower

Crew: 6- to 8-person active crew, 30 berths

Use: restaurant ship, maritime memorial

The *Vidar* was built as a sloop (a 1-masted freighter). In 1898 she received a galleass rig. She transported fish, wood, and bulk goods in European waters. The first engine was installed in 1919. Starting in 1922 she belonged to Alfred Synnevag of Florvag. In World War II the ship transported sand for the construction of German submarine bunkers.

In 1949 the *Vidar* was completely rebuilt and lengthened to the current size. In 1978 Alfred Synnevag sold the ship to Wilhelm Ehlers in Büsum. Her conversion into a club ship lasted until 1982. In the process the *Vidar* also received her current rig.

The ship had to be removed from service because of serious damage to the wood. In order to save the venerable ship and preserve her seaworthiness, a somewhat unconventional, but very long-lasting conservation method was attempted. The entire hull received a coat of sprayed concrete, which was covered with two coats of preservative for stability. The thickness of this coating is 7 centimeters on average. The improvement of the interior and of the engine alone reduced the weight by 40 tons.

Today the *Vidar* is moored as a floating restaurant in the harbor at Büsum.

White Dune

The 14-month conversion of the *White Dune* cost 2 million marks. In March 2000 the current owner had the ship brought to Harlingen in the Netherlands, where she is being converted into a luxury sailing ship. The masts stand on the hull, not on the deck.

A look back: In 1909 the *Neerlandia* was launched in Meppel in the Netherlands. Until 1939 she was the prop-

Previous names: *Klara Katharina, Neerlandia*

Type: fore-and-aft schooner

Nation: Germany

Owner: Brinkmann family, Leer

Home port: Leer

Year of construction: launched 1909

Dimensions:
Length of hull: 36.00 m
Width: 6.40 m
Draft: 1.40 m

Sail area: 440 square meters

Masts: mainmast: 16 meters; mizzenmast: 17 meters

Auxiliary engine: MAN diesel, 340 horsepower

Crew: size of crew not known, 24 overnight guests, 60 guests on day cruises

Use: day cruises, conferences, restaurant, chartered cruises

erty of the Priet family of Holterfehn. Then Karl Funk purchased her for 40,000 Reich marks, modified the ship, and named her *Klara Katharina.*

Two years later, in 1941, she sank in a heavy storm, but it was possible to raise her. In 1964 the ship, at that time a coasting vessel, received the name *White Dune,* and until 1999 she carried junk, bricks, and stone among the Rhineland, the Ruhr region, and the coast and islands of the North Sea.

Today the ship is cared for by the *White Dune* Sailing Schooner Association. She is moored in Leer next to the Town Hall Bridge.

White Shark

For many years the ship was stationed on the P-Buoy-Way as a seamark and lightship in the German Bay. On November 15, 1972, her location was shifted to the entrance of the Ems. Her new designation was *T/W Ems.* Her equipment included a beacon light, radio beacon, fog signal, and radar answering beacon, as well as red hull that functioned as a signal during the day. The crew at that time consisted of two groups of 14 people (first shift and second shift) that relieved each other every 14 days. In 1987 the lightship was retired from service and, starting in 1989, she was converted by her new owner, Willi Bolsmann, into a sailing ship for approximately 80 people.

The white color as well as the sharklike appearance of the unusual stem and the anchor hawse gave the ship the name *White Shark.*

Previous names: *T/W Ems, P8, FS Aussenjade*

Type: 3-masted fore-and-aft schooner, steel

Nation: Germany

Owner: Willi Bolsmann

Home port: Hamburg

Year of construction: 1902

Shipyard: J. L. Meyer Shipyard, Papenburg

Shipyards where modifications were performed: Rostock, Stralsund, Danzig, Motorworks, Bremen

Tonnage: 560 ts displacement; gross register tonnage 370; 149 tons net

Dimensions:
Length overall: 57.00 m
Length of hull: 47.20 m
Width: 8.20 m
Draft: 3.00 m

Sail area: 650 square meters

Masts: height of foremast: 31 meters; mainmast: 32 meters; mizzenmast: 31 meters

Auxiliary engine: two DMW Deutz diesel, 45 horsepower each

Crew: 18-person active crew

Use: chartered ship

The schooner now sails at the behest of the Bockhorner Tradition and Culture Association's *White Shark* Sailing Club. The main areas she visits are the waters off the Canary Islands and the Mediterranean.

Wyvern von Bremen

Type: fore-and-aft ketch, steel

Nation: Germany

Owner: Foundation for
Training Ships, Lübeck

Home port: Bremen

Year of construction: 1992

Shipyard: Bremer Vulkan,
Bremen-Vegesack

Tonnage: 59.45 ts
displacement

Dimensions:
Length overall: 24.60 m
Length at the
waterline: 16.35 m
Width: 5.45 m
Draft: 3.00 m

Sail area: 270 square meters

Rigging: 8 sails (with Genoa)

Masts: height of mainmast
over the deck: 24 meters

Auxiliary engine: Daimler-
Benz diesel, 175 kilowatt

Crew: 11 berths

Use: training ship for
commanders of historic ships,
youth work

The ketch is the steel reconstruction of the wooden sailing yacht *Wyvern*, which was built by the designer Colin Archer (1832–1921) at the end of the nineteenth century. The original belongs to the maritime museum in Stavanger and still sails today. Archer was especially famous for the design of his rescue ketches, which could be deployed reliably even under the worst weather conditions. The Wyvern is a winged dragon in English mythology.

This steel reconstruction was a shared project of the Bremen shipbuilding and shipbuilding supply industries led by the Worker Training Center in Bremen. The yacht designer Horst E. Glacer provided the plans.

Zuversicht

Previous name: *Leo*

Type: 2-masted fore-and-aft schooner, wood

Nation: Germany

Owner: Christian Youth Village Work Germany Association, Göppingen

Home port: Eckernförde

Year of construction: 1904

Shipyard: Kirsgard & Nielson, Troense, Denmark

Tonnage: 58 tons gross

Dimensions:
Length overall: 30.00 m
Length of hull: 22.00 m
Width: 5.60 m
Draft: 2.10 m

Sail area: 274 square meters

Rigging: 7 sails

Masts: height of the mainmast over the deck: 21 meters

Auxiliary engine: Volvo Penta diesel, 270 horsepower

Crew: 4-person active crew, 12-person guest crew

Use: youth sailing schooner

The *Zuversicht* was equipped in keeping with all of the conditions and legal requirements of the German maritime professional organizations. The ship does not have the task of undertaking recreational cruises. She supplements the work of the youth village Eckernförde. All preparatory and restorative work takes place there. This village's areas of activity include: intensive courses in personality development and work motivation; social work and therapeutic courses; and training and continuing education of employees.

Great Britain

Activ
Adix
Baboon
Carrick
Carrie
Cutty Sark
De Wadden
Discovery
Earl of Pembroke
Eye of the Wind
HMS Gannett
Glenlee
Golden Hinde
Grand Turk
Great Britain
Helga

Irene
Jean de la Lune
Ji Fung
Julia
Kaskelot
Kathleen & May
Lord Nelson
Matthew
Phoenix
Queen Galadriel
Raphaelo
Result
Return of Marco
   Polo
Ring-Andersen
Royalist

Saint Kilda
Søren Larsen
Spirit of
   Winestead
St. Barbara Ann
Stavros S. Niarchos/
   Prince William
Tenacious
HMS Trincomalee
HMS Unicorn
Unicorn
HMS Victory
HMS Warrior
Yankee Trader
Zamoura of Zermatt
Zebu

Previous names: *Svendborg, Mona*

Type: 3-masted topsail schooner, wood

Nation: Great Britain

Owner: Baltic Schooner Company Ltd., Guernsey

Home port: London

Year of construction: 1951; launched December 1951

Shipyard: J. Ring-Andersen, Svendborg (Denmark); modifications and new rig, 1980: Michael Kiersgaard Shipyard, Troense

Tonnage: 116.80 tons gross; 74.99 tons net

Dimensions:
Length overall: 42.00 m
Length of hull: 27.30 m
Width: 7.08 m
Depth in hold: 2.35 m
Draft: 3.00 m

Sail area: 536 square meters

Rigging: 13 sails; foremast: foresail, topsail, double topgallant

Masts: height of mainmast over the deck: 27 meters

Auxiliary engine: Saab-Scania, 230 horsepower, 6 cylinder

Crew: no set number, 8–18 berths

Use: private use, in part as a chartered film ship

The *Activ*, at that time called the *Mona*, was built in the winter of 1951–52 in Denmark as the last ship in a large series of similar schooners. She received only a one-and-a-half-mast rigging for auxiliary sails because from the beginning she was equipped with an engine for the Greenland trade. The ship was partially covered with iron plates for the Arctic waters. As the *Mona*, the ship traveled the Greenland route for 20 years and carried freight between Greenland's ports. After a 6-year respite, a re-rigging as a topsail schooner took place in 1980, resulting in a rig that fits exceptionally well with the hull. These "Baltic schooners" once sailed the Baltic in great numbers as freighters.

Previous names: *XXXX, Jessica*

Type: 3-masted fore-and-aft schooner, steel

Nation: Great Britain

Owner: Ocean Sailing Adventures Ltd., Guernsey

Home port: Guernsey

Year of construction: 1983

Shipyard: Astilleros de Mallorca S. A., Mallorca

Tonnage: 370 tdw

Dimensions:
Length overall: 64.50 m
Length of hull: 56.00 m
Length at the waterline: 42.40 m
Width: 8.60 m
Draft: 4.80 m

Sail area: 1720 square meters

Auxiliary engine: 540 PS MAN

Crew: 14-person active crew, 7 passengers

Use: private yacht

The Argentinean Carlos Perdomo commissioned the construction of the strikingly sporty yacht *Jessica,* which was named after his wife. The ship was originally rigged as a topsail schooner. The traditional appearance of the rig disguises the fact that modern deck equipment, for example, electric-powered winches, facilitate the sailing maneuvers. The interior of the ship likewise meets the highest standards. Her sailing properties have proven to be exceptional. In 1988 the schooner became the property of the Australian Alan Bond. The somewhat prosaic name *XXXX* that the ship was given at this time simply indicated that the ship was used to advertise the products of the Australian brewery bearing this name. After the Australians failed to win the America's Cup, the ship was put up for sale and passed into Spanish hands in 1990. The modification that followed amounted to a completely new construction. The poop was lengthened, the rooms rearranged, and the new aluminum masts received a pure fore-and-aft rig. The current name *Adix* is reminiscent of the previous name: "Add X."

Baboon

Type: 3-masted topsail schooner, steel	Tonnage: 444 tons gross; 134 tons net	Rigging: 13 sails
Nation: Great Britain	Dimensions:	Masts: wood
Owner: Drusberg Investments Ltd.	Length overall: 60.20 m Length between perpendiculars: 43.06 m	Auxiliary engine: Caterpillar, 2000 horsepower
Home port: Hamilton, Bermuda	Width: 8.40 m Depth to deck: 4.88 m Draft: 4.20 m	Crew: 14-person active crew, 14 guests
Year of construction: 1991	Sail area: 950 square meters	Use: for the company's own purposes
Shipyard: Marstrand, Sweden		

The *Baboon* is one of the most state-of-the art luxury yachts to be found on the world's oceans. The accommodations for the passengers are reminiscent of a first-class hotel. Central heating, air conditioning, as well as amenities of the most diverse kind are taken for granted.

 Carrick

Previous name: *City of Adelaide*

Type: former clipper full-rigged ship, composite construction

Nation: Great Britain

Owner: Scottish Maritime Museum

Home port: Irvine

Year of construction: 1864

Shipyard: William Pile, Sunderland, England

Tonnage: 791 tons gross

Dimensions:
Length between perpendiculars: 53.70 m
Width: 10.10 m
Depth in hold: 5.70 m

Rigging: originally double topsail, double topgallant, royals

Masts: top- and topgallant masts

Auxiliary engine: none

Use: museum ship

Only two composite clippers have been preserved from the golden age of the clippers. In London lies the *Cutty Sark* and in Glasgow the *Carrick,* formerly the *City of Adelaide.* Although the renowned English sailing-ship expert H. A. Underhill ascribed more elegance to the hull of the *Carrick,* today there is no comparison between the two ships. The *Cutty Sark* displays the full beauty of her rig, while the *Carrick* has become a hulk. At this point no bowsprit completes the elegant line of her bow. An unsightly deck, or rather roof, which furthermore overshadows the poop and forecastle decks, obscures the form completely. The sailing ship, which was formerly a full-rigged ship, was built for the Australian passenger line Devitt & Moore. A hundred years ago the passengers were primarily immigrants to Australia. She once sailed from London to Adelaide in the record time of 65 days.

When the passenger cruises ceased to be profitable because steamships were preferred, the shipping company used its ship in the wool trade. Shortly before World War I the British navy took over the clipper. The *City of Adelaide* became the HMS *Carrick,* named after the southwestern Scottish landscape of the same name. During the war she was probably a medical ship. After that she was used as a depot and school-ship.

Until 1947 she lay in the outer harbor of Greenock, at first as the Naval Gunnery School HMS *Carrick,* later as the headquarters ship of the Greenock Sub-Division, R.N.V.R. In 1946 the Royal Naval Volunteer Reserve was looking for appropriate accommodations for its officers' club. A year later the *Carrick* was selected for this purpose and equipped accordingly. For many years she was moored in the Clyde in Glasgow. She ran aground several times during this period.

Since then the ship has been towed to Irvine, where investigations are under way to determine whether the ship can continue to be used as a floating museum or needs to be brought into a dry dock.

A group has formed to promote the preservation of the ship, which has become extremely dilapidated. It is considering the possibility of transporting it to Australia for repairs.

The group includes the great-granddaughter of the first captain as well as the great-grandson of a passenger from 1874.

Carrie

Previous name: *Kenavo*

Type: 2-masted fore-and-aft schooner, wood

Nation: Great Britain

Owner: Mrs. Ellie M. Standen

Home port: Plymouth

Year of construction: 1947

Shipyard: M. Cornec, Carnaret, France

Tonnage: 62 ts displacement, 58.3 tons gross

Dimensions:
Length overall: 27.40 m
Length of hull: 20.00 m
Length between perpendiculars: 19.00 m
Width: 6.20 m
Draft: 2.80 m

Sail area: 325 square meters

Rigging: 7 sails

Masts: height of mainmast over the deck: 26.20 meters

Auxiliary engine: Baudoin diesel, 120 horsepower

Crew: 3-person active crew, 10 guests

Use: chartered ship

The ship, which is constructed of larch wood on oak, was built to transport spring lobster from the coasts of Mauritania and Brazil to France. For this purpose she was equipped with large saltwater tanks so that the animals could be delivered still living. For a time the ship was also employed as a fishing vessel. In 1986 the Square Sail organization of Charlestown, Cornwall, assumed ownership of the extremely run-down sailing vessel. Following a thorough overhaul the schooner received a new rig. The ship took on various film roles under the auspices of this organization. For example, she was converted to play the *Pinta* in the film *1492: Conquest of Paradise.* Since 1998 the schooner, with her wide upper deck, has been employed as a chartered ship.

In order to bring the Chinese tea harvests ever-more quickly to Europe, and especially to England, the tea merchants demanded ever-faster ships.

At that time this could not be achieved with steamships, but only with the streamlined and elegant clippers, the "race-horses of the sea." In 1869 the shipowner and captain John Willis of London had the clipper *Cutty Sark* built in order to defeat the *Thermopylae*, which was one year older, in the "tea race." The name *Cutty Sark* is of Scottish origin and means "short shirt." It refers to a piece of clothing belonging to the witch Nannie in the poem

Previous names: *Maria do Amparo, Ferreira (= El Pequina Camisola), Cutty Sark*

Type: full-rigged ship, composite construction

Nation: Great Britain

Owner: Cutty Sark Preservation Society, London

Home port: Greenwich (dry dock)

Year of construction: 1869; launched November 23, 1869

Shipyard: Scott & Linton, Dumbarton/Clyde; completed by Denny Bros., Leven

Tonnage: 2100 ts displacment; 963 tons gross; 921 tons net

Dimensions:
Length overall: 85.10 m
Length of hull: 70.50 m
Length between perpendiculars: 64.70 m
Length of keel: 61.80
Width: 10.90 m
Depth in hold: 6.40 m
Draft (with heavy cargo): 6.00 m

Sail area: 2970 square meters

Rigging: 34 sails; 4 foresails, all masts: double topsails, single topgallants, royals; mainmast: skysail, fore-, mainmast: studding sails

Masts, spars: bowsprit and jibboom: 18.20 meters; foremast: from the deck to the head of the mast: 39.40 meters; main yard: 23.70 meters; fore-royal yard: 11.50 meters; mainmast: from the deck to the head of the mast: 44.40 m; main yard: 23.70 meters; main-royal yard: 11.50 meters; sky yard: 10.30 m; mizzenmast: from the deck to the head of the mast: 33.10 meters; mizzen yard: 20.20 meters; mizzen-royal yard: 10 meters; mizzen boom: 15.80 meters

Crew: maximum 28 people, usually 23–24 people (the ship was also operated by 19 people)

136

"Tam o'Shanter" by Robert Burns. Until 1877 the full-rigged ship sailed almost exclusively as a tea clipper in the China trade. She frequently completed her voyages in record time. Speeds of up 17 knots were often logged. After 1877 the *Cutty Sark* was primarily engaged in Australia's wool trade. In 1880 the sail area was significantly reduced and the lower masts shortened by 3 meters. In the following years the ship sailed as a tramping vessel (oil in canisters, coal, iron, piece goods, etc.). From 1885 until 1895 the sailing ship once again carried mostly wool from Australia under the command of Captain Woodget. In 1895 she was sold to the firm J. A. Ferreira in Lisbon. The name changed to *Ferreira*. Mostly, however, one referred to her as *El Pequina Camisola*.

Little is known about the ship's use by the Portuguese. In 1916 a storm dismasted the ship because of an incorrect coal stowage. The clipper docked at Cape Town as an emergency port, and there she was rerigged as a barkentine. In 1920 the firm Ferreira sold her to the Cia de Navegacao de Portugal in Lisbon. The voyages under this flag were not profitable, however.

The famous ship was offered for sale in England without success. As the *Maria do Amparo* it finally went to Gibraltar. In 1922 Captain Wilfred Dowman of Falmouth bought the ship. The *Cutty Sark*, as she was now called, was restored at great expense and once again rigged as a full-rigged ship. Until Dowman's death in 1936 she remained moored as a stationary school-ship in Falmouth. In 1938 his wife donated the ship to the Nautical Training College Worcester in London.

In June 1938 the *Cutty Sark*, in tow, undertook her last voyage over open water to London. She was moored in Greenhithe next to the *Worcester*. During the war she was unrigged to her lower masts. In 1951 she underwent a thorough inspection in the dry dock of Millwall. The condition of the ship proved to be faultless. In 1952 the National Maritime Museum in Greenwich developed plans to restore the ship and use her as a permanent memorial to the great age of sailing-ship travel. In 1953 her period of use as a school-ship came to an end. The *Cutty Sark* Preservation Society was founded. The necessary overhaul work was undertaken in the East India Dock. On July 10, 1954, the *Cutty Sark* was hauled to her dry berth in Greenwich. On June 25, 1957, the queen presented the ship to the public.

The figurehead had already been altered. The exact appearance of the original figure is not known. The figure represents the witch Nannie.

In the hold there is now a museum with numerous figureheads. In addition the room is also used for instructional purposes.

De Wadden

Type: 3-masted fore-and-aft schooner, steel	Dimensions: Length of hull: 35.58 m Width: 7.44 m Depth in hold: 3.17 m Draft: 3.00 m
Nation: Great Britain	
Owner: Merseyside Maritime Museum, Liverpool	Rigging: 10 sails; 4 foresails, gaff- and gaff topsails
Home port: Liverpool, dry dock	Auxiliary engine: Stavwall diesel, 125 horsepower
Year of construction: 1917	
Shipyard: Brothers van Diepen, Waterhuizen, Holland	Crew: 9-person active crew
Tonnage: 251 tons gross; 190 tons net	Use: museum ship

Along with the schooners *De Dollart* and *De Lauwers*, *De Wadden* was built as a cargo-carrying schooner with an auxiliary engine for the relatively small company with the big name, Netherlands Steamship Company. In 1921 she was sold to the renowned Hall shipping company in Arklow, England.

At that time *De Wadden* was one of the best-known trading vessels traveling between England and Ireland. She primarily transported bulk goods such as fertilizer, ore, grain, kaolin, and coal, but she also carried mine timbers in her large holds. Repeated interior modifications and the installation of a new engine helped her remain a safe and reliable vessel. For 40 years *De Wadden* sailed in the service of the Hall shipping company. The firm eventually abandoned its fleet of schooners due to their insufficient speed. In 1961 the ship passed into private hands, after which only the lower masts were retained from the original rig. She transported sand for a construction company, served as a film ship (*The Onedin Line*), and finally became a floating platform for sport fishermen. Her sails had to be removed for financial reasons. Since 1984 the schooner has belonged to the Merseyside Maritime Museum in Liverpool. She lies in a dry dock at the museum and is supposed to be rerigged. Nonetheless, her sailing days are over.

Type: bark, wood

Nation: Great Britain

Owner: The Maritime Trust, London

Home port: Dundee, Discovery Point, Discovery Quay

Year of construction: 1901; launched March 21, 1901

Shipyard: Dundee Shipbuilder's Company, Steven's Yard, Dundee (Scotland); design: W. C. Smith, Naval Architect

Tonnage: 1620 ts displacement; 736 tons gross

Dimensions:
Length between perpendiculars: 52.20 m
Width: 10.30 m
Draft: 4.80 m

Sail area: 1144 square meters

Rigging: 18 sails; 3 foresails; double topsail, single topgallant, royals (the arrangement of the sails was not always the same)

Masts, spars: fore-, mainmast: top- and topgallant masts; topgallant mast: 1 topmast; bowsprit with jibboom

Auxiliary engine: triple-expansion steam engine, 450 horsepower

Crew: during the Scott expedition 38 people, not including scientists

Use: museum ship

At the International Geographical Congress that was held in 1899 in Berlin, the exploration of the Antarctic formed a topic of special interest. The participants agreed to strengthen international cooperation. The commission to build the *Dis-* *covery* was issued by the Royal Geographical Society in preparation for the Royal Antarctic Expedition. The crew consisted of members of the Royal Navy, mostly volunteers. Commander Robert Falcon Scott, himself an officer in the Royal Navy, took command in June 1900.

Special plans were developed for the *Discovery* in order to meet the special demands of the Arctic Ocean. The ship received a double-layered hull. Because of the dangers that could result from a freezing of the hull, no bilge keels were installed. The disadvantage of this was that the ship was not particularly protected against rolling and lurching. The stem was adapted to ice breaking. The wide, jutting stern protected the rudder blade and propeller from the effects of ice. The rudder blade could be replaced with a spare from the deck. In case of danger, it was also possible to remove the propeller and store it above in a vertical shaft.

The yards and sails of the two forward masts were interchangeable. The shrouds and backstays were set outboard to chain plates. At the time of her great voyage the ship had five 8-meter whaling boats and two Norwegian prams on board. In the top of the mainmast hung an ice lookout barrel. The only ornamentation was the beautifully carved scrollwork on the bow, which was crowned with the British coat of arms. The ship could carry two years'

worth of equipment and provisions. On July 31, 1901, the *Discovery* left London. In addition to the crew, five scientists were on board.

The ship proved to not be very fast under sail, because the sail area had intentionally been kept small. The expedition lasted until September 1904. Subsequently, the ship was sold to the Hudson Bay Company. It transported supplies for the company between Europe and North America. From 1912 until 1914 the bark was laid up. In 1914 she was chartered to the French government for the transport of munitions to Russia. Between the years 1920 and 1923 she was once again laid up. In 1923 the *Discovery* Committee purchased the ship and

once again had her equipped for voyages to the South Pole. From 1925 until 1927 the *Discovery* was used for research purposes in the whaling grounds around South Georgia and the South Orkneys.

In 1928 the ship was once again equipped for a great polar voyage. Sir Douglas Mawson used it for his South Polar expedition until 1931. From 1931 until 1937 the bark lay idle in the East India Dock in London. In 1937 she was turned over to the Boy Scouts' Association as a stationary school-ship. After 1955 the *Discovery* was a practice ship of the London Division, Royal Naval Volunteer Reserve, and after November 1, 1958, of the Royal Naval Reserve. At the same time she was the Royal

Naval Recruiting Headquarters and the Scott Museum.

In 1979 the ship was turned over to the Maritime Trust. For a long time afterward the ship was moored for a thorough refitting in St. Catherine's Dock under the Tower Bridge. In May 1985, she was once again rigged as a bark there. Following the removal of the yards, tugs maneuvered the ship out of the dock while the water was at its highest possible level on March 27, 1986. After a stay of a few days in the Thames, the special transporter *Happy Mariner* used the "piggyback system" (half-flooded transporter) to bring the *Discovery* to Dundee in two days' time, where she was finally rigged.

Earl of Pembroke

Previous name: *Orion*	Depth to deck: 2.90 m
	Draft: 3.20 m
Type: bark, wood	
	Sail area: 882 square meters
Nation: Great Britain	
	Rigging: 14 sails, single top-, single topgallant
Owner: Square Sail, Ltd.	
	Masts: height of mainmast over the deck: 28 meters
Home port: Charlestown, Cornwall	
	Auxiliary engine: MAN 6-cylinder diesel, 300 horsepower
Year of construction: 1948	
Shipyard: Albert Svenson, Pukavik, Sweden	Crew: 15-person active crew, 8 trainees, 12 guests
Tonnage: 350 ts displacement; 174 tons gross	

Dimensions:
Length overall: 44.20 m
Length of hull: 35.30 m
Width: 7.30 m
Depth in hold: 2.10 m

Built as the *Orion* out of oak, what was at that time a schooner primarily transported wood in the Baltic and to the east coast of Britain. In 1974 it

was laid up in Thisted, Denmark. Square Sail, Ltd., acquired the ship in 1979. A thorough overhaul followed, during which the former

schooner was rerigged as an eighteenth-century bark.

The ship's exterior is frequently modified so that it can serve as needed in different films. When it is not being used in films, the bark is available to be used for training purposes. A sail-training program is then offered. The *Kaskelot*, the *Carrie*, and the

Phoenix likewise belong to Square Sail, Ltd.

James Cook's (1728–79) ship, the *Endeavour*, originally bore the name *Earl of Pembroke*. She transported coal between England and Scandinavia before being modified and equipped for voyages around the world.

 Eye of the Wind

Previous names: *Merry, Rose Marie, Merry, Sam, Friedrich*

Type: brig, iron

Nation: Great Britain

Owner: "Adventure Under Sail" Syndicate, Annandale, NSW, Australia

Home port: Faversham

Year of construction: 1911

Shipyard: C. Lühring, Hammelwarden, Unterweser

Tonnage: 149.96 tons gross; 115.06 tons net

Dimensions:
Length overall: 40.00 m
Length of hull: 33.00 m
Length between perpendiculars: 29.00 m
Width: 7.00 m
Depth in hold: 2.40 m
Depth to deck: 3.60 m
Draft: 2.70 m

Sail area: 650 square meters

Rigging: 14 sails; double topsails; single topgallant

Masts: height of mainmast over the deck: 26 meters

Auxiliary engine: Gardner diesel, 8L3B, 230 horsepower

Crew: 8–9-person active crew

Use: chartered ship, sailing school-ship, film ship

Before the *Eye of the Wind* was acquired by her current owners in 1973, she sailed as a topsail schooner engaged in commercial trade. Until the beginning of World War I she made 2 voyages a year from Hamburg to Rio de la Plata. On the voyage out she carried piece goods, and on the voyage home she carried cowhides to England and Cornish argillaceous earth to Germany. A serious fire in the late 1960s almost completely destroyed her. Since assuming her new function, the ship has sailed around the world twice. As the flagship of Operation Drake, she welcomed over 400 young people from 27 nations on board, where they were mentored by scientists, doctors, and army personnel.

In 1999 the brig was put up for sale.

HMS Gannet

HMS *Gannet,* formerly HMS *President,* HMS *Mercury,* and HMS *Gannet,* was built in 1878 at the Sheerness shipyards. She has a displacement of 1,130 tons, with a length between perpendiculars of 51.70 meters and a width of 11 meters. The iron frames are planked with teakwood (a composite construction). The ship originally possessed a steam engine and an armament of two 17.5 breechloaders and four 64-pounders. The warship is typical of the middle of the Victorian era. At that time the steam engine was gradually replacing wind power, and as a result many ships used both types of propulsion in combination.

In 1888 HMS *Gannet* relieved the port city of Suakin in the Red Sea, in which the English had been besieged for more than 3 months, by firing upon the enemy fortifications. From 1904 on she served in London as a practice ship of the Royal Naval Reserve. From 1916 until 1968 she was moored as a stationary school-ship in the Hamble River near Southampton. Today the ship lies as a hulk in Portsmouth. She belongs to the Maritime Trust. Plans are under way to rerig and restore HMS *Gannet.*

Glenlee

In 1896 the ship was built as the freighter *Glenlee* for R. Ferguson & Company of Port Glasgow; as the *Islamount* the ship was transferred to R. Ferguson & Company of Dundee. The shipping company sold the sailing ship in 1905 to the Flint Castle Shipping Company in Liverpool. Until 1918 the ship sailed under this flag. Like many other sailing ships, the *Islamount* too came under state control because of the war. After the war the ship was sold to the Societa Italiana Di Navigazione "Stella d'Italia." After the ship had been thoroughly modernized, with the installation of two auxiliary engines, electric light, and modern navigational instruments, she was registered in 1920 as the *Clarastella* with Genoa as her home port. On March 29, 1922, she was sold to Spain. Previously the *Clarastella* had been equipped as a school-ship at the shipyard Cautieu Navale Triestino in Monfalcon (Trieste).

With the new name *Galatea* she became a school-ship for the sailors of the Spanish navy (Escuela de Maniobra). Much has changed on deck since her time as a freighter. A large deckhouse was built between the foremast and the mainmast. Aft of the mainmast stands the shaft house of the engine room, to the roof of which boats are lashed. A small bridge was built in front of the mizzenmast, from which the ship is steered. The former main steering wheel on the poop now serves only for emergency steering. The living and instructional areas for the

Previous names: *Galatea, Clarastella, Islamount, Glenlee*

Type: bark, steel

Nation: Great Britain

Owner: The Clyde Maritime Trust

Home port: Yorkhill Quay, Glasgow

Year of construction: 1896; launched December 1896

Shipyard: Anderson Rodger & Company, Glasgow

Tonnage: 2700 ts displacement; 2800 tons gross

Dimensions:
Length overall: 94.57 m
Length of hull: 83.07 m
Length between perpendiculars: 74.87 m
Width: 11.41 m
Depth in hold: 7.45 m
Draft, fore: 5.20 m
Draft aft: 6.20 m

Sail area: 2800 square meters

Rigging: 21 sails, 5 foresails; double topsail, double topgallant, no royals ("baldheader"); mizzenmast: mizzen sail, mizzen topsail

Masts, spars: height of the mainmast over the deck: 42.70 meters; long bowsprit with jibboom; 3 sprit nets, one behind the other

Auxiliary engine: two 2-stroke 4-cylinder Diesel Polar engines, 1360 horsepower together

Crew: while sailing, 75-person active crew, 150 boys

Use: museum ship

young men, as well as the work stations, are located on the between deck.

Until 1969 the *Galatea* served as a school-ship for the Spanish navy; then she was laid up in Seville until 1992. On June 30, 1992, the Clyde Maritime Trust acquired the ship at auction. Starting on June 1, 1993, she was towed to Greenock, a process that took 9 days.

The bark is being thoroughly overhauled and rerigged in Glasgow under her original name, *Glenlee*. At the end of the process she will once again have the appearance of the former freighter.

Golden Hinde

Type: galleon, wood (reproduction of a sixteenth-century warship)

Nation: Great Britain

Owner: Golden Hinde, Ltd., Salisbury

Home port: St. Mary Overie Dock, London

Year of construction: keel laid September 30, 1971; launched April 5, 1973

Shipyard: J. Hinks & Son, Appledore, Devon/England

Tonnage: 305 ts displacement

Dimensions:
Length overall: 37.00 m
Length of hull: 31.00 m
Length at the waterline: 23.00 m
Width: 6.10 m
Draft: 2.70 m

Sail area: 386 square meters

Rigging: 6 sails; bowsprit; sprit sail; fore- and mainmast: lower sail, topsail; mizzenmast: lateen sail

Masts: height of mainmast over the keel: 26 meters

Auxiliary engine: diesel engine, 140 horsepower

Use: museum ship

Equipped with the blessing and the letters of marques of his queen, Elisabeth I of England, Sir Francis Drake started off in the *Golden Hinde* in 1577 on his 3-year circumnavigation of the globe. Drake was one of the most dazzling figures of his time: a pirate, a hero, an explorer, an imperialist, and not least of all an outstanding seaman. His ship with its eighteen cannons was typical of the smaller warships of the mid-sixteenth century. All that remains of the original is a chair made from the planks of the ship. It can still be seen today in Buckland Abbey. On June 17, 1579, Drake became the first white person to set foot in California. He named the land Nova Albion. As a re-

sult, the English crown had a claim to the areas surrounding present-day San Francisco. In the eighteenth century Spanish colonization put an end to this state of affairs.

Drake's visit to California gave rise to the idea of creating a reconstruction of his famous ship. With the greatest care, all available historical sources were used in order to make the reconstruction as authentic as possible. Drawings, paintings, and manuscripts served as models. Building plans did not exist at that time. The shipbuilders had to rely on their own experience and on tradition. The result, the modern-day *Golden Hinde,* is convincing and impressive. Even the interior and the equipment correspond to

the models of that time. Oak, elm, and pine were used as building materials. The guns are cast iron and are well suited for firing salutes. The construction costs ran to approximately 5 million dollars.

Prior to its first voyage, which was to lead through the Panama Canal to its American owners in San Francisco, the ship was moored for several weeks at the Tower Pier in London, where she was visited by 200,000 people. In 1978, the *Golden Hinde* sailed to Japan by way of Hawaii, where she was used in the film *Shōgun.* She returned to England by way of Hong Kong in 1980. In 1984 she passed into British hands. The ship has proven herself to be exception-

ally seaworthy. During her visits to many ports she is an extraordinary attraction.

Today the *Golden Hinde* is moored in the harbor of London as a museum ship.

Grand Turk

Type: eighteenth-century frigate, wood, full-rigged ship rig, reproduction	perpendiculars: 29.56 m Width: 10.36 m Draft: 3.04 m
Nation: Great Britain	Sail area: 790 square meters
Owner: The Turk Phoenix, Ltd., Sunbury	Rigging: 12 sails
Home port: London	Masts: height of mainmast over the waterline: 35.60 meters
Year of construction: 1997; launched August 1997	Auxiliary engine: 2 Kelvin diesel engines, 450 horsepower each; 4 generators
Shipyard: Yalgingburs, Marmaris, Turkey	
Tonnage: 314 tons gross	Crew: 28-person active crew while deployed at sea
Dimensions: Length overall: 46.30 m Length of hull: 36.40 m Length between	Use: film ship, museum ship

The *Grand Turk* is a reconstruction of a French frigate that was commandeered by the English. Two hundred fifty cubic meters of high-quality wood were available for the reconstruction. The ship contains the most modern tech-

nology, including electric equipment. A bow thruster guarantees maneuverability in narrow waters. Her primary use in a film was as the HMS *Indefatigable* in a television series about Horatio Hornblower.

When not in use on the sea, the frigate is moored in the harbor at London, directly next to the Tower Bridge.

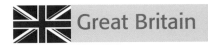
Type: schooner, iron, with steam engine; 1848: 6 masts; 1853: 4 masts; later 3 masts (square-rigger)

Nation: Great Britain

Owner: SS *Great Britain* Project, Bristol

Home port: Great Western Dock, Bristol

Year of construction: July 19, 1843

Shipyard: Messrs. Patterson and Sons, Bristol; design: Isambard Kingdom Brunel

Tonnage: 3675 ts displacement

Dimensions:
Length of hull: 97.90 m
Length of keel: 87.80 m
Width: 15.30 m
Depth to deck: 9.70 m
Draft: 5.50 m

Sail area: 1400 square meters (1865 as a 3-master, full-rigged ship)

Rigging: 16 sails as a 6-master

Masts: mainmast (total length without topmast): 22.50 meters; weight: 20 tons

Auxiliary engine: 1865; 4-cylinder steam engine, 500 horsepower

Use: museum ship

All three of the marvelous ship designs by the brilliant Isambard Kingdom Brunel were milestones of shipbuilding and far ahead of their time (*Great Western, Great Britain, Great Eastern*). Brunel was the first to use propellers rather than paddle wheels for trans-Atlantic steamers. As a result, the *Great Britain* was able to set several records simultaneously. She was the first propeller-driven trans-Atlantic ship. Up to that time, she was the largest ship with watertight bulkheads, double bottom, and balance rudder. And that was before the wooden wool clippers had reached their peak. The ship was built for Atlantic passenger travel. In terms of livestock alone, she was able to carry: 160 sheep, 40 pigs, and several hundred chickens. There was room for 600 passengers aboard the ship. A voyage from England to New York lasted approximately 15 days.

On her 5th voyage the *Great Britain* ran aground on the coast of Northern Ireland. She only managed to break free after more than a year. After spending 3 years in dock, she sailed the Australia route after 1851. During these years the rig was changed many times, until the original 6-masted schooner had become a 3-masted square-rigger. (The 6 masts had been named after the days of the week from Monday to Saturday.)

During the Crimean War the ship was deployed as a troop transporter. Forty-four thousand men traveled in both directions during this period. After the war Australia was once again the main destination, although the ship once again transported troops to suppress the uprising in India.

After 1880, the ship was enlarged. From now on the *Great Britain* sailed as a mailboat to Australia under wind power alone.

She sustained serious damage during a storm off Cape Horn in 1886. She succeeded in reaching the Falkland Islands, but there she was declared to be a total loss. In Port Stanley she served as a wool storage ship until 1937.

Subsequently she lay grounded for 30 years in Sparrow Cove near Port Stanley. Dr. Ewan Corlett, a shipbuilding engineer, is to thank for the fact that a rescue effort was undertaken. Under difficult technical conditions, the ship was loaded onto a pontoon in 1970 and towed "home" by three ships to Bristol. The restoration work is now proceeding rapidly in the same dock in which the *Great Britain* was originally built.

Type: 2-masted topsail schooner, wood

Nation: Great Britain

Owner: Patrick E. Keen

Home port: London

Year of construction: 1908

Shipyard: J. Hugerman, Viken, Malmöhuslän, Sweden

Tonnage: 53 tons gross; 29 tons net

Dimensions:
Length overall: 24.70 m
Length of hull: 19.30 m
Width: 5.90 m
Draft: 2.40 m

Sail area: 280 square meters

Rigging: 7 sails

Auxiliary engine: Scania diesel, 125 horsepower

Crew: 2-person active crew

Use: private ship, chartered ship

The *Helga* served for a long time as a freighter on the Swedish Vänern and Vättern lakes. The spoon bow and the transom stern have typical Swedish lines. The rig was removed in 1959, after which the schooner mast served only as a part of the loading gear. She subsequently sailed for 10 years as a motorized freighter.

After being used as a houseboat, the ship ended up in England in 1975. After many years of reconstruction work it once again became a commercial sailing ship for paying guests. The square topsail on the schooner mast is operated with a roller reefing system.

 Irene

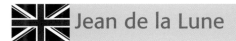 Jean de la Lune

Irene

Type: ketch, wood

Nation: Great Britain

Owner: Dr. Leslie Morrish

Home port: Bridgwater

Years of construction: 1904–7; launched May 31, 1907

Shipyard: Carver, Bridgwater, Somerset

Tonnage: 200 ts displacement; 98 tons gross; 66 tons net

Dimensions:
Length overall: 34.00 m
Length of hull: 28.00 m
Length between perpendiculars: 26.00 m
Width: 6.20 m
Depth in hold: 2.00 m
Draft: 3.00 m

Sail area: 500 square meters

Rigging: 9 sails

Masts: height of mainmast over the deck: 30 meters

Auxiliary engine: 2 Gardner engines, 130 horsepower

Crew: 5–6-person active crew, 10 guests

Use: chartered ship

From 1907 to 1960 the ketch was used in the freight trade. Under her current owner she sails in the charter service not only in European waters but also in the Caribbean.

Jean de la Lune

Type: brigantine, wood

Nation: Great Britain

Owner: John Reid

Home port: Leith, Scotland

Year of construction: 1957

Shipyard: Chantiers Navales de Cornouille, L'Orient, France

Tonnage: 160 ts displacement; 80 tons gross; 53 tons net

Dimensions:
Length overall: 32.00 m
Length of hull: 24.00 m
Width: 6.40 m

Depth in hold: 3.10 m
Depth to deck: 3.90 m
Draft: 3.30 m

Sail area: 400 square meters

Rigging: 10 sails

Masts: height of mainmast over the deck: 23.30 meters

Auxiliary engine: Scania DSI diesel, 300 horsepower

Crew: 6-person active crew, 14 trainees or 12 guests

Use: sailing school-ship, chartered ship

The brigantine started her life—the name refers to a French children's rhyme—as a tuna fishing vessel in the waters of the Azores. In the late 1960s she was converted into a staysail schooner. In 1983 the ship was equipped to be used for recreational diving.

In 1988 her current owner bought her and converted her to be used for training purposes. In 1993 the ship became a topsail schooner. Her operators are very proud to have the only Scottish square-rigger currently in service.

Type: brigantine, wood

Nation: Great Britain

Owner: Outward Bound Trust of Hong Kong, Ltd.

Home port: Hong Kong

Year of construction: launched November 1980; commissioned March 1981

Shipyard: Kong and Halvorsen

Tonnage: 196 ts displacement; 174 tons gross; 74 tons net

Dimensions:
Length overall: 40.20 m
Length of hull: 28.80 m
Width: 7.60 m
Depth in hold: 3.70 m
Depth to deck: 5.10 m
Draft: 3.90 m

Sail area: 598 square meters

Rigging: 10 sails; mainmast with Bermuda sail

Masts: height of mainmast over the deck: 30.50 meters

Auxiliary engine: Gardner 8-cylinder diesel, 230 horsepower

Crew: 5-person active crew, 40 trainees

Use: sailing school-ship

The name *Ji Fung* means "Divine Wind." The young men and women who are trained on board come primarily from large Chinese companies.

A unique type of ship was built in southern Denmark starting in 1864. The important characteristics of these sailing ships, which were used as freighters, were the round stern, the round stems, and the elegant lines. They became famous as "Marstal Schooners."

The *Julia* was originally a 3-masted topsail schooner. In 1976 she was converted into a sailing school-ship in Skagen, and later, in 1982, she was restored in order to be used for passenger cruises in the Baltic Sea. The ship is intended especially for "soft" tourism.

Previous names: *Jette Jan, Fraennenaes, Jütlandia*

Type: 2-masted topsail schooner, wood

Nation: Great Britain

Owner: Bambina, Ltd.

Home port: Denmark (without a fixed location)

Year of construction: 1938

Shipyard: Rasmus Møller, Fåborg

Dimensions:
Length overall: 38.00 m
Length of hull: 27.00 m

Width: 7.00 m
Depth in hold: 2.50 m
Draft: 2.30 m

Sail area: 500 square meters

Rigging: 10 sails

Masts: height of mainmast over the deck: 25 meters

Auxiliary engine: Alpha diesel, 120 horsepower

Crew: 3-person active crew, 10 guests

Use: sails for WWF and Greenpeace, guest cruises

Previous names: *Anne-Marie Grenius, Anne-Marie, Arctic Explorer, Kaskelot*

Type: bark, wood

Nation: Great Britain

Owner: Square Sail, Charlestown, Cornwall (Mr. Robert Davies)

Home port: Charlestown, Cornwall

Year of construction: 1948

Shipyard: J. Ring-Andersen, Svendborg, Denmark

Tonnage: 450 ts displacement; 226 tons gross

Dimensions:
Length overall: 46.50 m
Width: 7.60 m
Draft: 3.60 m

Sail area: 883 square meters

Rigging: 117 sails; single or double topsail, depending on use

Masts: height of mainmast over the deck: 31 meters

Auxiliary engine: B & W Alpha diesel, 375 horsepower

Crew: 14-person active crew, 12 passengers

Use: sailing school-ship, chartered ship, film ship

The *Kaskelot* ("sperm whale") was built as a ketch-rigged motor ship for the Royal Greenland Trading Company. As a trading and hospital ship she tended to the settlements on the coast of Greenland. In 1983 the current owners purchased her. She became one of the largest still extant wooden barks. Henceforth she was used as a film ship. She played a "leading role" in numerous films, in the process receiving the necessary new name in each case, such as *Terra Nova*, *Fram*, *John Howard*, and *Saracen*.

 # Kathleen & May

The *Kathleen & May* is the last British wind-powered freighter. Her first owner, John Coppack, gave the ship the name *Lizzie May* in honor of his two daughters. The schooner carried mass-produced goods around the British Isles. In 1908 Mr. J. Fleming of Youghal in the county of Cork purchased the ship and gave her her current name. These were the names of his daughters. In 1931 Captain T. Jewell from Appledore became the new owner. He re-duced the size of the rig and installed an engine. The ship continued to sail as a freighter for another 30 years.

After 1970 the *Kathleen & May* belonged to the Maritime Trust. She was restored and once again had her original rig. Since then the rig has once again been removed due to financial difficulties. In 1996 the Gloucester Tall Ship Trust became the new owner. There are plans to put the ship back into service under wind power.

Previous name: *Lizzie May*

Type: 3-masted topsail schooner, wood

Nation: Great Britain

Owner: Gloucester Tall Ship Trust, Gloucester

Home port: Gloucester Docks

Year of construction: 1900

Shipyard: Ferguson & Baird, Connah's Quay, near Chester

Tonnage: 136 tons gross; 99 tons net

Dimensions:
Length of hull: 29.80 m
Width: 7.00 m
Draft: 3.00 m

Sail area: 420 square meters

Masts: height of mainmast over the deck: 24 meters

Auxiliary engine: diesel engine, 80 horsepower

Use: museum ship, also sails

Type: bark, steel

Nation: Great Britain

Owner: Jubilee Sailing Trust, London

Year of construction: 1985; keel laid: October 19, 1984; launched: October 15, 1985

Shipyard: James W. Cook & Company, Ltd., Wivenhoe, Essex; completed by Vosper Thornycraft UK, Ltd., Southampton; design: Colin Mudie

Tonnage: 400 ts displacement

Dimensions:
Length overall: 52.10 m
Length of hull: 43.00 m
Length at the waterline: 37.20 m
Width: 8.50 m
Draft: 4.10 m

Sail area: 845 square meters

Masts: height of mainmast over the waterline: 33.50 meters

Auxiliary engine: two 195-kilowatt Mitsubishi Herald diesel engines

Crew: equipped for 40 boys and girls, of which 20 are physically handicapped

Use: sailing school-ship

The ship was equipped specially for physically handicapped young people, who often make up half of the crew. One handicapped person and one nonhandicapped person work together as a pair. For this reason, the bowsprit was made very wide. There are safety rails for wheelchairs on board. All the staysails and topsails can be operated with roller reefing systems. The command bridge is accessible to all. The ship can be steered from a seated position. There is an acoustic compass for the blind, a map table for people with prosthetic limbs, and a radio receiver with braille tuning controls. The radar has an especially large and bright screen for the benefit of people who are visually impaired. Because the construction costs were in the vicinity of 2 million pounds, the Jubilee Sailing Trust was dependent on the generosity of the entire British population for donations.

Type: square-rigged caravel (*caravella redonda*); reproduction of a trading vessel from the end of the fifteenth century

Nation: Great Britain

Owner: Bristol '96, Ltd.

Home port: Bristol

Year of construction: 1995; launched September 9, 1995

Shipyard: Bristol '96, Ltd., Redcliffe Quay, design: Colin Mudie, RDI

Tonnage: 81.3 ts displacement

Dimensions:
Length overall: 24.00 m
Length of hull: 22.30 m
Width: 6.20 m
Depth in hold: 2.13 m
Draft: 1.83 m

Sail area: 202 square meters

Rigging: 4 sails

Masts: height of mainmast over the deck: 17.68 meters

Auxiliary engine: diesel, 170 horsepower

Crew: 18-person active crew, 12 guests

Use: sailing museum ship

It was with a ship of this type that the Italian John Cabot (Giovanni Caboto; 1450–98), who sailed in the service of King Henry VII, rediscovered Newfoundland (1498), which Leif Erickson had found 500 years before. Cabot had been in search of a western sea route to China.

It was the special merit of the famous British ship designer Colin Mudie to undertake reconstructions of this kind. (Other Mudie designs include the *Royalist*, the *Varuna*, the *Lord Nelson*, the *Young Endeavour*, and the *Tunas Samudera*).

Caravels formed an important link between the ships of the Normans and the significantly larger ships of the Elizabethan era. The ships of that time were not built according to plans. Experience played the most important role. Only contemporary descriptions and visual representations provide us with information about the appearance of these vessels. The reconstruction is historically accurate only on the exterior. Naturally, the most modern navigational and safety equipment are available on board.

Previous names: *Gabriel, Adella, Skibladner, Karma, Jørgen Peter, Palmeto, Anna*

Type: brigantine, wood

Nation: Great Britain

Owner: Square Sail, Charlestown, Cornwall

Home port: Charlestown, Cornwall

Year of construction: 1929

Shipyard: Hjørne & Jacobsen, Frederikshavn, Denmark

Tonnage: 151 ts TM; 78 tons gross; 58 tons net

Dimensions:
Length overall: 31.00 m
Length of hull: 26.50 m
Width: 6.60 m
Draft: 2.00 m

Rigging: 14 sails; double topsail, single topgallant

Masts: height of mainmast over the waterline: 22 meters

Auxiliary engine: Volvo diesel, 240 horsepower

Crew: approx. 6-person active crew, 18 guests

Use: chartered ship, film ship

The *Phoenix* was built as a trading schooner. Her voyages took her to Iceland and into the North and Baltic seas. In 1970 she left the freight trade, was rerigged as a brigantine, and received her current name. She proved her excellent sailing capacities in numerous regattas. In 1976 the Mariners International Club chartered the ship. After crossing the Atlantic the *Phoenix* took part in the Great Sailing Ship Parade in New York. Already at that time she was used frequently as a film ship. In 1988 the ship was acquired in a sinking condition by the current owner in Miami. In Bristol she was thoroughly overhauled and prepared for her new use.

In 1991 the *Phoenix* was converted into a caravel for the film *1492: Conquest of Paradise,* but thereafter was returned to her original condition.

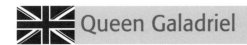

Queen Galadriel

Previous names: *Else of Thisted, Else*

Type: ketch, wood

Nation: Great Britain

Owner: The Cirdan Trust, Maldon, Essex

Home port: Ipswitch

Year of construction: 1937

Shipyard: J. Ring-Andersen, Svendborg

Tonnage: 122.70 ts displacement; 85.40 tons gross; 72.35 tons net

Dimensions:
Length overall: 31.40 m
Length of hull: 22.86 m
Length between perpendiculars: 21.34 m
Width: 6.71 m
Depth to deck: 3.42 m
Draft: 2.07 m

Sail area: 387 square meters

Rigging: 8 sails

Masts: height of mainmast over the deck: 30.50 meters

Auxiliary engine: Cummins diesel, 190 horsepower

Crew: 4-person active crew, 17 trainees

Use: sailing school-ship

Coal and grain were the main commodities that the *Else* transported in the Baltic and along the Norwegian coast. In 1956 she was sold to a buyer in Norway. She was transformed into a fully motorized coastal freighter, whereby the lower part of the mainmast was used as a place to attach the loading gear. After a short stay in the United States, the ship ended up in England. Attempts at restoring the vessel, which in the meantime had run aground and been raised, failed as a result of financial difficulties. Thisted in Denmark was its first home port. For this reason, its name was lengthened to *Else of Thisted*. When the Cirdan Trust acquired the ship in 1983, she got the new name *Queen Galadriel* after a character in J. R. R. Tolkien's *Lord of the Rings*. The ship is used primarily by young people and youth organizations.

Raphaelo

Previous names: *Taitu, Gerlando*

Type: 3-masted staysail schooner, wood

Nation: Great Britain

Owner: Raphaelo Marine, Ltd., Isle of Man

Home port: Cannes

Years of construction: 1938–41

Shipyard: Cantieri Navali Fratelli Benetti, Viareggio, Italy

Tonnage: 435 ts displacement; 282 tons gross

Dimensions:
Length overall: 49.40 m
Length of hull: 37.25 m
Length at the waterline: 31.58 m
Width: 8.47 m
Draft: 3.85 m

Sail area: 664–930 square meters

Auxiliary engine: Detroit diesel, 850 horsepower

Crew: 12-person active crew, 10 guests

Use: private yacht

The *Raphaelo* was one of the last Italian trading schooners. Until the end of the 1950s she transported primarily marble from Carrara to the Mediterranean region. Originally, she was rigged as a brigantine. With her conversion to a private yacht in 1961 the current rig was introduced. Taitu was an ancient Egyptian queen.

Result

Type: 2-masted topsail schooner	Shipyard: Paul Rodgers, Carrickfergus, Antrim/Northern Ireland
Nation: Great Britain (Northern Ireland)	Tonnage: 122 tons gross
Owner: Ulster Folk and Transport Museum, Cultra Manor	Dimensions: Length between perpendiculars: 31.00 m Width: 6.50 m Depth to deck: 2.70 m
Home port: Belfast	
Years of construction: 1892–93	Crew: museum ship

The *Result* was active as a trading ship from 1893 until 1967, first as a pure sailing ship, then, after 1914, with an auxiliary engine. Finally she sailed as a ketch-rigged motor ship. In 1916 she was deployed in the submarine defense. In 1946 a thorough overhaul took place, in the process of which a new engine was also installed. She is now being rapidly overhauled and rerigged as a museum ship.

Previous name: *Fyrskib XIX*

Type: 3-masted fore-and-aft schooner, wood

Nation: Great Britain

Owner: Argyll Smith (The Small School at Winestead Hall, Hull)

Home port: Hull

Year of construction: 1905

Shipyard: H. V. Buhl, Frederikshavn, Denmark

Tonnage: 380 ts displacement; 116.6 tons gross

Dimensions:
Length overall: 48.50 m
Length of hull: 36.25 m
Width: 6.58 m
Depth in hold: 4.86 m
Depth to deck: 3.50 m
Draft: 3.66 m

Sail area: 646.9 square meters

Rigging: 11 sails

Masts: height of mainmast over the deck: 28 meters

Auxiliary engine: Perkins diesel, 450 horsepower

Crew: 5-person active crew, 15 trainees

Use: sailing school-ship

The students who are accepted into the boarding school beginning at age 12 receive instruction in a great many subjects. Special emphasis is placed on sports and on training aboard the school's sailing ships (see also the *Spirit of Winestead*). Following the winter break the students themselves undertake the extensive reconditioning that needs to be done on the ship. They do everything, including the rigging, themselves.

After the necessary training period, the ships and their crews are prepared to take part in the competitions of the Sail Training Association.

A figurehead of Marco Polo holding the globe in his hand decorates the bow.

Ring-Andersen

Type: Baltic ketch

Nation: Great Britain

Year of construction: 1948

Shipyard: J. Ring-Andersen, Svendborg, Denmark

Tonnage: 155 ts displacement

Dimensions:
Length overall: 35.10 m
Length of hull: 28.60 m
Length at the waterline: 24.20 m
Width: 6.50 m
Draft: 3.00 m

Sail area: 395 square meters

Auxiliary engine: Detroit diesel 8V71, 300 horsepower

Use: private yacht

There are few ships that bear the names of the shipyards that built them. The *Ring-Andersen* does so for good reason. This relatively small shipyard in Svendborg is famous for the construction of freighters that had to earn their living in the Baltic and North sea region. Typical for the hull of these wooden ships is above all the exceptionally elegant sheer line of the deck. The *Ring-Andersen* was a freighter for many years and transported sugar, flour, beer, raw paper, curbstones, and wheat. In 1962 the ship was sold, modified, and put into charter service. In 1980 it returned with a new owner to Svendborg, where a large-scale conversion into a private yacht took place.

Royalist

Type: brig, steel

Nation: Great Britain

Owner: Sea Cadet Corps

Home port: Portsmouth

Year of construction: 1971; keel laid: October 21, 1970; launched July 12, 1971

Shipyard: Groves & Gutteridge, Ltd., Cowes

Tonnage: 110 ts TM; 83 tons gross; 67 tons net

Dimensions:
Length overall: 29.50 m
Length of hull: 23.20 m
Length between perpendiculars: 17.80 m
Width: 5.90 m
Draft: 2.60 m

Sail area: 433 square meters

Rigging: 10 sails, 2 foresails; foremast: foresail, topsails, topgallants; mainmast: topmast staysail, mainsail, topsail, topgallant, mizzen sail

Masts: height of mainmast over the waterline: approx. 22 meters; both masts are one piece

Auxiliary engine: two Perkins diesel engines, 230 horsepower each; speed with engine, 8 knots; speed with sails, 12 knots

Crew: 6 crew members, 26 cadets

Use: sailing school-ship

The Sea Cadet Corps offers British young people the opportunity to gain practical insights into their future careers as seamen. The Royal Navy, the merchant marine, and the fishery fleet can observe their young talent here. Formerly, the training took place only on smaller vessels. The *Royalist* now makes it possible to also hold training cruises for larger groups. The courses are distributed such that each year some 1000 young people spend time aboard the ship. The painted gun ports as well as the wide director top are reminiscent of a war brig of the nineteenth century. The lines of the hull, the material, and the navigational equipment, however, are more reminiscent of modern ship designs—one more example of the fact that even technologically a sailing ship can still hold its own in our age of supertankers.

The sails are made of terylene. Stainless steel and ropes made of synthetic fibers were used for both the standing and the running rigging. All modern navigational devices are found on board. Naturally, there is also central heating, a cold-storage chamber, and multiple generators to provide electricity.

The voyages last 1 or 2 weeks each, and in addition there are a number of weekend cruises for adults. They lead to the waters around England, and a change of cadets takes place in the appropriate destination ports. The ship also visits foreign ports, however. The minimum age for the young people is 14$^1/_2$ years. On most voyages 6 berths are reserved for female cadets from the Girl's Nautical Training Corps.

A number of courses are open exclusively to girls.

Saint Kilda

Previous names: *Starfish, Bielefeld*

Type: 3-masted fore-and-aft schooner, steel

Nation: Great Britain

Owner: (owner does not want to be identified)

Home port: St. Peter Port, Guernsey

Year of construction: 1957

Shipyard: Abeking & Rasmussen, Lemwerder, serial number 5169; modified: 1989–90 at Scheel & Jöhnk, Hamburg

Tonnage: 296.7 tons gross; 152.3 tons net (neither figure is definitive)

Dimensions:
Length overall: approx. 50.00 m
Length of hull: approx. 46.00 m (figures not final because of ongoing modifications)
Length between perpendiculars: 40.00 m
Width: 7.90 m
Draft: 3.60 m

Sail area: 650 square meters

Rigging: 4–5 sails

Masts: height of mainmast over the deck: approx. 32 meters

Auxiliary engine: KHD diesel engine, 600 horsepower

Crew: 2–4-person active crew, 4–6 guests

Use: private yacht

The schooner was formerly a fishing trawler that sailed under the German flag. She is very similar to the Greenpeace ship *Rainbow Warrior* and was modified at the same shipyard.

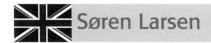# Søren Larsen

This formally beautiful brigantine was built as a motor ship. She was involved in the cargo trade until 1969. After being purchased by her current owner she was rerigged and equipped for her new use. She could be seen on television, especially on the series *The Onedin Line*. In 1982 the ship received an iron reenforcement for a new film about Shackleton. As the *Endurance*, the expedition ship of that period, she had to temporarily take on an additional mizzenmast.

In 1983 the *Søren Larsen* was chartered by the Jubilee Sailing Trust for three years. Primarily physically handicapped young people could be found on board during this time. In 1987 the brigantine joined the European fleet that came to Australia in honor of the 200th anniversary of the first settlement of the fifth continent.

In 1993 the ship was completely overhauled in England over a period of 7 months.

Today the *Søren Larsen* sails short cruises (up to 5 days) in the waters off New Zealand and longer cruises of 10 to 16 days in the Pacific. The guests can choose between "island hopping" in short stages or longer cruises on the open sea during which they are incorporated into the "watch" system.

Type: brigantine, wood	Location: Auckland, New Zealand	Dimensions: Length overall: 44.00 m Length at the waterline: 32.20 m	Auxiliary engine: B & W Alpha diesel engine, 240 horsepower
Nation: Great Britain	Year of construction: 1949	Width: 7.70 m Draft: 3.00 m	Crew: 12-person active crew, 22 guests
Owner: Square Sail, Charlestown, Cornwall (Robin and Tony Davies)	Shipyard: Søren Larsen & Sons, Nykøbing Mors, Denmark	Sail area: 627 square meters	Use: chartered ship, especially for film purposes
Home port: Charlestown, Cornwall	Tonnage: 300 ts displacement; 125 tons gross	Rigging: 12 sails; 3 foresails; double topsail, single topgallant, royal	

157

Spirit of Winestead

Previous names: *Den Lille Bjørn, Christian Bach*

Type: brigantine, wood

Nation: Great Britain

Owner: Argyn Smith (The Small School at Winestead Hall, Hull)

Home port: Hull

Year of construction: 1953

Shipyard: Gilleleje, Denmark

Tonnage: 178.4 ts displacement; 115 tons gross

Dimensions:
Length overall: 36.24 m
Length of hull: 28.26 m
Width: 7.00 m
Depth to deck: 2.86 m

Sail area: 421 square meters

Rigging: 13 sails; foremast: foresail, single topsails and topgallants, royal sail

Masts: height of mainmast over the deck: 23 meters

Auxiliary engine: Perkins diesel engine, 179 kilowatts

Crew: 5-person active crew, 15 trainees

Use: sailing school-ship

This brigantine was built as a trading schooner and converted into a school-ship in 1973–76 in Iverness. In the process she also received her present rig.

(On the topic of the "Small School at Winestead Hall," see also the *Return of the Marco Polo.*)

St. Barbara Ann

Previous name: *Vanessa Ann*

Type: 3-masted topsail schooner, steel

Nation: Great Britain

Owner: Kelly siblings

Home port: Lowestoft, England

Year of construction: 1951

Shipyard: Richard Ironworks, Lowestoft

Tonnage: 316 ts displacement; 153.5 tons gross; 80.1 tons net

Dimensions: 316 ts displacement; 153.5 tons gross; 80.1 tons net
Length overall: 44.20 m

Length of hull: 34.14 m
Length between perpendiculars: 31.39 m
Width: 7.01 m
Depth in hold: 2.70 m
Depth to deck: 3.40 m
Draft: 3.66 m

Sail area: 538 square meters

Rigging: 12 sails

Masts: height of mainmast over the deck: 27.70 meters

Auxiliary engine: Hundested diesel, 250 horsepower

Crew: 12-person active crew

Use: living and advertising ship

The ship was built as a trawler for the Dalby Steam Fishing Company. The area she fished lay in the waters around Iceland. She was actively involved in the "Cod War." During a collision with the Icelandic cannon boat *Thor* the ship's forecastle was seriously damaged. The subsequent attempt to convert the elegant hull at English expense into a trading vessel for use in the Pacific islands was unsuccessful. In 1984 Reg March and Jack Scott purchased the *Vanessa Ann*. In Padstow (Cornwall) the ship was made into a topsail schooner for chartered cruises in the waters of the West Indies. For financial reasons the ship had to be laid up for 4 years. Since 1994 it has belonged to the Kelly family.

Stavros S. Niarchos/Prince William

Type: brig, steel

Nation: Great Britain

Owner: The Sail Training Association

Home port: London

Year of construction: hull 1996; commissioned February 11, 2000

Shipyard: Abeking & Rasmussen, Lemwerder; completed: Appledore Shipbuilders, Appledore (UK)

Tonnage: 635 ts displacement; 493 tons gross; 198 tons net

Dimensions:
Length overall: 59.40 m
Length between perpendiculars: 50.20 m
Width: 9.90 m
Depth to deck: 5.80 m
Draft: 4.50 m

Sail area: 1162 square meters

Rigging: 18 sails, 4 foresails, double topsails, single topgallant, royals

Masts: height of mainmast over the deck: 39.20 meters

Auxiliary engine: 2 MTU engines, 330 kilowatts each

Crew: 6-person active crew, 13 volunteers, 45 trainees

Use: sailing school-ship

Two large sailing ship hulls were built in 1996 at Abeking & Rasmussen in Lemwerder. They were supposed to be rigged as brigantines and were intended for use as luxury cruisers in the Caribbean. Because of financial difficulties, the ships were not completed. Temporarily they received the names *Neptun Princess* and *Neptun Baroness*.

In 1997 the British Sail Training Association acquired the two hulls. They were towed to Appledore in the north of Devon. Rigged as brigs, they replaced the two schooners *Sir Winston Churchill* and *Malcolm Miller*. The *Stavros S. Niarchos,* aboard which physically handicapped young people could find appropriate training, was the first of the brigs to be completed.

Starting in 1940, Niarchos had built up a fast-growing, very large fleet of super-tankers. He died in 1996. A philanthropic foundation he had started made a large sum of money available for the construction of the school-ship. For this reason, it was named after him. In the future the ship will probably be known simply as the *Niarchos*.

In the year 2001 the second brig for the STA was also completed. She received the name *Prince William*.

Type: bark, wood

Nation: Great Britain

Owner: Jubilee Sailing Trust, Southampton

Home port: Southampton

Years of construction: 1996–2000; launched February 4, 2000; commissioned September 1, 2000

Shipyard: Jubilee Yard, Vosper Thornycraft, Southampton

Tonnage: 675 ts displacement; 500 tons gross

Dimensions:
Length overall: 65.00 m
Length of hull: 54.02 m
Length between perpendiculars 46.10 m
Width: 10.60 m
Depth in hold: 6.60 m
Draft: 4.50 m

Sail area: 1251 square meters

Rigging: 21 sails; 4 foresails, double topsails, single topgallants, royals; mizzenmast: lower mizzen sail, upper mizzen sail, mizzen topsail

Masts: height of mainmast over the waterline: 38.05 meters

Auxiliary engine: two diesel motors, 300 kilowatts each

Crew: 10-person active crew, 20 handicapped and 20 nonhandicapped young people

Use: sailing school-ship

The Jubilee Sailing Trust (JST) was founded in 1978 with a donation from the Queen's Silver Jubilee Appeal Fund. The idea was to create a charitable institution that would enable healthy and physically disabled young people to meet aboard a large sailing ship. The JST's first ship, which was outfitted with the necessary equipment to serve the handicapped, was the *Lord Nelson*.

The newly built *Tenacious* has had an interesting construction history. The hull was built keel-up in a large hall, a building method that was used frequently in earlier times. All of the wood used in the construction was covered with epoxy resins. The ribs consist of Siberian larch, while wood from the African sapelli tree was used for the multiple layers of planking. Five layers of fiberglass form the ship's outer shell.

In order to rotate the 250-ton hull the shipyard constructed two powerful steel rings like those used in the construction of submarines. The rotated hull was then placed on a 160-wheel transporter that deposited it on a floodable barge. The ship was hauled to the finishing quay at the Vosper shipyard. Once the barge was sunk, the *Tenacious* had been launched. The construction costs came to 14.3 million pounds, of which 6.5 million was provided by the British Lottery Sports Fund.

A distinguishing characteristic of the ship is the relatively high superstructure containing the bridge on the stern. Two mermaids decorate the elegant clipper bow.

Previous names: HMS *Foudroyant,* HMS *Trincomalee*

Type: frigate (full-rigged ship), teakwood; "Fifth Rate, 46 guns"

Nation: Great Britain

Owner: Foudroyant Trust

Home port: Gosport, Southampton

Year of construction: 1817; keel laid May 1816; launched October 19, 1817

Shipyard: Wadia Shipyard, Bombay

Tonnage: 1447 ts displacement; 1066 tons gross

Dimensions:
Length overall: 45.70 m
Length to keel: 38.20 m
Width: 12.20 m
Depth in hold: 3.90 m
Draft (during the construction with 30 t ballast)
  Fore: 3.80 m
  Aft: 4.10 m

Rigging: deep single topsail, topgallant

Crew: during active service approx. 300 men

Armament: until 1847, 45 cannons; from then on, 26 cannons; later, 24 cannons

Use: museum ship

After its completion in Bombay, the frigate, which got its name from the East-Ceylonean port city of Trincomalee, was sailed to England and subsequently laid up for 25 years in Portsmouth. The official launch did not take place until 1847, but with significantly reduced weaponry. Until 1852 she served in North American and West Indian waters. During the Crimean War the frigate patrolled the Pacific for four years beginning in June 1852. Until 1861 she was once again laid up in Chatham. In January 1861, the *Trincomalee* became a school-ship of the Royal Navy Reserve in Sunderland. On May 19, 1897, the Royal Navy Reserve sold the ship to the firm of J. Read for scrap. Shortly thereafter another change of ownership took place: the *Trincomalee* once again became a school-ship with the new name

Foudroyant. Wheatley Cobb had had a 74-cannon ship called *Foudroyant* restored in order to use it as a school-ship for young men. Unfortunately this ship was lost in a storm in 1893. Hence Mr. Cobb purchased the *Trincomalee* for the same purpose and gave her the name *Foudroyant* ("Thunderclap").

The ship lay in the harbor of Falmouth until Cobb's death. Later she was removed to Portsmouth, where she was moored next to HMS *Implacable.* After the *Implacable* was sunk in the Channel with all honors in 1949, the *Foudroyant* took over her training duties. She performs this service today.

From March until October courses for boys and girls ages 11 and up are held (sailing, boating, seamanship, etc.). All students sleep in hammocks. Between 1800 and 1830, 32

similar frigates were built. Of these ships, only the *Unicorn* in Dundee survives in addition to the *Foudroyant.*

After her 50-year stay in Portsmouth, the frigate was hauled to Hartlepool in a half-flooded transport ship in 1987. Restoration work began in 1990. In 1995 the mainmast was installed. The restoration was completed early in the summer of 2001.

Previous names: HMS *Cressy,* HMS *Unicorn II,* HMS *Unicorn*

Type: frigate (full-rigged), wood; "Fifth Rate, 46 guns"

Nation: Great Britain

Owner: Royal Naval Reserve, The Unicorn Preservation Society, Dundee

Home port: Dundee, Victoria Dock

Years of construction: 1794–1824; keel laid 1794; launched March 30, 1824

Shipyard: Naval Shipyard Chatham; design: R. Seppings

Tonnage: 1077 ts displacement

Dimensions:
Length overall: 50.50 m
Length over the deck: 46.10 m
Length between perpendiculars: 42.80 m
Width: 12.10 m
Depth in hold: 3.80 m
Draft: approx. 4.00 m

Rigging: deep, single topsail; single topgallant; royals

Masts, spars: height of mainmast over the deck: approx. 40 meters; main yard: 24 meters; main royal yard: 8 meters

Armament: originally 46 cannons

Use: museum ship

Although the *Unicorn* is not a "famous" ship and was never in active service, she has survived, because of her many uses, as one of the oldest still-existing sailing ships. Until the year 1554, when the English captured the Scottish galley *Unicorn,* all the flagships of the Scottish fleet bore this name. The English kept up the tradition of giving this name to one of their warships, so that the current *Unicorn* is the thirteenth ship to bear this name. Her keel was laid in 1794, but construction did not begin in earnest until February 1822. The frigate was never equipped to go to sea, however. From the beginning she was a stationary ship equipped to sail quickly in an emergency.

In 1855 she became a hulk and served until 1862 as a powder magazine in Woolwich. Until 1872 the *Unicorn* lay in Sheerness. In October 1871 she was offered to the Medway health agencies as a cholera hospital ship.

This plan was never realized, however, and instead the former frigate was converted into a practice ship for the Navy Reserve (HMS *Unicorn, Headquarters Tay Divisions, Royal Naval Reserve,* as its official designation ran until recently).

The ship received a permanent roof. Ten guns were available for artillery training at that time (1x9/, 1x6/, 4x64 pound, 4x32 pound). On November 9, 1873, the ship was towed to the Earl Grey Dock in Dundee. Obviously, the ship was constantly adapted to the needs of modern training over the course of time. The guns still stood on the top deck until very recently. When an aircraft carrier received the tradition-rich name *Unicorn* in 1939, the frigate received the official name *Unicorn II.* On November 20, 1941, she was renamed the *Cressy.* In 1959 she got her name back. The other bearer of the name was scrapped. During World War II the ship served as an administrative center for the naval base at Dundee.

From April 1946 on, the *Unicorn* was once again in the possession of the RNR.

In 1962 she was transferred from the Earl Grey Dock to the Camperdown Dock. Since September 17, 1963, she has lain in Victoria Dock, because her former berth had to be filled in for the new Tay Bridge.

In autumn 1968 the Royal Naval Reserve moved into a permanent building on land. The *Unicorn* was handed over to the *Unicorn* Preservation Society. Today she is a museum ship. It is not inconceivable that the ship will one day be rerigged.

What is astounding is that the ship is almost completely watertight after being in the water for a period of almost 150 years.

Unicorn

Previous name: *Eenhorn*	Dimensions:
	Length overall: 35.05 m
Type: 2-masted topsail schooner, steel	Length of hull: 26.70 m
	Length at the waterline: 23.76 m
Nation: Great Britain	Width: 6.00 m
	Draft: 2.59 m
Owner: Cocos Island Productions, St. Helier, Jersey	Sail area: 900 square meters
Year of construction: 1947	Auxiliary engine: Henschel diesel, 300 horsepower
Shipyard: De Vooruitgang, Gouwsluis, the Netherlands	Crew: 16 berths for crew and passengers; 60 guests on day tours
Tonnage: 95.26 tons gross; 56.53 tons net	Use: chartered ship

As a motorized vehicle the *Eenhoorn* fished in the waters off Iceland. In 1978 Pieter Kaptein of Hoorn purchased her.

After a complete modification, a topsail schooner with appropriate accommodations for guests emerged. In the process, unnecessary and distracting superstructures were removed from the deck. A unique characteristic is the steeply raised bowsprit with jibboom.

In 1986 the current owner purchased the ship and translated the name into the English *Unicorn*. She is engaged primarily in the charter service. The ship can accommodate up to 60 people on day cruises. Her main area of activity is the Caribbean. She also sails the Amazon.

HMS Victory

HMS *Victory* is the fifth ship of the Royal Navy to bear this name. The first *Victory* was built in 1559 and was Sir John Hawkins's flagship in the battle against the Spanish armada. In 1758 the ministers of King George II recommended the construction of twelve large warships to be led by a 100-cannon ship. The English victories in the Seven Years' War, above all in North America, were the occasion for giving this ship, too, the name *Victory*.

The ongoing favorable course of the war for England, including in sea battles, made a precipitous construction of the squadron unnecessary. Normally 5 years were needed for the construction of a large warship at that time. The *Victory* was laid on its keel in 1759 and launched in 1765. The construction costs came to 57,748 pounds. For 13 years she remained anchored without particular use in the Medway. With the entry of France into the American War of Independence the *Victory* was ordered to Portsmouth in 1778. Her first commission was as the flagship of the Channel fleet under Admiral Keppel. An indecisive engagement with a French squadron took place near Ushant.

The *Victory* was the flagship of admirals Hardy, Geary, Hyde Parker, and Kempenfelt in succession. Under Lord How she took part in the engagements off Gibraltar and Cape Spartel in 1782. After the Peace of Versailles (American Independence) the ship was temporarily retired from service. In 1793 England joined the first coalition against France. Lord Hood aboard the *Victory* led a formation of 22 ships into the Mediterranean.

Toulon was conquered but had to be surrendered again because of heavy French counterattacks led by the artillery officer Napoleon Bonaparte. The cannons of the *Victory* were put ashore for the siege of Calvi on Corsica. Captain Horatio Nelson led the artillery command. Subsequently the ship was brought to Portsmouth for improvements.

In 1795 Admiral Hotham was once again in the Mediterranean with the *Victory*, where she was victorious in the engagement off Cape Hyeres and in February 1797 took part in the victory in the battle of Cape Vincent under Admiral Sir John Jervis. In November 1797 the ship returned to Chatham and was released from service until further notice.

From 1798 until 1800 the *Victory* was a hospital ship for prisoners. In 1801 she was docked for two years. A thorough overhaul was urgently needed. In the process, in addition to other changes, the open stern galleries were removed and the figurehead changed. The ship took on its current appearance at that time. On Nelson's orders, all of his ships were painted with an ochre-colored band. The outside of the port lids remained black like the rest of the body of the ship. When the covers were closed, the famous chess board pattern thus came into being. (The insides of the port lids are red.)

In April 1803 the ship was once again ordered into service. Under the supreme command of Lord Nelson the flagship *Victory* was with the squadron in the Mediterranean in July 1803. After an 18-month blockade of Toulon, the French squadron under Admiral Villeneuve managed to break out. Nelson followed him into West Indian waters before turning back to England to lead the blockade of Cadiz. The decisive battle came at Trafalgar on October 21, 1805. The *Victory*, badly damaged, had to be towed to Gibraltar. In great haste she received makeshift repairs there. On November 3, 1805, she returned to England with Nelson's body on board.

After extensive repair work at the naval shipyard in Chatham, the ship once again went into service as of March 1808. In 1813 she once again had to be docked for improvements. The outcome of the Battle of Waterloo initially made it unnecessary for the ship to go back into service. The *Victory* remained in reserve until 1824. From then on until today, with the exception of the years 1869 to 1889, she has been the flagship of the Portsmouth command. Until 1922 she was anchored in the harbor of Portsmouth. Since then the *Victory* has lain in Portsmouth in the world's oldest dry dock. At great expense she was restored and returned to the condition of 1805. This work was completed on July 17, 1928. In order to preserve the hull, almost all of the cannons and the heavy anchors were replaced by wooden copies. The originals stand at the edge of the dock. One of the giant anchors lies on the beach at Southsea, on the spot where Nelson left England for

the last time. Every year on the anniversary of the Battle of Trafalgar a memorial service takes place on board the ship. During the extensive renovation work in the 1970s the entire stern was rebuilt out of teak wood.

The photo shows the *Victory* on October 21, 1995, the 150th anniversary of the Battle of Trafalgar. It is displaying Nelson's famous flag signal: "England expects every man to do his duty."

Type: "Ship of the Line" = three-decker, wood; "First-rate, 104 guns"

Nation: Great Britain

Owner: navy (flagship of the Portsmouth command)

Home port: Portsmouth (dry dock)

Year of construction: 1759; keel laid July 23, 1759; launched May 7, 1765; commissioned 1778

Shipyard: Single Dock, Chatham–Medway; design: Thomas Slade, Senior Surveyor of the Royal Navy

Tonnage: approx. 3500 ts displacement; aprox. 4000 ts displacement fully armed; 2162 t carrying capacity (tons burden)

Dimensions:
Length overall: approx. 100.00 m
Length of hull: 69.00 m
Length of gun deck: 56.50 m
Tonnage length: 46.30 m
Tonnage width: 15.30 m
Width: 15.70 m
Width overall (with studding sails): approx. 60.00 m

Depth to deck: approx. 10.00 m
Draft: approx. 6.00 m

Rigging: full-rigged ship rig; lower sail, single topsail, single topgallant, studding sails on fore- and mainmast

Masts, spars: all masts have a lower mast, topmast, topgallant; height of masts over the waterline: foremast 55 meters, mainmast 62 meters, mizzenmast 46 meters; bowsprit with jibboom approx. 35 meters, bowsprit yard 19.50 meters, main yard 31 meters, main topgallant yard 14.50 meters

Armaments: 104 cannons (1805); lower gun deck thirty 32-pound, middle gun deck twenty-eight 24-pound, upper gun deck thirty 12-pound, quarterdeck twelve 12-pound; stern two 12-pound and two 68-pound carronades (maximum range of the 32-pounders approximately 1.5 miles)

Crew: at Trafalgar 850 officers, regular crew, and soldiers

Use: museum ship (still in service as a stationary flagship)

Previous names: *C77, HMS Vernon III, HMS Warrior*

Type: steam frigate (full-rigged ship), (plate) iron

Nation: Great Britain

Owner: Warrior Preservation Trust, Portsmouth

Home port: Victory Gate, H. M. Naval Base, Portsmouth

Year of construction: keel laid May 25, 1859; launched December 29, 1860; commissioned August 1, 1861

Shipyard: Thames Ironworks & Shipbuilding Company, Blackwall, London

Tonnage: 9210 ts displacement

Dimensions:
Length overall: 127.40 m
Width: 17.60 m
Draft: 7.90 m

Sail area: 3488 square meters (without studding sails)

Armor: protective planking of the midsection: 63.9 meters long and 6.6 meters high, consisting of 11.4-cm thick slot and key steel plates on 45.7-cm teakwood

Armaments: original armaments: twenty-six 68-pound front-loader cannons, ten 110-pounds, and four 40-pound Armstrong rear-loading cannons with rifled barrels

Auxiliary engine: steam and sails; engine: horizontal steam engine, developed by John Penn, 1250 horsepower rated output; 10 boilers with 40 burn chambers (the current engine system is simulated)

Crew: 706 men, of those 50 officers, 93 petty officers, 441 sailors, including 66 stokers and cadets, as well as 122 naval soldiers

Use: museum ship

The construction of HMS *Warrior,* together with her sister ship HMS *Black Prince,* was Britain's response to France's naval armament, which sought to break England's maritime supremacy through the construction of several large, wooden warships with steel planking. The first ship was the *Gloire,* with 5700 tons displacement.

HMS *Warrior,* with her iron hull and steel planking, was the first ship of her kind, and also the largest and fastest warship of her time. The engines were designed largely for combat maneuvers. Napoleon III named the giant a "black snake among rabbits." The frigate was retired after only ten years. The rapid techno-logical progress of that period had rendered her obsolete. She spent the following period in the reserve fleet and in the coast guard, until she was removed from active duty in 1883.

In 1904 under the name HMS *Vernon* the ship was converted into a power station of the Royal Naval Torpedo School in Portsmouth, until the hull was towed to South Wales in 1929. In Milford Haven it served as the floating oil tank hulk *C77,* until it was turned over to the Maritime Trust for restoration in 1979. In June of the same year HMS *Warrior* was towed to Hartlepool, where 8 years and 9 million pounds were spent to restore her to her original con-dition of 1861. Along with HMS *Victory,* she had become an additional attraction of Portsmouth. A figurehead of a Roman warrior, with its wide, jutting head gear, ornaments the bow.

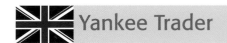

Yankee Trader

Previous name: *Hydrographer*

Type: 2-masted staysail schooner, steel

Nation: Great Britain (British Virgin Islands)

Owner: Turtle Dove Enterprise, Ltd.

Home port: Freeport, Bahamas

Year of construction: 1947

Shipyard: in Norfolk, Virginia, USA

Tonnage: 938 ts displacement; 812 tons gross; 360 tons net

Dimensions:
Length overall: 54.40 m
Length of hull: 43.10 m
Length between perpendiculars: 37.00 m
Width: 9.70 m
Draft: 3.90 m

Sail area: 579 square meters

Rigging: 4 sails

Masts: height of mainmast over the waterline: 42 meters

Auxiliary engine: two Baldwin Hamilton diesel engines, 810 horsepower; speed with engine, 12 knots

Crew: 26-person crew, accommodations for 84 guests

Use: chartered ship for cruises (Windjammer Barefoot Cruises, Miami Beach)

As the *Hyrdrographer,* the ship was built for the U.S. Coast Guard & Geodetic Survey. It became famous as a result of its numerous exploratory voyages to all corners of the world. Since 1971 the *Yankee Trader,* as she has been known since then, has belonged to the Windjammer Fleet in Florida. The luxuriously furnished cabins for the passengers are now located on two new decks. A 9-month circumnavigation of the globe is conducted yearly. In addition, the ship sales in the Caribbean.

Zamoura of Zermatt

Previous name: *Mavi*

Type: barkentine, iron

Nation: Great Britain

Owner: Swiss Holding Company

Home port: London

Year of construction: 1927

Shipyard: in Vienna

Tonnage: 250 ts displacement

Dimensions:
Length overall: 44.00 m
Length of hull: 36.00 m
Width: 7.00 m

Draft: 2.90 m

Sail area: 700 square meters

Rigging: 15 sails

Masts: height of mainmast over the deck: 27.40 meters

Auxiliary engine: two Caterpillar 336 TDAC engines, 400 horsepower each

Crew: 9-person active crew, 12 guests

Use: private yacht

The ship was originally built in 1927 at Bulgarian expense in Vienna. To this day she has her original magnet compass on deck, including the two compensating spheres. In terms of safety technology, the ship is equipped with high-tech navigational instruments and is capable of making voyages worldwide.

During cruises the *Zamoura* accommodates at most 12 guests in 6 double cabins, each of which is luxurious and has its own bathroom. During their stay on board, the guests have various opportunities to take part in sports. Since autumn 2000 the ship has been operated by the Swedish nonprofit organization the Grand Largue Association, which provides specially designed sailing courses for physically and visually handicapped people as well as young people with social problems. The deck is so spacious that wheelchairs also have sufficient space.

 Zebu

Previous name: *Ziba*

Type: brigantine, wood

Nation: Great Britain

Owner: Merseyside Heritage Trust, Liverpool

Home port: Southampton

Year of construction: 1938

Shipyard: A. B. Holmes, Råå, Sweden

Dimensions:
Length overall: 31.00 m
Length of hull: 21.90 m
Width: 6.10 m
Draft: 2.30 m

Sail area: 395 square meters

Rigging: 10 sails

Auxiliary engine: Gardner 6LW, 84 horsepower

Crew: 24 people

Use: chartered ship

The *Zebu* was built as a fore-and-aft ketch. Under the name *Ziba* she transported salt, wood, and grain until 1972. In the same year she passed into English hands. Now rigged as a Bermuda ketch, she was used as a charter ship. A few years later the current owner purchased her. She got the name *Zebu.* Her new rigging as a brigantine took place in 1983. In October 1984 in London a long voyage began that took the ship around the globe in four years. In the process she took part in Operation Raleigh.

The ship visited 30 countries, and more than 300 young people had the experience of sailing the world's oceans aboard a great sailing ship.

After the long voyage the owner at that time, Stephen Rodger, sold the ship. The new owner donated the brigantine to the Merseyside Heritage Trust, under whose direction it undertakes daylong excursions and short cruises leaving from Southampton.

Greece

Eugenios Eugenides

Eugenios Eugenides

The famous yacht *Sunbeam* was built for Lord Brassey in 1874. After 1922 she belonged to Sir Walter Runciman, who later became Lord Runciman von Shoreston. When this composite construction had to be retired and scrapped because of age, Lord Runciman had the steel *Sunbeam II* built. At first the yacht was rigged as a pure three-masted schooner, just like her predecessor, but already during her trials the foremast received square topsails and topgallants. The ship remained the private yacht of her owner until World War II. At the beginning of the war the British admiralty took the ship over and used her until the end of the war for various purposes.

In 1945 the *Sunbeam II* was sold to the Abraham Rydberg Foundation in Stockholm, which, contrary to its custom up to that point, did not name

Previous names: *Flying Clipper, Sunbeam II, Sunbeam*

Type: 3-masted topsail schooner, steel

Nation: Greece

Owner: merchant marine, national merchant marine academies

Home port: Piräus

Year of construction: 1929; launched August 1929

Shipyard: Messrs. W. Denny Brothers, Dumbarton; design: Messrs. G. L. Watson & Co. Glasgow

Tonnage: 1300 ts displacement; 634.34 tons gross; 225.71 tons net

Dimensions:
Length overall: 59.40 m
Length between perpendiculars: 49.60
Width: 9.10 m

Depth to deck: 6.00 m
Draft: 5.30 m

Sail area: 1540 square meters

Rigging: 12 sails; 3 foresails; foremast: boom foresail, single topsail, single topgallant; mainmast: mainsail, main topsail, main-topmast staysail; mizzenmast: mizzen sail, mizzen topsail, mizzen-topmast staysail

Masts, spars: height of mainmast over the deck: 39.95 meters; all masts with one topmast; lower masts, bowsprit: steel; topmasts, yards, gaffs: wood

Auxiliary engine: Polar diesel engine, type M34M, 400 horsepower

Crew: 22-person active crew, 70 cadets

Use: sailing school-ship

the ship after her founder, but rather left her old name intact. After the necessary modifications to prepare her for her new function, the former yacht became a school-ship for the foundation. She was the successor to the 4-masted bark *Abraham Rydberg,* which had been sold in 1942. The training cruises took place primarily in European waters. During a long voyage to the West Indies in 1949 the ship experienced serious weather damage to her rig.

In 1955 the Einer Hansen's Clipper Line in Malmö purchased the ship for use in training its recruits. The new name was the *Flying Clipper.* After overhaul work in Karlskrona she took part in the Tall Ships Race from Torbay to Lisbon in 1956. In 1958, too, she participated in the race. After 1960 the ship sailed primarily in the Mediterranean. This was also where, in 1961–62, the shooting of the film *Flying Clipper* took place. During its 10 years under the flag of the Clipper Line, more than 200 cadets were trained for careers as deck officers aboard the sailing ship, in addition to 60 engineering candidates and 27 trainees for careers in the cooking and catering trades.

On July 4, 1965, the ship was sold to the Greek Merchant Marine Ministry. Under the new name *Eugenios Eugenides* she sailed on June 12 to Piräus. Eugenios Eugenides was a Greek shipowner who died in 1954. His heirs made a donation in his honor to the fund for Greek nautical training. This fund was also the origin of the money for the purchase of the school-ship.

The individual academies of the Greek merchant marine are distributed over wide sections of the country. Cadets from these schools come to the *Eugenios Eugenides* for additional training. The curriculum includes instruction for deck officers, maritime engineers, and radio officers. Although the ship belongs to the merchant marine, the training is organized in a strictly military fashion. In the summer the ship undertakes a 3-month training voyage, while in the winter only short voyages take place.

For a number of years now the ship has lain idle in a run-down condition. Efforts are under way to put her back into service.

India

Tarangini   Varuna

Tarangini

Type: bark, steel

Nation: India

Owner: Indian navy

Home port: Cochin

Years of construction:
1995–96; launched
December 1995

Shipyard: Goa Shipyard, Ltd.

Tonnage: 420 ts
displacement; 360 tons gross

Dimensions:
Length overall: 54.00 m
Length of hull: 42.80 m
Width: 8.50 m
Draft: 4.00 m

Sail area: 1035 square meters

Rigging: 18 sails; lower sails,
single topsails and
topgallants, royal sails

Masts: height of mainmast
over the deck: approx.
30 meters

Auxiliary engine: 2 Kirloscar
Cummins diesel, 300
horsepower each

Crew: 15-person active crew,
45 trainees

Use: sailing school-ship

The *Tarangini* ("She Who Glides over the Waves") is another ship designed by the famous British ship designer Colin Mudie, this time for the Indian navy (see also *Tunas Samudera, Young Endeavour,* etc.). The training cruises take place primarily in Indian waters.

Varuna

Type: staysail schooner

Nation: India

Owner: Sea Cadet Council, Bombay, Marine

Home port: Bombay

Year of construction: launched August 27, 1980; commissioned April 20, 1981

Shipyard: Mazagon Dock, Ltd., Bombay

Tonnage: 100 ts displacement; 83 tons gross; 67 tons net

Dimensions:
Length overall: 29.50 m
Length of hull: 23.10 m
Length between perpendiculars: 17.80 m
Width: 6.00 m
Depth in hold: 3.90 m
Draft: 3.00 m

Sail area: 600 square meters

Rigging: 10 sails, 2 foresails; foremast: foresail, topsails, topgallants; mainmast: topmast staysail, mainsail, topsail, topgallant, mizzen sail

Masts: height of mainmast over the deck: 22.80 meters

Auxiliary engine: two Kirloscar Cummins diesel, 100 horsepower each

Crew: 36 officers and cadets

The sister ship of the British *Royalist* got her name from a sea god in Indian mythology.

The Ananta Nag, a sea snake in Indian mythology on whose back the lord of the seas and the winds rides, ornaments the bow.

The *Varuna* serves both the Indian navy and also the Sea Cadet Corps as a training ship.

Indonesia

KRI Arung Samudera   KRI Dewarutji

KRI Arung Samudera

Previous name: *Adventure*

Type: 3-masted fore-and-aft schooner, steel

Nation: Indonesia

Owner: Indonesian navy

Home port: Jakarta

Year of construction: 1991

Shipyard: hull: Auckland, New Zealand; equipment: Tauranga

Tonnage: 96 tons gross

Dimensions:
Length overall: 39.40 m
Length between perpendiculars: 31.63 m
Width: 6.45 m
Draft: 2.60 m

Sail area: 432 square meters

Rigging: 9 sails

Masts: height of mainmast over the deck: 28.20 meters; all masts are the same height

Auxiliary engine: two Ford diesel MK 2725 E engines, 108.8 kilowatts each

Crew: 20 people, including cadets

Use: sailing school-ship

The *KRI Arung Samudera,* or "ocean crosser" (also known as the *KRI Arsa*), was built as a fast luxury yacht at New Zealand's expense. Since January 9, 1996, she has officially belonged to the Indonesian navy.

The acronym KRI stands for Kapalerang Republic Indonsia, which means "warship of the Republic of Indonesia."

KRI Dewarutji

Type: barkentine, steel

Nation: Indonesia

Owner: Indonesian navy

Home port: Jakarta

Year of construction: 1953;
keel laid October 15, 1952;
launched January 24, 1953

Shipyard: H. C. Stülcken &
Son, Hamburg

Tonnage: 886 ts displacement

Dimensions:
Length overall: 58.27 m
Length of hull: 49.66 m
Length between
perpendiculars: 41.50 m
Width: 9.50 m
Depth to deck: 7.04 m
Draft: 4.05 m

Sail area: 1100 square meters;
foresail 108 square meters,
mainsail 145 square meters

Rigging: 16 sails; 4 foresails;
foremast: fore course, double
topsails, single topgallants,
royals; mainmast,
mizzenmast: gaffsail, gaff-
topsail; mainsail without
boom

Masts: all masts with one
topmast (wood); height of
mainmast over the deck: 35
meters

Auxiliary engine: 6-cylinder
4-stroke MAN diesel engine,
600 horsepower; speed with
engine, 10.4 knots

Crew: captain, 8 officers, 8
petty officers, doctor,
boatswain, sailmaker, 6
sailors, engineer, cook, 4
stewards, 78 cadets

Use: sailing school-ship

In 1932 the Stülcken shipyard in Hamburg built the sailing school-ship *Jadran* for the Yugoslavian navy. The Indonesian government wanted a similar ship for the training of its sea cadets and thus commissioned this shipyard with the construction. In Indonesian legends, Dewarutji is the ruler and guardian of the seas. He corresponds roughly to Neptune. The wooden figurehead of the *Dewarutji* represents this god. The barkentine possesses three decks. The uppermost, continuous spar deck came about through the connection of the poop deck with the forecastle and also includes the midships house. On the second deck are located the poop and the forecastle. The entire active crew lives here: in the poop the officers and in the midships house the petty officers, as well as the personnel. The kitchen is also located in this house.

The cadets live and sleep (hammocks) on the between decks in two separate rooms. Waterproof supply rooms are located on the aft between deck. The entire ship was equipped with elaborate ventilation and air-conditioning systems because of the tropical environment. The radio room and the charthouse are located in the poop-house. In front of this house stands the manual steering system, which has a double wheel. On the starboard side lies a stock anchor on a riding chock; on the portside a stockless anchor is carried in a hawse.

The only device on the deck is a combined windlass (hand and electrical power) for raising the anchor. In terms of boats, the *Dewarutji* possesses one motor jollyboat, three cutters, two jollies, and one gig (stern). The ship is naturally equipped with all modern navigational instruments.

Mainsails and mizzen sails can be set and handed both through hoisting and lowering of the gaffs and by means of outhaulers and inhaulers. These two sails run with slides along T-rails on the masts and gaffs. The topsails have hoops on the luff. The braces of the lower yards are connected to approximately 2.40-meter-high brass crossbeams so that the boat davits can also be operated while sailing. During test cruises the ship was able to reach up to five and a half points off the wind. Two hundred tons of permanent ballast provide the necessary stability.

The training cruises take place primarily in East Asian waters.

The initials "KRI" stand for Kapalperang Republic Indonesia, or "warship of the Republic of Indonesia."

Asgard II   Dunbrody   Jeanie Johnston

Asgard II

Type: brigantine, wood

Nation: Republic of Ireland

Owner: government property
(Irish navy)

Year of construction: 1981;
commissioned March 6, 1981

Shipyard: Jack Tyrell, Arklow,
County Wicklow, Ireland

Tonnage: 120 ts
displacement; 92.67 tons
gross; 50.06 tons net

Dimensions:
Length of hull: 25.50 m
Length between
perpendiculars: 21.20 m
Width: 6.40 m
Draft: 2.90 m

Sail area: 370 square meters

Auxiliary engine: Kelvin
Marine diesel, 160
horsepower

Crew: 5-person active crew,
20 trainees

Use: sailing school-ship

The first *Asgard*, which was named after the home of the gods in Nordic mythology, was a ketch designed by Colin Archer. She was built in 1905 and belonged to the wife of the English writer Erskine Childers (*The Riddle of the Sands*). He promoted the cause of the Irish freedom fighters, used the *Asgard* to smuggle weapons from Germany to Ireland in 1914, and was shot by political opponents in 1922. His son became the first prime minister of the independent Ireland, and in 1973 president.

The *Asgard a Do*, as the ship is called in Gallic, was designed and built exclusively for training purposes. The figurehead represents Grainne Mhaol, a female warrior of the sixteenth century from Irish and English history.

Dunbrody

The reproduction of this bark has an important background in Irish history. In 1845 a previously unknown fungus (*Phytophora infestans*) appeared in Ireland and destroyed the island's entire potato crop until 1849. The result was a famine of unthinkable proportions (An Gorta Mor). Approximately a million people died of malnutrition and related illnesses. Approximately the same number of Irishmen attempted to save their lives through emigration. These included the Kennedy family of New Ross, the ancestors of the later president of the United States.

Their destinations were primarily the United States and Canada. Admittedly, many people could not raise the money for the fare. The living conditions on many of the ships involved in the emigration were catastrophic. The state of hygiene defied description. For this reason these ships also received the nickname "coffin ships."

One of the few exceptions was the bark *Dunbrody*, built in 1845 in Quebec. The Irish lumber merchant William Graves of New Ross, who had a large fleet of trading vessels at his disposal, had commissioned the ship. In only 6 months she was ready to set sail. The *Dunbrody* was used to bring wood from Canada to Europe. Already in 1845 she was equipped to carry emigrants, who came on board in New Ross. From 1845 to 1851 she brought thousands of people to Canada, for whose relatively tolerable living conditions Captain Williams provided. There were 176 passengers per voyage.

The ship got her name from the Dunbrody Abbey. The abbey stands near New Ross on the banks of the Barrow, which flows through the city. The John F. Kennedy Trust contributed substantially to the construction of the current bark.

Another way to help finance the construction is to sponsor a tree (an oak or a larch) that is then part of a forest (25,000 trees) that is being planted near New Ross.

Type: bark, wood, reproduction	Shipyard: Ross Company Boatyard, Raheen, New Ross	Sail area: 786 square meters	Crew: 20-person active crew
Nation: Ireland	Tonnage: 458 ts displacement	Rigging: 18 sails, single topsail, single topgallant, royals	Use: ambassador and goodwill cruises, museum ship in New Ross
Owner: John F. Kennedy Trust	Dimensions: Length overall: 53.70 m	Masts: height of mainmast over the deck: 33.50 meters	
Home port: New Ross, County Wexford	Length of hull: 36.60 m Width: 8.50 m		
	Depth in hold: 5.80 m	Auxiliary engine: two Ford Mermaid diesel, 212 horsepower each	
Years of construction: 1997–2000; launched January 2001	Draft: 3.50 m		

Jeanie Johnston

Type: bark, wood, reproduction

Nation: Ireland

Owner: Jeanie Johnston Company, Tralee, County Kerry

Home port: Tralee

Years of construction: 1998–2000; launched May 6, 2000

Shipyard: Blennerville (old harbor of Tralee)

Tonnage: 450 tons gross

Dimensions:
Length overall: 45.00 m
Length of hull: 37.50 m
Width: 8.00 m
Draft: 4.20 m

Sail area: 643 square meters

Rigging: 18 sails, double topsails, single topgallants, royals

Masts: height of mainmast over the deck: 29.50 meters

Auxiliary engine: two Caterpillar diesels, 280 horsepower each

Crew: 4-person active crew, 29 trainees

Use: sailing school-ship;

The reproduction was built in remembrance of the great famine in Ireland (1845–49), during which well over a million people had to leave their island (see the *Dunbrody*). The original *Jeanie Johnston* was built in 1847 in Quebec. She crossed the Atlantic with emigrants on board sixteen times and in the process brought approximately 200 people to New York, Baltimore, and Quebec. No one was ever lost on board, not even in 1858, when she sank in the middle of the Atlantic.

The very expensive reproduction was built outdoors near the striking windmill of Tralee so that paying visitors could observe the progress of the work. Over 300 young people from several countries assisted with the construction of the ship under appropriate supervision and received training in the relevant trades. The reproduction makes use of an auxiliary engine and a bow thruster. The historically highly interesting ship carries the figure of a woman as its figurehead.

Israel

L'Amie

L'Amie

Type: gaff ketch, wood

Nation: Israel

Owner: Eitan Berber; Arie Eliyahu; Azaria Bernitzki; A. B. Services, Eilat

Home port: Eilat

Year of construction: 1951

Shipyard: A. Nilsen Skibsværft, Holbæk, Denmark

Tonnage: 99.1 tons gross

Dimensions:
Length overall: 26.50 m
Width: 6.60 m
Draft: 2.80 m

Auxiliary engine: Volvo diesel

Use: private yacht

Italy

Amerigo Vespucci
Croce del Sud

Palinuro

Puritan

Amerigo Vespucci

Type: full-rigged ship, frigate, steel

Nation: Italy

Owner: Marina Militare, Accademia Navale, Livorno

Home port: La Spezia

Year of construction: 1930; keel laid May 12, 1930; launched February 22, 1931

Shipyard: former royal shipyard in Castellamare di Stabia

Tonnage: 3550–4100 ts displacement

Dimensions:
Length overall: 101.00 m
Length of hull: 82.00 m
Length between perpendiculars: 70.00 m
Width: 15.50 m
Depth to deck: 11.30 m
Depth in hold: 6.90 m
Draft (midships): 6.50 m

Sail area: 2100 square meters

Rigging: 23 sails; 4 foresails; double topsail, single topgallant, royals

Masts, spars: height of mainmast over the deck: 46 meters; all masts with top and topgallant masts, bowsprit, jibboom, outer jibboom, spritsail yard

Auxiliary engine: two 950 horsepower Fiat Marelli electro-diesel engines driving one propeller

Crew: 24 officers, 34 petty officers, 205 regular crewmembers, 150 cadets, 40 boys of the cadets

Use: sailing school-ship

The Italian navy possessed two large sailing school-ships until the end of World War II: the *Cristoforo Colombo,* built in 1928, and its sister ship the *Amerigo Vespucci,* built in 1930. The *Cristoforo Colombo* had to be turned over to Russia at the end of the war. The ships belonged to the type of the large frigates of the nineteenth century. This was made especially clear by the high freeboard, the stern gallery, and the painted white streaks. The idea for the construction of these unusual ships came from a lieutenant colonel in the navy engineering corps, Francesco Rotundi.

The *Amerigo Vespucci* belongs to the Accademia Navale in Livorno. In the yard of this school stand 2 full-rigged masts with bowsprits and the corresponding headgear. Above a ground-level "main deck" the masts rise almost to their real height. The young men practice here, protected by large safety nets, until they switch over to the school-ship. Since entering service, the *Amerigo Vespucci* has continuously been used for the training of future officers from the naval academy. Until 1965, in addition to shorter cruises in the Mediterranean, she made 31 voyages on the high seas lasting from 3 to 5 months, including 4 trans-Atlantic voyages to North and South America. The frigate form was chosen so that the largest crew possible could be accommodated at a predetermined maximum size of the ship. Three through decks lie above the waterline. The instruments meet the most modern standards. All the belaying pins on board are identified by small brass plaques. The memorization of the individual lines and ends is not essential for the overall education.

Richly carved, gilded scrollwork ornaments the ship's bow and stern. The stern gallery is accessible only from the captain's quarters. The decor and the distinguished furnishings of the rooms almost allow one to forget that one is aboard a sailing ship. A complete figure of Amerigo Vespucci ornaments the bow as a figurehead.

The Florentine Vespucci undertook 4 exploratory voyages to South America from 1497 to 1504. His exact descriptions of the lands he had discovered, which were distributed throughout Europe, made him so famous that at that time he was seen as the true discoverer of America.

The sister ship of the *Amerigo Vespucci,* the *Christoforo Colombo,* received the name *Dunay* under the Soviet flag. She was laid up in 1962 and in 1971 removed from the navy list. In 1972 the ship was scrapped in Odessa.

Type: 3-masted fore-and-aft schooner, steel

Nation: Italy

Owner: M. Vela, Italy

Year of construction: 1931

Shipyard: Martinoli, Lussinpiccolo, Italy (today Mali Lošinj, Lošinj/Croatia)

Tonnage: 220 ts displacement; 175 tons gross

Dimensions:
Length overall: 37.70 m
Length of hull: 34.90 m
Length at the waterline: 27.80 m
Width: 7.20 m
Draft: 5.00 m

Sail area: 436 square meters

Rigging: mizzenmast: Bermuda sails

Auxiliary engine: two 240 horsepower Volvo Penta diesel engines

Crew: 9-person active crew

Use: private yacht

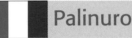

Palinuro

Previous names: *Jean Marc Aline, Commandant Louis Richard*

Type: barkentine, steel

Nation: Italy

Owner: Naval school in La Maddalena on the island of Maddalena (Sardinia)

Home port: La Maddalena

Year of construction: 1934

Shipyard: Anciens Chantiers Dubigeon, Nantes

Tonnage: 1041–1341 ts displacement; 835 tons gross

Dimensions:
Length overall: 68.95 m
Length between perpendiculars: 50.00 m
Width: 10.09 m
Depth to deck: 5.70 m
Draft (fully armed):
    Fore: 3.78 m
    Aft: 4.84 m

Sail area: 898.40 meters

Rigging: 14 sails; 3 foresails; foremast: double topsails; single topgallants; main, mizzenmast: gaff-sail, gaff-topsail

Masts: all masts are pole masts; height of foremast: 35 meters; mainmast: 34.50 meters; mizzenmast: 30 meters

Auxiliary engine: Fiat diesel, 450 horsepower

Crew: 5 officers, 12 petty officers, 44 regular crew members, approx. 50 boys

Use: sailing school-ship

Built in Nantes, the barkentine sailed under the French flag with the names *Jean Marc Aline* and *Commandant Louis Richard*. Because of her good nautical and technical qualities, the Italian navy purchased the ship in 1951. In the years 1954 to 1955 she was converted for future use as a school-ship and at the same time modernized. On July 1, 1955, she was put into service under the new name *Palinuro* (Palinuro was Aeneas's helmsman when he sailed to Italy). Primarily helmsmen are trained aboard the ship, and in addition also beginning personnel of the port administration (*portuali*). The barkentine is equipped with the most modern navigational instruments. Her poop reaches past the mainmast. There are bow and stern ornaments in addition to figureheads. The white streak runs under the deck line in the English manner. The training cruises lead mostly to the Mediterranean.

In the early 1980s there was talk of replacing the *Palinuro* with a newly built ship. The price comparison between overhauling the new *Palinuro* and building a new ship worked out in the *Palinuro*'s favor, however. From 1984 to 1986 she was thoroughly overhauled in Messina and subsequently put back into service.

Puritan

The *Puritan* was built as a luxury and racing yacht. In 1979 a thorough overhaul took place at the Camper & Nicholson shipyards in Hampshire. Yachts of this kind had up to 40 men on board during regattas. The ship was designed by the American yacht builder John G. Alden.

Type: 2-masted fore-and-aft schooner, steel

Nation: Italy

Owner: Arturo Feruzzi

Year of construction: 1926

Shipyard: Electric Boat Company, Groton, Connecticut, USA

Tonnage: 111.44 tons gross

Dimensions:
Length overall: 38.00 m
Length of hull: 31.30 m
Width: 6.90 m
Draft: 2.70 m

Sail area: 399 square meters

Auxiliary engine: General Motors diesel, 240 horsepower

Crew: 12-person active crew

Use: private yacht

Japan

Akogare
Belle Blonde
De Liefde
Kaisei
Kaiwo Maru II
Kanko Maru

Kanrin Maru
Meiji Maru
Nippon Maru I
   and Kaiwo
   Maru I
Nippon Maru II

Prins Willem
Sant Juan Bautista
Unyo Maru

Akogare

Type: 3-masted topsail schooner, steel

Nation: Japan

Owner: city of Osaka

Home port: Osaka

Year of construction: launched November 24, 1992; commissioned March 31, 1993

Shipyard: Sumitomo Heavy Industries, Ltd.

Tonnage: 108 ts displacement; 362 tons gross; 108 tons net

Dimensions:
Length overall: 52.16 m
Length between perpendiculars: 36.00 m
Width: 8.60 m
Depth to deck: 5.90 m

Draft: 3.90 m

Sail area: 824 square meters

Rigging: 14 sails; 3 square sails, 11 fore-and-aft sails

Masts: height of mainmast over the deck: 30 meters

Auxiliary engine: diesel engine, 320 horsepower

Crew: 13-person active crew, 40 trainees (passengers)

Use: sailing school-ship

It is very unusual for a city, in this case Osaka, to build and maintain a sailing school-ship. The citizenry's long-cherished desire to possess such a ship is also expressed in the ship's name: *Akogare* means "desire" or "longing." The ship is available to be used by all segments of the population.

The most modern navigational equipment guarantee a high level of safety. The figurehead represents the legendary hero Yamato Takeru, whose soul, according to the legend, was transformed into a white bird and flew to Osaka.

Belle Blonde

Previous name: *LV 88*

Type: brigantine, iron

Nation: Japan

Owner: Hokuku Kosan Kabushiki Kaisha, Tokyo, Japan

Home port: Tokyo

Year of construction: 1906

Shipyard: New York Shipbuilding Company, Camden, New Jersey, USA

Tonnage: 478 tons gross; 276 tons net

Dimensions:
Length overall: 50.10 m
Length of hull: 41.10 m
Length at the waterline: 39.30 m
Width: 9.10 m
Draft: 4.20 m

Sail area: 1300 square meters

Auxiliary engine: Washington diesel, 350 horsepower

Crew: 12-person crew

Use: chartered ship, company ship

The *Belle Blonde* was built as Light Vessel 88 with a staysail rig for the United States Coast Guard. An auxiliary engine supported the sails. She worked primarily in Astoria, Oregon. In 1962 she was donated to the Columbia River Maritime Museum in Astoria. In 1982 Captain Claude Lacerte of Canada purchased the ship and converted her into a brigantine.

In March 1998 the *Belle Blonde* was sold to a Japanese construction and real estate management company. She is used for advertising purposes.

De Liefde

Type: reproduction of a Dutch trading vessel of the seventeenth century, steel, wood

Nation: Japan

Owner: Nagasaki Holland Village Corporation

Home port: Oranda Mura near Nagasaki

Year of construction: 1992

Shipyard: Merwede Shipyard, Rivierdijk, the Netherlands

Dimensions:
Length overall: 39.00 m
Length between perpendiculars: 25.80 m
Width: 7.75 m
Depth in hold: 5.00 m
Draft: 2.50 m

Rigging: 6 sails, spritsail

Use: stationary museum ship

De Liefde ("love") is a reproduction of the first Dutch trading ship that sailed to Japan in the year 1600 in order to open up trade relations. The hull is made of steel and planked with wood. Erasmus of Rotterdam adorns the long, extended cutwater. The original figurehead is still on display today in Japan. The ship is one of the major exhibits at the Dutch village near Nagasaki and does not sail.

Kaisei

Previous name: *Zew*

Type: brigantine, steel

Nation: Japan

Owner: Kaoru Ogimi, Shogakukan, Inc., Yasunori Kobayashi

Home port: Miura, Kanagawa prefecture

Year of construction: 1990; launched August 1990

Shipyard: Interster S. A., Gdansk

Tonnage: 180 tons gross; 54 tons net

Dimensions:
Length overall: 46.00 m

Length of hull: 35.50 m
Length between perpendiculars: 31.00 m
Width: 7.56 m
Depth to deck: 5.34 m
Draft: 3.80 m

Sail area: 780 square meters

Rigging: 15 sails

Masts: height of mainmast over the deck: 28.40 meters

Auxiliary engine: ship's diesel engine, 200 horsepower

Crew: 9-person active crew, plus 4 voluntary trainees, 32 trainees, 50 passengers on short day cruises

Use: sailing school-ship

This brigantine was built as the schooner *Zew* for the Polish Sail Training Association. The current name means "Planet of the Ocean." The ship passed into Japanese hands in 1991. She is the first Japanese ship to sail for the Japanese Sail Training Association by means of a private endowment.

The ship's conversion and rerigging as a brigantine took place in Gdansk, Poland, and later in Weymouth, England.

Because of the international workers who were employed in this process and because of the fact that until the ship's arrival in Japan the trainees were always part of an international exchange, the *Kaisei* was the only ship at the Columbus Regatta in 1992 that was allowed to fly the flag of the United Nations. The ship's passage to Japan, during which numerous ports were visited, took 16 months. The ship is available for use to everyone over the age of 16.

Type: 4-masted bark, steel

Nation: Japan

Owner: The Training Ship Education, Support Association, Institute for Sea Training, Tokyo

Home port: Tokyo

Year of construction: launched March 7, 1989; commissioned September 16, 1989

Shipyard: Uraga Dockyard, Sumitomo Heavy Industries, Ltd.

Tonnage: 4654.7 ts displacement; 2879 tons gross; 865 tons net

Dimensions:
Length overall: 110.10 m
Length at the waterline: 86.00 m
Width: 13.80 m
Depth to deck: 10.70 m
Draft: 6.60 m

Sail area: 2760 meters

Rigging: 36 sails; double topsail, double topgallant, royal; mizzenmast: lower mizzen, upper mizzen, mizzen topsail

Mast: height of mainmast over the deck: 44.05 meters

Auxiliary engine: diesel, two 1500-horsepower engines

Crew: 69-person active crew, 130 cadets

Use: sailing school-ship

In contrast to her predecessor, the *Kaiwo Maru II* carries a figurehead. This figurehead is named "Konjo," and she is the younger sister to "Ronjo," who adorns the bow of the *Nippon Maru II*. She symbolizes innocence with classical dignity.

The predecessor in imitation of which the current *Kanko Maru* (*Kanko* means "one sees the light") was built was originally called the *Soembing* (Soembing is a mountain on Java). Armed with six cannons, she was a Dutch navy sailing ship that had been built in Holland in 1850 and had been propelled by steam-powered paddlewheels since 1875. King Willem III gave the ship to Japan as a gift in 1855.

The *Kanko Maru*, as she was now called, became a school-ship of the naval school in Nagasaki. She was the first school-ship of the developing Japanese navy and thus also Japan's first warship. In 1868 she became state property and was first scrapped in 1876.

The strikingly great width of the current *Kanko Maru* is a result of the fact that the wheel boxes for the former paddle wheels are included in the reproduction. A bare-breasted mermaid decorates the bow as a figurehead.

Type: 3-masted topsail schooner, steel (Jackass-bark/Polka-bark)	Shipyard: Verolme Shipyard, the Netherlands	Width: 14.50 m Depth in hold: 3.50 m Depth to deck: 5.80 m	Masts: height of mainmast over the deck: 29 meters
Nation: Japan	Tonnage: 781 ts displacement; 353 tons gross	Draft: 4.20 m Sail area: 650 square meters	Auxiliary engine: two 340-horsepower engines
Owner: Industrial Bank of Japan	Dimensions: Length overall: 65.80 m	Rigging: 12 sails; fore- and mainmast in addition to lower sail, topsail, and topgallant	Crew: 14-person active crew, 300 guests on day cruises
Home port: Tokyo	Length of hull: 49.00 m Length between perpendiculars: 45.00 m		Use: passenger ship
Year of construction: 1988			

The development of the Japanese navy during the 1850s and 1860s was heavily influenced by the Netherlands. In 1856 the Japanese had a sailing ship built at a Dutch shipyard that received the name *Japan*. While being delivered to Japan the ship rounded the Cape of Good Hope and reached Nagasaki in September 1857. There she received the name *Kanrin Maru* (*Kanrin* means approximately "the Emperor and his retinue ensure peace"). Aboard the ships *Kanko Maru* and *Kanrin Maru* instruction took place primarily in Dutch, because the instructors were from the Netherlands.

It was not until 1867 that the Meiji restoration ended the power of the shoguns, and after leading a shadowy existence for centuries, the Tenno could finally enter back into his hereditary rights. In 1868 the influential warlord family Tokugawa captured the *Kanrin Maru*. The entire crew was killed during the attack.

The ship was released from military service in 1866 and served as a sailing school-ship until 1867. The ship was employed as a freighter until 1870, when she was lost in a typhoon.

The modern *Kanrin Maru* was reconstructed according

to original plans that had been preserved in Amsterdam. The idea underlying the construction of the current ships *Kanko Maru* and *Kanrin Maru* was the motto "encounter between human beings and the sea."

Type: 3-masted topsail schooner, steel (Jackass-bark/Polka-bark)

Nation: Japan

Owner: Industrial Bank of Japan Leasing Company, Ltd.

Home port: Yokohama

Years of construction: 1989–90; launched December 1989

Shipyard: Merwede shipyard, Holland

Tonnage: 1050 ts displacement; 539 tons gross; 238 tons net

Dimensions:
Length overall: 65.84 m
Length of hull: 52.35 m
Length between perpendiculars: 47.35 m
Width: 10.50 m
Depth in hold: 4.00 m
Depth to deck: 6.82 m
Draft: 4.50 m

Sail area: 1295 square meters

Rigging: 13 sails; fore- and mainmast in addition to lower sails, top, and topgallants

Masts: height of mainmast over the deck: 29.70 meters

Auxiliary engine: two ship's diesel engines, 476 horsepower each

Crew: 21-person active crew; 290 guests on day cruises, 35 guests on longer cruises

Use: company passenger ship

Meiji Maru

Type: full-rigged ship

Nation: Japan

Owner: Merchant Marine Academy, Tokyo

Home port: dry dock on the grounds of the academy, Tokyo

Year of construction: 1874

Shipyard: Robert Napier, Glasgow, Scotland

Tonnage: 1038 tons gross; 457 tons net

Dimensions:
Length overall: 86.60 m

Length of hull: 76.00 m
Length between perpendiculars: 73.00 m
Width: 8.50 m
Depth to deck: 7.60 m

Rigging: 26 sails (full-rigged ship); double topsail; single topgallant; royals

Masts: height of mainmast over the deck: 31 meters; bowsprit with jibboom

Auxiliary engine: Kolben steam engine, 1530 horsepower

Use: museum ship

In March 1873, the Japanese government commissioned the shipyard R. Napier in Glasgow with the construction of a schooner-rigged, steam-powered lighthouse tender. *Meiji* ("enlightened government") was the motto of Emperor Mutsuhito (1867–1912). Under his government Japan became a great power. The Emperor used the *Meiji Maru* twice for voyages. In March 1875 he sailed on her from Yokosuka to Yokohama after taking part in the christening of a warship in Yokohama. In July 1876 he returned to Yokohama aboard the ship from an inspection trip in the north of Japan. Until November 1897 the *Meiji Maru* was operated by the Japanese lighthouse administration. Then she was given to the naval academy of Tokyo, the predecessor of the current university of the merchant marine. Her conversion and retackling as a full-rigged ship followed. From then on the sailing ship lay as a school-ship of the academy in the Tokyo harbor. In August 1927 her engines and tank were removed. The Americans confiscated the ship in September of 1945 and used her as a cantina for their troops. She was returned to the academy in 1951.

Distinctive features of the ship are the continuous flush deck with very little sheer and the continuous, open railing.

In March 1964 the *Meiji Maru* was overhauled and brought to her current berth. There are plans to expand the ship into a museum.

Type: 4-masted bark, steel

Nation: Japan

Owner: merchant marine, Unyusho (Ministry of Transport); operated by Kokai-Kunrensho/Tokyo (Institute for Maritime Training)

Home port: Tokyo

Year of construction: 1930; launched January 27, 1930

Shipyard: Kawasaki Shipyard, Kobe-Hondo

Tonnage: 4343 ts displacement; 2285.77 tons gross; 743.53 tons net

Dimensions:
Length overall: 97.00 m
Length of hull: 93.50 m
Length between perpendiculars: 79.25 m
Width: 12.95 m
Depth to deck: 7.85 m
Depth in hold: 5.39 m
Draft: 6.90 m

Sail area: 2397 meters

Rigging: 32 sails; 3 foresails, double topsails, double topgallants, royals; mizzenmast: mizzen and mizzen topgallant

Masts: height of mainmast over the deck: 44.60 meters; fore-, main-, and mizzen-mast with one topmast; mizzenmast one piece

Auxiliary engine: two 6-cylinder diesel motors, 600 horsepower each

Crew: 27 officers, 48 regular crew members, 120 cadets

Use: sailing school-ship (now stationary)

Japan is largely dependent on maritime trade due to its geographical location and topography. Even inner-state trade takes place primarily by sea.

In order to satisfy the growing demand for young seamen for the growing merchant marine, the two sister ships *Nippon Maru I* and *Kaiwo Maru I* were built in 1930. Aboard them future officers of the merchant marine were and are trained. The young men receive 3-year preparatory training at the country's various schools for seamen. This is followed by a 1-year period of service aboard one of the great sailing ships. After an additional year aboard motorized school-ships, the cadets can earn a second mate's certificate.

Before the war, military instruction in guns and torpedo tubes took place in addition to the general training in seamanship, navigation, and meteorology. The young officers could then be taken over by the naval reserve in an emergency.

Almost all Japanese ships of the merchant marine carry the extra designation *Maru,* which means "to. This simply serves to identify them as trading ships. In Japanese legends,

Kaiwo is the "king of the seas."

The sailing ships were designed to take on a large number of young men, in particular with the aim of providing all living and recreation areas with daylight. For this reason, the hull has a remarkably high freeboard. With her smokestack between the mainmast and the mizzenmast she is reminiscent of a well-designed passenger ship.

A 65-meter-long awning deck reaches from the stern to a point between the fore- and mainmasts. The short forecastle is for all practical purposes used only to operate the anchor equipment. Between the forecastle and the awning deck only a very short piece of the main deck remains open. A navigational bridge with wings is located on the awning deck between the fore- and the mainmast. One stands outside on the bridge, a second below in the wheelhouse. In addition, the cadets' sextants are stored here.

Behind the mizzenmast

stands a large deckhouse in which additional charthouses are located. The great double wheel for steering by hand is located behind the mizzenmast. In spite of the large size of the crew, all cadets sleep in cabins with eight berths. There are neither brace nor halyard winches. Even the most difficult tasks during sea maneuvers are completed only with the assistance of the six capstans. A boiler provides the power for the winches, the anchor windlass, and the steam-powered steering engine. Six lifeboats hang in davits, and in addition there is a motor cutter and a gig that are lashed to the awning deck.

The entire rig was provided by the firm Ramage & Ferguson of Leith. She is adapted to the short stature of many Japanese sailors. For this reason the sail area also seems small relative to the size of the ship by European standards. In order to give the hull with its high freeboard the necessary stability, 640 tons of copper in addition to 130 tons of reinforced concrete are stowed as permanent ballast. In addition there are five ballast water tanks in the double bottom. Before the war both sailing ships regularly made voyages, usually in the waters of the Pacific.

At the start of the war all of the yards were removed. The barks now became pure motorized ships with standing masts. The training operations were carried on in domestic waters. After the war the ships served to transport Japanese troops and civilians back into their homeland. Both were newly tackled in the course of the postwar years and once again put into operation, the *Nippon*

Maru in 1952 and the *Kaiwo Maru* in 1955. In the year 1954, the *Nippon Maru* again visited the United States for the first time since the end of the war. In 1960, she represented her country in New York, where the 100th anniversary of the first visit of a Japanese mission to this city was celebrated. The training voyages nowadays usually begin in May and lead to Hawaii and to the West Coast of the United States. During these voyages, the ships almost always sail separately.

A predecessor of the two 4-masters *Nippon Maru* and *Kaiwo Maru* was the 4-masted bark *Taisei Maru,* which was built in 1904. After the end of the war in 1945 she ran into a mine in the inner harbor of Kobe and was completely destroyed. The motor ship *Otaru Maru,* which today serves the Kokai Kunrensho (Institute for Maritime Training) as a school-ship, carries on her name. In 1924 the 4-masted barkentine *Shintoku Maru* was built as a school-ship. In 1943 she caught fire following an air attack and ran aground in a small harbor in Kobe. After the war she was raised and did service as a school-ship until 1962. The government is planning to preserve her as a museum ship. A motorized school-ship belonging to the institute that took part in Operation Sail in New York in 1964 now bears her name. The Kokai Kunrensho controls a total of six large school-ships, among them two sailing ships.

Following the construction of the ships *Nippon Maru II* and *Kaiwo Maru II,* instructional activities have been transferred to these two ships. Nothing about the system has changed.

Nippon Maru II

The *Nippon Maru I,* which had been built in 1930, was relieved of active training duty in September 1984. She has been replaced by a new ship with the same name.

As a result of the increased standard of living following World War II, young Japanese are significantly taller than their peers of the 1930s. As a result, the dimensions of the rig on the new bark had to be adapted to this development.

In contrast to her predecessor, the *Nippon Maru II* carries a figurehead. She bears the name *Ranjo.* Her elegance, smoothness, and dignity symbolize the Japanese woman. In literature the name also stands for the blue of the deep sea. Proposals for the figurehead came from all parts of Japan.

The same is true of the figure-head of the *Kaiwo Maru II*.

The weather deck has three deck superstructures. The forward one is overshadowed by the command bridge. The second wheel on the stern is occupied when the ship is under sail. The top deck contains the officers' quarters, the galley, a large classroom, and some of the crew's quarters. The lower deck houses the cadets' quarters—primarily eight-bed cabins as well as quarters for female cadets, the mess, and more of the crew's quarters. The between deck is filled with another classroom, the engine room, tanks, and holds.

The *Nippon Maru I* is moored in Yokohama as a museum ship.

Type: 4-masted bark, steel	Length at the waterline: 86.00 m
Nation: Japan	Width: 13.80 m Depth to deck: 10.70 m Draft: 6.50 m
Owner: Ministry of Transport, Institute for Sea Training, Tokyo	Sail area: 2760 meters
Home port: Tokyo	Rigging: 36 sails; double topsail, double topgallant, royal; mizzenmast: lower mizzen, upper mizzen, mizzen topsail
Year of construction: launched February 15, 1984; commissioned September 16, 1984	
Shipyard: Uraga Dockyard, Sumitomo Heavy Industries, Ltd.	Masts: height of mainmast over the deck: 44.05 meters
Tonnage: 4729.9 ts displacement; 2891 tons gross; 867 tons net	Auxiliary engine: two diesel engines, 1500 horsepower each
	Crew: 70-person active crew, 120 cadets
Dimensions: Length overall: 110.10 m	Use: sailing school-ship

● Prins Willem

The model for the current reproduction was the East Indian trader *Prins Willem,* which was built for the Verenigde Oost-Indische Compagnie (V.O.C.) from 1649 to 1651 in Middleburg. This ship brought the first Dutch settlers to the Japanese island of Hirado. They were allowed to pursue trade there. Armed with forty cannons, she belonged to the Dutch navy in 1652. After sustaining damage in battles against the English, the *Prins Willem* was returned to the company in 1653. Without dispensing with her cannons, she made multiple voyages to Batavia between 1653 and 1660. During the voyage from Batavia to Holland that began on December 23, 1661, she sank off the island of Brandon.

The reconstruction was undertaken in remembrance of the old trade relations between the Netherlands and Japan. In the Nagasaki Holland Village that was opened in 1983, imposing ships are displayed in addition to reproductions of Dutch houses and a windmill.

For the sake of durability, the hull of the reproduction is made of steel. The area above the waterline was covered with wooden planks. The gun decks and the numerous carvings on board are extremely impressive, above all the baroque poop with its sculptures and paintings. The transport to Japan took place by means of the heavy transport vessel *Happy Mammoth*. After a 6-week voyage the *Prins Willem* was carried to its final berth using the "piggyback" method in the middle of August 1985.

Type: reproduction of a Dutch trading vessel of the seventeenth century, steel, wood

Nation: Japan

Owner: Nagasaki Holland Village Corporation

Home port: Oranda Mura near Nagasaki

Year of construction: 1985; launched July 1985

Shipyard: AMELS B. V., Makkum, the Netherlands; supported by 21 supply companies (rig, wood ornaments, cannons, etc.)

Tonnage: 1000 ts displacement

Dimensions:
Length overall: 68.00 m
Length at the waterline: 51.25 m
Width: 14.32 m
Depth to deck: 5.90 m
Height of poop deck above the keel: 20.50 m
Draft: 3.70 m

Masts: height of mainmast over the keel: 54 m; bowsprit with spritsail yard, bowsprit and bowsprit topsail yard

Auxiliary engine: none

Use: stationary museum ship

 ## San Juan Bautista

Type: reproduction of a seventeenth-century galleon, wood

Nation: Japan

Owner: Keicho Diplomatic Mission Ship Association

Home port: Ishinomaki City, Miyagi prefecture, Japan

Year of construction: keel laid April 17, 1992; launched May 22, 1993

Shipyard: K. K. Murakami zosensho (hull), K. K. Yaminishi (rig)

Tonnage: 665 ts displacement; 387 tons gross

Dimensions:
Length overall: 55.35 m
Length of hull: 47.10 m
Length between perpendiculars: 34.28 m
Width: 10.91 m
Depth in hold: 5.00 m
Depth to deck: 4.55 m
Draft: 3.55 m

Sail area: 1059 square meters

Rigging: 6 sails, bowsprit with spritsail

Masts: height of mainmast over the keel: 48.12 meters; height of mainmast over the deck: 41.17 meters

Auxiliary engine: none

Crew: nowadays 6-person active crew, 144 guests

Use: sailing museum and representation ship

The original of the galleon, which was also called the *Saint John the Baptist*, was built in Sendai, Japan, in 1613 on the basis of Western models. The armed ship also had an important task as protection against the shoguns and vying Protestants.

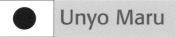

Unyo Maru

Type: bark, steel

Nation: Japan

Owner: University for the
Fishing Sciences, Tokyo

Location: university campus,
Tokyo

Year of construction: 1909;
launched February 2, 1909

Shipyard: Osaka Iron Factory
Co Ltd., Osaka

Tonnage: 448.25 tons gross;
197.46 tons net

Dimensions:
Length of hull: 45.90 m
Length between
perpendiculars: 41.00 m
Width: 8.10 m
Depth to deck: 5.00 m
Depth in hold: 4.50 m
Draft: 3.60 m

Sail area: 540 square meters

Rigging: 21 sails; double
topsail; single topgallant, royals

Crew: 25-person active crew,
15 to 30 boys

Use: museum ship

This small, steam-powered bark was built as a sailing school-ship and was under the control of the Ministry for Agriculture and Forests. After being released from service under sail as a training ship, she was moored along with the *Meiji Maru* for many years prior to World War II as a stationary ship in Tokyo.

Today the ship is moored as a museum ship at the campus of the University for Fishery Sciences in Tokyo.

Luxemburg

Royal Clipper

Star Clipper/
Star Flyer

Royal Clipper

Type: 5-masted full-rigged ship, steel

Nation: Luxemburg

Owner: Star Clippers, Mikael Krafft, Sweden

Home port: Cannes, Bridgetown, Barbados

Year of construction: hull as the *Gwarek,* 1990; launched February 8, 1991, Stoczina Gdanska S. A. (Gdansk Shipyard, Gdansk)

Shipyard: completed as a 5-masted full-rigged ship at the Merwede shipyard, Dordrecht, the Netherlands; launched July 15, 2000

Tonnage: 5050 gross register tonnage

Dimensions:
Length overall: 134.00 m
Length of hull: 119.40 m
Length between perpendiculars: 99.00 m
Width: 16.50 m
Draft: 5.60 m

Sail area: 5000 square meters

Rigging: 42 sails; double topsail, double topgallant, main and middle-masted with royals

Masts: height of mainmast over the deck: 54 meters

Auxiliary engine: two Caterpillar 16-cylinder engines, 1865 kilowatts each

Crew: 100-person active crew, 228 passengers

Use: cruise ship

The *Royal Clipper*, which belongs to the shipping company Star Clippers, is not only the largest sailing ship in the world today but also has accommodations otherwise found only in first-class hotels.

The initial launch took place in 1991 in Danzig. The ship was supposed to receive the name *Gwarek* (Polish for "miner") and be made available primarily for the use of the youth of upper Silesia. This would have made her a sister ship of the *Dar Mlodziezy*. The designer was the well-known Polish maritime architect Zygmunt Choren. Due to financial difficulties the ship was not completed.

In March 1998 the Swedish shipowner Mikael Krafft purchased the unfinished hull. The lengthening and widening of the ship, which thus took on its enormous current size, proceeded on site. The largely finished hull was brought to the Dutch city of Dordrecht with the help of a tow boat. Further interior construction and the rigging took place there. The powerful masts were not placed on the keel but instead attached to the deck so that the line of sight in the interior would be clear.

All of the sails can be furled or unfurled within minutes. The square sails are rolled up in the yards, and the staysail on the stay. An adjustable propeller and bow thruster are givens. The ship makes use of anti-roll tanks that hold 160 tons of water each. As a result, the maximum angle of heel is only five degrees.

Three swimming pools are available on deck, and the glass bottom of the middle pool is simultaneously the upper surface of the atrium in which the large dining room is also located.

In the Captain Nemo Lounge guests have the opportunity to view underwater life through portholes made of special glass.

A bare-breasted beauty representing the shipowner's daughter adorns the bow as a figurehead.

Star Clipper/Star Flyer

The hulls of these two luxury yachts (sister ships) were built in the style of the famous nineteenth-century shipbuilder Donald McKay. Four continuous decks distinguish the ships. They have bow thrusters and anti-rolling tanks. The yards are firmly mounted. There are no turnbuckles, only climbing aids on the masts. The square sails can be operated by three men. The roll reefing devices on the yards are operated with a joystick.

Type: 4-masted barkentine, steel	Shipyard: Langerbrugge Shipyards, Gent	Sail area: 3365 square meters	Auxiliary engine: Caterpillar 3512 de/TA, 1015 kilowatts
Nation: Luxemburg	Tonnage: 2300 tons gross	Rigging: 16-sail foremast: foresail, double topsail, single topgallant, royal sail	Crew: 70-person active crew, of them 10 for the nautical operations, maximum 170 passengers (85 cabins)
Owner: White Star Clipper N.V. Shipping Company, Brussels	Dimensions: Length overall: 111.50 m Length of hull: 91.40 m Width: 15.00 m Draft: 6.50 m	Masts: height of mainmast over the deck: 63 meters	
Home port: Antwerp			Use: chartered ship, cruise ship
Year of construction: 1991			

Madeira

Anny von Hamburg

Anny von Hamburg

Previous names: *Ringö, Kurt Both, Hanna, Anny*

Type: 3-masted fore-and-aft schooner, iron

Nation: Madeira

Owner: Anny Yachting Company

Home port: Thien & Heyenga, Ltd., Hamburg

Year of construction: 1914

Shipyard: C. Lühring, Hammelwerden, Unterweser

Tonnage: 242 ts displacement; 124 tons gross; 43 tons net

Dimensions:
Length overall: 38.00 m
Length of hull: 32.27 m
Length between perpendiculars: 28.40 meters
Width: 7.00 m
Depth in hold: 2.95 m
Draft: 2.35 m

Sail area: 520 square meters

Rigging: 12 sails, including square foresail

Masts: height of mainmast over the deck: 24 meters

Auxiliary engine: 6-cylinder Deutz diesel, 280 horsepower

Crew: 5-person active crew, 10 guests, 30 guests on day cruises

Use: chartered ship

The adventurous life of the *Anny von Hamburg* could almost have ended at a salvage company if her present owners had not discovered her in time.

The *Anny* was built as a freighter in response to a commission from Captain Diedrich Hasseldieck of Nordenham. A total of eight schooners with the same elegant lines left the wharf. The first voyage was to Petersburg. There the ship was immediately commandeered following the outbreak of World War I.

After the war the hull was returned to Germany. In 1925 the ship was rebuilt at the Ernst Harms shipyard in Hamburg. Among other things, the ship at that time received a smaller rig, her first engine, and the new name *Hanna*. The owner at that time, Captain Walter Richter of

Hamburg, sold his ship in 1936 to Captain Max Both of Glückstadt. From then on she was called *Kurt Both*. Until the outbreak of the war the motor schooner transported cement to Helgoland, where it was used to build fortifications. Later the ship sailed to Scandinavia as a tramping vessel. In 1940 she was converted into a 1½-master.

In 1950 the *Kurt Both* was lengthened by 8 meters in Hamburg-Wilhelmsburg. With the removal of the bowsprit in 1952, the former schooner had become a purely motorized ship.

In 1957 the Swedish shipping firm Oscar Abrahamson bought the ship and gave her the name *Ringö*. Later she was purchased by Paul Grönquist of Borga, Finland. Until 1970 the ship was employed as a sand

freighter in Finland. In 1980 members of the Germania Shipping Company (Germani Schiffahrt, Ltd.) of Hamburg discovered the ship, partially burned, in Karlskrona, Sweden. Since no new buyer could be found, the ship was to be sold as scrap. The hull was able to reach Hamburg without being hauled by another ship. For the next few years, the ship was registered as *Anny* in the Hamburg ship registry.

A thorough overhaul had become necessary. The lengthening was undone. The *Anny* got her old rig back in keeping with the original plans. Great attention was paid to the interior furnishings. In the hold, in addition to a great room, five double cabins, each with its own bathroom and shower, came into being. The captain's aft cabin as well as the crew's living quarters under the stern were carefully refurbished in the style of the period. In November 1982 the restoration work on this stunning ship was completed. Starting in 1987 the *Anny* sailed for 10 years under the flag of Antigua in the Caribbean.

Since 1998 she has been the property of the Anny Yachting Company. She was thoroughly overhauled in Wilhelmshaven and today sails the North Sea and the Baltic as a chartered ship. In the summer she is moored in Kiel near the Blücher Bridge.

Tunas Samudera

Type: brigantine, steel

Nation: Malaysia

Owner: Royal Malaysian Navy

Home port: Lumut-Perak

Year of construction: keel laid 1988; launched August 4, 1989

Shipyard: Brooke Yachts International, Ltd., Lowestoft, England; design: Colin Mudie

Tonnage: 250 ts displacement; 173 tons gross; 51 tons net

Dimensions:
Length overall: 44.00 m
Length of hull: 35.00 m
Length at the waterline: 28.30 m
Width: 7.80 m
Depth to deck: 5.60 m
Draft: 4.00 m

Sail area: 569 square meters

Rigging: 10 sails

Masts: height of mainmast over the deck: 32 meters

Auxiliary engine: two Perkins diesel M200 Ti engines, 185 horsepower

Crew: 16-person active crew, 36 trainees

Use: sailing school-ship

On October 16, 1989, the ship was handed over to the Malaysian navy in the presence of Queen Elizabeth II of England and H. M. The Yang Di-Pertuan Agong, Sultan Az-lan Shah, the head of the Malaysian federation. Twenty training missions a year are planned. Thirteen of these are reserved for the navy, while the others are open to youth groups.

The *Tunas Samudera* is a sister ship of the Australian *Young Endeavour,* which was built by the same designer and at the same shipyard. The name means "Offspring of the Ocean."

Malta

Black Pearl

Charlotte Louise

Sea Cloud
Sea Cloud II

Black Pearl

Previous names: *Aeolus, Black Opal*

Type: barkentine, wood

Nation: Malta

Owner: Vincent Vella Natal Azzopardi

Home port: Valletta (dry)

Year of construction: 1909

Shipyard: in Pukavisk, Sweden

Tonnage: 400 tons net

Dimensions:
Length: 45.00 m

Sail area: 840 square meters

Masts: height of mainmast over the deck: 27 meters

Crew: 16-person active crew, 40 guests (as a chartered ship)

Use: restaurant ship

The *Black Pearl* was built as a schooner. Her hull was planked with two layers of oak wood to allow for use in the icy winter waters of the Baltic. For 69 years the ship carried primarily grain, coal, and wood.

In 1969 she was converted into a barkentine with a luxurious interior. The ship was now called the *Aeolus* and sailed with passengers between Australia and the Pacific islands. After teredo had seriously damaged the hull, the *Aeolus* was supposed to be brought to England for repairs in 1976. Fire broke out in the machine room while the ship was in the Suez Canal. When the ship reached Malta, it sank in the harbor of Marsamxett.

In 1979 the current owners raised her in order to use her in films. The barkentine sank a second time during a heavy storm in 1981. She was raised again, received the name *Black Pearl*, and since then has served as a restaurant ship.

Charlotte Louise

Type: 2-masted topsail schooner, wood

Nation: Malta

Owner: Captain Morgan Leisure, Ltd.

Home port: Valletta

Year of construction: 1942

Shipyard: Frasers Yard, Western Scotland

Tonnage: 65 tons gross; 19 tons net

Dimensions:
Length overall: 33.30 m
Length of hull: 22.25 m
Width: 6.02 m
Depth in hold: 2.78 m

Draft: 2.20 m

Sail area: 485 square meters

Rigging: 10 sails; foremast: square foresail, fore-topsail, fore-topgallant

Masts: height of mainmast over the deck: 18 meters; each mast has 1 topmast

Auxiliary engine: Ford BSD 666T diesel, 360 horsepower

Crew: 8-person active crew, 4 trainees, 75 day guests

Use: day passenger cruises

The schooner originally belonged to the Royal Navy. In the early 1950s she was stolen by pirates in Singapore and in 1952 recaptured by the navy. The ship belongs to the type of the small nineteenth-century cargo-carrying schooner. Following a thorough modification and modernization, the *Charlotte Louise* now sails day tours in the waters off Malta. The figure of a young girl adorns the bow.

Sea Cloud

Previous names: *Antarna, Patria, Angelita, Sea Cloud, Hussar II*

Type: 4-masted bark, steel

Nation: Malta

Owner: Sea Cloud Cruises, Ltd., Hamburg

Home port: Valletta, Malta

Year of construction: 1931

Shipyard: Friedrich Krupp Germania Shipyard; keel designers: Gibbs and Cox of Cox & Stevens, New York

Tonnage: 3530 ts displacement; 2323 tons gross; 1147 tons net

Dimensions:
Length overall: 107.50 m
Length of hull: 96.10 m
Length between perpendiculars: 77.20 m
Width: 14.94 m
Draft: 5.00 m

Sail area: 3160 square meters

Rigging: 31 sails; 4 foresails; fore, mizzenmast: double topsail, single topgallant, royals; mainmast: double topsail, single topgallant, royal, skysail; mizzenmast: mizzen sail, upper mizzen sail

Masts: height of mainmast over the deck: 58.40 meters

Auxiliary engine: four 8-cylinder Enterprise diesel motors with a total of 5000 horsepower

Crew: approx. 30 people, maximum 80 passengers

Use: chartered yacht

This unusual ship is not only the last 4-masted brig built before World War II but is also unique in the sense that from the very beginning she was conceived as a pure yacht and built accordingly. For this reason the *Sea Cloud* scarcely resembles a freight-carrying 4-master or a large sailing ship, except in the rig. Yet even here there is an anomaly; on her large mast she sets a skysail above and in addition to the royal. Everything about this ship is oriented toward elegance and speed, from the sharp cut of the bow to the long stern. The sharp upward taper of the masts is likewise unmistakable. A large eagle adorns the bow. The *Sea Cloud* was built as the *Hussar II* for Edward F. Hutton of New York under the supervision of her first commandant, Captain C. W. Lawson. Every conceivable luxury allowed the interior of the ship to be more like a first-class hotel than a seafaring vessel. The construction costs came to nearly a million dollars. Admittedly, the somewhat ponderous superstructures and a short, thick smokestack do not match the elegance of the rest of the ship.

A few years before World War II the ship was acquired by the American ambassador to Russia, Joseph E. Davies, under the new name *Sea Cloud*. The *Sea Cloud* remained moored in the Leningrad harbor as a floating palace during the rest of the ambassador's period of service.

When Davies became ambassador to Belgium, his ship followed him to Antwerp. Until 1942, then, the ship lay partially unrigged in Jacksonville. In that year, Davies leased the ship for an unspecified period to the U.S. Coast Guard for a dollar a year. Subsequently she sailed as a patrol ship with a much-reduced sail area. At the end of the war the entire set of sails was nearly given to the Danish full-rigged ship *Danmark*, which at that time was likewise doing service with the Coast Guard. This was prevented because Davies reclaimed the ship in the knick of time. Nonetheless, the process of putting the ship back in order to serve as a yacht again cost nearly a million dollars.

The next owner of the *Sea Cloud* was General Rafael Trujillo, president of the Dominican Republic. Under Trujillo's ownership the ship remained family property and did not become a state-owned yacht. The 4-masted bark received the new name *Angelita* after the president's daughter.

In 1963 the ship was offered for sale for 2 million dollars. Corporation Sea Cruise, Inc., a law firm in Panama, had the *Angelita* entered in the Panamese shipping register under the name *Patria*. The new owner was John Blue of Florida.

From the end of 1967 until the middle of 1968 the 4-master underwent a thorough overhaul at a Neapolitan shipyard, after which it once again set sail.

In 1969 the *Patria* was acquired by Antarna, Inc. Under the new name *Antarna* she was available for chartered cruises around the globe. In 1978 Captain Paschburg found the ship in Colon in a state of neglect. He brought the *Sea Cloud*, as she was now called once again, to Europe and had her overhauled from the ground up by the shipyard of Scheel & Jöhnk in Hamburg. Since then she has been engaged in chartered service as the largest sailing yacht of our time.

Sea Cloud II

Type: bark, steel

Nation: Malta

Owner: Sea Cloud Cruises, Ltd., Hamburg

Home port: La Valletta

Year of construction: 2000; launched March 18, 1999

Shipyard: Astilleros Gondan, Figueras, Spain

Tonnage: gross register tonnage 3000; approx. 3300 ts displacement; approx. 3800 tons gross; 1500 tons net (figures from the shipyard)

Dimensions:
Length overall: 117.20 m
Length of hull: 102.36 m
Length between perpendiculars: 81.50 m
Width: 16.00 m
Depth to deck: 9.40 m
Draft: 5.35 m

Sail area: 2758 square meters

Rigging: 24 sails, double topsails, single topgallant, mainsail, skysail

Masts: height of mainmast over the deck: 51.20 meters

Auxiliary engine: two MAK diesel engines, 1280 kilowatts each

Crew: 54-person active crew, 98 guests

Use: cruises

The *Sea Cloud II* is a cruise ship of the most exclusive class. Her interior resembles a luxury hotel. Only the bark's rig is reminiscent of the golden age of the sailing freighters. Extravagance abounds wherever one looks. In the design of the luxury cabins, no color combination was left to chance. The combination of the fabrics with leather, rattan, brass, gold, marble, and rare woods produces an exquisite decor in the style of the 1930s. Individual pieces of carefully chosen furniture define the character of each room. A sauna and fitness facilities are available as a matter of course. In addition to individual passengers, many companies reward their employees with a cruise aboard the ship.

Mexico

Cuauhtémoc

Cuauhtémoc

Type: bark, steel

Nation: Mexico

Owner: Armada de Mejico

Home port: Acapulco

Year of construction: 1982

Shipyard: Astilleros y Talleres
Celaya S. A., Bilbao, Spain

Tonnage: 1800 ts displacement

Dimensions:
Length overall: 90.50 m
Width: 12.00 m
Draft: 4.80 m

Sail area: 2200 square meters

Rigging: 23 sails; 5 foresails,
double topsails, single
topgallants, royals, mizzen
topsail

Auxiliary engine: diesel engine,
1125 horsepower

Crew: 275 people

Use: sailing school-ship

The bark received her name from the last Aztec emperor, Cuauhtémoc, who after being captured was hanged on the orders of the conquistador Hernán Cortés in 1525. No expense was spared in the construction of the imposing ship. Thus the standing rigging, for example, is made of rustproof steel.

Monaco

Xarifa

Xarifa

Previous names: *Capitone, Georgette, Capitana, L'Oiseau Blanc, Radiant, Xarifa*

Type: 3-masted schooner, steel

Nation: Monaco

Owner: Belgian Baron Louis Empani

Home port: Monte Carlo

Year of construction: 1928

Shipyard: White & Company, Cowes, England

Tonnage: 275 tons gross

Dimensions:
Length overall: 47.20 m
Length of hull: 44.20 m
Width: 8.60 m
Draft: 4.57 m

Sail area: 548 square meters

Rigging: Deutz diesel, 230 horsepower

Use: private yacht

The *Xarifa* (Egyptian for "beautiful creation") was built as a steamship for the industrialist Singer of sewing machine fame. Multiple circumnavigations of the globe marked her life history until she was requisitioned by Germany in Hamburg in 1939. She became a coal transporter.

After World War II the underwater explorer Hans Hass purchased the ship. The *Xarifa* became world renowned as a research vessel.

In 1960 the current owner purchased her. In an Italian shipyard in La Spezia she was converted into a private luxury yacht. Many parts of the retired *Liberté*, formerly the *Bremen*, were used in this process.

The Netherlands

Abel Tasman
Abel Tasman
Albert Johannes
Amazone
Amsterdam
Antigua
Aphrodite
Artemis
Astrid
Atlantis
Atlantis
Batavia
Bisshop van Arkel
Bonaire
Brabander
Brandaris
Catherina
De Liefde
Eendracht II
Elegant
Elisabeth Smit
Elizabeth
Europa
Fleurtje
Frisius van Adel

Grootvorst
Hendrika Bartelds
Hoop doet Leven
Horizon
Ide Min
Jacob Meindert
Jantje
J. R. R. Tolkien
Koh-I-Noor
Linde
Loth Loriën
Luciana
Maartinus
Mare Frisium
Minerva
Mon Desir
Mondrian
Morgana
Nil Desperandum
Noorderlicht
Oosterschelde
Oostvogel
Pacific Swift
Pedro Doncker
Pollux

Radboud
Rainbow Warrior
Regina Maris
Rembrandt
 van Rijn
Sir Robert
 Baden-Powell
Sodade
Stad Amsterdam
Stedemaeght
Store Baelt
Swaensborgh
Swan fan Makkum
Tecla
Thalassa
Tsjerk Hiddes
Urania
Vliegende Hollander
Vrouwe Geertruida
 Magdalena
Willem Barentsz
Wytske Eelkje/
 Willem
Zeelandia
Zuiderzee

Abel Tasman

Previous names: *Hermann, Laksen, Atlantis*

Type: 2-masted fore-and-aft schooner, steel

Nation: the Netherlands

Owner: Hanse Charter Holland, Groningen

Home port: Groningen

Year of construction: 1913; launched May 1913

Shipyard: Patje, Waterhuizen

Dimensions:
Length overall: 40.50 m
Length of hull: 31.00 m
Length between perpendiculars: 29.65 m
Width: 6.66 m
Draft: 2.60 m

Sail area: 420 square meters

Rigging: 7 sails

Masts: height of mainmast over the deck: 29 meters

Auxiliary engine: Detroit diesel, 318 horsepower

Crew: 3-person active crew, 6 trainees, 24–30 guests, 70 guests on day cruises

Use: chartered ship

The former freighter got her name from the Dutch seafarer Abel Janszoon Tasman (1603–59). He discovered Tasmania and the south island of New Zealand in 1642, and in 1643 the Tonga and Fiji islands. She sails in the North Sea and the Baltic.

Previous name: *Graesholm*

Type: barkentine, iron

Nation: the Netherlands

Owner: Gerhard Veldhuizen, Enkhuizen

Home port: Hoorn

Year of construction: 1920

Shipyard: Friedrich Krupp—Germania Shipyard

Tonnage: 176 ts displacement; 224 tons gross; 69 tons net

Dimensions:
Length overall: 49.00 m
Length of hull: 40.00 m
Length between perpendiculars: 36.11 m
Width: 6.77 m
Depth to deck: 2.70 m
Draft: 1.80 m

Sail area: 620 square meters

Rigging: 10 sails

Masts: height of mainmast over the deck: 30 meters

Auxiliary engine: Scania diesel, 340 horsepower

Crew: 3-person active crew, 100 guests on day cruises

Use: chartered ship, party ship

The former freighter, which has been converted into a barkentine, has been in service since 1999. Her day cruises take her primarily to the Ijsselmeer. The ship is named after the Dutch seafarer Abel J. Tasman (1603–59). He discovered Tasmania and the south island of New Zealand in 1642, and in 1643 the Tonga and Fiji islands.

Albert Johannes

Previous names: *Martha, Eiland*

Type: 3-masted fore-and-aft schooner, steel

Nation: the Netherlands

Owner: Willem Sligting, Scheveningen

Home port: Scheveningen

Year of construction: 1930

Shipyard: Diepen Shipyard, the Netherlands

Tonnage: 128 ts displacement; 66 tons gross

Dimensions:
Length overall: 48.20 m
Length of hull: 35.20 m
Width: 5.60 m
Depth in hold: 2.00 m
Depth to deck: 2.20 m
Draft: 1.50 m

Sail area: 360 square meters

Rigging: 8 sails

Masts: height of mainmast over the deck: 27 meters

Auxiliary engine: Deutz diesel, 120 horsepower

Crew: 2–3-person active crew, 26 guests

Use: chartered ship

In the hold of the former freighter there are now cabins and a recreation room for the guests, who are allowed to help with the operation of the ship. The ship can be chartered for day or vacation-long cruises.

Amazone

Previous name: *Meyert Menno*

Type: 2-masted fore-and-aft schooner, steel

Nation: the Netherlands

Owner: L. N. Baars & Company

Home port: Enkhuizen

Year of construction: 1963; launched March 1, 1963

Shipyard: Laan & Kooy te Den Oever, Holland

Tonnage: 160 ts displacement; 132 tons gross; 63 tons net

Dimensions:
Length overall: 41.95 m
Length of hull: 35.04 m
Length between perpendiculars: 28.62 m
Width: 6.70 m
Depth to deck: 3.65 m
Draft: 2.74 m

Sail area: 440 square meters

Rigging: 5 sails

Masts: height of mainmast over the deck: 29.80 meters

Auxiliary engine: General Motors diesel, 250 horsepower

Crew: 2-person active crew, 24 guests

Use: chartered ship

Originally built as a fishing vessel, the ship's areas of activity are today the North and Baltic seas. The interior is luxurious. All ten cabins have central heating. Her splendid lines make the ship fast and safe.

Amsterdam

Type: East India trader, fully rigged, reproduction, wood

Nation: the Netherlands

Owner: N. V. Oostindiëvaarder

Home port: Amsterdam

Location: Oosterdock, at the maritime museum

Years of construction: 1985–89; launched October 27, 1989

Shipyard: Sonderhelling, Salt Harbor, Amsterdam

Tonnage: 1200 ts displacement

Dimensions:
Length between perpendiculars: 42.45 m
Width: 11.82 m
Depth to deck: 7.55 m
Depth in hold: 5.30 m
Draft: 4.50 m

Sail area: 1940 square meters

Rigging: 21 sails

Masts: height of mainmast over the deck: 48.45 meters

Crew: in 1750: 203 sailors, 127 soldiers; today: 70 role players, exchanging 12 roles

Use: museum ship, exhibit ship

Ships in the East India trade were the backbone of the Dutch merchant marine (V.O.C., Verenigde Oost-Indische Compagnie) in the seventeenth and eighteenth centuries. They were for the most part heavily armed and could carry a large cargo. In the course of these centuries, V.O.C. ships made approximately 4800 voyages from the Netherlands to Asia. Only about a hundred ships were lost in the process. Thus, the loss of the *Amsterdam* was an exception.

The ship was built in around 1745 in Amsterdam. (It took about a year and a half to build an East Indian trading vessel of this size.) Her first voyage to Asia sealed her fate. The voyage began in October 1748. Together with five other ships, she entered the Channel. Following a heavy storm and after running aground, the *Amsterdam* lost her rudder and sought refuge in a bay near Hastings. Within a few days forty seamen had died of an epidemic. The captain tried to land the ship on a beach. This attempt failed. The *Amsterdam* sank quickly. The remaining members of the crew were able to save themselves. Only the currency, about 300,000 silver guldens, could be retrieved. The entire cargo was lost.

When the water level is particularly low, the hull is still visible near Hastings. Attempts at raising the ship have remained unsuccessful.

A powerful lion's head adorns the cutwater of the current replica, and Mercury and Neptune flank the richly ornamented stern transom. Actors demonstrate what life was like at that time aboard this kind of ship.

Antigua

Type: barkentine, steel	Width: 7.30 m
	Draft: 3.30 m
Nation: the Netherlands	
	Sail area: 750 square meters
Owner: Antigua Shipping Company c/o Laboe Sail Tourism	Rigging: 12 sails
	Auxiliary engine: 380-horsepower diesel engine
Home port: Franeker	
Year of construction: 1956	Crew: 4-person active crew, 32–85 guests
Dimensions: Length overall: 48.00 m	Use: chartered ship

The *Antigua* was built as a motorized fishing vessel. Her conversion into a barkentine with comfortable accommodations took place form 1993 to 1995.

Aphrodite

This brig is exclusively a sailing ship. She has the classic and traditional rig of a square-rigged 2-masted ship. Admittedly, the interior is more like a first-class hotel. The whole idea for the reproduction came from the owner himself. The result was the *Aphrodite*, as beautiful as her namesake. The main areas in which she sails are the Ijsselmeer and the Wadden Sea. All eight of the double cabins have central heating as well as heated floors in the showers. Optimal nautical instrumentation is naturally a given.

Type: brig, steel

Nation: the Netherlands

Owner: Captain Aent Kingman (Zeilvloot Lemmer-Stavoren)

Home port: Stavoren

Year of construction: 1994; launched December 13, 1993

Shipyard: J. M. de Vries, Lemmer

Tonnage: 150 ts displacement; 94 tons gross

Dimensions:
Length overall: 31.00 m
Length of hull: 25.00 m
Length between perpendiculars: 21.55 m
Width: 6.60 m

Depth in hold: 2.89 m
Draft: 1.90 m

Sail area: 383 square meters

Rigging: 19 sails; both masts in addition to lower sail, double topsail, and double topgallant

Masts: height of mainmast over the deck: 23 meters; both masts with 2 topmasts

Auxiliary engine: Iveco diesel, 360 horsepower

Crew: 4–6-person active crew, 16–40 passengers

Use: chartered ship

Artemis

Type: bark, steel

Nation: the Netherlands

Owner: Gebr. Bruinsma, Easterlittens (Frisian Sailing Company BV, Lemmer)

Home port: Franeker

Year of construction: 1926 (christened as a bark April 20, 2001)

Dimensions:
Length overall: 60.00 m
Width: 7.01 m
Draft: 3.50 m

Sail area: 1050 square meters

Rigging: 18 sails

Auxiliary engine: 550-horsepower bowsprit rudder, 2 generators, 40 kilowatts each

Crew: unknown, 35 guests, 120 people on day cruises

Use: charter and cruise ship, hotel ship

Equipped as a whaling vessel, the ship was engaged in whaling until the end of the 1940s. Her sailing and whaling area included, in the first instance, the Arctic and Antarctic oceans as well as Spitzbergen and the Bering Sea. A steam engine and 2 auxiliary masts assisted in these activities. Her home port was Oslo. In the 1950s the *Artemis* was converted into a freighter. She sailed primarily as a tramp vessel. Her home port was Marstal (Denmark).

From the end of the 1990s until 2001 her conversion into a bark took place, and she was luxuriously equipped for chartered voyages and cruises.

Astrid

Previous name: *Wuta*

Type: brig, iron

Nation: the Netherlands

Owner: Tallship Astrid B. V., Harlingen

Home port: Harlingen

Year of construction: 1918; commissioned 1921

Shipyard: Greg van Leeuwin, Sheveningen, Holland

Tonnage: 271 ts displacement; 170 tons gross; 120 tons net

Dimensions:
Length overall: 42.00 m
Length of hull: 32.90 m

Length between perpendiculars: 30.80 m
Width: 6.70 m
Depth in hold: 2.40 m
Depth to deck: 3.30 m
Draft: 2.50 m

Sail area: 488 square meters

Rigging: 17 sails; double topsails, double topgallants

Masts: height of mainmast over the deck: 23 meters

Auxiliary engine: Scania diesel, 290 horsepower

Crew: 9-person active crew, 25 trainees

Use: sailing school-ship

The ship was built as a freight lugger with a schooner rig. Characteristic of this type of vessel, built in Holland, is the almost vertical stern. The first name, *Wuta,* meant "Patience, wait for better days." For 17 years the *Wuta* sailed under the Dutch flag in the freight trade. In 1937 the Swede John Jeppson purchased the ship and gave her the name *Astrid.*

The chief cargoes were wheat, barley, and rapeseed for Scandinavia; during the war, also coal and wood between Poland and Sweden. In 1957 the ship was unrigged and continued to sail as a coasting vessel. In 1976 she was sold to a buyer in Lebanon. After serious fire damage that the ship sustained in a canal in July 1977, she was supposed to be scrapped. The *Astrid* was towed to Newhaven and re-

mained there for several years without being cared for.

In 1984 the newly founded *Astrid* Trust started to restore the ship and retackle her as a brig. The iron hull had remained in exceptional condition. Eighty tons of ballast (railroad rails) give the ship the necessary stability. From autumn through spring, the *Astrid* made school trips for young people to the United

States. The rest of the year she was used as a chartered ship.

Since 1998 the brig has belonged to her current owner. The entire rig had to be overhauled for her present use as a school-ship. A number of yards were also replaced. Today the ship is in excellent condition.

Atlantis

Type: 2-masted fore-and-aft schooner, steel

Nation: the Netherlands

Owner: R. J. de Waard (de Zeilvaart Enkhuizen)

Home port: Groningen

Year of construction: 1913

Shipyard: J. J. Pattje, Waterhuizen, the Netherlands

Tonnage: 137 tons gross; 93 tons net

Dimensions:
Length overall: 38.50 m

Length of hull: 31.00 m
Length between perpendiculars: 26.90 m
Width: 6.66 m
Draft: 2.50 m

Sail area: 421 square meters

Rigging: 7 sails

Masts: height of mainmast over the deck: 26 meters

Auxiliary engine: Detroit VF 71, 318 horsepower

Crew: 2–3-person active crew, 22 guests in berths

Use: chartered ship

The former freighter today sails primarily in the Baltic Sea and in the Canary Islands.

Atlantis

Previous name:
Bürgermeister Bartels

Type: barkentine, steel

Nation: the Netherlands

Owner: Rederij Atlantis, Hoorn

Home port: Hoorn

Year of construction: 1985 (except the hull); launched 1905 as the *Bürgermeister Bartels*

Shipyard: J. N. H. Wichhorst, Hamburg; shipyard where modified: Ship Repair Yard, Szczecin (Poland)

Tonnage: 299.1 tons gross; 191.7 tons net

Dimensions:
Length overall: 57.00 m
Length of hull: 49.70 m

Length between perpendiculars: 43.40 m
Width: 7.40 m
Draft: 4.70 m

Sail area: 742 square meters

Rigging: 15 sails; 4 foresails; foremast: foresail, double top sail, single topgallant

Masts: height of mainmast over the waterline: 33 meters

Auxiliary engine: two Mercedes diesel engines, 135 kilowatts each

Crew: 15 people, 70 guests (not staying overnight)

Use: passenger sailing ship

After the former light-ship was retired from active duty, the fire department used her for fire-extinguishing exercises.

Thanks to her elegant and stable hull, she was converted into a square-rigged ship. The restoration and modification work was carried out between 1984 and 1985 at the Scheel & Joehnk shipyard in Hamburg and in Stettin.

Seventeen two-bed external cabins are available to guests. The lodgings resemble a hotel: wide double beds, television set, refrigertor, shower, and toilet.

The *Atlantis* sails with passengers all over the world.

Batavia

Type: East India trader, seventeenth century, full-rigging, reproduction, wood

Nation: the Netherlands

Owner: Stichting Nederland bouwt V.O.C. retourschip

Home port: Lelystad, the Netherlands

Years of construction: 1985–95; keel laid October 4, 1985; launched April 7, 1995

Shipyard: Batavia shipyard, Lelystad

Tonnage: 1200 ts displacement; 600 tons gross

Dimensions:
Length overall: 56.60 m
Length between perpendiculars: 45.28 m
Width: 10.50 m
Depth to deck: 5.09 m
Draft: 5.10 m

Sail area: 1190 square meters

Rigging: 10 sails

Masts: height of mainmast over the keel: 53 meters; bowsprit with bowsprit topmast and bowsprit top yard

Auxiliary engine: none

Use: sailing museum ship, sailing ambassador

The original *Batavia* was built in 1628 in Amsterdam. The heavily armed trading vessel of the Verenigden Oost-Indischen Compagnie (V.O.C.) was lost on her first voyage. She ran into a reef in 1629 on the Australian coast. The Dutch master shipbuilder Willem Vos made it his goal to rebuild this ship in a manner true to the original in remembrance of the golden age of Dutch shipbuilding. This reproduction is the most ambitious of its kind in our age. From the construction materials to the technical equipment, everything is correct. The state supported the project and financed the training of unemployed young people, who today are in demand as skilled workers. During the 10-year period of construction 1.7 million people visited the shipyard. Their entrance fees contributed significantly to the financing of the project. The crowning feature of the ornamentation is the red Dutch lion on the cutwater and especially the artfully formed transom and the sides of the ship's stern. On April 7, 1995, Queen Beatrix performed the christening.

Since 1994 an additional reproduction has been under way at the same shipyard. This is the flagship of the famous Dutch admiral Michiel Adriaansz de Ruyter, of the *Zeven Provincien* ("seven provinces").

On the occasion of the Olympic Games that took place in the year 2000 in Sydney, the powerful *Batavia* was brought to Sydney for a visit aboard an even more powerful transport vessel.

Bisshop van Arkel

The ship was built in Holland at German expense. In 1910 the sale to Jakob Noldt of Hohenhort took place. Since 1943, the schooner has sailed with an engine. In 1945 the Fa. Junge in Rellingen took over ownership of the ship. From 1953 to 1963 she was registered under the name *Antje Adelheit* on the island of Amrum, from 1963 to 1977 under the same name in Husum. In 1977 she was finally sold to a buyer in Enkuizen.

Previous names: *Adelheit van Enkhuizen, Antje Adelheit, Adelheit*	Home port: Vlieland, Makkum	Dimensions: Length overall: 33.00 m Length of hull: 26.00 m	Masts: height of mainmast over the deck: 24 meters
Type: 2-masted topsail schooner, steel	Year of construction: 1900	Length between perpendiculars: 23.00 m Width: 5.50 m	Auxiliary engine: Volvo Penta TD 100, 200 horsepower
Nation: the Netherlands	Shipyard: J. J. Pattje & Zoon, Waterhuizen	Depth in hold: 2.50 m Draft: 2.00 m	Crew: 2-person active crew, 16 guests or 16 trainees
Owner: Erik Querngester, Harlingen	Tonnage: 66 tons gross; 21 tons net	Sail area: 700 square meters	Use: chartered ship and sailing school-ship
		Rigging: 13 sails	

Bonaire

Previous names: *Abel Tasman, Bonaire*

Type: former barkentine with steam engine, iron

Nation: the Netherlands

Home port: Den Helder

Year of construction: 1876

Shipyard: Nederlandse Stoombootmaatschappij Fijenoord

Tonnage: 824 ts displacement

Dimensions:
Length overall: 53.60 m
Width: 9.00 m
Draft: 3.55 m

Sail area: 746 square meters

Auxiliary engine: steam engine

Use: museum ship
(after restoration)

The *Bonaire* is the oldest surviving Dutch naval ship. During her period of active service she cruised primarily in the waters off Surinam and the Dutch Antilles. The iron hull received a second layer of teakwood planks above the waterline, and below the waterline a layer of zinc plates. It was possible to retract the smokestack like a telescope and to raise the propeller while the ship was sailing purely under wind power. Her period as a naval vessel came to an end in 1902, and she became a barracks ship in Hellevoetsluis for members of the torpedo service. In 1923 the ship left the navy. As a hulk with the new name *Abel Tasman*, she became a dormitory ship for the merchant marine school at Delfzijl. In 1995 she was towed to Den Helder to receive restoration work.

Brabander

Type: 2-masted topsail schooner, iron

Nation: the Netherlands

Owner: Fred & Nell Franssen, Drimmelen

Home port: Drimmelen

Year of construction: 1977; launched April 7, 1977

Shipyard: rigged 1980 at Spencer's Dockyard, Isle of Wight

Dimensions:
Length overall: 36.00 m
Length of hull: 23.11 m
Length between perpendiculars: 22.00 m

Width: 6.06 m
Depth in hold: 4.04 m
Draft: 3.00 m

Sail area: 540 square meters

Rigging: 11 sails; foremast: square foresail, top-, topgallants

Masts: height of mainmast over the deck: 28 meters; both masts with 1 topmast, wood

Auxiliary engine: two Deutz diesel engines, 101 horsepower each

Crew: 5-person active crew, 12 guests

Use: private ship for guests

The elegant hull with its sharp bow lines is decorated with a streak. The stern has a nearly flat transom. Paying guests are taken aboard primarily for the purpose of lowering the maintenance costs.

Brandaris

The schooner sailed the coastal waters of Western Europe as a freighter until the 1940s. Subsequently she served as the mother ship of a Berlin sailing club. Since 1986 the *Brandaris* has sailed with her current rig. A high weather rail provides the guests with safety even when the sea is rough.

Previous names: *Hoop op Zegen, Deltana*

Type: 3-masted fore-and-aft schooner

Nation: the Netherlands

Owner: E. A. Jansen

Home port: Elburg

Year of construction: 1905

Shipyard: Niestern Sander, Delfzijl

Tonnage: 91 tons gross; 53 tons net

Dimensions:
Length overall: 45.00 m
Length of hull: 33.00 m
Length between perpendiculars: 27.50 m
Width: 6.00 m
Depth in hold: 1.90 m
Depth to deck: 1.40 m
Draft: 2.10 m

Sail area: 500 square meters

Rigging: 13 sails

Masts: height of mainmast over the deck: 26 meters

Auxiliary engine: DAF diesel, 220 horsepower

Crew: 2–3-person active crew, 26 guests, 40 guests on day cruises

Use: chartered ship

Catherina

The schooner was built for the German navy in 1920 as a sailing mine sweeper with wooden planking on a steel frame. Her first name is not recorded. In 1955 the ship was lengthened in Belgium, and her wooden outer surface was replaced with steel. Until 1982 the ship served as a fishing vessel. Starting in 1985 she was employed as a passenger vessel with the name *Vlieland* under the Dutch flag. In 1996 the current owners acquired the schooner and gave her the name *Catherina*. The two large deckhouses are a distinguishing characteristic of the ship. The port of departure for her voyages in the Baltic and North seas is Kiel-Holtenau.

Previous names: *Vlieland, Kamina*

Type: 2-masted fore-and-aft schooner, steel

Nation: the Netherlands

Owner: V. O. F. Europe Sailing, The Hague

Home port: Rotterdam

Year of construction: 1920

Shipyard: German naval shipyard

Tonnage: 145 ts displacement; 97 tons gross; 20 tons net

Dimensions:
Length overall: 39.50 m
Length of hull: 31.00 m
Length between perpendiculars: 25.53 m
Width: 6.24 m
Depth in hold: 3.10 m
Draft: 2.85 m

Sail area: 440 square meters

Rigging: 8 sails

Masts: height of mainmast over the deck: 26.50 meters

Auxiliary engine: DAF-diesel, 220 horsepower

Crew: 2-person active crew, 23 guests

Use: chartered ship

De Liefde

Previous names: *Thalatta*

Type: 3-masted topsail schooner, steel

Nation: the Netherlands

Owner: Quo Vadis Vof

Home port: Kampen

Year of construction: 1916; modified 2000

Shipyard: SRF—Harlingen (modification)

Tonnage: 260 tons gross; 220 tons net

Dimensions:
Length overall: 50.10 m
Length of hull: 42.00 m
Length between perpendiculars: 38.00 m
Width: 7.00 m
Depth in hold: 3.00 m
Draft: 2.50 m

Sail area: 720 square meters

Rigging: 9 sails

Masts: height of mainmast over the deck: 29.50 meters

Auxiliary engine: Mitsubishi, 520 horsepower

Crew: 6-person active crew, 60 day guests, 24 overnight guests

Use: one- or multiple-day chartered cruises on the Ijsselmeer and Wadden Sea

The current topsail schooner was originally a Baltic trading vessel. Under the name *Thalatta* she transported her cargo between various ports all over the Baltic beginning in 1916. At the end of the 1980s the ship was removed from freight service and transferred to the Netherlands. There was no longer any use for the schooner with her powerful lines. A new owner was finally found in 1998. By 2000 she had been transformed into a sailing hotel ship with every conceivable comfort.

The Eendracht II replaced the *Eendracht* (*I*), which with the new name *Johann Smidt* now belongs to the association CLIPPER—German Youth Works at Sea. The ship can be expanded into a topsail schooner by adding a yard to the foremast.

The ship is supposed to provide everyone with the opportunity to sail. Young people in particular can spend their vacations aboard the ship. The

Type: 3-masted fore-and-aft schooner, steel

Nation: the Netherlands

Owner: Stichting Het Zeilende Zeeschip

Home port: Scheveningen

Year of construction: 1989; launched May 1989

Shipyard: Damen Shipyards, Gorinchem, the Netherlands

Tonnage: 470 ts displacement; 608 tons gross; 181 tons net

Dimensions:
Length overall: 59.40 m
Length of hull: 55.00 m
Length between perpendiculars: 41.90 m
Width: 12.30 m
Depth to deck: 5.80 m
Draft: 5.00 m

Sail area: 1047 square meters

Rigging: 9 sails; mizzenmast: Bermuda sails

Masts: height of mainmast over the deck: 38.70 meters

Auxiliary engine: Caterpillar diesel, 550 horsepower (403 kilowatts)

Crew: 13-person active crew, 40 trainees

Use: school and chartered ship

most modern nautical equipment and exceptional underwater lines make the ship a fast and safe sailing vessel.

The *Eendracht* is a typical de Vries Lentsch yacht: rated, with a strong sheer line and large deckhouses. The bridge with the enclosed wheelhouse is similar to that of a motorized ship, while the sailing bridge behind it is raised so that the person at the helm can see over the wheelhouse. The entire between deck is occupied by the living and sanitary facilities of the crew and trainees.

A strong storm on October 21, 1998, caused the *Eendracht* to run aground on a beach on the coast of Sussex. Rescue helicopters saved the guests and crew. In a difficult operation, a tug succeeded in freeing the ship and bringing her to the harbor in Dover. The damage to the hull was limited.

Elegant

Type: 2-masted fore-and-aft schooner, steel

Nation: the Netherlands

Owner: Gotze van der Velde

Home port: Lemmer

Year of construction: 1989

Shipyard: Duivendykle Lekkerkerk

Tonnage: 200 ts displacement; 126 tons gross; 76 tons net

Dimensions:
Length overall: 37.80 m
Length between perpendiculars: 33.40 m
Width: 6.25 m
Depth in hold: 2.01 m
Draft: 1.65 m

Sail area: 440 square meters

Rigging: 4 sails

Masts: height of mainmast over the deck: 23.50 meters

Auxiliary engine: DAF diesel, 155 kilowatts

Crew: 2-person active crew, 30 guests, 50 guests on day cruises

Use: chartered ship

The luxuriously constructed, flat-bottomed 2-masted schooner with leeboards lives up to her name with her elegant appearance. The ship was specially designed to be sailed in the Baltic and on the Wadden Sea and Ijsselmeer. Kiel is often her port of departure.

Elisabeth Smit

Previous name: *Z. S. Marken*

Type: barkentine, wood

Nation: The Netherlands

Owner: Smit Tall Ship B. V.

Home port: Amsterdam

Year of construction: 1938

Shipyard: McKinsey

Tonnage: 240 ts displacement

Dimensions:
Length overall: 52.00 m
Length of hull: 35.00 m
Length between perpendiculars: 7.50 m
Width: 6.00 m
Draft: 3.00 m

Sail area: 1025 square meters

Rigging: 13 sails; foremast: double topsail, single topgallant

Masts: height of mainmast over the deck: 31 meters

Auxiliary engine: Dormann 560-horsepower diesel engine

Crew: 4-person active crew, 75 guests

Use: party ship

The sailing ship was built in Scotland as a freighter and fishing vessel. In World War II she served the British navy as a mine sweeper and in the North Sea. After the war she served the Dutch navy in the same capacity in the east branch of the Schelde. In 1981 she was converted into a party ship. The barkentine is the Netherlands' largest wooden sailing ship.

Elizabeth

Type: 3-masted fore- and aft-schooner ("clipper"), steel

Nation: the Netherlands

Owner: Jan Bruinsma (Zeilrederij Friesland)

Home port: Lemmer

Year of construction: 1914; launched April 30, 1914

Shipyard: De Boer, Rode Vaart

Tonnage: 225 ts displacement

Dimensions:
Length overall: 51.50 m
Length of hull: 39.90 m
Length between perpendiculars: 36.50 m
Width: 6.50 m
Depth in hold: 3.10 m
Draft: 1.45 m

Sail area: 470 square meters

Rigging: 7 sails

Masts: height of mainmast over the deck: 27.50 meters

Auxiliary engine: Gardner diesel, 200 horsepower

Crew: 3-person active crew, 30 guests

Use: chartered ship

The *Elizabeth* was built as a 2-masted schooner with a flat bottom and leeboards for the freight trade in shallow waters and also in rivers. She received an auxiliary engine in the 1930s in order to keep up with the competition. In 1960 a larger engine was installed. The ship was then employed as a purely motorized freighter without masts until 1990. Under the current owner an extensive conversion into a 3-masted passenger ship with the appropriate luxury accommodations followed. Her main area of activity is the Ijsselmeer.

Europa

From 1911 to 1914 the *Senator Brockes* was moored as a lightship at Position 4 in the Elbe. From 1916 until 1918 she was a pilot station, and then from 1918 to 1936 she once again did service as *Lightship Elbe 3*. After October 1942 the ship was under the command of the navy in the Baltic.

In July 1945 she was returned once again to the Maritime Office in Hamburg. Until her retirement in 1974 she was employed as reserve lightship *Elbe 2* and *Elbe 3*.

After another period of unmanned use in the German Bay, the current owner acquired the ship in 1987. After seven years of conversion work, during which the ship was rigged as a bark, the *Europa*, as she was now called, was able to undertake her first voyage in 1993. The studding sails, which can be set in an aft wind, are unusual and extremely rare. A voluptuous figure of a woman adorns the bow as a figurehead.

Previous name: *FS Senator Brockes*

Type: bark, iron

Nation: the Netherlands

Owner: Harry Smit (Stichting het vaarend Museumschip)

Home port: Amsterdam

Years of construction: 1910–11

Shipyard: H. C. Stülcken & Son, Hamburg

Dimensions:
Length overall: 55.10 m
Length between perpendiculars: 45.40 m
Width: 7.50 m
Depth in hold: 5.10 m
Draft: 4.00 m

Sail area: 1020 square meters

Rigging: 22 sails; in addition 4 studding sails; fore-, mainmast: double topsail, double topgallant

Masts: height of mainmast over the deck: 36 meters

Auxiliary engine: Caterpillar diesel engines, 460 horsepower each

Crew: 14-person active crew (maximum), 50 trainees or 50 guests

Use: sailing school-ship

Fleurtje

Previous names: *Argonaftis, Carita*

Type: 3-masted staysail schooner, steel

Nation: the Netherlands

Year of construction: 1959; launched April 1959

Shipyard: Amsterdamsche Scheepswerf, G. de Vries Lentsch Jr., Amsterdam

Tonnage: 485 ts displacement; 336.18 tons gross; 154.42 tons net

Dimensions:
Length overall: 51.90 m
Length between perpendiculars: 36.90 m
Width: 8.50 m

Depth to deck: 6.00 m
Depth in hold: 4.60 m
Draft: 4.70 m

Sail area: 870 square meters (mainsail 230 square meters)

Rigging: 7 sails; 2 (3) foresails; foremast: foresail (jib-headed sail); mainmast: main staysail, mainsail (jib-headed sail); mizzenmast: mizzen sail (jib-headed sail)

Masts, spars: Height of mainmast over the waterline: 40.20 meters; fore-staysail and main staysail with boom; no bowsprit

Auxiliary engine: two Davey-Paxman diesel motors, 597 horsepower each

Crew: 14 people

Use: private yacht

Frisius van Adel

The original freighter with a flat bottom and leeboards was modified in 1971 and equipped to undertake day tours. The main areas in which she sails are the Ijsselmeer, the Wadden Sea, and the interior lakes.

The name *Frisius van Adel* comes from the centuries-old history of the Frisians, which began shortly after Christ's birth. Adel was Friso's oldest son. Adel became famous by holding festive banquets.

Type: 3-masted fore-and-aft schooner, steel

Nation: the Netherlands

Owner: Jappie Bandstra, Stavoren (Zeilvloot Lemmer-Stavoren)

Home port: Stavoren

Year of construction: 1906

Tonnage: 300 tons gross

Dimensions:
Length overall: 46.80 m
Length of hull: 38.80 m
Length between perpendiculars: 37.60 m
Width: 6.10 m
Depth in hold: 2.10 m
Depth to deck: 1.90 m
Draft: 1.40 m

Sail area: 485 square meters

Rigging: 9 sails

Masts: height of mainmast over the deck: 29.50 meters

Auxiliary engine: Scania diesel engine, 165 horsepower

Crew: 3-person active crew, 75 day guests

Use: chartered ship for day cruises

Grootvorst

Previous names: *Cornelia, Pieternella, Leentje, Onderneming*

Type: 3-masted fore-and-aft schooner, steel

Nation: the Netherlands

Owner: C. W. Velthuys

Home port: Enkhuizen

Year of construction: 1895; launched March 15, 1895

Shipyard: Bodewes, Martenshoek, Groningen

Tonnage: 160 ts displacement; 40 tons net

Dimensions:
Length overall: 46.00 m
Length of hull: 40.00 m

Length between perpendiculars: 37.50 m
Width: 1.30 m
Depth in hold: 1.30 m
Depth to deck: 2.10 m
Draft: 1.35 m
With sideboard: 5.00 m

Sail area: 500 square meters

Rigging: 10 sails

Masts: height of mainmast over the waterline: 29.80 meters

Auxiliary engine: General Motors diesel engine (8V7), 250 horsepower

Crew: 2–3-person active crew, 29 guests

Use: chartered ship

The Ijsselmeer, the Wadden Sea, and the lakes of the Netherlands are the main areas sailed by this large ship with a flat bottom and leeboards. This type of schooner was also referred to as a clipper in the Netherlands. The *Grootvorst* began her career as an engineless 2-masted freighter until, following multiple changes of ownership, she was acquired by her current owner in 1985 and modified and equipped for upscale chartered cruises.

Hendrika Bartelds

The ship was built in 1917 as the fish lugger *Johan Last.* Several changes of ownership occurred over the years. After her retirement from service as a trading ship the vessel was converted into a 3-masted schooner and fitted with comfortable accommodations for charter service. In May 1989 the schooner received her current name, *Hendrika Bartels,* and entered her new line of work.

Previous names: *Elise, Dolfyn, Johan Last*

Type: 3-masted fore-and-aft schooner

Nation: the Netherlands

Owner: Frank and Wieke Flaun, Amsterdam

Home port: Amsterdam

Year of construction: 1917

Shipyard: in Leeuwarden

Tonnage: 167 tons gross; 87 tons net

Dimensions:
Length overall: 49.00 m
Length of hull: 36.40 m
Width: 6.60 m
Depth in hold: 2.80 m
Depth to deck: 3.30 m
Draft: 3.00 m

Sail area: 643 square meters

Rigging: 13 sails

Masts: height of mainmast over the deck: 30.20 meters

Auxiliary engine: Caterpillar diesel, 385 horsepower

Crew: 3-person active crew, 70 guests on day cruises

Use: chartered ship

Hoop doet Leven

Previous names: *Jaweg, Herzogin Ilse Irene*

Type: fore-and-aft ketch, iron

Nation: the Netherlands

Owner: A. Valk, Groningen

Home port: Groningen

Year of construction: 1892

Shipyard: Wed Duivendijk, Papendrecht

Tonnage: 276 ts displacement; 158 tons gross; 97 tons net

Dimensions:
Length overall: 33.00 m
Length of hull: 27.90 m
Width: 5.80 m
Draft: 1.30 m

Sail area: 450 square meters

Rigging: 8 sails

Masts: height of mainmast over the deck: 21.50 meters

Auxiliary engine: DAF diesel, 165 horsepower

Crew: 2-person active crew, 24 guests

Use: chartered ship

The *Hoop doet Leven* ("Hope Gives Life"), a flat-bottomed clipper with leeboards, transported primarily coal and gravel in her early years. Since 1982 she has been employed in the charter service. The Ijsselmeer, the Wadden Sea, and the interior lakes are her main areas of activity.

Horizon

The *Horizon* was one of the first Dutch freighters to be converted and equipped for passenger service. The work began in the 1950s. Her main areas of activity are the Ijsselmeer, the Wadden Sea, and the interior lakes of the Netherlands.

Type: 2-masted tjalk

Nation: the Netherlands

Owner: Wim Patist

Dimensions:
Length overall: 21.78 m
Width: 5.12 m
Draft: 1.00 m

Crew: 2-person active crew, 14 passengers

Use: chartered ship

Ide Min

Previous name: *Stanislaw*

Type: 2-masted fore-and-aft schooner, steel

Nation: the Netherlands

Owner: Thomas R. de Nijs, Paul M. de Jong

Home port: Amsterdam

Year of construction: 1957

Shipyard: VEB Shipyard Edgar André, Magdeburg

Tonnage: 160 ts displacement; 105 tons gross; 58 tons net

Dimensions:
Length overall: 39.60 m
Length of hull: 30.00 m
Length between perpendiculars: 24.80 m
Width: 6.98 m
Depth in hold: 2.60 m
Depth to deck: 3.00 m
Draft: 2.40 m

Sail area: 564 square meters

Rigging: 8 sails

Masts: height of mainmast over the deck: 31.50 meters

Auxiliary engine: DAF diesel, 6 cylinder, 260 horsepower

Crew: 3-person active crew, 26 guests or trainees

Use: chartered ship

The elegant lines of the modern schooner would hardly lead one to believe that the ship was originally built as a purely motorized tug. Until 1990 she was employed as a harbor tug in a fleet of tugboats in Danzig. Now under the Dutch flag, her conversion into a schooner began in 1991. All of the steel work was carried out at a small shipyard in Danzig; the technology, interior, and rigging were added in Harlingen. The ship, which is maintained in keeping with tradition, has proven to be very fast.

Jacob Meindert

Previous name: *Oldeoog*

Type: 2-masted topsail schooner, steel

Nation: the Netherlands

Owner: Willem F. Sligting

Home port: Makkum (summer location: Kiel)

Year of construction: 1952

Shipyard: Jade Shipyard Wilhelmshaven; modified 1989–1990, Stocnia Wiswa, Gdansk

Tonnage: 96 tons gross; 29 tons net

Dimensions:
Length overall: 36.50 m
Length of hull: 29.00 m
Length between perpendiculars: 26.50 m
Width: 7.30 m
Depth to deck: 2.50 m
Draft: 2.40 m

Sail area: 630 square meters

Rigging: 8 sails

Masts: height of mainmast over the deck: 28.30 meters

Auxiliary engine: DAF 1160 turbo diesel, 260 horsepower

Crew: 2-person active crew; guests: 27 on multiple-day cruises, 42 day guests

Use: chartered ship, passenger sailing ship

The ship was built as a motorized tug. Because of her good waterlines, the hull was well suited to be rigged as a schooner. The elegant lines and the rake of the masts are highly reminiscent of the famous American Baltimore clippers.

The *Jacob Meindert* is a very fast sailing ship. Beneath the deck the accommodations meet the most modern standards with regard to safety and comfort.

Jantje

Previous names: *Zwarte Rat, Johanna Maria, Ennie & Appie*

Type: 2-masted topsail schooner, steel

Nation: the Netherlands

Owner: H. Müter, Ijmuiden

Home port: Ijmuiden

Year of construction: 1929

Shipyard: Van Goor, Monnickendam

Tonnage: 96 ts displacement; 54 tons gross; 16 tons net

Dimensions:
Length overall: 28.00 m
Length of hull: 20.00 m
Length between perpendiculars: 16.50 m
Width: 5.90 m
Depth in hold: 2.40 m
Depth to deck: 3.10 m
Draft: 2.40 m

Sail area: 380 square meters

Rigging: 12 sails, square foresail

Masts: height of mainmast over the deck: 21 meters

Auxiliary engine: Scania D 11, 180 horsepower

Use: sailing school-ship, chartered ship

Previous name: *Dierkow*

Type: 2-masted topsail schooner, steel

Nation: the Netherlands

Owner: Anna and Jaap van der Rest

Home port: Amsterdam

Year of construction: 1964 (converted into a sailing ship 1996–98)

Shipyard: VEB Shipyard "Edgar Andre," Magedburg

Tonnage: 138 tons gross

Dimensions:
Length overall: 41.70 m
Length of hull: 26.00 m
Width: 7.80 m
Draft: 3.20 m

Sail area: 628 square meters

Rigging: 8 sails, 3 foresails; foremast: topsail and topgallant

Masts: height of mainmast over the deck: 32.50 meters

Auxiliary engine: Caterpillar diesel, 365 horsepower

Crew: 3-person active crew, 34 guests, on day cruises 90 guests

Use: chartered ship

The current schooner was built in 1964 in Magdeburg to be used for sounding, towing, and raising. The ship was employed in Rostock by the Dredging, Towing, and Raising Shipping Company, Inc. She was subsequently sold to the Netherlands. The current owners found the ship at a junkyard after she had been marked to be scrapped, and they acquired her on December 29, 1995.

In the autumn of 1996 the entire hull was removed from the water and with a heavy transporter hauled to an unused hall at a shipyard in Amsterdam. Within two years she had been converted and equipped as a schooner for the charter service. Characteristic, and already recognizable from a distance, is the almost tublike sheer line of the deck.

The ship was named after the British writer John Ronald Reuel Tolkien (1892–1973), who became famous primarily for his book *The Lord of the Rings*.

Koh-I-Noor

Previous name: *Petrus*

Type: 2-masted topsail schooner

Nation: the Netherlands

Owner: Jan Duinmeijer

Home port: Harlingen

Year of construction: 1909

Shipyard: Johannes Thormähler & Company, Elmshorn

Tonnage: approx. 140 ts displacement; 113 tons gross; 59 tons net

Dimensions:
Length overall: 37.00 m
Length of hull: 27.00 m
Length between perpendiculars: 24.80 m
Width: 6.90 m
Depth in hold: 1.90 m
Draft: 2.45 m

Sail area: 540 square meters

Rigging: 10 sails; foremast: fore topsail, fore topgallant

Masts: height of mainmast over the deck: 28 meters

Auxiliary engine: Mercedes diesel, 320 horsepower

Crew: 2-person active crew, 4 trainees, 20 guests, 38 guests on day cruises

Use: chartered ship

The former coastal sailing ship *Petrus* (originally a yacht with an engine) sailed as a freighter, primarily in Scandinavian waters. Her home port was Næstved on Zealand. In 1994 the current owner purchased the ship and christened it *Koh-I-Noor* (Persian for "Mountain of Light").

Her conversion into a topsail schooner with luxurious accommodations took two years. In the process a keel was welded on in 1997 and gave the ship a deeper draft. The areas in which she sails are the Ijsselmeer and the Wadden Sea.

Linde

Previous names: *Rival, Quo Vadis*

Type: 3-masted fore-and-aft schooner, steel

Nation: the Netherlands

Owner: V. O. F. Rederij Fokkelina-Linde

Home port: Stavoren

Year of construction: 1910

Shipyard: v. d. Adel, Papendrecht

Dimensions:
Length overall: 50.00 m
Length of hull: 39.65 m

Width: 6.39 m
Depth in hold: 2.11 m
Draft: 1.40 m

Sail area: 425 square meters

Rigging: 6 sails

Masts: height of mainmast over the deck: 28 meters

Auxiliary engine: Scania diesel, 296 horsepower

Crew: 3-person active crew, 30 passengers

Use: chartered ship

Until 1990 the schooner, which has a flat bottom and leeboards, sailed under her first two names in the freight trade, initially as a 1-masted ship and later as a purely motorized vessel. In the 1960s she was lengthened by seven meters. The ship was finally converted into 3-master in 1990 and equipped for the charter service. The main areas in which she sails are the Ijsselmeer, the Wadden Sea, and the interior lakes.

Loth Loriën

The ship was built as a Norwegian fishing vessel.

Previous name: *Njord*

Type: Bermuda ketch, steel

Nation: the Netherlands

Owner: Jaap van der Rest

Home port: Amsterdam

Year of construction: 1907

Shipyard: Asselem & Karsten

Tonnage: 148 tons gross;
44 tons net

Dimensions:
Length of hull: 37.60 m
Width: 5.80 m
Draft: 2.80 m

Sail area: 450 square meters

Rigging: 5 sails

Masts: height of mainmast over the deck: 30 meters

Auxiliary engine: Deutz diesel 716, 365 horsepower

Crew: 3-person active crew, 34 trainees or 34 guests, 70 guests on day cruises

Use: chartered ship

Luciana

Previous names: *Frisiana, Sjoborrun, Kerstin, Twee Gebroeders II, Marcus Aurelius, Cornelia en Petronella, Katwijk 66, Vlaardingen 173 (VL 173)*

Type: 2-masted fore-and-aft schooner, steel

Nation: the Netherlands

Owner: V. O. F. Europe Sailing, The Hague

Home port: Rotterdam

Year of construction: 1916

Shipyard: Gebroeders Pot, Elshout, the Netherlands

Tonnage: 165 ts displacement; 111 tons gross; 55 tons net

Dimensions:
Length overall: 39.00 m
Length of hull: 29.00 m
Length between perpendiculars: 25.06 m
Width: 6.54 m
Depth in hold: 3.10 m
Draft: 2.50 m

Sail area: 485 square meters

Rigging: 9 sails, also a square foresail

Masts: height of mainmast over the deck: 25.65 meters

Auxiliary engine: KHD diesel, 150 horsepower

Crew: 3-person active crew, 22 guests

Use: chartered ship

The colorful history of the *Luciana* began in 1916 with her deployment as a sailing herring lugger with no engine. Following the installation of an auxiliary engine, she was sold to a buyer in Sweden in 1928 and until the 1970s sailed as a freighter for various owners in the waters of Scandinavia. At the end of the 1970s the ship was laid up in Göteborg.

In 1981 she was sold to a buyer in the Netherlands and used as a sailing passenger ship. Characteristic features of the schooner are her two deckhouses. The main areas in which she sails are the North Sea and the Baltic, but in the winter she also sails in the Mediterranean and the southern Atlantic.

Maartinus

Type: 2-masted staysail schooner

Nation: the Netherlands

Owner: S. P. M. Ineveld

Home port: Hoorn

Dimensions:
Length overall: 24.40 m
Width: 5.40 m
Draft: 2.30 m

Sail area: 300 square meters

Rigging: 5 sails

Crew: 2-person active crew, 12 passengers

Use: chartered ship

The ship, with her elegant lines, was built as a fishing vessel. In 1986 she was converted for the charter service. The main areas in which she sails are the Ijsselmeer, the Wadden Sea, and the Dutch interior lakes.

Mare Frisium

Previous name: *Helmut*

Type: 3-masted topsail schooner, steel

Nation: the Netherlands

Owner: the Bruinsma brothers (Traditional Sailing Charter, Lemmer)

Home port: Harlingen

Year of construction: 1916

Shipyard: in Weert, the Netherlands

Tonnage: unknown

Dimensions:
Length overall: 52.00 m
Length of hull: 40.00 m
Length at the waterline: 36.00 m
Width: 6.70 m
Draft: 2.80 m

Sail area: 634 square meters

Auxiliary engine: 18 Kva Mitsubishi and 28 Kva Perkins

Engine: Scania, 339 horsepower

Crew: size of active crew not known; 36 passengers in berths, 90 guests on day cruises

Use: chartered ship

The ship's original name is not known. She was originally built as a 1½ masted fishing lugger that was primarily employed to fish on the Dogger Bank. By the end of the 1940s this fishing was no longer profitable. The ship came to Germany with the name *Helmut*. In 1960 the hull was lengthened to its current length of 40 meters. As a freighter the *Helmut* sailed from Hamburg to Sweden and St. Petersburg. She regularly transported wood from Scandinavia to Belgium and England. She was ultimately laid up in Sweden and started to rot there.

In 1995 the current owners started work on her conversion into a 3-masted passenger ship with all available sailing licenses. On April 4, 1997, she was put into service.

Minerva

Previous name: *Uwe Ursula*

Type: 3-masted fore-and-aft schooner, steel

Nation: the Netherlands

Owner: Resto-Sail B. V., Scheveningen

Home port: Scheveningen

Year of construction: 1935

Shipyard: C. Lühring, Hammelwarden, Unterweser

Tonnage: 250 ts displacement

Dimensions:
Length overall: 50.00 m
Length of hull: 40.00 m
Length at the waterline: 37.00 m
Width: 7.10 m
Depth in hold: 2.20 m
Draft: 2.20 m

Sail area: 900 square meters

Rigging: 9 sails

Masts: height of mainmast over the deck: 33 meters

Auxiliary engine: MAK diesel, 180 horsepower

Crew: 8-person active crew, 75 guests (on day tours)

Use: chartered ship

The *Uwe Ursula* was built for Captain Johann Peter Henning of Wischhafen on the Elbe. Her home port at that time was Hamburg. The ship changed owners several times. In the middle of the 1960s her rig was removed. Until 1987 the ship was employed as a coasting vessel. In the same year she was sold to a buyer in the Netherlands and converted into a charter ship.

Mon Desir

Previous names: *Vertrouwen, Hoop, Berendina, Adriana-Johanna*

Type: fore-and-aft ketch, steel

Nation: the Netherlands

Owner: A. van der Cingel, Lemmer

Home port: Akkrum

Year of construction: 1903

Shipyard: T. v. Duyvendijk Lekkerkerk

Tonnage: 100 ts displacement; 87 tons gross; 53 tons net

Dimensions:
Length overall: 37.50 m
Length of hull: 29.65 m
Length between perpendiculars: 27.68 m
Width: 5.56 m
Depth in hold: 1.90 m
Draft: 1.20 m

Sail area: 300 square meters

Rigging: 4 sails

Masts: height of mainmast over the deck: 24 meters

Auxiliary engine: Gardner diesel 6L3B

Crew: 3-person active crew, 25 guests on day cruises

Use: chartered ship

The flat-bottomed ship with leeboards served as a freighter under her previous name. In 1987 she was converted for the charter service she provides today.

Mondrian

Type: 2-masted fore-and-aft schooner, steel

Nation: the Netherlands

Home port: Middelburg

Year of construction: modification took place in 1995

Shipyard: A en van G Jachtbouw (modification)

Dimensions:
Length overall: 44.40 m
Length of hull: 36.50 m
Length between perpendiculars: 30.25 m
Width: 6.65 m
Depth in hold: 2.25 m
Depth to deck: 3.20 m
Draft: 2.65 m

Sail area: 650 square meters

Rigging: 8 sails

Masts: height of mainmast over the deck: 34 meters

Auxiliary engine: Detroit diesel, 365 horsepower

Crew: 10-person active crew, 22 guests

Use: chartered ship

Morgana

Previous name: *De Hoop*

Type: 3-masted fore-and-aft schooner, steel

Nation: the Netherlands

Owner: Morgana Charters BV Harlingen

Home port: Harlingen

Year of construction: 1924

Shipyard: SRF Shipyard Harlingen (modification 1998–99)

Tonnage: 168 ts displacement; 116 tons gross; 62 tons net

Dimensions:
Length overall: 43.30 m
Length of hull: 35.90 m

Width: 6.40 m
Depth in hold: 2.50 m
Draft: (without leeboards): 1.30 m

Sail area: 450 square meters

Rigging: 7 sails

Masts: height of mainmast over the deck: 28.50 meters

Auxiliary engine: Scania diesel, 340 horsepower (new 1999), bow motor, 80 horsepower

Crew: 2–3-person active crew, 32 guests, 70 guests on day cruises

Use: chartered ship at the TSC Traditional Sailing Charter shipping company

The flat-bottomed ship was built as a motorized ship with auxiliary sails. Until 1997 she was in service on the Rhine and the Maas.

In 1998 she was converted into a luxuriously equipped passenger ship. Harlingen is her port of departure for voyages to the offshore islands of the Wadden Sea. Additional areas of activity are the Ijsselmeer and the Frisian seascape with its interior canals.

Nil Desperandum

Type: 3-masted fore-and-aft schooner, iron

Nation: the Netherlands

Owner: Gert van Wijk

Home port: Woubrugge

Year of construction: 1894

Shipyard: in Duyvendijk

Tonnage: 130 ts displacement

Dimensions:
Length overall: 45.00 m
Length of hull: 35.50 m
Width: 6.25 m
Depth in hold: 1.15 m
Draft: 1.15 m

Sail area: 435 square meters

Rigging: 8 sails

Masts: height of mainmast over the deck: 28 meters

Auxiliary engine: General Motors Diesel, 110 horsepower

Crew: 2-person active crew, 28 guests

Use: chartered ship

Until 1986 the flat-bottomed ship with leeboards carried cargo in Holland, Belgium, and Germany. Then she was converted into an upscale chartered ship. The Ijsselmeer, the Wadden Sea, and the interior lakes of the Netherlands are her preferred areas of activity. The ship belongs to the Zeilvloot Lemmer-Stavoren.

Noorderlicht

Previous names: *FS Kalkgrund, FS Flensburg*

Type: 2-masted fore-and-aft schooner, steel

Nation: the Netherlands

Owner: Ribro B. V.

Home port: Enkhuizen

Year of construction: 1910

Shipyard: Flensburger Ship Building Association

Tonnage: 260 ts displacement; 140 tons gross; 60 tons net

Dimensions:
Length overall: 46.50 m
Length of hull: 36.50 m
Length between perpendiculars: 30.00 m
Width: 6.50 m
Depth to deck: 4.00 m
Draft: 3.10 m

Sail area: 550 square meters

Rigging: 8 sails

Masts: height of mainmast over the deck: 30 meters

Auxiliary engine: Caterpillar diesel, 320 horsepower

Crew: 4-person active crew, 20 guests

Use: chartered ship

The ship was built as the lightship *Kalkgrund* with serial number 300. At the time the construction costs came to 184,000 marks. In 1925 she received the new name *Feuerschiff Flensburg*. In 1953–54 the ship was overhauled and modernized. On June 11, 1963, her duties as a lightship were taken over by the lighthouse "Kalkgrund." In 1963 the firm of Holm & Molzen purchased her and had her towed to the firm's pier in the harbor at Flensburg. The ship became a home for Greek workers. From 1967 to 1985 it was the clubhouse of the Möltenort sailing club. Attempts by two Dutchmen to make a sailing ship from the elegant hull failed.

It was not until 1991 that the current owner converted the ship into a 2-master. A female bust adorns the sporty bow as a figurehead. The girl has no particular significance. According to the owner, she is simply "young and beautiful."

In April 1994, the *Noorderlicht* was completed and now sails in the summer off Spitzbergen and in the winter off the Canary Islands.

Previous names: *Sylvan, Fuglen, Oosterschelde*

Type: 3-masted topsail schooner, steel

Nation: the Netherlands

Owner: BV Rederij Oosterschelde, Rotterdam

Home port: Veerhaven in Rotterdam

Year of construction: 1918

Shipyard: Appelo, Zwaartsluis

Tonnage: 226 tons gross; 93 tons net

Dimensions:
Length overall: 34.49 m

Length of hull: 40.12 m
Length between perpendiculars: 34.49 m
Width: 7.50 m
Depth in hold: 3.40 m
Depth to deck: 4.40 m
Draft: 3.00 m

Sail area: 891 square meters

Rigging: 12 sails; foremast with top and topgallant

Masts: height of mainmast over the deck: 34 meters

Auxiliary engine: Deutz 6-cylinder diesel, 360 horsepower

Crew: 6-person active crew, 24 trainees or 24 guests, 120 guests on day cruises

Use: sailing school-ship, chartered ship

The ship was built as a cargo-carrying 3-masted fore-and-aft schooner with her current name. She primarily transported clay, stones, wood, and foodstuffs such as herring and bananas. In 1930 the ship was unrigged, equipped with a powerful engine, and converted into a motorized coastal ship. In 1939 she was sold to a buyer in Denmark. With the name *Fuglen,* the ship belonged to the most modern vessels of the Danish merchant marine.

In 1954 she was sold to a buyer in Skärhamn, Sweden. After further modifications the *Sylvan,* as she was now called, sailed as a freighter in the Baltic Sea.

In 1988 Dick van Andel bought the ship in order to return the *Oosterschelde* to her former glory. Once she was restored, the sailing ship was supposed to serve as the last remaining representative of a large fleet of 3-masted topsail schooners that sailed under the Dutch flag at the beginning of this century.

The extensive modifications took place in Leeuwarden and Rotterdam. On August 21, 1992, the schooner was officially put into service by Princess Margaret.

Oostvogel

The ship, which was built as a freight schooner with a flat bottom and leeboards, sails in the passenger service today. Spacious salons and comfortable cabins are available for the guests. Her main areas of activity are the Ijsselmeer and the Wadden Sea.

The 3-masted fore-and-aft schooner *Sanne Sophia* also belongs to the Zeilvloot Hollands Glorie. Built in 1886, her dimensions are similar to those of the *Oostvogel.* Her home port is Muiden.

Previous names: *VgF Gezusters, Aldor, Karino, Christa*

Type: 3-masted fore-and-aft schooner, iron

Nation: the Netherlands

Owner: Oostvogel Charters, Rotterdam (Zeilvloot Hollands Glorie)

Home port: Rotterdam

Year of construction: 1898

Shipyard: Kalkman, Capelle A/D Yssel

Tonnage: 166.15 ts displacement; 47 tons gross

Dimensions:
Length overall: 48.00 m
Length of hull: 39.12 m
Width: 6.28 m
Depth in hold: 2.10 m
Draft: 1.40 m

Sail area: 1010 square meters

Rigging: 7 sails

Masts: height of mainmast over the deck: 29 meters

Auxiliary engine: Scania diesel, 220 horsepower

Crew: 2-person active crew, 24 guests, 75 guests on day cruises

Use: chartered ship

Pacific Swift

Previous names: *Barmines, Sansibar, Terje Viken*

Type: brigantine, steel

Nation: the Netherlands

Owner: Cees Koeman, Thredbo Village, Australia

Home port: Hoorn

Year of construction: 1904

Shipyard: in Alesund near Trondheim, Norway

Dimensions:
Length overall: 39.00 m
Length of hull: 31.00 m
Width: 5.20 m

Sail area: 600 square meters

Rigging: 12 sails

Auxiliary engine: Normo diesel, 210 horsepower

Use: private ship, chartered ship

Under her first name the schooner, which had been built as a brigantine, was active as a fishing vessel and a coastal trader under the Norwegian flag. Before the outbreak of World War I, she had been converted into a purely motorized ship with the corresponding superstructures. In 1985 Cees Koeman purchased the ship. Her expensive conversion into a brigantine took place at a Dutch shipyard. In the process she also received a clipper bow.

Pedro Doncker

Previous name: *Maverick*

Type: 3-masted staysail schooner, steel

Nation: the Netherlands

Owner: Vlaun shipping company

Home port: Amsterdam

Year of construction: 1974

Shipyard: Veldhuis Shipyard, Groningen

Tonnage: 242 tons gross; 91 tons net

Dimensions
Length overall: 42.00 m

Length of hull: 34.00 m
Length between perpendiculars: 30.66 m
Width: 7.50 m
Depth in hold: 3.85 m
Draft: 3.60 m

Sail area: 570 square meters

Rigging: 8 sails

Masts: height of mainmast over the deck: 34.50 meters

Auxiliary engine: Mercedes diesel V10, 450 horsepower

Crew: 3–4-person active crew, 32 guests, 80 guests on day cruises

Use: chartered ship

The former freighter was modified in 1993 for its current use. V & S Charters Holland in Noordwijk operates the charter cruises.

Pollux

Type: bark, steel

Nation: the Netherlands

Owner: International Maritiem Training Instituut, Nederland

Home port: Ijmuiden (Forteiland)

Year of construction: 1940; launched April 1940; commissioned January 1941

Shipyard: Verschure, Amsterdam

Tonnage: 746.89 tons gross; 272.86 tons net

Dimensions:
Length of hull: 61.40 m
Width: 11.03 m
Depth in hold: 3.00 m
Draft: .60 m

Rigging: double topsail, single topgallant yards

Masts, spars: height of mainmast: 31.50 meters, fore- and mainmast with topsail and topgallant masts, mizzenmast with 1 topmast, bowsprit with jibboom: 10 meters

Crew: commander, boatswain, 2 boatswain's mates, cook, trainer, approximately 80 boys

Use: stationary school-ship

In 1849, an educational association was founded in Amsterdam with the goal of training professional sailors for the Netherlands. The government contributed to the endeavor and put the retired troop transport ship *Z. M. Dordrecht* at the group's disposal. Numerous retired navy ships were used for this purpose in succession. The last of them was the HM *Pollux*. She served until 1940.

The name *Pollux* had become so renowned within the merchant marine that from the beginning there were plans to give the name to a new ship. When changes in the training system made a new school name necessary, the entire school received the name Elementary Seafaring School Pollux (Lagere Zeevaartschool Pollux).

The current *Pollux* was built as a stationary school-ship. She has a flat bottom and thus cannot sail. Much additional space was created by the use of the flat bottom, however. The ship received a mermaid as a figurehead. The young men come on board at the age of 14 to 16 years. Their period of training lasts 1 year. Afterward they are integrated into the various shipping lines. A large percentage of them earn a helmsman's certificate. The title "commander" for the captain comes from the time of the early whaling ships.

In 1943 the *Pollux* was towed to Ijmuiden by the German occupation forces. There she did service, completely unrigged, for the former navy. In 1945 the bark was found in a very bad condition. For a time yet she provided shelter for the British and Dutch navies. Late in the year 1945 the *Pollux* returned to Amsterdam, but was at first not returned to her old place. The steamship company Nederlande (Stoomvaart Maatschappij) carried out the extensive restoration work.

In 1993 the *Pollux* was brought to Ijmuiden. There she meets training and practice needs, above all for safety equipment used in the oil industry. Following needed modifications to the ship below the waterline, the *Pollux* might sail again.

Radboud

Previous names: *Philippina Johanna, Hoop op Zegen*

Type: 3-masted fore-and-aft schooner, steel

Nation: the Netherlands

Owner: P. W. Kaptein

Home port: Medernblik

Year of construction: 1909

Shipyard: Boot–Leiderdorp

Tonnage: 187 ts displacement

Dimensions:
Length overall: 52.00 m

Length of hull: 46.40 m
Width: 7.60 m
Depth in hold: 2.20 m
Draft: 1.60 m

Sail area: 525 square meters

Rigging: 6 sails

Masts: height of mainmast over the deck: 31 meters

Auxiliary engine: Detroit diesel, 360 horsepower

Crew: 3-person active crew, 32 guests

Use: chartered ship

The former flat-bottomed freighter with leeboards sailed in the shallow waters off the Dutch coast. Following her conversion into a chartered ship, the *Radboud* today undertakes sailing excursions for guests with refined tastes.

Rainbow Warrior

The *Rainbow Warrior* was made from the former Scottish fishing trawler *Grampian Fame* as a replacement for the Greenpeace ship that was blown up by the French secret service on July 10, 1985, in New Zealand. The ship has computerized sail and engine systems. Solar collectors provide warm water. A water-purification system cleans the waste water. Distinguishing characteristics of the ship's exterior are the lack of a bowsprit and the horizontal gaff. A Bermuda sail is set on the mizzenmast.

Previous name: *Grampian Fame*

Type: 3-masted fore-and-aft schooner, steel

Nation: the Netherlands

Owner: Greenpeace Association, Hamburg

Year of construction: 1957;

modification 1988–89

Shipyard: Cochrane Shipbuilders

Tonnage: 555 tons gross

Dimensions:
Length of hull: 55.50 m
Length between perpendiculars: 48.90 m
Width: 8.50 m

Draft: 3.60 m

Sail area: 650 square meters

Rigging: 4 sails

Masts: height of mainmast over the deck: 32 meters

Auxiliary engine: two KHD MWM diesel motors, 500 horsepower each

Crew: 9–13-person active crew, maximum 16 guests

Use: fulfilling the tasks of Greenpeace

Regina Maris

Type: 3-masted fore-and-aft schooner

Nation: the Netherlands

Owner: Martin Duba

Home port: Amsterdam

Year of construction: 1970

Shipyard: Topsel shipyard, Gdansk (Danzig)

Tonnage: 153 tons gross; 84 tons net

Dimensions:
Length overall: 48.00 m
Length of hull: 36.00 m
Length between perpendiculars: 31.00 m
Width: 6.90 m
Depth in hold: 3.20 m
Draft: 3.00 m

Sail area: 600 square meters

Rigging: 9 sails

Masts: height of mainmast over the deck: 29 meters

Auxiliary engine: MTU diesel, 500 horsepower

Crew: 3-person active crew, 36 guests (70 on day cruises)

Use: chartered ship

Following extensive modifications, the schooner has sailed in the charter service since 1991. Exquisite accommodations are available for the passengers. The figure of a crowned woman with a lapdog under her arm adorns the bow as a figurehead.

Rembrandt van Rijn

Previous names: *Klaus D., Minde, Anna Marta (Martha)*

Type: 3-masted fore-and-aft schooner, steel

Nation: the Netherlands

Owner: Blader Nieuwland

Home port: Middelburg

Year of construction: probably 1924

Shipyard: Gebroeders Boot, Leiderdorp, the Netherlands

Tonnage: 400 ts displacement

Dimensions:
Length overall: 56.00 m
Length of hull: 45.00 m
Length between perpendiculars: 39.90 m
Width: 6.75 m
Depth in hold: 2.20 m
Depth to deck: 3.20 m
Draft: 2.85 m

Sail area: 654 square meters

Rigging: 12 sails

Masts: height of mainmast over the deck: 32 meters

Auxiliary engine: Cummins diesel, 370 horsepower

Crew: 12-person active crew, 36 passengers in berth, 120 passengers on day cruises

Use: chartered and passenger ship

The former freight schooner was built in Holland at German expense, probably in 1924. She sailed under the German flag until 1962, at which point she became Danish and took on the name *Minde*. The penultimate change of name, this time to *Klaus D.*, also took place under the Danish flag.

From 1990 to 1993 the ship was completely restored and equipped as a luxurious fore-and-aft schooner for passenger cruises. Only about 20 percent of the hull was retained in the process.

Sir Robert Baden-Powell

Previous name: *Robert*

Type: 2-masted topsail schooner, steel

Nation: the Netherlands

Owner: Karsten Börner (Zeilvloot Lemmer-Stavoren)

Home port: Lemmer

Year of construction: 1957

Shipyard: Shipyard Edgar André, Magdeburg-Rothensee

Tonnage: 250 tons gross

Dimensions:
Length overall: 42.00 m
Length of hull: 36.00 m
Width: 6.50 m
Depth in hold: 2.50 m
Depth to deck: 2.00 m
Draft: 2.40 m

Sail area: 600 square meters

Rigging: 10 sails; foremast with topsail and topgallant

Masts: height of mainmast over the deck: 29 meters

Auxiliary engine: Mitsubishi diesel, 300 horsepower

Crew: 4–5-person active crew, 22 guests

The schooner was built as the sea tug *Robert* for export to Poland. In 1991 the current owner purchased the ship and completely modified her on both the exterior and the interior. The tug became a topsail schooner. The models for the modification were the Baltimore clippers and their traditional rigs.

Named after Sir Robert Baden-Powell, the founder of the worldwide Boy Scout movement, who lived from 1857 to 1941, the ship has sailed primarily in the Mediterranean and the Red seas since March 1993. The most modern technical equipment is a matter of course.

Sodade

Previous names: *Tradewind, Aaltje en Willem, Sophie Theresia*

Type: 2-masted topsail schooner, steel

Nation: the Netherlands

Owner: Trop-Scan-Sailing—Charters and Consulting Lda., Kees Rol and Hanna Kluvtenaar

Home port: Santa Maria, Sal, Kapverden

Year of construction: 1911

Shipyard: Van Wijk Shipyard, Capelle a/d Ijssel

Tonnage: 195 ts displacement; 99 tons gross; 52 tons net

Dimensions:
Length overall: 37.00 m
Width: 6.85 m
Draft: 2.95 m

Sail area: 540 square meters

Rigging: 11 sails; schooner mast: foresail, topsail, and topgallant

Masts: height of mainmast over the deck: 33 meters; schooner mast: 30.50 meters; 1 topmast each

Auxiliary engine: Caterpillar, 440 horsepower

Crew: 5 crewmembers (captain, helmsman, boatswain, cook, stewardess), 16 guests

Use: sailing tours for tourists, chartered ship

The *Sophie Theresia* cruised the North and Baltic seas under the Dutch flag as an engineless sailing freighter. The first engine was installed in 1952. Because the freight trade had ceased to be profitable, the ship was retired and henceforth served as a dormitory ship in a canal in Amsterdam.

In 1981 three Dutch enthusiasts purchased the former sailing ship and started converting her back into a schooner. A new owner, Mark Hammond from New Zealand, completed this work in 1986. The *Tradewind*, as the ship was known at that time, began her career. She sailed around the world twice, crossed the Atlantic several times, and sailed to the Antarctic. She also starred in many films.

The relatively large sail area and the sharp underwater lines make the schooner an unusually fast ship, and she has left many competitors in her wake during regattas. For example, she won the Sydney Tall Ship Regatta. In 1992 the *Tradewind* was the flagship during the Columbus-related festivities. Beginning in 1993 she belonged to the Finn Christian Johansson and has been employed in the northern Baltic as a school-ship. In 1998 the ship was sold to her current owner, and in 1999 she underwent a refitting.

The *Sodade* is used for sailing cruises for tourists around the islands of Cape Verde. The ship is equipped with every conceivable comfort and technical safety device.

Stad Amsterdam

Type: full-rigged ship, steel

Nation: the Netherlands

Owner: Rederij Clipper Stad Amsterdam

Home port: Amsterdam

Years of construction: 1997–2000; launched December 1998

Shipyard: Damen shipyard, Amsterdam

Tonnage: 1083 ts displacement; 698 tons gross; 277 tons net

Dimensions:
Length overall: 78.00 m
Length of hull: 60.50 m
Width: 10.50 m
Depth in hold: 6.40 m
Draft: 4.80 m

Sail area: 2200 square meters (with studding sails)

Rigging: 26 sails (31 with studding sails), 4 foresails, standard square sails; foremast: foresail, lower-, uppertopsails, single topgallant, royal; mainmast: mainsail, lower-, upper-topsails, single topgallant, royal, skysail; mizzenmast: crossjack, single topsail, single topgallant, royal

Masts: height of mainmast over the waterline: 46.25 meters

Auxiliary engine: Caterpillar diesel, 1014 horsepower; bow thruster

Crew: 25-person active crew (maximum), 6 trainees, on day cruises 120 guests, on cruises 32 guests, on youth cruises 70 guests

Use: business cruises, cruises, private events, day trips, participation in large sailing-ship races

"The clipper *Stad Amsterdam* is a one-of-a-kind ship: a modern 'extreme' clipper, that from a historical perspective was built as a tribute to the fast sailing clippers of the 1850–60 period. Historical data about the frigate *Amsterdam* (1854), the first iron clipper ever built in Amsterdam, inspired the architect in his design for the *Stad Amsterdam.*

"An additional source of information was the timetable of the Dutch clipper *California* from the year 1853. The final design of the *Stad Amsterdam* combines the best features of a number of famous clippers from past centuries, including the famous *Cutty Sark*" (from a report of the Rederij Clipper Stad Amsterdam).

The famous clippers were built to sail fast because it was necessary to carry people and goods across the world's oceans quickly. The voyages of the streamlined ships were featured in the daily press. Ship and crew were pushed to their limits in order to complete a profitable voyage in record time.

Because the new *Stad Amsterdam,* which is not a reproduction, does without excess superstructures, the ship, with her powerful sail towers, presents a picture of the utmost elegance. Because the clipper, obviously, doesn't carry any commercial cargo, the large hull is available for accommodations for passengers and crew. And here no expense was spared. One can rightly describe the accommodations as luxurious.

In order to avoid top-heaviness, the stems and yards were made of aluminum. Two hundred ten tons of lead ballast give the ship the necessary stability. Brace winches (Jarvis winches) on the main deck assist with setting the sails on the lower yards. With her bow thruster the ship can also sail in narrower waters, for example, in harbors, without help from tug boats. The figure of a woman with arms stretched wide adorns the elegant bow as a figurehead. She symbolizes tolerance and freedom.

Stedemaeght

Previous names: *Alf, Bent Flinot, A. Fabricius, Cito, Viskan, Galeon* (1957), *Kinnekulle* (1952), *Gribb II, Pool, Pol IV*

Type: bark, steel,

Nation: the Netherlands

Owner: Hanzestad Compagnie BV, Kampen

Home port: Nylands Verksted, Oslo

Year of construction: 1926

Shipyard: Nylands Verksted, Oslo

Tonnage: 340 ts displacement; 298.13 tons gross; 108 tons net

Dimensions:
Length overall: 58.90 m
Length of hull: 44.10 m
Width: 7.05 m
Depth in hold: 2.90 m

Sail area: 900 square meters

Rigging: 19 sails

Masts: height of mainmast over the deck: 32 meters

Auxiliary engine: Volvo diesel, 450 horsepower

Crew: 4-person active crew, 10 stewards, 150 guests on day cruises

Use: chartered ship

The current bark, which is the largest Dutch sailing ship, is part of a series of whaling vessels built in Oslo. In 1949 the ship was converted into a freighter in Halmstad, Sweden. In 1957 in Wilhelmshaven the hull was lengthened by 7.5 meters. *Alf* was her final name during her time as a freighter.

In 1991 the Dutchmen Toon Slurink and Gerard Veldhuizen purchased the vessel. The hull, which had been designed for speed, was exceptionally well suited to be converted into a large sailing ship. Because all of the square sails can be made fast by means of roller reefing systems, very few people are needed to operate the ship. "Stedemaeght," the patroness of Kampen, formerly stood on a bridge above the Ijssel.

The stylish and luxurious accommodations almost allow one to forget that one is aboard a large sailing ship.

Store Baelt

Previous name: *Drittura*

Type: fore-and-aft ketch, steel

Nation: the Netherlands

Owner: J. Baaijens & V. Roos, Amsterdam

Home port: Monnickendam

Year of construction: 1928

Shipyard: Vos, Groningen

Tonnage: 190 tons gross

Dimensions:
Length overall: 43.00 m
Length of hull: 34.50 m
Width: 6.25 m
Depth to deck: 3.10 m
Draft: 2.10 m

Sail area: 407 square meters

Rigging: 5 sails

Masts: height of mainmast over the deck: 28.50 meters

Auxiliary engine: Mercedes diesel, 325 horsepower

Crew: 2-person active crew, 40 guests (32 berths)

Use: chartered ship (Holland Zeilcharters)

Although the current schooner was built as a motorized ship, she was built with the lines of a sailing ship. Her trade routes led to and from the Baltic. In 1994 she was converted into a luxurious schooner. The high bulwark and the 200 square meters of deck surface make her very comfortable and especially well suited for young sailors. A long jibboom is a distinguishing feature of the fast schooner.

Swaensborgh

The topsail schooner was built as a stern boat with two masts for service in the Elbe, the Weser, and the Wadden Sea. In 1950 the masts were removed, an engine was installed, and the ship was lengthened and elevated by 5 meters. In 1957 she was once again lengthened by 5 meters.

In 1990 the current owner purchased the ship. With a new rig and accommodations for passenger travel, she has since then served as an upscale chartered ship.

Previous names: *Mira II, Adele Raap, Eleonore, Anna*

Type: 3-masted topsail schooner, steel

Nation: the Netherlands

Owner: Claes Tolman, Monnickendam

Home port: Monnickendam

Year of construction: 1907

Shipyard: J. Jacobs, Moorregge

Tonnage: 275.30 ts displacement; 165 tons gross; 78 tons net

Dimensions:
Length overall: 47.00 m
Length of hull: 41.00 m
Length between perpendiculars: 37.15 m

Width: 5.85 m
Depth in hold: 2.56 m
Depth to deck: 3.26 m
Draft: 2.30 m

Sail area: 500 square meters

Rigging: 11 sails

Masts: height of mainmast over the deck: 29.50 meters

Auxiliary engine: Deutz BF 12M 716, 380 horsepower

Crew: 3-person active crew, 30 guests, 60 guests on day cruises

Use: chartered ship

The ship is one of the largest brigantines ever to have sailed the seas. She was built in accordance with historical models and equipped with the most modern technology and much comfort. Eight double cabins and large salons are available for the guests. Her main areas of activity are the Baltic and North seas during the summer, and in the winter the Caribbean. A powerful white swan decorates the bow as a figurehead.

Type: brigantine, steel

Nation: the Netherlands

Owner: Swan Compagnie Holland

Home port: Makkum

Year of construction: 1993

Shipyard: REF shipyard, Gdansk (Danzig)

Tonnage: 404 tons gross; 147 tons net

Dimensions:
Length overall: 61.00 m
Length of hull: 51.00 m
Length between
perpendiculars: 39.67 m
Width: 9.20 m
Draft: 3.70 m

Sail area: 1300 square meters

Rigging: 14 sails; foremast: foresail, double topsail, single topgallant, royal sail

Masts: height of mainmast over the deck: 44.60 meters

Auxiliary engine: Caterpillar diesel, 480 horsepower

Crew: 10-person active crew, 36 passengers, 120 guests on day voyages

Use: chartered ship

Tecla

Type: fore-and-aft ketch

Nation: the Netherlands

Owner: Jaap Vreeken, Jenny Pierik

Home port: Enkhuizen

Year of construction: 1915

Crew: chartered ship

The former herring lugger was modified for her current use in 1989. Her areas of activity are the Ijsselmeer, the Wadden Sea, and the coastal waters of Europe.

Thalassa

Previous names: *HD 99-Relinquenda, Theodore*

Type: barkentine, steel

Nation: the Netherlands

Owner: Barketyn V. O. F. (Zeilvaart Enkhuizen)

Home port: Haak Shipyard, Zaandam

Year of construction: 1980

Shipyard: Haak Shipyard, Zaandam

Tonnage: 350 ts displacement; 282 tons gross; 116 tons net

Dimensions:
Length overall: 48.00 m
Length of hull: 38.00 m
Length between perpendiculars: 32.60 m
Width: 8.00 m
Depth to deck: 4.44 m
Draft: 4.00 m

Rigging: 15 sails

Masts: height of mainmast over the deck: 36 meters

Auxiliary engine: General Motors diesel, 650 horsepower

Crew: 5-person active crew, 36 passengers, 80 guests on day cruises

Use: chartered ship

In 1995 the former deep seas trawler was converted into a barkentine and equipped to carry passengers.

Tsjerk Hiddes

Previous names: *Linquenda, Avontuur*	Length of hull: 40.00 m Width: 6.30 m Depth in hold: 2.70 m
Type: 3-masted fore-and-aft schooner	Draft: 1.60 m
Nation: the Netherlands	Sail area: 540 square meters
Owner: F. Bruinsma (de Zeilvaart Enkhuizen)	Rigging: 7 sails
	Masts: height of mainmast over the deck: 27 meters
Home port: Franeker	
Year of construction: 1881	Auxiliary engine: General Motors diesel, 240 horsepower
Shipyard: Kinderdyk	Crew: 2-person active crew, 30 guests
Tonnage: 240 ts displacement	
Dimensions: Length overall: 50.00 m	Use: chartered ship

The former flat-bottomed freighter was refitted and equipped for her current use in 1993. The ship was named after a seafaring Frisian hero. Her main areas of activity are the Ijsselmeer and the Wadden Sea.

Urania

Previous name: *Tromp*	Draft: 3.20 m Freeboard: 1.40 m
Type: ketch, steel	Sail area: 234.5 square meters (in the wind); in addition a Genoa (136 square meters), spinnaker (260 square meters), Aap (105 square meters)
Nation: the Netherlands	
Owner: Koninklijk Instituut voor de Marine, Den Helder	
Home port: Den Helder	Rigging: 4 sails (in the wind); 2 foresails, mainsail (Bermuda), mizzen sail (Bermuda)
Year of construction: 1928	
Shipyard: Haarlemse Scheepsbouw Mij.	Masts: height of foremast over the deck: 23.50 meters; height of mizzenmast over the deck: 19.50 meters
Tonnage: 38 ts displacement; 50.96 tons gross; 38.36 tons net	
	Auxiliary engine: diesel engine, 65 horsepower
Dimensions: Length overall: 23.75 m Length of hull: 19.00 m Length between perpendiculars: 16.50 m Width: 5.50 m	Crew: 17 people, 3 officers, 2 sailors, 12 cadets
	Use: sailing school-ship

Urania was built in 1928 as the schooner yacht *Tromp* for the Dutchman Nierstratz. On April 23, 1938, the Royal Naval Institute (Koninklijk Instituut voor de Marine) acquired the ship. Since then the *Urania* has served as a sailing school-ship for the training of sea cadets. During World War II the schooner was brought to Germany and was rerigged as a ketch after her return. The ship regularly takes part in high-seas regattas and is classified in the R.O.R.C.-I class at these events (Royal Ocean Racing Committee).

Vliegende Hollander

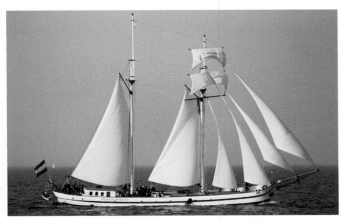

The schooner, with her elegant lines, sailed for many years as a freighter, primarily in the Dutch coastal waters. Her conversion into a luxurious sailing ship for the passenger service took place very recently. Her area of deployment is primarily the Ijsselmeer. According to legend, the Flying Hollander was a wicked captain who is condemned to sail against the wind with his ghost ship for eternity. Whoever encountered him was lost. The theme inspired an opera by Richard Wagner (1843).

Previous names: *Martha, Broedertrouw, Jatum Jerenda*

Type: 2-masted topsail schooner, iron

Nation: the Netherlands

Owner: Klaas van Twillert

Home port: Lemmer—summer; Spakenburg—winter

Year of construction: 1892; reconstruction 1996–2000; launched April 21, 2000

Shipyard: Geertman—Zwartsluis

Dimensions:
Length overall: 50.00 m
Length of hull: 40.00 m
Width: 6.10 m
Draft: 1.30 m

Sail area: 540 square meters

Rigging: 10 sail, foremast with lower and upper topsail

Masts: height of mainmast over the deck: 31.50 meters

Auxiliary engine: main engine Scania diesel, 260 horsepower; bow engine, 200 horsepower

Crew: 2 persons, 34 overnight guests, 60 day guests

Use: chartered ship, passenger ship

Vrouwe Geertruida Magdalena

The ship, which was originally built using the composite-construction method, became an all-steel ship through the introduction of a layer of steel. She had initially worked for the pilots of Texel and was then sold to a buyer in Germany. In 1943 the ship entered service as a patrol cutter for weather and airplane observation in the German Bay. In the 1970s the current owner once again converted the ship into a schooner. Many years in the charter service followed. From 1991 until May 1992 *Vrouwe Geertruida Magdalena,* as she has been called since 1976, was thoroughly overhauled and modified in Zaandam for luxury charter cruises. In the process the original form of the stern was also re-created, which caused the hull to be lengthened somewhat. Today the ship has a white hull.

Previous names: *Flevo, Weser Nr. 3*

Type: 2-masted fore-and-aft schooner, steel

Nation: the Netherlands

Owner: Berend P. Groen

Year of construction: 1910

Shipyard: Bodewes, Groningen, the Netherlands

Tonnage: 128 tons gross (prior to 1992 modification)

Dimensions:
Length overall: 37.00 m
Width: 6.20 m
Draft: 3.20 m

Sail area: 550 square meters

Auxiliary engine: Caterpillar diesel, 375 horsepower

Crew: 4-person active crew, 14 passengers, 35 day guests

Use: chartered ship

Willem Barentsz

Previous names: *Maria Becker, Landsort fa de Vriendschap*

Type: 3-masted fore-and-aft schooner, steel

Nation: the Netherlands

Owner: Zeilvaart Enkhuizen

Home port: Enkhuizen

Year of construction: 1931

Shipyard: Visseryhaven

Tonnage: 230 ts displacement; 166 tons gross; 110 tons net

Dimensions:
Length overall: 49.70 m
Length of hull: 39.79 m
Width: 6.10 m
Draft: 1.80 m

Sail area: 460 square meters

Rigging: 11 sails

Masts: height of mainmast over the deck: 27 meters

Auxiliary engine: Mitsubishi diesel, 300 horsepower

Crew: 5-person active crew, up to 100 guests on day tours

Use: chartered ship

The ship can be rented by the day. The cruises take place primarily in Dutch coastal waters. The guests are able to take part in setting the sails, steering, and navigating. The *Willem Barentsz* has accommodations for large groups, including a restaurant.

Wytske Eelkje/Willem

Type: brigantine, steel

Nation: the Netherlands

Owner: Reederij Vlaun

Home port: Amsterdam

Year of construction: 1968

Shipyard: in Gdansk

Tonnage: 74 tons gross; 51 tons net

Dimensions:
Length overall: 29.00 m
Length of hull: 19.11 m
Width: 6.10 m

Depth in hold: 2.90 m
Draft: 3.10 m

Sail area: 430 square meters

Rigging: 8 sails

Masts: Height of mainmast over the deck: 22 meters

Auxiliary engine: DAF diesel engine, 149 horsepower

Crew: 2-person active crew, 16–24 guests on multiple-day cruises, 36 guests on day cruises

Use: chartered ship

The Two brigantines, which can easily be recognized by their painted strakes, were built to be absolutely identical. The intention was to be able to engage in "match racing' with these two sister ships. The desire of sailors to test their ships and their skills against those of others is as old as sailing itself.

Zeelandia

Rigged as a ketch, the *Oceaan II* sailed out of Scheveningen in order to fish in the North Sea. For financial reasons, all Dutch sailing vessels of this type were laid up in 1967. With the new name *Zeelandia,* the ship was subsequently engaged in the sport-fishing industry.

In 1975 the current owner purchased the vessel, which had decayed almost to the level of a hulk. After an ambitious modification, a 3-master came into being. Because the individual sails are smaller as a result, it is even possible to sail the relatively large ship "with one hand."

Previous name: *Oceaan II (Sch 47)*

Type: 3-masted fore-and-aft schooner, steel

Nation: the Netherlands

Owner: Marnix van der Wel

Home port: Rotterdam

Year of construction: 1931

Shipyard: Vuyck shipyard, Capelle a/d Ijssel

Tonnage: 280 ts displacement; 142 tons gross; 23 tons net

Dimensions:
Length overall: 40.00 m
Length of hull: 33.00 m

Length between perpendiculars: 30.18 m
Width: 7.00 m
Depth in hold: 2.20 m
Depth to deck: 2.90 m
Draft: 2.90 m

Sail area: 440–780 square meters

Rigging: 10 to 15 sails

Masts: height of mainmast over the deck: 26 meters

Auxiliary engine: industry diesel 3V06, 120 horsepower

Crew: 2-person active crew, up to 10 trainees

Use: private ship

Zuiderzee

Previous names: *Ernst-Wilhelm, Hans, Peter, Pirat, Genius*

Type: 2-masted fore-and-aft schooner

Nation: the Netherlands

Owner: Stormvogel bv, Enkhuizen

Home port: Enkhuizen

Year of construction: 1909

Shipyard: Pattje, Waterhuizen

Tonnage: 200 ts displacement; 131 tons gross; 62 tons net

Dimensions:
Length overall: 40.00 m
Length of hull: 30.04 m
Length between perpendiculars: 27.56 m
Width: 6.70 m
Depth to deck: 2.92 m
Draft: 2.30 m

Sail area: 540 square meters

Rigging: 9 sails

Masts: height of mainmast over the deck: 30 meters

Auxiliary engine: Detroit diesel, 280 horsepower

Crew: 2–3-person active crew, 22 guests

Use: chartered ship, school-ship

The *Zuiderzee* was engaged in the freight trade for decades. Her sailing area was the "Grote Kustvaart" (Atlantic Ocean, the Mediterranean, the Baltic, and the North Sea).

She is one of the few authentic 2-masted schooners still sailing in the Netherlands.

In 1992 the ship was converted for the passenger service and luxuriously furnished. In the process special emphasis was placed on maintaining the ship's historic character. The passengers are encouraged to assist with the maintenance of the schooner.

New Zealand

Breeze
Edwin Fox
R. Tucker Thompson

Spirit of New Zealand
Tui

Breeze

Type: brigantine, wood

Nation: New Zealand

Owner: Auckland Maritime Museum (Friends of the Breeze)

Home port: Auckland

Year of construction: 1981

Shipyard: Ralph Sewell, Coromandel, New Zealand

Tonnage: 25 ts displacement

Dimensions:
Length of hull: 18.30 m
Width: 5.00 m
Draft: 1.80 m

Sail area: 216 square meters

Masts: height of mainmast: 17.50 meters

Auxiliary engine: Lister diesel, 54 horsepower

Crew: 6-person active crew, 12 berths for guests

Use: sailing school-ship

The *Breeze* is the flagship of the Auckland Maritime Museum, to which she has belonged since 1989. The hull was built from the wood of the copal tree. The very small brigantine is the faithful reproduction of vessels that sailed the coastal waters of New Zealand until the end of the nineteenth century.

Edwin Fox

Type: former full-rigged ship (later a bark), currently a hulk, wood (teak)

Nation: New Zealand

Owner: Edwin Fox Restoration Society, Blenheim, New Zealand

Home port: Picton Sound, Marlborough, New Zealand

Year of construction: 1853

Shipyard: in Sulkeali, Bengal

Tonnage: 891 tons gross; 836 tons net

Dimensions:
Length between perpendiculars: 43.90 m
Width: 9.00 m
Draft: 7.20 m

Auxiliary engine: none

Use: museum ship

During the almost 1-year blockade of the fortress Sebastopol in the Crimean War the western powers lost twenty transport ships that were lying in the roadstead to a serious storm in November 1854. The *Edwin Fox* was the only ship that came away unscathed.

Many documents related to the history of this ship were lost in fires in London and New Zealand. Her life was so colorful and eventful, however, that her trail was never lost.

The *Edwin Fox* was commissioned by the East India Company but was sold to Sir George Hodgkinson of Cornhill, London, while still under construction. The shipyard used exclusively the best teak wood in her construction. The ship got her name from the well-known Quaker from Southampton.

The *Edwin Smith* sailed to London with a cargo of tea on her first journey and was then acquired by the shipowner Duncan Dunbar for the record price of 30,000 English pounds, following the dissolution of the company. Immediately afterward the English government chartered the ship and sent her as a troop transporter to the Black Sea. Sebastopol was under siege. For eighteen months the *Edwin Fox* flew the British war flag in the Crimean War. After 3 consecutive East Indian voyages the government once again chartered the sailing ship, this time to bring political prisoners to Western Australia.

The *Edwin Fox* once again set sail for military purposes when she transported troops against the great Indian rebellion of 1856–58. In 1861 she passed back into the hands of her civilian owner. A full cargo, which had just been taken aboard in Bombay, had to be unloaded again at Indian request. All available capacity was needed to combat the great famine in the northwest provinces. Sixteen times the *Edwin Fox* sailed with rice on board from Bangkok to the area of the catastrophe. After Dunbar's death in 1862, the shipping company Gellatly & Company in London purchased the ship. The *Edwin Fox* has now become a tea ship. Her somewhat squat and rounded form earned her the nickname "Teatub."

The next period of her life is closely connected with the European settlement of New Zealand. For this reason, she is also being preserved in New Zealand for the benefit of future generations. In 1873 the firm Shaw Savill chartered the ship for immigrants' voyages to New Zealand. On her first departure the ship encountered a heavy storm in the Atlantic that claimed several lives on board. Towed by the steam-powered American mailboat *Copernicus,* the *Edwin Fox* reached Brest as an emergency port. After 4 weeks of repair, the voyage resumed. The second trip with emigrants also began with the ship encountering a storm, sustaining losses, and touching bottom. Only the extraordinarily strong construction saved the ship from being completely lost.

Up to 259 emigrants were on board for the voyages. In 1878 the full-rigged ship was rerigged as a bark. The last colonialists she carried left their English home in 1880. Competition from steamships in this business was increasingly intense. For this reason the bark was outfitted with refrigeration units and sailed to New Zealand. There she lay alternately in Gisborne, Lyttleton, Bluff, and Port Chalmers. In a single day 500 sheep could be frozen and a total of up to 20,000 sheep stored, which were then transported to England aboard refrigeration ships. In 1897 the *Edwin Fox* was towed to Picton. She had only her lower masts at this point. She served for three more years in Picton as a freezing ship. She was subsequently used as a coal hulk until 1950.

Since 1964 there have been plans to restore the *Edwin Fox.* In 1965 the Edwin Fox Preservation Society purchased the ship for a shilling from the Picton Meat Company. As of today the restoration has still not been completed. Since 1999 the ship has lain in a dry dock and is supposed to be restored gradually. The project is dependant on donations. If the restoration is completed, the *Edwin Fox* will be the only emigrant ship that has been preserved.

Type: 2-masted topsail schooner, steel

Nation: New Zealand

Owner: Tod Thompson, Russel Harris, Opua, New Zealand

Home port: Whangarei

Year of construction: 1985

Shipyard: Mangawhai Heads, New Zealand

Tonnage: 60 ts displacement; 45 tons gross; 33 tons net

Dimensions:
Length overall: 25.80 m
Length of hull: 18.20 m
Length at the waterline: 16.70 m
Width: 4.60 m
Draft: 2.40 m

Sail area: 280 square meters

Rigging: 11 sails

Masts: height of mainmast over the deck: 21.30 meters

Auxiliary engine: Ford diesel, 120 horsepower

Crew: 6-person active crew, 8 berths, 41 day guests

Use: chartered ship

Following a circumnavigation of the globe in 1986 and her subsequent participation in the 200th anniversary of the discovery of Australia, the *R. Tucker Thompson* sails primarily in the South Seas.

Beautiful woodwork from the bulwarks up further empha-sizes the elegant lines of the steel hull. The deck, the bul-wark, the masts, and the spars are likewise made of wood.

In 1986 the ship was char-tered for use in a children's film shot in New Zealand. In the film she appeared as the *Sea Wolf*.

Spirit of New Zealand

Type: barkentine, steel

Nation: New Zealand

Owner: Spirit of Adventure Trust

Home port: Auckland

Year of construction: 1986

Shipyard: Thackwray Yachts, Ltd., Auckland

Tonnage: 244.3 ts displacement; 184.4 tons gross; 55.3 tons net

Dimensions:
Length overall: 45.20 m
Width: 9.10 m
Draft: 3.80 m

Sail area: 736 square meters

Rigging: 17 sails

Masts: height of mainmast over the deck: 31.30 meters

Auxiliary engine: Gardner 8L 3B diesel, 250 horsepower

Crew: 12-person active crew, 42 trainees

Use: sailing school-ship

The barkentine is primarily for the use of male and female students from New Zealand. The young people's usually 10-day stay aboard the ship can be compared to a field trip to a house in the country. The communal life and work are in-comparably more intensive aboard the ship, however. Toward the end of the course the students choose their own "officers." They then operate the ship themselves with the least possible supervision. The ship is also available for groups of adults. Many companies and organizations in New Zealand made the construction of the ship possible through assistance of various kinds.

Tui

In Waitangi, near the city of Whangarei (north island), the wooden bark *Tui* lies on dry land. She belongs to the local shipwreck museum. The ship has a flat bottom. Her sides are decorated with a streak.

Norway

Anna Kristina
Christian Radich
Christiana

Fram
Johanna
Sørlandet

Statsraad
Lehmkuhl
Svanen

Anna Kristina

Previous name: *Dyrafield*

Type: gaff-rigged topsail ketch, wood

Nation: Norway

Owner: Sollerudstranda skole, Lysaker, Norway

Home port: Bergen, Norway

Year of construction: 1889

Shipyard: John Børve, Stankvik, Norway

Tonnage: 72 tons gross; 51 tons net

Dimensions:
Length overall: 32.00 m
Length of hull: 23.00 m
Width: 6.40 m
Depth in hold: 2.60 m
Draft: 2.90 m

Sail area: 402 square meters

Rigging: 10 sails; mainmast (square sail), lower sail, and topsail

Masts: height of mainmast over the deck: 24 meters

Auxiliary engine: Volvo Penta/TMD 100, 238 horsepower

Crew: 6-person active crew, 16 passengers

Use: 1- and 2-week cruises in the waters of the Canary Islands (whale observations)

Approximately 600 carefully chosen pine trees were used in the construction of a Hardanger Jakt like the *Anna Kristina*. (The Hardanger-Fjord Region was well known for the construction of these ships.) These well-built ships transported trading goods on many seas. They were also employed as fishing vessels.

The *Dyrafield* found her current owner in 1977. He had the ship thoroughly overhauled, rerigged, and equipped for the current use. Modern nautical equipment is a matter of course.

In 1987 the *Anna Kristina* was chartered to take part in the First Fleet Reenactment, which led from Portsmouth to Sydney in honor of Australia's bicentennial. After a longer stay in the South Sea and after taking part in the Columbus Regatta in 1992, the ship returned to Norwegian waters in 1993.

Type: full-rigged ship, steel

Nation: Norway

Owner: Østlandets Skoleskib, Oslo

Home port: Oslo

Year of construction: 1937

Shipyard: Framnaes Mek. Verksted, Sandefjord

Tonnage: 696 tons gross; 207 tons net

Sail area: 1234 square meters

Rigging: 26 sails; 4 foresails, double topsail, single topgallant, royals

Auxiliary engine: General Motors diesel, 450 horsepower; speed with engine, 8 knots

Crew: captain, first, second, and third mates, 6 instructors, doctor, mechanical engineer, cook, steward, approximately 100 boys

Use: sailing school-ship

The *Christian Radich* is the replacement for the brig *Staatsraad Erichsen* of the former Kristiania School-ship Society. She received her name from one of her important donors and promoters. Prior to World War II the sailing ship made two longer voyages. The last one took it, together with the Danish *Danmark,* to the world exhibition in New York. At the end of 1939 the *Christian Radich* left New York, while the *Danmark* remained there. After her return she served with the Norwegian navy at the naval base at Horten. In April 1940, she was requisitioned by German troops.

The Norwegian government decisively rejected the German proposal to use her as a school-ship in the Baltic under Norwegian administration. Until the end of the war the ship was a submarine depot ship. At the end of the war it lay half sunk and without masts and yards in Flensburg. After being raised by the Allies it was returned to its owner. There followed an extensive repair at the shipyard in Sandefjord. The costs for this came to 70,000 pounds. Since 1947, the *Christian Radich* has once again been in service. In 1956–57 the film *Windjammer* was shot with and on her. The voyage for the film led from Oslo to Madeira—Trinidad—New York—Boston, and back to Oslo.

In the spring of 1963 thorough renovation work was carried out at the naval shipyard (Marinens Hovedverft) in Horten. The ship received a more powerful engine. The kitchen and the washrooms were modernized, and the standing and running rigging were replaced. In 1983 another thorough overhaul and modernization took place. Permanent berths replaced the hammocks. The ship also takes paying guests on board.

The normal school-ship program for young women and men, including those preparing for maritime careers, begins in August and runs until the following June.

In 1992 the full-rigged ship took part in the Columbus regatta.

Christiana

While the former trading vessel *Christiana* was being converted and equipped for her current use, special care was taken to preserve the ship in her original condition. Her berth is immediately in front of the Oslo Town Hall.

Previous name: *Helga*

Type: 3-masted fore-and-aft schooner

Nation: Norway

Owner: Norway Yacht Charter A/S

Home port: Oslo

Year of construction: 1946; launched 1948

Shipyard: Paul Grönquist & Company, Valax, Finland

Tonnage: 126 tons gross; 38 tons net

Dimensions:
Length overall: 45.70 m
Length of hull: 33.20 m
Width: 7.45 m
Draft: 2.61 m

Sail area: 550 square meters

Rigging: 10 sails

Masts: height of mainmast over the deck: approx. 25 meters

Auxiliary engine: Caterpillar 6-cylinder diesel, 365 horsepower

Crew: 5–9-person active crew, 150 guests on day cruises

Use: lunch and dinner cruises in the Oslo Fjord

Fram

Type: 3-masted topsail schooner

Nation: Norway

Owner, location: Fram Museum, Oslo Bygdøy

Year of construction: 1892

Shipyard: Colin Archer's Shipyard, Rekevik near Larvik; design: Colin Archer

Tonnage: 800 ts displacement (fully equipped); 402 tons gross; 307 t carrying capacity

Dimensions:
Length of hull: 39.00 m
Length at the waterline: 34.50 m
Length keel: 31.00 m
Width (without ice lining): 11.00 m
Depth in hold: 5.20 m
Draft (fully equipped): 4.70 m

Sail area: 600 square meters

Rigging: 7 sails; 2 foresails; foremast: square foresail, single topsail, schooner sail; main-, mizzenmast: gaff-sail

Masts: fore- and mainmast with snow mast; mainmast with one topmast; height of mainmast over the keel: 40 meters

Auxiliary engine: triple expansion engine 200 indiz. horsepower; speed with engine 6 to 7 knots

Crew: 13 people during Nansen's polar expedition

Use: museum ship

Although as a custom construction and a pure research ship the *Fram* ("Forward") cannot be counted among the authentic great sailing ships, considered in terms of her rig she belongs to this group. The ship was built exclusively for voyages in polar waters. This explains her small size and also her shape. Everything was designed so as to offer the expected ice pressure little resistance. The length-to-width ratio is approximately 3:1. The forms are round and smooth. Thus the keel only protrudes 7 centimeters from the exterior surface. The hull itself naturally was built to be especially strong. A multiplicity of beams, supports, and diagonal buttresses were supposed to catch and distribute the expected pressure of the ice. The sides of the ship consist of multiple layers and are 70 to 80 centimeters thick. The final external layer consists of the 15-centimeter-thick ice lining. The rudder and propeller could be raised into a shaft during the passage to prevent them from being damaged by the ice.

The poop extends almost to the mainmast. The cabins for all the expedition participants are located under her strong deck. All the walls of the living quarters, including the decks and floors, are equipped with numerous layers of insulation. The ship already had electricity on board at the time of her construction. The electricity was provided by a dynamo that was powered either by a steam engine or by a large windmill on the main deck. There were a total of eight boats on board, of which the two largest had been built 8.8 meters in length and 2.1 meters in width. The lookout platform on the mainmast was originally approximately 32 meters above the surface of the water.

The ship became famous through the great polar expedition of the Norwegian Fritjof Nansen from 1893 to 1896, for which it was built. A second voyage followed, to the North Sea. From 1910 until 1912 the *Fram* was Roald Amundsen's expedition ship. During this Antarctica expedition Amundsen reached the South Pole in 1911. The *Fram* is the ship that has penetrated farthest north and farthest south.

A special house has been built for the *Fram* in Oslo-Bygdøy—the Fram Museum.

Type: brigantine, wood

Nation: Norway

Owner: Norway Yacht Charter A/S

Home port: Oslo

Year of construction: 1892

Shipyard: G. Øverik, Tustna, Norway

Tonnage: 200 ts displacement; 115 tons gross; 54 tons net

Dimensions:
Length overall: 38.10 m
Length of hull: 28.30 m
Width: 6.55 m
Depth to deck: 2.91 m
Draft: 3.00 m

Rigging: originally 11 sails (today usually only 3 sails)

Masts: height of mainmast over the deck: 28 meters

Auxiliary engine: Callesen 3-cylinder, 260 horsepower

Crew: 5–6-person active crew, 200 guests on day cruises

Use: lunch and dinner cruises in Oslofjord

The brigantine is one of the oldest Norwegian ships that is still in use. She has served three different owners in her long life, but always under the same name. For many years she sailed as a fishing vessel in the waters of northern Norway. She was also used as a freighter, however.

In 1992 the ship was acquired by the Norway Yacht Charter A/S. An extensive restoration followed. Distinguishing features are the large deck and the spacious salons in the interior of the ship.

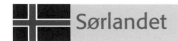

Type: full-rigged ship, steel

Nation: Norway

Owner: Stiftelsen Fullriggeren Sørlandet, Kristiansand S.

Home port: Kristiansand S.

Year of construction: 1927

Shipyard: Høivolds Mek. Versted A/K, Kristiansand S.

Tonnage: 568 tons gross

Dimensions:
Length overall: 65.00 m
Length of hull: 56.80 m
Length between perpendiculars: 52.30 m
Width: 9.60 m
Draft: 4.80 m

Sail area: 1000 square meters

Rigging: 26 sails; 4 foresails, double topsail, single topgallant, royals

Auxiliary engine: Deutz diesel, 564 horsepower; until winter 1959–60 last active sailing ship without an engine

Crew: captain, first, second, third, and fourth mates, doctor, steward, cook, approx. 85 boys

Use: adventure school-ship, chartered ship

The construction of this ship was made possible by a donation from the Norwegian shipowner A.O.T. Skjelbred, who made it a condition, however, that she be built as a pure sailing ship. In 1933 the Sørlandet ("South Land") visited the World Exhibition in Chicago. The voyage took her down the St. Lawrence and across the Great Lakes. She regularly made training voyages until World War II.

At the outbreak of the war, the Norwegian navy took control of the ship. In Horten she was immediately requisitioned by the German occupation authorities. In 1942 the Sørlandet was towed to Kirkenes, where she was used as a military prison facility.

Shrapnel from an Allied bomb damaged the surface of the ship just above the waterline, which ultimately caused the ship to sink. Later she was raised by the Germans, towed to Kristiansand, and used there as a submarine depot ship until the end of the war. For this purpose all of her masts were removed and another large house was constructed on the deck.

The ship was returned to her owner in very bad condition at the end of the war. The extensive repair and modernization work that was immediately begun lasted until 1947. After that the sailing ship was once again used for regular training purposes.

Until 1973 the ship was operated by the Sørlandets Seilende Skoleskibs Institution, whose young people were trained on board. After lying idle for a number of years, the full-rigger was thoroughly overhauled (new rig, new sails, a new engine, new living quarters, etc.). In 1980 the current owner acquired the ship.

The *Sørlandet* has been available for diverse uses since this time. Because she is also used for charter cruises, a regular training program cannot be carried out. The city of Kristiansand has a great interest in preserving the ship as a landmark of the harbor.

Statsraad Lehmkuhl

The German School-Ship Association had the bark *Grand Duke Friedrich August* constructed in 1914 as an addition to its two existing schoolships, the *Grand Duchess Elis-* *abeth* and the *Princess Eitel Friedrich*. Because of the outbreak of World War II, however, it was not possible to undertake any long voyages. After the end of the war she was given to England as a reparations payment. Formally, she was registered at the shipping company of J. Council & Sons in Newcastle upon Tyne. In reality, however, there was no use for her, because as a pure school-ship she was not suited for carrying freight. In 1922 the Bergen Steamship Company purchased the ship and gave her to the association Bergens

Previous names: *Westwards, Statsraad Lehmkuhl, Grand Duke Friedrich August*

Type: bark, steel

Nation: Norway

Owner: Seilskip STATSRAAD LEHMKUHL foundation, Bryggen, Bergen (Norway)

Home port: Bergen

Year of construction: 1914

Shipyard: J. C. Tecklenborg, Geestemünde (Bremerhaven)

Tonnage: 1701 tons gross

Dimensions:
Length overall: 98.00 m
Length of hull: 87.50 m
Length between perpendiculars: 75.50 m

Width: 12.60 m
Depth in hold: 7.10 m
Draft: 5.10 m

Sail area: 2200 square meters

Rigging: 21 sails; 4 foresails, double topsail, single topgallant, royals; mizzenmast only mizzen sails

Masts: height of the mainmast over the waterline: 50 meters; fore- and main-mast with topmast and topgallant mast, mizzenmast with one topmast

Auxiliary engine: diesel engine, 450 horsepower

Crew: 24-person active crew, 150 trainees and sailing enthusiasts

Use: "adventure school-ship"

Skoleskip in 1923. She received the new name *Statsraad Lehmkuhl* and became a substitute for the retired corvette *Alfen*. The bark made her regular training cruises, which usually lasted from April to September, until 1939. In 1940 German troops requisitioned the sailing ship in Bergen. Under the name *Westwards* she was a depot ship for the navy until her return to her owner in 1945. The ship immediately got her old name back. The repair and overhaul work lasted until April 1946. For three years the normal training voyages were continued.

By the 1949 season the maintenance costs for the ship had become so high that the association resolved to stop sailing her. For a year the *Staatsrad* became a stationary training ship of the Norwegian Fishery School. After that she served the Bergens Skoleskib, likewise as a school-ship. In 1952 she was once again allowed to set sail and remained in service until the end of 1967. The Norwegian government cut back on her maintenance at the end of 1967 because the costs of the great ship had become too great and because enough other training facilities were available. After plans to sell the ship to a foreign buyer became known, the shipowner Hilmar Reksten of Sjøsanger near Bergen intervened as a patron of the ship and purchased her so that the city of Bergen could retain her. In 1969 Reksten had the ship thoroughly overhauled and modernized. Since then the training activity has once again been taken up in its full breadth.

As in many sailing school-ships, the poop here extends to the mainmast. The large deckhouse stands behind the foremast. The bark carries nine boats and has stock anchors on both sides. The main wheel stands on the poop in front of the charthouse and the emergency wheel behind it, immediately adjacent to the rear edge. Both are double wheels. As the *Grand Duke Friedrich August* the ship had a full figurehead. Today very tastefully colored scrollwork with the coat of arms of Norway and of the city of Bergen ornaments the bow and stern.

Since 1979 the bark has belonged to a foundation. For paying guests, primarily young boys and girls, she is once again available as a training ship. She is the largest sailing bark in the world. At windjammer parades she is always viewed with much interest. Since the guests come from many nations, she promotes the mutual understanding of peoples to an especially great degree.

Svanen

Previous names: *Smart, Aina, Jason*

Type: 3-masted fore-and-aft schooner, wood

Nation: Norway

Owner: Norsk Sjøfartsmuseum, Oslo

Home port: Kristiansand

Year of construction: 1916

Shipyard: J. Ring-Andersen, Svendborg, Denmark

Tonnage: 102 tons gross

Dimensions:
Length overall: 33.00 m
Length of hull: 28.50 m
Length between perpendiculars: 26.10 m
Width: 6.70 m
Draft: 2.50 m

Sail area: 350 square meters

Rigging: 11 sails

Masts: height of mainmast over the deck: 22 meters

Auxiliary engine: General Motors diesel, 240 horsepower

Crew: 5-person active crew, 25 students

Use: museum ship, sailing school-ship, research vessel

Built as the *Jason*, the schooner received the name *Smart* soon thereafter. During this time the ship sailed for various Norwegian owners as a trading ship. In 1921 the *Smart* was sold to a buyer in Sweden and received her current name, *Svanen*. In 1964 she returned to Norway. Until 1972 she belonged to the Selskapet Skonnerten Svanen in Kristiansand; after 1972 to the Norsk Sjø- fartsmuseum in Oslo. During the summer months entire school classes can take 6-day cruises aboard her. During these trips the young people are supposed to be able to get their first experiences of life at sea. The rest of the time she is at the disposal of the museum, which uses her as a base from which divers explore ship- wrecks near the coast.

Oman

Shabab Oman

Shabab Oman

The ship was built as the *Captain Scott* for the Dulverton Trust in the Scottish city of Buckie. During the period in which she still sailed her old home waters, the training did not serve only nautical purposes. Expeditionlike excursions into the mountainous land were supposed to revive the spirit of the Antarctic explorer Robert Scott, after whom the ship was named.

In 1977 the schooner was sold to Sultan Qaboos bin Said of Oman. The name of the ship can be translated "Youth of Oman."

The figurehead depicts the young Sultan of Oman.

German and British seamen, including the later commandant of the *Gorch Fock*, Immon von Schnurbein, were employed as captain and officers and supported by officers from Oman.

In addition to the naval trainees, places are reserved for young civilians from the population of Oman who are sponsored by the Ministry of Youth Affairs.

In 1984 the ship was refitted. The schooner was converted into a barkentine with a foresail and without a boom foresail.

Previous names: *Youth of Oman, Captain Scott*

Type: 3-masted barkentine

Nation: Oman

Owner: Sultanate Oman

Home port: Maskat

Year of construction: 1971; launched September 7, 1971

Shipyard: Herd & Mackenzie, Buckie, Banffshire, Scotland

Tonnage: 380 ts displacement; 265.35 tons gross; 54.97 tons net

Dimensions:
Length overall: 52.10 m
Length of hull: 44.00 m
Length between perpendiculars: 36.60 m
Width: 8.50 m
Depth to deck: 4.70 m
Depth in hold: 4.10 m
Draft (aft): 4.50 m

Sail area: 1020 square meters

Rigging: 14 sails; 4 foresails; foremast: foresail, lower topsail, upper topsail, topgallant; mainmast: mainsail, main gaff topsail, main topmast staysail; mizzenmast: mizzen sail, mizzen-gaff topsail, mizzen-topmast staysail

Masts: height of mainmast over the deck: 30.20 meters; lower masts: aluminum alloy; topmast and spars: rattan plywood

Auxiliary engine: two Gardner diesel engines, 230 horsepower each

Crew: 6-person active crew, 3 rotating instructors, 36 trainees

Use: sailing school-ship

Poland

Dar Mlodziezy
Dar Pomorza
Fryderyk Chopin

General Zaruski
Iskra II
Kapitan Glowacki

Oceania
Pogoria
Zawisza Czarny II

Dar Mlodziezy

The *Dar Mlodiezy* ("The Gift of Youth") relieved the long-serving *Dar Pomorza,* which has now become a museum ship. The new ship was arranged so that training operations can be carried out year-round. In addition to the top deck the ship possesses three through decks. The cadets sleep in hammocks in three large rooms for 50 men each.

Great attention was given to the external features. Mostly weather-resistant material was used, for example, synthetic rope on the running rigging and rustproof steel for the belaying pins. The stern is shaped in a very original manner—four windows of the drawing room break through the unusual square stern. A starboard and portside forecastle yardarm facilitates maneuvers in har-

bor waters. In addition to the two stockless anchors, a backup stockless anchor lies on the forecastle.

A large percentage of the financial means for the construction of the new school-ship was raised by the youth of Poland. On her maiden voyage, the *Dar Mlodziezy* sailed in the STA-regatta of 1982 from England to Portugal and back. Her size alone was enough to awaken

great interest everywhere she went. To cover the high cost of her upkeep, the ship also takes paying passengers on board. In 1990, for example, she undertook cruises in the Mediterranean, and at the Columbus Regatta in 1992 the full-rigged ship also hosted paying trainees from Western countries.

Type: full-rigged ship, steel

Nation: Poland

Owner: Wyzsza Szkola Morska

Home port: Gdynia

Year of construction: launched March 4, 1981; commissioned 1982

Shipyard: Stoczinia Gdanska (Danzig shipyard), Gdansk

Tonnage: approx. 2950 ts displacement

Dimensions:
Length overall: 105.40 m
Length of hull: 91.00 m
Length between perpendiculars: 79.40 m

Width: 14.00 m
Depth to deck: 10.00 m
Draft: 6.00 m

Sail area: 2780 square meters

Rigging: 4 foresails; all masts double topsail, single topgallant, royal

Masts: height of mainmast: 49 meters

Auxiliary engine: two Sulzer 8 AL20/24 diesel, 750 horsepower each, 1 propeller with adjustable blades

Crew: 42-person active crew, 4 teachers, 150 cadets

Use: sailing school-ship

Dar Pomorza

In 1909 the German School-Ship Association put its second sailing school-ship, the *Princess Eitel Friedrich*, in service. Her design was very similar to that of the *Grand Duchess Elisabeth* (today the *Duchesse Anne*), which had been built in 1901 as the association's first school-ship. The training at that time was for the benefit of deck boys and officer cadets. A unique feature of the ship is the long poop that extends to the mainmast.

After World War I the ship had to be given to France, which had no use for it. Until 1921 the sailing ship remained laid up in St. Nazaire. The Société Anonyme de Navigation "Les Navires Ecoles Francais" at this time owned the 4-masted bark *Richelieu* to meet its training needs. The *Princess Eitel Friedrich* was supposed to join her in the training service. She received the new name *Colbert*. But even after the loss of the *Richelieu* this never happened. The ship remained in St. Na-

zaire. In 1926 she was sold to Baron de Forrest, who wanted to make a yacht out of her. But this undertaking, too, did not get past the planning stages.

The Polish State Merchant Marine School at that time still used the bark *Lwow* to meet its training needs, but because of her age this ship was scheduled for retirement. A replacement ship was needed. The *Colbert* seemed well suited for this purpose.

With the means assembled through voluntary donations

Previous names: *Pomorze, Colbert, Princess Eitel Friedrich*

Type: full-rigged ship, steel

Nation: Poland

Owner: *Dar Pomorza* foundation

Home port: Gdynia

Year of construction: 1909; commissioned April 6, 1910

Shipyard: Blohm & Voss, Hamburg

Tonnage: 1561 tons gross

Dimensions:
Length overall: 91.00 m
Length between perpendiculars: 72.60 m
Width: 12.60 m
Depth in hold: 6.30 m
Draft: 5.70 m

Sail area: 1900 square meters

Rigging: 25 sails; 4 foresails, double topsail, single topgallant, royals

Masts: topmast and topgallant mast

Auxiliary engine: MAN 6-cylinder diesel engine, 430 horsepower

Crew: 30-person active crew, 150 boys

Use: museum ship in Gdynia

from the population of Pomorze, it was possible to purchase the ship in 1929. She first received the name *Pomorze* and, after her arrival in Poland, the name *Dar Pomorza* ("Dar" means gift, "Pomorza" is the genitive form of Pomorze). The ship bore the name *Pomorze* only on her voyage from St. Nazaire to Nakskov.

On December 26, 1929, the *Pomorze* left St. Nazaire, towed by the *Poolzee.* On December 29 she had to drop anchor in a heavy storm. The crew entered the boats, because a total loss was feared. Only with the help of a second towboat was it possible to bring the *Pomorze* under control again. On January 9, 1930, she reached Poland. The sailing ship now received an auxiliary engine and soon thereafter could be given to the merchant marine school. Training voyages, which repeatedly led across the Atlantic, took place regularly until 1939. At the outbreak of World War II the *Dar Pomorza* entered Swedish waters in search of protection. She then lay interned in Stockholm during the war. After the end of the war she was returned to Poland and once again sailed regularly in the training service, often visiting foreign ports. In 1972 she became the first ship from the Eastern Block to take part in the Tall Ships Race. She continued to do so regularly until her retirement. In 1980 she received the regatta's highest honor, the Cutty Sark Trophy, which is awarded in recognition of exceptional contributions to international understanding. Since the *Dar Mlodziezy* entered service in 1982 the *Dar Pomorza* has been moored as a stationary ship.

Fryderyk Chopin

Type: brig, steel	Shipyard: Dora Shipyard, Gdynia	Sail area: 1200 square meters	Crew: 17-person active crew, 39 trainees (students)
Nation: Poland		Rigging: 23 sails; both masts in addition to lower sail, double topsail, single topgallant, royal and skysail	Use: sailing school-ship
Owner: International Class Aflot Foundation	Tonnage: 305 tons gross; 91 tons net; 400 tdw		
Home port: Gdansk	Dimensions: Length overall: 55.50 m Length of hull: 44.80 m Width: 8.50 m Draft: 3.80 m	Masts: height of mainmast over the deck: 37 meters	
Year of construction: 1990; launched November 11, 1990; commissioned November 1991		Auxiliary engine: Wola diesel, 400 horsepower	

The rig, which is strikingly high in relation to the size of the ship, and the elegant lines of the hull make the brig a square-rigger with the qualities of a racing yacht.

Like all Polish-built tall sailing ships, the *Fryderyk Chopin* comes from the drawing board of the world-famous designer Zygmunt Choren. She is the ninth square-rigger that Choren had built in Gdansk and Gdynia. Most of these ships are full-rigged ships belonging to either Russia or the Ukraine. She got her name from the famous Polish composer.

The captain of the brig, Krzyztof Baranowski, had the idea of establishing floating classrooms aboard sailing ships. Initially high seas yachts were used, and later the *Pogoria*. Today the *Fryderyk Chopin* is used for this purpose.

General Zaruski

The ketch was built at a Swedish shipyard at Polish expense according to the plans for the yacht *Kaparen* of the "Svenska Segler Skolan." Because of the war, her delivery to Poland was no longer possible. For this reason, Sweden used the ship under the name *Kryssaren* until 1945, when she was taken into training service by Poland under the name *General Zaruski*. In 1948 the ketch received the name *Mloda Gwardia* ("Young Guard"), which was then changed to *Mariusz Zaruski*. Zaruski was a pioneer of Polish competitive sailing.

Previous names: *Mariusz Zaruski, Mloda Gwardia, General Zaruski*	Dimensions: Length overall: 28.00 m Length between perpendiculars: 25.30 m Width: 5.80 m Draft: 3.50 m
Type: ketch	
Nation: Poland	Sail area: 310 square meters
Owner: Liga Obrony Kraju	Rigging: 7 sails
Home port: Gdansk (Danzig)	Auxiliary engine: two 6-cylinder Albin diesel engines, 150 horsepower total, 2 propellers
Year of construction: 1930	
Shipyard: B. Lund in Ekenäs near Kalmar (Sweden)	Crew: 3-person active crew, 25 boys
Tonnage: 71 tons gross	Use: sailing school-ship

Iskra II

Type: barkentine, steel	Year of construction: launched March 6, 1982; commissioned August 11, 1982	Dimensions: Length overall: 49.00 m Length at the waterline: 42.50 m Width: 8.00 m Draft: 3.70 m	Masts: height of mainmast: 30.20 meters
Nation: Poland			Auxiliary engine: diesel engine
Owner: Marine Wyzsza Szkola Marynarki	Shipyard: Stocznia Gdanska (Danzig Shipyard), Gdansk; design: Zygmunt Choren		Crew: 18-person active crew, 45 cadets
Home port: Gdynia		Sail area: 1035 square meters	Use: sailing school-ship
	Tonnage: 381 ts displacement		

The *Iskra* ("spark") belongs to the Pogoria class (like the *Kaliakra* and the *Oceania*). A typical characteristic of this class is the flat stern. The ship has a Bermuda sail on her mizzenmast.

Kapitan Glowacki

Previous name: *Henryk Rutkowski*

Type: brigantine, composite construction

Nation: Poland

Owner: Polish Yacht Union, Trzebiez

Home port: Gdansk (Danzig)

Year of construction: 1944

Shipyard: Swinemünde

Tonnage: gross register tonnage 99; 24 tons net

Dimensions:
Length overall: 29.70 m

Length of hull: 24.30 m
Length at the waterline: 21.40 m
Width: 6.43 m
Draft: 3.20 m

Sail area: 337 square meters

Rigging: 3 square sails on the foremast

Masts: steel (one piece), height of mast: 21 meters

Auxiliary engine: Delfin diesel, 121 horsepower

Crew: 3-person active crew, 15 boys (girls)

Use: sailing school-ship

The ship was built as a purely motorized German patrol boat. Poland claimed her as a war prize in 1945.

She got her name from a well-known fighter in the resistance from 1939 to 1945. In 1950–51 she was converted into a fore-and-aft ketch at the Rybacka shipyard in Gdynia. As a school-ship with the designation GDY-180 she served the trainees of the Polish fishing fleet. From 1976 to 1984 the ketch did not find any particular use. In 1984 her conversion into a brigantine began with an extensive modification of the entire ship. Since 1986 the *Henryk Rutkowski* has sailed for the Polish Yacht Association. Mostly clubs and youth groups book the cruises. There is no age limit. The ship also hosts paying guests from Western countries. Already prior to the political changes in the former Eastern Block the *Hendryk Rutkowski* made frequent cruises to Western European coasts. Today the ship sails under the name *Kapitan Glowacki*.

Oceania

The ship has the hull of the Pogoria class with the typical flat stern. It has no bowsprit. The square sails, which are tapered at the bottom, are hoisted to the yards, which are mounted rigidly at the tops of the masts. The furling of the sails takes place by rolling them downwards into a long "basket."

Type: 3-master, steel

Nation: Poland

Owner: Polish Academy of Sciences

Year of construction: 1985

Shipyard: Stocznia Gdanska (Danzig Shipyard), Gdansk

Tonnage: 550 ts displacement; 396 tons gross

Dimensions:
Length overall: 48.50 m
Length of hull: 41.00 m
Width: 9.00 m

Sail area: 650 square meters

Rigging: automatic rig; all masts with one very high and relatively narrow square sail

Masts: all masts are the same height

Auxiliary engine: auxiliary engine

Use: research vessel

Pogoria

Type: barkentine, steel

Nation: Poland

Owner: Polish Yachting Association, Warsaw (Iron Shackle Fraternity)

Home port: Gdansk

Year of construction: 1980

Shipyard: Stocznia Gdanska (Danzig shipyard), Gdansk

Tonnage: 342 ts displacement

Dimensions:
Length overall: 47.00 m
Length of hull: 40.00 m

Length at the waterline: 35.40 m
Width: 8.00 m
Draft: 3.50 m

Sail area: 1000 square meters

Masts: height of mainmast: 33.50 meters

Auxiliary engine: diesel engine, 310 horsepower

Crew: 18-person active crew, 45 trainees

Use: sailing school-ship, chartered ship

The *Pogoria* is a sailing school-ship that was built for the youth of the Iron Shackle Association. The four crossed shackles on the square sails of the foremast are the symbol of this association.

In addition to the training voyages during the summer vacation from June until September, the ship undertakes chartered cruises that can take her as far as the Caribbean. In the winter of 1980–81 the *Pogoria* sailed to the Antarctic Ocean on a commission of the Academy of Sciences to bring scientists who had spent the winter at the South Pole back to Poland. From September 1983 to May 1984 she sailed around Africa with young Poles and also trainees from the West for the project "Floating Classrooms." From 1985 to 1991 the ship was continuously chartered, serving the Canadian Educational Alternative of Ottawa and Montreal as a floating school.

In her appearances in regattas the barkentine has acquitted herself exceptionally well.

The ship got her name from a Polish lake. An essential feature of the ship is her flat stern. Other sailing ships of the Pogoria class are the *Kaliakra*, the *Oceania*, and the *Iskra II*.

Zawisza Czarny II

Previous name: *Cietrzew*

Type: 3-masted staysail schooner

Nation: Poland

Owner: Zwiazek Harcerstwa Pulsing (Union of Polish Boy Scouts)

Home port: Kolobrzeg

Year of construction: 1952

Shipyard: Stocznia Polnocna, Gdansk (Danzig)

Tonnage: 164 tons gross

Dimensions:
Length overall: 42.00 m
Length of hull: 35.50 m
Length between perpendiculars: 33.00 m
Width: 6.80 m
Draft: 4.60 m

Sail area: 550 square meters (with square foresail)

Rigging: 10 sails (with square foresail); 4 foresails (forestaysail with boom); foremast: foretrysail, square foresail; mainmast: main staysail, main trysail; mizzenmast: mizzen staysail, mizzen (jib-headed) sail; main staysail and mizzen staysail with boom

Masts: pole masts

Auxiliary engine: DKW diesel engine, 300 horsepower

Crew: 5-person active crew, 47 boys

Use: sailing school-ship

The current *Zawisza Czarny* must not be confused with the wooden 3-masted fore-and-aft schooner of the same name, formerly the *Petra,* that was built in 1902 at the shipyard of Holm & Gustafsson in Raa, Sweden. After 1934 the ship sailed under the Polish flag. After the occupation of Poland in August 1939, the schooner was probably brought to Lübeck, renamed the *Black Hussar,* painted black, and used by the naval Hitler Youth for training purposes. In 1946 the ship was returned to Poland. Her condition was so bad, however, that she had to be scrapped in 1947.

The *Zawisza Czarny II* was built in 1952 as fishery vessel. In 1961 she was converted into a school-ship for the Boy Scouts. In the winter of 1967 another modification took place, in the course of which the ship was lengthened by 3 meters to its current size.

Staysail rigging on a 3-master is something extremely rare nowadays. An additional peculiarity distinguishes the ship. Each of the trysails is set between two curved gaffs. By this means the sails achieve the most favorable curvature. This type of rig is also known as a "wishbone rig." Staysails make it possible to reduce the weight of the gaffs and are also supposed to facilitate the handling of the sails.

Zawisza is the family name of a knightly family from the fifteenth century. "Czarny," the "Black One," is the surname of a famous member of this family who fought against the Order of Teutonic Knights. His steel-clad bust stands in a bracket-like holder on the bow of the ship.

274

Portugal

Boa Esperança
Condor de
  Vilamoura

Creoula
D. Fernando II
  e Gloria

Leão Holandês
Sagres II
Santa Maria Manuela

Boa Esperança

Type: caravel, fifteenth century, reproduction, wood

Nation: Portugal

Owner: Associaçao Portuguesa de Treino de Vela (APORVELA)

Home port: Lisbon

Years of construction: 1989–1990; launched April 28, 1990

Shipyard: Samuel & Filhos, Vila do Conde, Portugal

Dimensions:
Length overall: 23.20 m
Length between perpendiculars: 21.72 m
Width: 6.59 m
Depth to deck: 3.60 m
Draft: 3.25 m

Sail area: total sail area, 220 square meters; mainsail, 150 square meters; mizzen sail 70 square meters

Rigging: 2 sails (lateen sails)

Masts: height of mainmast over the keel: 21 meters

Auxiliary engine: Volvo Penta diesel engine

Crew: 22 people

Use: sailing school-ship

From the beginning, the square sail was in use in Northern Europe as well as in the Mediterranean region. While in the north it evolved into the series of sails characteristic of the powerful sail towers of large modern sailing ships, in southern latitudes it disappeared for no apparent reason. After the ninth century the lateen sail appeared there, which was set on a lateen yard that was extraordinarily long in relation to the size of the ship. The golden age of this type of sail was the era of the caravels, the galleys, and the galleasses. Columbus's *Niña* even had 3 masts with this type of rigging. In Northern Europe the lateen sail was still set aft of the square-rigged masts on the mizzenmast well into the eighteenth century. Today the boom and gaff on this mast are used to maneuver the mizzen sail.

The *Boa Esperança* was built in commemoration of the pioneering achievements of Portuguese seafarers 500 years ago. On the orders of John II of Portugal, Bartolomeu Dias set off in 1487–88 in search of a sea route to India by way of the west coast of Africa and sailed around what he called the "Cape of Storms" (the Cape of Good Hope).

Because the ship is used for educational purposes, it was impossible to do without modern navigational aids and an engine. The reproduction proved herself admirably during its voyage across the Atlantic in 1992 commemorating Columbus's voyage of discovery 500 years before.

Type: 2-masted schooner, steel

Nation: Portugal

Owner: Atlântico Lda.

Home port: Vilamoura

Year of construction: 1986

Shipyard: Marina de Vilamoura

Tonnage: 106.86 tons gross; 72.88 tons net

Dimensions:
Length overall: 34.77 m
Length of hull: 25.99 m
Width: 7.12 m
Draft: 2.60 m

Rigging: 7 sails; 3 foresails; foremast: square foresail, foretrysail; mainmast: main staysail, Bermuda sail

Auxiliary engine: Cummins, 235 horsepower

Crew: 8-person active crew, 120 guests on day cruises

Use: chartered ship

The schooner is a reproduction of an American fishing vessel. She is luxuriously furnished with a large salon and air conditioning and is used exclusively for tourism on the coast of the Algarve.

The *Creoula* belonged to the famous fleet of Portugal's bank schooners. At that time she belonged to the Parceria Geral de Pescarias. As of 1973 she had sailed a total of thirty-seven times to the cod-fishing grounds in the waters off New Foundland. The fifty-four fishermen among the crew of seventy-two would then sail in their dories to the actual fishing spots. Often they were out of view of the mother ship for the entire day while engaged in the task of laying out the four-hundred-meter-long fishing line with its four hundred hooks and, after the catch,

pulling it back into the little boat.

The demands that were placed on the fishermen in the process were exceptional. A superb sense of direction, a perfect knowledge of the weather and the sea, courage, and presence of mind were the most important preconditions for a happy and successful fishing expedition. The school-ship *Creoula* is today operated by the Aporvela (Associação Portugueasa de Treino de Vela).

Type: 4-masted fore-and-aft schooner, steel

Nation: Portugal

Owner: Defense ministry

Home port: Lisbon

Year of construction: launched March 1937; commissioned May 1937 (construction time 62 days)

Shipyard: Estaleiros Navais de Lisbao (CUF)

Tonnage: 818 ts displacement; 1055 tons gross

Dimensions:
Length overall: 67.40 m
Length at the waterline: 52.70 m
Width: 9.90 m
Draft: 4.10 m

Sail area: 1364 square meters

Rigging: 11 sails

Masts: height of mainmast over the deck: 29 meters

Auxiliary engine: 6-cylinder diesel, 480 horsepower

Crew: 37-person active crew, 50 trainees

Use: sailing school-ship

D. Fernando II e Gloria

Type: frigate (full-rigging), wood

Nation: Portugal

Owner: maritime museum, Lisbon

Location: Lisbon

Year of construction: 1843

Shipyard: Damão Shipyard, Goa

Tonnage: 1849.16 ts displacement

Dimensions:
Length overall: 86.75 m
Width: 12.80 m
Draft (maximum): 6.40 m

Sail area: 2052.21 square meters

Auxiliary engine: none

Crew: 143–379 people

Armaments: twenty-eight guns on the gun deck, twenty-two guns on the main deck

Use: museum ship

The ship was the Portuguese navy's last sailing frigate. The hull was built entirely of teakwood and covered with a layer of copper to protect against teredo.

The maiden voyage in 1845 led from Goa to Lisbon. Ferdinand of Saxony, the husband of Queen Maria I of Portugal, performed the christening.

The *D. Fernando,* as the frigate was called, was an important link between the motherland and the colonies. During the long voyages not only military personnel and the corresponding equipment were on board, but also colonists, so that up to 650 souls could be on board. In 1878 the frigate ended her active service. Until 1938 she was an artillery school-ship.

Subsequently she became a school and dormitory ship for young men from poor families. In 1963 a fire partially destroyed the ship. She ran aground in the mud of the Mar da Palha, Tagus. In January of 1992 she was raised, and in September of the same year she entered a floating dock. There the restoration began.

In April 1998 the restored ship was brought to the maritime museum in Lisbon, where she was open to visitors of the Expo.

Today conferences also take place on the ship; there is also room for traveling exhibitions.

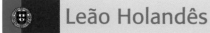

Previous names: *Sepha Vollaars, Ibaek, Peterna, Mojenhörn, Rönndik, Marie Hilck, Martha Ahrens, Amalie*

Type: 3-masted fore-and-aft schooner, steel

Nation: Portugal

Owner: Dirk Willem Gesink

Home port: Olhao, Portugal

Year of construction: 1910

Shipyard: Brothers Bodewes, Martenshoek, Holland

Tonnage: 150 ts displacement; 89.8 tons gross; 47.0 tons net

Dimensions:
Length overall: 44.00 m
Length of hull: 31.10 m
Length at the waterline: 28.10 m
Width: 6.10 m
Depth in hold: 2.30 m
Depth to deck: 3.90 m
Draft: 2.80–3.20 m

Sail area: 5075.5 square meters

Rigging: 12 sails

Masts: height of mainmast over the deck: 27 meters

Auxiliary engine: Caterpillar diesel, 253 horsepower

Crew: 5-person active crew, 12–14 guests

Use: chartered ship, tourist ship

There are certainly not many ships that, even in the course of a long life, have changed owners and names as often as the *Leão Holandês* ("Dutch Lion").

She was built as the 2-masted schooner *Amalie* at German expense and deployed as a freighter in the coastal trade. In 1922 the ship received her first engine, and in 1923 the hull was lengthened by 5 meters. The 2-master became a 3-masted fore-and-aft schooner. As the *Peterna* the ship sailed under the Danish flag after 1957. She had become a motorized schooner. In 1975 the *Peterna* was sold to Holland. There her rerigging as a 3-master with the name *Sepha Vollaars* took place.

From 1983 until 1987 the sailing ship was in Swiss hands. She was supposed to be used in the tourist business in Tahiti under the same name.

The venture fell through. After the ship's return to Europe, the current owner purchased her in 1987. The necessary restoration took place in Belgium and Portugal. The *Leão Holandês* today sails the Portuguese coastal waters.

In 1998 it was learned that the ship is up for sale.

The *Albert Leo Schlageter* was built in 1937 as the last and most modern sailing school-ship of the former German Reich navy. Because of the war that soon followed, the bark was able to make voyages for only a few months. At that time an eagle ornamented the bow. The crew consisted of 298 men.

During the war the ship suffered an engine breakdown. At the end of the war the United States took the ship over in Bremerhaven. Because it had no use for the ship, however, the United States gave her to Brazil in 1948. Under the new name *Guanabara* she was, with some interruptions, a school-ship of the Brazilian navy until 1961. In October 1961, the Portuguese navy purchased the bark as a replacement for the retired *Sagres I*. She received the name *Sagres II*.

Sagres is a port city in the south of Portugal from which famous Portuguese exploratory missions were launched. The city is closely associated with Prince Henry the Navigator, who here established the world's first merchant marine school. His bust decorates the bow of the *Sagres II*.

On April 24, 1962, the ship's first voyage under the Portuguese flag took her from her previous home port of Rio de Janeiro to Lisbon. The captain was Capt. Lt. Henrique Alfonso Silva da Horta.

The ship, like her predecessor, bears a red cross on all her square sails (no longer on the spanker as was the case with the *Sagres I*). Normally two training missions a year are undertaken.

The *Sagres II* regularly takes part in tall ship regattas.

Previous names: *Guanabara, Albert Leo Schlageter*

Type: bark, steel

Nation: Portugal

Owner: Armada Portuguesa

Home port: Alfeite near Lisbon

Year of construction: 1937; launched October 30, 1937

Shipyard: Blohm & Voss, Hamburg

Tonnage: 1869 ts displacement

Dimensions:
Length overall: 89.48 m
Length of hull: 81.28 m
Length between perpendiculars: 70.10 m
Width: 12.02 m
Draft: 5.30 m

Sail area: 1796 square meters

Rigging: 23 sails; 4 foresails, double topsail, single topgallant, royals; mizzenmast: lower mizzen, upper mizzen, mizzen topsail

Masts: fore- and mainmast with 1 topmast; height of mainmast masthead truck over the waterline: approx. 45 meters

Auxiliary engine: MAN diesel engine, 750 horsepower; speed with engine, approx. 10 knots

Crew: 10 officers, 19 lower officers, 131 regular crew members, approx. 90 cadets

Use: sailing school-ship

Santa Maria Manuela

Type: 4-masted fore-and-aft schooner, steel

Nation: Portugal

Owner: Fundação Santa Maria Manuela

Home port: Viano do Castelo, Aveiro

Year of construction: 1937 (construction time 62 days); launched March 10, 1937

Shipyard: Estaleiros Navais de Lisboa (CUF)

Tonnage: 1237 tons gross

Dimensions:
Length overall: 67.40 m
Length of hull: 57.70 m

Length between perpendiculars: 52.80 m
Width: 9.90 m
Depth in hold: 5.10 m
Depth to deck: 5.90 m
Draft: 5.20 m

Sail area: 1244 square meters

Rigging: 11 sails

Masts: height of mainmast over the deck: 36.90 meters

Auxiliary engine: Burmeister diesel, 380 horsepower

Crew: 75, of which 55 are fishermen

Use: still active as fishing vessel, conversion into a sailing school-ship is planned

Like her sister ship the *Creoula*, the *Santa Maria Manuela* also sailed to the waters off Newfoundland in order to catch cod with her small fishing boats (dories). Greenland and the Davis Strait were also among her fishing areas. The voyages lasted from April until August or the beginning of September. When fully loaded, the ship sailed home with 750 tons of deep-frozen fish and 60 tons of liver oil. There are plans to convert the schooner into a school-ship for 50 trainees.

Romania

Mircea

Mircea

Previous names: *Rion, Mircea*

Type: bark, steel

Nation: Romania

Owner: Maritime School Constanza

Home port: Constanza

Year of construction: 1938, launched September 1938

Shipyard: Blohm & Voss, Hamburg

Tonnage: 1760 ts displacement (fully equipped); 1312 tons gross

Dimensions:
Length overall: 82.10 m
Length of hull: 73.70 m
Length between perpendiculars: 62.00 m

Width: 12.00 m
Depth to deck: 7.30 m
Draft: 5.20 m

Sail area: 1748 square meters

Rigging: 23 sails; 4 foresails, double topsail, single topgallant, royals; mizzenmast: lower mizzen, upper mizzen, mizzen topsail

Masts: height of mainmast over the deck: 41.38 meters; height of mainmast over the bottom edge of the keel: 49.16 meters

Auxiliary engine: MaK diesel engine, 1100 horsepower

Crew: 40 officers and lower officers, 50 active crew members, 120 pupils

Use: sailing school-ship

The *Mircea* was built for Romania in 1938 with exactly the same dimensions as the *Gorch Fock I,* the current *Towarischtsch.* She was a replacement ship for the retired brig *Mircea I.* The other sailing school-ships of the former German Reich navy, the *Horst Wessel* (1936), now the *Eagle,* and the *Albert Leo Schaefer* (1938), now the *Sagres II,* as well as the *Gorch Fock II* (1958) of the German Federal Navy, are of exactly the same type but have been lengthened by 8 meters. It is a little-known fact that yet another sailing school-ship of the same class was built at the same shipyard. The ship had been launched in Hamburg, but still had no official name. After the end of the war she came to Kiel, was loaded with munitions, and subsequently sank in the Baltic. Thus a total of six sailing school-ships were built according to the same basic plan at the Blohm & Voss shipyard.

The *Mircea* received her name from Duke Mircea, who in the fourteenth century, after long battles against the Turks, won back the Dobrugea and thus opened sea trading routes for the Walachia. The ship carries a magnificent depiction of the duke as a figurehead.

In April 1939 the ship was transferred to the Black Sea port of Constanta. Her maiden voyage subsequently took her to the Mediterranean. After the war the ship was temporarily in Russian hands but was soon given back to Romania. From January until September 1966, the ship remained at a shipbuilding yard in Hamburg for rebuilding and renovation work. The rebuilding included routine work, replacement of the standing and running rigging and of the sails, installation of a MaK diesel engine, and the addition of new lifeboats and tenders, refurbishment of the living quarters (including the deck flooring, the cabin walls, the furniture, and the medical facilities), renewal and modernization of the navigational and electrical equipment, and changes in the watertight compartments to increase the level of safety in case of a leak.

Russia

Alevtina and Tuy
Alpha
Courier
Elena Maria
  Barbara
Horisont

Kronwerk
Kruzenshtern
Meridian/Sekstant/
  Tropik
Mir
Nadeshda

Pallada
Sedov
Shtandart
Sviatitel Nikolai
Triumph
Yunyi Baltiets
Zarja

Alevtina and Tuy

Type: 2-masted topsail schooner, wood

Nation: Russia

Owner: Ekron company

Home port: Saint Petersburg

Year of construction: 1995

Shipyard: Askold, Petrosawodsk, Lake Onega

Tonnage: 58 ts displacement

Dimensions:
Length overall: 29.50 m
Length of hull: 18.70 m
Length between perpendiculars: 16.00 m
Width: 4.67 m
Draft: 2.25 m

Sail area: 240 square meters

Rigging: 7 sails

Masts: height of mainmast over the deck: 17.70 meters

Auxiliary engine: Volvo Penta TAMD 41 HD, 145 horsepower

Crew: 4–5-person active crew, 5–8 trainees, 6–8 guests, on day cruises, 20 guests

Use: sailing school-ship, chartered ship

The schooner is an authentic reproduction of a type of trading vessel used in Europe in the middle of the eighteenth century. The figure of a woman on the cutwater and the plentiful carvings on the transom decorate the ship in a distinctive manner. A sister ship is the *Elena Maria Barbara*. Additional sister ships are the *Anna* (1994) and the *Volchista*. Each of the ships can be distinguished by her unique figurehead and stern ornamentation.

After a collision with a Kuwaiti freighter in the outer Elbe during the night of June 8, 1996, the *Alevtina* had such a serious leak that she ultimately had to send out an SOS by radio. The German emergency cruisers *Hermann Helms*, based in Cuxhaven, and *Wilhelm Kaisen*, based in Helgoland, immediately rushed to her aid. With the help of pumps, the emergency cruisers escorted the seriously damaged ship to Cuxhaven.

Alpha

Like several other Soviet sailing school-ships, the *Alpha* was built by Finland for the Soviet Union after World War I as a reparations payment. Her distinguishing signal is UOJV (Roman alphabet). In Saint Petersburg's main ship registry she is entered under the number M-16566.

Type: barkentine

Nation: Russia

Owner: Ministry of the Maritime fleet, Moscow

Home port: Saint Petersburg

Year of construction: 1948

Shipyard: Finnish shipyard

Tonnage: 322 tons gross; 41 tons net; 55 tdw

Dimensions:
Length overall: 44.00 m
Length of hull: 8.90 m
Depth to deck: 4.00 m
Draft: 3.30 m

Auxiliary engine: 4-stroke diesel engine, built in 1958 (German Democratic Republic); speed with engine, 7 knots

Crew: sailing school-ship (existence is questionable)

Courier

Type: coastal frigate, eighteenth century, wood, reproduction

Nation: Russia

Owner: Avantgarde shipyard, Petrosawodsk, Lake Onega

Home port: Saint Petersburg

Year of construction: 1993

Shipyard: Avant Garde Shipyard, Petrosawodsk

Tonnage: 56.82 ts displacement

Dimensions:
Length overall: 26.50 m
Width: 5.20 m
Draft: 1.80 m, maximum 2.56 m

Sail area: 260 square meters

Rigging: 6 sails, bowsprit with spritsail

Auxiliary engine: K161M1 diesel, 100 horsepower

Crew: 5-person active crew, 8 (11) passengers

Use: chartered, museum ship

The *Courier* is the reproduction of a war frigate from czarist Russia in the period of Peter the Great. The ship is armed with guns and bears the ornamentation of a ship of that time.

The shipbuilders on Lake Onega constructed a robust and well-crafted sailing ship. During her first voyages on a rough sea she proved to be surprisingly fast and seaworthy.

Elena Maria Barbara

Type: 2-masted topsail
schooner, wood

Nation: Russia

Owner: STS Elena Maria
Barbara, Saint Petersburg

Home port: Saint Petersburg

Year of construction: 1995;
launched July 16, 1995

Shipyard: Askold,
Petrosawodsk, Lake Onega

Tonnage: 58 ts displacement

Dimensions:
Length overall: 29.40 m
Length of hull: 19.40 m
Length between
perpendiculars: 16.00 m

Width: 4.60 m
Depth in hold: 2.30 m
Draft: 2.30 m

Sail area: 234 square meters

Rigging: 7 sails

Masts: height of mainmast over
the deck: 18 meters

Auxiliary engine: Volvo Penta
TAMD 41 HD, 145 horsepower

Crew: 4–5-person active crew,
5–8 trainees, 6–8 guests,
20 on day cruises

Use: sailing school-ship,
chartered ship

The schooner is the authentic reproduction of a type of trading vessel used in Europe in the middle of the eighteenth century. The figure of a blue-clad woman on the cutwater and prolific carving on the transom decorate the ship in a distinctive manner. Her sister ships are the *Alevtina* and the *Tuy*.

Horisont

Type: barkentine, wood

Nation: Russia

Owner: merchant marine

Year of construction: 1948

Shipyard: Laivateollisuus, Åbo, Finland

Tonnage: 322 tons gross; 41 tons net; 55 tdw

Dimensions:
Length overall: 39.40 m
Width: 8.90 m
Depth to deck: 4.00 m
Draft: 3.40 m

Rigging: 14 sails; 3 foresails; foremast: foresail, double topsail, single topgallant, royal; mainmast: gaff-sail, gaff-topsail, main staysail, main topmast staysail; mizzenmast: gaff-sail, gaff-topsail

Auxiliary engine: diesel engine

Use: sailing school-ship (existence questionable)

Kronwerk

Previous name: *Sirius*

Type: barkentine, wood

Nation: Russia

Home port: Saint Petersburg

Year of construction: 1948

Shipyard: Laivateollisuus, Åbo, Finland

Tonnage: 322 tons gross; 41 tons net

Dimensions:
Length overall: 44.00 m
Width: 8.90 m
Draft: 3.30 m

Auxiliary engine: removed, originally an East German auxiliary diesel engine

Use: restaurant ship

Like several other Soviet sailing school-ships, the *Kronwerk* was built by Finland after World War II as a reparations payment to the Soviet Union.

She lies moored today as a restaurant ship in Saint Petersburg.

Previous name: *Padua*

Type: 4-masted bark, steel

Nation: Russia

Owner: Academy of the Fishing Fleet (Fishing Ministry), Kaliningrad

Home port: Kaliningrad

Year of construction: 1926; launched June 24, 1926

Shipyard: J. C. Tecklenborg, Wesermünde

Tonnage: 3545 tons gross; 1162 tons net; 1976 tdw

Dimensions:
Length overall: 114.50 m
Length between perpendiculars: 95.00 m
Width: 14.00 m
Depth to deck: 8.50 m
Depth in hold: 7.80 m

Sail area: 3400 square meters

Rigging: 34 sails; 4 foresails, double topsail, double topgallant, royals; mizzenmast: lower mizzen, upper mizzen, mizzen topsail

Masts, spars: height of mainmast over the deck: 55.30 meters; main yard 29.10 meters; main royal yard: 14.50 meters; fore-, main-, and mizzenmast with topgallant mast; mizzenmast with mizzen topmast

Auxiliary engine: two SKL 8-cylinder diesel engines, 736 kilowatts each

Crew: 74 people under the German flag, 40 of them boys

Use: sailing school-ship, opportunities for guests to sail

The *Padua* was built in 1926 for the Hamburg shipping company F. Laeisz as the last of all the cargo-carrying 4-masted barks. Although the shipping company had already repurchased the majority of its barks after the world war, it chose to undertake this remarkable new construction project. Four-masted barks of about 3000 tons gross were the most profitable sailing ships of that time. Like most of the Laeisz sailing ships, the *Padua* too sailed in the saltpeter trade and later also hauled wheat from Australia. She had no engine. The ship belonged to the "3 island type" of the Laeisz fleet. The upper three decks were connected to one another by gangways. Special ballast tanks were built into the ship. There is room for 437 tons of ballast water in the cell-like compartments of the double bottom. In addition there are 16 tons of water in the afterpeak tanks. Laeisz had had the large bark equipped from the beginning as a combined freighter and school-ship. Under his flag the 40 places for young sailors were always filled. On her maiden voyage it took the *Padua* 87 days to cover the distance between Hamburg and Talcahuano (Chile); on her return voyage from Taltal to Delfzijl it took 94 days. Her record voyage took her in 1933–34 from Hamburg to Port Lincoln, South Australia, in 67 days. Although the ship still possessed no engine at that time, she sailed at remarkably regular intervals between Europe and South America. In 1930 the *Padua* lost four men overboard in a heavy storm off Cape Horn. In 1932 she was laid up in Hamburg, but with the support of the German government was able to be put back into service. The *Padua* made her last long journey under the German flag in 1938–39. Captain Richard Wendt had the command. The *Padua* left Bremen on October 15, 1983, and reached Port Lincoln (Australia) by way of Valparaiso on March 8, 1939. She departed on April 3, 1939, with a full cargo of wheat. After a voyage of 93 days she entered the Clyde on July 8, 1939.

At the end of the war the ship lay at Flensburg. In January 1946, the *Padua* arrived in Swindemünde and there was delivered to Russia. She received her new name in honor of the famous Russian seaman and explorer Adam Johann Ritter v. Krusenstern (Novermber 19, 1770, to August 24, 1846). The *Kruzenshtern* has been a familiar guest in many ports of the world for years. With her vast dimensions, she will always be a main attraction whenever large sailing ships hold a rendezvous.

Since then it has become possible to sail aboard the ship as a paying guest. "Friends of the Kruzenshtern" in Bremerhaven handle these bookings, which provide the ship with vital revenue. Starting in 1980, the ship was registered in Tallinn. When Estonia gained its independence from the Soviet Union in April of 1991, the Kruzenshtern's registration was transferred to Kaliningrad (Königsberg). The fisheries ministry of the USSR was dissolved in November of 1991, but its responsibilities, including the management of the Kruzenshtern, were taken over by the Russian fisheries ministry in February of 1992.

Meridian/Sekstant/Tropik

Type: barkentine, wood

Nation: Russia

Owner: Ministry of Fishing, Moscow (in the case of the *Meridian* also the Kaliningrad merchant marine school)

Home port: Meridian, Kaliningrad; Tropik, Riga; Sekstant, Nachodka (near Vladivostok)

Shipyard: Finnish shipyard

Tonnage: 322 tons gross; 41 tons net; 55 tdw

Dimensions:
Length overall: 39.40 m
  Tropik: 44.00 m
Width: 8.90 m
Depth to deck: 4.00 m
Draft: 3.40 m
  Tropik 3.30 m

Auxiliary engine: 2-stroke and 4-stroke diesel engines; speed with engine, 6.5 knots (Tropik, 7 knots)

Use: sailing school-ship

Like several other Soviet sailing school-ships, the *Meridian, Sekstant,* and *Tropik* were built by Finland for the Soviet Union after World War II as a reparations payment.

Their distinguishing signals are, in the Roman alphabet, UTCW, UZUU, and UWLZ. In Saint Petersburg's main ship registry they are entered under the numbers M-16574, M-16651, and M-16577.

The *Mir* ("Freedom," "World") belongs, with her sister ships, the *Druzhba*, the *Pallada*, the *Khersones*, and the Polish *Dar Mlodziezy*, to a new generation of large sailing ships. Typical of the hull is above all the flat poop. Many technical features, such as the steering system, are similar to those of modern motorized ships. Multiple copies of all of the navigational systems are present to facilitate training exercises. During some of the training cruises the ship is also open to a certain number of paying guests. The *Mir* is also supposed to be used for charter purposes in the winter.

Type: full-rigged ship

Nation: Russia

Owner: State Maritime Academy, Saint Petersburg

Home port: Saint Petersburg

Year of construction: launched March 31, 1987; commissioned November 30, 1987

Shipyard: Stocznia Gdanska (Danzing Shipyard), Gdansk

Tonnage: 2824 ts displacement; 2256 tons gross; 677 tons net

Dimensions:
Length overall: 109.40 m
Length of hull: 94.20 m
Length at the waterline: 79.40 m
Width: 14.00 m
Depth to upper deck: 8.40 m
Draft: 6.60 m

Sail area: 2771 square meters

Rigging: 26 sails (Dracon)

Masts: height of mainmast over the waterline: 49.50 meters (all 3 masts)

Auxiliary engine: two Cegielski Sulzer diesel engines on one axle, type 6AL20/24 engines, 570 horsepower each

Crew: 55-person active crew, 144 cadets

Use: sailing school-ship

Nadeshda

Type: full-rigged ship, steel

Nation: Russia

Owner: Far Eastern State Maritime Academy (FESMA)

Home port: Vladivostok

Years of construction: 1989–90

Shipyard: Stocznia Gdanska (Danziger shipyard), Gdansk

Tonnage: approx. 2800 ts displacement

Dimensions:
Length overall: 109.40 m
Length of hull: 94.20 m
Length at the waterline: 79.40 m
Width: 14.00 m
Depth to upper deck: 10.60 m
Depth to deck: 8.40 m
Draft: 6.60 m

Sail area: approx. 2700 square meters

Rigging: 26 sails; all masts double topsails, single topgallants, royal sails

Masts: height of mainmast over the waterline: 49.50 meters

Auxiliary engine: two diesel engines on one axle, 450 kilowatts each

Crew: 55-person active crew, 140 cadets (trainees)

Use: sailing school-ship

The *Nadeshda* ("Hope") is the fifth sailing school-ship to be built according to plans by the designer Zygmund Choren. Many of her technical systems, for instance, the steering system, are similar to those of modern motorized ships.

For instructional purposes, multiple copies of all of the navigational systems are present. A blue-painted band at the height of the deck decorates the hull. From a distance the ship can be recognized by the initials of the school in Vladivostok, which are painted on the sides of the hull.

Pallada

Type: full-rigged ship, steel

Nation: Russia

Owner: fishery school, Vladivostock

Home port: Vladivostok

Year of construction: launched July 20, 1988; commissioned June 30, 1989

Shipyard: Stocznia Gdanska (Danzig shipyard); Gdansk

Tonnage: 2987 ts displacement; 2264 tons gross; 667 tons net

Dimensions:
Length overall: 109.40 m
Length of hull: 94.20 m
Length at the waterline: 79.40 m
Width: 14.00 m
Depth to upper deck: 10.60 m
Depth to main deck: 8.40 m
Draft: 6.60 m

Sail area: 2771 square meters

Rigging: 26 sails

Masts: height over the waterline: 49.50 meters (all 3 masts)

Auxiliary engine: two Ciegielski Sulzer diesel engines on one axle, type 6AL20/24, 570 horsepower each

Crew: 56-person active crew, 143 cadets

Use: sailing school-ship

The *Pallada* is a sister ship to the new Soviet sailing ship *Mir*. Externally she distinguishes herself very significantly from her sister by means of her black hull with a painted white streak. In Russian her name means "Pallas" (Athena). In 1992 she took part in the Columbus Regatta, and in 1997 in the Hong Kong–Osaka Regatta.

Sedov

Previous names:
Kommodore Johnsen,
Magdalene Vinnen

Type: 4-masted bark, steel

Nation: Russia

Owner: State Fishing Academy,
Murmansk

Home port: Murmansk

Year of construction: 1921

Shipyard: Friedrich Krupp,
Germania Shipyard, Kiel

Tonnage: 5300 ts
displacement; 3476 tons
gross; 3017 tons net (under
the German flag)

Dimensions:
Length overall: 117.50 m
Length of hull: 109.00 m
Length between
perpendiculars: 100.20 m
Width: 14.60 m
Depth in hold: 8.10 m

Sail area: 4192 square meters

Rigging: 34 sails; 4 foresails,
double topsails, double
topgallants, royals;
mizzenmast: lower mizzen,
upper mizzen, mizzen topsail

Masts: height of mainmast
over the deck: 54.50 meters

Auxiliary engine: SKL
8-cylinder diesel,
1160 horsepower

Crew: 64-person active crew,
180 trainees

Use: sailing school-ship,
opportunities for guests to sail

Before World War I the F. A. Vinnen shipping company in Bremen owned a fleet of twelve large sailing freighters, among them the *Magdalene Vinnen I,* formerly the *Dunstaffnage,* which had to be given to Italy as a reparations payment after the war. The second *Magdalene Vinnen* was commissioned in Kiel soon after the war and built as a freight-carrying school-ship with an auxiliary engine. Like most of the 4-masted barks of that time, she sailed primarily to South America in the saltpeter trade during the 1920s. The synthetic process developed by Haber-Bosch to bind nitrogen gradually made Europe independent of saltpeter supplies from Chile. For that reason the large saltpeter ships often sailed to Australia in order to transport wheat.

The *Magdalene Vinnen* was built according to the "three-island principle" (forecastle, maindeck, poop). The main wheel stands midships on the main deck in front of the charthouse; the emergency wheel is located under the poop with a skylight to allow for observation of the sails. The main deck is covered with steel plates. Hatch 3 opens onto the main deck in front of the main wheel. (That is a peculiarity that is seldom found in ships of the "three-island" type.

Usually all of the hatches lie on the main deck.) The ship does not possess any special ballast tanks. The double bottom can take in a total of 345 tons of ballast water in three separate sections. (The problem of stability is probably solved differently today, since the ship no longer carries any cargo).

In 1936 the *Magdalene Vinnen* was sold to the North German Lloyd, Bremen, and received the new name *Kommodore Johnsen,* From this time until the outbreak of World War II she sailed only in the wheat trade to Australia. During a storm in 1937 the ship nearly capsized because the load of wheat shifted. Before the ships that had been summoned by the SOS could bring help, the crew managed to restabilize the ship by trimming the load. The sailing ship made her last great voyage in 1939. She left Port Lincoln, Australia, on March 26 and reached Queenstown on July 11, after 107 days. During the entirety of the war the *Kommodore Johnsen* sailed in the Baltic in the warm months and was laid up in the Flensburger Förde in the winter. That is where she was in 1945 at the end of the war. At the command of the Allies, she had to be brought to Hamburg and was handed over to the British authorities in 1949. Later a German-English crew brought her to Kiel, where she was taken over by the Russians. She remained moored in Swinemünde a while longer before being towed, probably to Odessa, in 1950. She got the name *Sedov* from the Russian polar explorer Georgij J. Sedov (February 20, 1877, to May 5, 1914), who attempted to reach the North Pole in 1911. He died in the ice after spending two winters in the polar region. For a long time it was not known whether the *Sedov* was once again sailing under wind power. Accordingly, the surprise was great when the 4-masted bark once again set off on journeys abroad in the spring of 1982 and visited Hamburg in May 1982. In 1983 the *Sedov* was at the windjammer rendezvous in Bremerhaven, where many of her former officers and crew members were invited aboard.

Since then she has been a frequent and much appreciated guest during visits to foreign ports and at tall ship rendezvous. It has also become possible to enroll as a paying guest. This is an important source of funding for the ship.

Shtandart

Type: early-eighteenth-century frigate, wood, reproduction	Length between perpendiculars: 24.20 m Width: 6.95 m Depth in hold: 2.45 m Draft: 2.50 m
Nation: Russia	
Owner: Shtandart Project, Saint Petersburg	Sail area: 660 square meters
Home port: Saint Petersburg	Rigging: 14 sails
Year of construction: keel laid November 4, 1994; launched September 4, 1999	Masts: height of mainmast over the deck: 33 meters
Shipyard: Shtandart Shipyard, Saint Petersburg	Auxiliary engine: two Volvo Penta engines, 250 horsepower
Tonnage: 180 ts displacement; 134 tons gross; 80 tons net	Crew: 10-person active crew, 26 trainees, 4 guests
Dimensions: Length overall: 34.50 m Length of hull: 25.40 m	Use: sailing school-ship, ambassador ship, museum ship

Peter the Great (1672–1725) traveled incognito with a large delegation to Holland and England to learn the European countries' shipbuilding methods. He presented himself as a servant of the embassy and worked for 4 months as a carpenter at a shipyard in the English city of Deptford. In the Nordic War (1700–21), Peter I succeeded in winning an access route to the Baltic from Sweden. As a result Russia had access to four seas.

The czar started to build up a fleet in accordance with European models. The first ship of the new Russian navy was the twenty-eight-cannon *Shtan-*

dart ("Standard"), which the czar himself had designed and in whose construction he participated. A new flag was designed for this ship. She shows the Russian double eagle in the center, surrounded by the outlines of the four seas, which are held by the beaks and claws of the eagle.

The frigate was repeatedly deployed in battle against Sweden, and during these engagements the czar himself commanded the ship. The ship did service as the symbolic backbone of the Russian navy until 1728. After that she was moored as a monument in the Kronwerk Canal behind the Peter and Paul Fortress. Because the ship increasingly rotted below the waterline, she ultimately had to be scrapped. A reconstruction planned at that time never came into being. The name, admittedly, was passed on to many of the fleet's ships. Ultimately it was born by the yacht *Czar Nicholas II.*

The current reconstruction of the *Shtandart* is based on a model that was completed after careful investigations of plans and visual representations from that time. Young people from different countries, under the supervision of professional shipbuilders, were employed in the construction. The larch wood for the planking comes from the Lindulovskaya Forest near Reschino, which Peter I had planted especially for shipbuilding. On the reproduction, too, the standard adorns the artfully executed stern. The head of a lion on the cutwater, with the year 1703 beneath it, leads the ship over the seas.

Sviatitel Nikolai

Type: reproduction of a trading vessel (Lodya) of the eighteenth to nineteenth centuries, wood

Nation: Russia

Owner: Historical Maritime and Culture Center in Petrosawodsk, Karelia

Home port: Petrozavodsk, Lake Onega

Year of construction: 1991

Shipyard: A/O NPK Karelien TAMP

Tonnage: 45 ts displacement; 52.6 tons gross

Dimensions:
Length overall: 21.00 m
Length of hull: 16.00 m
Length between perpendiculars: 15.00 m
Width: 5.20 m
Draft: 1.90 m

Sail area: 185 square meters

Rigging: 3 sails

Masts: height of mainmast over the deck: 13.80 meters

Auxiliary engine: diesel, 40 horsepower

Crew: 2–6-person active crew, 10 guests

Use: chartered ship, sailing museum ship

The 3-masted *Saint Nicholas* represents an important stage in the evolution of the square-riggers. The fore- and mainmasts set one square sail each, whose sail area can be modified by means of laced studding sails. A lug sail is set on the mizzenmast. As ships, along with the corresponding sail areas, became larger, the square-sail areas had to be distributed over several yards.

Triumph

Type: brig, steel

Nation: Russia

Owner: Boris Sidorovsky, Saint Petersburg

Home port: Saint Petersburg

Year of construction: 1954

Shipyard: in Petrozavodsk

Tonnage: 80 ts displacement; 55 tons gross

Dimensions:
Length overall: 25.00 m
Length of hull: 21.80 m
Length between perpendiculars: 19.00 m
Width: 5.42 m
Depth in hold: 2.25 m
Draft: 1.90 m

Sail area: 220 square meters

Rigging: 11 sails

Masts: height of mainmast over the deck: 14 meters

Auxiliary engine:
Russian diesel engine, 180 horsepower

Crew: 2-person active crew, guests, trainees

Use: private ship, film ship

Originally the *Triumph* was a trawler that had been built using the composite construction method and with a 2-masted Bermuda rig. In 1986 the current owner purchased the heavily decayed vessel from a fishing enterprise in Lomonosov. As the first step in the renovation process the wooden planks were replaced with steel plates. Within a year, largely by means of the owner's own labor, a brig with bow and stern ornamentation as well as a painted streak came into being that could have been part of Czar Peter the Great's fleet. The name too is reminiscent of a ship of that time. The double-headed Russian eagle adorns the cutwater.

The *Triumph* is a consistently popular attraction in the harbor of St. Petersburg.

"Young Man of the Baltic," as the ship is called in translation, offers the highest safety standards in combination with a large amount of space. She was supposed to be a floating school for the Young Pioneers of the former USSR.

Even after perestroika, nothing about the ship's use as a school changed. A striking feature is the lower rigging on the heavy hull. The relatively small draft allows the ship to also approach smaller harbors. Increasingly, guests are also taken aboard to help finance the voyages.

The schooner has also made appearances in Bremerhaven in the context of Sail '90 and Sail '95.

In 1999 she took part in the windjammer rendezvous in Rouen.

Type: 2-masted Bermuda schooner, steel

Nation: Russia

Owner: Palace of the Youth (Marine Club Yunea), Saint Petersburg

Home port: Saint Petersburg

Year of construction: 1989

Shipyard: Baltic Shipyard

Tonnage: 495 ts displacement

Dimensions:
Length overall: 49.40 m
Width: 8.40 m
Draft: 3.17 m

Sail area: 506 square meters

Rigging: 6 sails; foremast gaff-sail, mainmast Bermuda sail

Masts: height of mainmast over the deck: 28.30 meters

Auxiliary engine: 408-horsepower diesel engine

Crew: 18-person active crew including teachers, 34 trainees

Use: sailing school-ship

Zarja

Type: 3-masted fore-and-aft schooner, wood

Nation: Russia

Owner: presumably the Oceanographic Institute Saint Petersburg

Home port: presumably Saint Petersburg

Year of construction: 1952

Shipyard: Finnish shipyard

Tonnage: ; 580 ts displacement; 333 tons gross

Rigging: 9 sails (with topsails); 3 foresails (forestaysails with boom); foremast: schooner sails, running square foresail (attached like a curtain to the middle of the yard and fastened to the lower mast); main- and mizzen-mast: gaff-sail (topsails are not set, but may be used in the future)

Masts, spars: all masts with 1 topmast; hoisting gaffs

Auxiliary engine: diesel engine, 300 horsepower; speed with engine, 9 knots

Use: sailing school-ship

The *Zarja* was built at a Finnish wharf as a reparations payment. She sails with a civilian crew and is used as a nonmagnetic ship for oceanographic research.

The Seychelles

Sea Pearl   Sea Shell

Sea Pearl

Previous names: *Regina Chatarina, Spica, Frisk, Fri, Carlsö LL 324, Drochtersen, Dirk KW 44*

Type: 2-masted fore-and-aft schooner, steel

Nation: the Seychelles

Owner: Silhouette Cruises shipping company

Home port: Victoria, Mahé, Seychelles

Year of construction: 1915

Shipyard: Gebroeders de Windt, Vlaardingen, the Netherlands

Tonnage: 155 ts displacement; 99.8 tons gross; 70.4 tons net

Dimensions:
Length overall: 35.00 m
Length of hull: 27.00 m
Length between perpendiculars: 24.50 m
Width: 6.62 m
Depth in hold: 2.98 m
Draft: 2.75 m

Sail area: 540 square meters

Rigging: 7 sails

Masts: height of mainmast over the deck: 27 meters

Auxiliary engine: Cummins diesel, NTCE 365, 300 horsepower

Crew: 7-person active crew, 22 guests

Use: tourist sailing ship

The current schooner was built as a sailing fish lugger. Until 1930 she belonged—at the end as its final sailing ship—to the Dutch herring fishing fleet under the name *Dirk*. The ship returned to the Netherlands in 1978 by way of Germany, Sweden, and Denmark.

Anton Jacobsen purchased the ship in 1991 and converted her into a passenger ship with a schooner rig. The fully air-conditioned ship sails the Caribbean in the winter and in the summer primarily Canadian waters.

In 1999 the ship was renovated and today sails with guests around the Seychelles. The ship is equipped for diving cruises.

Previous names: *Elisabeth Louw, Tonijn*

Type: 2-masted topsail schooner, iron

Nation: the Seychelles

Owner: Silhouette Cruises shipping company

Home port: Victoria, Mahé, the Seychelles

Year of construction: 1910 (modified 1985–86)

Shipyard: Vigé Shipyard, Haarlem, the Netherlands

Tonnage: 160 ts displacement; 110 tons gross; 33 tons net

Dimensions:
Length overall: 36.17 m
Length of hull: 28.70 m
Length between perpendiculars: 25.00 m
Width: 6.60 m
Draft: 2.90 m

Sail area: 520 square meters (on the wind, 374 square meters)

Rigging: 7 sails

Masts: height of mainmast over the deck: 32 meters

Auxiliary engine: Henschel diesel, 300 horsepower

Crew: 8-person active crew, 23 passengers

Use: tourist sailing ship

In 1985–86 the current owner converted the former pilot schooner *Tonijn* (tuna fish) into a chartered yacht. The riveted steel hull has four bulkheads. During the conversion a false clipper bow was attached and the steel deck was covered with iroko planks. The main wheel and the compass house stand behind the wheelhouse on the quarterdeck. The masts are made of larch, the gaffs and yards of aluminum. Both yards remain at position. Twenty-three guest berths are distributed over eight cabins. From 1986 to 1988 the schooner was chartered by a Belgian sailing school.

Since 1997 she has carried tourists around the Seychelles under her current name. Guests have the opportunity to undertake two or three diving sessions a day.

Spain

America II
Carmen Flores
Don Juan
  de Austria

Gefion
Juan Sebastian
  de Elcano
Niña

Pinta
Santa Maria

America II

Type: 2-masted fore-and-aft schooner, wood

Nation: Spain

Owner: Ramon Mendoza

Home port: Hamilton

Year of construction: 1967; launched May 3, 1967

Shipyard: Messrs. Goudy & Stevens, East Boothbay, Maine; design: George Steers and William Brown (original); Sparkman & Stevens (reproduction)

Tonnage: 149 ts displacement; 92.24 tons gross; 66.0 tons net

Dimensions:
Length overall: 39.50 m
Length of hull: 31.90 m
Length at the waterline: 27.60 m
Width: 6.90 m
Draft (maximum): 3.50 m

Sail area: 500 square meters

Rigging: 4 sails; 1 foremast (with boom); foremast: gaff-sail; mainmast: gaff-sail, gaff-topsail

Masts: height of mainmast over the deck: 22.70 meters; mainmast with topmast

Auxiliary engine: General Motors 8 V-71 diesel engine, 350 horsepower

Crew: 7 people

Use: private yacht

The story of the schooner *America* is one of the most exciting in all of competitive sailing. For the opening of the first World's Exhibition in 1851 a regatta was supposed to take place off the coast of England to which the newly founded New York Yacht Club was invited. England, the stronghold of competitive sailing, was considered the favorite from the beginning. The Americans could at best take part with a sailing ship that had not yet been built. Work began at the William Brown shipyard in New York City in the winter of 1850. All existing experience in the construction of fast ships was analyzed and used for this new construction. The ship was launched on May 3, 1851. She had to repre-

sent the nation and bore its name: America.

The Royal Yacht Squadron donated a silver tankard as a prize, which since then has become world famous as the America's Cup.

The historic contest began on August 22, 1851, at ten o'clock in the morning. The Royal Yacht Squadron entered 14 schooners and cutters. The United States was represented only by the *America*. But this ship achieved the unimaginable. It sailed the 58-mile course, which led around the Isle of Wight, in 10½ hours and crossed the finish line 8 minutes before its closest competitor. The queen followed the regatta from state yacht *Victoria and Albert*. When she asked during the race who was

in second place, she was told: "Madame, there is no second place."

The cup went to America and remained there for 132 years. It was not until 1983 that the Australians won in the 26th America's Cup. The English have tried many times to bring the coveted cup home. As of today they have not succeeded. Many millions have been spent on the construction of the ships and the training of the crews. Many a patron has lost his fortune in the process. Nowadays such enormous sums can be raised only by syndicates of millionaires.

It was possible to preserve *America I* as a national treasure until 1944. The *America II*, an exact replica, was launched on May 3, 1967, in Maine, exactly 116 years after the original. R. J. Schaefer, president of the T & M Schaefer Brewery in New York, had had the schooner reconstructed at 25 times the cost of the original. During the America's Cup competition off Newport, Rhode Island, in September 1967, the *America* was part of the spectator fleet.

Today the yacht belongs the Spaniard Ramon Mendoza.

Carmen Flores

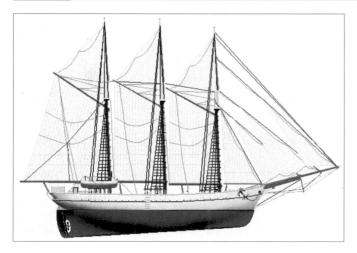

Previous names: *Sayremar Uno* (1975–99), *Cala San Vicenç* (1936–75), *Puerto de Palma* (1931–36), *Carmen Flores* (1919–31)

Type: 3-masted fore-and-aft schooner, wood

Nation: Spain

Owner: Museu Marítim, Barcelona

Home port: Barcelona

Year of construction: 1918; launched January 14, 1919

Shipyard: Astilleros Mari, Torrevieja, Spain

Tonnage: 271 ts displacement; 167 tons gross; 155 tons net

Dimensions:
Length overall: 46.00 m
Length of hull: 34.00
Length between perpendiculars: 27.70 m
Width: 8.50 m
Depth in hold: 4.60 m
Depth to deck: 4.50 m

Sail area: 515 square meters

Rigging: 11 sails

Masts: height of mainmast over the deck: 27 meters

Auxiliary engine: Volvo Penta diesel, 397 horsepower

Crew: 8-person active crew

Use: museum ship, sailing school-ship

The *Carmen Flores* was built for the Cuba trade. The later name *Puerto de Palma* indicates that the schooner belonged to the large fleet of the Naviera Mallorquina at that time. She remained a freighter, but the rig was reduced to 2, and later to 1 mast.

After a long period as a trading vessel the ship returned to Torrevieja in the 1960s as a mother ship for divers. During caulking work at dock it was revealed that the wood of the hull is remarkably well preserved. After she had performed work on artificial reefs off the coast of the province of Alicante, the Spanish authorities took the ship out of service for financial reasons. An auction for the by now run-down ship took place in Cartagena.

The Museu Marítim in Barcelona acquired her as an important part of Spanish shipbuilding history. Extensive restoration work followed and is still taking place, and a change of name is planned.

Don Juan de Austria

In the sea battle of Lepanto (Gulf of Corinth) on October 7, 1571, the fleet of the Holy League, assembled by Pope Pius V and consisting of Spain, Venice, and Malta, defeated the Turkish fleet decisively. The battle was a direct response to the Turks' conquest of Cyprus. The victory meant the end of Ottoman hegemony in the Mediterranean. The league's most important ship was the galley. Driven by a large number of oars and by large lateen sails, these ships could be deployed rapidly and effectively provided the sea was relatively calm. The fleet that ultimately

secured the victory at Lepanto was created and commanded by Don Juan de Austria, born on February 24, 1547, in Regensburg. He was the illegitimate son of Charles V and Barbara Blomberg. The flagship of his fleet was the *Sphinx*, a 2-masted royal galley. She had been built in 1568. An exact reproduction of this ship was built in 1971 at the same shipyard. She received the name *Don Juan de Austria* and can be seen in the maritime museum in Barcelona (Museu Marítim). The barrel vault in which she is housed resembles the ship halls of that time, some of which can still be seen today (on Crete, for example).

The reproduction has a total length of 60 meters, deck length of 52.5 meters, and a width of 8.40 meters. Four hundred men originally populated the ship. Of those, 236 were rowers, who had to work in groups of four chained to the 59 oars.

The oars have a length of 11.4 meters and a weight of 180 kilograms. For the reproduction, heights of 22 meters for the mainmast and 15 meters for the foremast were calculated. The lateen yard on the mainmast has a length of 50 meters. The lateen yard on the foremast measures 26.8 meters. With these dimensions, the mainmast could set 565 square meters and the foremast 126 square meters of sail area. The masts and the lateen yard were usually laid down with the sails rolled up while the ship was in the hall; hence in the case of the modern reproduction they also cannot be displayed in their working positions.

With the galleys the lateen sails reached their maximum sail area, because unlike the classic square sails they cannot be divided among multiple lateen yards on the same mast.

Gefion

The *Gefion* was built out of oak as a robust freighter. Stability and cargo capacity were the main considerations in the construction of the ship, which went into service in the Newfoundland trade. In 1928 the first engine was installed. In order to remain competitive, the ship had to be able to meet schedules. During the war the ship sailed with a reduced sail area as a freighter in the Baltic. In 1948 a thorough overhaul took place. The *Gefion* became a pure motorized freighter with a powerful engine. Bulk goods such as corn, cement, and salt were her cargo. In 1970 the Baltic Schooner Association acquired the schooner. The ship was rerigged according to original drawings. Within 2 years a seaworthy sailing vessel had again taken shape. The schooner made passenger cruises through the Danish islands. Today the ship sails primarily in the Caribbean.

In Nordic mythology, Gefion was the virginal goddess who looked after girls who died unmarried.

Type: 2-masted topsail schooner, wood	Width: 7.50 m
	Draft: 2.90 m
Nation: Spain	
	Sail area: 500 square meters
Owner: Joop Hooghienstra, Holland	Rigging: 10 sails; 4 foresails; foremast: topsail and topgallant
Home port: registered in Las Palmas	
	Masts: height of mainmast: 33 meters
Year of construction: 1894	
	Auxiliary engine: diesel engine, 120 horsepower
Shipyard: Sölvesborg, Sweden	
Tonnage: 189 ts displacement; 92 tons gross	Crew: 6-person active crew, 12 guests
Dimensions: Length overall: 40.00 m	Use: private ship for passenger cruises

The schooner was built in 1927 for what was at that time the Royal Spanish Navy. The ship's name comes from the Spanish seafarer Juan Sebastian de Elcano, who in 1526, following Magellan's death, completed the first circumnavigation of the globe.

The ship has the old, "original" schooner rig: All gaffs are hoisted and lowered. The sails are bent to the mast with cringles. As a school-ship it has a very long poop. The large deckhouse, located midships, carries a small navigational bridge on its roof.

Below the boat skids this house was later expanded to the bulwark. In this respect, through the short forecastle, and in that the square sails are gathered to the middle of the yard, the *Juan Sebastian De Elcano* differs in some significant respects from her sister ship, the *Esmeralda*. The schooner has the most modern navigational devices at her disposal. She carries a total of twelve boats (two motorized lifeboats, four rowing lifeboats, one captain's launch, one officers' launch, one cutter, one cadets' gig, two ding-

hies). In addition there are ten fully equipped rubber dinghies, of which eight are lashed over the bulwark, and several automatic life rafts. A crowned female figure ornaments the bow as a figurehead. The training voyages take place in many different seas.

At the start of Race No. 3 of "Operation Sail '76," the large ship collided with the Argentinean *Libertad*. The jibboom, several jib stays, and the topmast were broken. By the time of the parade on July 4, 1976, the damage had been repaired.

Type: 4-masted topsail schooner, steel

Nation: Spain

Owner: Buque Escuela De Guardias Marinas

Home port: San Fernando, Cádiz

Year of construction: 1927; launched March 1927

Shipyard: Messrs. Echevarrieta y Larringa, Cádiz; design: Camper & Nicholsons, Ltd., Naval Architects and Yacht Building, Southampton

Tonnage: 3750 ts displacement

Dimensions:
Length overall: 106.80 m
Length of hull: 88.10 m
Length between perpendiculars: 79.10 m
Width: 13.10 m
Depth to deck: 9.00 m
Draft: 6.90 m

Sail area: 2467 square meters

Rigging: 20 sails; 5 foresails; foremast: fore-, double topsail, single topgallant, schooner sail, fore-gaff topsail; the other masts: gaff-sail, gaff-topsail, topgallant

Masts: all masts have the same height; height over the deck: 45.60 meters; height over the waterline: 48.70 meters; lower masts, bowsprit, fore-yard: steel; topmasts and all remaining spars: Oregon pine; mizzen lower mast only serves to expel exhaust; length of bowsprit: 19.20 meters

Auxiliary engine: Sulzer Bazán (Cartegna) diesel engine, 1500 horsepower; speed with engine, approx. 9 knots

Armaments: four 5.7-centimeter rapid-fire cannons

Crew: 243 officers, petty officers, and regular crew members, 89 cadets

Use: sailing school-ship

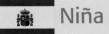

Niña

Type: caravel, reproduction of Columbus's ship (1492), wood

Nation: Spain

Owner: Muelle de las Carabelas, La Rabida, Palos de la Frontera

Home port: Palos de la Frontera

Years of construction: 1989–90

Shipyard: Naval Shipyard Cartagena

Tonnage: 100.30 ts displacement

Dimensions:
Length overall: 21.40 m
Length of keel: 15.55 m
Width: 6.28 m
Depth to deck: 2.00 m

Sail area: 178.85 square meters

Rigging: 3 sails

Auxiliary engine: none

Crew: 1990—4 officers, 12 regular crew members

Use: museum ship

Pinta

Type: caravel, reproduction of Columbus's ship (1492), wood

Nation: Spain

Owner: Muelle de las Carabelas, La Rabida, Palos de la Frontera

Home port: Palos de la Frontera

Years of construction: 1989–90

Shipyard: Reunidos Shipyard, Isla Cristina (Huelva)

Tonnage: 115.50 ts displacement

Dimensions:
Length overall: 22.75 m
Length of keel: 16.12 m
Width: 6.60 m
Depth to deck: 2.21 m

Sail area: 186.62 square meters

Rigging: 3 sails

Auxiliary engine: none

Crew: 1990—4 officers, 13 regular crew members

Use: museum ship

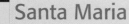

Type: carrack (caravel), reproduction of Columbus's ship (1492), wood

Nation: Spain

Owner: Muelle de las Carabelas, La Rabida, Palos de la Frontera

Home port: Palos de la Frontera

Years of construction: 1989–90

Shipyard: Viudes Shipyard, Barcelona

Tonnage: 223.88 ts displacement

Dimensions:
Length overall: 29.60 m
Length of keel: 16.10 m
Width: 7.96 m
Height of sails: 3.24 m

Sail area: 269.85 square meters

Rigging: 5 sails; bowsprit with spritsail

Auxiliary engine: none

Crew: 1990—6 officers, 20 regular crew members

Use: museum ship

Following their completion, the three reproductions of Columbus's ships, the *Santa Maria,* the *Pinta,* and the *Niña,* visited numerous ports in Spain, France, and Italy in 1990 and 1991. In the process they logged 9500 nautical miles, mostly under wind power.

Three other reproductions of the Columbus ships, built in Spain, sailed across the Atlantic in 1990 for the large Columbus Regatta in 1992. Today they are moored as museum ships in Corpus Christi, Texas.

On his first voyage in 1492, Columbus tried to reach India by sea. He died in the belief that he had found this route. His contemporaries also had not recognized that in reality America had been discovered.

With the three ships *Santa Maria, Pinta,* and *Niña,* Columbus left the port of Palos on August 3, 1492, and reached the island of Guanahani, which he named San Salvador on October 12, 1492. It is very probably Watling Island of the Bahamas. No visual representation or exact measures, much less plans, have survived of any of these ships. It was only in the seventeenth century that people started to build ships according to plans. Columbus sailed as an admiral aboard the flagship *Santa Maria,* which

for this reason became one of the most famous ships in maritime history. Numerous attempted reconstructions of this ship have been undertaken, of which the most recent and certainly the best was initiated in 1963 by Captain de Corbeta José Maria Martinez-Hidalgo, the director of the Museo Marítimo in Barcelona. It has since been destroyed by arson.

Another reproduction of the *Santa Maria* was built in 1963 for the World Exhibition in New York and brought to America aboard the German freighter *Neidenfals.* After the end of the World Exhibition the ship was brought to Washington, where for a number of years it lay moored in the Potomac as the main exhibit of the Museum for History of American Exploration. On the way to an exhibit in Saint Louis this ship capsized and sank in the Mississippi in 1969.

The *Santa Maria* was a normal trading ship that Columbus chose for his journey. He intentionally chose small ships, because they were easier to handle and because it was easier to cruise with them in the steady westerly wind.

Strangely, many reconstruction attempts and descriptions neglected the fact that the *Santa Maria* was a nao and not a caravel. The resulting errors and misinterpretations are obvious. Columbus uses the term "nao" 81 times to refer to the ship and designates the *Pinta* and the *Niña* explicitly as caravels by contrast.

In Columbus's time a nao used the complete rig of a large ship, namely five sails. In terms of square sails, there were a spritsail, a foresail, a mainsail, and a main topsail; on the mizzenmast there was a lateen sail. A nao had a round stern and a high forecastle. It is very probable that there was a hut on the half deck. The classic proportion of greatest width to the length of the keel and to the length of the deck at the time of the *Santa Maria* was called 1:2:3 (as-dos-tres). By contemporary standards these were quite ponderous ships, as Columbus himself had noted. Caravels were built in a more streamlined manner, had a flat stern, no forecastle, and in the beginning probably set only lateen sails on 1 or 2 masts.

In establishing the dimensions of his reproduction, Martinez-Hidalgo worked from the fact that in the surviving literature the *Santa Maria* is described repeatedly as a ship of slightly over 100 tons (*toneles*). This specification is a measurement of volume and refers to the number of barrels of wine of a particular size that the ship could have loaded. A *tonele* corresponds to approximately five-sixths of a registered ton. Extensive experiments with models and the careful examination of surviving visual representations and models produced a ship of 105 *toneles* cargo capacity with the corresponding dimensions. Martinez-Hidalgo had his version built according to these results.

The *Santa Maria* had two boats on board, a longboat and a small jolly. Four bombards for stone shot stood on the half deck. The gun ports had no covers. The remaining weaponry consisted of guns mounted on the railings (falconets) and the typical hand armaments of the time for the crew.

The topsail was rectangular and not trapezoidal, as it is often represented. It was sheeted to the crow's nest and not to the main yardarms. When furled, the sprit-sail was taken in to the yard, and this was then lashed parallel to the bowsprit. One may assume that in the case of the *Santa Maria,* too, large red crosses were painted on the square sails, as was the custom at that time for Portuguese and Spanish ships. A ship with this rig could sail within approximately 7 points of the wind. In the log, speeds of up to 9.5 knots are noted, even for long stretches. During the great sailing-ship parade in 1976 in the harbor of New York a second reconstruction of the *Santa Maria* took part, one which had been built during the same year in St. Petersburg, Florida. This ship too was wrecked in the Mississippi.

St. Vincent/Grenadines

Peace

Peace

Previous name: *SWI 180 Goplo*

Type: barkentine, steel

Nation: St. Vincent/ Grenadines

Owner: Kings Lake Shipping Company, Ltd., Malta

Home port: Kingstown, St. Vincent

Year of construction: 1962

Shipyard: in Gdansk (Danzig)

Dimensions:
Length overall: 79.80 m
Width: 10.60 m
Draft: 5.40 m

Sail area: 2280 square meters

Rigging: 16 sails; foremast: foresail, double topsail, single topgallant, royal sail

Masts: height of foremast over the waterline: 49.80 meters; mizzenmast expels exhaust

Auxiliary engine: Klöckner Humboldt Deutz diesel, 1380 kilowatts

Crew: 30-person active crew, 52 trainees, passengers

Use: sailing school-ship, sailing cruise ship

The hull of the *Peace* was built as an ocean trawler for fishing. Afterward the ship was employed worldwide for expeditions and research purposes. In 1990 Captain Heinz Hoss purchased the ship in order to convert her into a barkentine. This work was carried out in Danzig. Her use as a sailing cruise ship is possible because of her comfortable accommodations. A restaurant with 100 seats, a bar on deck, and a large sundeck as well as 26 double cabins with showers and toilets are available.

Sweden

Af Chapman
Älva
Amorina
Baltic Beauty
Blå Marité af Pripps
Blue Clipper
Falken and Gladan
Götheborg III

Gratia of Gothenburg
Gratitude of
   Gothenburg
Gretel
Gunilla
Hamlet
Hawila
Jarramas

Lady Ellen
Lady Ellen IV
Najaden
Najaden
Shalom
Vida
Viking
Wasa

Af Chapman

Previous names: *G. D. Kennedy, Dunboyne*

Type: full-rigged ship, iron

Nation: Sweden

Owner: city of Stockholm

Home port: Stockholm, Skeppsholmen

Year of construction: 1888; keel laid 1885; launched March 1888

Shipyard: Shipbuilding Company, Whitehaven, England (city of Cumberland)

Tonnage: 2300 ts displacement; 1425 tons gross; 1380 tons net

Dimensions:
Length overall: 85.40 m
Length of hull: 71.10 m
Length between perpendiculars: 71.10 m

Width: 11.40 m
Draft: 5.60 m

Sail area: 2207 square meters

Rigging: 26 sails, 4 foresails; all masts: double topsail, single topgallant, royal

Masts, spars: height of mainmast over the deck 41.60 meters; length of main yard: 25.70 meters

Auxiliary engine: none

Crew: as a naval school-ship 50-person active crew and 200 cadets

Use: youth hostel ship

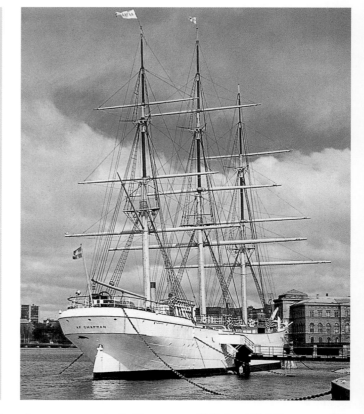

Because of the shipbuilding crisis at that time, the construction time took more than 3 years. Only then did the ship find a buyer. As a pure trading ship she sailed under her original name, the *Dunboyne*, from 1888 to 1908, for the Dublin shipping company Charles E. Martin & Company, primarily in the Australian trade. In 1909 the Norwegian shipowner Leif Gundersen of Porsgrund purchased the full-rigged ship without changing her name. The *Dunboyne* remained a trading ship. Before World War I she also belonged for a short time to the shipowner Emil Knutsen of Lillesand.

On July 30, 1915, the ship was sold to the Swedish shipping company A.-B. Transatlantic in Göteberg for 8300 pounds. Under the new name *G. D. Kennedy* the ship became a freight-carrying school-ship for the shipping company with room for 30 young men. For this purpose she was equipped with modern technical devices. The Swedish crown purchased the ship in November 1923 for 128,000 crowns. She was supposed to become a pure school-ship for the Swedish navy. For this purpose there followed a complete interior renovation. Since no cargo was carried any longer, living quarters for 200 cadets were built on the between deck and lit through numerous portholes cut in the sides. The sailing ship received the name *Af Chapman*. (Frederic Henric af Chapman, 1721–1808, was a master ship-builder and vice admiral in Karlskrona. His most important work is the *Architectura Navalis Mercatoria,* which first appeared in 1786).

Until 1937 the school-ship made numerous voyages in all the world's oceans (1934 was her last great overseas voyage). In 1937 the *Af Chapman* was retired as a school-ship and served until 1947 in Stockholm as a naval barracks. Subsequently the city museum

of Stockholm purchased the ship and put her at the disposal of the Svenska Turist Foreningen as a hostel ship. The *Af Chapman* has served this purpose since early 1949. The necessary modifications hardly changed the external appearance. Every mast still contains

the following yards: lower yard, topsail yard, topgallant yard.

The ship is not only a youth hostel, but can be used by guests of all ages.

 # Älva

Type: 3-masted Bermuda schooner

Nation: Sweden

Owner: AB ALVA shipping company (Captain Claes Stenestad)

Home port: Stockholm

Year of construction: 1939

Shipyard: Lödöse Shipyard (near Göteberg)

Tonnage: 470 ts displacement (including water ballast); 286 tons gross; 85 tons net

Dimensions:
Length overall: 52.00 m
Length of hull: 44.00 m
Width: 7.20 m
Depth in hold: 2.56 m
Depth to deck: 3.62 m
Draft: 3.00 m

Sail area: 500 square meters

Rigging: 6 sails

Masts: height of mainmast over the deck: 27.50 meters

Auxiliary engine:
Caterpillar diesel D-343,
400 horsepower

Crew: 4-person active crew, 38 guest berths, 80 guests on day cruises

Use: chartered ship

The *Älva* was built as a motor schooner for the cargo trade in Swedish waters and in the Baltic. The hull was lengthened by 7.8 meters in 1951 in Bremerhaven. During the installation of the powerful engine in 1961 the rig was removed. From 1967 to 1979 the motorized ship belonged to Rolf Pettersson of Stockholm and then became the property of Claes and Håkan Stenestad of Stockholm. The ship was newly rigged in Marstal and until 1990 sailed as the last wind-powered freighter in northern European waters. The steelwork for the ship's subsequent conversion into a school-ship took place in Stettin. In the process the structures were strengthened to such an extent that a planned conversion into a 4-masted bark is now feasible. At the moment the ship, with her extravagant interior, is used primarily for chartered cruises.

Amorina

Type: barkentine, steel

Nation: Sweden

Owner: Jan Lagerfeld & Association, Örebro, Sweden

Home port: Hurghada, Egypt

Year of construction: 1934; modification 1977–81

Shipyard: Götaverken, Göteberg

Tonnage: 530 ts displacement

Dimensions:
Length overall: 48.50 m
Length of hull: 34.30 m
Length at the waterline: 30.30 m

Width: 7.70 m
Draft: 4.10 m

Sail area: 650 square meters

Rigging: 16 sails (Dacron); foremast: double topsail, single topgallant, royal

Auxiliary engine: Deutz diesel engine, 420 horsepower

Crew: 11-person active crew; total of 59 berths in 20 cabins for guests

Use: chartered ship

The *Amorina* was built as a lightship. After years of deployment, the ship was modified and rerigged in Lisbon between 1977 and 1981. The bulging stern as well as the generous amounts of space in the interior of the ship are especially reminiscent of her earlier use. The sauna on the main deck is a Swedish "must." The Caribbean and the Mediterranean are the main travel destinations of this unusual ship, which is also used for diving vacations in the Red Sea.

Baltic Beauty

The ship was employed for many years as a fishing vessel. In 1980 the current owner modified the ketch so that she could be used for the passenger service.

A streak adorns the elegant hull, and a female figurehead points the ship's way.

Previous names: *Dominique Fredion, Sven Wilhelm, Hans II*

Type: gaff-rigged topsail ketch, steel

Nation: Sweden

Owner: Captain Yngve Victor Gottlow

Home port: Ronneby, Sweden

Year of construction: 1926; launched August 1, 1926

Shipyard: N. V. Capello, Zwartsluis, the Netherlands

Tonnage: 115 ts displacement; 75 tons gross; 37 tons net

Dimensions:
Length overall: 40.00 m

Length of hull: 29.29 m
Length between perpendiculars: 26.20 m
Width: 4.95 m
Draft: 2.50 m

Sail area: 345 square meters

Rigging: 7 sails; mainmast with topsail

Masts: height of mainmast over the deck: 19 meters

Auxiliary engine: Scania DSI 11, 245 horsepower

Crew: 3-person active crew, 20 guests (trainees)

Use: chartered ship

Type: 3-masted topsail schooner, wood	Tonnage: 450 ts displacement; 170 tons gross; 51 tons net	Rigging: 13 sails
Nation: Sweden	Dimensions: Length overall: 47.00 m	Masts: height of mainmast over the deck: 30 meters
Owner: H. B. Ambrått	Length of hull: 35.00 m Length between perpendiculars: 32.50 m	Auxiliary engine: Isuzu diesel, 460 horsepower
Home port: Stockholm	Width: 8.00 m Depth in hold: 3.60 m	Crew: 12-person active crew, 24 guests
Year of construction: 1921	Draft: 4.20 m	
Shipyard: in Fécamp, France	Sail area: 600 square meters	Use: conference ship, chartered ship, sailing school-ship

The *Marité* was built as a 3-masted topsail schooner to be used for fishing off Newfoundland. Her strong oak hull was able to deal with the often rough waters of the North Atlantic. She was the mother ship for ten dories, whose fishermen caught cod with long lines in the traditional manner. It could take up to 6 months to catch a full load of fish.

In 1929 the ship stopped fishing under wind power because it was no longer profitable. The *Marité* was sold to a buyer in Denmark and unrigged. As a motorized ship she was then used as a fishing vessel again until her retirement in 1974. Tvöroyri on the Faroe Islands was her base and homeport during this period.

In 1979 the current owner acquired the ship. She was in a truly desolate condition. Only the naked hull remained as a basis for the reconstruction and rerigging as one of the last remaining banks schooners.

In 1992 the schooner took part in the Columbus Regatta.

In 1999 the schooner was put up for sail.

Blue Clipper

Type: 3-masted fore-and-aft schooner, steel

Nation: Sweden

Owner: Svenska Skonertkompaniet, Torslanda

Home port: Torslanda

Year of construction: 1990

Shipyard: Marstrandsverken FEAB; Marstrand

Tonnage: 137 tons gross

Dimensions:
Length overall: 43.90 m
Length of hull: 31.90 m
Length at the waterline: 27.00 m
Width: 7.40 m
Draft: 4.00 m

Sail area: 675 square meters

Rigging: 10 sails

Auxiliary engine: Caterpillar diesel, 315 horsepower

Crew: 8-person active crew, 14 passengers, 45 guests on day cruises

Use: chartered ship

This luxuriously furnished schooner is the former *Spirit of Hennessy*. In 1872 the ship *Alfred* brought the first load of cognac from France to Shanghai. With the same name and painted white, the *Blue Clipper* repeated this memorable voyage in 1992.

In the construction of the hull modern elements are mixed with traditional elements, such as a clipper bow, an elegant yacht stern, and a long ballast keel. The teak deck was built on top of steel plates. An unusual feature is the placement of the auxiliary engine. Because there was no room for the engine in front of the propeller shaft, it was mounted above the shaft. A series of belts links the two elements.

Type: 2-masted fore-and-aft schooner, steel

Nation: Sweden

Owner: Royal Swedish Navy

Home port: Karlskrona

Year of construction: 1946 (Falken) and 1947 (Gladan)

Shipyard: Naval Shipyard, Stockholm

Tonnage: 220 ts displacement

Dimensions:
Length overall: 39.30 m
Length of hull: 34.40 m
Length between perpendiculars: 28.30 m
Width: 7.20 m
Draft: 4.20 m

Sail area: 519 square meters (working rig); in addition, fisherman's staysail, 97 square meters; square foresail, 87 square meters

Rigging: 9 sails; 3 foresails; fore-, mainmast: gaff-sail, gaff-topsail; square foresail, main fisherman's staysail

Masts: both masts with 1 topmast; height of mainmast over the waterline: 31.40 m

Auxiliary engine: 6-cylinder Scania Vabis diesel, 128 horsepower

Crew: 15-person active crew, of which 3 to 4 are officers, 38 boys

Use: sailing school-ship

The *Falken* ("falcon," sailing number S 02), together with her sister ship, the *Gladan* ("kite," sailing number S 01), was built by the Swedish navy as a replacement for the full-rigged ships *Jarramas* and *Najaden*. The *Falken* was chartered by the Rydberg-Stiftung for half a year in 1952 as a school-ship. On both ships, the forward deckhouse contains the galley, the after deckhouse primarily the officers' mess. The young men sleep in bunks and in hammocks. The gaffs are lowered to take in the sails. Approximately 60 tons of permanent ballast give the ship the necessary stability. Officer candidates of the merchant marine are trained in addition to those for the navy. The voyages lead mostly to the Baltic and North seas. The two schooners normally undertake 4-week voyages with cadets from the naval school in Karlskrona. The ships can also be chartered for civilian purposes, for example, for school outings.

Götheborg III

The Swedish East India Company was founded in 1731 and existed until 1813. Its most important trade relations were with China. One of its large ships, the *Götheborg,* which was built in 1738 at the Terra Nova shipyard in Stockholm, returned, heavily laden, to her home port of Götheborg on September 12. She was carrying tea, large quantities of porcelain, and five tons of silver. Shortly before reaching the harbor the ship collided with a cliff near the Älvsborg Fortress and sank. It was possible to raise a large portion of the cargo at that time, so that the long voyage was profitable nonetheless.

In 1984 the wreck was rediscovered. In the course of a number of years, divers recovered large quantities of valuable porcelain, which since then has been put on display in many exhibits. During the diving operations it was also possible to learn a great deal about the appearance of the ship. In October 1992 a group of sponsors formed and set itself the goal of reconstructing the ship as the *Götheborg III.* (The *Götheborg II* set off on her first trading voyage on February 2, 1788, and was wrecked on May 12, 1795, off the Shetland Islands.)

The reproduction is currently being completed at its own shipyard in Götheborg, which has in turn received the name Terra Nova. The ship weighs in at 1350 tons displacement. With a hull length of 40.55 meters and a keel length of 33.5 meters, she has a width of 10.7 meters. The height of the hull is 9.9 meters.

The *Götheborg III* will make her first voyage to China in October 2005. She will be used as a seagoing ship for research and educational purposes. In addition to an auxiliary engine, she will have a sail area of 1450 square meters.

Gratia of Gothenburg

Previous names: *Blue Shadow, Cinderella*

Type: fore-and-aft schooner, wood

Nation: Sweden

Owner: Stiftelsen Svenska Kryssarklubbens Seglarskola, Göteberg

Home port: Göteberg

Year of construction: 1900

Shipyard: Camper & Nicholsons, Gosport, England

Tonnage: 45.24 tons gross; 34.86 tons net

Dimensions:
Length overall: 29.85 m
Length of hull: 25.63 m
Length between perpendiculars: 20.48 m
Width: 5.08 m
Depth in hold: 2.77 m
Draft: 3.30 m

Sail area: 350 square meters

Rigging: 8 sails

Masts: height of mainmast over the waterline: 25.80 meters

Auxiliary engine: Volvo Penta diesel engine, 164 horsepower

Crew: 6–7-person active crew, 18 students

Use: sailing school-ship

The *Gratia* was built as a schooner and was sailed as a yacht by her previous owners, until in 1964 she came to the Stiftelsen Svenska Kryssarklubbens Seglarsko.

Gratitude of Gothenburg

Previous name: *Östervag*

Type: fore-and-aft ketch

Nation: Sweden

Owner: Stiftelsen Svenska Kryssarklubbens Seglarskola, Göteberg

Home port: Göteberg

Year of construction: 1907

Shipyard: in Portleven, England

Tonnage: 103 ts displacement; 60 tons gross; 31 tons net

Dimensions:
Length overall: 29.10 m
Length of hull: 23.00 m
Length between perpendiculars: 21.10 m
Width: 5.90 m
Draft: 2.90 m

Sail area: 350 square meters

Rigging: 8 sails

Masts: height of mainmast over the deck: 20.50 meters

Auxiliary engine: Volvo Penta diesel, 184 horsepower

Crew: 6–7-person active crew, 20 students

Use: sailing school-ship

The *Gratitude* was built as a Brixam trawler. Her homeport was Lowestoft until 1930, after which she sailed under the Swedish flag as a fishing vessel and a motorized freighter.

Since 1957 she has belonged to the Stiftelsen Svenska Kryssarklubbens Seglarsko, which had been recently founded at that time.

Gretel

This wooden 3-masted Bermuda schooner was built in Finland shortly after the end of World War II. She now belongs to Swedish owners. The ship is used for cruises. From 1974 to 1975 a circumnavigation of the globe was undertaken with the *Gretel*.

Type: 3-masted Bermuda schooner, wood

Nation: Sweden

Owner: Per Hagelin & Partners, Sweden

Year of construction: 1946

Shipyard: Einar Gustafson, Borga, Finland

Tonnage: 160 ts displacement

Dimensions:
Length overall: 27.30 m
Length of hull: 23.50 m
Width: 6.40 m
Draft: 2.10 m

Sail area: 230 square meters

Auxiliary engine: 120-horsepower Albin diesel

Crew: 5-person active crew, 10 guests

Use: chartered ship

Gunilla

Type: bark, steel

Nation: Sweden

Owner: AB Gunilla shipping company, Öckerö (Mott Bättre Vetande)

Home port: Öckerö

Year of construction: 1940 (last modification, 1997–99 in Öckerö)

Shipyard: Oskarshamn

Tonnage: 402 tons gross

Dimensions:
Length overall: 61.00 m
Length of hull: 49.96 m
Length between perpendiculars: 42.05 m

Width: 8.23 m
Depth in hold: 3.00 m
Depth to deck: 3.76 m
Draft: 3.20 m

Sail area: 1040 square meters

Rigging: 20 sails; 3 foresails, double topsail, single topgallant, royals

Masts: height of mainmast over the deck: 34 meters

Auxiliary engine: Caterpillar, 550 horsepower

Crew: 10 people, 38 trainees; for day cruises, up to 50 guests can come on board

The *Gunilla,* a 3-masted bark with a Bermuda rig intended for use in the freight trade, came into being in 1940 at a shipyard in the Swedish city of Oskarshamn. The ship was not put into service until the end of World War II. Under various owners she transported piece goods and bulk goods such as autos, lead, wheat, and sludge.

In 1954 the hull was lengthened by 8 meters and the schooner was converted into a pure motor ship. Following her last voyage with a cargo of grain, the organization Mot Bättre Vetande (Sailing Schools for Better Knowledge) purchased the ship. Within 2 years it had been converted and equipped as a bark to be used for educational purposes. Allan Palmer of the Åland islands designed the rig.

The original of the figurehead, which represents the daughter of the first owner, is located in the maritime museum in Oskarshamn. An exact copy was carved for the current bark.

The students of the organization remain affiliated with the ship for 3 years, spending a third of each school year aboard the bark. Depending on how advanced the students are, the voyages lead either to Swedish waters or, later, to the Atlantic, the Caribbean, and as far as South America.

Hamlet

Type: 2-masted fore-and-aft schooner, composite construction

Nation: Sweden

Owner: Trade Wind Cruises

Home port: Skärhamn, Sweden

Year of construction: 1936

Shipyard: Sjötorp, Sweden

Dimensions:
Length overall: 34.00 m
Length of hull: 24.70 m

Length at the waterline: 23.30 m
Width: 6.80 m
Draft: 2.70 m

Sail area: 320 square meters

Rigging: 8 sails

Masts: height of mainmast over the deck: 25 meters

Auxiliary engine: Volvo Penta TMD 10A, 220 horsepower

Crew: 4-person active crew, 14 berths, 75 day guests

Use: chartered ship

Hawila

Type: ketch, wood

Nation: Sweden

Owner: AB Gunilla shipping company (Mot Bättre Vetande)

Home port: Öckerö

Year of construction: 1935

Shipyard: Lindstöl

Tonnage: 120 ts displacement; 87 tons gross

Dimensions:
Length overall: 36.80 m
Length of hull: 25.60 m
Width: 6.20 m
Depth to deck: 3.10 m
Draft: 2.90 m

Sail area: 520 square meters

Rigging: 9 sails

Masts: height of mainmast over the deck: 25.50 meters

Auxiliary engine: Volvo Penta Tamd 102, 370 horsepower

Crew: 10-person active crew, 30 trainees

Use: sailing school-ship

The fore-and-aft-rigged ketch is a typical representative of this type of Baltic trading vessel, which could often be found as late as the 1930s. The very pious owners gave the ship the name *Hawila* after a passage in the Old Testament (Genesis 2:11), which says: "And a river went out of Eden to water the garden; and from thence it was parted, and be- came into four heads. The name of the first is Pison: that is it which compasseth the whole land of Havilah, where there is gold." The name was supposed to bring the ship luck.

In 1978 the organization Mot Bättre Vetande acquired the ketch. Her conversion into a sailing school-ship followed and was completed in 1984.

From the beginning of May until the end of October the *Hawila* undertakes training cruises. In the process approx- imately 400 young people re- ceive training in seamanship as well as school instruction.

Jarramas

Type: full-rigged ship

Nation: Sweden

Owner: city of Karlskrona

Home port: Karlskrona, Borgmästarekajen

Year of construction: 1899; keel laid March 18, 1899; launched February 1, 1900

Shipyard: Polhamsdocken, Karlskrona

Tonnage: 350 ts displacement (fully armed)

Dimensions:
Length overall: 49.00 m
Length of hull: 39.15 m
Length between perpendiculars: 33.30 m
Width: 8.38 m
Depth in hold: 3.98 m
Draft (not armed): 3.20 m

Sail area: originally approx. 800 square meters (without studding sails), 1002 square meters with lee sails

Rigging: originally 17 sails (without studding sails); 4 foresails; single topsail, single topgallant, royals; mainmast: gaff-sail without boom

(spencer); studding sails on fore- and mainmast

Masts, spars: top and topgallant masts; bowsprit with jibboom, angled spritsail yard, dolphin striker; height of mainmast over the deck 25.25 meters

Auxiliary engine: none

Crew: 4 officers, 1 doctor, 7 petty officers, 15 corporals, 92 boys ages 13 1/2 to 15

Use: museum ship

In 1716, Carl XII of Sweden had two frigates built in Karl- skrona. They were given the names *Illerim* and *Jarramas* on his command. The words are of Turkish origin ("light- ning" and "thunder"). After Carl XII had lost the battle near Poltawa to the Russians in July 1709, he fled with only 500 men to Bender in Turkey. Carl succeeded in convincing the Sublime Porte in Constan- tinople to declare war on Czar Peter. Through intrigues, the czar prevented the annihilation of his army and his own cap- ture. In the peace of Husch,

Carl was guaranteed free passage through Russia. Carl, however, resisted the request that he leave Turkish territory because he still wanted to bring about a Turkish-Russian war. The sultan finally resorted to force. Carl entrenched himself in Bender with 300 soldiers and defied the relentless attacks of several thousand janissaries for an entire day. After much effort, he was finally captured. This reckless behavior earned Carl the Turkish nickname Illerim and Jarramas, which he then proudly transferred to his ships.

The frigate *Jarramas* was still in service long after Carl's death. Her later fate is not known. From 1825 to 1859 a corvette served in the Swedish navy that was likewise called *Jarramas*. The iron *Jarramas* was built for the turn-of-the-century Swedish navy as a second school-ship modeled after the wooden *Najaden*. They are sister ships with substantial similarities in their details.

Both the *Jarramas* and the *Najaden* originally had a black hull with a white streak. During changes to the rigs in the 1930s, the royals were removed and the topgallant masts shortened accordingly. The fore- and main topsails had three, the mizzen topsail two rows of reef points. The standing rigging is fastened to chain plates outboard with tackle ropes. Because of the small size of the ship, the boats were carried outboard, one on each side next to the mizzenmast and one in davits across the stern. The two stock anchors also remained outboard because of the lack of space on deck. As was generally the case with the sailing warships of the nineteenth century, the hammocks were stowed between the outer and inner bulwarks.

In contrast to the *Najaden*, the *Jarramas* has a completely continuous main deck. Both ships sailed primarily in the North and East seas. The *Jarramas* made its final voyage in 1846 around Sweden.

In 1950 the city of Karlskrona purchased the ship. Today she is a museum ship with a café on board. Both full-rigged ships were replaced in 1947 by the schooners *Gladan* and *Falken*.

Lady Ellen

Type: 3-masted topsail schooner, steel	Year of construction: 1980; launched August 10, 1980; commissioned October 3, 1982	Dimensions: Length overall: 49.00 m Length of hull: 38.90 m	Rigging: 13 sails; double topsails, single topgallant
Nation: Sweden		Length at the waterline: 36.00 m	Masts: height of mainmast over the deck: 30 meters
	Shipyard: Kockums Shipyard, Malmö, and Vindö Marin, Sweden	Width: 7.80 m Draft: 3.90 m	
Owner: Tradewind Cruises AB, Skärhamn			Auxiliary engine: Iveco diesel, 550 horsepower
Home port: Skärhamn	Tonnage: 410 ts displacement; 229 tons gross; 130 tons net	Sail area: 685 square meters	Crew: 9-person active crew, 12 guests
			Use: chartered ship

The *Lady Ellen* certainly occupies a special place among recently constructed large chartered sailing ships. The technical design of the ship, its equipment, along with its luxurious accommodations are of the most exceptional quality. The rig and the lines of the ship are reminiscent of the trading schooner *Ellen*, which was built in 1890 for the Johansson family and was used in the wood trade as well as in trade with England.

The schooner is typical of the Baltic, with her pronounced sheer and her clipper bow. She is equipped with extensive electronics and modern technology. Voyages with this elegant sailing ship can be undertaken in all the world's oceans, including circumnavigations of the globe.

Lady Ellen IV

Type: 3-masted topsail schooner, steel

Nation: Sweden

Owner: Lars Johansson Shipping, Skärhamn

Home port: Skagen, Denmark

Year of construction: launched September 1989;

commissioned June 1990

Shipyard: FEAB Marstrandsverken, Marstrand, Sweden

Tonnage: 580 ts displacement; 380 tons gross; 220 tons net

Dimensions:
Length overall: 62.00 m
Length of hull: 51.30 m

Length at the waterline: 42.40 m
Width: 8.50 m
Draft: 4.00 m

Sail area: 820 square meters

Rigging: 13 sails; foremast: schooner sail, double topsail, single topgallant

Masts: height of mainmast over the deck: 36 meters

Auxiliary engine: Caterpillar V16, 2000 horsepower

Crew: 12-person active crew, 14 guests in 7 double cabins

Use: chartered ship

Najaden

Type: full-rigged ship

Nation: Sweden

Owner: city of Halmstad

Home port: Halmstad, in the Nissan on the Castle Quay

Year of construction: 1897; launched February 12, 1897

Shipyard: Royal Naval Shipyard Karlskrona

Tonnage: 350 ts displacement (fully armed)

Dimensions:
Length overall: 48.80 m
Length of hull: 40.06 m
Length between perpendiculars: 33.95 m
Width: 8.38 m
Draft (armed): 3.70 m

Sail area: originally 740 square meters (without studding sails)

Rigging: originally 17 sails (without studding sails); 4 foresails; single topsail, single topgallant, royals; mainmast: gaff-sail without boom (spencer); studding sails on fore- and mainmast

Masts, spars: topmast and topgallant mast; bowsprit with

jibboom, angled spritsail yard, dolphin striker; height of mainmast over the deck: 25 meters (today the topgallant masts are shortened)

Auxiliary engine: none

Crew: 3 officers, 1 doctor, 2 petty officers, 6 junior officer corporals, 10 sailors, 100 boys

Use: museum ship

The *Najaden* was built as a school-ship for the Swedish navy. The ship corresponds to the type of the nineteenth-century sailing frigate. She is one of the smallest full-rigged ships ever built.

In 1900 a sister ship, the *Jarramas,* was constructed—but in contrast to the *Najaden,* out of iron. The *Najaden* served actively as a school-ship until the summer of 1938 and was unrigged in the autumn of that year. During the war she was probably a barracks ship. In 1945 she lay in a very bad condition as a hulk in Torekov and was supposed to be scrapped there. An action by the city of Halmstad rescued the ship. At the naval shipyard in Karlskrona she was completely restored and rerigged on a large scale. On July 29, 1946, to the great interest of the population, the *Najaden* was towed to Halmstad and there moored to her berth in the Nissan. In the winter there is an art school on board, and in the summer a café.

Najaden

Following a very long period as a merchantman, the ship was rerigged in 1987–88 and equipped as a chartered ship. She sails primarily in the Baltic.

Previous names: *Nora, Harlingen, Möeve, Vadder Gerrit, Inspe, Utskär, Nora, Najaden*

Type: 3-masted fore-and-aft schooner, steel

Nation: Sweden

Owner: Baltic Sail Ship AB

Home port: Stockholm

Year of construction: 1918

Shipyard: J. J. Pattje & Zoon, Waterhuizen, the Netherlands

Tonnage: 250 ts displacement; 175 tons gross; 90 tons net

Dimensions:
Length overal : 45.00 m
Length of hull: 34.00 m
Length between perpendiculars: 30.00 m
Width: 7.05 m
Depth in hold: 3.15 m
Draft: 2.90 m

Sail area: 600 square meters

Rigging: 11 sails

Masts: height of mainmast over the deck: 26 meters

Auxiliary engine: Caterpillar (1987), 353 horsepower

Crew: 8-person active crew; 82 guests on day cruises

Use: chartered ship

Shalom

The 2-masted Bermuda schooner, which today is at home in the Swedish port of Oskarshamn, was built in 1896 as the lugger *BV 8 St. Magnus* in Vegesack. In 1906–7 the hull was lengthened. In 1921 she was sold to a buyer in Hamburg and given the new name *Bertha*. In 1931 the ship was sold to a buyer in Sweden.

In the course of several changes of ownership, the ship bore the name *Thellef* starting in 1949 and after 1972 patrolled the coast as *TV 015* under the Swedish flag.

Vida

Previous names: *Spirit of Merseyside, Marie, Sudersand, Grimsö, Elsa*

Type: 3-masted topsail schooner, iron

Nation: Sweden

Owner: Vida Shipping AB, Stockholm

Home port: Stockholm

Year of construction: 1916

Shipyard: in Vlaardingen, the Netherlands

Tonnage: approx. 200 ts displacement

Dimensions:
Length overall: 42.36 m
Width: 6.60 m
Draft: 2.70 m

Sail area: 660 square meters

Rigging: 10 sails

Masts: height of mainmast over the deck: 27 meters

Auxiliary engine: Scania diesel, 230 horsepower

Use: chartered ship

In her early years the ship was employed as a fishing vessel in the North Sea. In 1931 she was sold to a buyer in Karlskrona in Sweden. In spite of a powerful engine and a correspondingly reduced sail area, the freight trade was no longer profitable for the ship by the mid-1960s. The ship was laid up and subsequently converted and equipped for charter service by the present owner.

Viking

The 4-masted bark was built as a cargo-carrying school-ship for the Danish merchant marine. The owner at that time was the A/S Den Danske Handelsflades for Befalingsmaend. On March 18, 1907, a strong gale caused the ship to capsize shortly before her delivery to the shipyard where she was supposed to be outfitted. At this point not enough water had yet been pumped into the ballast tanks. (Total water ballast 1390 tons, of which 456 tons in the double bottom, 864 tons in the midship deep tank, 44 tons in the forepeak tanks, and 26 tons in the afterpeak tanks.) Luckily the ship tipped over on the side closest to the quay, so that she couldn't run aground. Nonetheless, her entry into service was delayed by months. The construction costs came to 591,000 Danish crowns. The *Viking* was built for a large number of sailors. The connection of the poop with the main deck produced a total length of 61 meters for the deck. All the living quar-ters could thus be located above the main deck. This deck consists of steel plates that are covered with teak planks. A continuous between deck originally divided the hold.

On June 16, 1907, a short trial voyage was undertaken. On July 19, 1907, the *Viking* was towed to Hamburg, where she loaded coke bound for Peru. Her first departure took place on August 29, 1907. Until World War I she undertook several voyages in the saltpeter trade. At the beginning of the war the *Viking* was laid up in Copenhagen. In 1916 De forende Dampskibs-selskab purchased the ship for 320,000 crowns in order to continue to use her as a school-ship. Yet cargoes were very difficult to find after the war. Even at that time a ship of this size had to earn her money as a school-ship. This was possible only with great effort, so that the *Viking* was once again laid up in 1925. Occasionally she made short voyages.

Type: 4-masted bark, steel	Width: 13.90 m
	Draft: 7.06 m
Nation: Sweden	
	Sail area: 2850 square meters
Owner: Utbildningsförvaltningen Göteberg	Rigging: 32 sails; 4 foresails, double topsail, double topgallant, royals; mizzenmast: mizzen sail, mizzen topsail
Home port: Göteberg	
Year of construction: 1906; launched December 1, 1906; armed March 1907	Masts: fore-, main-, and mizzen-mast with 1 topmast; mizzenmast one piece; height of mainmast over waterline: 47 meters
Shipyard: Burmeister & Wain, Copenhagen	Auxiliary engine: none
Tonnage: 2959 tons gross; 2665 tons net	Crew: as a school-ship up to 150 men, including about 80 boys; on the final voyage 32 people
Dimensions: Length overall: approx. 105.00 m Length of hull: 97.30 m Length between perpendiculars: 89.20 m	Use: Professional school for hotel and restaurant training, with affiliated hotel and restaurants

In 1929 the Finish shipowner Gustaf Erikson purchased the ship. Her new home port was Mariehamn. During her grain-carrying voyages to Australia, the *Viking* always had many young men on board. When the war broke out in 1939, the voyages had to be canceled. With other sailing ships the *Viking* went to Stockholm to serve as a granary.

After the end of the war, Erikson got the ship back. A much-noted departure for Australia took place in 1946 with a crew of 32 men. The ship had wood for South Africa aboard and brought 4000 tons of sacked wheat back to Europe. After her return home the ship was overhauled in Antwerp for additional voyages. G. Erikson's death put an end to these plans, however.

In 1949 the city of Göteberg decided to purchase the *Viking*. As a stationary school-ship she was supposed to become part of the Göteborg merchant marine school. In the process, however, the *Viking* also became the much admired "ship of the city," something one often finds in Scandinavia. On May 28, 1951, the ship was towed to Göteborg with 2000 tons of coke on board. Her entry into the harbor resembled a triumphal procession. Subsequently there was a large-scale conversion of the entire hull into classrooms, workstations, and so forth, in which young people are today instructed in all nautical subjects and also in the study of maritime engineering. On the between deck there are sleeping and living areas for 120 students.

A few years ago the *Viking* was given a completely different use. She now houses an upscale school for the hotel, restaurant, and hairdressing trades (HRS, Hotell-Restaurangoch Frisörskolan). The students are able to demonstrate what they've learned in the hotel and restaurant area of the ship. Approximately 2500 students a year graduate from the school. Conferences also take place aboard the ship.

 # Wasa

Type: seventeenth-century warship, 64 cannons, 2 battery decks, wood

Nation: Sweden

Owner: Statens Sjöhistorika Museum, Stockholm

Home port: Stockholm, Wasa Museum

Year of construction: 1628; royal commission in the year 1625; launched presumably in 1627

Shipyard: royal naval shipyard Stockholm (on the modern Blasieholmen)

Tonnage: 1210 ts displacement

Dimensions:
Length overall: 69.00 m
Length of hull: 57.00 m
Length between perpendiculars: 47.50 m
Width: 11.70 m
Draft: 4.80 m
Height of stern: 19.30 m

Sail area: 1275 square meters

Rigging: 10 sails; spritsail, bowsprit topsail; fore- and mainmast: single topsail, single topgallant; mizzenmast: lateen sail, in addition a single topsail

Masts, spars: height of mainmast over the keel: 52.50 meters; bowsprit with spritsail yard; bowsprit topmast with upper spritsail yard

Crew: 145 people plus 300 sailors

Armaments: sixty-four cannons; forty-eight 24-pounders, eight 3-pounders, three 35-pounders, two 62-pounders, two 1-pounders, one 16-pounder; all barrels made of bronze; total weight about 80 tons

Use: museum ship

During the Thirty Years' War, the imperial troops reached the Baltic Sea in the summer of 1628. Emperor Ferdinand II had already named their supreme commander Wallenstein as Great Admiral of the Baltic Sea. The futile siege of Stralsund then slowed their northward march significantly. Sweden had won Stralsund as an ally. King Gustavus II Adolphus responded with interest to its plea for assistance, because by this means he could gain a firm foothold in German territory. For his future endeavors he needed a strong fleet. On the other side, meanwhile, Wallenstein likewise sought to arm a fleet, which was furthermore to be supported by the Spanish squadron.

A series of large warships were commissioned by the Swedish king. Among these ships was the *Wasa*, which was already under construction and which was supposed to bear the name *Ny Wassan*. The Dutch master Henrik Hybertsson de Groot was commissioned with her construction. He died in 1627. His successor, who completed the *Wasa*, was Hein Jacobsson. The total costs came to approximately 100,000 Reich talers. On July 31, 1628, all cannons were on board, and on August 10, 1628, between three and four o'clock in the afternoon, the *Wasa* set off on her maiden voyage under the command of Captain Söfring Hansson. At first the ship was warped. After she had gotten free of the land somewhat, she also got wind in her sails, of which the fore and the main topsails, the fore as well as the lateen sails were already standing.

Already at this point the *Wasa* demonstrated a strong angle of heel toward the leeward side. Only a few minutes later a sudden gust forced the ship onto her side. Attempts at trimming commenced immediately, but were without success. Through the open gun ports, of which the lower row was only 1.2 to 1.5 meters above the surface of the water, large quantities of water came rushing in. Near the island of Beckholmen the *Wasa* ran aground in water 32 meters deep. Of the crew, not all of which was on board yet, some 30 people drowned. When the ship was raised, 15 skeletons were found in the hull. On September 5, 1628, a maritime court proceeding began. It was not possible, however, to identify a guilty party for the loss of the ship.

One assumes that the main cause was that the hull at the bottom of the ship was too narrow and sharp to take on ballast and that the lower gun ports lay too close to the surface of the water. The ship was top-heavy. The first attempts at

326

raising it began on August 13, 1628. They brought the *Wasa* to an even keel. In 1664 and 1683 approximately 54 cannons were raised with the help of diving bells.

In August 1956, Anders Franzén rediscovered the wreck after 2 years of searching. In the course of the centuries, twenty-nine large anchors had had been caught in the ship. The divers of the 64-man team assigned to raise the ship dug six 24-meter-long tunnels under the hull through which the raising hawsers had to pass. The first raising succeeded on August 20, 1959, with the help of two pontoons. In 28 days a tug towed the *Wasa* 550 meters in shallow water. In the process the ship had to be set down 18 times in order to be lifted again. Countless individual parts, including sculptures from the ornamentation on the stern, were found

next to the ship and retrieved. The lower foremast was still standing at the time of the ship's rediscovery.

On April 24, 1961, all of the preparatory work was advanced enough that the *Wasa* could be removed from the water. She floated into the dry dock on her own keel on May 4, 1961. In the meantime a giant concrete pontoon had been built, upon which the ship found its final berth a short time later.

Great difficulties were involved in preserving the wood. In a lengthy process, the water was replaced by a high molecular alcohol. A shower system that covered the entirety of the ship prevented her from drying out too quickly. Smaller pieces of wood could be treated in baths. Only original parts were supposed to be used during the restoration. In the 100 cubic meters of mud that was re-

moved from the hull, archeologists found 16,000 original parts.

It is only thanks to the circumstance that due to the cold waters of the Baltic Sea no teredo are able to live there that the *Wasa* still exists today. She is the oldest preserved and completely identified ship that we know of to date.

Today she lies in the Wasa Museum. A building was erected around her. It is a completely airtight concrete construction that guarantees exact temperature and humidity.

In February 2002 it was announced that up to five tons of sulfuric acid endanger the museum ship. The corrosive liquid is forming in the wood because of sulfuric waste products from bacteria. These waste products built up in the 333 years prior to the raising of the ship.

Ukraine

Druzhba   Khersones   Towarischtsch

Druzhba

Type: full-rigged ship, steel

Nation: Ukraine

Owner: Academy for Navigation, UKR, Odessa

Home port: Odessa

Year of construction: commissioned August 1987

Shipyard: Stocznia Gdanska (Danzig Shipyard), Gdansk

Tonnage: 2987 ts displacement; 2264 tons gross; 677 tons net

Dimensions:
Length overall: 109.40 m
Length of hull: 94.20 m
Length at the waterline: 79.40 m
Width: 14.00 m
Height of sides to the upper deck: 10.60 m
Height of sides to the main deck: 8.40 m
Draft: 6.60 m

Sail area: 2936 square meters

Rigging: 26 sails

Masts: height of mainmast over the waterline: 49.50 meters

Auxiliary engine: two Cegielski-Sulzer diesel engines on one shaft, type 6AL20, 420 kilowatts, 570 horsepower each

Crew: 50-person active crew, 144 cadets

Use: sailing school-ship, tourist use

The *Druzhba* ("Friendship") belongs, with her sister ships, the *Mir,* the *Pallada,* and the *Khersones,* to a new generation of tall sailing ships. Typical of the hull is above all the flat stern. Many technical features, such as the steering system, correspond to those of modern motorized ships. Multiple copies of all of the navigational systems are present to facilitate the training exercises.

Following extensive renovation and modification work in 1996–97 the ship is now also used for tourist purposes under the auspices of International Cruise and Hotel Management (I.C.H.).

In addition to the cabins for the guests, there is now also a restaurant with room for 75, the Captain's Bar, and a bar on the sundeck.

The *Druzhba* continues to serve as a sailing school-ship. In the summer she cruises in Greek and Turkish waters, and in the winter in the Mediterranean.

Khersones

The *Khersones* is a sister ship to the tall sailing ships *Mir, Druzhba,* and *Pallada.* She got her name from the ancient city of Chersones, which was located on the site of the current Sevastopol. Originally the ship was supposed to have the name *Aleksandr Grin.*

A special feature of the ship is an extra, fully equipped navigation bridge used exclusively for training purposes. Passenger cruises take place under the auspices of the Inmaris Perestroika Sailing Maritime Service, which also administers the *Mir* and the *Sedov.* On October 27, 1996, the *Khersones* left Kiel on a voyage around South America in a counterclockwise direction. On January 26, 1997, she passed Cape Horn at a distance of 5.2 nautical miles off the coast. For the first time since the *Pamir* and *Passat* in 1949 a windjammer had made the passage around Cape Horn from 50 degrees south in the Pacific to 50 degrees south in the Atlantic under wind power alone.

The full-rigged ship then visited Rostock on her voyage home.

In May 1999 the *Khersones* was beautified with a classic figurehead.

Previous name: *Aleksandr Grin*

Type: full-rigged ship, steel

Nation: Ukraine

Owner: Naval Technological Institute, Kerch

Home port: Kerch

Year of construction: launched June 10, 1988; commissioned March 21, 1989

Shipyard: Stocznia Gdanska (Danzig Shipyard), Gdansk

Tonnage: 2987 ts displacement; 2264 tons gross; 667 tons net

Dimensions:
Length overall: 109.40 m
Length of hull: 94.20 m

Length at the waterline: 79.40 m
Width: 14.00 m
Depth to upper deck: 10.60 m
Height of sides to the main deck: 8.40 m
Draft: 6.60 m

Sail area: 2771 square meters

Rigging: 26 sails

Masts: height of mainmast over the waterline: 49.50 meters (all 3 masts)

Auxiliary engine: two Cegielski Sulzer diesel engines on one shaft, type 6AL20/24, 570 horsepower each

Crew: 40-person active crew, 48–72 cadets, up to 94 trainees/guests

Use: sailing school-ship, guest ship

Towarischtsch

Previous name: *Gorch Fock I*

Type: bark, steel

Nation: Ukraine

Owner: merchant marine

Home port: Cherson (Black Sea)

Year of construction: 1933; launched May 3, 1933

Shipyard: Blohm & Voss, Hamburg

Tonnage: 1392 tons gross; 230 tons net; 292 tdw; 1760/1350 ts displacement

Dimensions:
Length overall: 82.10 m
Length of hull: 73.70 m
Length between perpendiculars: 62.00 m
Width: 12.00 m
Depth to deck: 7.30 m
Draft: 5.20 m

Sail area: 1750 square meters

Rigging: 23 sails; 4 foresails, double topsail, single topgallant, royals; mizzenmast: lower mizzen, upper mizzen

Masts: height of mainmast over the deck: 41.30 meters

Auxiliary engine: Skoda diesel, 550 horsepower

Crew: 51-person active crew, 134 cadets

Use: sailing school-ship

The German Reich navy was in need of a new sailing school-ship because the school-ship *Niobe* was completely lost on July 26, 1932, during a thunder squall in the Fehmarn Belt. The *Gorch Fock* was the first sailing school-ship of her kind in the Reich navy. She was replicated in the same dimensions only once, as the *Mircea* for Romania. The subsequent ships of this type, the current *Eagle,* formerly the *Horst Wessel* (1936), the *Sagres II,* formerly the *Leo Schlageter*

(1938), and the *Gorch Fock II* of the federal navy correspond to this prototype in their construction down to the details but are 8 meters longer. The ship was built for the highest classification of the German Lloyd. All of the decks consist of steel plates that are covered with 6-centimeter-thick teakwood planks. The forecastle is connected to the forward deckhouse. As the *Gorch Fock,* the sailing ship carried a stockless anchor on the starboard and a stock anchor on the port side. The decoration of the bow at that time consisted of a scroll and a coat of arms with the na-

tional emblem. (Everything except the national emblem has been changed today.) The large eagle first appeared on the navy's two subsequent sailing school-ships. Originally only mizzen sail and mizzen topsails were set on the mizzenmast.

Until 1939 the ship made extended voyages as well as shorter cruises together with her sister ships. In May 1945 the *Gorch Fock* was sunk near Stralsund. In 1948 the Soviet Union raised and salvaged the ship. The reconstruction work lasted until 1951. As the *Towarischtsch II,* the ship subse-

quently became a school-ship of the Soviet navy. (The *Towarischtsch I* was a 4-masted bark, formerly the *Lauriston.*) Almost nothing about the exterior of the ship has changed. Instead of the starboard stock anchor a stockless anchor is now carried here too. The home port is now Odessa.

In May 1995 the ship entered the harbor of Newcastle, where urgently needed and extensive repairs were supposed to be carried out. Among other things, the replacement of steel plates on the outer surface is necessary. Unfortunately, the project, costing

millions, was and is not sufficiently supported by the Ukrainian government. With the exception of the captain and four other members of the crew, all of the men were sent home. With the approval of the Blohm & Voss shipyard, a circle of friends in Newcastle and "The Tall Ships Friends e. V." of Hamburg are trying to raise the funds for the thorough overhaul.

Uruguay

Capitan Miranda

Capitan Miranda

Type: 3-masted Bermuda schooner, steel

Nation: Uruguay

Owner: Armada de Uruguay

Home port: Montevideo

Year of construction: 1930

Shipyard: Astilleros de Matagorda, Cadiz

Tonnage: 715 ts displacement

Dimensions:
Length overall: 61.00 m
Length of hull: 54.60 m
Width: 8.40 m
Draft: 3.20 m

Sail area: 722 square meters

Rigging: 8 sails; all masts Bermuda rigged; fore-trysail

Auxiliary engine: 1 MAN diesel engine, 368 kilowatts

Crew: 49 people

Use: sailing school-ship

The ship was built as a motorized ship for hydrographic research expeditions. Saved from being scrapped, in 1977 she was converted into a sailing school-ship for the Uruguayan navy.

Captain Francisco P. Miranda (1869–1925) was a famous naval officer who made his name primarily through his research work in the waters off Uruguay.

USA

Adventure
Alabama
Alvei
America III
American Pride
American Rover
Amistad
Ariel
Balclutha
Barba Negra
Beaver II
Bill of Rights
Black Pearl
Bounty II
Bowdoin
C. A. Thayer
Californian
Caribee
Carthaginian II
Charles W. Morgan
Clipper City
Constellation
Constitution
Coronet
Corwith Cramer
Denis Sullivan
Eagle
Elissa
Falls of Clyde

Friendship
Gazela of
    Philadelphia
Half Moon
Harvey Gamage
Hawaiian Chieftan
Jamestown Ships
    (replicas)
Joseph Conrad
Kalmar Nyckel
L. A. Dunton
Lady Maryland
Lady Washington
Le Pelican
Lettie G. Howard
Liberty
Liberty Clipper
Lisa
Margaret Todd
Mary Day
Maryland Dove
Mayflower II
Moshulu
Mystic Whaler
Nathaniel Bowditch
New Way
Niagara
Niña
Ocean Star

Peking
Perseus
Pilgrim
Pioneer
Polynesia
Pride of
    Baltimore II
Providence
Regina Maris
Rose
Sea Lion
Shenandoah
Soundwaters
Spirit of
    Massachusetts
Star of India
Stephen Taber
Swift of Ipswich
Tabor Boy
Te Vega
Timberwind
Tole Mour
Unicorn
Victory Chimes
Wavertree
Wawona
Westward
Windy
Young America

Adventure

Type: 2-masted fore-and-aft
schooner, wood

Nation: USA

Owner: Captain Jim W. Sharp,
Camden, Maine

Home port: Camden, Maine

Year of construction: 1926;
keel laid April 1926; launched
September 16, 1926

Shipyard: James Yard, Essex,
Massachusetts; design:
Thomas F. McManus

Tonnage: 134 tons gross;
62 tons net

Dimensions:
Length overall: 36.90 m
Length on the deck: 36.20 m
Length between
perpendiculars: 32.50 m
Width: 7.60 m
Depth in hold: 3.40 m
Draft: 4.00 m

Sail area: 480 square meters

Rigging: 4 sails; 2 foresails,
1 gaff-sail each

Masts: height of mainmast
over the deck: 25 meters; no
topmasts today; no bowsprit

Auxiliary engine: none

Crew: 5-person active crew

Use: private ship for
passenger cruises

The *Adventure* was one of the most successful bank schooners that ever fished off Newfoundland. She was the last dory schooner to be built at an American shipyard. For her construction, the architect, Thomas F. McManus, used all the experience that had been collected in the long years of this specialized type of ship construction.

The unparalleled success of this Gloucesterman confirmed the correctness of his calculations. Because of the strong storms in the North Atlantic, the bank schooners not only had to be built very strong but also had to be able to carry their perishable cargo to its markets with the greatest possible speed. In addition, however, the cargo hold could not be too small; otherwise, the dangerous voyages would not be profitable. There are only a few branches of maritime activity in which the shipyards must meet this extreme combination of requirements when undertaking the design of a new ship. The *Adventure* originally had topmasts on both masts. The number of sails was thus increased by a gaff-topsail each on the foremast and mainmast. The first auxiliary diesel engine of 120 horsepower was later replaced by a 230-horsepower engine, which was in turn removed completely in 1953, so that today the ship is a pure sailing vessel.

Captain Jeff Thomas led the *Adventure* on its first fishing mission on October 16, 1926. Thomas fished for halibut in the summer and shellfish in the winter. The voyages left from either Boston or Gloucester. On her first voyages the schooner returned with record catches. On October 3, 1927, this amounted to 100,000 pounds of halibut, which brought a price of 11,770 dollars. Fourteen dories were found on board, which were manned by 28 dorymen. In a strong storm in December 1933 the *Adventure* sustained very heavy damage. Only with the utmost exertion was it possible to keep the ship above water. In the process, 40,000 pounds of fish had to be thrown overboard.

On March 24, 1934, Captain Thomas suffered a heart attack on board while all of the dories were at sea. His successor was Captain Leo Hynes. The *Adventure* rammed the auxiliary schooner *Adventure II*, formerly the *Mary P. Goulart*, in Boston Harbor on March 20, 1943, and the *Adventure II* immediately sank. With great effort, the crew was able to rescue itself in the dories. Both ships belonged to the same owner.

Captain Hynes usually had twelve dories and 27 men on board. He had the sail area reduced and a 230-horsepower engine installed. Under his leadership the schooner registered catches that toppled all previous records. The record year was 1943, when the *Adventure* landed fish worth a total of 364,000 dollars. Hynes commanded the ship for 19 years. In this time she earned approximately 3.5 million dollars. This amount has never been achieved by any other fishery vessel on the entire American Atlantic coast. It was not for nothing that the *Adventure* received the enviable predicate "High Liner." In 1953 her fishing time came to an end. None of the crew members were under the age of 70 at that time. Young men were no longer willing to take part in these demanding fishing voyages. With the ship's retirement, one of the most glorious periods of high seas fishing came to an end.

As if through a miracle, the schooner was preserved after her retirement. Donald P. Hurd purchased the ship and converted her into a passenger ship but made absolutely no changes to her exterior. A drawing room and luxury cabins were installed in the former hold, and the kitchen was enlarged. The engine had to be removed, but in exchange the sail area was enlarged again. The schooner's old equipment is still located on board today.

The *Adventure* now belongs to Captain Jim W. Sharp. All summer she sails for the benefit of paying passengers from Monday to Saturday in the waters off Maine. At night the schooner lies at anchor in a protected place. The guests are allowed to take part in the operation of the ship if they wish.

Alabama

Previous name: *Alabamian*

Type: 2-masted fore-and-aft schooner

Nation: USA

Owner: Vineyard Haven

Home port: Vineyard Haven

Year of construction: 1926; June 12, 1926

Shipyard: Pensacola Shipbuilding Company, Pensacola, Florida

Tonnage: 150 ts displacement; 70 tons gross; 35 tons net

Dimensions:
Length overall: 36.50 m
Length of hull: 27.40 m
Length between perpendiculars: 25.80 m
Width: 6.50 m
Depth in hold: 2.80 m
Draft: 3.80 m

Sail area: 418 square meters

Rigging: 8 sails

Masts: height of mainmast over the waterline: 28.60 meters

Auxiliary engine: two General Motors diesels, 250 horsepower each

Crew: 5-person active crew, 24 trainees (students), 49 guests on day cruises

Use: training ship for young people between the ages 10 and 14 years

This maneuverable and fast ship is a typical representative of the Gloucester fishing schooner. She was designed by the famous shipbuilding engineer Thomas F. McManus. Prior to her acquisition by her current owner, the *Alabama* sailed as a pilot schooner for the Mobile Bar Pilot Association in Pensacola. A 3-year modification for use as a schoolship for students ages 10 to 14 followed in Vineyard Haven. The young people must pay a daily fee.

334

Alvei

Previous names:
Rovedefjord, Vaarvind, Mostring, Brith Marith, Alvei

Type: 3-masted fore-and-aft topsail schooner, steel

Nation: USA

Owner: Evan Logan, Albany, California

Home port: no fixed home port

Year of construction: 1920

Shipyard: in Montrose, Scotland

Tonnage: 140 ts displacement; 103 tons gross; 51 tons net

Dimensions:
Length overall: 35.00 m
Length of hull: 28.00 m
Length between perpendiculars: 26.20 m
Width: 5.80 m
Depth in hold: 2.28 m
Depth to deck: 2.74 m
Draft: fore 2.00 m, aft 3.00 m

Sail area: 529 square meters

Rigging: 16 sails; foremast: square foresail, topsail, and topgallant; mainmast: mainsail, main, and topgallant

Masts: height of mainmast over the deck: 26 meters

Auxiliary engine: Wichmann diesel, 2 ACA, 160 horsepower

Crew: 18 berths for crews of varying composition

Use: private ship

The original name of this schooner, which has an exceptionally rare type of rig, is not known. Rigged as a ketch, the *Alvei* ("Alvei" means someone who travels all roads) was employed as a herring lugger in her early years. Typical for this type of vessel is the nearly vertical stern. After that she sailed as a motorized coasting ship.

Her current owner acquired her in 1986. In the course of 8 years of work, the ship was completely converted in Portugal and rigged as a schooner. In October 1995 the *Alvei* was able to leave the shipyard and undertook a 5-year voyage around the world.

Type: 2-masted fore-and-aft schooner, wood

Nation: USA

Owner: Schooner America USA, Inc.

Home port: none (constantly on the move)

Year of construction: 1995; launched August 30, 1995

Shipyard: Scarano Boat Building, Albany, New York

Tonnage: 120 ts displacement; 100 tons gross

Dimensions:
Length overall: 42.40 m
Length of hull: 32.00 m

Length at the waterline: 27.60 m
Width: 7.60 m
Draft: 3.00 m

Sail area: 595.2 square meters

Rigging: 5 sails

Masts: height of mainmast over the deck: 33 meters

Auxiliary engine: two John Deere diesel engines, 220 horsepower each

Crew: 7-person active crew, accommodations for 8 overnight guests, 49 day passengers

Use: ambassador ship for the USA and for the shipbuilding industry

This ship is modeled on the schooner *America*, which in 1851 left fourteen British competitors in her wake during a spectacular race around the Isle of Wight and thus brought the One Hundred Guinea Cup (America's Cup) to America. It was a singular demonstration of the development of technology in the New World. The ship was seriously damaged on Palm Sunday in 1942 when the roof of her shelter house collapsed under the weight of the snow.

The new *America* is also an extraordinarily fast ship. At a top speed of 18 knots she defeated thirty-one other schooners in October 1995 at the Great Chesapeake Bay Schooner Race from Baltimore to Norfolk. She once again gained the attention of the public on July 9, 1996, when she brought the Olympic flame to the sailing competitors in the harbor of Savannah, Georgia.

American Pride

Previous names: *Natalie Todd, Lady in Blue, St. Catherine, Alaho, Virginia*

Type: 3-masted fore-and-aft schooner, wood

Nation: USA

Owner: Heritage Marine Institute, California

Home port: Rainbow Harbor, Long Beach, California

Year of construction: 1941

Shipyard: Muller Boat Works, Brooklyn, New York

Tonnage: 200 ts displacement; 98.9 tons gross

Dimensions:
Length overall: 39.20 m
Length of hull: 30.70 m
Width: 6.40 m
Draft: 2.90 m

Sail area: 362 square meters

Rigging: 6 sails

Masts: height of mainmast over the deck: 25 meters

Auxiliary engine: General Motors diesel 671, 150 horsepower

Crew: 4-person active crew, berths for 38 people, 100 day guests

Use: chartered ship, passenger service

Hardly anyone would guess that this 3-master was once a 2-masted fishing vessel. Originally called the *Virginia*, she fished with dragnets off the East Coast of the United States. After she had completed 40 years of active service, Captain Steven F. Pagels purchased her in 1986 in Gloucester. The ship was converted in Thomaston, Maine, by experienced carpenters using traditional construction methods. This work lasted a year.

Prior to the ship's conversion into an elegant schooner with a great deal of ambience, only the completely empty hull remained.

American Rover

Type: 3-masted fore-and-aft schooner

Nation: USA

Owner: Rover Marine, Inc., Norfolk

Home port: Norfolk, Virginia

Year of construction: 1986

Shipyard: Kolsar & Rover Marine, Panama City, Florida

Tonnage: 110 ts displacement, 96 tons gross

Dimensions:
Length overall: 41.10 m
Length of hull: 29.90 m

Width: 7.30 m
Draft: 2.90 m

Sail area: 465 square meters

Rigging: 11 sails; 4 foresails, square foresail

Masts: height of mainmast over the deck: 24 meters

Auxiliary engine: two American diesel engines, 130 horsepower each

Crew: 4-person active crew, 4 trainees, 149 guests on day cruises

Use: passenger cruises, floating classroom for secondary school and university students

The ship is modeled after the sailing freighters of the nineteenth century. A very long bowsprit and the soft sheer of the hull accentuate the elegance of the schooner. The two propellers are arranged one above the other. The ship specializes in cruises of approximately 2 hours around the large harbor area of Norfolk. She also offers educational cruises of an hour and a half. On these tours the guests can learn how to set sails, steer the ship, or tie knots. A figurehead of Matilda provides good luck.

Amistad

Type: 2-masted topsail schooner, wood, reproduction

Nation: USA

Owner: Amistad America, Inc.

Home port: New Haven, Connecticut

Years of construction: 1998–2000; launched March 25, 2000

Shipyard: Mystic Seaport Museum

Tonnage: 137 ts displacement, 90 tons gross, 81 tons net

Dimensions:
Length overall: 39.30 m
Length of hull: 24.40 m
Width: 7.00 m
Draft: 3.20 m

Sail area: 483 square meters

Rigging: 8 sails

Auxiliary engine: two Caterpillar diesel engines, 135 horsepower each

Crew: 9-person active crew, 49 trainees, 49 guests

Use: sailing school-ship, museum ship, passenger ship, floating classroom

The first *Amistad* (Spanish for "friendship") became famous in 1839 when 53 slaves from what is now Sierra Leone who were supposed to be sold in Cuba overpowered the crew, killed the captain, and thus took control of the ship. They wanted to sail back to their homeland. Off the East Coast of the United States, at the latitude of Long Island, the ship was captured by the brigantine *Washington*. The mutineers were brought to trial. Following prolonged court proceedings, the Supreme Court under the former president John Quincy Adams secured their release. The freed slaves were allowed to return to their homeland.

The current reproduction was christened with water from Cuba, Long Island, and Sierra Leone. The rake of the masts is a charming feature of this streamlined and fast ship. Today a figurehead of a golden eagle symbolizes freedom.

Ariel

Type: 2-masted fore-and-aft schooner, steel

Nation: USA

Owner: Walter J. Nacey, Elyria, Ohio

Home port: Bermudas

Year of construction: 1969; launched August 28, 1969

Shipyard: Schlichting Shipyard, Lübeck-Travemünde

Tonnage: 154 ts displacement; 150 tons gross

Dimensions:
Length overall: 41.40 m
Length of hull: 33.60 m
Length between perpendiculars: 27.25 m
Width: 7.00 m

Depth in hold: 2.70 m
Draft: 2.67 m

Sail area: 544 square meters, in addition to a square foresail with 90 square meters

Rigging: 11 sails; typical schooner rig with square foresail

Masts: height of mainmast over the deck: 29.50 meters; masts and topmasts made of wood

Auxiliary engine: Mercedes Benz MB 846 A, 240 horsepower; speed with engine, 10 knots

Crew: 5-person active crew, 10 guests

Use: private ship, chartered ship

This 2-million-dollar ship was the largest new yacht construction to be undertaken in Germany after the war. The rooms in the ship have modern equipment and are luxuriously furnished. The sails are operated only by hand. The *Ariel* is part of the fleet of large private yachts that for the most part are used in America as charter ships for paying guests.

Balclutha

Previous names: *Pacific Queen, Star of Alaska, Balclutha*

Type: full-rigged ship, steel

Nation: USA

Owner: U.S. Department of the Interior; National Park Service Golden Gate National Recreation Area

Home port: San Francisco, Pier 43—Fisherman's Wharf

Year of construction: 1886; launched December 9, 1886

Shipyard: Charles Connell & Company, Glasgow

Tonnage: 2660 ts displacement; 1689 tons gross

Dimensions:
Length overall: 91.50 m
Length of hull: 78.00 m
Length between perpendiculars: 74.00 m
Width: 11.70 m
Depth in hold: 6.90 m

Sail area: approx. 1900 square meters

Rigging: 25 sails; double topsail, single topgallant, royals

Masts: all masts with 1 topmast; height of foremast over the deck: 42.80 meters; height of mainmast over the deck: 43.70 meters; height of mizzenmast over the deck: 39.20 meters; main yard: 26.30 meters; main royal yard: 12.20 meters

Auxiliary engine: none

Crew: as a trading vessel, 26 people

Use: museum ship

The *Balcutha* was built in Glasgow for Robert McMillan of Dumbarton on Clyde. The gallic word means "City (Bal) on the Clutha (Clyde)" and is the old name for Dumbarton. The ship was employed in general trade, an authentic "deep-water man," as the oceangoing sailing ships were called. The maiden voyage led around Cape Horn to San Francisco. In total the ship sailed around the Cape 17 times. She brought grain from California, guano from Chile, wool from New Zealand, and rice from Rangun to Europe. The *Balclutha* sailed under the British flag until 1899. From 1899 until 1902 she flew the flag of Hawaii. She brought wood to Australia for a company in San Francisco and coal from Newcastle to the United States for the Southern Pacific Railroad. In 1902 Pope & Talbot of San Francisco purchased the ship. Since this time the *Balcutha* has sailed under the American flag. She now found use in the salmon trade. The crew consisted of sailors, fishermen, and cannery workers, often totaling up to 300 men. The voyages lasted from spring until autumn and led into the waters of Alaska. In 1904 she ran aground near the Kodiak islands and subsequently suffered a serious leak. The Alaska Packers Association acquired the ship for 500 dollars, organized the difficult raising, and integrated her into its Star fleet as the *Star of Alaska*. The repair work took place in San Francisco. The poop was greatly lengthened in front in order to create living quarters for the large crew.

She was one of the fastest ships in this fleet and, in Sep-tember 1930, was the last of its ships to return to port. The time of the Alaska Packers was over. For 3 years the ship was laid up in the shallow bay of Alameda. In 1933 show business took over the ship. As the *Pacific Queen* she was used in the shooting of films, appearing as a pirate ship in many of them. In 1952 she ended up on the mud banks of Sausalito near San Francisco. Through the initiative of K. Kortum, the director of the maritime museum of San Francisco, the museum purchased the ship in 1954 for 25,000 dollars. Numerous firms contributed materials and labor to the reconstruction efforts free of charge. (The costs otherwise would have come to 250,000 dollars.) After 1 year's work the *Balclutha* (she had gotten this name back) could be towed to her berth. Her current condition corresponds to that of the period of her first construction. A typical feature is the white streak. A female figure ornaments the beautiful bow as a figurehead.

Barba Negra

Type: barkentine, wood	Tonnage: 55.64 tons gross; 120 ts TM	Masts: height of mainmast over the deck: 22.80 meters	The *Barba Negra* was built as a galleass. For four years she sailed as a whaling ship in Arctic waters. She was one of the first whaling ships to be equipped with a harpoon gun. After 1900 the ship sailed as a fish transporter. In 1956 the first engine was installed. Until 1971 the *Barbra Negra* earned money in the coastal trade. Then a thorough overhaul took place, and the ship was no longer used to kill
Nation: USA			
Owner: J. Seidl, Savannah, Georgia	Dimensions: Length overall: 33.40 m Length between perpendiculars: 21.20 m Width: 6.40 m Draft: 3.60 m	Auxiliary engine: Scania diesel, 230 horsepower	
Home port: Savannah		Crew: 8-person active crew	
Year of construction: 1896		Use: research vessel for Save our SEAS, Inc.	
Shipyard: John Lekve, Hemme, Norway	Sail area: 400 square meters		
	Rigging: 16 sails; double topsail, single topgallant		

whales but rather to protect them from extinction. A complete laboratory for this purpose, which occupies itself primarily with marine biology, is located on board.

The *Barba Negra* has been involved in many films and television programs, and she has also served as the camera ship for a number of programs.

She carries a harpoon gun on her forecastle and a crow's nest on her mainmast. Captain Seidel is not only a shipbuilder but also a painter of seascapes who uses the *Barba Negra* as a floating artist's studio. In 1992, in addition to other substantial restoration work, she got a new mast that allowed her to sail under wind power again.

Beaver II

Type: brig	Dimensions: Length overall: 34.00 m Length of deck: 23.10 m
Nation: USA	Width: 6.60 m Depth in hold: 1.90 m
Owner: Boston Tea Party Ship, Inc.	Draft: 2.40 m
Home port: Boston, Congress Street Bridge	Rigging: 11 sails
Year of construction: 1973; launched May 1973	Masts: height of mainmast over the deck: 21.80 meters
Shipyard: G. Clausen, Marstal, Denmark; design: W. A. Baker, naval architect	Auxiliary engine: Volvo Penta diesel, 120 horsepower (improved after crossing the Atlantic in 1974)
Tonnage: 130 ts displacement	Crew: 10 people
	Use: museum ship

The reconstruction of the *Beaver* was sailed under her own power from Denmark to Boston on the occasion of the 200th anniversary of the Boston Tea Party. The original ship, which belonged to Hezikiah Coffin of Nantucket, sailed from London to Boston on October 2, 1773, with 112 crates of tea on board. On December 7 she reached the entrance to Boston Harbor but had to remain at the Rainsford Island quarantine station because of a pox infection on board. Following the type of disinfection by smoke available at that time, the ship was towed to Griffin's Wharf. The following night a group of men who called themselves the Sons of Liberty and who were disguised as Indians entered the ship and threw the cargo into the water. This was a protest against the high duties England had placed on the young colonies in America.

With this act began the Revolutionary War, which led to the Declaration of Independence of the United States of America in 1776.

Bill of Rights

The schooner was built as a trading ship.

The Bill of Rights was added to the U.S. constitution in 1791. This catalogue of basic rights guarantees freedom of religion, speech, press, and assembly, protection against arbitrary search, arrest, and seizure, as well as the right to bear arms.

Type: 3-masted topsail schooner	Year of construction: 1971
	Shipyard: in Bristol, Maine
Nation: USA	Tonnage: 160 tons gross
Owner: Los Angeles Maritime Institute	Dimensions: Length overall: 42.90 m Length of hull: 35.00 m
Home port: Los Angeles	

Width: 7.40 m
Draft: 3.00 m

Sail area: 585 square meters

Auxiliary engine: none

Use: school-ship for young people, also for at-risk youth

Black Pearl

Type: brigantine, wood

Nation: USA

Owner: Aquaculture Foundation, Bridgeport, Connecticut

Home port: Bridgeport, Connecticut

Year of construction: 1951; launched April 18, 1951

Shipyard: C. Lincoln Vaughn Shipyard, Wickford, Rhode Island

Tonnage: 36 ts displacement; 27 tons gross; 23 tons net

Dimensions:
Length overall: 22.03 m
Length of hull: 17.93 m
Length between perpendiculars: 11.55 m

Width: 4.71 m
Depth to deck: 4.86 m
Depth in hold: 2.22 m
Draft: 2.50 m

Sail area: 185 square meters

Rigging: 10 sails; 2 foresails; foremast: double topsail, single topgallant; mainmast: gaff-sail, gaff-topsail, main staysail, main-topmast staysail

Masts: foremast with topmast and topgallant mast; mainmast with one topmast; height of mainmast over the deck: 17 meters

Auxiliary engine: Hercules diesel engine, 150 horsepower

Crew: 6 people, including 4 boys

Use: sailing school-ship

This yachtlike brigantine was built by C. Lincoln Vaughn as a private yacht. Her summer voyages took place mostly along the mid-Atlantic coast of the United States. In August 1959, Barcley H. Warburton of Boston purchased the sailing ship. Under his command the brigantine sailed from the West Indian islands to Nova Scotia. Although she continued to be a private yacht, young sailors were also sometimes trained on the ship.

During the summer of 1962, the *Black Pearl* was in Boy's Harbour, a summer camp for boys in East Hampton (Long Island), for a month. The brigantine was the only private yacht to take part in the parade of tall sailing ships at Operation Sail 1964 in New York. At that time there were 3 officers and 5 cadets on board. During a voyage of 1160 sea miles in the summer of 1965 the ship logged an average of 8.1 knots. In an emergency the ship could be operated under sail by only 2 men. In total there are living accommodations for 9 people.

The *Black Pearl* has proven to be a ship with excellent sailing attributes. A thorough overhaul took place in 1985.

Bounty II

Type: full-rigged ship, wood, reproduction of an eighteenth-century trading vessel

Nation: USA

Owner: Metro Goldwyn Mayer, Inc., New York

Home port: St. Petersburg, Florida

Year of construction: 1960; keel laid February 1960

Shipyard: Smith & Rhuland, Ltd., Lunenburg, Nova Scotia

Tonnage: 415 tons gross; 111 tons net

Dimensions:
Length overall: 51.40 m
Length of hull: 40.50 m
Length between perpendiculars: 33.60 m
Width: 9.20 m
Depth to deck: 6.30 m
Depth in hold: 5.40 m
Draft: 4.20 m

Sail area: approx. 950 square meters

Rigging: 18 sails; 2 foresails, single topsail, single topgallant, royals

Masts, spars: height of mainmast over the deck: 31.60 meters; all masts with top- and topgallant masts; bowsprit with jibboom

Auxiliary engine: two Caterpillar marine diesel engines, 220 horsepower each (2 propellers)

Crew: for the film *Mutiny on the Bounty* a total of 26 people; original crew in 1789, a total of 45 people

Use: museum ship

The history of navigation records mutinies in all epochs. Yet none has moved people's minds and imaginations to the same extent or provided as much material and as many storylines for books and films as the mutiny on the HMS *Bounty* in the year 1789. This may especially be the case because the events took place in the South Sea, because it was possible for the mutineers to escape discovery for years, and, not least, because Captain Bligh managed, through unparalleled seamanship and luck, to sail 3600 sea miles in an open boat, to return to England, and to bring about the punishment of some of the mutineers.

On one of his voyages, Captain James Cook described the fruit of the breadfruit tree (Artocarpus) found on the Polynesian Islands as a very tasty and nourishing food. This occasioned the settlers of the British West Indian possessions to petition King George III to introduce the plant as a form of nourishment for the black slaves in the West Indies.

In 1787 the British admiralty purchased the cargo vessel *Bethia*, which had been built in 1785 and belonged to Duncan Campbell, for 1950 pounds. The ship was converted and armed in Deptford on the Thames for 4456 pounds. Lieutenant William Bligh received the command and was given orders to sail to Tahiti (Otaheite) and bring saplings of the breadfruit tree to the West Indies. Because this attempt to improve the nutrition of the slaves was seen as an especially humane act, the ship received the name *Bounty*.

Bligh left England from Spithead on December 23, 1787. The plan to round Cape Horn had to be abandoned because of constant bad weather.

The *Bounty* did not reach Tahiti until October 26, 1788. Bligh left the island on April 4, 1789, with 1105 plants on board and a course set for Jamaica. At the latitude of the island of Tofua near the Tonga Islands, mutiny broke out on April 28, 1789. Fletcher Christian, the 24-year-old first mate, assumed command and put Bligh out to sea with 18 men in the 7-meter-long longboat. After 41 days the boat reached Timor, having covered a distance of 3618 sea miles.

Bligh returned to England and brought it about that the frigate *Pandora* sailed to Tahiti to hunt down the mutineers. He himself had to appear in front of a naval court, which acquitted him, but nonetheless reprimanded him for his harsh and inhumane command. Bligh was then governor of New South Wales from 1805 to 1808 and later became a vice admiral. The entire incident helped bring about a substantial improvement in the living conditions of sailors aboard British warships. Fletcher Christian returned to Tahiti at first. With a number of natives and women he reached the uninhabited island of Pitcairn in January 1790. Not until 18 years later, in 1808, did the American sealing vessel *Topaz* from Boston accidentally discover the few survivors. They had burned the *Bounty* shortly after their arrival. Direct descendants of the mutineers still live on the island today. About a third of the approximately 150 inhabitants are named Christian.

In 1957 Louis Marden of the National Geographic Society discovered the remains of the *Bounty* and raised an anchor, nails, and ballast iron, among other items. The great irony is that the slaves of the West Indies ultimately refused to eat the breadfruit because it didn't taste good to them.

Metro-Goldwyn-Mayer, Inc., had the ship reconstructed according to the original London plans for its big film *Mutiny on the Bounty*. Planning and construction cost 700,000 dollars. The ship had to be built approximately 9 meters longer in order to give the large film cameras enough freedom of movement. The installation of an auxiliary engine was also necessary. The figurehead was carved according to the original specifications. It depicts a woman in a riding costume.

After the completion of the film, the *Bounty* visited a number of American ports, traveled to London in October 1962, and sailed in April 1964 to the World Exhibition in New York. Everywhere she went she was met with great interest, and she was visited by hundreds of thousands of people. Today the sailing ship lies as an exhibition ship in the harbor of St. Petersburg in Florida.

A second reconstruction of the *Bounty,* likewise built to be used in a film, arose in 1978 in Whangarei, New Zealand. The ship, which was built at great expense, has a wood-covered steel hull. The planned film was never made, so that the ship has to find another use.

Bowdoin

Type: 2-masted fore-and-aft schooner, wood	perpendiculars: 22.97 m Width: 6.15 m Depth to deck: 2.83 m Depth in hold: 1.90 m Draft: 2.88 m
Nation: USA	
Owner: Maine Maritime Academy, Castine	Sail area: 230 square meters
Home port: Castine	Rigging: 4 sails; 2 foresails (forestaysail with boom); fore-, mainmast: gaff-sail
Year of construction: 1921; launched September 9, 1921	
Shipyard: Hodgdon Brothers, East Boothbay, Maine; design: Admiral MacMillan	Masts, spars: height of mainmast over the deck: 19.80 meters; pole masts; no bowsprit
Tonnage: 66 tons gross; 15 tons net	Auxiliary engine: diesel engine
Dimensions: Length overall: 27.63 m Length of hull: 26.44 m Length between	Crew: 4-person active crew, 10 cadets Use: sailing school-ship

Admiral MacMillan designed the schooner while he was trapped in the ice with a ship 700 miles from the North Pole. The schooner was supposed to be built so strong that it could resist even the most powerful ice pressure. And indeed, MacMillan's construction proved itself exceptionally well in many dangerous situations.

The *Bowdoin* got her name from Bowdoin College in Brunswick, Maine, where MacMillan had earned an academic degree. Until World War II the *Bowdoin* sailed reliably every year under MacMillan's command into the waters around the North Pole.

During these voyages there were always scientists on board who worked in different branches of geography, geology, and mineralogy. In the years 1923–24 the ship lay trapped in the ice for 320 days in Refuge Harbor (Northern Greenland). The *Bowdoin* also encountered difficulties on many other voyages, but thanks to her sturdiness she was always able to extricate herself. She normally spent the winter in Boothbay Harbor.

During World War II the schooner sailed with the U.S. Navy patrol in the waters off Greenland. Her base at that time was the South Strom Fjord on Greenland. After the war MacMillan was able to continue his expeditions. In 1947 he made a voyage in the name of the Chicago Geographic Society on which he reached the 79th parallel with the ship. An ice barrier prevented further progress northward. In 1948, at the age of 72, Macmillan still held the command on a very successful expedition in which scientists from Bowdoin College and the Cleveland Museum of Natural History took part. Until the end of 1968, the *Bowdoin* belonged as a museum ship to the famous nautical museum in Mystic Seaport, Connecticut.

In 1986 a modification and thorough overhaul took place. Since then the *Bowdoin* has once again been sailing as an active school-ship. The training cruises lead primarily to Arctic waters.

 ## C. A. Thayer

Type: 3-masted fore-and-aft schooner, wood

Nation: USA

Owner: U.S. National Park System, Golden Gate National Recreation Area, National Maritime Museum, Hyde Street Pier

Home port: San Francisco, Hyde Street Pier

Year of construction: 1895; launched July 9, 1895

Shipyard: Hans Bendixsen, Eureka, California

Tonnage: 452 tons gross; 390 tons net

Dimensions:
Length overall: 66.60 m
Length between perpendiculars: 47.40 m
Width: 11.10 m
Depth in hold: 3.50 m
Draft: 2.40 m

Rigging: 9 sails; fore-, mainmast: gaff-sail, gaff-topsail; mizzenmast: jib-headed sail

Masts: height of mainmast over the deck: 28.90 meters

Auxiliary engine: none

Crew: 8 to 9 people in the lumber trade, 30 to 40 people as a fishing vessel

Use: museum ship

The extraordinarily rapid settlement of California at the end of the nineteenth century and the growth of the already existing cities and settlements led to a situation in which larger quantities of lumber were used than the state itself could provide. Almost all of the houses in these boomtowns were still built entirely of wood at that time. Most of the necessary lumber came to California by water. The trees were felled in the northwestern states and cut into lumber at sawmills near the coast. A fleet of more than a hundred schooners like the *C. A. Thayer* provided transportation south.

The ship was originally built for the E. K. Wood Lumber Company and got her name from its secretary, Clarence A. Thayer. For 17 years the schooner carried only wood. In 1912 the firm sold her to Peter Nelson. The *C. A. Thayer* sailed from now on in the summer in the salmon trade to Alaska. The large forward deckhouse that had to be built for the enlarged crew also dates from this period.

In 1925 the schooner changed owners again. For several years the *C. A. Thayer* spent the fishing season in the Bering Sea as a cod-fishing ship with one-man dories and hand lines. When the prices for salted cod began to fall, she had to be laid up. From 1942 until the end of the war the navy used her as a barge. She was later equipped as a fishing vessel one more time. In 1950 she made her final voyage in the Bering Sea. After she had lain idle for 7 years, it was possible to convince the government of the historical significance of the ship. The *C. A. Thayer* was completely restored and today lies as a museum ship in San Francisco.

Californian

Type: 2-masted topsail schooner, wood

Nation: USA

Owner: Nautical Heritage Society, San Clemente, California

Home port: Sacramento, California

Years of construction: 1983–84; launched May 28, 1984

Shipyard: in San Diego, California (Spanish Landing)

Tonnage: 130 ts displacement

Dimensions:
Length overall: 44.00 m
Length of hull: 28.40 m
Length between perpendiculars: 26.20 m
Width: 7.40 m
Draft: 2.80 m

Sail area: 650 square meters

Rigging: 9 sails; foremast with single topsail and topgallant

Masts: height of mainmast over the deck: 30 meters

Auxiliary engine: Caterpillar diesel engine, 100 horsepower

Crew: 8-person active crew, 16 trainees, 49 guests

Use: sailing school-ship

The *Californian* is an exact reproduction of the customs cutter *C. W. Lawrence,* which was built in 1848. This ship was the fastest and largest sailing ship of her kind at that time. Charming features of the reproduction, as of the original, are the elegant lines of the hull and the sharp bow that bears Queen Califia as a figurehead.

The schooner is intended primarily for the use of young people from California. The *Californian*'s first assignment was to serve as a flagship during the Olympic Games in Los Angeles in 1984.

Caribee

In the eighteenth and early nineteenth centuries very streamlined and thus fast ships were often used on privateering missions and in the slave trade. These ships were relatively heavily armed in spite of their often small size. In addition, this type of ship was also used by the coast guard and the customs services (see the *Centurion*).

The *Caribee* is in her exterior and in her rigging an exact reproduction of such a sailing ship. The painted gun ports give her a charming appearance. For many years the ship belonged to Windjammer Cruises in Miami Beach.

Type: 2-masted topsail schooner, wood

Nation: USA

Year of construction: 1942

Shipyard: shipyard in Ipswich, Massachusetts; construction: Howard I. Chapelle

Tonnage: 20 ts displacement; 180 tons gross; 102 tons net

Dimensions:
Length overall: 36.50 m
Length between perpendiculars: 29.80 m
Width: 7.40 m
Living quarters (height): 2.40 m
Draft: 3.60 m

Sail area: 450 square meters

Rigging: 9 sails; 3 foresails; foremast: square foresail, single topsail, foretrysail; mainmast: main staysail, mainsail, main gaff-topsail

Masts: height of mainmast over the deck: 30 meters; both masts with 1 topmast

Auxiliary engine: 6-71 gasoline engine, 180 horsepower

Crew: 8-person active crew, living quarters and accommodations for 20 people

Carthaginian II

Previous names: *Komet, Familiens Haab, Mary*

Type: brig, riveted steel

Nation: USA

Owner: Lahaina Restoration Foundation, Lahaina, Maui, Hawaii

Home port: San Francisco, Hyde Street Pier

Year of construction: 1920

Shipyard: Fr. Krupp Germania Shipyard, Kiel

Tonnage: 140 tons gross

Dimensions:
Length of hull: 29.00 m
Width: 6.70 m
Draft: 2.10 m

Masts: Each mast consists of three parts; height of mainmast: 26.40 meters; both masts double topsail, single topgallant, royal

Auxiliary engine: Scania Vabis diesel, 275 horsepower

Use: museum ship

The ship was built at the Krupp shipyard as the 2-masted schooner *Mary*. According to the regulations of the Allies, the shipyard at that time was not allowed to build any ships that were longer than 30 meters. The *Mary* was sold to Sweden soon thereafter and sailed as a cement carrier in the Baltic Sea.

In 1972 the Lahaina Restoration Foundation purchased the ship. After a 105-day voyage, the *Carthaginian*, as the ship was called from then on, reached Lahaina. There she was supposed to replace the first *Carthaginian*, which was scrapped. Over the course of many years of work the ship was rigged as a brig.

This type of ship was often used by whalers based in Lahaina. The whalers from New Bedford and Mystic Seaport at that time had to round Cape Horn if they wanted to reach the whaling grounds in the Arctic Ocean. Lahaina on Maui was the first base at which supplies of fresh water and food could be replenished. From here the voyage continued northward. In the winter, when weather conditions necessitated a pause in the catch, many ships returned to Lahaina in order to sail northward again the following year.

Because the whalers at sea obeyed only their own laws, there were often conflicts between them and the missionaries on the Hawaiian Islands. The story of these is related in the novel *Hawaii* by James Michener. Once, a whaling captain had a missionary fired upon with the ship's guns because the missionary had forbidden the Hawaiian girls from setting foot on the ship.

The *Carthaginian* houses a whaling museum in which visitors can view films about whales in addition to exhibits of historical objects.

Charles W. Morgan

Type: full-rigged ship, wood	Year of construction: 1841; launched July 21, 1841; first fishing voyage September 4, 1841	Dimensions: Length overall: 51.30 m Length between perpendiculars: 32.00 m Width: 8.40 m Depth to deck: 5.30 m	Masts: all masts with top- and topgallant masts
Nation: USA			Auxiliary engine: no auxiliary engine, even in later years
Owner: Marine Historical Association Inc., Mystic, Connecticut	Shipyard: Brothers Jethro & Zacariah Hilmann, Fairhaven, near New Bedford, Massachusetts		Crew: 28 people on average
Home port: Mystic Seaport		Rigging: 20 sails; single topsail, single topgallant, royals	Use: sailing museum ship
	Tonnage: 313 tons gross; 298 tons net		

The *Charles W. Morgan* is the only one of the famous wooden whaling ships that has been preserved for us. Her first owner was the Quaker businessman Charles W. Morgan. The next owners were Edward Mott Robinson; I. Howland & Company; J. & W. R. Cleveland; John A. Cook, and Whaling Enshrined. The ship has a painted streak that at the time of the ship's construction and even later served the purpose of deterring pirates from an attack. During her 80 years of whaling activity the *Charles W. Morgan* sailed on 37 whaling expeditions in all the oceans of the world. These voyages often lasted several years. Only when the ship was fully loaded did she return to her home port. More than a thousand whalers found a home aboard the *Charles W. Morgan*. In all, more than 2500 whales were harpooned and captured by her boats.

On board there were up to seven boats, which were usually occupied by 6 men each—4 men on the oars, a harpooner, and a helmsman. From 1841 to 1866 her home port was New Bedford; from 1867 to 1906, San Francisco. Subsequently she returned to New Bedford. From here the ship made its final 7 whaling expeditions until 1921. In 1921 she set sail one more time for the film *Down to the Sea in Ships*.

In November 1941, the *Charles W. Morgan* was towed from Round Hills, Dartmouth (Massachusetts), to Mystic. Today she is one of the main tourist attractions in Mystic Seaport. She has almost always been rigged as a full-rigged ship. The walled oven with the rendering pots in which the whale blubber was extracted still stands on deck.

Clipper City

Type: 2-masted topsail schooner, steel	Width: 8.30 m Draft: 1.70 m–4.20 m
Nation: USA	Sail area: 916 square meters
Owner: Clipper City, Inc., Baltimore	Rigging: 9 sails; foremast with topsail and topgallant
Home port: Baltimore	Masts: height of mainmast over the deck: 38 meters
Year of construction: 1985; launched September 11, 1985	Auxiliary engine: Diesel Cat 3208, 210 horsepower
Tonnage: 210 ts displacement	Crew: 7-person active crew, 143 guests on day cruises
Dimensions: Length overall: 48.00 m Length of hull: 39.21 m Length between perpendiculars: 18.54 m	Use: chartered ship

The model for this reproduction was a topsail schooner from the year 1854. The *Clipper City* is the largest sailing ship from the United States that can take passengers aboard. It is used primarily to take large groups on cruises in the harbor area of Baltimore and in the Chesapeake Bay.

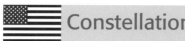

Constellation

Type: sloop-of-war (full-rigged ship), wood

Nation: USA

Owner: city of Baltimore

Home port: Baltimore, Inner Harbor

Years of construction: 1853–55; launched August 28, 1854

Shipyard: Gosport Navy Yard, Norfolk, Virginia

Tonnage: 1400 ts displacement

Dimensions:
Length overall: 86.00 m
Length of hull: 56.50 m
Length between perpendiculars: 53.50 m
Width: 12.50 m
Depth in hold: 6.40 m
Depth to deck: 9.20 m
Draft: 6.40 m

Sail area: 2000 square meters

Rigging: 38 sails, including studding sails, single topsail, single topgallant, royals

Masts: height of mainmast over the deck: 50 meters

Crew: 300 people, including soldiers

Armaments: sixteen 8-inch guns (20.30 cm), four 32-pounders

Use: museum ship

The *Constellation* is the second wind-powered warship of the U.S. Navy to bear this name. For a long time there was uncertainty even among experts as to whether this ship was actually the frigate of the same name that the young United States of America built in 1797 along with five additional frigates. It is a documented fact, however, that the frigate *Constellation* was scrapped at the Gosport Navy Yard at the same time as the current ship was being built there. It is likely that some parts of the old ship, which

had acquitted herself very well during her period of service, were used in the new construction for reasons of tradition.

In the terminology of the American navy, a sloop-of-war is a heavily armed wooden sailing ship on which all guns are located on a single deck. This is in contrast to a frigate, on which one and a half decks are equipped with guns. The German word *Schaluppe* ("sloop") refers to a completely different type of vessel.

Instead of the flat stern that was typical of the earlier frigates, the *Constellation* was

built with a round stern that gave her hull significantly greater strength. This type of stern became ever-more prevalent. The ship got her name from the "constellation" of stars on the early American flag.

Following a period of service in the Mediterranean, the *Constellation* was deployed to combat the slave trade. Between 1859 and 1861 she captured three slave ships and in the process liberated 700 men, women, and children who had been on their way to the United States as slaves. The slave ship *Triton* was the first ship captured in the American Civil War. Two more years of service in the Mediterranean followed. After the war the ship transported humanitarian relief to Ireland during the great potato famine. In 1878 she carried valuable American artworks destined for the World's Exhibition in Paris. From 1873 to 1893 she trained

naval cadets as a school-ship for the Naval Academy.

At the outbreak of World War II the ship lay almost forgotten in a very bad condition in Newport, Rhode Island. It was President Franklin Delano Roosevelt who in 1940 designated the *Constellation* as the auxiliary flagship of the Atlantic fleet and as the flagship of Battle Ship Group 5. This was her last great command.

In 1955 the *Constellation* was officially retired from active service and donated to the "Star-Spangled Banner" Flag House Association of Baltimore. She arrived in Baltimore from Boston in a floating dock. Following restoration work, the ship lay fully rigged in the city's inner harbor from 1968 to 1994 and was open to tourists.

Renewed investigations uncovered a rupture in the keel, so that the yards, masts, and the powerful jibboom with the bowsprit had to be removed for safety reasons. Serious damage to the hull was also discovered. The *Constellation* had to be closed to the public. In November 1996 the hull was towed into a dry dock in Baltimore. There rotted planks were replaced with composite materials. This form of repair proved to be more economical than using real wood. Frames also had to be replaced. In spite of efforts to save money, the costs of the restoration approached 9 million dollars.

Since August 21, 1998, the *Constellation* has been back in her element. It has been possible to start the rigging work.

She is the only ship to have survived the Civil War and was the last pure sailing ship to be built by the U.S. Navy.

Constitution

After the end of the War of Independence in 1783 the young United States gradually succeeded in opening the channels of maritime trade to their own merchant marine. In the Mediterranean, however, the ships were attacked constantly by pirates from the Barbary states and their crews were taken prisoner. In order to protect these sailing ships and the new nation, Congress decided in 1794 to have six frigates built. Three of these were commissioned immediately. Of these ships, only the *Constitution* in Boston still survives.

In the war with England (1812–14), the *Constitution* took part in a victorious engagement with the thirty-eight-cannon frigate *Guerriere*, and likewise with the frigate *Java*. Because the gun deck lies high over the waterline (approximately 2.5 meters) the *Constitution* could be sailed hard even through rough water. This ability gave her an advantage over her foes in many situations. Speeds of up to 13½ knots were logged.

In February 1815, she made her last voyage as an active naval vessel. On February 20, 1815, the ship fought a victorious engagement with the British frigate *Cyane* and the cannon sloop *Levant*. From 1815 until 1821 the ship was laid up in Boston. Extensive repairs followed. On May 13, 1821, the *Constitution* became the flagship of the Mediterranean squadron. In July 1828, her period of service was supposed to come to a provisional end. A commission declared that the ship was not seaworthy. As a result, the government decided on her demolition. A poem that appeared in many newspapers, "Old Ironsides," by Oliver W. Holmes, brought about the preservation of the ship. (A story reports that a sailor saw how the enemy's shot bounced back off of the sides of the *Constitution*. The nickname Ironsides arose from this story).

The thorough overhaul at a shipyard in Boston lasted from 1833 to 1834. In 1835 the ship was once again deployed in the Mediterranean squadron. In 1839 the frigate made a trip around Cape Horn in the South Pacific, and in 1844 she traveled to China. In 1848 there followed a voyage in the Mediterranean.

In 1852 the frigate cruised off the West Coast of Africa to monitor and combat the slave trade. From 1855 to 1860 the ship was extensively renovated in Portsmouth (New Hampshire). On July 1, 1860, the naval academy in Annapolis acquired the *Constitution*. This academy had to be moved to Newport (Rhode Island) in 1861 for reasons of security arising from the Civil War. The frigate became a school-ship and returned to Annapolis in 1865. In 1871 the ship lay docked at Philadelphia. In 1878 the ship brought trade goods to France for the Paris World's Exhibition. In the 1880s the *Constitution* was used for receptions in Portsmouth. Through the influence of John F. Fitzgerald, the great grandfather of President Kennedy, the heavily damaged frigate was restored for her hundredth birthday in 1897. Some of the earlier repair work had been carried out inappropriately.

In 1905 the condition of the ship was once again worrisomely bad. For this reason, the *Constitution* was supposed to be used as a practice target for the fleet. Once again it was the public who protested against the ship's destruction and brought about her preservation. The costs for the reconstruction ran to 100,000 dollars in 1906.

For 20 years the frigate was then a museum ship. Her further decay could not be prevented, however. In 1925 Congress agreed to her complete reconstruction, but at first did not provide any funds. The costs were covered to a great extent by money raised through citizens' initiatives. Later, state funds were added. On June 16, 1927, work began on the *Constitution* Dry Dock in Boston. Douglas firs for the masts came all the way from the West Coast. This time the total cost came to 92,100 dollars.

The frigate lay at dock until March 16, 1931. Then, on July 2, 1931, there began a 3-year voyage during which the ship was brought in tow to 90 American ports. During this period 4,614,792 visitors came on board. A total of about 22,000 sea miles were covered. Since 1934 the *Constitution* has been moored in Boston Harbor. She is the flagship of the commandant of the First Naval District and thus the oldest active warship in the world. Once a year the ship is ceremoniously rotated in Boston Harbor in order to change the side that is exposed to the weather.

For her 200th birthday, the *Constitution* sailed with some of her sails set from Marblehead to Boston. On board was a crew of 60, plus 4 U.S. admirals in historic uniforms. The event became a large maritime spectacle. In preparation for its mini-cruise, the frigate had previously been towed north to Marblehead.

Type: frigate, wood, full-rigged ship

Nation: USA

Owner: U.S. Navy

Home port: Boston, Charlestown Navy Yard

Year of construction: 1797; launched October 21, 1797

Shipyard: Hartt's Shipyard, Boston, Massachusetts, design: Joshua Humphreys

Tonnage: 2200 ts displacement

Dimensions:
Length overall: 93.00 m
Length of hull: 62.00 m
Length between perpendiculars: 53.50 m
Width: 14.00 m
Width main deck: 11.70 m
Depth to deck: 11.00 m
Draft: 6.00 m

Sail area: 3970 square meters (with studding sails); main topsail, 315 square meters

Rigging: 36 sails (with studding sails, original rig); single topsail, single topgallant, royals, skysail, studding sails

Masts, spars: height of mainmast over the deck: 52 meters; length of main yard: 28 meters; length of main royal yard: 9 meters; bowsprit with jibboom: 29 meters

Crew: about 475 people, including soldiers

Armaments: at the time of construction: forty-four guns; in the war of 1812: gun deck: thirty 24-pounders, spar deck: sixteen 32-pounders, forespar deck: two 24-pounders, one 16-pounder, six 32-pounders; a total of fifty-five guns

Use: stationary flagship, museum ship

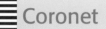

Coronet

Type: 2-masted fore-and-aft schooner, wood

Nation: USA

Owner: International Yacht Restoration School

Home Port: Newport, Rhode Island

Year of construction: 1885; launched August 17, 1885

Shipyard: C. & R. Poillon, Brooklyn, New York

Tonnage: 174 tons gross; 152.67 tons net

Dimensions:
Length overall: 57.90 m
Length of hull: 52.70 m
Length between perpendiculars: 36.10 m
Width: 8.20 m
Depth in hold: 3.00 m
Draft: 3.40 m

Sail area: 770 square meters

Rigging: 9 sails

Masts: height of mainmast over the deck (with topmast): 53 meters

Auxiliary engine: originally no engine

Crew: as a yacht 15–19 people

Use: sailing passenger ship, museum ship

The *Coronet* is one of the largest wooden racing yachts ever built. A striking feature is the vertical stern. Since at the moment the jibboom and stems are missing, the ship only partially resembles a seagoing yacht. In order to demonstrate the speed of the ship, the first owner, the New York businessman Rufus T. Bush, organized a trans-Atlantic race in which the *Coronet* defeated the famous racing yacht *Dauntless* by 30 hours.

The ship twice undertook a circumnavigation of the globe, in the process becoming the first yacht to sail around Cape Horn. In 1895 she hosted a group of American and Japanese scientists who observed and measured a total eclipse.

From 1905 to 1995 the yacht was employed as a mission ship. In 1995 the International Yacht Restoration School (IYRS) acquired the ship. The *Coronet* is being carefully restored as a national maritime memorial, after which she will once again be used as a flagship for sailing cruises.

Corwith Cramer

Type: brigantine, steel

Nation: USA

Owner: Sea Education Association, Woods Hole, Massachusetts

Home port: Woods Hole, Massachusetts

Year of construction: 1987

Shipyard: ASTACE shipyard, Bilbao, Spain

Tonnage: 280 ts displacement

Dimensions:
Length overall: 40.70 m
Length of hull: 29.70 m
Width: 7.90 m
Draft: 3.90 m

Sail area: 725 square meters

Rigging: 8 sails with foresails

Auxiliary engine: Cummins diesel, 500 horsepower

Crew: 11-person active crew, including scientists, 25 students (trainees)

Use: sailing school-ship

The founder of the Sea Education Association gave the ship her name. In addition to instruction in seamanship and navigation, natural sciences and oceanography are emphasized in the curriculum. During the summer semester, for example, the students first spend 4 weeks in their classrooms and then 4 weeks at sea. In the process they log up to 2000 sea miles.

Denis Sullivan

Type: 3-masted fore-and-aft schooner, wood

Nation: USA

Owner: Wisconsin Lake Schooner Education Association

Home port: Milwaukee, Wisconsin

Years of construction: 1995–2000; keel laid October 1995; launched June 22, 2000

Shipyard: Wisconsin Lake Schooner Education Association

Tonnage: 156 ts displacement; 100 tons gross

Dimensions:
Length overall: 40.50 m

Length of hull: 28.30 m
Width: 7.20 m
Draft: 2.60 m

Sail area: 550 square meters

Rigging: 10 sails

Masts: height of mainmast over the deck: 29 meters

Auxiliary engine: 2 diesel engines, 180 horsepower each

Crew: 7-person active crew, overnight accommodations for 18 guests, 45 guests on day cruises

Use: floating classroom, passenger ship, ambassador ship

This large schooner was built outdoors so that spectators and visitors could observe the progress of the work during the 5-year construction period. More than 300 volunteers, including young people, took part in the communal work under the supervision of experienced shipbuilders.

As Wisconsin's flagship, the ship commemorates a period in the 1880s when the transportation system on the Great Lakes operated entirely on the basis of sailing ships. At times during this period up to two thousand ships were in service.

The main function of the sailing ship is to provide instruction to young people and adults in the most diverse disciplines. She is named after a famous and influential ship's captain of that period.

Eagle

Previous name: *Horst Wessel*

Type: bark, steel

Nation: USA

Owner: Department of Transportation, U.S. Coast Guard, Washington, D.C.

Home port: New London, Connecticut

Year of construction: 1936; launched June 30, 1936

Shipyard: Blohm & Voss, Hamburg

Tonnage: 1634/1816 ts displacement

Dimensions:
Length overall: 89.70 m
Length of hull: 80.70 m
Length between perpendiculars: 70.20 m
Width: 11.90 m
Draft (armed): 5.20 m
Freeboard: 2.70 m

Sail area: 2065 square meters

Rigging: 22 sails; 4 foresails, double topsails, single topgallants, royals; mizzenmast: mizzen sail, mizzen topsail

Masts, spars: fore- and mainmast masthead truck: 45.70 meters; mizzenmast masthead truck: 40.10 meters over the waterline; length fore- and main rah: 23.90 meters

Auxiliary engine: MAN 8-cylinder four-stroke diesel engine, 750 horsepower; speed with engine, 10 knots

Crew: 5 officers, 30 regular crew members, about 150 cadets, including women

Use: sailing school-ship

In 1790 Alexander Hamilton, who was secretary of the Treasury at that time, founded the Coast Guard. He ordered the construction of several boats that were supposed primarily to monitor coastal smuggling. Until 1798 the fleet of the Coast Guard was the United States' only navy. Today the Coast Guard supervises the entire coastal security system, including navigational aids (lighthouses, lightships, buoys, etc.). In peacetime it is subordinated to the Treasury Department, whereas during a war it is part of the navy.

During World War II the Coast Guard used the Danish full-rigged ship *Danmark* as a school-ship for its cadets. The war had overtaken the *Danmark* while it was visiting America, and it was not able to return. At the end of the war the Coast Guard acquired the ship now known as the *Eagle* from Germany as a reparations payment. This bark was built with the name *Horst Wessel* as the second school-ship for what was at that time the Reich navy. Only a few training voyages could be undertaken prior to the outbreak of the war. The ship was used all the more extensively for the transport of people and provisions in the Baltic region during the first years of the war. The United States acquired the ship in 1946 in Bremerhaven. The spanker, which was originally divided into an upper and a lower sail, was replaced by a single spanker. Both anchors are today stockless. The *Horst Wessel,* by contrast, carried a stock anchor as her portside anchor.

The original bow ornamentation, a large eagle, was replaced by a smaller eagle that fit better with the lines of the bow. The original is located today in the Marine Museum of Mystic Seaport (Connecticut).

The *Eagle*'s yearly main voyage takes her to European or Central American waters from June until August with the first and third classes of the academy. This is followed by a shorter voyage with the second and fourth classes in the western Atlantic. All the cadets sleep in hammocks. Three hundred forty-four tons of iron bars serve as ballast and give the ship the necessary stability.

Three 75-kilowatt diesel generators provide electricity.

From 1981 to 1982 the *Eagle* was equipped with additional watertight bulkheads. At the same time she also got a new engine, the cadets' hammocks were replaced with permanent bunks, and the cafeteria was separated from the sleeping quarters.

She has taken part in numerous regattas and windjammer rendezvous. She can easily be recognized by the vertical stripes typical of U.S. Coast Guard ships.

Elissa

Previous names: *Pioneer, Achaios, Christophoros, Gustaf, Fjeld, Elissa*

Type: bark, iron

Nation: USA

Owner: Galveston Historical Foundation, Inc., Galveston, Texas

Home port: Galveston, Texas

Year of construction: 1877

Shipyard: Alexander Hall & Company, Aberdeen, Scotland

Tonnage: 430 tons gross

Dimensions:
Length overall: 61.40 m
Length over deck: 45.40 m
Width: 8.50 m
Draft: 4.80 m

Sail area: 1115 square meters

Rigging: 19 sails; double topsail, single topgallant, royals

Masts: height of mainmast over the deck: 31 meters

Auxiliary engine: none

Crew: not fixed

Use: museum, school-, and chartered ship

For Henry F. Watt, her first owner, the *Elissa* sailed all the freight trade routes of that time with the most diverse cargoes, sometimes also as a tramping vessel. In 1897 she was sold to the Norwegian firm Bugge & Olsen and received the name *Fjeld.* In 1919 the sailing ship got an auxiliary engine and, in order to save money, the rig of a barkentine. The flag had now become Swedish, as had the new name, *Gustaf* (shipowner: Carl Johansson). In the 1920s the rig was further reduced.

When the *Gustaf* finally passed into Finnish hands in 1930 the bark had become a fore-and-aft schooner from which the sailing bow had also been removed.

A new engine, deckhouse, and bridge completed the ship's conversion into a purely motorized ship. As the *Christophoros,* the ship now belonged to a Greek owner and had Piraeus as her home port. The American George Throckmorton discovered the *Elissa* in 1961 while in search of an old sailing

ship and finally purchased her in 1970—she was to take on her old appearance again.

First, however, she changed her name two more times. As the *Achaios,* she sailed in the legal freight trade; she was active as a smuggling ship under the name *Pioneer.*

The *Elissa* was towed to Galveston in 1979 by way of Gibraltar, where she spent the winter. At great expense and with much expertise the ship

was thoroughly overhauled and rerigged as a bark. The rebirth of this beautiful ship cost about 1 million dollars. Since 1982 she has once again sailed under wind power.

Type: 4-masted full-rigged ship, iron

Nation: USA

Owner: Hawaii Maritime Center, Honolulu

Home port: Honolulu, Pier 4

Year of construction: 1878

Shipyard: Russel & Company, Port Glasgow, Scotland

Tonnage: 1195 ts displacement; 1809 tons gross; 1748 tons net

Dimensions:
Length overall: approx. 98.00 m
Length of hull: approx. 85.00 m
Length between perpendiculars: 80.10 m
Width: 12.20 m
Depth to deck: 7.10 m
Depth in hold: 7.00 m
Draft (fully loaded): 6.40 m

Rigging: 32 sails (as a full-rigged ship); double topsail, single topgallant, royals

Masts: height of mainmast over the deck: 41 meters

Auxiliary engine: none

Use: museum ship

The firm Wright & Breakenridge (later Wright, Graham & Company) controlled a fleet of nine large square-rigged ships in 1878, the famous Glasgow Falls Line. Six of these sailing ships were 4-masted full-rigged ships. Of these, only the *Falls of Clyde* survives today.

Even before the turn of the century the ship sometimes sailed under the Hawaiian flag. In 1900 Captain William Matson purchased the ship and had her rerigged as a 4-masted bark. For 7 years the *Falls of Clyde* sailed cargo and passengers between California and Hilo (Hawaii). In 1907 she became the property of Associated Oil (now the Tidewater Oil Company) and was converted into a wind-powered tanker. For the next 15 years the ship sailed between the American West Coast and Honolulu with 19,000 barrels of oil on board each time.

From 1926 to 1959 the *Falls of Clyde* lay without masts as a fuel depot ship for the General Petroleum Company in the harbor of Ketchikan, Alaska. A private buyer later had her towed to Seattle in the hope that some organization would intervene to provide for the preservation of the ship. Several large cities of the West Coast attempted in vain to raise the necessary funds. Finally a bank in Alaska that had lent the money for the last purchase determined that the hull should be sold for 18,950 dollars on May 31, 1963, in order to be sunk as a breakwater off Alaska. Shortly before this date, Karl Kortum, the director of the San Francisco Maritime Museum, took up contact with Honolulu. Immediately thereafter a collection began throughout Hawaii to which industrialists, newspaper people, and various trade delegations contributed but in which the general public played the largest role. The goal was to save a ship that had played a significant part in the recent history of the island. The Matson Navigation Company in the meantime succeeded in negotiating a 30-day deferral of the deadline with the bank. The collection raised not only the necessary sum of 18,950 dollars, but also an additional 5000 dollars for the transport of the *Falls of Clyde* to Hawaii. The ship initially belonged in trust to the B. P. Bishop Museum in Honolulu but has since been donated to the Hawaii Maritime Center in Honolulu.

The restoration work has been largely completed. In spite of the high costs, the full-rigged ship has been rerigged. Soil samples in the dry dock into which the *Falls of Clyde* was towed in July 1981 showed that the outer surface was in relatively good condition. Nonetheless, the rudder blade had to be replaced because of rust damage. The *Falls of Clyde* is the only still-existing 4-masted full-rigged ship.

Friendship

Type: full-rigged ship, wood, reproduction

Nation: USA

Owner: U.S. government, National Park Service

Home port: Salem, Massachusetts

Years of construction: 1996–2000

Shipyard: Scarano Boats, Albany, New York (hull); Dion's Yacht Yard, Salem (technical equipment)

Tonnage: 350 ts displacement

Dimensions:
Length overall: 52.10 m
Length of hull: 35.30 m
Length between perpendiculars: 31.70 m

Width: 9.10 m
Depth to deck: 6.10 m
Draft: 3.30 m

Sail area: 874 square meters (studding sails, 809 square meters)

Rigging: 21 sails, single topsail, single topgallant, royals

Masts: height of mainmast over the deck: 32.30 meters

Auxiliary engine: two Cummins diesel engines, 330 horsepower each

Crew: 20-person active crew, 149 guests

Use: museum ship, exhibit ship

The original *Friendship* was built in 1796–97 as a trading ship in Salem, Massachusetts.

Her 16 voyages carried goods to China, Java, Sumatra, Madras, London, Hamburg, Archangel, St. Petersburg, and other European ports. At that time it was completely normal to arm a trading ship with cannons so that it could also be employed as a privateer.

In the war of 1812–14, in which control of Canada was at stake, the ship was captured by the English and later sold. Nothing is known about her fate after that point.

At that time Salem was an important center of the maritime trade. Because a model of the *Friendship* exists from that period, and because three paintings testify to her appearance, she was chosen for a reproduction.

The hull, which was built in Albany, New York, was rigged in Boston. One hundred fifty tons of lead provide the ship with the necessary stability. Modern technology allows her to sail safely on the open sea. A figurehead depicts a classically dressed woman offering a bouquet of flowers with open arms as a sign of friendship.

Gazela of Philadelphia

Previous name: *Gazela Primeiro*

Type: barkentine, wood

Nation: USA

Owner: Philadelphia Marine Museum

Home port: Philadelphia (Penn's Landing, Delaware River)

Year of construction: 1883

Shipyard: in Cacilhas, Portugal

Tonnage: 323.89 tons gross; 220.96 tons net; as a banker: 5193 quintels (311,580 kg) fish loading capacity

Dimensions:
Length overall: 54.00 m
Length of hull: 47.40 m

Length between perpendiculars: 41.10 m
Width: 8.20 m
Depth in hull: 5.00 m
Draft: 5.20 m

Sail area: 828 square meters

Rigging: 13 sails; 3 foresails; foremast: fore-, double topsail, topgallant

Masts, spars: height of foremast over the deck: 28.30 meters;

foremast with top- and topgallant mast; main and mizzenmast with one topmast.

Auxiliary engine: 4-cylinder Mannheim diesel, 180 horsepower

Crew: as a banker, 42 people, 31 dories

Use: sailing school-ship and museum ship

The *Gazela Primeiro* belonged to the Portuguese fleet of bank schooners since the time of her construction. She is thus the oldest ship to have fished for cod off Newfoundland from a port in Europe. She left Europe under wind power in May 1971 in order to relocate to the United States. Today she belongs to the Philadelphia Marine Museum.

Half Moon

Type: merchantman, seventeenth century, wood, reproduction (bark rigging)	Dimensions: Length overall: 28.80 m Length of hull: 25.50 m Width: 5.30 m Depth in hold: 2.40 m Draft: 2.50 m
Nation: USA	
Owner: Holland Villages, Inc., Princeton, New Jersey	Sail area: 256 square meters
Home port: Croton-on-Hudson, New York	Rigging: 6 sails
Years of construction: 1988–89; launched June 10, 1989	Masts: height of mainmast over the waterline: 23.70 meters
Shipyard: Snow Dock, Albany, New York; design: Nick Benton	Auxiliary engine: Cummins diesel, 250 horsepower
	Armaments: six small cannons
Tonnage: 130 ts displacement; 112 tons gross	Use: museum ship, tourist cruises, film ship

The original *Halve Maan* ("Half Moon") was built in 1608 by the Dutch East India Company. She was Henry Hudson's ship, with which he undertook 4 voyages between 1609 and 1611. He was searching for a shorter sea route to China by way of the Arctic Ocean. In the process he discovered the Hudson River and the Chesapeake Bay. In 1610 he reached the Hudson Strait and Hudson Bay. Together with his son and seven companions he was put ashore by a mutinous crew in June 1611 and never found.

The reproduction is based on plans for a sister ship that were preserved in the Dutch maritime archives in The Hague.

Following her completion, the ship visited numerous ports on the American and Canadian coasts as well as in the Great Lakes. The *Half Moon* has appeared in the films *Pocohantas: The Legend, The Scarlet Letter,* and Disney's *Squanto.*

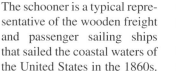

Harvey Gamage

Type: 2-masted fore-and-aft schooner, wood

Nation: USA

Owner: Schooner Harvey Gamage Foundation, Inc., Cornwall, New York

Home port: Islesboro, Maine

Year of construction: 1973

Shipyard: Harvey Gamage Shipyard, South Bristol, Maine

Tonnage: 129 ts displacement; 94 tons gross; 91 tons net

Dimensions:
Length overall: 39.90 m

Length of hull: 28.90 m
Width: 7.30 m
Draft: 2.90 m

Sail area: 650 square meters

Rigging: 7 sails

Masts: height of mainmast over the deck: 29 meters

Auxiliary engine: Volvo Penta diesel, 220 horsepower

Crew: 8–12-person active crew, 20–26 trainees (secondary and university students)

Use: sailing school-ship, sailing classroom

The schooner is a typical representative of the wooden freight and passenger sailing ships that sailed the coastal waters of the United States in the 1860s. Her namesake is the master shipbuilder Harvey Gamage, who had already built several ships of the same type.

The designation High School Ocean Classroom refers to the educational program that is offered to secondary and university students. In addition to various school and academic subjects, the young people are instructed primarily in seamanship. Thus the elegant schooner is a floating classroom and at the same time an active school-ship.

In the summer the *Harvey Gamage* sails off the coast of New England, and in the winter the Caribbean becomes her area of activity.

Hawaiian Chieftan

Type: topsail ketch, steel

Nation: USA

Owner: Central Coast Charters

Home port: Sausalito, California

Years of construction: 1985–88; launched June 12, 1988

Shipyard: Mala Wharf, Lahaina, Maui, Hawaii

Tonnage: 84 ts displacement; 60 tons gross

Dimensions:
Length overall: 31.50 m
Length of hull: 23.40 m
Length between

perpendiculars: 19.80 m
Width: 6.70 m
Draft: 1.80 m

Sail area: 418 square meters

Rigging: 10 sails, single topsail, single topgallant, royal

Masts: height of mainmast over the deck: 22.80 meters

Auxiliary engine: 2 Volvo Penta TMDI engines, 150 horsepower each

Crew: 8-person active crew, 12 trainees, 45 guests

Use: sailing school-ship, chartered ship, day cruises

360

The ketch is a coastal sailing ship of the type that was used in the freight trade in northern European waters during the 1890s. Her launch served the locals in Lahaina as the occasion for a popular festival. Two Caterpillars dragged the hull, which was decorated with a large wreath, through a freshly dug sand ditch filled with water from the shipyard to the open sea.

The ship represents an exceptional mixture of old shipbuilding art and new shipbuilding technology. The small draft allows for cruises in shallow waters as well. The bust of a Hawaiian chief adorns the bow as a figurehead.

In addition to university students, children receive instruction aboard in various subjects having to do with seafaring.

Jamestown Ships (replicas)

In Jamestown lies a group of outstanding replicas that were built in 1956–57. English settlers sailed with the originals to America in 1606–67 and founded the first permanent English-speaking colony. In 1984 the *Godspeed* and the *Discovery* were replaced by new reproductions because the first replicas had rotted extensively.

Susan Constant II

Dimensions:
Length overall: 33.40 m
Length between
perpendiculars: 24.00 m
Width: 7.20 m
Draft (aft): 3.00 m

Sail area: 240 square meters

Masts: height of mainmast over the waterline: 26 meters

Crew: 17-person crew (probably); passengers: 54 people (probably)

Godspeed II

Dimensions:
Length overall: 20.60 m
Length between
perpendiculars: 15.10 m
Width: 4.70 m
Draft (aft): 2.10 m

Sail area: 71 square meters

Masts: height of mainmast over the waterline: 17 meters

Crew: 13 people (probably); passengers: 39 people (probably)

Discovery II

Dimensions:
Length overall: 15.00 m
Length between
perpendiculars: 11.50 m
Width: 3.40 m
Draft (aft): 1.60 m

Sail area: 36 square meters

Masts: height of mainmast over the waterline: 10.90 meters

Crew: 9 people (probably); passengers: 12 people (probably)

Previous name: *Georg Stage I*

Type: full-rigged ship, iron

Nation: USA

Owner: Marine Historical Association, Inc., Mystic, Connecticut

Home port: Mystic Seaport

Year of construction: 1882

Shipyard: Burmeister & Wain, Copenhagen

Tonnage: 203 tons gross; 187 tons net; 400 tdw

Dimensions:
Length overall: 46.80 m
Length of hull: 36.00
Length between perpendiculars: 30.60 m
Width: 7.60 m
Depth to deck: 4.50 m
Draft: 3.60 m

Rigging: 20 sails; 4 foresails, deep, single topsail, single topgallant, royals; studding sail on fore- and main mast

Mast, spars: height of mainmast from keel to masthead truck: 30 meters; masts, yards, and spars: wood, bowsprit with jibboom

Auxiliary engine: diesel engine, 265 horsepower

Crew: as an active sailing school-ship: captain, first and second mates, 1 teacher, 5 petty officers, cook, about 80 boys

Use: museum ship, stationary training ship

The Danish shipowner Frederik Stage had the full-rigged ship *Georg Stage* built in 1882 in remembrance of his deceased son Georg. The Stiftelsen Georg Stages Minde, which still operates the full-rigged ship *Georg Stage II* today, arose in Copenhagen with the help of this shipowner. The *Georg Stage* had an auxiliary steam engine with a vertical boiler as well as a removable propeller, which were distinguishing features at that time. The need for these elements can be explained by the fact that a large percentage of the sailing warships of the ship's era possessed an auxiliary engine. The young men needed to become acquainted with this equipment during their training period.

The ship was and is constantly designated as a former steamer. This categorization is false. The sailing ship was rigged as a full-rigged ship and made use of the engine only under special circumstances.

The *Georg Stage* was built with a small, high forecastle. The anchor windlass stood on the main deck and was operated with a "pump handle" motion (up and down movements of the handle). The bulwark was doubled over the pin-rail. Thus a classic stowage space for the young men's rolled-up hammocks was formed. The young men's living quarters lay on the between deck, and for this reason there were skylights and companionways in the main deck.

The original wooden figurehead of Georg Stage had to be replaced by a bronze bust in the course of time, because the young men had used it to practice their carving. Today two small brass cannons, which at that time were used for salutes, still stand on the poop.

The ship was designed for voyages in the North and Baltic seas only. At the end of the season she was unrigged by the young men themselves. During the winter she was laid up in Copenhagen. On June 25, 1905, the *Georg Stage* was rammed at night in the Øresund by the British steamship *Ancona of Leith*. The ship had no bulkheads and sank in less than three minutes. Twenty-two young men lost their lives in the accident. Repair and reconstruction work took place after the ship was raised. The old steam engine with the removable propeller was expanded, and four watertight bulkheads were introduced. After the completion of this

work she continued her training voyages as a pure sailing ship. Not until 1916 did she once again receive a 52-horsepower engine. In 1922 a new deck was built and the anchor windlass was replaced by a capstan on the forecastle. Over time the ship had become too small for the training program, however. The construction of the *Georg Stage II* was being planned. On August 29, 1934, the *Georg Stage* was sold to the maritime writer Alan Villiers.

Villier subsequently had her equipped and furnished for a voyage around the world. Because she didn't carry any cargo, she wasn't a trading vessel, and although paying cadets served aboard her, she wasn't an official school-ship. For this reason she was registered at the Royal Harwich Yacht Club. The sailing ship received the name *Joseph Conrad*.

On October 22, 1934, her great voyage began. In New

York the ship was damaged and almost lost. The sailing ship returned to New York on October 16, 1936. Villiers sailed a total of 57,000 sea miles. On November 10, 1936, the *Joseph Conrad* was sold to Huntington Hartford. He had her furnished as a yacht with every conceivable comfort. In addition to many changes to the interior, the ship received a 265-horsepower diesel engine. In 1939 Hartford donated the ship to the U.S. Maritime Commission.

The *Joseph Conrad* was an oceangoing training ship of the merchant marine until 1945, with her home port in St. Petersburg, Florida. From 1945 until 1947 she lay there as a gift to the Marine Historical Association. Since the summer of 1948 she has lain in Mystic Seaport as a museum ship. In addition, training courses for boys and girls from the Sea Scouts take place aboard the full-rigged ship.

Kalmar Nyckel

Originally a pinnace, the *Kalmar Nyckel* was built in the 1720s in Holland. Typical features of a pinnace were its full-rigged ship rig and the usually richly ornamented square stern.

In 1629 the two Swedish cities Kalmar and Jönköping purchased the ship, which subsequently took up service as an armed trading vessel for the Swedish navy. The ship got the name *Nyckel* (Swedish for "key") from the fortress Nyckel, which that has protected and marked the entrance to the harbor of Kalmar since the twelfth century. In November 1637 the *Kalmar Nyckel* left the harbor of Götheborg with a group of 24 emigrants: Swedes,

Type: pinnace, full-rigged ship, wood, reproduction	Dimensions: Length overall: 42.40 m Length of hull: 33.50 m Length between perpendiculars: 28.30 m Width: 7.60 m Depth in hold: 2.10 m Depth to deck: 4.30 m Draft: 3.60 m	Armaments: 2 6-pounders, 8 3-pounders, 2 guns mounted on railings	
Nation: USA			
Owner: Kalmar Nyckel		Auxiliary engine: 2 Caterpillar engines, 180 horsepower each	
Home port: Wilmington, Delaware			
		Crew: 35-person active crew, including 3 professional sailors and 32 volunteers, 60 passengers on day cruises	
Years of construction: 1995–97; keel laid April 1995; launched September 28, 1997	Sail area: 706 square meters		
	Rigging: 8 sails, 3 laced studding sails, single, large topsail, bowsprit with spritsail and bowsprit topsail	Use: museum ship, educational ship, passenger ship, ambassador ship	
Shipyard: Kalmar Nyckel Shipyard, Wilmington			
Tonnage: 300 ts displacement; 168 tons gross; 50 tons net	Masts: height of mainmast over the deck: 32 meters		

Finns, Dutchmen, and Germans who wanted to seek a new home in America. The ship

was escorted by the *Fogel Grip*. Following an extremely heavy storm in the North Sea

the two ships met after a week's time at the island of Texel. On December 31, 1637,

it became possible to continue the voyage. In the middle of March 1638, both ships reached the Delaware Bay, where the colony of New Sweden ultimately arose.

The *Kalmar Nyckel* crossed the Atlantic four more times in both directions, a feat that no other ship had achieved at that time. As a ship of the Swedish navy she was lost in an engagement off the Swedish coast during the Swedish–Danish War.

In 1986 the *Kalmar Nyckel* Foundation was created with the goal of launching a reproduction of the famous ship. An extremely impressive ship came into being, which charms viewers primarily by means of its rig, its colors, and its rich ornamentation. Fourteen tons of lead, which serve as external keel ballast, provide the pinnace with the necessary stability. A red lion adorns the extended cutwater.

L. A. Dunton

Type: 2-masted fore-and-aft schooner, wood	Tonnage: approx. 175 tons gross	main gaff-topsail, fisherman's staysail
Nation: USA	Dimensions: Length overall: 48.20 m Length of hull: 37.70 m Length at the waterline: 31.60 m Width: 7.60 m Depth in hold: 3.50 m Draft: 4.20 m	Masts: height of mainmast over the deck: 34.30 meters; diameter of mainmast at the deck: 0.45 meters; each mast has 1 topmast
Owner: Marine Historical Association, Inc., Mystic, Connecticut		
Home port: Mystic Seaport		Auxiliary engine: Fairbanks Morse diesel engine, 160 horsepower
Year of construction: 1921; launched March 23, 1921	Sail area: 800 square meters	Crew: 22 people as a fishery schooner
Shipyard: Arthur Story, Essex, Massachusetts; design: Thomas F. McManus	Rigging: 8 sails; 3 foresails; foremast: foresail, fore gaff-topsail; mainmast: mainsail,	Use: museum ship

The fishing schooners of New England were some of the most famous sailing ships of the American coast. Their voyages to the Great Banks and their unusually hard-fought races were some of the most exciting episodes in the history of wind-powered deep sea fishing. One of the few survivors from this era is the schooner *L. A. Dunton*, a fishing vessel from Gloucester. The audacity with which these ships were sailed earned the ships and the men aboard them the shared name "Gloucestermen"—a term of respect that consistently evoked feelings of appreciation and admiration. In spite of their purely commercial purpose, these ships were constantly improved. The speed with which the catch could be carried home was the main concern of the designers, who in part also built pure yachts. The races home ultimately took on more and more the character of a sport.

The *L. A. Dunton* received her name from a famous sail-

maker from Boothbay (Maine), Louis A. Dunton. Initially the schooner sailed without an engine, as was normal. Her home port was Gloucester (Massachusetts). The fishing was done from ten 4-meter-long dories that were piled in "nests" on deck during breaks in the fishing. Three hundred cod-hooks were fastened with bait to 500-meter-long fishing lines. During the daily fishing period only the captain and the cook remained on board the schooner. Every dory was occupied by 2 men. The caught fish were salted or—less often—also stored frozen.

At the end of the 1920s the spars were removed from the *L. A. Dunton* and a gasoline-powered auxiliary engine was added. Until 1935 she sailed to the banks under the American flag; after that she was sold to Canada. The number of "bankers" decreased steadily. After additional changes of ownership, J. B. Foote & Sons purchased the ship. She became a cargo ship for bulk goods in the American–Canadian coastal waters. The bowsprit disappeared, and the mainmast was significantly shortened. The gasoline engine gave way to a 160-horsepower diesel engine. The schooner had become a motorized ship with auxiliary sails.

On October 8, 1963, the Marine Historical Association acquired the schooner. Since then she has been restored to her original condition.

Lady Maryland

Type: 2-masted fore-and-aft schooner, wood	Dimensions: Length overall: 31.60 m Length of hull: 21.80 m Width: 6.60 m Draft: 2.10 m
Nation: USA	
Owner: Living Classrooms Foundation, Baltimore	Sail area: 278 square meters
Home port: Baltimore, Maryland	Rigging: 4 sails
Year of construction: 1986; launched June 4, 1986	Masts: height of mainmast over the deck: 25.50 meters
Shipyard: Lee Street Shipyard	Auxiliary engine: two Cummins diesel engines, 85 horsepower each
Tonnage: 75 ts displacement; 60 tons gross; 40 tons net	Crew: 6–8-person active crew, 12–14 trainees
	Use: sailing school-ship

The schooner embodies the type of ship known as a "pungy," which was used in the Chesapeake for 150 years. Characteristic of this type of ship is the drop-shaped hull, which enables the ship to glide easily through the water. Pungies were used primarily to transport highly perishable foodstuffs. Students from all parts of Maryland are instructed in various subjects aboard the ship.

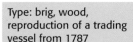

Lady Washington

Type: brig, wood, reproduction of a trading vessel from 1787

Nation: USA

Owner: Grays Harbor Historical Seaport

Home port: Grays Harbor, Washington

Year of construction: 1989; launched March 7, 1989

Shipyard: Aberdeen, Washington

Tonnage: 170 ts displacement

Dimensions:
Length overall: 34.00 m
Length between perpendiculars: 21.80 m
Width: 6.60 m
Draft: 3.30 m

Sail area: 408 square meters

Rigging: 12 sails; bowsprit with spritsail

Masts: height of mainmast over the deck: 27 meters

Auxiliary engine: none

Crew: 45 passengers on day cruises

Use: ambassador ship of the state of Washington, chartered ship, sailing school-ship

In 1787 Captain Robert Gray sailed around Cape Horn to the West Coast of North America in the *Lady Washington,* which at that time was still rigged as a sloop. Boston was the port of departure for this voyage. By this means, Captain Gray paved the way for the settlement of the later state of Wash-ington. The ship was also engaged in the fur trade with China. She was converted into a brig in Macao.

Subsequently the brig became the first American ship to visit a Japanese port. The reproduction is a source of much wonderment during her visits to various ports.

Le Pelican

The model for this reproduction, which cannot be sailed, was the warship of the French buccaneer Pierre Le Moyne d'Iberville, who fought against the English off the East Coast of North America. In 1697 he sank two British warships off Baffin Island. Because of his successes, Louis XIV sent him on an expedition into the Mississippi region. Le Moyne d'Iberville thus became one of the founders of the state of Louisiana. His brother was one of its first governors. For two years the reproduction could be seen in Montreal, and in 1995 she came to New Orleans.

Type: reproduction of a forty-four-cannon ship of the seventeenth century, wood

Nation: USA

Owner: New Orleans Treasure, Inc.

Home port: New Orleans

Year of construction: 1992

Dimensions:
Length overall: 45.00 m

Masts: 3 masts (bark rigging) with bowsprit mast

Use: museum ship

Lettie G. Howard

The man who commissioned and became the first owner of what at that time was a fishing vessel, Fred Howard of Beverly, Massachusetts, named his ship after his daughter Lettie because she celebrated her twenty-second birthday during the month in which the ship's keel was laid. After 73 years of active service as a fishing vessel, the schooner was acquired by the South Street Seaport Museum in New York in August 1968. She was subsequently moored in New York Harbor for nearly 20 years as a museum ship devoted to the fishing industry.

Extensive restoration work was necessary before the ship,

with her elegant lines, could be employed for her current use. Her character as a former fishing vessel has been preserved to a great extent.

Previous names: *Caviare, Mystic C., Lettie Howard*

Type: 2-masted fore-and-aft schooner, wood

Nation: USA

Owner: South Street Seaport Museum, New York, New York

Home port: New York

Year of construction: 1893; launched March 22, 1893

Shipyard: Arthur D. Story, Essex, Massachusetts

Tonnage: 110 ts displacement; 59.74 tons gross; 56.76 tons net

Dimensions:
Length overall: 39.20 m
Length of hull: 26.75 m
Length between perpendiculars: 22.55 m
Width: 6.40 m
Depth in hold: 2.55 m
Draft: 3.20 m

Sail area: 466 square meters

Rigging: 7 sails

Masts: height of mainmast over the deck: 27 meters

Auxiliary engine: twin diesel engines, 2 propellers, 84 horsepower each

Crew: 5-person active crew, 2 instructors, 13 trainees

Use: sailing school-ship

Liberty

Previous name: *Schooner Liberty*

Type: 2-masted fore-and-aft schooner, steel

Nation: USA

Owner: Schooner Liberty, Inc., Boston, Massachusetts, Gregory E. Muzzy

Home port: Boston

Year of construction: 1993

Shipyard: Treworgy Yachts, Palm Coast, Florida

Tonnage: 49 tons gross

Dimensions:
Length overall: 24.40 m
Length of hull: 18.60 m
Width: 5.20 m
Draft: 2.10 m

Sail area: 186 square meters

Rigging: 5 sails

Masts: height of mainmast over the deck: 19.70 meters

Auxiliary engine: Perkins diesel

Crew: 4-person active crew, 6 guests, 49 guests on day cruises

Use: chartered ship, day cruises

The schooner is a typical representative of the sailing freighters that were used in the nineteenth century on the coast of New England.

In the summer these waters are sailed by the reproduction. The large harbor area of Boston itself is a primary destination. In the winter, Key West in Florida is the point of departure for the ship's cruises.

Liberty Clipper

Previous name: *Mystic Clipper*

Type: 2-masted fore-and-aft schooner, steel

Nation: USA

Owner: Schooner Liberty Clipper, Inc., Boston, Massachusetts, Gregory E. Muzzy

Home port: Boston

Year of construction: 1983

Shipyard: Blount Marine Corp., Warren, Rhode Island

Tonnage: 145 tons gross; 99 tons net

Dimensions:
Length overall: 38.10 m
Length of hull: 26.20 m
Width: 8.20 m
Draft:
　Centerboard up: 2.40 m
　Centerboard down: 3.90 m

Sail area: 465 square meters

Rigging: 8 sails

Masts: height of mainmast over the deck: 30.70 meters

Auxiliary engine: Detroit diesel

Crew: 6–10-person active crew, 26 guests, 125 guests on day cruises

Use: chartered ship, day cruises

The schooner corresponds exactly to the type of the Baltimore clippers which in the nineteenth century became famous for their fast voyages around Cape Horn to the West Coast of the United States of America.

In the summer the reproduction sails along the coast of New England; in the winter Key West in Florida is the point of departure for her cruises.

Lisa

The small brig (snow) offers girls and boys the opportunity to sail and also to participate in instruction in history, geography, and mathematics.

Naturally, the ship is not armed. The streak circling the hull is reminiscent of times in which even trading vessels had cannons on board to defend themselves against pirates.

Type: brig, steel

Nation: USA

Owner: Snow Lisa, Inc.

Home port: Wilmington, Delaware

Years of construction: 1981–85; launched September 1985

Shipyard: Fenton Marina

Tonnage: 50 ts displacement; 40 tons gross

Dimensions:
Length overall: 22.00 m
Length of hull: 15.20 m
Width: 5.50 m
Depth in hold: 1.80 m
Depth to deck: 3.00 m
Draft: 1.20 m

Sail area: 278 square meters

Rigging: 16 sails; single topsail and topgallants

Masts: height of mainmast over the deck: 15.20 meters

Auxiliary engine: diesel, 100 horsepower

Crew: 4-person active crew, 6 trainees

Use: sailing school-ship

Margaret Todd

The *Margaret Todd,* with her clear, elegant lines, continues the tradition of the schooner with multiple masts, a type of ship a great number of which traded or fished off the coast of New England at the turn of the century.

The twin centerboards make it possible for the schooner, with her large sail area, to come to hard. With her small draft and her high boards, the ship can also sail in shallow waters and bays.

The ship primarily undertakes day cruises with large numbers of passengers to the coasts of Acadia National Park.

Type: 4-masted fore-and-aft schooner, steel

Nation: USA

Owner: Captain Steven F. Pagels, Cherryfield, Maine

Home port: Bar Harbor, Maine

Years of construction: 1997–98; launched April 11, 1998

Shipyard: Schreiber Boats, St. Augustine, Florida

Tonnage: 150 ts displacement; 136 tons gross; 53 tons net

Dimensions:
Length overall: 46.00 m
Length of hull: 36.80 m
Length at the waterline: 32.00 m
Width: 7.00 m

Depth in hold: 2.50 m
Depth to deck: 2.50 m
Draft: 1.70 m (2 centerboards up)

Sail area: 445 square meters

Rigging: 9 sails

Masts: height of mainmast over the deck: 25 meters

Auxiliary engine: Cummins diesel, 400 horsepower

Crew: 6-person active crew, 150 guests on day cruises

Use: passenger ship

Mary Day

1962 marked the first time in almost 30 years that a sailing ship of this type and size had been built in Maine. The plans originated with the owner, Captain H. S. Hawkins, himself, to whom the *Alice S. Wentworth* had previously belonged. The exterior of the *Mary Day* resembles that of the traditional coastal schooners.

Her interior furnishings were designed for passenger travel from the very beginning,

Type: 2-masted fore-and-aft schooner, wood

Nation: USA

Owner: Captains Jen Martin & Barry King

Home port: Camden, Maine

Year of construction: 1962; launched January 20, 1962

Shipyard: South Bristol, Maine

Tonnage: approx. 100 ts displacement; 86 tons gross

Dimensions:
Length overall: 25.20 m
Width: 7.10 m
Depth in hold: 1.80 m
Draft: 1.90 m

Sail area: 335 square meters

Rigging: 4 sails; 2 foresails, 1 gaff-sail each

Masts: height of mainmast over the deck: 19.50 meters

Auxiliary engine: none

Crew: 4-person active crew: captain, helmsman, cook, cook's assistant; 28 passengers

Use: private ship for passenger cruises

however. Two one-bed, six double-bed, two three-bed, and four four-bed cabins are located on board. The large "salon," which is located aft, serves as a community room. The schooner received her name from Mrs. Hawkins.

A large motorboat, which can also be used to tow the engineless sailing ship, hangs in davits across the flat stern. During the summer the *Mary Day* makes 1-week voyages, each of which leaves on a Monday from Camden, Maine.

The ship has belonged to the current owner since 1998.

Recently the schooner has had topmasts installed on both of her masts.

Maryland Dove

Type: pinnace, wood (bark rig), reproduction of a square-rigger of the seventeenth century

Nation: USA

Owner: State of Maryland, Historic St. Mary's City

Home port: St. Mary's City, Maryland

Year of construction: 1978; launched August 14, 1978

Shipyard: James K. Richardson Boatyard, Cambridge, Maryland

Tonnage: 42 ts displacement

Dimensions:
Length overall: 23.10 m
Length of hull: 17.02 m
Length between the leads: 15.50 m

Width: 5.16 m
Draft: 2.10 m

Sail area: 182 square meters

Rigging: 6 sails; bowsprit with spritsail; mizzenmast with lateen sails

Masts: height of mainmast over the deck: 18 meters

Auxiliary engine: two Lehmann Super 90 diesel 4-cylinder

Crew: 7-person active crew

Use: museum ship; occasionally cruises with volunteer trainings

The model for this reproduction was the pinnace *Dove*, which brought provisions to the settlers in Maryland in 1634. Costumed crewmembers act out the life of that time in the harbor museum. The pinnace visits the ports of the Chesapeake Bay as a goodwill ship of the state of Maryland.

371

Type: bark (galleon), wood, reproduction

Nation: USA

Owner: Plymouth Plantation, Inc., Plymouth, Massachusetts

Home port: Plymouth, Massachusetts

Years of construction: 1955–56; keel laid July 1955; launched September 1956

Shipyard: Stuart Uphams' Shipyard, Brixham, Devonshire; design: William Avery Baker, naval architect

Tonnage: 365 ts displacement; 260.12 tons gross; 223.29 tons net; (voyage 1957); 181 ts burden (from 1620)

Dimensions:
Length overall: approx. 40.10 m
Length of hull: 32.40 m
Length at the waterline: 24.25 m
Width (wales): 7.85 m
Depth in hold: 3.31 m
Depth to deck: 5.57 m
Draft (1957 voyage): 3.87 m
Freeboard (1957 voyage): approx. 2.00 m

Sail area: 470 square meters

Rigging: 6 sails; bowsprit with spritsail; fore-, mainmast: lower sail, deep single topsail; mizzenmast: lateen sail

Masts: fore- and mainmast with 1 topmast

Crew: 33 people (1957 journey)

Use: museum ship

In 1620, 105 Puritans, the Pilgrims, left England in order to settle in New England. Together with the crew of the ship, there were approximately 125 to 130 people on board. The *Mayflower*, the ship that they had at their disposal, was a normal freight galleon of the Elizabethan period that was not built specifically for this purpose.

Starting in 1947, the Plymouth Plantation, an association in Plymouth (Massachusetts) was interested in a reconstruction of the *Mayflower* to be moored in Plymouth Harbor as a museum ship and memorial. Two Englishmen, Warwick Charlton and John Lowe, decided upon and made possible the production. In the process, the ship was promised to the Plymouth Plantation following its successful crossing of the Atlantic. The original plans were not available. All that was known was the type of ship and its approximate dimensions. The reconstruction had to be larger, because the original design of the ship would not even have provided adequate standing room, which was a condition that naturally had to be met in order for the ship to be used as a museum open to the public.

On the building slip the *Mayflower II* was completed only as far as the between deck. It was finished in the shipyard's dry dock. The building material for the entire hull was English oak. Canadian pine was used for the masts and yards. The ropes and the linen for the sails came from Scottish workshops. One hundred thirty-five tons of iron ballast made the ship stable but also somewhat stiff on her voyage across the Atlantic. For the sake of increased safety, the steering was done with the wheel and not with the tiller.

Great strain on the standing rigging and the masts resulted from the fact that the bowsprit could not be stayed because of the spritsail and the fact that the braces were led to the stays. But this was the only way one knew how to do it at the time of the Pilgrims. Staysails and jibs did not become known until later. The yards of the lower sails could be lowered from on deck; it was not possible to reef the sails.

In 1620 the *Mayflower* sailed across the Atlantic in 67 days under the command of Captain Christopher Jones. Captain Alan Villiers managed it in 53 days in 1957. The voyage lasted from April 20, 1957, to June 12, 1957. In the process 5420 nautical miles were covered at an average speed of 7.7 knots and an average day's run of 106 nautical miles.

Following her triumphant arrival at Pilgrim's Rock in Plymouth the *Mayflower* sailed to New York, and subsequently made a tour of a number of ports on the American East Coast. At the end of June 1958, she returned to her permanent berth in the harbor of Plymouth, Massachusetts.

Previous names: *Oplag, Moshulu, Dreadknought, Kurt*

Type: 4-masted bark, steel

Nation: USA

Owner: HMS Ventures, Inc., Philadelphia

Home port: Pier 34, Columbus Boulevard, Philadelphia

Year of construction: 1904; launched April 20, 1904

Shipyard: William Hamilton & Company, Ltd., Port Glasgow, Scotland

Tonnage: 3116 tons gross; 2911 tons net

Dimensions:
Length overall: 122.00 m
Length of hull: 111.00 m
Length between perpendiculars: 101.90 m
Width: 14.20 m

Height of side: 8.50 m
Depth in hold: 8.00 m

Sail area: 4180 square meters

Rigging: former rig 34 sails; 4 foresails, double topsails, double topgallants, royals; mizzenmast: lower mizzen, upper mizzen, mizzen topsail

Masts, spars: height of mainmast over the deck: 50.10 m; length of main yard: 29.40 meters; length of main royal yard: 14.80 meters

Auxiliary engine: diesel engine

Crew: on 1 voyage in the year 1937, 19-person active crew, 6 young men, 8 deck boys

Use: restaurant and museum ship

A significant percentage of the large 4-masted barks were built around the turn of the century in the three-island style, with a forecastle and a poop deck, and a main deck lying approximately midships between them. This deck and the gangways between it, the forecastle, and the poop enhanced the safety of the crew, especially rough water. The rooms beneath were living and work areas. The midship superstructure divided the otherwise extraordinarily large surface of the main deck. The main advantage consisted in the fact that when the ship was at a sharp angle of heel, life-threatening quantities of water could not be taken on board. The *Moshulu,* formerly the *Kurt,* was built as this type of ship for the German shipping company G. J. H. Siemers of Hamburg. She was named after Dr. Kurt Siemers, who

headed the firm until World War II. While under the German flag, the ship was used only to carry saltpeter. During her 9 voyages the *Kurt* brought coal to South America or Mexico and returned to Germany loaded with saltpeter. Her tenth voyage took her to Santa Rosalia, Mexico. After the coal had been unloaded, the ship sailed with ballast to Portland, Oregon, in order to load grain there. During this voyage World War I broke out, and the *Kurt* entered Astoria, Oregon, as a safe harbor. She was interned and handed over to the U.S. Shipping Board Emergency Fleet Corporation.

All of the ships seized in this manner were supposed to remain in service and were renamed after famous American clippers. The *Kurt* was rechristened the *Dreadnought* and sailed for a period of time in the Pacific between the Philip-

pines, Australia, and the United States. It soon became clear, however, that many of these clipper names had already been given to other ships. Another name change was necessary. The First Lady, Mrs. Woodrow Wilson chose names for the individual ships from the Native American languages. Hence the *Dreadnought* was known after September 18, 1917, as the *Moshulu,* which has approximately the same meaning.

In 1922 the shipping company Charles Nelson Company of San Francisco purchased the ship for 40,000 dollars and employed her to carry wood to Australia and Africa. The *Moshulu* made her last voyage under the American flag in

1927–28 with a load of lumber to Melbourne and Geelong, Australia. Subsequently the sailing ship lay for 7 years without work, first in Union Lake, Seattle, Washington, and later in Winslow, Washington. In February 1935 the Finnish shipowner Gustaf Erickson of Mariehamn, Åaland, purchased the *Moshulu* for 20,000 dollars. Captain Gunnar Boman, the head of the maritime museum in Mariehamn, traveled to Winslow, took control of the *Moshulu,* sailed her to Port Victoria, Australia, and returned to Europe in 1936 with a load of wheat.

At that time Erikson owned the largest fleet of cargo-carrying sailing ships in the world. Counting the newly acquired *Moshulu,* it consisted of a total of twenty-five ships (three schooners—including two 4-masted schooners; three barkentines—including two 4-masted barkentines; eight barks and eleven 4-masted barks) with a total of 44,728 tons gross. A large portion of these ships, including the *Moshulu,* sailed in the grain trade to Australia. On May 22, 1940, she returned from her fifth and final wheat-carrying voyage under the Erikson flag. The cargo was unloaded in Kristiansand, Norway.

From March until July 1942, the ship was requisitioned by German troops. In November of the same year the *Moshulu* was towed to Horten, Oslo-Fjord, and there unrigged. She then sailed to Kirkenes. After being stranded, having capsized, and being raised in September 1947, she was purchased by Gisken Jacobsen of Narvik for approximately 20,000 dollars. Jacosen's plans to make a pure motorized ship out of the former sailing ship could not be realized. She sold the *Moshulu* in 1948 to Trygve Sommerfeldt of Oslo, who brought her to Bergen. The ship then served as a granary in Stockholm for the next 4 years.

In the summer of 1952 T. Sommerfeldt sold his ship to the German shipowner Heinz Schliewen of Lübeck. The *Moshulu* came to Germany. Under the name *Oplag,* she was supposed to serve along with the *Pamir* and the *Passat* as the third wind-powered cargo ship of the Schliewen fleet. Schliewen had to discontinue his payments soon thereafter. This also brought an end to all preparations to rerig the *Moshulu.* She was brought back to Stockholm. In 1961 the Finnish government purchased the ship in order to use her as a granary in Naantali. In 1970 the *Moshulu* was taken over by an American owner. She was towed to Amsterdam.

In 1972 she was towed to New York, where her rerigging took place.

In 1975 the *Moshulu* arrived in Philadelphia. She was moored at Penn's Landing as a restaurant ship. A fire in 1989 caused serious damage. After her yards and topmasts had been removed, the ship was brought in a very bad condition to Camden, New Jersey, for repairs. The current owner acquired her in 1994. Since July 1996 the newly rigged 4-masted bark has once again been moored in Philadelphia. The interior resembles that of a turn-of-the-century luxury liner.

Mystic Whaler

Type: 2-masted fore-and-aft schooner, steel

Nation: USA

Owner: John and Marelda Eginton, Mystic

Home port: Mystic, Connecticut

Year of construction: 1967

Shipyard: George Sutton Boatworks, Tarpon Springs, Florida

Tonnage: 100 ts displacement; 97 tons gross; 93 tons net

Dimensions:
Length overall: 33.50 m
Length of hull: 25.30 m
Width: 7.60 m

Draft:
Centerboard up: 2.10 m
Centerboard down: 3.90 m

Sail area: 280 square meters

Rigging: 4 sails

Masts: height of mainmast over the deck: 25.90 meters

Auxiliary engine: General Motors diesel, 175 horsepower

Crew: 5-person active crew, 36 guests, 65 guests on day cruises

Use: chartered ship, passenger cruises

Until 1990 the schooner sailed as a coastal freighter in the waters off New England. In 1994 the current owner, a former captain of the ship, acquired her. Her conversion and equipping as a luxurious passenger ship followed. All cruises begin with a visit to the famous Mystic Seaport Museum.

Nathaniel Bowditch

Previous names: *La Donna, Jane Doré, Joseph Hawkins, Nathaniel Bowditch*

Type: 2-masted fore-and-aft schooner, wood

Nation: USA

Owner: Gib Philbrick

Home port: Rockland, Maine

Year of construction: 1922

Shipyard: Hodsdon Brothers, East Boothbay, Maine

Tonnage: 52 tons gross

Dimensions:
Length overall: 32.80 m
Length of hull: 24.90 m
Width: 6.60 m

Depth in hold: 2.30 m
Depth to deck: 4.80 m
Draft: 3.30 m

Sail area: 344 square meters

Rigging: 6 sails

Masts: height of mainmast over the deck: 18.80 meters

Auxiliary engine: Detroit diesel, 150 horsepower

Crew: 6-person active crew, 1 trainee, 24 guests

Use: chartered ship, passenger ship

During World War II the schooner served as a patrol ship for the U.S. Coast Guard under the name *Jane Doré*.

For more than 20 years she has fulfilled her current purpose, sailing in the Gulf of Maine.

New Way

Previous names: *Western Union, La Amistad*

Type: fore-and-aft schooner, wood

Nation: USA

Owner: Vision Quest National, Exton, Pennsylvania

Year of construction: 1939

Shipyard: in Key West, Florida

Tonnage: 91.91 tons gross

Dimensions:
Length overall: 39.50 m
Length at the waterline: 26.10 m
Width: 7.20 m
Draft: 2.40 m

Sail area: 460 square meters

Masts: height of mainmast over the waterline: 36 meters

Auxiliary engine: two General Motors diesel engines, 100 horsepower each

Crew: approx. 20 people

Use: sailing school-ship

The ship is used to resocialize young people who have been convicted of a crime.

Type: brig, wood, reproduction of the ship from 1813

Nation: USA

Owner: state of Pennsylvania (Pennsylvania Historical and Museum Commission)

Home port: Erie, Pennsylvania

Year of construction: 1988; launched September 10, 1988

Shipyard: Erie (special shipyard)

Tonnage: 297 ts displacement

Dimensions:
Length overall: 60.19 m
Length of hull: 37.39 m
Length at the waterline: 33.59 m
Width: 9.72 m
Draft: 3.19 m

Sail area: 1176 square meters

Rigging: 15 sails; both masts lower sail, topsail, topgallant, royal sail (optional)

Masts: height of mainmast over the waterline: 35.60 meters; bowsprit with jibboom

Auxiliary engine: two diesel engines, 180 horsepower each

Crew: 1813: 155 officers and regular crew members; today: 40-person active crew (16 professional seamen, 24 volunteers)

Armaments: 1813: two 12-pound, eighteen 32-pound carronades; today: two 12-pounders, eighteen 32-pounders

Use: ambassador ship for the state of Pennsylvania, museum ship

In the War of 1812–14 between the USA and England, both powers sought to gain control of the Great Lakes. For the United States the immediate goal was to prevent a further southward advance by the English, while the English made the attempt to penetrate into Canada. The Peace of Ghent ended the war on December 24, 1814. At the very beginning of the war the United States started to build a small fleet for Lake Erie, the largest ships in which were the *Niagara* and her sister ship the *Lawrence*. The fleet stood under the command of Captain Oliver Hazard Perry.

On September 10, 1813, an engagement took place in the Put-in-Bay (Ohio) in which the English were defeated. Two brigs, four cannon boats, and four additional, smaller armed vessels fought on the American side. The English led two full-rigged ships, two brigs, a schooner, and a sloop into the battle. The *Niagara* was Captain Perry's flagship. During the battle he had the signal "Don't Give Up the Ship" displayed.

The original *Niagara* remained in service until 1820 and was then sunk in Misery Bay in Lake Erie. In 1913, a hundred years after the battle,

citizens of Erie raised the ship and started to restore her. At that time many of the old wooden pieces could not be used. Additional restorations took place between 1913 and 1963. The most recent work on this ship began in 1980.

The *Niagara* was set up as a monument on a solid foundation in Niagara Park in Erie. In 1987 she was scrapped, although original wooden pieces were preserved. Some of these could be used in the current reproduction.

Type: caravel, wood, reproduction

Nation: USA

Years of construction: 1989–91

Shipyard: in Valenca, Brazil

Tonnage: 100 ts displacement; 57 tons gross

Dimensions:
Length overall: 28.00 m
Length of hull: 21.40 m
Length between perpendiculars: 19.10 m
Width: 6.10 m
Depth in hold: 1.90 m
Depth to deck: 2.80 m
Draft: 2.10 m

Sail area: 140 square meters

Rigging: 3 sails

Masts: height of mainmast over the deck: 16.20 meters

Auxiliary engine: Caterpillar, 180 horsepower

Crew: 3-person active crew, 15–20 trainees

Use: sailing museum ship

The Columbus Foundation, which was founded in 1986 in the Virgin Islands, collected money to build reproductions of three of Columbus's ships on the occasion of his 500th birthday. For 2 years the history and construction of the three ships *Pinta, Niña,* and *Santa Maria* were researched. For financial reasons the Columbus Foundation decided to build the *Niña.*

In 1988 the American engineer and expert on Portuguese caravels John Patrick Sarsfield was commissioned to design and construct the *Niña.* In the process, early discoveries of Spanish shipwrecks from the fifteenth and sixteenth centuries in the Caribbean, in addition to other sources, yielded valuable pieces of information, such as the number of masts.

The caravel was then ultimately built in Valenca, Brazil. Only traditional tools were used in the construction, such as axes, hand saws, hatchets, and chisels.

In December 1991 the 4-master left Valenca and reached Puntarenas, Costa Rica, on January 23, 1992. There she served as a film ship for the film *1492* starring Gerard Depardieu.

Since June 1992 she has served as a sailing museum and is constantly on the way to new ports. She has visited 300 ports on the East Coast of the United States, on the Great Lakes, and on various rivers.

In 1996 the ship left Texas, sailed through the Panama Canal, and reached the West Coast of the United States. There she visited additional ports in her capacity as a sailing maritime museum. She offers daylong cruises for passengers and is also used for scientific research.

Ocean Star

Type: 2-masted fore-and-aft schooner, steel

Nation: USA

Owner: Greg Walsh, Ocean Navigator Magazine

Home port: Portland, Maine

Year of construction: 1990; launched April 1991

Shipyard: Marine Metals, Inc., Norfolk, Virginia, Howdy Bailey Custom Yachts

Tonnage: 60 ts displacement; 68 tons gross

Dimensions:
Length overall: 26.70 m
Length of hull: 22.40 m
Width: 5.70 m

Rigging: 7 sails (full rigging); foremast with gaff-sails; mainmast with Bermuda sails

Auxiliary engine: Caterpillar diesel, 3208N, 210 horsepower

Crew: 6-person active crew, 6 trainees

Use: private ship, sailing school-ship

Peking

The *Peking* was built as the sister ship of the *Passat* for the F. Laeisz shipping company in Hamburg. She was originally 85 tons gross smaller than her sister. Although she also represents the "three island type" (forecastle–main deck–poop deck), she was steered from the main deck. The helmsman stood at the wheel in front of the poop. Characteristic of the Laeisz ships, as for many other German sailing ships, were the divided spankers.

From 1911 to 1921 the *Peking* was employed along with the other Laeisz ships in the saltpeter trade. After World War I she had to be delivered to Italy as a reparations pay-

ment on May 10, 1921. There was no use for the ship there, however. In 1923 Laeisz purchased his ship back for 8500 pounds. She then sailed in the saltpeter trade again until 1932. In 1926 she was converted into a cargo-carrying school-ship belonging to the shipping company.

After 1932 the saltpeter trade was no longer profitable. Laeisz sold his ship to the Shaftesbury Homes and Training Ship. The *Peking* was renamed the *Arethusa* and served as a replacement for the wooden warship of the same name. A shipyard in Rochester converted the ship for about 40,000 pounds. After that she

served as a stationary school-ship in Lower Upnor on the Medway near Rochester. The *Arethusa*'s old berth near Greenhithe, Thames, was no longer appropriate because of the increased shipping traffic on the river.

The future King George VI performed the official opening on July 25, 1933. The ship had space for 200 to 300 young men of ages 13 to 15 years. The students were trained and educated in a half-military fashion. Because of the powerful movements of the ship during the changing of the tides, almost all of the yards were removed. Only the foreyard, the lower topsail yard, and the

lower topgallant yard remained on the foremast. Some of the removed yards were transferred to the school-ship *Worcester*, which was anchored near Greenhithe in the Thames. In spite of the conversion, no important additional superstructures were built on the deck. The former deckhouse between hatch I and hatch II was lengthened beyond hatch II to the main deck. The deckhouse between hatch III and hatch IV as well as hatch IV itself were removed and closed. By this means a large roll-call and training space was created. In keeping with tradition, the *Arethusa* bore a white streak.

Previous names: *Arethusa, Peking*

Type: 4-masted bark, steel

Nation: USA

Owner: South Street Seaport Museum, New York

Home port: South Street Seaport Museum, New York

Year of construction: 1911

Shipyard: Blohm & Voss, Hamburg

Tonnage: 3100 tons gross; 2883 tons net

Dimensions:
Length overall: 115.00 m
Length of hull: 106.00 m
Length between perpendiculars: 97.80 m
Width: 14.30 m
Depth in hold: 8.00 m

Sail area: 4100 square meters

Rigging: 32 sails; 4 foresails, double topsail, double topgallant, royals; mizzenmast: lower mizzen, upper mizzen, mizzen topsail

Masts: fore-, main-, and mizzenmasts with 1 topmast

Use: museum ship

Arethusa was the name of numerous springs in antiquity. The most famous of them flowed on the island of Ortigia off Syracuse. In mythology the nymph Arethusa is a daughter of Nereus and Doris. She was persecuted by the river god Alpheus and fled into the sea. She reappeared in Sicily as a spring.

In 1974 the upkeep of the *Arethusa* became too expensive. The South Street Seaport Museum in New York purchased her for more than 1 million dollars. In July 1975, she was towed to the United States.

The rigging work was completed just in time for Operation Sail '76. The ship's old name, *Peking*, now stands once again on her bow and stern.

Perseus

Type: 3-masted topsail schooner, wood

Nation: USA

Owner: Marc A. Schützer, Olympia, Washington

Home port: Olympia, Washington

Year of construction: 1907

Shipyard: J. Ring-Andersen, Svendborg

Tonnage: 180 tons gross

Dimensions:
Length overall: 38.00 m
Length of hull: 32.00 m

Length between perpendiculars: 29.80 m
Width: 6.80 m
Depth in hold: 2.70 m
Draft: 2.70 m

Rigging: 12 sails (possibly a square foresail)

Masts: height of mainmast over the deck: 24 meters

Auxiliary engine: Caterpillar diesel, 6-cylinder, 290 horsepower

Crew: 12-person active crew, 15 cadets or guests

Use: private ship, sailing school-ship

The *Perseus* embodies the classic type of a Baltic schooner. The rig was overhauled around 1970. Until that point the ship had been engaged in the freight trade. After a stay in Los Angeles, her current owner purchased her in the mid-1960s.

Perseus, a sword in his right hand, adorns the bow as a figurehead.

Pilgrim

Type: snow brig, wood, reproduction

Nation: USA

Owner: Orange County Marine Institute, Dana Point

Home port: Dana Port, California

Year of construction: 1945

Shipyard: A. Nielsen, Holbaek, Denmark

Tonnage: 99 tons gross; 64 tons net

Dimensions:
Length overall: 39.60 m
Length of hull: 29.80 m
Width: 7.50 m
Draft: 2.70 m

Sail area: 706 square meters

Rigging: 14 sails; 3 foresails, single top- and topgallant, royals, foremast with spencer

Masts: height of mainmast over the deck: 29.20 meters

Auxiliary engine: B & W Alpha diesel

Crew: 24–35-person active crew, 30–50 trainees

Use: sailing school-ship, event ship, advertising ship for her homeport

The original *Pilgrim,* which was built in 1825, was immortalized in the classic novel *Two Years Before the Mast* by Richard Henry Dana Jr. Following a serious illness, Dana did not sail aboard the ship as a passenger but rather enlisted as a sailor. Dana distinguished himself by advocating the rights of seamen. The *Pilgrim* often sailed around Cape Horn to reach the coast of California. Departing from Boston, she brought trade goods such as shoes, iron products, and food to the West Coast. On her voyages home she was loaded with thousands of cowhides and barrels of tallow, which was used to make lubricants and candles. The leather-goods factories in New England were dependant on these deliveries of hides.

The current *Pilgrim* started her life in 1945 as a freight schooner with a Danish owner. In 1975 she was purchased by a California consortium whose intention was to convert and rerig her as Dana's brig. These modifications took place in Lisbon. Since 1981 the ship has been an attraction in her home port, hosting many events and educational programs. Every year in the late summer she undertakes an extended voyage along the coast of California.

Pioneer

Type: 2-masted fore-and-aft schooner, steel

Nation: USA

Owner: South Street Seaport Museum, New York, New York

Home port: New York

Year of construction: 1885

Shipyard: Pioneer Iron Works, Marcus Hook, Pennsylvania

Tonnage: 43 tons gross

Dimensions:
Length overall: 31.00 m
Length of hull: 19.40 m
Length at the waterline: 17.30 m
Width: 6.40 m
Draft: 1.40 m

Sail area: 254 square meters

Masts: height of mainmast over the waterline: 24 meters

Auxiliary engine: diesel, 85 horsepower

Use: sailing school-ship, chartered ship

The former trading schooner was completely converted and modernized from 1966 to 1968. In the process the older external surface was replaced by steel plates. The *Pioneer* sails from April to October with students of the Pioneer Marine School. In addition she is also deployed in the waters around New York for the benefit of paying passengers.

Previous name: *Elk*

Type: 2-masted staysail schooner, steel

Nation: USA

Owner: Windjammer Cruises, Inc., Miami Beach, Florida, Captain Mike Burke

Home port: Miami Beach, Florida

Year of construction: 1928

Shipyard: Scott Shipbuilding

Tonnage: 350 ts displacement; 180 tons gross; 108 tons net

Dimensions:
Length overall: 46.00 m
Length of hull: 39.80 m
Width: 7.60 m
Headroom: 3.10 m
Draft: 4.90 m

Sail area: 890 square meters

Masts: height of mainmast over the deck: 33.50 meters

Auxiliary engine: two gasoline engines, 180 horsepower each

Crew: 12-person active crew, living quarters and accommodations for 46 people

Use: private ship for passenger cruises

The *Polynesia* was built as the *Elk* for Sir Oliver Simmonds. She is one of the largest staysail schooners in the world. Like the *Yankee Clipper* and the *Caribee*, she belongs to the Windjammer Cruises enterprise that Captain Mike Burke built up after World War II. The ship sails year-round on 10-day cruises from Miami Beach to the Bahamas for paying guests.

Type: 2-masted topsail schooner, wood

Nation: USA

Owner: state of Maryland

Home port: Baltimore

Year of construction: 1988; launched April 30, 1988;

commissioned October 23, 1988

Shipyard: building site: Inner Harbor, Baltimore

Tonnage: 185.5 long tons; 97 tons gross; 67 tons net

Dimensions:
Length overall: 47.70 m

Length of hull: 32.80 m
Width: 7.90 m
Draft: 3.70 m

Sail area: 970 square meters

Rigging: 10 sails

Masts: height of mainmast over the deck: 31.30 meters

Auxiliary engine: two diesel engines, 140 horsepower each

Crew: 12-person active crew, 6 guests

Use: ambassador ship

Ships like the *Pride of Baltimore* were the backbone of the young American navy and merchant marine at the beginning of the nineteenth century. In the war against England, the fleet's only hope of competing with the superior British fleet lay in its speed, which was admired and feared. After the victorious homecoming of Captain Thomas Boyle, who had erected a naval blockade against England with his clipper *Chasseur*, to Baltimore in the year 1814, the people of the city gave this ship the name *Pride of Baltimore*.

The Baltimore clippers were exceptionally streamlined and made use of an extremely large sail area. An additional distinguishing feature is the strong rake of the masts.

Because no ship of this type has survived from that era, a replica was built in Baltimore, which was the major center of clipper construction at that time. The ship was built using classic methods of wooden ship construction. From an observation deck the public could watch the progress of the work. For 9 years the clipper voyaged to many American and also European ports to raise awareness of the legacy of American maritime history. In May 1986 the ship was tragically lost during a storm north of Puerto Rico.

The *Pride of Baltimore II* was built in Baltimore in the same manner as the original, although the new ship is in fact about a third larger than her predecessor. In the process particular emphasis was placed on the safety features of the ship. The clipper received watertight bulkheads and heavy ballast. The task of "showing the flag" as a goodwill ship has remained the same.

Providence

Type: sloop (fiberglass hull)

Nation: USA

Owner: Seaport '76 Foundation, Ltd., Newport, Rhode Island

Home port: Newport, Rhode Island

Year of construction: 1975; commissioned October 24, 1976

Shipyard: in Newport, Rhode Island

Tonnage: 67.5 ts displacement

Dimensions:
Length of hull: 18.0 m
Width: 6.0 m
Draft: 1.80 m

Sail area: 320 square meters

Auxiliary engine: General Motors diesel, 170 horsepower

Crew: 35 people (original)

Use: museum ship, exhibit ship, chartered ship, sailing school-ship

The original of the *Providence*, a twelve-cannon sloop (4-pound guns) became the first ship of the U.S. Navy and its first flag ship on October 13, 1775. John Paul Jones had his first command aboard her.

The first marines embarked aboard her and ultimately captured Nassau in 1776. The reconstruction is based directly on contemporary representations, and even the guns on board are ready to fire salutes.

Regina Maris

Previous name: *Regina*

Type: barkentine, steel

Nation: USA

Owner: Save the Regina Maris, Ltd., Greenport, Long Island

Home port: Greenport, Long Island

Year of construction: 1908

Shipyard: J. Ring-Andersen, Svendborg

Tonnage: 186 tons gross

Dimensions:
Length overall: 42.50 m
Length of hull: 35.00 m
Length between perpendiculars: 30.50 m
Width: 7.60 m
Draft: 3.30 m

Sail area: 550 square meters

Rigging: 16 sails (in addition, 6 studding sails); 4 foresails; foremast: double topsails, single topgallants, royal; main- and mizzenmast: gaffsail, gaff-topsail

Masts, spars: foremast with top- and topgallant mast; main- and mizzenmast with 1 topmast; all masts made of pitch-pine wood; bowsprit with jibboom; height of mainmast over the deck: 33 meters

Auxiliary engine: diesel engine, 242 horsepower

Crew: 16 people

Use: museum ship

In 1908 the *Regina* was built as a 3-masted schooner with a square foresail for P. Reinhold of Råå in Sweden. She was designed primarily for the arctic waters and accordingly built to be strong. Later the ship was also used in the saltpeter trade. In 1931 she belonged to the shipowner O. B. Bengston of Råå. Since about 1932–33 the ship has sailed with an auxiliary engine.

A fire in the engine room damaged the ship significantly in 1962. In 1963 the two Norwegian shipowners and brothers Siegfried and John Aage Wilson (Ocean Transport Lines) of Arendal purchased the *Regina*, which at that time was laid up in Ystadt, and had her converted at Høivolds Mek. Verksted A/S in Kristiansand for 299,000 dollars. A very well made brigantine emerged from the schooner. Because of her great age, no north European country wanted to have her entered in its ship registry. It was possible to get her entered in Malta, however. This explains why the Norwegian ship was registered in Valletta.

It is probably unprecedented that on a sailing ship of this size all of the running rigging is made of terylene. The standing rigging is fastened outboard on chain plates with turnbuckles. A crowned female figure decorates the bow as a figurehead. The ship carries two stock anchors. The exhaust is expelled through the lower mizzenmast, which is the only mast that is made of steel.

The conversion work was completed in the summer of 1966. In August of the same year a new voyage began, which led around the world in the course of a year.

The *Regina Maris* sank in 1996 while performing research work for the Ocean Research Society in Boston. It was possible to raise the ship. The city of Greenport has made 100,000 dollars available to repair the ship. Following her successful restoration she will serve as a museum ship.

Type: frigate, wood, reproduction

Nation: USA

Owner: Kaye Williams, Groton, Connecticut

Home port: Bridgeport, Connecticut

Year of construction: 1970; keel laid August 1, 1969; launched March 28, 1970

Shipyard: Smith & Rhuland, Lunenburg, Nova Scotia

Tonnage: 500 ts displacement; 380 tons gross

Dimensions:
Length overall: 51.80 m
Length of hull: 38.10 m
Length between perpendiculars: 33.20 m
Width: 9.30 m
Draft: 3.90 m

Sail area: 1200 square meters

Rigging: originally 17 sails; 2 spritsails, 2 foresails; foremast: foresail, topsail, topgallant; mainmast: 3 staysails, mainsail, topsail, topgallant; mizzenmast: 2 staysails, topsail, mizzen sail

Masts: height of mainmast over the deck: 36.50 meters

Auxiliary engine: none

Armaments: originally twenty-six 9-pounders, six 3-pounders

Crew: wartime crew in the eighteenth century: 160 people; peacetime crew in the eighteenth century: 80 people; today when sailing: 30 people

Use: museum and film ship, sailing school-ship

In 1976 the United States celebrated the 200th anniversary of its Declaration of Independence. For this occasion the second frigate *Rose* was built according to the original plans in Greenwich. The original ship played a decisive role in the events surrounding the American Revolution.

Her keel was laid on June 5, 1756, at the Hugh Blaydes Shipyard in Hull, and she was launched on March 8, 1757.

Led by a crowned lion, which once again decorates the bow of the reproduction, the *Rose* fought in England's Seven Years' War against France and Spain.

In 1768 she was supposed to become James Cook's expedition ship for a trip around the world. At the last minute Cook decided on the *Endeavour*. The *Rose* was ordered to Boston and from 1774 to 1776 to Newport, Rhode Island. She became the flagship of a small squadron that was supposed to combat large-scale smuggling. The smugglers, who were attempting to circumvent English taxes, used armed force to prevent the provisioning of English ships. As a result, the squadron's commodore, Sir James Wallace, declared a complete blockade of the entire Bay of Newport. This provoked the Americans to found their own fleet, the U.S. Navy, in October 1775. When the *Rose* had to leave harbor in order to secure provisions, the general assembly of Rhode Island became the first of the colonies to declare its independence from the English crown. For two years there-

after the *Rose* protected British trading vessels along the American coast. In 1779 she brought news of the arrival of a French invasion fleet to Savannah. Orders were given to sink the *Rose* along with other ships at the entry to the harbor. This made a French landing at this spot impossible. Hence, the *Rose* was never an American ship. But her presence strengthened the young America's strivings for liberty to such an extent that she became a symbol for this portion of American history.

During dredging work many parts of the original frigate were found, which today are shown in the onboard museum.

Since 1991 the *Rose* has been a school-ship licensed by the U.S. Coast Guard.

Sea Lion

Following an inspiring visit by the *Mayflower II*, the American Ernest Cowan decided to reconstruct a seaworthy trading vessel from the same epoch. Approximately 70,000 hours of work were needed to build the ship. Original plans from the year 1586, which were found in England, provided the basis for the construction of the handmade vessel. The ship was named after C. E. Lyon, a friend of Cowan. She sails only on Lake Chautauqua in New York State.

Type: reproduction of a sixteenth-century British trading vessel, wood

Nation: USA

Owner: Sea Lion Project, Ltd., Mayville, New York

Home port: Mayville, New York (Lake Chautauqua)

Year of construction: keel laid 1977; launched 1984

Tonnage: 90 ts displacement

Dimensions:
Length overall: 19.00 m
Length of hull: 12.00 m

Sail area: 120 square meters

Masts: height of mainmast over the deck: 17 meters

Use: tourist and museum ship

Shendandoah

In the United States it has become very popular in recent years to spend one's vacation on board a large sailing ship. For this reason the demand for appropriate ships has also grown. This was the occasion for the construction of the sporty schooner *Shenandoah*, which can take 37 vacationers on board in addition to the 8 crew members. The monthly cruises take place in the waters off Cape Cod.

Plans for the swift American customs cutter *Joe Lane*, which was built in 1849, served as the basis for the construction of the ship.

The ships of the coastal smugglers were not of a single kind. What they all had in common were agility, speed, and the best sailing skills. Since the "hot" goods for the most part did not require a large cargo space, smaller ships were preferred. With them one could also sail in narrow waters. If one wanted to catch them, one had to deploy ships against them that also possessed all of these qualities, but which in addition were large and strong enough to carry the necessary weaponry. In the *Shenandoah* we have a classic representative of this exceptional type of ship.

Type: 2-masted topsail schooner, wood

Nation: USA

Owner: Captain Robert S. Douglas, Coastwise Packet Company, Vineyard Haven, Massachusetts

Home port: Vineyard Haven, Martha's Vineyard, Massachusetts

Year of construction: 1964; launched February 15, 1964

Shipyard: Harvey F. Gamage, South Bristol, Maine

Tonnage: 172 ts displacement; 85 tons gross

Dimensions:
Length overall: 46.20 m
Length of hull: 34.60 m

Length between perpendiculars: 30.40 m
Width: 7.00 m
Depth in hold: 2.10 m
Draft: 3.30 m

Sail area: 630 square meters

Rigging: 8 sails; 3 foresails; foremast: double topsail, schooner sail; mainmast: gaff-sail, gaff-topsail

Masts, spars: height of mainmast over the deck: 27.50 meters; both masts with topmast; bowsprit with jibboom

Auxiliary engine: none

Crew: 8 people, 30 overnight guests

Use: private ship for passenger cruises

Soundwaters

Previous name: *Eagle*

Type: 3-masted fore-and-aft schooner, steel

Nation: USA

Owner: SoundWaters, Inc., Stamford, Connecticut

Home port: Stamford

Year of construction: 1986

Shipyard: Marine Metals, Norfolk, Virginia

Dimensions:
Length overall: 24.40 m
Length of hull: 19.80 m
Length between perpendiculars: 17.90 m

Draft:
Centerboard up: 0.90 m
Centerboard down: 2.60 m

Sail area: 140 square meters

Rigging: 4 sails

Masts: height of mainmast over the deck: 18.20 meters

Auxiliary engine: Perkins diesel, 135 horsepower

Crew: 8-person active crew, 20 trainees, 45 guests on day cruises

Use: instruction ship (marine biology, environmental protection, general curriculum)

As the *Eagle*, the schooner originally undertook day cruises for tourists leaving from Baltimore. The hull was built as a sharpie with twin centerboards. This means that the frame was put together out of straight parts. In the process, it was possible to do without a steam room for bending the wood. This type of ship was used especially for oyster fishing in the Chesapeake Bay. In 1992 the organization SoundWaters purchased the ship and equipped it as a "floating classroom." The word "Sound" in the name refers to the Long Island Sound, the ship's home waters.

Spirit of Massachusetts

Type: 2-masted fore-and-aft schooner, wood

Nation: USA

Owner: Schools for Children, Inc., Arlington, Massachusetts

Home port: Boston

Year of construction: 1984

Shipyard: Charlestown Navy Yard, Boston

Tonnage: 138 ts displacement; 90 tons gross; 83 tons net

Dimensions:
Length overall: 38.00 m
Length of hull: 31.70 m

Width: 7.30 m
Depth in hold: 3.00 m
Draft: 3.20 m

Sail area: 910 square meters

Rigging: 8 sails

Masts: height of mainmast over the deck: 29 meters

Auxiliary engine: General Motors diesel 250 horsepower

Crew: 8-person active crew, 22 trainees

Use: sailing school-ship, chartered ship, ambassador ship for Massachusetts

The model during the construction of this ship was the *Fredonia*, a famous Gloucester fishing schooner built in 1889 that fished in the North Atlantic with great success at the end of the nineteenth and the beginning of the twentieth centuries.

The beauty of her lines, her robustness, and the high speeds she can reach made the ship well known worldwide. Secondary school and university students are instructed aboard, not only in seamanship and navigation but also in marine biology, ecology, history, and other subjects, which likewise form part of the curriculum.

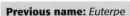

Star of India

Previous name: *Euterpe*

Type: bark, iron

Nation: USA

Owner: Maritime Museum Association of San Diego, California

Home port: San Diego, Embarcadero

Year of construction: 1863; launched November 14, 1863

Shipyard: Gibson, McDonald & Arnold, Ramsey, Isle of Man

Tonnage: 2200 ts displacement; 1197 tons gross

Dimensions:
Length overall: 84.50 m
Length of hull: 65.70 m
Length between perpendiculars: 62.40 m
Width: 11.80 m
Depth in hold: 6.70 m
Draft (loaded): 6.60 m

Sail area: 2050 square meters

Rigging: 19 sails; 3 (4) foresails, double topsail, single topgallant, royals; mizzenmast: mizzen sail, mizzen topsail

Masts, spars: fore- and main-mast with topmast and topgallant mast; mizzenmast with one topmast; height of mainmast over the deck: 38 meters; length of large yard: 22 meters; length of main royal yard: 12 meters

Auxiliary engine: none

Crew: originally 38 people

Use: sailing museum ship

The British shipping company Wakefield, Nash & Company of Liverpool had the *Euterpe* built as a full-rigged ship in 1863. The ship sailed two voyages to Calcutta under this flag, during which she sustained serious damage through collisions and storms. During her last voyage home, the captain died on board. Because of the unprofitable voyages, the company decided to sell the sailing ship to the East Indian businessman David Brown of London in 1867. The *Euterpe* was once again involved in India trade until she was sold to the shipping company of Shaw, Savill & Albion in 1871. She sailed under the same flag for the next 27 years. Most of the voyages led around the Cape of Good Hope to South Australia and New Zealand, often also to the Pacific Coast of the United States and around Cape Horn back to Europe. One of the company's captains, Th. E. Phillips, sailed this route around the world ten times in a row.

In addition to the trading goods, there were often also immigrants to Australia and New Zealand on board. The ship did not prove to be particularly fast on any of these voyages. In 1899 J. J. Moore (Pacific Colonial Ship Company) of San Francisco bought the ship. Subsequently the *Euterpe* sailed for 2 years under the Hawaiian flag in the lumber trade between the United States (Puget Sound) and Australia; two loading ports had to be cut in the stern for the long trunks and beams. She usually brought coal back from Australia.

In the winter of 1901 the ship was brought to a shipyard. Extensive conversion work had to be done, because the Alaska Packers Association had taken the *Euterpe* into its Star fleet as the *Star of India*. The full-rigged ship became a bark. Living quarters had to be created for the crew of often 200 men. In addition, the poop was lengthened almost to the mainmast, and the forward deckhouse was widened. The gross tonnage increased to 1318 tons in the process.

With the Star fleet, the bark sailed every year to the large fish canning works in Alaska's Bristol Bay. Seamen, fishermen, and cannery works could be found on board. In 1923 she sailed under the flag of the Alaska Packers for the last time. J. Wood Coffroth purchased the ship in 1926 for the Zoological Society of San Diego. He wanted to make her the centerpiece of an oceanographic museum and aquarium in San Diego. The Great Depression of the 1920s put an end to these plans.

By the end of World War II the ship was in a very bad condition. The upper topmasts and yards had to be removed because of the heavy air traffic over San Diego. This work was unfortunately carried out incompetently, so that almost none of the standing rigging could be used in the later restoration.

In 1959 a group of citizens decided to rebuild the ship once and for all as a monument to a decisive period of maritime history. Thus arose the Star of India Auxiliary. The restoration work had been largely completed by the 100th birthday of the ship. "Euterpe" has been retained as a figurehead since the time of the ship's construction. Today the ship lies at the Embarcadero in San Diego. An oceanographic museum is being installed on the between deck. Since 1976 the ship has sailed under wind power again from time to time.

Stephen Taber

Type: 2-masted fore-and-aft schooner, wood	Length of hull: 20.70 m
	Width: 6.80 m
	Draft:
	    Centerboard up: 1.50 m
	    Centerboard down: 4.30 m

Nation: USA	
Owner: Captains Ken and Ellen Barnes, Camden	Sail area: 325 square meters
Home port: Rockland, Maine	Rigging: 4 sails
Year of construction: 1871	Masts: height of mainmast over the deck: 17.40 meters
Shipyard: Van Cott Shipyard, Glenhead, New York	Auxiliary engine: none
Tonnage: 72 ts displacement; 50.30 tons gross; 41 tons net	Crew: 4-person active crew, 24 guests
Dimensions: Length overall: 35.00 m	Use: chartered ship, passenger ship

This ship can claim to be unique and to have set a record. With the exception of short periods of time for repairs, the schooner has remained in service continuously for 130 years under the same name and with the same rig. For the largest part of its life it earned its money as a freighter.

Equipped with a centerboard, but otherwise with a small draft, the ship could be loaded or unloaded in shallow waters as well. The care of her various owners guaranteed that she was always highly seaworthy and had a long life. The last, very extensive overhaul took place in 1981–82.

Instead of cargo, passengers are taken aboard today, with whom the sailing ship cruises off the island-rich coast of Maine.

The design of the ship is based on the American privateer *Swift,* a brigantine that was built in 1778 in Baltimore. The entire design and ornamentation correspond to the taste in the period of its predecessor. The ship has a window in the stern; her shrouds are fastened to outboard chain plates with deadeyes and tackle ropes. The large aft cabin is another distinguishing feature. The figurehead today represents the wife of the builder, Mrs. Robinson.

From 1940 to 1958 the *Swift of Ipswich* belonged to the actor James Cagney. At that time she was moored across from the actor's house in Newport Beach. Cagney sold the ship to the Newport Dunes, Inc., from whom the Swift Associates, Ltd., purchased the ship in 1963 and had her equipped for passenger cruises. Since then the schooner has sailed on shorter voyages in the waters off California.

Type: 2-masted sailing schooner, wood

Nation: USA

Owner: Los Angeles Maritime Institute

Home port: San Pedro, Los Angeles

Year of construction: 1937; launched spring 1937

Shipyard: William A. Robinson, Inc., Ipswich, Massachusetts; design: Howard I. Chapelle, naval architect

Tonnage: 64 ts displacement

Dimensions:
Length overall: 31.40 m
Length of hull: 21.00 m
Length between perpendiculars: 19.20 m
Width: 5.50 m

Depth to deck: 5.30 m
Depth in hold: 4.10 m
Draft: 2.70 m

Sail area: 530 square meters

Rigging: 7 sails; 3 foresails; foremast: foresail, topsail, schooner sail; mainmast: gaff-sail

Masts, spars: height of main-mast over the deck: 21.30 meters; bowsprit with jibboom

Auxiliary engine: General Motors diesel engine 671, 165 horsepower

Crew: 4-person active crew, 42 passengers, 12 beds

Use: private ship for passenger cruises

Tabor Boy

The ship was built as the *Lotsenschoner II* to serve as a pilot ship in Amsterdam. In 1923 the Dutch merchant marine acquired her for use in the training of its officer candidates. The name changed to *Bestevaer.* In 1939 the German navy requisitioned the ship and used her until the end of the war. Then the schooner passed into Russian hands for a short time before being reclaimed by Holland. After her return she became private property. In 1950 the owners equipped the *Bestevaer* as a yacht, although she was then never really sailed as a yacht.

Shortly thereafter R. C. Allen of R. C. Allen Business Machines in Holland, Michigan, purchased the ship and donated her to the Tabor Academy in Marion, Massachusetts, in 1954. Now called the *Tabor Boy,* the schooner is the fourth ship belonging to the academy to bear this name. The Tabor Academy is a college preparatory boardingschool for boys. It was founded in 1876 and named after Mount Tabor in Palestine, which was once a famous Christian holy place. According to tradition it was the site of Christ's transfiguration.

Rowing and sailing occupy a special place in the life of the academy. During the school year the *Tabor Boy* undertakes weekend cruises along the coast of New England. Every student can take part in these cruises. During the spring and summer vacations the schooner makes cruises to South Carolina, Florida, and Bermuda, or to Nassau in the Bahamas.

Te Vega

Previous names: *Vega, Etak*

Type: 2-masted fore-and-aft schooner, steel

Nation: USA

Owner: Landmark School of Pride's Crossing, Massachusetts

Home port: unknown

Year of construction: 1930

Shipyard: Fr. Krupp Germania shipyard, Kiel

Tonnage: 400 ts displacement; 243 tons gross; 113 tons net

Dimensions:
Length overall: 47.40 m
Length of hull: 41.30 m

Length between perpendiculars: 30.40 m
Width: 8.50 m
Draft: 5.20 m

Sail area: 966 square meters

Rigging: 7 sails; 3 foresails, gaff-sail, gaff-topsail

Masts: height of mainmast over the deck: 39.20 meters; both masts with 1 topmast

Auxiliary engine: Mirrless diesel engine, 225 horsepower

Crew: 17 girls, 28 boys

Use: school and sailing school-ship

The design for this former private yacht came from Cox and Evans. Her commissioner and first owner was Walter G. Ladd, after whose first wife the ship received the name *Etak*. Until the war she changed owners a number of times and then became the property of the navy. She frequently demonstrated her exceptional sailing qualities during the shooting of the film *South Seas Adventure*. Runs of 270 nautical miles a day were not unusual. In the Pacific this earned her the admiring nickname *Te*, which essentially means "large" or "wondrous."

These record-setting voyages, moreover, have been repeated quite recently. In 1958 the schooner was thoroughly overhauled and sailed as a yacht for a number of years, until it was acquired by Stanford University to be used as an oceanographic research vessel. Since being purchased by her current owner, the ship has sailed mostly in the Mediterranean.

Timberwind

Previous name: *Portland Pilot*

Type: 2-masted fore-and-aft schooner, wood

Nation: USA

Owner: Bill, Julie, and Dan Alexander, Albion, Maine

Home port: Rockport, Maine

Year of construction: 1931; launched March 10, 1931

Shipyard: Brown's Wharf, Portland, Maine

Tonnage: 85 ts displacement; 85 tons gross; 49 tons net

Dimensions:
Length overall: 30.40 m
Length of hull: 21.30 m
Width: 5.70 m
Depth in hold: 2.70 m
Draft: 3.00 m

Sail area: 223 square meters

Rigging: 5 sails

Masts: height of mainmast over the deck: 25 meters

Auxiliary engine: none

Crew: 5-person active crew, 20 guests

Use: vacation cruises on the coast of Maine

The *Portland Pilot* was a pilot-ship in the waters off Portland from 1931 to 1969. During the war years she was also deployed to maintain the submarine nets protecting the entrance to Portland's harbor. At that time the ship had an auxiliary engine. The *Timberwind*, as she is now called, sails for paying guests during the warm months of the year in the waters off Maine.

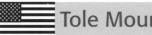

Tole Mour

Type: 3-masted topsail schooner, steel

Nation: USA

Owner: Marimed Foundation, Honolulu and Majuro, Marshall Islands

Home port: Honolulu

Year of construction: launched July 14, 1987; commissioned October 4, 1988

Shipyard: Nichols Brothers Boat Builders, Freeland, Washington

Tonnage: 340 ts displacement (ready for deployment); 229 tons gross; 151 tons net

Dimensions:
Length overall: 47.40 m
Length of hull: 37.20 m
Width: 8.80 m
Depth in hold: 3.60 m
Draft: 4.10 m

Sail area: 790 square meters

Rigging: 15 sails

Masts: height of mainmast over the deck: 33.40 meters

Auxiliary engine: Deutz SBA 8M816, 564 square meters

Crew: 11-person active crew, plus a 15-person medical crew

Use: medical support, sailing school-ship

In the language of the Marshall Islands, the name *Tole Mour* means "the Gift of Life and Health." The ship is probably unique among large sailing vessels. She serves exclusively to provide for the medical care of the people of the Marshall Islands. Wind power was chosen in the interest of saving en-ergy. In shallow and reef-filled coastal waters it is naturally impossible to do without the help of an engine.

The *Tole Mour* has all the medical equipment on board that is necessary for this ser-vice. The types of care offered include prenatal care, dental care, and the prevention and treatment of adult illnesses. An additional important task is to provide for the cultural needs of the people on the for the most part widely separated is-lands and atolls.

Previous name: *Lyra*

Type: brig, wood

Nation: USA

Owner: Robert Elliot, St. Lucia

Home port: Castries, St. Lucia

Year of construction: 1948

Shipyard: Helge Johansson, Sibbo, Finland

Tonnage: 190 ts TM

Dimensions:
Length overall: 39.20 m
Length of hull: 7.40 m
Draft: 2.80 m

Rigging: 13 sails

Masts: height of mainmast over the deck: 22.90 meters

Auxiliary engine: Caterpillar diesel, 335 horsepower

Crew: 22 people

Use: chartered ship

Rigged as a brig, the *Unicorn* is one of the very few sailing ships of her kind. She was built by Finland as the freighter *Lyra* and after the war transported primarily sand and lumber for the ruined cities of that country. Later she was un-rigged and sailed as a sand transporter. In 1971 the American Jaques Thiry purchased the ship. He rigged the hull as a traditional brig according to the plans for the sailing ship *Adolph et Laura*, which was built in France in 1867. A layer of copper protects the ship from teredo.

Following an additional change of owners, which resulted in the ship's being put to use in films (*Roots, Ghost of Cape Horn*), the English hotelier Robert Elliott purchased her in 1980. Castries on St. Lucia became her new homeport. From there the *Unicorn* sails with passengers and a steelband on board in the Caribbean.

Victory Chimes

Previous name: *Edwin and Maud*

Type: 3-masted fore-and-aft schooner, wood

Nation: USA

Owner: Victory Chimes America Windjammer, Rockland

Home port: Rockland, Maine

Year of construction: 1900; launched April 1900

Shipyard: Phillips & Company, Broad Creek

Tonnage: 208.48 tons gross; 178 tons net

Dimensions:
Length overall: 51.70 m

Length of hull: 40.10 m
Length between perpendiculars: 38.30 m
Width: 7.30 m
Depth in hold: 2.60 m
Draft: 2.30 m

Sail area: 695 square meters

Rigging: 6 sails; all masts with gaff-sails only

Masts: height of mainmast over the deck: 25.20 meters (all masts are the same height); pole masts without topmasts

Auxiliary engine: none

Crew: 9 people, 43 passengers

Use: private ship for passenger cruises

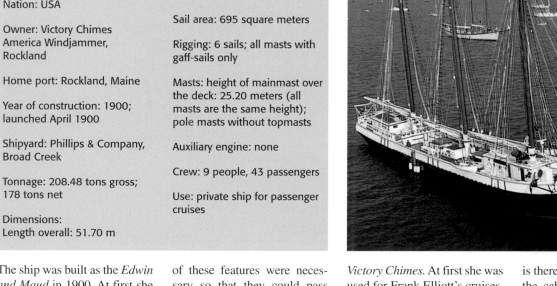

The ship was built as the *Edwin and Maud* in 1900. At first she was a pure freighter, which was used especially to transport lumber. Ships of this type were rigged as pole-mast schooners, which meant that they didn't have any topmasts and thus only gaff-sails. Their width could not exceed 7.5 meters, and they had flat bottoms; both of these features were necessary so that they could pass through the Chesapeake and Delaware canals. Nevertheless, these ships were highly seaworthy and were easily able to cross the Atlantic.

In 1954 the *Edwin and Maud* was converted into a passenger ship. She moved to Rockland (Maine) and received the name *Victory Chimes*. At first she was used for Frank Elliott's cruises. Today she belongs to Captain F. B. Guild of Castine, Maine. *Victory Chimes* is one of the largest American passenger sailing ships and the only 3-masted schooner that still sails without an engine. The ship is equipped with electric lights. There is no cooling system, nor is there running water in any of the cabins. There are thirteen two-bed, one three-bed, and three four-bed cabins for the guests. From the middle of June until the middle of September the schooner undertakes a 1-week cruise from Rockland every Monday in the waters off Maine.

Wavertree

Previous name: *Southgate*

Type: full-rigged ship, iron

Nation: USA

Owner: South Street Seaport Museum, New York, New York

Home port: South Street Seaport Museum, New York

Year of construction: 1885

Shipyard: Oswald, Mordaunt & Company, Southampton, England

Tonnage: 2170 tons gross; 2118 tons net

Dimensions:
Length overall: 99.10 m
Length of hull: 89.40 m
Length between perpendiculars: 81.80 m
Width: 12.20 m
Depth to deck: 8.10 m
Depth in hold: 7.40 m
Draft (loaded): 6.20 m

Sail area: 2926 square meters

Rigging: 28 sails; double topsails, single topgallants, royals

Masts: height of mainmast over the deck: 42.80 meters; topmast and topgallant mast

Auxiliary engine: none

Crew: 29 people

Use: museum ship

The freighter was originally commissioned as the *Southgate* by the Liverpool shipping firm of R. W. Leyland & Company. The ship changed owners while she was still under construction. Following her completion, the *Southgate* sailed for the shipping company of Chadwick, Pritchard on the trade routes with India from 1886 to 1888. After that R. W. Leyland bought her back. Under Leyland's "hungry goose" flag, the ship for the most part sailed long distances. She transported primarily saltpeter, sawn timber, barrels of oil, and jute to all parts of the world. In September 1910 the *Southgate* was badly damaged during a storm off Cape Horn. She returned to Montevideo for repairs.

In November of the same year she lost her mainmast off Cape Horn; it broke off above decks. She sought safety in the Falkland Islands. Another repair was apparently not considered worthwhile, because she was brought to Punta Arenas in 1911, where she was used as a storage ship for wool. In January 1948 she was towed to Buenos Aires. There

she was supposed to be scrapped. In the meantime, however, Señor Alfredo Numeriani had bought the ship and had her converted into a barge for hauling sand.

The South Street Seaport Museum, founded in 1966, purchased the mastless ship in 1968. In August 1970 the *Wavertree* was towed to New York. Since then repairs have been under way, which, with the exception of the hull, amount to a reconstruction.

Wawona

Type: 3-masted fore-and-aft schooner, wood	Width: 10.90 m
	Depth to deck: 3.70 m
Nation: USA	Rigging: 7 sails; 4 foresails (forestaysail with boom), 1 gaff-sail per mast
Owner: Northwest Seaport, Seattle, Washington	
Home port: Seattle, Washington	Masts, spars: all masts are the same height; height over the deck: 34.50 meters; no topmasts, gaffs are not used
Year of construction: 1897	
Shipyard: Hans Bendixsen, Fairhaven, Connecticut	Auxiliary engine: none
Tonnage: 630 ts displacement; 468 tons gross; 413 tons net	Crew: 8 people as a wood transporter; more than 30 people as a cod-fishing schooner
Dimensions: Length between perpendiculars: 47.50 m	Use: museum ship

For a number of years, interested circles in Seattle have been making an effort to preserve and restore the *Wawona*. Since a complete overhaul with a replacement of the masts is necessary, significant funds are needed.

The schooner was built in 1897 for Dolbeer & Carson of Eureka and San Francisco and was specially equipped to transport sawed timber. Even today the large "wood hatches" beneath the starboard anchor hawse, designed to allow for the loading of long beams, testify to that use. The ship could load 630,000 board feet of wood.

In 1913 the *Wawona* was converted to fish for cod. Storage rooms for the fish and additional living quarters for the now larger crew had to be installed. It is probable that the schooner holds the world record in fishing results for this type of ship. In 1947 the *Wawona* sailed on a fishing voyage for the last time. During the war she was chartered by the government to transport wood.

The word "Wawona" comes from the Native American language and refers to a tree that is native to California.

Westward

Type: 2-masted staysail schooner, steel

Nation: USA

Owner: Sea Education Association, Woods Hole, Massachusetts

Home port: Woods Hole, Massachusetts

Year of construction: 1961

Shipyard: Abeking & Rasmussen

Tonnage: 138 tons gross; 98 tons net

Dimensions:
Length overall: 38.00 m
Length of hull: 31.00 m
Length between perpendiculars: 25.20 m
Width: 6.53 m
Depth to deck: 5.10 m
Draft: 3.90 m

Sail area: 650 square meters

Rigging: 8 sails

Masts: height of mainmast over the deck: 30 meters

Auxiliary engine: Cummins diesel, 500 horsepower

Crew: 10-person active crew, 24 students

Use: oceanographic research and training ship

The ship's first owner, Mr. Drayton Cochran of Oyster Bay, New York, sailed the *Westward* around the world as a private yacht. At the end of the 1960s, the Oceanographic Institute of Makapuu on Hawaii purchased the schooner. The ship became a research ship for the institute and was employed especially to observe fish populations in the Pacific. In 1971 the Sea Education Association purchased the ship. During six voyages a year, scientists from universities and research institutes instruct students in marine biology and oceanography.

Windy

Type: 4-masted fore-and-aft schooner, steel

Nation: USA

Owner: Captain Robert Marthai, Windy of Chicago, Ltd.

Home port: Chicago

Years of construction: 1995–96

Shipyard: Charleston, South Carolina

Tonnage: 140 ts displacement

Dimensions:
Length overall: 45.10 m
Length of hull: 33.20 m
Length between perpendiculars: 28.90 m

Width: 7.60 m
Depth in hold: 3.10 m
Draft: 2.50 m

Sail area: 445 meters

Rigging: 11 sails

Masts: height of the mainmast over the deck: 26.20 meters

Auxiliary engine: Cummins diesel, 300 horsepower

Crew: 10-person active crew, 26 trainees

Use: charter ship, passenger ship, sailing school-ship

This 4-masted schooner belongs to a modern type of sailing ship, equipped with all the necessary technology for training and passenger service. The guests are allowed to take part in the operation of the ship.

The voyages lead not only across Lake Michigan but also to the other Great Lakes, down the Erie Canal to the Hudson, Long Island Sound, and Chesapeake Bay. The ship also takes part in tall-ship events.

Young America

Previous name: *Enchantress*

Type: brigantine, reinforced concrete

Nation: USA

Owner: Young America Marine Education Society

Home port: Atlantic City, New Jersey

Year of construction: launched May 20, 1975

Shipyard: David M. Kent, Port Jefferson; design: Charles Wittholz

Tonnage: 196 tons gross; 76 tons net

Dimensions:
Length overall: 39.50 m
Length of hull: 29.80 m
Length between perpendiculars: 26.60 m
Width: 7.40 m
Depth in hold: 2.40 m
Draft: 2.80 m

Sail area: 489 square meters

Rigging: 10 sails

Masts: height of mainmast over the deck: 28.50 meters

Auxiliary engine: diesel engine, 200 horsepower

Crew: 5-person active crew; 30–40 boys

Use: sailing school-ship

This is the largest sailing ship ever built out of reinforced concrete. This mode of construction involves layers of chicken wire and cement; its primary advantages are that it offers protection against corrosion and damage from teredo.

Originally, the former *Enchantress* was used for private passenger cruises. As with all American ships, the Coast Guard sets the ship's safety standards.

Venezuela

Simon Bolivar

Simon Bolivar

Type: bark, steel

Nation: Venezuela

Owner: Marina de Guerra de Venezuela

Home port: La Guaira

Year of construction: launched November 21, 1979; put in service August 12, 1980

Shipyard: Astilleros y Talleres Celaya S. A., Bilbao, Spain

Tonnage: 1260 ts displacement

Dimensions:
Length overall: 82.40 m
Width: 10.60 m
Draft: 4.35 m

Sail area: 1650 square meters

Rigging: 23 sails; double topsail, single topgallant, royals

Auxiliary engine: General Motors diesel, 750 horsepower

Crew: 92-person active crew, 102 cadets (male), 18 cadets (female)

Use: sailing school-ship

The ship was named after Simon Bolivar (1783–1830), the most significant leader in the Creoles' struggle for independence from Spanish domination. The figurehead symbolizes freedom. She wears the Phrygian cap of the French Revolution. In her right hand she carries a sword, and in her left hand the flag that Bolivar flew during the war.

The *Simon Bolivar* undertakes one long training voyage per year. On these voyages she often has the opportunity to participate in tall-ship regattas as well as windjammer events.

Yugoslavia

Jadran

Jadran

Previous names: *Marco Polo, Jadran*

Type: 3-masted topsail schooner, steel

Nation: Yugoslavia

Owner: Bakar Naval School

Home port: Tivat (Montenegro)

Years of construction: 1931–32; launched June 25, 1931; commissioned June 1933

Shipyard: H. C. Stülcken & Son, Hamburg

Tonnage: 700 ts displacement

Dimensions:
Length overall: 58.00 m
Length of hull: 48.00 m
Length between perpendiculars: 41.00 m
Width: 8.90 m
Depth to deck: 4.55 m
Draft: 4.00 m

Sail area: 800 square meters

Rigging: 12 sails; 4 foresails; foremast: square foresail (150 square meters), single topsails, single topgallants, gaff sail; mainmast, mizzenmast: gaff-sail, gaff-topsail

Masts: height of mainmast over the deck: 34 meters

Auxiliary engine: Linke-Hofmann-Busch works diesel engine, 375 horsepower; speed with engine, 8 knots

Crew: accommodations for commandant, 10 officers, 1 doctor, 20 officer candidates, 8 warrant officers, 16 petty officers, 132 petty officer candidates

Use: sailing school-ship

The *Jadran* was built for the Yugoslavian fleet association Jadranska Straza. The name of the sailing ship means "Adriatic." During her period of construction, work was interrupted for 19 months. In her main dimensions the ship is identical to the *Niobe,* a ship of the former German Reich Navy that sank in 1932. The aft main deck is lowered by 50 centimeters in the area of the officers' living quarters. The between deck reaches from the front machine room bulkhead to the stern. A second continuous deck is the maneuver deck, which reaches from the poop deck to the stern and covers the midship house. Because of the large size of the crew,

the rank-and-file crewmembers and the petty officers sleep in hammocks. A topsail schooner was chosen so that the young men could be trained on different types of sails. In order to further expand the range of seamanship skills, the topsails were made so that they could be raised and lowered, and this task is carried out by the young men themselves.

The *Jadran* carries seven boats: three sailing cutters, one jollyboat, two dinghies, and one gig. Five of these boats hang outboard in davits. This preserves space on deck. The exhaust gasses from the engine are directed out through the high mizzenmast. Because of the stony bottom of the Adri-

atic coast, the ground tackle had to be made especially strong. During World War II the ship was commandeered by Italy and sailed as the *Marco Polo* under the Italian war flag. At the end of the war the ship was given back to Yugoslavia. The ship's training voyages take place primarily in the Mediterranean.

Glossary

Aft–Toward the back of the ship.

Awning deck–*See* hurricane deck.

Bachstays–Stays for the masts and topmasts that stand aft of the shrouds.

Baldheader–Square-rigger, usually 4-masted, with no royals.

Ballast–Material added to a ship in order to achieve an optimal stability (for example, sand, stone, or water). Especially important on voyages without cargo.

Bark, or barque–Originally only 3-masted square-rigged ship with 2 full-rigged masts and the last mast with a fore-and-aft sail. In addition, 4- or 5-masted square-rigged ships, which except for the last mast with its fore-and-aft sails rigging have full-rigged masts only.

Belting–Particularly strong layer of planking on wooden ships. It rises above the outer skin, stabilizes the ship, and prevents damage during docking.

Bermuda rig–Rig containing jib-headed sails, especially on modern yachts. Refers to boats in the Bahamas that use this type of rig.

Between deck–On large sailing ships, usually only a single deck between the main deck and the bottom of the ship.

Bilge–The lowest point in a ship, in which all water that has leaked in or all water that has formed through condensation can gather.

Bilge keel–A humplike keel on the bilge of the hull in order to reduce rolling; often found on large, flat-bottomed ships.

Boom–A round piece of wood to which the lower edge (foot) of a fore-and-aft sail (for example, a gaff-sail) is attached.

Bow–The front end of a ship's hull.

Bow ornamentation–When there is no figurehead, carved scrollwork or baroque fiddle-heads often adorn the bow.

Bowsprit–A spar that is firmly attached to the body of the ship that extends forward above the stems. The forestays, to which the staysails are attached, leads to the bowsprit.

Bowsprit topsail yard–A small yard to which the bowsprit topmast is attached; a small mast that stands on the bowsprit or the jibboom. Primarily on old warships.

Brace–Rope with which the position of a yard with respect to the ship's axis is changed. It is attached to the end of the respective yard.

Brail–To haul a sail up to the yard with the brails.

Brails–All parts of the running rigging that serve to haul a sail up to the yard or gaff.

Brig–A square-rigged ship with 2 full-rigged masts.

Brigantine–A 2-masted square-rigged ship that sets only square sails on its foremast but only fore-and-aft sails on its mainmast.

Bulkhead–A dividing wall that separates one part of the interior of a ship from another.

Bulwark–Solid wall surrounding an open deck.

Cap–Spectacle-shaped fixture at the point where the mast and topmast (or two topmasts) are connected.

Capstan–A winch with a vertical axis.

Carvel build–Build in which the external planks lie next to each other such that a smooth surface results.

Chain plates–The metal fittings used to connect the shrouds with the outer hull.

Clew lines–The two brails that lead to the clews (lower corners) of a square sail.

Chocks–Structures for storing boats on dock, adapted to the shape of the boat. Also used to store rope.

Classification–Every larger ship is placed in a "class" based on the way it was built, its level of safety following its construction, and in what condition it is maintained.

Clinker build–Build in which the external planks overlap each other like shingles on a roof.

Clipper–Sharply built, fast sailing ship of American origin. Later and currently a general term for a fast, large sailing ship. Even 4-mast barks are referred to as clippers.

Coamings–Raised edge around hatches and at the thresholds of doors to prevent water from entering.

Cringles–Iron or wooden rings around masts or stays to which staysails are fastened.

Composite construction–Shipbuilding method in which the frames and the keel are made of iron or steel and the planks are made of wood.

Corvette–Smaller than the frigate. Usually rigged as a full-rigged ship. Guns on the upper deck. Used for reconnaissance, escorting convoys, and privateering.

Cross-trees–On square-riggers and large schooners the thin wooden or iron beams on the mast parallel and perpendicular to the hull upon which the top rests. They are also used to spread the shrouds and backstays.

Crow's nest–A protected platform on the mast used for lookout duties.

Cutter–A naval utility boat with a transom stern that can be rowed or sailed.

Davit–Gibbetlike crane on which boats are hung. Davits always occur in pairs.

Deadweight–The cargo carrying capacity of a ship (deadweight all told), whereby provisions, etc., that the ship needs for the voyage are included.

Deck beams–Beams supporting the deck that run perpendicular to the hull and rest on the frame heads.

Depth in hold–A vertical measure taken in the hold. Upper edge of the floor plate to the lower edge of the deck beams (uppermost continuous deck) midships.

Depth to deck–Measured at the ship's midpoint from the bottom of the hull to the upper edge of the deck beams of the uppermost continuous deck.

Dhow–Term for an Arabian sailing vessel with one or more masts and lateen sails. Admittedly, the word "dhow" is unknown in the Arab world.

Dinghy–A small boat that can be operated by one person.

Displacement–The amount of water displaced by a ship.

Dolphin striker–Downward-pointing iron or wooden spar mounted below the bowsprit to spread the jibboom stays.

Donkey boiler–Boiler aboard sailing ships to power equipment that assists with heavy work.

Dory–A rowboat for one or two people with which cod is caught off Newfoundland.

Draft marks–Indicators of depth on the stern and stem. The units used are decimeters or English feet.

Dromon–Byzantine warship with at least two banks of oars.

End–Seaman's term for every type of rope.

Figurehead–A figure that is attached below the bowsprit and that seems to "grow" organically out of the forecastle. Usually related to the name of the ship.

Fisherman's staysail–A light sail whose head is attached to the top of the main topmast and whose tack is attached to the cap of the foremast.

Flat stern–*See* transom stern.

Floor plate–Reinforcement of the floor that lies athwartships.

Flush deck–Continuous upper deck with no superstructures.

Flute–An important, primarily Dutch trading ship of the seventeenth and eighteenth centuries. Flat-bottomed and rather narrow.

Foot–Unit of length. For measuring ships the English foot, which is equivalent to 304 millimeters, is usually taken as the standard unit.

Fore-and-aft sail–All sails that run parallel to the length of the ship.

Forecastle–Front superstructure of a ship, reaching from one side to the other.

Foremast–The first mast on all ships with more than 1 mast (but not on 1½-masters).

Foresail–On square-rigged ships the lower sail on the foremast. On yachts the foremost sail set next to the mast (the stayforesail).

Frames–The "ribs" of the hull. They stand perpendicular to the keel and rise from the floor plate.

Frigate–An older type of ship with 3 full-rigged masts (usually a warship).

Full-rigged ship–Originally only a 3-masted square-rigged ship on which all masts were fully rigged. In addition, every ship with more than 3 masts with the same type of rigging. More precise designation: 4- or 5-masted full-rigged ship.

Full sail–The condition of a sailing ship when it has set all available sails.

Gaff–The upper spar of a gaffsail. The lower end clutches the mast from behind like a fork.

Galleass–A coastal trading vessel rigged as a 1½-master.

Genoa–Overlapping foresail that is set on the forestay.

Gig–Small, narrow, quick-moving boat.

Gun ports–Openings in the side of the ship through which the muzzles of guns protrude.

Halyards–Ropes with which yards or sails are hoisted.

Halyard winch–Winch with which yards or sails are hoisted or lowered.

Hawse–Round or oval opening in the side of a ship or in the deck through which lines or chains pass (for example, an anchor hawse).

Helmsman–The person who stands at the wheel and steers the ship.

Hoist–To run up a sail or a flag.

Hulk–The hull of a retired, unrigged ship, often used for storage.

Hurricane deck–Continuous deck above the main deck. The bulwark reaches to this deck, producing a continuous superstructure.

Ice doubling, ice lining–Special external planking on ships that sail in Arctic waters.

Jacob's ladder–The ladder to the top of the top of the topgallant mast.

Jibboom–An extension of the bowsprit. In contrast to the bowsprit itself, the jibboom is designed to be removable. In many cases the jibboom can be further extended by an outer jibboom. This causes the staysails to be farther apart, better utilizing the power of the wind.

Jib-headed sail–Also called a Bermuda sail. A high fore-and-aft sail with no gaff, the head of which reaches to the mast top.

Jolly–A flat boat with a transom stern.

Keel–The backbone of the hull. On wooden ships a beam that runs along the center of the bottom of the hull. The floor plate is attached perpendicular to the keel and supports the frames.

Ketch–A 1½-master. The smaller mizzenmast stands aft, but in front of the ship's rudder.

Knot–One knot (kn) is equal to one nautical mile per hour. Knots appear as marks on the log line.

Laid up–Temporarily taken out of service.

Lateen sail–A triangular sail that is set on a lateen yard (something in between a yard and a gaff). It probably originated in the Mediterranean.

Lee–The side of the ship that is toward the wind.

Log–To measure the ship's speed from on board.

Longboat–A large lifeboat that is always lashed on deck or to the deckhouse.

Lower sail–The lowest square sail on a full-rigged mast (foremast, mainsail, etc.).

Luff–The forward edge of a fore-and-aft sail.

Mainmast–The second mast on a ship with 2 or more masts (but not on a 1½-master).

Mainsail–The lower sail on a full-rigged mainmast or the sail on the mainmast in the case of a fore-and-aft rig.

Mess–Living and eating room on trading ships or warships.

Mizzen boom–Boom of the mizzen sail. On a large ship it usually extends above the stern rails.

Mizzenmast–The last mast on all ships with 3 or more masts as well as ketches and yawls.

Mizzen sail–The sail on the mizzenmast as well as the last fore-and-aft sail on all ships with more than 2 masts as well as on ketches and yawls.

Moon sail–Triangular sail above the highest yard with the point upward.

Nautical mile–The sixtieth part of a degree of longitude; equal to 1852 meters.

Patent anchor–A stockless anchor that can be partially retracted into the hawse.

Peak–Designation for the extremities of a ship; peak rooms (forepeak, afterpeak).

Pinnace–Smallish, fully rigged trading ship or warship with a flat stern. Primarily from the seventeenth century.

Pin rail–Benchlike structure on the bulwark and around the masts to which the running rigging is made fast with belaying pins.

Planks–More or less wide boards that are attached to the frames in the case of the body of the ship or to deck beams in the case of the deck.

Pole mast–A mast consisting of one piece, with no topmasts.

Poop–The rear superstructure of the ship, extending from one side to the other.

Port–The left side of a ship.

Port lids–Flaps that cover the gun ports from the outside on old warships.

Pram dinghy–A box-shaped transport or work boat.

Quarterdeck–An elevated portion of the main deck in the rear of the ship.

Railing–The "fence" running around an open deck.

Rake of mast–Downward slope of a mast or masts. Allows the masts to sustain a higher wind pressure.

Rabbet–Grooves running the length of either side of the stem and the keel into which the planks are fitted.

Reef–The part of the sail that can be shortened (to shorten is "to reef"). The reef runs parallel to the yard or to the boom.

Reef points–Small lines that are attached to the bottom of a sail in one or more rows with which the sail can be tied up.

Rig–The sails and masts of a ship considered as a whole.

Royal(-sail)–A single square sail that is set above the topgallant sail(s).

Run (day's run)–Distance covered by a ship from noon one day until noon the following day.

Running rigging–All ropes that are used to operate sails and to move the yards, gaffs, and other spars.

Schooner–Sailing vessel with 2 or more masts that doesn't have a full-rigged mast. Frequently, it only has fore-and-aft sails. In the case of 2-masters, the larger mast stands aft.

Schooner sail–The fore-and-aft sails of the foremast, even when this mast also has square sails.

Shrouds–Ropes of the standing rigging that support the masts and topmasts on the sides.

Skysail–Simple square sail that is set above the royal.

Sloop–1. The rigging of a boat with 1 mast, a mainsail, and a forestaysail. The most common rigging of recreational vessels. 2. A 1-masted freight vessel (also a "jolly-boat").

Snow mast–Light lower mast that stands aft of the mainmast.

Sound–To measure the depth of the water.

Spars–Round wooden pieces on board except for masts and topmasts.

Spencer–A gaff-sail without a boom.

Spinnaker–A large, light, balloon-like sail that en route is set with the true direction of the wind anywhere from dead astern to about abeam.

Spritsail yard–On older sailing ships a yard that is attached below the bowsprit.

S.T.A.–Sail Training Association. English association that promotes sailing-ship regattas and sailing instruction.

Stability–The ability of a ship to right itself from a horizontal position.

Standing rigging–All of the ropes and cables that serve to support the masts and topmasts and that are not moved.

Starboard–The right side of the ship.

Stays–The ropes of the standing rigging that support the masts and topmasts in front.

Staysail–Any sail that is attached to the stays.

Staysail schooner–A schooner that sets a staysail rather than a schooner sail on its foremast.

Stem–More or less vertical extension of the keel on the front and back of the ship.

Stern–The back end of a ship.

Stern gallery–Often richly ornamented, balconylike structure around the stern found on many old warships and also on many trading ships.

Stock anchor–A very old type of anchor. The stock is fastened perpendicular to the main shank.

Streak–Usually white-painted band running around the otherwise black-painted hull at the level of the row of the gun ports in order to highlight (or give the impression of) the ports.

Studding sail–Sails that square-riggers set in light, rough winds. First the studding sail spars are pushed out to lengthen the yards, and then the studding sails are set on the studding sail spars. Very rare nowadays.

Tack–On triangular fore-and-aft sails the front corner of the sail. On square sails, depending on the placement of the sail, the lower front corner.

Tiller–A horizontal lever running along the ship with which the rudder is turned. On large ships replaced by a rudder wheel.

Topmast–Extension of the lower mast that can be raised or lowered. Large sailing ships often have two topmasts, the topmast and the topgallant mast.

Tonnage–Measurement of a ship's cargo-carrying capacity (a measurement of volume and mass).

Top–Platform on the mast that rests on the crosstrees.

Topgallant–A single or double square sail that is set above the topsail (or topsails) on a square-rigged mast.

Topsail–General term for the square sails on square-rigged schooner (topsail schooner). On fore-and-aft schooners the sails above the gaff-sails (gaff-topsails).

Topsail schooner–A schooner that sets one or more square sails on its foremast in addition to the schooner sails.

Tramp–A commercial trading vessel that picks up cargo wherever it happens to be rather than following a regular trade route.

Transom stern–A flat back end of a ship (as opposed to a round stern).

Trim–1. Trimming is the process of putting the ship into a good position (through proper setting of the sails, proper positioning of the cargo on board, etc.). 2. To move cargo from one spot on board to another.

Trireme–A Greek galley with three banks of oars.

Trysail–A fore-and-aft sail on staysail schooners that is set between the stay and the mast in front of it.

Warp–The forward movement of a ship in which, with the help of a kedge and of the smaller warp anchor, the ship is moved from one anchoring place to another.

Windlass–A winch with a horizontal axis.

Yacht–A sailing vessel that is not used for commercial purposes but rather for sport, recreation, or out of love for sailing.

Yard–Spar perpendicular to the ship's length axis on a mast to which a square sail is attached.

Yard-arm–The end of a spar (yard, gaff, or boom).

The Museum Harbor of Oevelgönne

This museum harbor is located in the Hamburg district of Oevelgönne on the Elbe. There the nonprofit association Museum Harbor of Oevelgönne maintains a small harbor in which wind- and steam-powered former commercial vessels are housed. The ships, which are for the most part privately owned by members of the association, sail primarily under wind power (or under steam) and occasionally undertake voyages on the Elbe or on the North or Baltic sea. In many cases expensive restoration work was necessary to restore the ships in a manner as true to the originals as possible. The following ships are moored in the museum harbor, among others:

Präsident Freiherr von Maltzahn (HF 294) of Oevelgönne, a Finkenwerder high seas cutter built of wood at the J. Sietas shipyard in 1929, rigged as a 1½-master with a sail area of 210 square meters. The cutter belongs to the association and was restored at the Joachim Behrens shipyard in Finkenwerder. Length: 22.55 meters (30 meters overall); width: 6.60 meters; draft: 1.90 meters; 50.96 tons gross.

Catarina von Hamburg (ALT 287), a wooden cutter-lighter, built in 1889 at the Johann Brandt shipyard in Neuhof near Hamburg for the fisherman H. Rübke of Altenwerder. The ship was completely restored in a manner true to the original at the Joachim Behrens shipyard in Finkenwerder in 1976–78. Rigged as a mizzen-lighter with a sail area of 120 square meters; length: 16.10 meters; width: 5.25 meters: draft: 1.20 meters; 13.3 tons gross.

Moewve of Hamburg, steel freight-lighter, built in 1907 at the Heinrich Fack shipyard in Itzehoe for an Elbe shipper from Wilster. In her dimensions the ship is a so-called Lägerdorfer lighter, because she fits exactly through the locks and bridges of the Lägerdorf Canal and is thus able to transport cement from the factory there to Hamburg. Restored 1977–80. Length: 17.86 meters (24 meters overall); width: 4.10 meters; draft: 1 meter; 31.84 tons gross; rigged as a mizzen-lighter with a sail area of 150 square meters.

Fortuna of Oevelgönne, a Dutch "Skûtsje" (small tjalk), built of steel in 1914 as a freighter, extensively restored in Holland in 1974. Length: 15.79 meters; width: 3.35 meters; draft: 0.60 meters; rigged as a fore-and-aft sloop with a sail area of 100 square meters; 17.79 tons gross.

Hoop op Welvaart. The tjalk (Boeierschuit) was built of iron (riveted) in 1883 in Lekkerkerk in the Netherlands. The 13.08-meter-long, 3.61-meter-wide fore-and-aft rigged ship provided feeder service between Rotterdam and Lekkerkerk for a long time. The modified ship was rediscovered in 1977 in Billwerder, Hamburg, as a dented and rusted garbage barge and in 1978–79 restored to her original dimensions. Sail area: approx. 140 square meters; draft: 0.95 meters; displacement: 24.91 ts; engine: 68 horsepower; owner: private.

Elfried. This lighter was built in 1904 (steel, riveted) and sailed the lower Elbe and its tributaries (Lühe, Stör, Oste) with different cargoes depending on the season. In 1984–1990 the owner, the Altonaer Museum in Hamburg, had the ship restored at Blohm & Voss in Hamburg. Since 1998 the ship has once again been moored in Oevelgönne. Rigging: fore-and-aft sloop; sail area in the wind: 72 square meters; length of hull: 14.75 meters; width: 4.75 meters; draft: 1.09 meters; displacement 27 ts; engine: 60 horsepower.

Anna. The *Anna* (riveted steel) transported vital goods such as milk, fruit, grain, cement, and coal on the lower Elbe starting in 1910. In 1970 the ship was no longer listed in the ship register as a sailing mizzen-lighter, but rather as a motorized transport ship (without masts). Following a restoration in 1976 the ship again has 2 masts, and one can charter the ship for vacations or to sail. Length of the hull: 16.18 meters; width: 4.06 meters; draft: 1.39 meters; sail area: 145 square meters; engine: 70 horsepower; owner: private.

Vertrouwen is a tjalk that was built in 1893 in the Netherlands. She originally carried peat for the draining of the wetlands of Friesland; later she served a workshop, living, and storage ship as well as a barge. In 1990 she was restored in Hamburg. Length of hull: 22.70 meters; width: 4.70 meters; draft: 0.80 meters; rigging: fore-and-aft sloop; sail area in the wind: 110 square meters; engine: 205 horsepower; owner: private.

The *Elbe 3* of Hamburg, former light-ship; *see* the appropriate entry
Tiger of Hamburg, steam tug
Claus D of Hamburg, steam tug
Otto Lauffer of Hamburg, steam launch
Walter Hävernick of Hamburg, former firefighting boat for the Hamburg harbor
Präsident Schäfer, customs steam launch
Stettin, ice breaker
Fiete, open mooring boat
Bergedorf, HADAG guest ship (Type IIIb) as a café
Saatsee, pontoon with steam-driven outrigger
Karl Friedrich Steen, floating crane HHLA I

The Sail Training Association (STA)

Windjammers from all over the world gather at races sponsored by the STA. Pictured here are the KAISEI, *the* AMERIGO VESPUCCI, *the* GUAYAS *and the* CHRISTIAN RADICH.

At the beginning of 1954 the Englishman Bernard Morgan proposed bringing the still-existing sailing school-ships together for a regatta in order to promote the mutual understanding of the youth of the world. For this purpose, Captain John Illingworth founded a Sail Training Ships International Race Committee that was supposed to plan a regatta for 1956. This regatta left from the Tor Bay near Torquay and ended in Lisbon. Not only the large sailing ships were allowed to participate, but also schooners and smaller sailing vessels. The requirement for participation was that at least half the crew consist of young people between the ages of 16 and 25 years who had no or only very little experience sailing—the ships had to be school-ships. Twenty ships took part in this first regatta, of which seven were larger than 250 tons. Prior to the main regatta, competitions in rowing, swimming, and sailing with small vessels had taken place. The event was so popular that the committee decided to repeat the regatta every 2 years. The next race took place in 1958; it led from Brest to the Canary Islands. The Sail Training Association, which the responsible parties had united to form, became a permanent organization and was supposed to organize the regattas from then on. Since England didn't own a large sailing school-ship at that time, the *Sir Winston Churchill* was built in 1965 and was followed by the *Malcolm Miller* in 1968.

The participants in the regatta are divided into three classes. Square-rigged ships constitute the A class, schooners are in the B class, and smaller vessels such as ketches or cutters are in the C class. In addition a special formula is created for each ship, in which, in addition to other factors, primarily sail area, displacement, and length are taken into consideration. As a result, there cannot be an "absolute" winner.

Because the number of participants grew continuously, the costs of holding the regatta also climbed. In 1971 the STA found itself in a financial crisis that called the 1972 race into question. The British company of Berry Bros. & Rudd, Ltd., which owned Cutty Sark Scotch Whisky, came to the rescue as a sponsor. It was not and is not only the financial support that filled the STA's sails with the necessary "wind," but also the fact that the company donated the Cutty Sark Trophy. This is a silver model of the famous clipper *Cutty Sark,* which can still be seen today in London–Greenwich.

It is not the fastest ship that receives this prize at the end of a regatta, but the one whose crew has done the most to promote international understanding. The captains of all of the participating vessels choose this winner, who then gets to hold on to the prize for 2 years. The first ship that was allowed to take the trophy on board was the Russian 4-masted bark *Kruzenshtern* in 1974, which at that time, along with the *Towarischtsch,* became the first Soviet ship to take part in an international regatta. Hospitality on board and helpfulness on every occasion brought the *Kruzenshtern* the prize.

The largest rendezvous of large sailing ships took place in 1976 in New York on the occasion of the bicentennial of the United States and in 1992 in Cadiz on the occasion of the 500th anniversary of Columbus's discovery of America.

Pamir and Passat

With great difficulty and just in the knick of time, the shipowners Heinz Schliewen and Captain Helmut Grubbe succeed in rescuing the two large 4-masted barks from being scrapped in Antwerp. The sailing ships were towed to Travemünde on June 20, 1951. From there they arrived in Kiel shortly after. Here Schliewen had the ships equipped and expanded into sailing schoolships at great expense at the Howaldt Works. An auxiliary engine was installed, in addition to waterproof bulkheads, two deckhouses, gangways, and so forth.

For safety reasons the brace and halyard winches were removed from the maindeck. The modification was completed at the end of 1951. The subsequent classification resulted in the best possible score.

PASSAT

PAMIR

The 4-masted bark *Pamir* left Hamburg on January 10, 1952, for her first postwar voyage under the German flag. She had 4000 tons of cement intended for Brazil aboard; that corresponds to about 400 freight cars. The *Passat* followed her on February 12, 1952, departing from Brake/Weser. She too carried a cargo of cement destined for Brazil. With some interruptions, the two square-rigged ships sailed this route until 1957. They were the last great windpowered freighters to sail the world's oceans.

Following the tragic loss of the *Pamir* on September 21, 1957, the *Passat,* which was on her return voyage at the same time, was removed from service after arriving at her home port. Today she is moored at the Priwall in Travemünde.

Acknowledgments

Without extraordinarily generous help from all parts of the world it would not have been even remotely possible to complete this work. Only in this way was it possible to use really authentic material. I would like to take this opportunity to express my heartfelt thanks for this generous support.

Argentina
Botschaft der Bundesrepublik Deutschland, Buenos Aires
Botschaft der Republik Argentinien, Bonn
Generalkonsulat der Republik Argentinien, Hamburg

Australia
The Adelaide Steamship Company, Ltd., Adelaide
Graeme K. Andrews, Sydney
Albany Travel Centre, Albany
I. Hawrylow, Melbourne
Australian Outward Bound Foundation
Mr Nick Burningham, Fremantle
HM Bark *Endeavour* Foundation Pty. Ltd.
Cees Koeman, Thredbo Village
Tim & Jillian Lloyd, Sydney
National Trust of Australia (Victoria), Melbourne
Queensland Sail Training Association Inc.
Mr Bruce Reid, Bounty Cruises, Sydney
Sail & Adventure Ltd., Victoria
Pastor Lawrence Shave, Fremantle
Mrs Stephanie Symes, Williamstown
City of Albany, Western Australia
Sydney Maritime Museum

Bahamas
West Island College International Inc., Montreal

Belgium
A. S. B. L. Vent Debout, Lüttich
Philippe Vanthournout, Gullegem
walk about nv, Deerlijk

Brazil
Ministerio da Marinha, Rio de Janeiro

Germany
Alferra, Allgemeine Verwaltungsgesellschaft mbH & Co., Hamburg
Amphitrite Schifffahrts-KG
Ariadne Windjammer S. A., Hamburg
Baltic Schooner Association, Lübeck
M. Beil
Blohm & Voss AG, Hamburg
Christliches Jugenddorfwerk e. V., Göppingen
CLIPPER—Deutsches Jugendwerk zur See e.V., Bremen
Deutscher Schulschiff-Verein, Bremen
Der Hafenkapitän im Wasser- und Schifffahrtsamt, Emden
Der Kommandant des Segelschulschiffs *Gorch Fock*
Kapitän Harry Freidank, Berlin
Germania Schifffahrt GmbH, Hamburg
Hanse-Koggewerft e. V., Bremerhaven
Hapag-Lloyd Kreuzfahrten GmbH, Hamburg
Howaldtswerke, Kiel
Hygrapha GmbH, Hamburg
Verein Jugend in Arbeit Kiel e. V.
Verein Jugendschiff Corsar e. V., Beverstedt
Horst Krumke Verwaltungs-GmbH & Co., Berlin
Kings Lake Shipping Co. Ltd.
Harald Koppisch, Neu-Ulm
LebenLernen auf Segelschiffen e. V., Hamburg
Lürssen Werft, Bremen
Segeltouristik Meyer zur Heyde Mary-Anne GmbH & Co. KG, Laboe
Museumshafen Oevelgönne
Morgenstern-Museum, Bremerhaven
Reederei Zerssen & Co., Rendsburg
Hans Edwin Reith, Hamburg
Der Senat der Hansestadt Lübeck
Schleswig-Holsteinische Seemannsschule, Lübeck-Travemünde
Schlichting-Werft, Lübeck-Travemünde
Hartwig Schröder, Ekenis
SSD Segelschifffahrtsgesellschaft Deilmann GmbH & Co.
Stadt Wolgast
Stiftung Deutsches Schifffahrtsmuseum, Bremerhaven
Schiffergilde Bremerhaven
Verein Segelschiff F. Nansen e. V., Wolgast
Oliver Wipperfürth, Kiel
Matthias Zeug, Trasbol

Chile
Armada de Chile, Buque Escuela *Esmeralda*, Talcahuano
Ministerio de Defensa Nacional, Santiago

Denmark
Amba Thomas Brocklebank
FDF Aalborg Søkreds
Svend + Gitte Hansen, Helsingør
Herning-Holstebro Kommuner & Ringkjøbing
Holbæk Skibs- & Baadebyggeri, Holbæk
Kogtved Søfartsskole, Kogtved
Reederei J. Lauritzen, Kopenhagen
Otto Bjørn Leth, Århus
Kaj Lund, Kopenhagen
Kristian Lund, Svendborg
Mercandia Rederniere, Kopenhagen
National Museet, Kopenhagen
Navigations-Uddannelsesradet Statens Skoleskib *Danmark*
Orlogsmuseet, Kopenhagen
J. Ring-Andersen, Skibsværft, Svendborg
Sømandshøjskolen, Svendborg
Stiftelsen *Georg Stage Minde,* Kopenhagen
O. Stoltenberg, Kalundborg
Per K. Thuesen, Holte

Dominican Republic
Botschaft der Dominikanischen Republik, Bonn
Secretaria de Estado de las Fuerzas Armadas, Santo Domingo

Ecuador
Armada del Ecuador

Finland
Ålands Sjöfarts Museum,
Mariehamn
The *Albanus* Association
Lars Grönstrand, Åbo
Christian Johansson, Helsinki
Rederi AB LINDEN
Sail Training Association
Valtion Merimie-Sammattik-
oulu, Åbo

France
Association Bisquine Canca-
laise, Cancale
Association du Cotre Corsaire,
St. Malo
Association Goélette *La
Recouvrance*
Association pour un Grand
Volier-Ecole Français, Paris
Ateliers et Chantiers du Havre
Club Méditerranée et Societé
Havraise Services et Transports
Marine National, Ecole
Navale, Lanveoc-Poulmic
(Brest)
Ministère Des Armées, Paris

Greece
Messrs. A. Lusi, Ltd., London
Ministry of Merchant Marine,
Seamen's Training Division,
Piräus
Niarchos (London) Ltd.

Great Britain
Baltic Schooner Company
Ltd., Guernsey
Bristol '96 Ltd.
Camper & Nicholsons Ltd.,
Dockyard, Southampton
The Cirdan Trust, Maldon
Drusberg Investments Ltd.
The Dulverton Trust, London
Training Ship *Foudroyant,*
Gosport
General Register and Record
Office of Shipping and Sea-
men, Cardiff
J. Hinks & Son, Yacht and
Boat Builders, Appledore
Capt. Stephen Gibb, N. Fer-
riby, E. Yorks
F. P. V. Latham, Arcadian

Restaurant, Morecambe
Lawrie D. Johns, Emsworth
Lloyd's Register of Shipping,
London
The Marques Sailing Society
Merseyside Maritime
Museum, Liverpool
Ministry of Defence (Naval),
Dr. Leslie Morrish, Windsor
Royal Naval Reserve, Dundee
National Maritime Museum,
Greenwich
Outward Bound Moray Sea
School, Burghead
Outward Bound Trust, London
John Reid
The Sail Training Association,
Gosport
S. S. *Great Britain* Project,
Bristol
The Schooner Office,
Achdalieu, Fort William
Commander H. F. M. Scott,
Tunbridge Wells
R. Simper, Ramsholt
Salztrust Ltd., Guernsey
The Small School at
Winestead Hall, Hull
Mrs Ellie M. Standen,
Plymouth
Thames Nautical Training
College, Greenhithe
Ulster Folk and Transport
Museum, Cultra Manor
The Turk Phoenix Ltd.,
Sunbury

India
Goa Shipyard Ltd.
Sea Cadet Council, Bombay

Indonesia
Indonesische Marine

Ireland
The Jeanie Johnston Project,
Tralee

Italy
Adriatic Mercantile & Trad-
ing, Trieste
Italienisches Konsulat, Stuttgart
Marina Militare, Accademia
Navale, Livorno
Ministero Della Difesa-
Marina, Ufficio Storico
M. M., Rome

Japan
Industrial Bank of Japan
Leasing Co. Ltd.
Capt. K. Sano, Tokyo
Nagasaki Holland Village
Corporation
Kaoru Ogimi, Shogakukan
Inc.
Keicho Diplomatic Mission
Ship Association
City of Osaka

Canada
Brigantine Incorporated,
Kingston, Ontario
Bytown Brigantine Inc.,
Ottawa
Oland & Son Ltd., Halifax
Toronto Brigantine Incorpo-
rated, Adelaide, Toronto
Albert J. Seidl, Vancouver

Columbia
Embajada de Columbia, Bonn

Luxemburg
Reederei White Star Clipper
N. V., Brüssel

Malta
Captain Morgan Leisure, Ltd.

New Zealand
New Zealand Information
Service, Wellington

The Netherlands
L. N. Baars & Co.
Capt. Joop Bosshardt, Harlin-
gen
A. van der Cingel, Lemmer
Martin Duba
Damen Shipyard, Gorinchem
Jan Duinmeijaer, Harlingen
Fred & Nell Franssen, Drim-
melen
F. Goldenbeld, Franeker
Reederei Halfland, Rotterdam
Hanse Charter Holland,
Groningen
Hanzestad Compagnie BV,
Kampen
Holland Zeilcharters
H. J. Hoogendoorn
Koninklijk Institut voor de
Marine, Den Helder
Peter Lazet, Amsterdam

Maritiem Museum Prins
Hendrik, Rotterdam
Matrozen-Opleidingsschip
Pollux, Amsterdam
H. Müter, IJmuiden
N. V. Oostindiëvaarder
Peter de Groote, Amsterdam
Erik Querngester, Harlingen
V. O. F. Europe Sailing, Den
Haag
V. O. F. Rederij Fokkelina-
Linde
BV Rederij Oosterschelde,
Rotterdam
Reederei Vlaun
Rederij Clipper Stad Amster-
dam
Anna und Jaap van de Rest
Ribro BV
Willem F. Sligtin
Smit Tall Ship BV
Stichting Het Vaarend
Museumschip
Stichting Het Zeilende
Zeeschip, s'Gravenhage
Stichting Nederland bouwt
V. O. C. retourschip
Swan-Compagnie-Holland
Claes Tolman, Monnickendam
TSC-Traditional Sailing Char-
ter, Harlingen
Klaas van Twillert, Lemmer
A. Valk, Groningen
Gerhard Veldhuizen,
Enkhuizen
C. W. Velthuys
Marnix van der Wel
Gert van Wijk
Zeilrederij Friesland
de Zeilvaart Enkhuizen
Zeilvloot Hollands Glorie,
Rotterdam
Zeilvloot Lemmer-Stavoren
Zuiderzee-Museum,
Enkhuizen

Norway
Bergens Skoleskipet, Bergen
Fram Museum, Bygdøy
Hardanger Jakt Sailing Ltd.
Norsk Sjøfartsmuseum, Oslo
Østlandets Skoleskip, Oslo
Sørlandets Seilende Skole-
skips Institution, Kristian-
sand
Wilson Shipping Company,
Arendal

Poland

International Class Aflot Foundation
Maritime Branch of Polish Chamber of Foreign Trade, Gdynia
Wydawnictwo Morskie, Gdynia

Portugal

Associacao Portuguesa de Treino de Vela (Aporvela)
Comissao Consultiva National das Pescarias do Noroeste do Atlântico, Lissabon
Grémio dos Armadores De Navios da Pesca do Bacalhau, Lissabon
Ministério da Marinha, Lissabon
Pascoal & Filhos, Lda., Aveiro

Russia

Avantgarde-Werft, Petrosawodsk
Kapitän Boris Krishtal
Boris Sidorovsky, St. Petersburg
STS Elena-Maria-Barbara, Sankt Petersburg
Marineclub Yunea, Sankt Petersburg

Sweden

Kapitän Jens Andersson, Öckerö
Baltic Sail Ship AB
Broströms Tekniska AB, Göteborg
K. Carlsson, Karlskrona
Halmstads Stad, Fastighetskontoret, Halmstad
Jan Hagenfeld & Assoc., Örebro
Kapitän Yngve Victor Gottlow
Marinmuseum Karlskrona
Pederiaktiebolaget Clipper, Malmö
Rederi AB Gunilla, Öckerö
Sjömansskolan Viking, Göteborg
Statens Sjöhistoriska Museum, Wasavarvet, Stockholm
Capt. Claes Stenestad
Svensk Sjöfarts Tidning, Göteborg

Svenska Skonarkompaniet, Torslanda
Vandrarhemmet af Chapman, Stockholm
Stiftelsen Svenska Kryssarklubbens
Seglarskola, Göteborg
Vida Shipping AB, Stockholm

Spain

Astilleros Talleres Celaya S.A., Bilbao
Elcano De La Marina Mercante, Madrid
Escuela Maniobra Galatea, Comandancia, El Ferrol de Caudillo
Museo Maritimo, Barcelona
Juan Sebastian de Elcano, Buque Escuela
De Guardias Marinas, Comandante

South Africa

Dias-Museum, Mosselbai

Tahiti

W. A. Robinson, Papeete

Uruguay

Botschaft der Bundesrepublik Deutschland, Montevideo

United Arab Emirates

Boys Marine Training Establishment
Ras-El-Tin, Alexandria
The United Arab Company For Maritime Transport, Cairo

USA

Schooner America USA, Inc.
W. A. Baker, Naval Architect, Hingham, MA
Bounty Exhibit, St. Petersburg, Florida
Boston Tea Party Ship, Inc.
Capts. Ken and Ellen Barnes, Camden
Capt. Brook
Capt. Jonathan Boulware, Stamford
J. Smith, Norfolk
Capt. M. Burke, Windjammer Cruises Inc., Miami Beach

The City of Baltimore
Clipper City, Inc., Baltimore
U. S. Frigate Constellation, Commanding Officer U. S. S. Constitution, Boston, Mass.
Coast Cruises, Castine, Maine
U.S. Coast Guard Academy, New London, Conn.
Corpus Christi Museum of Science and History, Corpus Christi, Texas
Thomas J. Coughlin, Boston
Department of Commerce, Harrisburg, Penn.
Department of Conservation and Economic Development, Trenton, NJ
Roger Dawson, Doylestown, PA
R. S. Douglas, Coastwise Packet Co., Vineyard Haven
Mr Hary Dring, San Francisco
Capt. John Eginton, Mystic
Friends of Friendship, Salem, MA
Goudy & Stevens. Dockyard, East Boothbay, Maine
Grays Harbor Historical Seaport
Capt. F. B. Guild, Maine
Capt. Richard Headley, Santa Barbara, Calif.
Harvey Gamage Foundation Inc., Cornwall, NY
Hawaiian Chieftain, Sausalito
Capt. H. S. Hawkins, Coastal Cruises, Edgwick, Maine
Historic St. Mary's City, MD
Holland Village, Inc., of Princeton, New Jersey
International Yacht Restoration School, Newport, Rhode Island
Jamestown Foundation, Williamsburg, Virginia
Mr Gordon Jones, Seattle
Kalmar Nyckel Foundation, Wilmington
Thomas M. Kelly, Suttons Bay
Capt. A. M. Kimberly, Kimberly Cruises. St. Thomas, U.S. Virgin Islands
Lahaina Restoration Foundation, Lahaina. Maui, Hawaii
Mills B. Lane Jr., Bank President, Atlanta, Georgia
Larmont Geological Observa-

tory, Pallisades, NY
Captain John Leibolt, Altamonte Springs
The Living Class Rooms Foundation, Baltimore, MD
Evan Logan, Albany, CA
Long Beach Island Board of Trade, Ship Bottom, NJ
Larry Mahan, Marstons Mills
Marine Historical Association, Inc. Mystic Seaport, Mystic, CT
The Maritime Museum Association, San Diego, CA
Maritime State Historic Park
Capt. Robert Marthai, Windy of Chicago
Metro-Goldwyn-Mayer International Inc., New York, NY
J. F. Millar, Newport, RI
The Mirish Corporation, Hollywood, CA
Jerry Mac Mullen, San Diego
Gregory E. Muzzy, Schooner Liberty, Inc.
National Geographic Society, Washington, DC
National Maritime Historical Society, Washington, DC
Nautical Heritage Society
Orange County Marine Institute, Dana Point
Pennsylvania Historical and Museum Commission, Harrisburg, PA
Capt. Gib Philbrick, Rockland
Mr Leon D. Polland, Baltimore, MD
David E. Robinson, Picton Castle Office
The Golden Hinde Corporation of San Francisco
Plimoth Plantation, Plymouth
The Flint School, Sarasota
San Francisco Maritime Museum, San Francisco
F. & M. Schaefer Brewing Company, New York, NY
Capt. Jim Sharp, Camden
Sea Education Association, Woodshole, MA
Seaport '76 Foundation Ltd., Newport, RI
Smithsonian Institution, Washington, DC

South Street Seaport Museum, New York, NY
S/V Spirit of Massachusetts, Boston
Capt. Steven F. Pagels, Cherryfield
The Pennsylvania Historical and Museum Commission
Star of India, San Diego
Tabor Academy, Marion

Port Jefferson Packet Co.
Unicorn Inc., Fort Lauderdale
Philadelphia Maritime Museum
The Penn's Landing Corporation, Philadelphia
United States Merchant Marine Academy, Kings Point
Lawrence H. M. Vineburgh, Washington, DC

Greg Walsh, *Ocean Navigator* Magazine, Portland, ME
B. H. Warburton, Nassau
Yachting Magazine, New York
Wisconsin Lake Schooner Education Association

Venezuela
Marina de Guerra de Venezuela

The Photographs

The following people and organizations deserve thanks for providing photographs.

I. Aaserud Billedsentralen, Oslo
A.B.C. (*La Cancalaise*)
Abeking & Rasmussen, Lemwerder
Erik Abranson
Ålandia, Mariehamn
City of Albany, Western Australia
Albany Travel Centre, Albany
Frédéric Allain
Alma Doepel Supporter's Club, Lower Plenty
Amba Thomas Brocklebank
Graeme K. Andrews, Sydney
Anthony's Pier 4 Restaurant, Boston, MA
Archiv Edition Maritim, Hamburg
Armada de Argentinia
Armada de Chile
Armada de Colombia
Armada del Ecuador
Armada Portuguesa, Lissabon
E. M. Da Armanda, Servicio De Fotografia, Lissabon
Ashronia Christian Cadet & Mission Ship Association, Fremantle
Association du Cotre Corsaire, Saint Malo
Association Maritime Belge, Oostende
Astace Celaya, Bilbao
A.S.B.L. Vent Debout, Lüttich
Avantgarde-Werft, Petrosawodsk

Baltic Sail Ship AB, Stockholm
Jappie Bandstra, Stavoren
G. Barkowsky, Berlin
Ken and Ellen Barnes, Camden
William Bartz
M. Beil, Lübeck
Beken of Cowes Maritime Services Ltd., Cowes
Bergens Skoleskip
Hansjörg Beyer, Berlin
J. Bichard, Harlingen

Palle Blinkenberg
Blohm & Voss AG, Hamburg
John Blue
Herbert H. Böhm, Hamburg
Robert Boehme, Seattle, WA
Karsten Börner, Lemmer
Boston Tea Party Ship, Inc., Boston, MA
Bounty Cruises, Sydney
Kenneth Brack, Forked River
Catherine Braem, Brüssel
Warren Brawn, Sydney
Brigantine Incorporated, Kingston
Martina Brinkmann, Leer
Norman Brouwer, New York
Patrick J. Browne, New Ross
Wolfgang Bühling
Buque Escuela *Esmeralda*
Buque-Museo Fragata A. R. A.
Nick Burnigham, Fremantle

Christliches Jugenddorfwerk e. V., Göppingen
A. van der Cingel, Lemmer
The Cirdan Trust, Maldon
The City of Baltimore, Baltimore, MD
Clipper City Inc., Baltimore
CLIPPER—Deutsches Jugendwerk zur See e. V., Bremen
Club Méditerranée et Société Havraise Services et Transports, Le Havre
Coastwise Packet Company, Vineyard Haven, MA
Comissao Consultiva National Das Pescarias do Noreste do Atlantico, Lissabon
Maurice Crosby Photography Ltd., Halifax
Crowley Maritime Corporation of San Francisco, CA

Davies Brothers Ltd.
De Fotoboot, Rotterdam
De Zeilvaart, Enkhuizen

Peter Deilmann Reederei, Neustadt
Deutscher Schulschiff-Verein, Bremen
Deutsches Schifffahrtsmuseum, Bremerhaven
Jos Le Doaré, Chateaulin
Hans van Donkersgoed
Helmut Dose, Kiel
Downeast Windjammer Cruises
A. Duncan, Gravesend, Kent
Paul Dziuban, Toronto

Gerhard Eckardt, Bremen
Erwin Ehlers
Joachim Eicke, Barkelsby
Basil G. Emmerson
Patrik Eriksson
Escuela De Maniobra,

Anton Fercher
El Ferrol de Caudillo
The Flint School, Sarasota, FL
Flying Focus, Castricum, the Netherlands
Gert Fopma, Harlingen
Daniel Forster
Fotoboat Company, Santa Barbara, CA
Fototeca Uff. Propaganda, Stato Maggiore Marina, Rome
The Foudroyant Trust, Portsmouth
Fram-Museum, Oslo
Fred & Nell Franssen, Drimmelen
Arved Fuchs, Bad Bramstedt

Galveston Historical Foundation, Inc., Galveston TX
Georg Stage-Stiftung, Kopenhagen
Germania Schifffahrt GmbH, Hamburg
H.-J. Gersdorf, Hamburg
Capt. J. S. Gibt
Hanny & Leo van Ginderen, Antwerpen

Segelschulschiff *Gorch Fock,* Kiel
Dr. L. Gosse
Günther Gräfenhain
Peter Grage, Hamburg
S. S. *Great Britain* Project, Bristol
Kai Greiser, Hamburg
Gremio Dos Armadores de Navios da Pesca do Bacalhau, Lissabon
Volker Gries
Bob Grieser
Lars Grönstrand, Åbo
Capt. Frederick B. Guild

Jan Hagenfeldt, Orebro
Hanse-Koggewerft e. V., Bremerhaven
Hanze Charter Holland, Groningen
Hanzestad Compagnie BV, Kampen
Hardanger Jakt Sailing Ltd.
Harmstorf-Werften—Flensburger Schiffbau-Gesellschaft, Flensburg
C. W. Hawkins, Auckland
Hawrylow, Melbourne
Per Henriksen, Kopenhagen
Antje Herbst
Historic St. Mary's City, MD
Hollands Glorie, Rotterdam
Holland Zeilcharters, Monnickendam
H. J. Hoogendoorn, Hoorn
Howaldtswerke—Deutsche Werft AG, Kiel
Howell's Photo Studio, Vineyard Haven, MA
Huis Ten Bosch Co., Ltd./ J-1812, Amsterdam
Hygrapha GmbH, Hamburg
Indonesische Marine, Jakarta
Industrial Bank of Japan Leasing Co., Ltd., Yokohama
Industrie-Photo Schilling, Lübeck
Institut for Seatraining, Tokyo
Häkan Isefjord, Oskarshamn
Jakobstads Wapen

The Jeanie Johnston Project, Tralee
Chr. Jensen, Jamestown Foundation, Williamsburg, VA
Ove Jensen, Struer
Christian Johansson, Helsinki
Rita Jokiranta, Mariehamn
Richard de Jonge, Sneek
Gordon Jones, Seattle, WA

Henry Kabot, Gdynia
Todd N. Kamp
Theo Kampa, Vågåmo
Kenter, Neu-Ulm
A. F. Kersting, London
Capt. Arthur Kimberly, Woodmont
Monika Kludas, Hamburg
F. u. G. Köhler, Weinheim
G. F. de Kok, Dordrecht
Koninklijk Instituut voor de Marine, Den Helder
Koninklijke Marine, Den Haag
Karl Kortum, San Francisco
Kapt. Boris Krishtal, St. Petersburg

F. A. Mac Lachlan, Kingston
Lahaina Restoration Foundation, Lahaina, Maui, Hawaii
Lamont Geological Observatory, New York, NY
John Lancaster, Sydney
Landesbildstelle Schleswig-Holstein, Kiel
H. M. Lawrence, Vineburgh, Washington DC
LebenLernen auf Segelschiffen e. V., Wolgast
A. C. Littlejohns, Bideford
The Living Classrooms Foundation, Baltimore, MD
Lloyd's Register of Shipping, London
Loch Eil Trust
Løtvedt
Evan Logan, Albany, CA
Mike Louagie, Oostende
Kaj Lund, Kopenhagen
Kristian Lund, Svendborg
Foto-Lusarte, Lissabon
A. Lusi Ltd., London
Lynn-Photo-Service, Ship Bottom

Maine Coast Cruises, Castine
Jerry Mac Mullen, San Diego
Larry Mahan, Marstons Mills
Chris McLuckie, Kailua, Oahu, Hawaii
Manitoba-Museum, Winnipeg
Volkwin Marg, Hamburg
Marina de Guerra de Venezuela

Marine-Foto, Schweden
Marineministerium Athen
Maritime Museum, Vancouver
Maritime Museum Association of San Diego, CA
The Maritime Trust, London
Jan Mark Marinfoto
Capt. Bob & Janine Marthai
The *Marques* Sailing Society
L. S. Martel, Mystic Seaport, Mystic, CT
MAX Photographer, Lymington, Hants
MCS Film KG, München
Lex de Meester, Middelburg
Benjamin Mendlowitz, Brooklin, ME
Harald Mertes, Koblenz
Metro Goldwyn Mayer Inc., New York, NY
MGM's *Bounty* Exhibit, St. Petersburg
Miche LE COZ, Brest
Ministère des Armées, Paris
Ministerio da Marinha, Rio de Janeiro
Ministerio de Defensa Nacional, Santiago, Chile
Ministero Difesa Marina, Centro Fotografico dell Ufficio Documentazione, Rom
Miyagi Prefectural Govt., Ishinomaki City
T. Morgan
Rosemary Mudie, Lymington
Muelle de las Carabelas, Palos de la Frontera
Museo Maritimo, Barcelona
Museu de Marinha Arquivo Fotográfico
Mystic Seaport Museum, Mystic, CT
The Mystic Whaler, Mystic

National Maritime Historical Society, Washington, DC
National Maritime Museum, Greenwich
Nautical Heritage Society, Sacramento, CA
Navigations-Uddannelsesradet
Statens Skoleskib *Danmark*
Nederlands Scheepvaartmuseum, Amsterdam
Reinhard Nerlich, Hamburg
New Zealand Information Service, Wellington
Niarchos (London) Ltd., London
Pieter Nijdeken, Amsterdam
Bill Nimke, Education Director, Milwaukee, WI
Thomas R. de Nijs, Amsterdam
Kapt. J. P. Nørgaard

Norsk Sjøfartsmuseum, Oslo
Norway Yacht Charter A/S, Oslo

Ocean Navigator Magazine, Portland, ME
The Ocean Research and Education Society, Inc., Boston
Ocean Wide Film and TV Productions, Berlin
Østlandets Skoleskip, Oslo
Official Plimoth Plantation Photo, Plymouth, MA
Oland & Son, Halifax
Operation Drake, Round the World, London
G. A. Osbon
Flor van Otterdyk, Burcht
Outward Bound Foundation, Australia
Outward Bound Moray Sea School
L. B. Owen, Georgetown, Maine

Franco Pace, Triest
Paradise Consult, Hannover
Parceria Geral de Pescarias, Lissabon
Ted Parrish, Grays Harbor, WA
Pascal & Filhos, Aveiro
Clifford Patterson, Orleans
Pennsylvania Historical and Museum Commission, Harrisburg, PA
Andrew Pine, Savannah, GA
Pressebureau APN, Kopenhagen

Chris Queeney, Wilmington
Queensland Sail Training Association, Inc., Brisbane
Erik Querngester, Harlingen

Bo Rasmussen, Nørresundby
Peter Rath, Rostock
BV Reederij Oosterschelde, Rotterdam
Reederij Vlaun, Amsterdam
John Reid, Leith
Hans-Edwin Reith, Hamburg
Jaap van der Rest, Amsterdam
W. A. Robinson, Papeete
Rover Marine, Inc., Norfolk
Sarah Ruppert

Sail Training Association, Gosport
Salztrust Ltd., Guernsey
San Francisco Maritime Museum, San Francisco, CA
F. u. M. Schaefer Brewing Co., New York, NY
Otmar Schäuffelen, Ulm
Wolfhard Scheer, Bremerhaven
Schooner *America* Inc.

Marc Schützer, Olympia, WA
Schulschiffverein *Großherzogin Elisabeth* e. V., Elsfleth
Königl. Schwedische Marine
Les Scott, Virgin Islands Tourist Bureau
Sea Cadet Corps
Sea Cadet Council, Bombay
Sea Education Assoc., Woodshole, MA
Seaport '76 Foundation
Seefahrtsmuseum Lissabon
Segeltouristik Meyer zur Heyde *Mary-Anne* GmbH & Co. KG, Laboe
Albert J. Seidl, Vancouver
Capt. J. Sharp
Shogakukan Inc., Yasunori Kobayashi
Schooner Liberty, Inc., Boston
Schooner Liberty Clipper, Inc., Boston
Sjöhistoriska Museet vid Åbo, Ålandsinseln
Skyfotos, Lympne Airport, Kent
The Small School at Winestead Hall, Hull
The Small School/The Sailors, Nyborg
South Street Seaport Museum, New York, NY
Sozialwerk für Seeleute e. V., Hamburg
STA-Finnland, Helsinki
Statens Sjöhistoriska Museum, Stockholm
Star Clipper Kreuzfahrten, Brüssel
Star Clippers Monaco SAM
Star Spangled Banner Flag House Association of Baltimore, Baltimore, MD
Stato Maggiore della Marina, Ufficio Propaganda, Rom
Capt. Claes Stenestad, Stockholm
Stichting Het Vaarend Museumschip
Stichting Het Zeilende Zeeschip
Stiftelsen Fullriggeren *Sørlandet,* Kristiansand
Stiftung für Ausbildungsschiffe—Lübeck, Hamburg
Peter Stone, Seadive Photographics
Tony Stone Assoc., London
sTs Foto, Amsterdam
Stülcken-Werft, Hamburg
Studio Michel Sieurin, Le Havre
Stuurman Drykwerk, Sneek
Success-Treuhand GmbH
Svenska Turistföreningen, Stockholm
Hans Strand, Schweden
Swift Associates Ltd., Santa Barbara, CA

Tabor Academy, Marion
Tall Ship Cruising, Hamburg
The Turk Phoenix Ltd., Sunbury
Per K. Thuesen, Holte
Claes Tolman, Monnickendam
Toronto Bigantine Inc., Toronto

Ulster Folk and Transport
Museum, Cultra Manor
Universität für Fischerei-
Wissenschaften, Tokyo
U.S. Coast Guard Official Photo
U.S. Navy Photo

A. Valk, Groningen
Philippe Vanthournout, Gullegem
Verein Segelschiff F. Nansen
e. V., Wolgast
Victory-Museum, Portsmouth
Vida Shipping AB, Stockholm
Alan Villiers, Oxford
V&S Charters, Noordwijk

Barclay H. Warburton, Boston
Hagen Weihe, Alt-Duvenstedt
Marnix van der Wel, Rotterdam
Wilhelm Werst, Bremen
West Island College, Montreal

Windjammer Cruises Inc., Miami
Beach, FL
Windjammer Barefoot Cruises
Ltd.
Malcolm J. Wood & Associates,
Antibes
WWF/Ch. Eggers

YPS/Seephotographie, Hamburg

Sten Zackrisson, Ronneby
Zeilrederij
Zeilvloot Hollands Glorie,
Franeker
Zeilvloot Lemmer—Stavoren

Register of Ships

A. Fabricius 244
Aaltje en Willem 242
Aaron 43
Abel Tasman 204
Abel Tasman 205
Abel Tasman 214
Abraham Rydberg 169
Achaios 356
Activ 132
Adele Raap 245
Adelheit 213
Adelheit van Enkhuizen 213
Adella 151
Add x 133
Adix 132f.
Adolf 16f.
Adolph et Laura 395
Adriana-Johanna 231
Adventure 172
Adventure (USA) 333
Adventure II 333
Älva 311
Aeolus 197
Af Chapman 310f.
Afaneti 87
Agnete 48
Aina 266
Akogare 182
Alabama 334
Alabamien 334
Alaho 337
Albanus 67
Albatros 83, 106
Albert Johannes 206
Albert Leo Schlageter 27, 98, 115,
    280, 281, 282, 330
Albin Köbis 83
Aldor 236
Aleksandr Grin 329
Alevtina 283, 285
Alexander von Humboldt 84
Alf 244
Alfen 265
Alfred 314
Alice S. Wentworth 370
Allan Juel 97
Allerton 40
Alma Doepel 4

Alpha 284
Alphea 81
Alta 48
Alvei 335
Amalie 279
Amazone 206
America 301, 336
America II 301
America III 336
American Pride 337
American Rover 337
Amerigo Vespucci 178, 407
Amistad 338
Amity 5
Amorina 312
Amphitrite 85
Amsterdam 207
Ancona of Leith 363
Anette S. 73
Angelita 199
Anna (Deutschland) 406
Anna (Großbritannien) 151
Anna (Niederlande) 245
Anna (Russland) 283
Anna Elisabeth 97
Anna Kristina 258
Anna Marta (Martha) 241
Anne-Marie 148
Anne-Marie Grenius 148
Annelies 124
Annemarie Grenius 92
Anny 195
Anny von Hamburg 195
Antarctic 3
Antarna 199
Antigua 208
Antje Adelheit 213
Aphrodite 208f.
Aquarius 86
Arctic Explorer 148
Arctic Freezer 51
Arethusa 378, 379
Argonaftis 220
Argus 65
Argus 46
Ariadne 103
Ariel 339
Arny Maud 86

Artemis 209
Aschanti IV 87
Aschanti IV of Vege-
    sack 87
Aschanti of Saba 87
Asgard a Do 174
Asgard II 174
Assen 28
Assen II 28
Astarte 88
Astrid 210
Atalanta 88f.
Atlantic Tramp 89
Atlantide 26
Atlantis 204
Atlantis (Niederlande) 210f.
Atlantis (Niederlande) 211
FS Außenjade 128
Avontuur 248
Baboon 133
Balclutha 339f.
Baltic Beauty 312
Bandi 120
Barba Negra 340f.
Barden 18
Barmnes 237
Bartele Rensink 90
Batavia 212
Beaver II 341
Bel Espoir II 73
Belem 74f.
Belle Blonde 183
Bent 17
Bent Flinot 244
Berendina 231
Berge 97
Bergedorf 406
Bertha 323
Bestevaer 392
Bethia 6, 324
Bielefeld 156
Bill of Rights 342
Birgitte 90
Bisshop van Arkel 213
Blå Marité af Pripps 313f.
Black Douglas 86
Black Jack 29, 31
Black Opal 197

Black Pearl (Malta) 197
Black Pearl (USA) 342
HMS Black Prince 165
Blue Clipper 314
Blue Shadow 316
Blue Sirius 91
Bluenose I 30
Bluenose II 30
Boa Esperança 275
Bonaire 214
Bonavista 44
HMS Bounty 343
Bounty II 343f.
Bounty III 6
Bowdoin 344
Brabander 214
Brandaris 215
Breeze 253
Bremen 252
Bremer Hausekogge 91 Hanseatic
    Cog
Brita 45
Brita Leth 45
Brith Marith 335
British Governor 111
Broedertrouw 249
Buddi 103
FS Bürgermeister Abendroth 94
FS Bürgermeister Bartels 211
BV 2 Vegesack 126
BV 8 St. Magnus 323
Bygda 117
C. A. Thayer 345
C. W. Lawrence 346
C77 165
Cala San Vicenç 302
Californian 346
Cap Nor 3
Capitan Miranda 331
Capitana 202
Capitone 202
Captain Scott 267
Carene 46
Carene Star 46
Caribee (Äquatorialquinea) 66
Carribee (USA) 346f., 382
Carita 220
Carlsö LL 299, 312

Carmelan 92
Carmen Flores 302
Carola 92
Carrick 134
Carrie 135, 139
Carthaginian II 347f.
Catharina 406
Catherina 215f.
Caviare 368
Challenge of Outward Bound 7
Charles W. Morgan 348f.
Charlotte Louise 197f.
Chasseur 384
Christa 236
Christian Bach 158
Christian Radich 259f., 407
Christiana 260
Christophoros 256
Cietrzew 274
Cinderella 316
Cisne Branco 27
Cito 244
City of Adelaide 134
Clan Macleod 11
Clarastella 141
Claus D. 406
Clipper City 349
Club Med I 22, 75
Club Med II 75
Club Mediterranee 38
Colbert 269
Commandant Louis Richard 180
Comte de Smet Naeyer 23
Concordia 21, not mentioned
Condor de Vilamoura 276
Confidentia 84
Constellation 350f.
Constitution 350, 351f.
Copernicus 254
Cornelia 221
Cornelia en Petronella 229
Coronet 353
Corwith Cramer 354
Courier 284
Creole 25
Creoula 277, 281
Cressida 66
HMS Cressy 162
Cristoforo Colombo 178
Croce del Sud 180
Cuauhtémoc 61, 201
Cutty Sark 49, 134, 136f., 243, 407
Cuxhaven 88f.
Cyane 352
D. Fernando 278
D. Fernando II e Gloria 278
Dagmar 56
Dagmar Aaen 93
Dagmar Larssen 83
Danmark 46f., 53, 199, 260, 356
Daphne 111
Dar Mlodziezy 194, 268f., 270, 290, not mentioned

Dar Pomorza 76, 209f.
Dauntless 353
De Dollart 137
De Hoop 232
De Lanwers 137
De Liefde (Japan) 183
De Liefde (Niederlande) 216
De Maas RO 16, 116
De Wadden 137
Deliana 215
Den Lille Bjørn 158
Den Store Bjørn 48
Denis Sullivan 354
Dewarutji 118
Dierkow 226
Dirk KW 44 299
Discovery 138f.
Discovery II 361
Dolfyn 223
Dolmar 42
Dolores 85
Dominique Fredion 312
Don Juan de Austria 302f.
Dora av Raa 94
Dorthea 108
Dove 371
Dreadnought 373
Drittura 245
Drochtersen 299
Druzhba 290, 292, 328, 329
Duchesse Anne 76, 269
Dunay 178
Dunboyne 310
Dunbrody 175, 176
Dunstaffnage 262
Duyfken 7f.
Dyrafjeld 258
Eagle (Bark) 27, 47, 282, 329, 355f.
Eagle (Schoner) 388
Earl of Pembroke 8, 139
Edith 96
Edvord Hansen 54
Edwin and Maud 396
Edwin Fox 254
Eendracht 106, 217
Eendracht II 106, 217f.
Eenhorn 163
Eiland 206
El Pequina Camisola 136, 137
Elbe 2 220
Elbe 3 94
Elbe 3 (FS Weser) 94
Elbe 3 (Senator Brockes) 220
Elbe 4 253
Elegant 218
Elena Maria Barbara 282, 285
Eleonore 245
Elfriede 406
Elinor 48
Elisabeth Bandi 120
Elisabeth Louw 300
Elisabeth Smit 219

Elise 223
Elissa 356
Elizabeth 218f.
Elk 66, 382
Ellen 321
Elsa 324
Else 152
Else Dorothea Bager 58
Else of Thisted 152
Enchantress 399
Endeavour 139, 386
Endeavour (Australien) 8
Endurance 157
Ene 92
Ennie & Appie 225
Enterprise 9 sp. Enterprize
Erika 113
Ernst-Wilhelm 252
Esmeralda 39f., 40
Esther Lohse 83
Etak 393
Eugenios Eugenides 168f.
Europa 220
Euterpe 389, 390
Evermore 76
Eye of the Wind 140
Fair Jeanne 29, 31
Falado 95
Falie 10
Falken 315, 320
Falls of Clyde 357
Familiens Haab 347
Fantome II 74, 75
Ferreira 136, 137
Feuerschiff Nr. 18 48
Fiete 406
Finkampen 86
Fjeld 356
FS Flensburg 233
Fleurtje 220
Flevo 250
Flevo I 116
Flores 114f.
Flying Clipper 169
Flying Cloud 62, 63, 65
Fogel Grip 363
Fortuna 92
Fortuna 406
HMS Foudroyant 161
Fraennenaes 147
Fram 148, 261
Fram (Filmschiff) 148
France II 63
Franziska 124
Frederik Fischer 96
Freedom 95
Fredonia 388
Freia (Dänemark) 49
Freia (Frankreich) 77
Frem 59
Fremad 108
Fri 299
Fridtjof Nansen 96, 116

Friederike 97
Friedrich 140
Friendship 358
Frisiana 229
Frisius van Adel 221
Frisk 299
Frya 77
Fryderyk Chopin 270f.
Fuglen 235, 236
Fulton 50
Fulvia af Anholt 97
Fürst Felix Schwarzenberg 56
Fuur 48
Fylla 51
Fyn 51
Fyrskib XIX 154
G. B. Pattie 29
G. D. Kennedy 310
Gabriel 151
Galatea 141, 142
Galeon 244
HMS Gannet 141
Garcia 95
Gazela of Philadelphia 358f.
Gazela Primeiro 358
Gdynia 16 95
Gefion 303f.
General Zaruski 271
Genius 252
Georg Stage I 52f., 362
Georg Stage II 46, 52, 362, 363
Georgette 202
Gerd-Ute 124
Gerlando 152
Gertrud II 96
Gesine von Papenburg 98
VgF Gezusters 236
Giorgio Cini 75
Gladan 315, 320
Glenlee 141f.
Gloire 165
Gloria 41, 61
Godspeed II 361
Götheborg II 316
Götheborg III 316
Golden Hinde 142f.
Golden Plover 11
Gorch Fock I 98, 41, 282, 329
Gorch Fock II 98, 119, 76, 267, 282, 330
Gorianin 28
Graesholm 205
Grampian Fame 239, 240
Grand Turk 143
Gratia of Gothenburg 316
Gratitude of Gothenburg 317
Great Britain 144
Great Eastern 144
Great Western 144
Greif 100
Greta 90
Gretel 317
Grethe Witting 101

Gribb II 244
Grimsø 324
Grönland 102, 110
Grootvorst 221
Großherzog Friedrich August 76, 264, 265
Großherzogin Elisabeth (Deutschland) 103
Großherzogin Elisabeth (Frankreich) 76, 264, 269
Guanabara 27, 115, 280, 281
Guayas 61, 41
Guerriere 252
Gudrun 97
Gunilla 318
Gustaf 356
Gwarek 194
H. C. Andersen 14
Half Moon 359
Halmø 53
Halve Maan 359
Hamlet 318
Hanna 195
Hanne Hansen 46
Hans 252
Hans II 312
Hansekogge-Kiel 91, 104
Happy Mammoth 190
Happy Mariner 138
Harlingen 323
Harvey Gamage 360
Havet (Dänemark) 54
Havet (Deutschland) 121
Hawaiian Cieftain 360f.
Hawila 319
HD 99-Relinquenda 247
Hector 31f.
Heinz Helmut 90
Helena 67f.
Helga (Deutschland) 116
Helga (Großbritanien) 145
Helga (Finnland) 260
Helge 59
Helmut 230
Hendrika Bartelds 222f.
Henryk Rutkowski 272
Herbert Norkus 282
Hermann 204
Hermann Helms 283
Herzogin Ilse Irene 223
Hilfred 45
Hinemoa 85
Hollands Frouw 10
Hoop 231
Hoop doet Leven 223
Hoop op Welvaart 406
Hoop op Zeegen 215, 239
Hordatral, 105
Horisont 286
Horizon 224
Horst Wessel 27, 47, 98, 282, 329, 355, 356
Huascar 40

Hussar 64
Hussar II 199
Hydrographer 166
Ibaek 279
Ida 35
Ide Min 224
Ifka of Odense 101
Illerim 319
HMS Implacable 146
HMS Indefatigable 143
Inspe 323
Irene 146
Iris 80
Iris Thy 83
Ironsides 352
Isefjord 54
Iskra II 271f., 274
Islamount 141
J. R. R. Tolkien 226
Jachara 105
Jacob Meindert 225
Jacobstads Wapen 68
Jacqueline 58
Jadran 173, 401
James Craig 11
Jamestown-Schiffe 361
Jane Doré 375
Jantje 225
Japan 186
Jarramas 315, 319f., 321
Jason 266
Jatum Jerenda 249
Jaweg 223
Jean de la Lune 146
Jean Marc Aline 180
Jeanie Johnston 176
Jens Krogh 55
Jessica 132, 133
Jette Jan 147
Ji Fung 147
Jødnafjell 109
Jørgen Peter 151
Joe Lane 387
Johan Last 222, 223
Johann Smidt 106, 217
Johanna 262
Johanna Jacoba 59
Johanna Maria 225
John Howard 148
Joseph Conrad 52, 53, 362f.
Joseph Hawkins 375
Joy Farer 85
Juan D'Austria 39f.
Juan Sebastian de Elcano 2, 39, 304f.
Jules Verne 107
Julia 147
Jütlandia 147
Jylland 56f.
Kaisei 13, 184, 407
Kaiwo Maru I 188f.
Kaiwo Maru II 185, 189
Kaliakra 28, 272, 274

FS Kalkgrund 233
Kalmar Nyckel 363f.
Kanko Maru 186, 187
Kanrin Maru 186f.
Kaparen 271
Kapitan Glowacki 272
Karino 236
Karl Friedrich Steen 406
Karma 151
Karna 46
Kaskelot 139, 148
Kathleen 109
Kathleen & May 148
Katwijk 229
Kenavo 135
Kerstin 229
Khersones 290, 292, 328, 329
FS Kiel 84
Kinnekulle 244
Klara Katharina 127
Klaus D. 241
København 46
Koh-I-Nor 227
Komet 347
Kommodore Johnsen 112, 293, 294
Kon-Tiki 122
KRI Arsa 172
KRI Arung Samudera 172
KRI Dewarutji 173
Kristian 92
Kronwerk 287
Kruzenshtern 288f. 407
Kryssaren 271
Kurt 373
Kurt Both 195
L. A. Dunton 364f.
L'Amie 177
L'Avenir 23
L'Etoile 78
L'Oiseau Blanc 202
La Amistad 375
La Argentina 2
La Belle Poule 78
La Cancalaise 79
La Donna 375
La Recouvrance 80
La Sirena 40
Lady Ellen 320
Lady Ellen IV 321
Lady in Blue 337
Lady Maryland 365
Lady Nelson 12
Lady Washington 366
Laennec 72
Laksen (Deutschland) 86
Laksen (Niederlande) 204
Landsort fa de Vriendschap 250
Lars 46
Lasca II 26
Lawedua 17
Lawrence 376
Le Pelican 367
Le Renard 81

Leão Holandês 279
Leentje 221
Leeuwin 13
Legacy? 63
Leo 130
Lettie G. Howard 367f.
Levant 352
Libertad 1f, 3, 41, 305
Liberté 202
Liberty 368
Liberty Clipper 369
Lili 126
Lili Marleen 107
Lilla Dan 57
Lilleholm 108
Lilli 126
Linde 227
Linden 69
Linlithgowshire 23
Linquenda 248
Lisa 369
Lizzie May 148
Lord Nelson 149, 150, 160
Los Andes 3
Loth Loriën 228
Lotsenschoner II 392
Lotte Nagel 90
LT 685 101
Luchtstraal 90
Luciana 229
LV 88 183
Lwow 269
Lyra 395
M. A. Flyvbjerg 45
Maartinus 229
Madonna 58
Magdalene Vinnen 293
Meiji Maru 187, 192
Malcolm Miller 159
Mandalay 63, 64, 65
Marco Polo 401
Marcus Aurelius 229
Mare Frisium 230
Marga Henning 122
Margret Todd 370
Maria Becker 250
Maria do Amparo 136, 137
Marie 324
Marie af Sæby 53
Marie Hilck 279
Marie Pierre 87
Marij 77
Marilyn Anne 59
Marité 313
Mariusz Zaruski 271
Martana 108
Martha 206
Martha 249
Martha Ahrens 279
Martin 108
Mary 347
Mary Day 370f.
Mary P. Goulart 333

Mary-Anne 108
Maryland Dove 371
Mathilde 14f.
Matthew 150
Maverick 237
Mavi 166
Max 114f.
Mayflower 372
Mayflower II 372, 387
Meiji Maru 187, 192
Mercantic II 58
Mercator 23f.
HMS Mercury 141
Meridian 289
Merry 140
Mervede 116
Meta Buck 116
Meteor III 26
Meyert Menno 206
Midsummer 59
Milka 28
Minde 241
Minerva 231
Minna 54
Minnow 122
Minstrel 36
Mir 290, 292, 328, 329
Mira II 245
Mircea 98, 282, 329
Mistral 25
Mistralen 46
Mloda Gwardia 271
Mneme 70
Möeve 323
Möwe 400
Mojenhörn 279
Mon Desir 231
Mona 46, 132
Mondrian 232
Monika Harssen 126
Morgana 233
Moshulu 373f.
Mostring 335
Mystic C. 368
Mystic Clipper 369
Mystic Whaler 374
N. I. Vaptsarov 28
Nadeshda 291
Najaden 315, 321f.
Najaden 322f., 323
Natalie Todd 337
Nathaniel Bowditch 375
Neerlandia 127
Neidenfels 307
Neptun Baroness 159
Neptun Princess 159
Nette S. 73
New Endeavour 15, 19
New Way 375
Niagara 376
Nil Desperandum 233
Niña (Spanien) 306, 307
Niña (USA) 377

Niña (von Kolumbus) 275
Niobe 329
Nippon Maru I 188f., 189
Nippon Maru II 185, 189, 192
Njord 228
Nobile 109
Nonsuch 32f.
Noona Dan 121
Noorderlicht 234
Nora 323
Nordboen 60
Norden 110
Nordstrand 1 124
Norford Suffling 101
Nostra 126
Ny Wassan 326
Oceaan II 51, 52
Ocean Star 378
Oceania 272, 273, 274
Östervag 317
Oiseau des Iles 62
Olaf Petersen 77
Oldenburg 72
Oldeoog 225
Onderneming 221
One and All 14
Oosterschelde 235f.
Oostvogel 236
Oplag 373, 374
Orion 139
Otaru Maru 189
Otto Lauffer 406
Our Svanen 14f.
P8 128
Pacific 14
Pacific Queen 339, 340
Pacific Swift (Niederlande) 237
Pacific Swift (Kanada) 33
Padua 288, 289
Palinuro 180f.
Pallada 290, 292, 328, 329
Palmeto 151
Palmyra 124
Pamir 112, 329, 374, 408
Pandora 343
Passat 111f., 329, 374, 408
Pathfinder 34
Patria 199
Patriot 28
Peace 309
Peder Most 73
Pedro Doncker 237
Peking 111, 378f.
Perle 79
Perseus 380
Peter 252
Peterna 279
Petrea 274
Petrus 227
Petsmo 77
Philippina Johanna 239
Phocea 38
Phoenix 139, 151

Picton Castle 42
Pieter Albrecht Koerts 120, 121
Pieternella 221
Pilgrim 380f.
Pinta 306, 307
Pinta (Filmschiff) 135
Pioneer 356
Pioneer (Schoner) 381
Pippilotta 113
Pirat 252
Playfair 34
Plover 11
Pogoria 28, 273f., 271, 272
Pol IV 244
Polar Freeze 51
Pollux 238
Polly Woodside 15f.
Polynesia 382
Polynesia II 63, 65
Pommern 70f.
Pomorze 269f.
Pool 244
Poolzee 269f.
Portland Pilot 393
Präsident Freiherr von
   Maltzahn 405
HMS President 141
Presidente Sarmiento 2f.
Pride of Baltimore II 383f.
Prince Louis I 73
Prince Louis II 73
Prince William 159
Prins Willem 190 f.
Prinzess Eitel Friedrich 76, 117,
   264, 269
Privateer 36
Providence 384
Puerto de Palma 302
Puritan 181
Queen Galadriel 152
Quo Vadis 227
R. Tucker Thompson 255
Radboud 239
Radiant 202
Ragnborg 24
Rainbow Warrior 156, 239
Rakel 113f.
Raphaelo 152f.
Rara Avis 81
Rauna 92
Regina 385
Regina Chatarina 299
Regina Maris (Niederlande) 240
Regina Maris (USA) 385
Rembrandt van Rijn 241
FS Reserve Holtenau 84
FS Reserve Sonderburg 84
Result 153
Return of Marco Polo 154, 158
Richelieu 269
Rickmer Rickmers 114f.
Ring-Andersen 155
Ringö 195

Rion 282
Rival 227
Roald Amundsen 115f.
Robert 241
Robertson II 34f.
Rönndik 279
Rona 15
Rosborough 36
Rose 386
Rose Marie 140
Rovedefjord 335
Royal Clipper 193f.
Royalist 150, 155f., 171
Ryvar 116
Saatsee 406
Sælør 117
Sagres I 115, 280
Sagres II 115, 280f., 282, 329
Saint John The Baptist 191
Saint Kilda 156
Sam 140
San Antonio 103
San Juan Bautista 191
Sanne Sophia 236
Sansibar 237
Santa Maria 307f.
Santa Maria Manuela 281
Santo André 115
Santoni 103
Saracen 148
Sayremar Uno 302
Schooner Liberty 368
Schulschiff Deutschland 118f.
Sea Cloud 198f.
Sea Cloud II 200
Sea Lion 387
Sea Pearl 299
Sea Shell 300
Sea Wolf 255
Sedov 112, 293f.m 329
Sekstant 289
Senator Brockes 220
Sepha Vollaars 279
Seute Deern 120f.
Seute Deern II 121
Sha Nijma 7
Shabab Oman 267
Shalom 323
Shenandoah (Bermuda) 26
Shenandoah (USA) 387
Shintoku Maru 189
Shtandart 294f.
Sigyn 71
Silke 122
Simon Bolivar 61, 400
Sir Robert Baden-Powell 241
Sirius 287
Sjoborrun 229
Skagen 54
Skarvholmen 105
Skibladner 151
Smart 266
Sodade 242

Soembing 186
Sörkyst 48
Solvang 122
Solway Lass 16f.
Sophie Theresia 242
Søren Larsen 157
Sørlandet 263f.
Soundwaters 388
South Passage 17
Southgate 396, 397
Sovereign of the Seas 18
Spica 299
Spirit of Adventure 19
Spirit of Chemainus 35
Spirit of Hennessy 314
Spirit of Massachusetts 388
Spirit of Merseyside 324
Spirit of New Zealand 256
Spirit of the Pacific 19
Spirit of Winestead 154, 158
St. Barbara Ann 158f.
St. Catherine 337
HMS St. Lawrence 36
St. Lawrence II 34, 36
St. Roch 37
Stad Amsterdam 27, 243
Stanislaw 224
Star Clipper 194
Star Flyer 194
Star of Alaska 339, 340
Star of India 389f.
Starfish 156
Statsraad Erichsen 260
Statsraad Lehmkuhl 76, 264f.
Stavros S. Niarchos 159
Stedemaeght 244
Stephen Taber 390
Stettin 406
Stina 16f.
Store Baelt 245
Strela 28
Sudersand 324
Sunbeam 168f.
Sunbeam II 168f.
Sundeved 16f.
Suomen Joutsen 72
Susan Constant II 361
Svanen (Australien) 14
Svanen (Norwegen) 266
Svegrunn 116
Sven Wilhelm 312

Svendborg 132
Sviatitel Nikolai 295
Swaensborgh 245
Swan fan Makkum 246
SWI 180 Goplo 309
Swift 391
Swift of Ipswich 391
Sylvan 235, 236
Syveren 44
T/W Ems 128
Tabor Boy 392
Taisei Maru 189
Taitu 152
Talata 58
Tarangini 170
Tenacious 160
Te Quest 86
Te Vega 393
Tecla 247
Terje Viken 237
Terra Nova 148
Thalassa 247
Thalatta 216
Thellef 323
Theodore 247
Thermopylae 136
Thomas 44
Thor 159
Thor Heyerdahl 122
Tiger 406
Timberwind 393
HMS Tinderbox 12
Tinka 122
Tole Mour 394
Tonijn 300
Topaz 344
Towarischtsch 282, 329f., 407
Towarischtsch I 330
Towarischtsch II 330
Tradewind 242
HMS Trincomalee 161
Triton 350
Triumpf 296
Tromp 248
Tropik 289
Tsjerk Hiddes 248
Tui 257
Tui-Na-Savu Savu 16f.
Tunas Samudera 20, 150, 170, 196
Tuxtla 62
Tuy 283, 285

TV 015 323
Twee Gebroeders II 229
Ubena 123
Ubena von Bremen 91, 123
Ulla Vita 55
Undine 124
HMS Unicorn
    (Großbritannien) 162
HMS Unicorn
    (Großbritannien) II 162
Unicorn (Großbritannien) 163
Unicorn (USA) 395
Unyo Maru 192
Urania 248
Ursel Beate 90
Uruguay 3
Utskär 323
Uwe Ursula 231
Vaarvind 335
Vadder Gerrit 323
Valdivia 125
Vanadis 125
Vanessa Ann 158, 159
Varuna 150, 171
Vega 393
Vegesach BV2 126
Vema 64
HMS Vernon III 165
Vertrouwen (Deutschland) 220
Vertrouwen (Niederlande) 231
Veslets 28
Vest 59
Vestvåg 59
Victoria and Albert 301
HMS Victory 163f., 165
Victory Chimes 396
Vida 324
Vidar 127
Viking 46, 324f.
Vilm 115f.
Virginia 337
Viskan 244
Vlardingen 229
Vliegende Hollander 249
Vlieland 215
Vola 28
Volchitsa 283
Vrouwe Geertruida Magdalena 249
Walter Hävernick 406
HMS Warrior 165

Wasa 326f.
Washington 338
Wavertree 396f.
Wawona 397
Weiße Düne 127f.
FS Weser 94
Weser Nr. 3 250
Western Union 375
Westwärts 265
Westward 398
White Shark 128
Wilhelm Kaisen 283
Wilhelm Pieck 100
Willem 250f.
Willem Barentsz 250
Wind Song 22
Wind Spirit 22
Wind Star 22
Wind Surf 22, 75
Windeward Bound 19
Windy 399
Worcester 378
Wuta 210
Wytske Eelkje 250f.
Wyvern 129
Wyvern von Bremen 129
Xarifa 202
XXXX 132, 133
Yankee Clipper 63, 65, 66, 382
Yankee Trader 166
YH 45 101
Young America 399
Young Endeavour 20, 150, 170, 196
Youth of Oman 267
Yunyi Baltiets 297
Z. M. Dordrecht 238
Z. S. Marken 219
Zamoura of Zermatt 166f.
Zar Nikolaus II 295
Zarja 298
Zawisza Czarny II 274
Zebu 167
Zeelandia 251f.
Zeven Provincien 213
Zew 184
Ziba 167
Zuiderzee 252
Zuversicht 130
Zwarte Rat 225